Internet Multimedia Communications Using SIP

The Morgan Kaufmann Series in Networking

Series Editor, David Clark, M.I.T.

Internet Multimedia Communications Using SIP
Rogelio Martínez Perea

Bluetooth Application Programming with the Java APIs, Essentials Edition
C. Bala Kumar, Paul Kline, and Tim Thompson

Information Assurance: Dependability and Security in Networked Systems
Yi Qian, James Joshi, David Tipper, and Prashant Krishnamurthy

Network Simulation Experiments Manual, 2e
Emad Aboelela

Network Analysis, Architecture, and Design, 3e
James D. McCabe

Wireless Communications & Networking: An Introduction
Vijay K. Garg

Ethernet Networking for the Small Office and Professional Home Office
Jan L. Harrington

IPv6 Advanced Protocols Implementation
Qing Li, Tatuya Jinmei, and Keiichi Shima

Computer Networks: A Systems Approach, 4e
Larry L. Peterson and Bruce S. Davie

Network Routing: Algorithms, Protocols, and Architectures
Deepankar Medhi and Karthikeyan Ramaswami

Deploying IP and MPLS QoS for Multiservice Networks: Theory and Practice
John Evans and Clarence Filsfils

Traffic Engineering and QoS Optimization of Integrated Voice & Data Networks
Gerald R. Ash

IPv6 Core Protocols Implementation
Qing Li, Tatuya Jinmei, and Keiichi Shima

Smart Phone and Next-Generation Mobile Computing
Pei Zheng and Lionel Ni

GMPLS: Architecture and Applications
Adrian Farrel and Igor Bryskin

Network Security: A Practical Approach
Jan L. Harrington

Content Networking: Architecture, Protocols, and Practice
Markus Hofmann and Leland R. Beaumont

Network Algorithmics: An Interdisciplinary Approach to Designing Fast Networked Devices
George Varghese

Network Recovery: Protection and Restoration of Optical, SONET-SDH, IP, and MPLS
Jean Philippe Vasseur, Mario Pickavet, and Piet Demeester

Routing, Flow, and Capacity Design in Communication and Computer Networks
Michał Pióro and Deepankar Medhi

Wireless Sensor Networks: An Information Processing Approach
Feng Zhao and Leonidas Guibas

Communication Networking: An Analytical Approach
Anurag Kumar, D. Manjunath, and Joy Kuri

Internet Multimedia Communications Using SIP

A Modern Approach Including Java® Practice

Rogelio Martínez Perea

ELSEVIER

AMSTERDAM • BOSTON • HEIDELBERG • LONDON
NEW YORK • OXFORD • PARIS • SAN DIEGO
SAN FRANCISCO • SINGAPORE • SYDNEY • TOKYO

Morgan Kaufmann is an imprint of Elsevier

MORGAN KAUFMANN PUBLISHERS

Acquisitions Editor: Rick Adams
Publishing Services Manager: George Morrison
Project Manager: Mónica González de Mendoza
Assistant Editor: Greg Chalson
Production Assistant: Lianne Hong
Design Direction: Joanne Blank
Cover Design: Anne Carter
Cover Image © iStockphoto
Composition: Charon Tec
Interior printer: Sheridan Books, Inc.
Cover printer: Phoenix Color Corporation

Morgan Kaufmann Publishers is an imprint of Elsevier.
30 Corporate Drive, Suite 400, Burlington, MA 01803, USA

This book is printed on acid-free paper.

Library of Congress Cataloging-in-Publication Data
Martínez Perea, Rogelio.
Internet multimedia communications using SIP : a modern approach including Java practice / Rogelio Martínez Perea.
p. cm. — (Morgan Kaufmann series in networking)
Includes bibliographical references and index.
ISBN 978-0-12-374300-8 (hbk. : alk. paper) 1. Computer network protocols. 2. Internet. 3. Multimedia systems. I. Title. II. Title: Internet multimedia communications using Session Initiation Protocol.

TK5105.55.M373 2008
004.6′2—dc22
2007039431

ISBN: 978-0-12-374300-8

For information on all Morgan Kaufmann publications, visit our Web site at www.mkp.com or www.books.elsevier.com

Transferred to Digital Print 2011

Printed and bound in the United Kingdom

To my parents, for their love and support

Contents

Preface xv
About the Author xx
Foreword xxi

PART I FUNDAMENTALS 1

CHAPTER 1 Introduction 3
1.1 IP Multimedia Communication Services 3
1.2 The Role of Signaling and Media 6
1.3 Type of Services Enabled by SIP 10
1.4 Examples of SIP Applications 13
1.5 The Internet Engineering Task Force (IETF) 16
1.6 Summary 20

CHAPTER 2 A Bit of History 21
2.1 The Third Revolution in the Internet 21
2.2 The Next Revolution in the Telecommunication Industry 23
2.3 A Brief History of Internet Multimedia 26
2.4 Summary 29

CHAPTER 3 IP Multimedia Fundamentals 31
3.1 Internet Concepts 31
3.2 TCP/IP Protocol Architecture 34
3.3 Architecture for Internet Multimedia Communications 39
3.4 Summary 42

CHAPTER 4 SIP Overview 43
4.1 What is SIP? 43
4.2 SIP Addressing 44
4.3 SIP Functions 45
4.4 SIP Entities 50
4.5 Summary 58

CHAPTER 5 Multimedia-Service Creation Overview 59
5.1 What are SIP Services? 59
5.2 SIP Services and SIP Entities 60
5.3 Terminal-Based or Network-Based SIP Services 62
5.4 SIP Programming Interfaces 64
5.5 Media-Programming APIs 69
5.6 APIs Used in This Book 70
5.7 Summary 70

PART II CORE PROTOCOLS 73

CHAPTER 6 SIP Protocol Operation 75
6.1 SIP Mode of Operation 75
6.2 SIP Message Format 83
6.3 SIP Routing 95
6.4 SIP Detailed Call Flows 103
6.5 Summary 112

CHAPTER 7 SIP Protocol Structure 113
7.1 Protocol Structure Overview 113
7.2 SIP Core Sublayer 116
7.3 SIP Transaction Sublayer 117
7.4 SIP Transport Sublayer 129
7.5 SIP Syntax and Encoding Function 132
7.6 SIP Dialogs 132
7.7 Summary 136

CHAPTER 8 Practice with SIP 137
8.1 What Is JAIN SIP? 137
8.2 JAIN SIP Architecture 140
8.3 The SipStack, SipProvider and ListeningPoint 144
8.4 The SipListener 146
8.5 Other Factories: MessageFactory, HeaderFactory, AddressFactory 148
8.6 Programs and Practice 152
8.7 Summary 174

CHAPTER 9 Session Description 177
9.1 The Purpose of Session Description 177
9.2 The Session Description Protocol (SDP) 179
9.3 Example IP Communication Sessions Described with SDP 184
9.4 The Offer/Answer Model with SDP 187
9.5 SDP Programming 191
9.6 Summary 199

CHAPTER 10 The Media Plane 201
10.1 Overview of the Media Plane 201
10.2 Real-time Transport Protocol (RTP) 203
10.3 Messaging Service Relay Protocol (MSRP) 209
10.4 Summary 224

CHAPTER 11 Media Plane Programming 225
11.1 Overview 225
11.2 JMF Entities 228

11.3 JMF Operation 237
11.4 Putting It All Together: The VoiceTool 245
11.5 Putting It All Together: The VideoTool 248
11.6 Putting It All Together: The TonesTool 254
11.7 Using the Components. Example 6 255
11.8 Summary 256

CHAPTER 12 The SIP Soft-Phone 257
12.1 Scope 257
12.2 Architecture 258
12.3 User Interface and Configuration 263
12.4 State Model 267
12.5 Implementation Aspects 271
12.6 Summary 281

CHAPTER 13 Sip Proxies 283
13.1 What Is a SIP Proxy? 283
13.2 Transaction Stateful Proxies 285
13.3 Stateful Proxy Behavior 289
13.4 Transaction Stateless Proxies 293
13.5 Stateless Proxy Behavior 293
13.6 Practice: SIP Server 294
13.7 Summary 312

CHAPTER 14 Securing Multimedia Communications 313
14.1 Review of Basic Encryption Concepts 314
14.2 Attacks and Threat Models in SIP 319
14.3 Security Services for SIP 320
14.4 Security Mechanisms for SIP 320
14.5 Best Practices on SIP Security 327
14.6 Securing the Media Plane 330
14.7 Summary 334

PART III ADVANCED TOPICS 335

CHAPTER 15 Extending SIP 337
15.1 Defining New Extensions 337
15.2 SIP Architectural Principles 338
15.3 Extensibility and Compatibility 338
15.4 Reliability of Provisional Responses 344
15.5 UPDATE 347
15.6 SIP-specific Event Notification 348
15.7 History-Info 355
15.8 Globally Routable User Agent URIs (GRUUs) 356
15.9 Summary 360

CHAPTER 16 Presence and Instant Messaging 361
16.1 Overview of Presence and Instant Messaging 361
16.2 The Presence Model 363
16.3 Presence with SIP 365
16.4 Presence Information 368
16.5 Address Resolution 370
16.6 Resource Lists 370
16.7 XCAP 372
16.8 Instant Messaging 372
16.9 IM Servers 374
16.10 Practice: Softphone3 375
16.11 Summary 379

CHAPTER 17 Call Control 381
17.1 What Is Call Control? 381
17.2 Peer-to-Peer Call Control 383
17.3 Third Party Call Control (3PCC) 389
17.4 Remote Call Control 390
17.5 Summary 394

CHAPTER 18 Interworking with PSTN/PLMN 395
18.1 Motivation 395
18.2 Architecture 396
18.3 Telephone Addressing: The TEL URI 400
18.4 ENUM: The E.164 to URI Dynamic Delegation Discovery System 401
18.5 Protocol Translation 403
18.6 Protocol Encapsulation 406
18.7 Translation or Encapsulation? 407
18.8 Summary 408

CHAPTER 19 Media Servers and Conferencing 409
19.1 Basic Media Services 410
19.2 About KPML and the User Interaction Framework 417
19.3 Enhanced Conferencing 418
19.4 Framework for Conferencing with SIP 419
19.5 XCON Framework 423
19.6 Media Server Control 429
19.7 Other Media Services 435
19.8 Summary 436

CHAPTER 20 SIP Identity Aspects 437
20.1 Identity Management in SIP 437
20.2 Basic Identity Management 439
20.3 Private Header for Network Asserted Identity 441

20.4 Enhanced Identity Management....444
20.5 Summary....445

CHAPTER 21 Quality of Service....447
21.1 Quality of Service in IP Networks....447
21.2 Mechanisms for QoS....449
21.3 Policy-based Admission Control....453
21.4 SIP Integration with Resource Reservation: The Preconditions framework....454
21.5 SIP Integration with Policy Control: Media and Qos Authorization....460
21.6 Summary....465

CHAPTER 22 NAT Traversal....467
22.1 NAT Overview....467
22.2 Behavior of NAT Devices....470
22.3 SIP Traversal through NAT....474
22.4 RTP Traversal through NAT....479
22.5 Session Border Controllers....485
22.6 NAT Traversal Using SBCs....488
22.7 Summary....493

CHAPTER 23 SIP Networks....495
23.1 The Role of the Network....495
23.2 Mobility and Routing....497
23.3 Authentication, Authorization, and Accounting....497
23.4 Security....498
23.5 Interworking and Border Functions....498
23.6 Provision of Network-Based Services....499
23.7 Summary....500

CHAPTER 24 The IMS....501
24.1 3GPP and IMS....501
24.2 High-Level IMS Requirements....504
24.3 Overview of IMS Architecture....510
24.4 IMS Concepts....520
24.5 New Requirements on SIP....529
24.6 IMS Services....532
24.7 ETSI TISPAN NGN....536
24.8 Next Trends in IMS....538
24.9 Summary....539

Appendix A Source Code 541
Acronyms 545
References 551
Index 563

Preface

Why This Book

In the late 1990s, I was engineering manager at the switching department in a mobile telecom operator. The mobile switches we dealt with were based on circuit-switched technology. They were big, complex, and proprietary pieces of hardware and software involved almost exclusively in the provision of voice service. By that time, ATM (Asynchronous Transfer Mode), a packet-switched technology that followed the virtual circuit approach, started to gain maturity as a suitable way for carrying media traffic with QoS requirements. Media transport was only part of the problem. The other part, signaling, did not have, by then, a mature candidate. The industry response was to strip the existing circuit switches off their switching matrix and provide them with the interfaces to control an external packet-based switching matrix in the so-called soft-switch approach. It was kind of throwing out the old-fashioned hardware but retaining the software. That was a pragmatic approach that the market took in order to rapidly respond to the operator's needs. However, it still took several years for the telecom operators worldwide to implement these architectures. By that time, we knew there was work in the IETF about a protocol called SIP, whose first version was published in 1995, but the main focus of the industry was on H.323 for enterprise networks and in the soft-switch approach for public telecom networks. In the meantime, Internet and the web were increasing their popularity, but this fact seemed, by then, unrelated to our challenge of evolving the network. Being intrigued about the possibility of using a packet-based network for media transport, that was the first time I built an IP soft-phone. I just developed a simple Windows program over the Win32 API on a standard PC. I made up a simple signaling protocol consisting of a bunch of messages and sent them over TCP/IP using the Winsock interface. Regarding the media, I just got the raw voice samples from the Wave API and put them directly on UDP packets that I sent over the network using Winsock. Surprisingly enough, it worked, and I could test it over a medium-sized LAN. I needed no voice network equipment (neither voice switch nor soft-switch), just a dumb IP network and a Windows program that I developed in a few weeks and ran on a cheap PC. The simplicity and the flexibility of the solution convinced me that voice technology as we knew it was meant to change sooner or later, and that the new technology would be one that advocated simplicity in the network and flexibility in the endpoints as well as cheap and off-the-self hardware and software.

In the next years, I changed roles and became manager for a team doing mobile services design and development. By that time, I had already built a new version of my softphone, only that then I used a beta version of a SIP stack, an Internet protocol that was destined to revolutionize multimedia communications both in the Internet and in the telecom environment. As will be explained in this book,

SIP follows the flexible Internet approach that advocates moving intelligence to the endpoints and keeping the network as simple as possible.

During that time, I became convinced that understanding, even if it is at a high level, how SIP software works helps to understand its simplicity, flexibility, and potential. And that is the reason why, when years later I decided to write a book on a state-of-the-art approach for multimedia communications, I went for an approach that combined theory with practice. And the result is this book.

Approach

This book's aim is to let readers understand what Internet multimedia communications are and how they are enabled by using the Session Initiation Protocol and other related technologies. The approach I have taken in writing this book has three main characteristics.

First, it is *Internet-orientated*. That is, it is focused on the Internet technologies, protocols, and practices for delivering these services. In the last two chapters, it also touches upon how these Internet technologies can be used in controlled network scenarios such as those present in telecom operators' multimedia networks. In fact, the bodies involved in the standardization of telecom networks, such as ETSI or 3GPP, have adopted the ideas coming from the Internet in order to design the next generation of telecommunication networks.

Second, it follows a *fully modern and up-to-date* approach where the latest Internet developments are analyzed and discussed. In addition to providing a thorough explanation of the basic concepts, it also presents the most recent proposals for utilization of SIP and related technologies in the remit of multimedia communications. The book tackles new and innovative technologies and services such as MSRP, NAT traversal, STUN, ICE, session border controllers, TCP-based media transport, XCON conferencing framework, media server control, GRUUs, RPID, latest approaches for RTP security, XCAP, Text over IP, remote call control, floor control, conference control, Fax over IP, enhanced identity management, IMS, TISPAN next generation networks, voice call continuity, IMS centralized services, and so forth.

Following a modern approach implies that the book contains not just references to official standard or informative documents (e.g., Request For Comments), but also many references to the latest IETF Internet Drafts that represent current work in progress.

Third, the book is unique in its kind by the fact that it not only *contains theory but also practice*. The practical nature of the book is twofold. On one hand, the book tackles multimedia service creation, both at SIP level and at media level. It contains a comprehensive description of the state-of-the-art technologies for multimedia service creation. More than that, the book explains in detail how to program multimedia services using Java. Readers will learn how to programmatically use an open-source SIP stack and a popular Java API for media development. Many examples and Java practices are included in the book. Readers are guided step-by-step to build a simple yet functional soft-phone supporting voice, video, and messaging, plus a simple SIP proxy and registrar to be used with the soft-phone. The main purpose for the inclusion of code in the book is derived from my experience when dealing with multimedia technology: being able to take a look, even if you are not a Java programmer, at code that illustrates how services are done facilitates the comprehension of the technical concepts and the simplicity and potential in the technology. Another aspect of the practicality of the book refers to the fact that it also contains explanations of the situations where the different technical solutions may be used in real deployments.

Audience

The book is targeted at several types of audiences. In any case, all readers should have a technical background, an interest in technology, or a passion for Internet-related topics.

First, this book is targeted at the professional in the telecom or IT industry who needs to gain an understanding of the newest Internet Protocol–based technologies for delivering voice, video, messaging, and data services, and to acquire the skills and tools to successfully design and implement multimedia solutions in different environments (from small enterprise deployments up to Internet-wide deployments). IT architects will use the book to understand how their existing enterprise IP networks can be leveraged for delivering voice, video, and messaging, and what technologies the products that they choose must support. Telecom architects will use the book to gain an understanding of how SIP and other Internet technologies can be used to evolve their networks and offer innovative services (or offer existing services but with a reduced CAPEX and OPEX!). SIP related technologies play a key role in the movement into Fixed Mobile Convergence and Total Communication propositions that most telecom operators are embracing nowadays. IT and telecom engineers will find the necessary information in the book to understand how technology works, and will be referred to the appropriate technical documents for further detail. The book is also very useful for IT and telecom managers that want to understand how their business needs to be evolved toward an all-IP infrastructure and what are the benefits and challenges in doing so.

Second, this book is targeted at the academic community, where it can be used as base material for a one-semester theoretical course on Internet multimedia communications or as support material for practices in a laboratory course.

Third, software developers will find in the book the necessary theoretical and practical information that allows them to learn how to build basic SIP applications and sets the grounds for more-complex application design and development.

And last but not least, any person who has a technical background and has a passion for being informed about the hottest stuff around the Internet is also a potential candidate for enjoying the book.

Organization

The book is organized in three parts and 24 chapters.

The first part, "Fundamentals," comprises the first five chapters in the book. These give the necessary background information on Internet multimedia architecture, protocols, and service creation tools for understanding the rest of the book.

Above all, this first part explains the rationale behind the design of the multimedia protocols and the remit in which they are used. Setting the scope of the technology is crucial for using it successfully.

The second part, "Core Protocols," is the central part of the book, and is dedicated to explaining how the main protocols work in concert to deliver multimedia services. In order to enhance the comprehension of the theory, the reader is also guided into the elaboration of simple Java-based programming practices that allow him or her to better comprehend the theoretical concepts. As part of these practices, readers will learn to build, step-by-step, a simple yet functional soft-phone supporting voice, video, and messaging. Those readers who are not interested in the programming practice can simply skip the related chapters and just focus on the theory. However, I would recommend that even these readers take a quick look at some of the code snippets so that they can get a high-level understanding of how applications can be developed.

The third part, "Advanced Topics," deals with the latest and most innovative usages of the technology. Readers who already have professional experience with the technology, either designing or developing solutions, might want to skip the first two parts and dive directly into this part. In addition to tackling the most recent advances in the technology, Part III also shows how hot issues that every multimedia deployment faces are resolved. An example of that is the hot NAT traversal topic, of which a very thorough analysis is done and several possible solutions are detailed.

Additionally, the last two chapters in the book explain how Internet multimedia technology can be used in network scenarios where a tighter relationship with the service provider exists. A paradigmatic example of this concept is the 3GPP IMS, to which a long chapter is exclusively dedicated. The approach used in this book to present the IMS architecture and concepts is very different from the traditional one used by other books on the subject. Instead of first introducing an overwhelming architecture diagram full of unintelligible names and then explaining what the role is of the various components, a different approach is followed. It is based on leveraging the Internet concepts learned throughout the book, and explaining how they naturally evolve to support additional requirements that telecom operators may have, and that are not strictly relevant in a pure Internet environment.

Code Examples

This book does not intend to teach programming. The code examples are included just for the shake of illustrating how the protocols work. Readers can build simple examples where they can test the concepts learned. I have purposely omitted the bulk of error checking and recovery so as not to deviate the reader's attention from the functional concepts. I am convinced this has resulted in more comprehensive programs that show clearly how protocols operate. On the other hand, it means that programs are not fit for commercial use, and that they need to be fed with consistent data; otherwise, they will fail. Additionally, when I have thought that good OO practice made the functional concepts more difficult to understand, I have preferred to sacrifice perfect OO programming techniques.

Acknowledgments

I wish to thank Rogier Noldus, from Ericsson, and David Page, chief scientist at OpenCloud, for their impressive work in reviewing the manuscript. Their comments and suggestions have greatly contributed to the possible quality of the final product. Also, Nick Hudson, a former colleague at Vodafone, reviewed the manuscript and provided useful feedback. Santiago Borrero, a colleague of mine at Vodafone, reviewed the first introductory chapters and contributed to making the technical concepts in them easier to understand for readers with different backgrounds.

I also want to thank Rick Adams, Greg Chalson and Mónica González de Mendoza, my editors at Elsevier, who believed in the project from the very beginning and who provided timely help and assistance that allowed us to overcome the hurdles encountered during the manuscript delivery process.

My biggest thanks go for my wife, whose encouragement, support, patience, and understanding have been crucial for the successful accomplishment of this project.

About the Author

Rogelio Martínez has an M.S. in Telecommunications Engineering from Universidad Politécnica de Madrid, Spain. He has worked for the Vodafone Group for more than 12 years and has held various responsibilities there. Martínez was Switching Department Engineering Manager for 4 years. For the past 5 years, as Design Manager, he has led a team of technical specialists devoted to mobile applications design and implementation. More specifically, for the past 2 years, as a Senior Manager, he has led the design and evolution of the Vodafone Group multimedia service layer. At Vodafone, Martínez has been deeply involved in the deployment of SIP-based technology in operators all around the world.

Rogelio Martínez lives in Madrid with his wife and two children, and is very fond of playing tennis and skiing.

Foreword

Jorge Gató, Vodafone España

At the end of last century—to quote Thomas L. Friedman's excellent book, *The World Is Flat*—I was part of the unflat old world, specifically the old telephony world. I was reading (and listening to) the new flat world boys coming at the speed of light to re-do and improve things in months, weeks or even days that had previously taken us years to develop.

I was able to witness the initial days of the Voice over Packets (although, to be precise, voice was over packets when it became digital, years before), the initial trials and the early deployments of Voice over ATM and over IP. It was the time of the "Internet bubble" and a lot of fast innovation was happening, with many new small and smart start-up companies created, mainly in the USA and Scandinavia. It was a beautiful, creative time.

However, things were not so simple. The initial efforts to quickly replace the old telephony (SS7) world failed, and only the strongest companies survived. Once again, the technique of copying and using the best of both worlds (SS7 and IP), was used. SIP protocol was born (congratulations SIP!). It was, and still is, difficult to find people really skilled in both (SS7 and IP telephony) areas, and interdisciplinary teams were formed, with people bringing what they had, in many cases with high personal effort. I was lucky to be part of one of these teams in IETF (with a very modest contribution) and learned a lot from it.

Such technologies have evolved a lot and, still, there are not many people with complete knowledge of the SIP (and Internet Multimedia) technology, including all aspects: from theory, prototyping, and development, to implementation. Rogelio is one of the few people I know with such broad (covering theoretical and practical aspects) and deep knowledge, based on years of work in different managerial positions in the communications area (steering and inspiring key projects in different technology units).

I strongly believe the Multimedia Internet (mainly mobile and ubiquitous) is here to stay. It is starting to happen, and I honestly do not know where it will take us within the next five years, but I dream of a richer instant multimedia communication, making our lives more comfortable, allowing us more time to enjoy the company of our family and friends.

For such dream, I am sure that protocols like SIP are the way forward. But they are nothing without innovative, high quality applications adapted to our (customer) needs (and with a sustainable business model).

This book covers both areas needed to move into my dreams. It covers in depth SIP (and many IP related) protocols and networks and how to develop applications using its full potential. This is the reason I like Rogelio's book and I think it is an excellent guide to any engineer willing to plan, deploy or operate a SIP network and to any developer wishing to build efficient applications making use of the potential of a SIP network.

I am sure you will enjoy reading the book and I hope it helps you to contribute to enrich the Multimedia Mobile Internet world.

Rogier Noldus, Ericsson, Netherlands

When the Internet was developed in the 1970s of the previous century (long before my personal involvement with this technology!), it was targeting data services. Remote users could—in a convenient way according to the standards of that time—share electronic data files, establish simple message exchange sessions or establish machine-to-machine data communication sessions. Even so, the Internet had limited usage and was applied mainly in the academic world and by research institutes. The ARPANET, as the data connection network was known in those days, was gradually replaced by the NSFNET. The main transmission protocol used by NSFNET remained TCP/IP, inherited from the ARPANET. TCP and IP have undergone a number of iterations up to the current TCP v4, IP v4 and IP v6.

Along with the rapid growth of the number of Internet based applications, initially mainly person-to-content applications, emerged the concept of Internet based *communications*. Obviously, all Internet based applications constitute some form of communication. However, this new trend relates rather to person-to-person communication. One prominent example of this is Voice over IP (VOIP) between two Internet users. There are currently a large number of VOIP applications in operation on the public Internet. A current trend is to extend VOIP to include also multimedia, i.e. *Internet multimedia communications*, encompassing voice, video, text etc.

The Session initiation protocol (SIP) was developed by the Internet engineering task force (IETF) as the artery of Internet voice and multimedia communications. SIP is considered the successor of the H.323 protocol which was developed by the ITU-T for similar application.

The third generation partnership project (3GPP) has adopted SIP as the protocol for the IP multimedia system (IMS). This underscores the faith that the industry has in the long-term usability of SIP for multimedia communications. It also gives substance to the expectation that there will be widespread deployment of SIP-based communication for the foreseeable future. Thorough understanding of SIP is therefore quintessential for anyone involved in Internet based multimedia communication such as IMS. It must be emphasized here that *Internet based communication* encompasses the public Internet (e.g. peer-to-peer VOIP), enterprise networks (e.g. IP based office communication) and telecommunications networks (e.g. IMS). SIP and the accompanying media transport protocol RTP, have even found their way in the more traditional architectures like Wireline networks and mobile networks.

The book from Rogelio Martínez, *Internet Multimedia Communications Using SIP*, is an excellent source of information for anybody working in this field. During the period that Rogelio and I were closely involved in the development of architecture of an Internet based communication system, I came to appreciate Rogelio's wealth of knowledge in this field of technology. This book leaves no doubt about that! The book takes the reader through essentials of VOIP and IMS. It has an easy-to-follow step-by-step approach, starting with a brief history of the Internet. When reading chapter 1 of the book, one will almost feel part of the Internet development scene. The reader is then taken gradually from 'plain SIP' to advanced techniques. Brand new topics like Presence, IMS messaging and multimedia conferencing are covered. NAT Traversal, being an important issue when running SIP through border gateways, is extensively described in a separate chapter. Quality of service is traditionally a cornerstone of the telecommunications industry. Developers of Internet based communication systems will therefore gain ample advantage of the dedicated chapter on that topic. User identification and data security are essential to any communication system and are therefore covered in-depth as well. The book shows that there is continuing development in these areas. The reader is further enticed to put theory into practice. This is accomplished through the JAVA based SIP terminal that the reader is invited to build, using the example software code contained in the book. This combination of theory and practice makes the book unique in its class.

This book is an excellent contribution to the Internet communications industry. It not only provides a good explanation of the fundamentals of VOIP and IMS, but it also includes ample references to relevant standards for further reading. This book is therefore strongly recommended to anyone who needs to build up knowledge in this area of technology.

The book further strikes a bridge between the 'old technology' (GSM, Intelligent networks) and the 'new technology' (IMS, SIP). Having worked in the area of GSM and Intelligent networks for a substantial number of years, I appreciate the links that one can draw between well-known techniques and principles from GSM on the one hand and methods applied in the Internet communications on the other hand. Quite appropriately, the book closes with a dedicated chapter on IMS, placing SIP and related techniques in a mobile context and showing the additional challenges that the mobile environment brings. The book is therefore also an ideal guide for professionals who come from a telecommunications background.

PART

Fundamentals

I

CHAPTER

Introduction

1

There is a growing interest, both in the Internet and in the telecommunication industries, in multimedia communication services. An increasing number of Internet users who used to just surf the web or send emails are now becoming addicted to services such as Instant Messaging (IM), online gaming, and voice and video on the Net. These are examples of multimedia communication services delivered over the Internet that are enabled by the Session Initiation Protocol (SIP) in conjunction with other protocols.

In this first introductory chapter, we will explain what we mean by multimedia communication services. We will position these services in the context of the rest of the applications provided over the Internet.

We also want to give the reader a first hint of why SIP plays so crucial a role in the Internet communications space. That will lead us to dive into the importance of the signaling concept. We will underline the relevance of the signaling concept by looking at a very simple example of voice communication.

SIP not only enables voice on the Internet, but also a completely new universe of Total Communication services. To let the reader grasp the possibilities of SIP, we will show some examples of services and commercial products that currently use SIP.

SIP is, like any other Internet protocol, defined and developed by the Internet Engineering Task Force (IETF). More specifically, the core SIP specification is documented in [RFC 3261], and we will be referring throughout this book to this and other Internet specifications. So, in this chapter, we will also try to understand a bit better the SIP-related working groups in the IETF and the specifications they produce.

1.1 IP Multimedia Communication Services

A lot of very different services can be offered on top of the Internet and, in general, on top of an Internet Protocol (IP) network—a network based on the Internet Protocol.[1] It is not at all easy to find a categorization of those services

[1] Internet Protocol and IP networks are reviewed in Chapter 3.

from the user's perspective, but we will try to offer a simple one here, with the purpose of allowing us to understand what the remit of IP multimedia communication services is.

A very high-level approach might split the services offered on the Internet into three different categories or domains from the end-user perspective. A first category might include the infotainment services—that is, those services that give the user access to information and entertainment applications typically stored and executed in remote servers. The web would represent the paradigm for this kind of services. A second category would include the streaming services. These allow the user to access, in real-time, either live or stored time-based media content. Video-on-Demand (VOD) or the hot Internet Protocol Television (IPTV) service would fall into this category. The third service type includes the communication services—that is, those that allow people to communicate with each other using different types of media. A voice call or an email exchange would be examples of communication services (Figure 1.1).

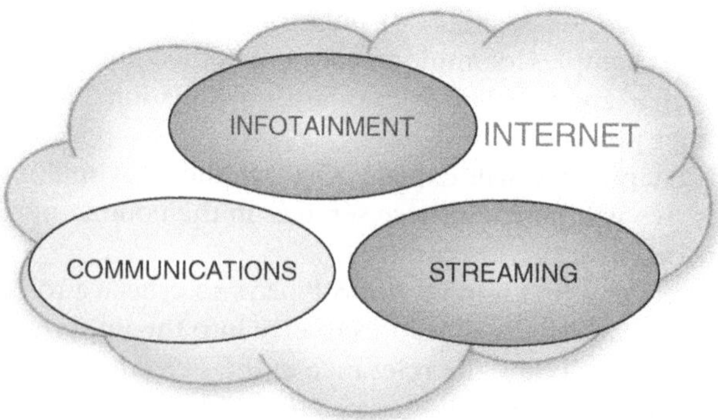

FIGURE 1.1

Communication services can be further classified into offline and online. In online communications, both originator and recipient need to be "connected" simultaneously for communication to happen, and the exchange of information occurs immediately between them. Examples of this include a voice call, an IM exchange, or a chess game.

In offline communication services, the involved parties do not necessarily need to be "connected" simultaneously for communication to happen. The popular email service is a good example of this. In the email service, the submission of information is decoupled from its reception by a store and forward mechanism, so the parties can communicate with each other even if they are not connected at the same time. Let us imagine that John wants to send an email to Alice. He switches on his computer, starts the email program, and sends the message. At that point, John closes the program and switches off his computer. Sometime later, Alice starts her email application and checks if new mail has arrived. She sees John's email and reads it. As we can see, John and Alice do not need to be connected simultaneously for the communication to happen.

The type of information (i.e., media) that can be exchanged in online communication services can be quite diverse. For instance, we might want to exchange real-time media such as voice or video, which have very stringent timing requirements. Packets containing voice samples should be received at regular intervals of some milliseconds so as to allow the receiver to play them back at the appropriate rate.

We might also want to exchange quasi-real-time information—that is, information that has requirements for timely delivery, but not as strong as in the case of voice. An example is an IM session or a chess game. In order to keep the interactivity in the session, data needs to arrive quickly enough—though, in this case, one or two seconds' delay would not impact the end user's experience.

Another type of information that we might want to exchange in online communication services is a prestored image or file. This scenario typically occurs in combination with an exchange of other types of media. Take, for instance, the case of John and Alice, who are engaged in a Voice over Internet Protocol (VoIP) conversation. John is at his 3G (third-generation) IP multimedia-enabled phone. Meanwhile, Alice is sitting at home in front of her PC. While talking to Alice, John takes a picture of a beautiful landscape with the camera integrated into his phone. He decides to show the picture to Alice. The image file would, in this case, be sent online and conveyed immediately to the recipient while both parties are talking so that they can comment on it (Figure 1.2).

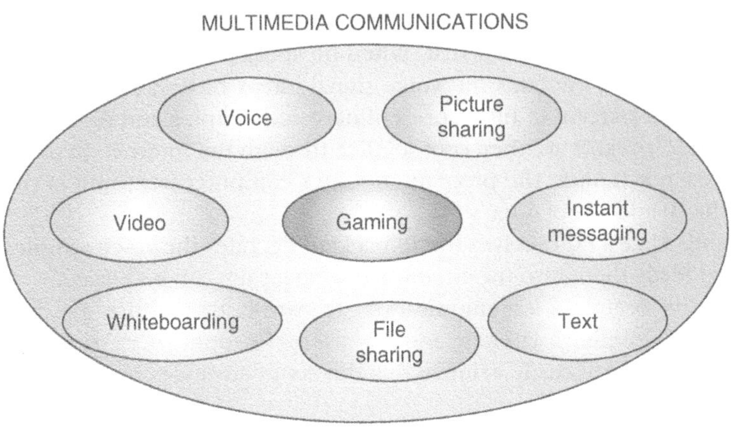

FIGURE 1.2

Online IP communication services are typically referred to as IP multimedia communication services, and that is the term that we will use throughout this book.

Unlike what occurs in other type of services, signaling plays a key role in IP multimedia communication services. SIP is typically used as the application-level signaling protocol in that remit, and therefore its role is crucial.

It is important to understand that SIP has not been designed to replace existing Internet application-level protocols such as those used in web (Hypertext Transfer Protocol, or HTTP) or email (Simple Mail Transfer Protocol, or SMTP; Post

Office Protocol version 3, or POP3; Internet Message Access Protocol version 4, or IMAP4). On the contrary, SIP covers a piece that was originally missing in the Internet architecture—that is, the signaling mechanism for multimedia communication services. SIP was designed in such a way as to fit smoothly with the existing Internet services and protocols such as web or email, so that, when combined with them, the promise of an all-IP total communications system encompassing all type of services can be made a reality.

It is also important to understand that SIP, all by itself, is not capable of delivering multimedia communication services. It needs to work alongside other protocols to accomplish that function. Most importantly, because SIP is a signaling protocol, it needs to work together with other protocols at the media layer.

1.2 The Role of Signaling and Media

In order to get a first understanding of the role of signaling and media protocols in IP multimedia communications, let us start by looking at a very simple example of voice communication on the Internet.

Let us assume that John and Alice, who are both in front of their PCs connected to the Internet, want to have a voice conversation. Each of them has a microphone and a loudspeaker connected to the soundcard in his or her computer. John is running a program such that, when he speaks on the microphone, the soundcard samples and encodes the voice signal into a bitstream. The computer program takes this stream of bits representing voice samples, and puts them into IP packets. These packets are then sent to Alice through the Internet. In order to make the packets reach Alice, the program in John's computer has to fill in the IP packets with the IP address of Alice's PC.

At the other end, Alice's PC receives the IP packets, decodes the voice samples in the payload, and feeds them into the soundcard so that they can be played.

In order for this real-time communication to work, this entire process has to be done with minimal latency, and it has to be done very regularly. Fortunately, PC programs can easily achieve this thanks to advances in computer technology.

In our example, we have considered that the voice samples are carried over IP protocol. Instead of conveying the samples directly over IP, an upper-level protocol is generally used. The information exchanged between the communicating parties (in this case, the voice) is typically referred to as media; thus, these protocols are referred to as media transport protocols. Different media transport protocols are specially suited to the type of media that needs to be conveyed. For instance, if the media is voice, a protocol called RTP (Real-time Transport Protocol) is typically used, which runs on top of User Datagram Protocol (UDP)/IP. RTP contains features that facilitate the transport of pure real-time traffic, such as voice, over IP networks. RTP and other media transport protocols are further described in Chapter 10.

Figure 1.3 depicts the previous example.

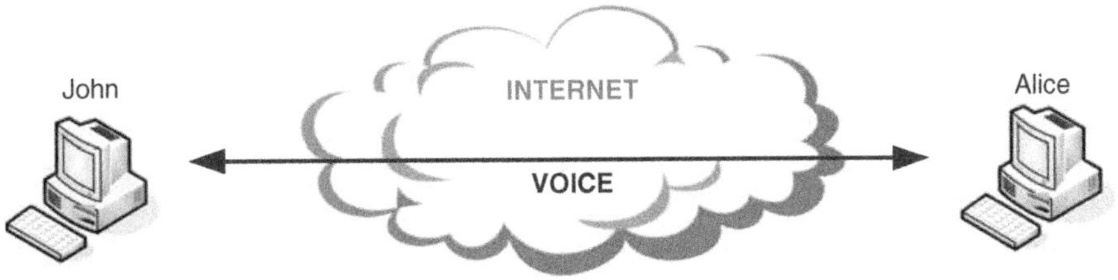

FIGURE 1.3

So we have seen in the example how a simple voice communication might be enabled in the Internet, and we have understood the need for:

- A media transport protocol to carry the real-time user information (media). In our example, we were using RTP to transport voice, but there are also other protocols more suited for other types of traffic.
- An application (computer program) in the endpoints able to:
    - capture the voice samples from the microphone and send them over the network using a media transport protocol; and
    - receive the media transport protocol packets, get the voice samples, and feed them to the soundcard to be played.

Are these two aspects enough, or do we need something more in order to enable fully fledged online communications? In order to answer this question, let us look at some of the additional challenges that the previous scenario presents.

First of all, we were assuming that both John and Alice were already available, prepared, and sitting in front of their PCs at the time communication started. Of course they might have agreed sometime before, through other means, that they both would have this communication at a specific date and time so they could be prepared for it—but that is not really a practical approach. Also, it is not efficient, from the resource-utilization perspective, to have the microphone, the loudspeaker, the soundcard, and software program permanently activated and processing the voice signals in the environment or listening for the voice packets being transmitted in the network. What is needed here is a mechanism by which John can first signal to Alice his desire to start a communication with her. This would be like an invitation signal sent from John's PC to Alice's. When this signal reaches Alice's PC, it would need to trigger some alerting mechanism—for example, a ringing audio signal—that can attract Alice's attention even if she happens not to be in front of the PC at that precise moment. This would be analogous to the ringing of the phone in the traditional, legacy phone system.

Secondly, John may want to be informed about the progress of the communication process. For instance, he may need to know that his invitation went through and that Alice is being alerted. Most importantly, he needs to know when Alice accepts the communication so that he knows when he can start speaking. This event is also very important for the computer program because it will trigger the activation of the necessary resources in the PC (soundcard, IP resources, and so on) just at the precise moment when they will be needed, thus optimizing resource usage.

The third aspect refers to the fact that in order to send voice samples over the network, they first need to be encoded. Likewise, the encoded data needs to be decoded at the receiving end. This coding or decoding process can be done by specialized hardware (the soundcard) or within the communication software running on top of the operating system, which is termed software CODEC (COder/DECoder). In any case, there are quite a few standard ways to code and decode the voice signals, and it is crucial that the codec used in John's PC matches the one used by Alice. Because there may typically be many different codecs installed in both PCs, it is necessary that, prior to starting the voice communication itself, John and Alice agree on the codecs that they will use for this particular communication. In other words, there is the need to agree on some voice-related parameters (e.g., the voice codecs) before communication can start.

The fourth aspect refers to the way addressing is done. In our example, we said John's program needed to add Alice's computer IP address as the destination address in the IP packets that it sent to Alice. This is actually cumbersome because it forces John to learn Alice's IP address as a set of four numbers, each of them ranging from 0 to 255.[2] Most importantly, a true communication system should be available for the user irrespective of his or her actual location (IP address). Alice would expect to be able to use the service from her PC at home connected to the Internet through Asymetric Digital Subscriber Line (ADSL), but also when at the office or, when traveling with her laptop, or with her Internet Multimedia Subsystem (IMS)-enabled mobile phone. The problem is that, as location changes, so does the IP address of the device. So how can we guarantee that Alice will be able to receive the call from John irrespective of her location?

All the aspects highlighted above call for the need to exchange some extra information between John and Alice. This is not actually voice information (media), but rather, information that helps John and Alice to control the way voice communication occurs. This control information is called signaling, and is sent in messages between Alice's and John's computers according to some signaling protocol. SIP is one such signaling protocol that can convey this type of information, but there are also others.

The relevance of signaling in this context is huge—not just in order to cope with the basic call scenarios, but also to enable more-complex multimedia value-added services. Accordingly, SIP plays a major role in making all these new services possible.

So we now have a clearer picture of what a true multimedia communication system requires in terms of information exchanges:

- Exchange of media information (voice or others). This is governed by an media transport protocol such as RTP or others.
- Exchange of control information (signaling). This is governed by a signaling protocol such as SIP or others.

---

[2]For an IPv4 address.

The set of functions and elements that participate in the processing and exchange of the media are said to form the media plane (also called user plane). The set of functions and elements that participate in the processing and exchange of the signaling are said to constitute the Control (or signaling) Plane. Both the media plane and the control plane are integral parts of an IP multimedia communication system.

Figure 1.4 shows the two planes in a multimedia communication.

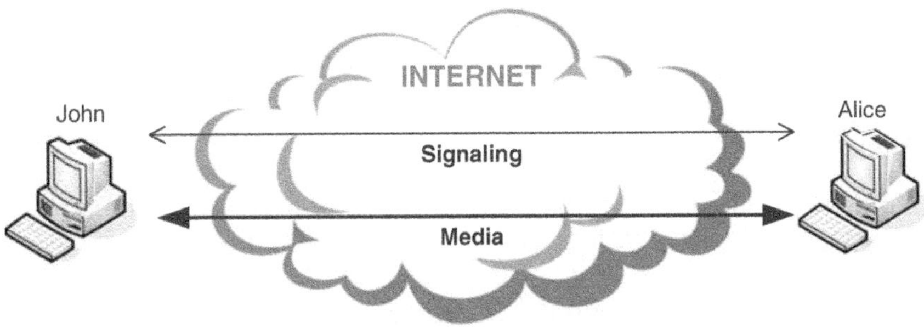

FIGURE 1.4

Both SIP and RTP are IP application-level protocols, meaning that they are sitting on top of the TCP/IP stack, and therefore they use the services provided by transport protocols such as UDP or TCP. Chapter 3 further explains the TCP/IP stack, and shows how the different protocols used in multimedia communications fit with it.

Media and control protocols are independent. For example, in the recent past, a lot of IP multimedia communication systems were using RTP in the media plane. Meanwhile, in the control plane, International Telecommunication Union (ITU) H.323 signaling protocols were used. Today, SIP is becoming commonplace as the signaling protocol in IP networks, and it is very often used with RTP in the media plane. Nevertheless, SIP can also be used with other Media Transport Protocols. For instance, some session-based Instant Messaging systems use SIP as the signaling protocol and Message Session Relay Protocol (MSRP) as the media transport protocol.

The previous example of voice communication between John and Alice was just meant to help the reader grasp the key concepts around signaling, and does not show all the power of SIP-enabled IP communications. More -sophisticated examples might be built with SIP. For example, communication between John and Alice might start out by being just voice, but after some minutes, Alice might want to add video so that she can show John the cake she is preparing for her birthday. At some point in time, they may even want to start playing a chess game through the Internet while they still talk to each other, or they may decide to stop voice communication but exchange real-time text messages while playing chess. Once they stop playing, Alice may want to show John a map of the new house she has recently bought, and write on top of it in order to mark where, for instance, the different rooms are located.

This would be an example of an IP multimedia call. Throughout this book, we will use the term "call" to refer to IP multimedia calls enabled by SIP. Obviously, this call concept is different from the traditional (voice communication only) telephone call that we are all used to. It is not only that the underlying technologies are completely different (the telephone call is supported by the legacy circuit-oriented telephone system, whereas the multimedia call is supported by the Internet), but also that the amount of services and communication experiences that SIP-enabled IP communications can offer does not have a match in the legacy telephone system.

1.3 Type of Services Enabled by SIP

In this section, we intend to give an overview of the different types of services that can be enabled by SIP. The list is not intended to be exhaustive.

1.3.1 Basic Session Management Services

In the previous section, we explained that SIP is a crucial element to provide the main control functions needed in multimedia communication scenarios. So, first of all, SIP can be used to enable communications based on a variety of media, such as:

- *Voice* communication.
- *Video* communication.
- *Instant Messaging* communication: interactive online exchange of (typically short) messages.
- *Text over IP*: exchange of real-time text.
- *Peer-to-peer gaming*: exchange of conversational data in order to implement peer-to-peer games (e.g., a chess game).
- *Whiteboarding*: exchange of conversational data to implement a whiteboard service. In this type of service, each user sees a whiteboard on the screen of their device and can draw or write over it. Changes on the whiteboard made by the users are kept in sync with one another.
- *File transfer*: exchange of peer-to-peer data.

Moreover, SIP provides off-the-self support for combining different type of media on the same communication. All the combinations one can imagine are possible; the most common are:

- *Voice combined with video*, so called video-telephony.
- *Voice combined with IM*: Users can talk to each other while they also exchange messages.
- *Voice combined with real-time text*: Users can talk to each other. For example, at some point in the conversation, one of the parties does not understand the word the other is pronouncing, and asks the other participant to write it and send it in realtime.
- *Voice combined with online transfer of a picture*: The users can share a live picture while they are talking to each other. Imagine Alice and John talking

to each other. At some point in time, Alice tells John about the house she has bought, and sends online a picture to him so they can share it while talking.

- *Voice combined with the online transfer of a generic file.*
- *Voice combined with gaming*: John and Alice can play a chess game while talking to each other.
- *Voice combined with whiteboarding:* Users share a whiteboard while having a voice conversation.

These are just some possible examples; there are many others. As we can see, in most cases, the main media component is voice, but an additional data media is added. These particular scenarios are sometimes referred to as "rich voice."

1.3.2 Enhanced Control Services

SIP signaling, as defined in the core SIP specification [RFC 3261] and its extensions, is a powerful tool to provide new services. SIP and Session Description Protocol (SDP) signaling convey useful information that can be used to provide enhanced services. Next follow some examples (the list is by no means exhaustive):

- *Identification of the originator of a session*: SIP includes information about the identity of the caller that can be presented to the called party. Likewise, SIP also provides the means for the caller to prevent his or her identity from being shown to the recipient.
- *Multimedia identification of the originator*: The originator can include multimedia content in the session initiation request so that it is rendered to the recipient when alerting is done. The multimedia content might consist of a picture, a personalized ringtone, a business card, and so on.
- *A call-blocking* application might decide to block a call based on a combination of different signaling parameters—for example, originator, destination, media type, or other external parameters such as date or time of day.
- *A call-hold* service can very easily be offered with SIP/SDP because SDP already provides the semantics for activating and deactivating the media being sent or received.
- *A call-forwarding* service can also very easily be offered by modifying specific SIP parameters that represent the destination of the call when certain conditions are met (e.g., original recipient does not answer).

The previous examples highlight some of the features that can be offered based on core SIP signaling parameters. These types of services can typically be applied irrespective of the media being exchanged.

SIP also offers a number of primitives that can be used to deliver *call-control* services. These types of services typically involve complex manipulation of the signaling relationships between participants or a more-complex processing of different signaling fields. Examples of these services are:

- *Call transfer*: John and Alice are communicating with each other, and then John decides to transfer the call to Bob so that Alice and Bob can communicate with each other.

- *Hunting groups*: A call to a group number may be distributed according to different algorithms between a set of individuals pertaining to the group.
- *Call queuing*: Calls to a group number can be queued before they are distributed among the agents.
- *Closed-user-group dialing:* Users within a group can use short codes to call each other.
- *Ring back when free*: Call from John to Alice is unsuccessful because Alice is busy with another call. As soon as Alice hangs up, a call is immediately placed back to John.
- *Simultaneous ringing*: Several devices can share the same number and can ring in parallel when someone dials that number.
- *Call pickup*: Two or more users can be part of a group that can pick up each other's calls. For instance, a call is placed to John, who is not currently at his PC. Alice hears his PC ringing and instructs her phone to take John's incoming call.
- *Click to dial*: by pressing a button in a web page, a two-party call is initiated.

A comprehensive list of SIP call-control services is provided in [draft-ietf-sipping-service-examples].

1.3.3 Media Services

Not all the services are delivered just through manipulation of the signaling. In other cases, there is a need for specific functions at the media plane, which are controlled through SIP. Examples of such services are:

- *Voice mail*: Allows users to have their calls redirected to the Voice Mail System (VMS), where the callers can leave their messages. The mailbox owner can later retrieve those messages.
- *Music on hold*: Whenever a user puts another user on hold, the first party can select the music to be played to the other party while waiting.
- *Ringback tones*: The called user can decide what ringback tone the caller will hear during the alerting phase.
- *Do not disturb*: The caller is redirected to specific announcements or menus based on configuration parameters, called-user preferences, and so forth.

1.3.4 Conferencing Services

Conferencing services deserve a separate consideration given their relevance and complexity. In order to provide a fully featured conferencing service, other protocols, in addition to SIP, need to be supported. Still, SIP provides the key call-signaling features.

Examples of conferencing services that can be enabled by SIP are:

- *Multiparty call*: John is in a call with Alice and decides online to join Bob to the conversation.

- *Dial-in conferences*: Participants in the conference just dial a predetermined identifier and are automatically connected to the conference.
- *Dial-out conferences*: Conferencing servers can be configured to start a conference at a specific time and automatically initiate the establishment of the corresponding sessions with all the participants.

1.3.5 Presence

SIP offers the tools for publishing, subscribing, and notifying the information about availability and willingness of users to set up multimedia communications. This feature is particularly useful when used in conjunction with other services such as IM and voice. A typical example of presence-enabled voice service is a multidevice application. It allows the user to have a set of different devices (PC, mobile, laptop, and so on.), all with the same identity. When a call is addressed to the common identity, a presence check could be done in order to determine at what device the user is available and/or willing to take the incoming call. Then the call is routed to the appropriate device.

Moreover, the presence service is typically related to other services that are responsible for managing lists of groups of users (buddy lists). Presence information can typically be transparently shared only within these groups of users. These capabilities allow the development of community-based services.

1.4 Examples of SIP Applications

In order to illustrate the concepts in the previous section, we will describe a few examples of commercial SIP applications that group some of the features previously mentioned.

In the web pages www.pulver.com and www.sipforum.org, the user can find a list of SIP commercial products in different categories:

- Gateways
- Severs
- Firewalls and NATs
- Software components
- Software tools
- Terminals
- PBXs (Private Branch Exchanges)
- Application servers

A list of SIP service providers can be also found at www.pulver.com.

Within the SIP environment, there are a lot of open-source initiatives. We recommend that the reader visit www.sipforum.org, where he or she will be able to find more information on open-source SIP products and components.

1.4.1 SIP Communicator Applications

An SIP communicator is an SIP-based multimedia application hosted in the endpoint (i.e., PC, mobile device, laptop, and so on) that provides the capability to establish communications in different media such as voice, video, messaging, and file sharing—all of them integrated with presence and contact-list management. The typical interface that these applications provide shows a list of contact names. Associated to each contact is typically an icon showing the presence information for that contact. By clicking in a contact, a menu is displayed that asks for the type of communication requested (voice, video, messaging). The user clicks on the desired option, and the application sets up the required media session.

These types of services, though strongly based on the terminals, do frequently also require some back-end infrastructure, for instance, in order to store the presence and contact information.

SIP communicator applications allow for building on the "community" concept, and are becoming increasingly popular across the Internet. Such Internet players as Microsoft and Yahoo! have a significant customer base of SIP-based communicator customers.

Figure 1.5 shows the layout of one example of these applications.

FIGURE 1.5

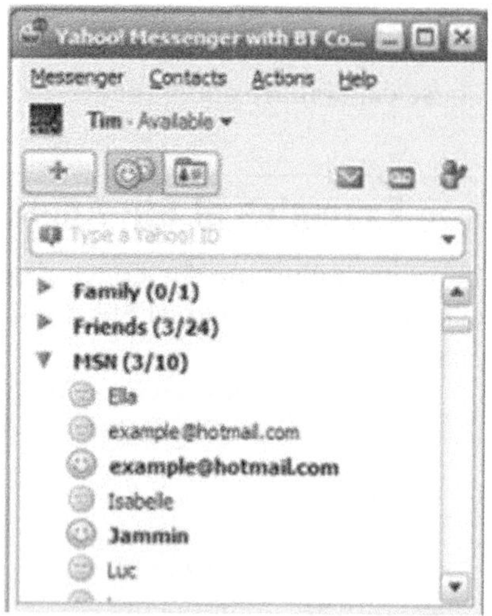

FIGURE 1.6

1.4.2 IP PBX Applications

In the enterprise environment, an alternative to traditional circuit-switched PBXs is becoming increasingly popular: the IP PBX. An IP PBX offers enterprises three main benefits:

- It allows them to converge their voice and data infrastructure over a unique IP network, thus resulting in OPEX (Operational Expenditure) reduction.

- It supports the existing TDM (Time Division Multiplex) PBX services, but adds additional ones, plus the capability to integrate other media components and data services.
- IP PBXs are cheaper, as well as easier to install and maintain, than traditional TDM PBXs.

Initial IP PBXs were not based on SIP, but on protocols such as H.323[3] and SCCP (Skinny Client Control Protocol).[4] Today, SIP IP PBXs are becoming commonplace in the market and are rapidly replacing the legacy PBXs. Big PBX providers that play in this space include Alcatel-Lucent, Avaya, Siemens, and Cisco Systems, although there are also many other smaller companies. Moreover, SIP-based open-source PBX applications are also becoming increasingly popular. The most famous example in this remit is the open-source Asterisk IP PBX (www.asterisk.org).

1.4.3 Enterprise Total Communication Systems

In order to cover enterprise communication needs, voice is a must, but also other applications are becoming increasingly in demand—applications such as IM, video, conferencing, remote control from the PC of the desk phone, and presence. Moreover, there is an increasing demand to integrate this communication infrastructure with existing data applications such as email, text editors, and spreadsheets. In this kind of environment, the user might be writing a document with a text editor and come to a point where he or she needs to discuss something with some colleagues. By clicking on a menu item within the text editor, the user can select two colleagues and ask the application to set up a video conference with them.

Products such as the Microsoft Office Communications Server are becoming increasingly popular in this remit.

1.4.4 IP Centrex Applications

Many companies do not want to bother with managing a PBX infrastructure. They just want to outsource their communication services to a reliable partner. An ideal solution for service providers in these cases is to use IP Centrex (Central Office Exchange Service) applications. These applications are situated within the partners' premises, and an IP network is integrated into the customer's premises for connectivity with IP phones. A typical IP Centrex application can offer PBX-like features to several companies.

Some typical features offered by IP centrex solutions are:

- Calling Line Identification Presentation (CLIP)
- Calling Line Identification Restriction (CLIR)
- Call forwarding
- Call blocking

---

[3]H.323 is an umbrella specification from the ITU (International Telecommunication Union) that defines protocols to provide packet-based multimedia services, originally targeted more toward a LAN environment.

[4]SCCP is a proprietary terminal-control protocol owned by Cisco Systems, Inc.

- Call return
- Call pickup
- Call hold
- Call park
- Music on hold
- Hunt groups
- Closed user groups
- Conferencing
- Call transfer
- Dual ringing
- Barge in
- Call toggle

Vendors such as BroadSoft, Sylantro Systems, and Netcentrex (which was acquired by Converse Converged IP Communications) have popular products in this space.

1.4.5 PSTN Emulation Applications

The evolution of the Public Switched Telephone Network (PSTN) implies changing to an SIP network infrastructure. In order to leverage the full power of SIP, intelligent terminals are needed with full SIP capability. However, this is not yet a reality in the fixed operators' environment. While this happens, some operators are starting to change their network infrastructure toward an SIP-based one while still not changing the end-user terminal and access. In this scenario, there is a need to offer the basic PSTN services (call forwarding, CLIR,[5] CLIP,[6] and so on) on the new SIP infrastructure. This is typically referred as PSTN emulation services.

1.5 The Internet Engineering Task Force (IETF)

According to [RFC 3233], the IETF is an "open global community of network designers, operators, vendors, and researchers producing technical specifications for the evolution of the Internet architecture and the smooth operation of the Internet." The IETF is the main body responsible for defining Internet standards.

The IETF is formally an activity that falls under the umbrella of the Internet Society (ISOC). The society is an international nonprofit organization with individual and corporate members all around the world whose aim is to promote Internet use and access. Among other things, the ISOC provides insurance service and some financial and logistical support to the IETF.

The IETF is organized into eight study areas. These are:

- Applications
- General

[5]CLIP is a PSTN service that allows the called party to know the identity of the caller.
[6]CLIR is a PSTN service that allows the calling party to hide his or her identity from the called party.

- Internet
- Operations and management
- Real-time applications and infrastructure
- Routing
- Security
- Transport

The study areas are broken down into Working Groups (WGs). Each WG focuses on a specific topic, and is intended to complete work on that topic and then shut down. Most of a WG's work is done via email. Anyone can participate in an IETF Working Group, and decisions are made by rough consensus.

The Internet Standards process is defined in [RFC 2026].

1.5.1 The IETF Publications: RFCs and I-Ds

There are two types of IETF publications: Requests for Comments (RFCs) and Internet Drafts (I-Ds). The RFC series contains the Internet specifications, whereas Internet Drafts are just draft specifications made available for informal review and comment—an I-D may or may not become a RFC. There are three types of RFCs: Standards Track, non-Standards Track, and Best Current Practice (BCP). Every RFC has a unique number and is stored permanently at the IETF web site: http://www.ietf.org.

Standards Track RFCs

This category of RFCs includes those specifications that are intended to become Internet Standards. In the process of becoming an Internet Standard, these RFCs evolve through a set of maturity levels known as the Standards Track. These maturity levels are proposed standard, draft standard, and standard.

When a specification in a Working Group becomes stable, it turns into a proposed standard RFC for which a number is assigned. Proposed standard is the entry maturity level into the Standards Track. In addition to being stable, "a proposed standard has to be well-understood, must have received significant review, and must enjoy enough community interest."

Proposed standards must remain in that level for at least six months before they become draft standards. In order for a RFC to become a draft standard, it must have at least two interoperable implementations with sufficient operational experience. An RFC that becomes a draft standard is assigned a new RFC number. The old RFC is not deleted from the RFC series, but it is made clear that the old RFC has been made obsolete by a new RFC. An example would be the SIP specification. It was first published as a draft standard in RFC 2543, which then was made obsolete by RFC 3261, which has, at the time of this writing, the status of proposed standard. Both of them can be found in the IETF directory for RFCs: http://www.ietf.org/rfc.html.

Draft standards must remain in that level for at least four months, and at least one IETF meeting has to be held before the draft can become an Internet Standard. If the specification has achieved a very high maturity level and has obtained significant implementation and successful operational experience, it may become an Internet Standard.

Internet Standards are published in the STD series, but they also retain their RFC number. For instance, the Real-time Transport Protocol (RTP) is Internet Standard STD 64 and [RFC 3550].

Non–Standards Track RFCs

Non–Standards Track RFCs do not define a standard in any sense. These specifications can be further classified into "Experimental," "Informational," and "Historic."

Experimental specifications contain the conclusions and the experiences of some research-and-development (R&D) effort.

Informational specifications contain general information for the Internet community. They do not represent an Internet community consensus or recommendation.

The term "Historic" applies to those specifications that have been superseded by a more recent one or that are considered to be obsolete for any other reason.

Best Current Practice RFCs

BCP RFCs standardize practices and the results of community deliberations. BCP RFCs are subject to the same basic set of procedures as Standards Track documents, but do not have maturity levels. BCP RFCs are published in the BCP series, but they also retain their RFC number. For instance, the IETF specification "SIP Basic Call Flow Examples" is [RFC 3665] and also BCP 75.

Internet Drafts (I-Ds)

Internet Drafts are draft versions of specifications that are under development. These draft specifications may or may not become RFCs. Internet drafts represent the current status of work and discussion within a Working Group regarding a particular topic. The IETF makes them public so as to obtain informal review and comments.

An Internet draft is valid for only six months. After that time, it either becomes an RFC, a new version of the draft is generated, or it is deleted.

Internet drafts are named using the following format: draft-ietf-working group-title-xx, where xx is the version of the draft starting from 00. For example, the Internet draft from the SIPPING WG called "Session Initiation Protocol Call Control - Transfer" is named draft-ietf-sipping-cc-transfer-07.

The IETF recommends that Internet drafts are referred to simply as "work in progress."

1.5.2 SIP in the IETF

Work on SIP in the IETF started in the MMUSIC Working Group, which produced RFC 2543 in March 1999. In September of that year, a new SIP Working Group was created. Later, that group was further split into two Working Groups: the SIP WG and the SIPPING WG.

The SIP WG is devoted to the SIP core protocol and its extensions, whereas the SIPPING WG is more focused on investigating new SIP applications and setting requirements for new SIP extensions.

In June 2002, the SIP WG published RFC 3261, which revises RFC 2543. It is mostly backward compatible with RFC 2543. RFC 3261 adds some modifications, and presents the protocol in a much cleaner layered approach. This book uses RFC 3261 (not RFC 2543) as the source of information for SIP.

Next follows a list that includes some of the working groups that, at the time of this writing, are to some extent related to SIP and multimedia communications.

SIP WG

The Session Initiation Protocol (SIP) Working Group is chartered to maintain and continue the development of SIP, currently specified as proposed standard RFC 3261, and its family of extensions

SIPPING WG

The Session Initiation Protocol Project INvestiGation (SIPPING) Working Group is chartered to document the use of SIP for several applications related to telephony and multimedia, and to develop requirements for extensions to SIP needed for those applications.

MMUSIC WG

The Multiparty MUltimedia SessIon Control (MMUSIC) Working Group was originally chartered to develop protocols to support Internet teleconferencing and multimedia communications. It produced the first SIP specification as RFC 2543. After that, responsibility for the SIP specification was moved to the SIP Working Group. The SIP WG created RFC 3261, which renders RFC 2543 obsolete.

Among other things, the MMUSIC WG is now responsible for maintaining and continuing the development on the Session Description Protocol (SDP), currently specified as proposed standard [RFC 4566].

SIMPLE WG

The SIP Instant Messaging and Presence Leveraging Extensions (SIMPLE) Working Group focuses on the application of the Session Initiation Protocol to the suite of services collectively known as Instant Messaging and Presence (IMP).

ENUM WG

The TElephone NUmber Mapping (ENUM) Working Group has defined a DNS[7]-based architecture and protocol [RFC 3761] by which a telephone number[8] can be expressed as a Fully Qualified Domain Name (FQDN)[9] in a defined Internet domain (e164.arpa).

---

[7] DNS is an Internet system that is used to associate several types of information (e.g., IP addresses) with meaningful high-level names (so-called domain names).

[8] Telephone number as defined in ITU Recommendation [E.164].

[9] FQDN is an unambiguous domain name for an entity within the Domain Name System.

IPTEL WG

The focus of the IP Telephony (IPTEL) Working Group is on the problems related to naming and routing for Voice over Internet Protocol (VoIP) protocols. In particular, this Working Group is responsible for [RFC 3966], which defines the tel URI format for telephone numbers.

AVT WG

The Audio/Video Transport (AVT) Working Group was formed to specify a protocol for real-time transmission of audio and video UDP/IP. In particular, this Working Group is responsible for [RFC 3550], which corresponds to Internet standard STD 64 and defines the Real-time Transport Protocol (RTP).

1.6 Summary

We have, in this chapter, understood what multimedia communications are and the role that SIP plays in this remit. We also looked at some examples of services that might be delivered through SIP. The way SIP and related protocols work is defined in Internet specifications generated by the IETF. We also learned a bit about how the IETF is organized and the types of documents that it generates. In the next chapter, we will review the past history of multimedia services in the Internet. As happens in other areas of knowledge, understanding the history can help us understand why things are as they are today.

CHAPTER

A Bit of History

2

The Internet's origins stretch back to the late 1960s, when the Advanced Research Projects Agency of the U.S. Department of Defense funded a project for the investigation of packet-switching[1] technologies. This gave birth to the ARPANET (Advanced Research Projects Agency Network), one of the first packet-switched networks ever. This chapter overviews the history of the Internet, explains how SIP (Session Initiation Protocol) was born, and positions it in the historical context of other technologies that have also been used to deliver real-time IP (Internet Protocol) communication services. We will also explain how SIP popularity and acceptance is growing, and how it is revolutionizing not only the Internet environment, but also the traditional telecommunications landscape.

2.1 The Third Revolution in the Internet

Unknown to the majority of the world, on August 30, 1969, several dozen of researchers, engineers, and students at UCLA managed to send the first bits of information between an SDS Sigma 7 computer acting as a host and a Honeywell DDP-516 acting as an IMP (Interface Message Processor). The IMP was the first node of the ARPANET, the network that would later become the Internet. At the time, little did these pioneers realize that they were giving birth to a reality that would change the lives of millions of people and become one of the most relevant sociological phenomena of the end of the 20th century and beginning of the third millennium.

At the very beginning, ARPANET was conceived as a tool for resource sharing among scientists and researchers, and the first nodes of the network were deployed in universities. However, it soon became apparent that the nature of the traffic was different from what ARPA (which funded the project) had expected. The scientists in the network were using it predominantly for personal communication via electronic messages. In 1972, Ray Tomlinson, an engineer at

[1]Packet switching is a communication paradigm by which different data traffics are divided into packets and sent over the same data link. This is as opposed to circuit switching, where a physical circuit is established prior to transmission of traffic and is not shared by other communications.

Bolt Beranek and Newman (today known as BBN Technologies),[2] wrote the first email program. Tomlinson is regarded as the inventor of email. He designed an addressing format that required a symbol in order to separate the name and the location of the computer of the recipient. When trying to discern what the best choice was for such a symbol, Tomlinson looked at the keyboard in front of him and came up with a quick decision: "The one that was most obvious was the @ sign, because this person was @ this other computer," he later explained. "At the time, there was nobody with an @ sign in their name that I was aware of."

By 1978, 75% of the ARPANET traffic was email and when ARPANET became Internet at the beginning of the 1980s with the adoption of the TCP/IP protocol suite, email became popular even among nonscientists. The first TCP/IP-based email protocol standard, SMTP (Simple Mail Transfer Protocol), which was instrumental to the success of email, was published in 1981. It is still in use today.

Email was the first revolution within the Net, and it is a revolution whose effects have stretched to the present day.

The second revolution in the Internet started in 1990, when Tim Berners-Lee, a British physicist working at the CERN (European Organization for Nuclear Research) facility near Geneva, Switzerland, conceived the World Wide Web (WWW), an application running on top of TCP/IP. Before that, the Internet provided only screens full of text—and not in a very aesthetic way.

The Web was made out of four key building blocks:

- the URL (Uniform Resource Locator), a standard addressing scheme to name sites and resources in the Internet.
- HTML (Hypertext Markup Language), a standard language that allowed pages to display different fonts and sizes, pictures, colors, and so on.
- HTTP (Hypertext Transfer Protocol), the protocol that defined the set of rules governing the delivery of the files.
- the hypertext concept, which allowed the creation of multiple paths for exploration by enabling the embedding, in each file, of automatic links or references to other files.

It was actually this last concept that gave the web its name. As Berners-Lee said, "There was a power in arranging ideas in an unconstrained, web-like way."

In fact, though the web revolution started in 1990, it truly materialized three years later, when Marc Andreessen and Eric Bina created a program called Mosaic, which made web browsing very easy and graphically intuitive. Also in 1993, CERN declared that they would claim no fees for the use of the technology. This proved to be a visionary decision—by 1994, there were a million browser copies in use.

That year signaled the beginning of the Internet era. From that timeonward, the Internet has experienced a massive growth, the likes of which had never been seen before.

Soon huge amounts of information started to move to servers. Initially, people used the web just to display information—but then came the search engines,

[2]A Massachussets-based technology company, Bolt Beranek and Newman was involved in the development of ARPANET.

followed by applications such as online shopping. Yahoo! and Amazon started in 1994, and Google in 1998.

In 1994, the web grew by an incredible 2,300 percent. By 1998, there already existed 750,000 commercial sites. From then, the Internet started to change people's lives—the way they worked, communicated, managed their bank accounts, bought cinema tickets, arranged trips, looked for jobs, enjoyed themselves, went to the supermarket, just to name a few examples. And even today, with the advent of Web 2.0, a new cultural shift around the web is being materialized. Web-based communities and social networking sites are positioning end users as key players in the generation of content. The new environment based on collaboration and sharing of information between end users is boosting innovation on the web. The web revolution was the second Internet revolution.

By that time, Vinton Cerf, one of the Internet's principal designers, said: "Revolutions like this don't come along very often." However, the third Internet revolution was already being conceived. In December 1996, the first Internet Draft (I-D) of the Session Initiation Protocol (SIP)—authored by Mark Handley, Henning Schulzrinne, and Eve Schooler—was submitted to the IETF in San Jose, California. SIP was conceived as a signaling protocol for inviting users to multimedia conferences. With this, the third Internet revolution silently started. This was the revolution that would end up converting the Internet into a Total Communications system that would allow people to talk to each other, see each other, work collaboratively, or send messages in real-time. Internet telephony and, in general, Internet multimedia, is the new revolution today, and SIP is, behind the scenes, the key protocol that is materializing this revolution.

In the same way that SMTP and HTTP made Internet email and the web, respectively, possible, so SIP is also the key enabler for the new era of Internet multimedia. Before SIP, multimedia transmission on IP networks was already a reality; however, SIP brought all the power of the signaling concept to IP networks in order to enhance the multimedia communications experience. To quote Vinton Cerf again: "SIP is probably the third great protocol of the Internet, after TCP/IP and HTTP."

2.2 The Next Revolution in the Telecommunication Industry

One of the interesting things about the SIP standard and Internet multimedia ideas is that the revolution that they entail is even more far-fetched than the previous ones. It is not only changing the way people use the Internet, but is also driving the evolution of the telecommunications industry. The concepts behind Internet multimedia and SIP are revolutionizing the traditionally closed telecom environment.

From their inception, the telecommunication networks (e.g., the PSTN,[3] or Public Switched Telephone Network) were designed to carry primarily voice. When data standards were born, different data networks, such as X.25 and frame

[3]PSTN refers to the legacy circuit-switched telephone network.

relay, were deployed alongside those already existing for voice. This led to the telecommunication operators having to design, deploy, and maintain separate networks for voice and for data. In the same way, the end users needed separate infrastructures for accessing each of these disparate networks.

A first attempt to provide a converged (voice and data) access for the end user came with the ISDN (Integrated Services Digital Network), which, in addition, brought forward the digitalization of the telephone network. The ISDN never became widespread, and the new applications that it provided, such as videotelephony, never gained extensive adoption. Interestingly enough, at the end of the 1990s, ISDN technology did raise some interest, but as a mere access method to the Internet.

In the early 1990s, the GSM (Global System for Mobile communications)[4] standard was introduced. GSM was based extensively on ISDN and used circuit switching. This had a tremendous success that continues to this day. In some western European countries, mobile subscriptions now exceed the number of fixed lines. Thanks to GSM, mobile telephony has changed our lives and has become a sociological phenomenon—most people think of the mobile phone as an indispensable element in their lives. The flourishing business within the GSM industry has driven the evolution of mobile technology significantly faster than that of the fixed networks. In order to demonstrate this statement, the reader need only compare the GSM terminals of 1992 with the fancy smart phones of today, which feature a number of technologies such as GSM, GPRS (General Packet Radio Service),[5] UMTS (Universal Mobile Telecommunications System),[6] XHTML (Extensible Hypertext Markup Language), MMS (Multimedia Messaging Service), WLAN (Wireless Local Area Network), Bluetooth, MP3, and IMS (Internet Multimedia Subsystem). In no other field of engineering has such a huge technological leap taken place in such a short period as in the technology for the mobile terminals.

Following GSM, a number of technological advances have occurred in the remit of mobile networks, such as GPRS and UMTS. With UMTS, the so-called third generation of mobile networks, we have seen a number of significant improvements—for example, an important increase of bandwidth in the radio access through the utilization of CDMA (Code Division Multiple Access)[7] techniques or the adoption of a converged packet-switched network to converge the transport of both voice and data traffic through the UMTS Release 4 split architecture. The UMTS Release 4 architecture for the core network moves away from the circuit-switched technology that GSM embraced, and adopts the convergence ideas based on a packet-switched backbone.

As important a step as this may be, it does not represent a revolution, but rather, an evolution where the fundamental concepts regarding central intelligence

---

[4]GSM is the most popular standard in the world for second-generation mobile-phone systems.

[5]GPRS is a packet-based (as opposed to circuit-based) mobile data service.

[6]UMTS is a third-generation mobile system that uses CDMA radio technology and an evolved GSM core network.

[7]CDMA is a radio technology that uses spread-spectrum techniques and is characterized by its high capacity.

in the network and coupling between call-control signaling and media description still remain mostly unchanged. From PSTN to ISDN, from ISDN to GSM, and from GSM to UMTS Release 4, the paradigm continued to be basically the same, and the new network was always designed with the clear objective of smoothing the integration with the existing one. With UMTS Release 5, which includes the IMS, this trend is broken, and a true revolution ensues. The IMS is designed with the Internet paradigm in mind, and its objective is to bring the Internet flexibility for delivering multimedia services into the mobile handsets. It is believed that by merging the two most successful technologies of the past 15 years, synergies will be created and the amount of business greatly increased. Moreover, 3GPP (3rd Generation Partnership Project), the standardization body behind UMTS and IMS, took the design decision to base the IMS architecture around the SIP structure, and it is impossible to understand the next-generation IP multimedia networks without understanding what functionality SIP provides. Thus the new IMS telecommunication network no longer resembles the previous telecom networks, but now resembles the Internet, and uses SIP as the basis for that convergence!

Meanwhile, what about the fixed-operator networks? Several attempts to evolve their fixed networks into the packet-switched domain, such as the ATM (Asynchronous Transfer Mode)[8]-based B-ISDN (Broadband Integrated Services Digital Network),[9] have failed ostentatiously. These approaches still attempted to use the paradigm of old telecom networks even though they were using a packet-based transport. In 2005, the ITU (International Telecommunication Union) declared the principles for the NGN (Next Generation Network), embracing the end-to-end IP connectivity and the Internet principles [ITU Y.2001] and [ITU Y.2011]. Today, ETSI (European Telecommunications Standards Institute), after merging the TIPHON (Telecommunications and Internet Protocol Harmonization Over Networks) and SPAN (Services and Protocols for Advanced Networks) Working Groups and creating the TISPAN (Telecoms and Internet converged Services and Protocols for Advanced Networks) group, is materializing the NGN concept. As it happens, Release 1 of the TISPAN NGN architecture has already been published, and is based largely on the IMS core network as defined by 3GPP. Thus, also in the remit of fixed networks, we see SIP being adopted as the base protocol and the architecture for delivering the next-generation multimedia services, but also for replacing the still-existing PSTN (in the so-called ETSI TISPAN PSTN emulation approach).

Summarizing, SIP was not created to evolve the telecom networks nor to make them converge. SIP was born in a pure Internet environment—at the beginning, mainly as a medium to invite users to participate in multimedia conferences. However, SIP has evolved, and what we are seeing today is not only how SIP is revolutionizing the Internet, but also how SIP is about to change for all time the old telecom environment.

---

[8]ATM is a connection-oriented packet-switching technology that encodes data traffic into small cells of a fixed size.

[9]B-ISDN was conceived as a logical evolution of the ISDN to offer broadband end-to-end circuit-oriented services.

2.3 A Brief History of Internet Multimedia

The recent adoption of the Voice over Internet Protocol (VoIP) technology in the Internet by the mass market might lead many people to believe that the technology that allows the transmission of voice on packet-based networks is relatively new. That is, however, not the case.

Soon after the birth of ARPANET in 1969, several students and researchers who were already familiar with the tools to transmit text and data on that network started to explore the possibility of using it to carry real-time voice. In August 1974, the first real-time packet voice transmission was demonstrated in ARPANET between the University of Southern California (USC) and the Massachussets Institute of Technology (MIT). This was not yet "Voice over IP" because the Internet Protocol (IP) had not yet been invented; however, these experiments demonstrated that voice communication over packet networks was feasible. The protocol used for this experiment was called NVP (Network Voice Protocol), and was built on top of the protocol that ARPANET used by that time, which was known as "BBN Report 1822." The NVP specification would later, in 1977, become [RFC741].

More experiments of this sort followed during the rest of the 1970s between universities connected to ARPANET in the United States. In 1978, the first intercontinental experiment of Voice over Packet (VoP) networks was conducted between the United States, the United Kingdom, and Norway. Also by that time, the first patents were granted in connection with this technology. Although these experiments were successful, they gave birth to no product that might be widely used.

During the 1980s, ARPANET became Internet, and workstations increased their processing power so as to allow voice transmission between two workstations connected to the Net. Researchers at universities created a number of tools for Internet telephony; however, these tools were never widespread. At the time, few people had access to workstations connected to the Internet, and the tools were too difficult to use. On top of that, the Internet of the 1980s did not yet have the necessary capacity (the web revolution had not yet occurred), and voice quality was an issue.

By the beginning of the next decade, things started to change. New tools were released: the VAT (Visual Audio Tool), VT (Voice Terminal), and VTALK. VAT was using version 0 of a protocol, RTP (Real-time Transport Protocol), that would later become the standard for voice and video transport on IP networks. And in 1991, the first audiocast in MBone (Multicast Backbone)[10] took place in San Diego, California.

From then onward, the experiments in MBone helped to improve RTP, a new version of which, version 1, was produced with the appearance of the first drafts in the IETF AVT Working Group.

At that time, the web revolution (with the release of Mosaic), together with the commercialization of the Internet and the creation of new ISPs (Internet Service

[10]The MBone was an experimental virtual network for IP multicast traffic over the Internet.

Providers), made the Internet more and more popular and increased the capacity of the Net. This was crucial for the success of Internet telephony because in order to obtain acceptable voice quality in packet networks, these must have excess capacity.[11] Another key enabling factor for the take-up of Internet telephony was the growth in the processing power of PCs and the proliferation of multimedia-enabled PCs and high-speed modems.

A key year in the history of Internet telephony was 1995. Before that time, no commercial product had really yet appealed to the market, but in 1995, more than a dozen commercial products were released. The first of these was the "Internet Phone," released by the Israeli company VocalTec in March 1995. In less than one year, more than 600,000 downloads of VocalTec's trial software took place. Ordinary people started to believe that the Internet could also be used to provide real-time voice calls with acceptable sound quality. Other products were Maven, CU-SeeMe, and or Netphone.

In the remit of the IETF, 1995 saw version 2 of the RTP specification become RFC 1889. Also in 1995, Eve Schooler developed the Multimedia Conference Control (MMCC), a tool that provided point-to-point and multipoint teleconferences, including audio, video, and whiteboarding. Three years before, in 1992, Thierry Turletti had developed the INRIA Videoconferencing System (IVS). It was a software system for audio- and videoconferencing on the Internet, and incorporated PCM (Pulse-Code Modulation), ADPCM (Adaptive Differential Pulse-Code Modulation), and H.261 software-based codecs.

These first multimedia systems gave way to the design of the first version of the Session Invitation Protocol (SIPv1) by Mark Handley and Eve Schooler, in February 1996. By that time, the ideas around Internet multimedia were becoming clear with the growing usage of MBone, and new protocols were being defined. One particular bit that was still missing was a mechanism to invite people to participate in an MBone session. In MBone, if som one wanted to know what conferences would be multicast on a particular day, there already existed the SAP (Session Announcement Protocol) [RFC 2974], which announced the sessions (one could compare it with a TV program guide). However, if someone was listening to an interesting videoconference in the MBone and wanted to invite a friend, there was no mechanism for doing that. That was, really, the original purpose of the Session Invitation Protocol (hence the name) when it was submitted to the IETF in 1996.

On February 22, 1996, Henning Schulzrinne submitted an I-D to the IETF specifying the Simple Conference Invitation Protocol (SCIP), which was also conceived as a mechanism for inviting users to point-to-point and multicast sessions.

At the 35th IETF meeting in Los Angeles, it was decided to merge the two protocols into a new protocol—one that kept the SIP acronym, but now stood for Session Initiation Protocol. Also, the second version of the protocol, SIPv2—co-authored by Hanley, Schulzrinne, and Schooler—was submitted to the IETF at the 37th meeting in December 1996.

---

[11] As opposed to what happens in circuit-switched networks, where a congested network prevents the user from establishing new calls, the Internet of the time did not reject any call in congested situations, although the voice quality diminished dramatically.

That same year, another relevant event took place. The first version of H.323 was released by the ITU. H.323 was meant to be a packet-based, LAN-only standard for audiovisual conferences. Unlike SIP, which was quite limited in scope and followed from the very beginning the Internet principles and ideas, H.323 had a very big scope and took a lot of ideas from existing ITU protocols from the ISDN remit, which resulted in unnecessary heaviness.

One area where the International Telecommunication Union adopted the Internet Standards was in the transport protocols, where the ITU embraced IETF RTP within the H.323 framework.

In the years from 1996 to 2000, several important things occurred. First of all, interest in H.323 grew, especially after VocalTec and Cisco founded the Voice Over IP Forum in order to set the standards for VoIP products. The industry tried to tune H.323 v1 into the specificities of the most popular WAN (Wide Area Network) environment: the Internet. In February 1998, version 2 of H.323, now renamed Packet-Based Multimedia Communications Systems, was approved by the ITU.

In the meantime, in the IETF, the multimedia concepts on the Internet were well understood, and work started at the same time to extend the Internet multimedia architecture for use in telephony—and, by doing so, to re-engineer the telephone system. Due to the enormous complexity and richness of the voice services on the PSTN, this was not an easy job. It was not until the end of 2000 that this matter was well understood. The years from 1997 to 2000 saw new SIP drafts being submitted before March 17, 1999, when it became a proposed standard and was published as RFC 2543 in the remit of the MMUSIC Working Group. In addition to the SIP specification itself, many other drafts were published during this period. These drafts were aimed at extending SIP in order to address many of the voice services that were already present in the PSTN, and also new ideas such as presence, Instant Messaging (IM), and so on.

By 2000, it was clear to the research and academic community that "H.323-based VoIP networks could not deliver the IP telephony service on a par with feature rich existing networks" [draft-tiphon-background]. On the other hand, interest in SIP was growing, especially when the 3GPP adopted SIP as the main protocol for the establishment of multimedia sessions within the IMS. According to the first version of 3GPP TS 22.228, which set up the requirements for the new IMS concept:

> *IP has opened up a whole range of communication applications, which may allow service providers to develop totally new value added applications as well as to enhance their existing solutions. The open architecture and platforms supported by IP and operating systems may lead to applications and new opportunities that are more difficult to replicate using a standard switched centralized solution.*

From then, SIP has grown considerably, evolving from the initial MMUSIC Working Group. Two additional WGs devoted to SIP have been created in IETF (SIP and SIPPING). In June 2002, a revised version of the standard was published as RFC 3261 by the SIP WG. Since then, the SIP capabilities have been expanded to incorporate not only voice and video, but also presence, IM, data sharing, and so forth, so that SIP has become the key IP signaling protocol for enabling a true real-time peer-to-peer total communications experience for end users.

A completely new paradigm for VoIP, different from H.323 and SIP, was born in 1999, when some new and incumbent carriers declared their urgent need to converge their voice and data infrastructure. The industry response was the IETF MGCP (Media Gateway Control Protocol), later to become the IETF and ITU MEGACO (Media Gateway Control). MEGACO gave birth to the concept of the call server, which has now been implemented in the networks of quite a few operators.

Whereas H.323 is already considered legacy, and SIP clearly represents the future-proof approach that is already a reality today, the MEGACO concepts have found their way into some interim architectures—for example, the 3GPP R4 core network split architecture conceived as an evolution of the circuit-switched domain for GSM/UMTS operators.

Already in 2007, there are millions of Internet users subscribed to SIP-based VoIP or messaging services. Very popular communicator applications such as Microsoft's or Yahoo!'s are based on the Session Initiation Protocol, and software providers are clearly betting on SIP. Also, most companies are looking into this protocol in order to cover their enterprise communication needs—not only voice, but also video, presence, IM, whiteboarding, and so on. Moreover, open-source initiatives in the SIP domain have been extremely successful—for example, the Asterisk IP PBX (Private Branch Exchange), which is being adopted by more and more corporate customers every year.

What's more, the traditional fixed-network providers are now starting to move toward SIP in order to offer their corporate and residential customers advanced services at the same time that they pave the way for the PSTN replacement.

Even though starting with VoIP and IM, SIP is advancing at a rapid pace in order to deliver the promise of unified IP communications.

2.4 Summary

This review of the past history of Internet and multimedia communications has allowed us to better comprehend the state of today's technology. Now our focus will turn toward the technology itself. In the next chapter, we will try to give the reader the global picture of multimedia communications, highlighting the different Internet Protocols that contribute to making it possible. This will set the scene for the rest of the book.

CHAPTER

3 IP Multimedia Fundamentals

IP multimedia communication services are built on top of the TCP/IP (Transmission Control Protocol/Internet Protocol) protocol suite. In this chapter, we will briefly review the fundamental concepts around IP networks and the TCP/IP protocols. After that, we will describe the architecture and the application-level Internet protocols that have been defined to enable multimedia communications. It is crucial to understand that SIP (Session Initiation Protocol) is not the only protocol involved in delivering multimedia communication services. It is just one additional component, though fundamental, in the whole architecture.

For a comprehensive description of the TCP/IP protocol suite, I recommend the excellent *Internetworking with TCP/IP, Volume 1* by Douglas E. Comer.

3.1 Internet Concepts

The core of the internetworking (or "internet") concept is that of being able to provide end-to-end connectivity on top of a variety of underlying network technologies. The tool to accomplish this concept is the Internet Protocol. The IP protocol provides a homogeneous network layer that enables the interconnection of many different types of networks while at the same time hiding the details of these networks to the applications above. The networks below can support a variety of technologies such as Ethernet, ATM (Asynchronous Transfer Mode), frame relay, and PSTN (Public Switched Telephone Network). It is interesting to note that no internal change is required in each of these physical networks for them to be part of an internet[1] (this was a ground rule in the early design of the Internet back in the early 1970s).

Figure 3.1 shows an internet composed of three different physical networks that are interconnected through IP routers (R). Routers help to route the packets from source to destination. The end systems are called hosts (H). Hosts are the entities where the end-user applications reside. They are connected to the network through

[1]Throughout this book, the term "internet" (with the first letter in lowercase) is used to refer to a collection of interconnected networks using the IP protocol. On the other hand, the term "Internet" (with the first letter in uppercase) refers to the well-known network, which represents a global instantiation of the internetworking (or internet) concept.

interfaces that are identified by an IP address. The IP address is the main parameter in the IP protocol, which is used for routing datagrams to their destination.

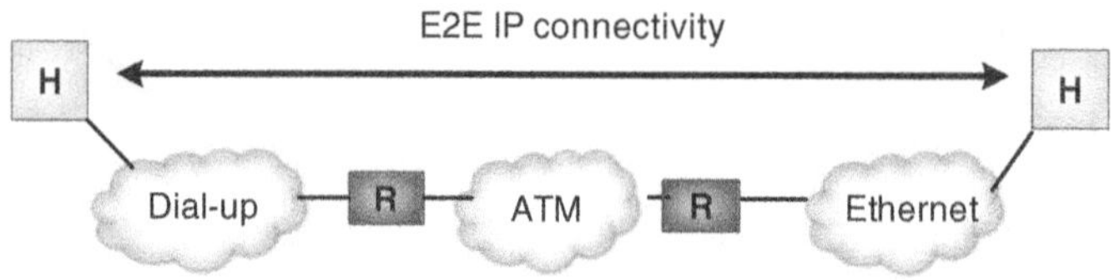

FIGURE 3.1

Both hosts and routers implement the IP protocol, and thus create a virtual-network layer that makes the applications in the hosts believe that they are sitting on top of a homogeneous network. This is shown in Figures 3.2 and 3.3.

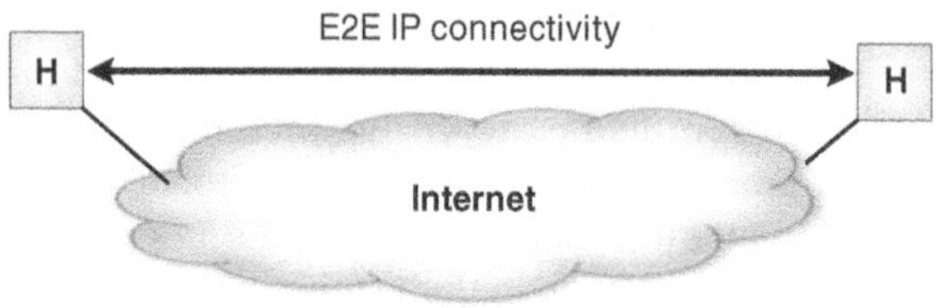

FIGURE 3.2

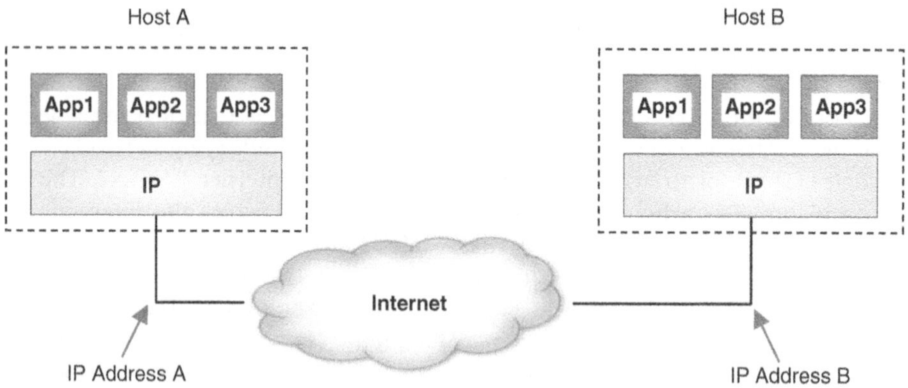

FIGURE 3.3

3.1.1 Internet Protocol

We will now look at the main functions provided by the Internet Protocol.

The most basic service that the IP layer provides is defined as an unreliable, connectionless packet-delivery service. The service is called unreliable because delivery is not guaranteed. The network will do its best to deliver the packets, but under congestion or faulty situations, packets may be lost, duplicated, or delayed. This concept is also sometimes referred to as best-effort delivery.

The service is called connectionless because each packet is treated independently from all others. The packet itself contains all the information needed by the network in order to route it to the destination. There is no "connection" concept or connection state stored in the network. A sequence of packets sent from one computer to another may travel over different paths—so some packets may be delivered out of order, or some may be lost while others are delivered.

The lack of state makes IP networks very robust in cases of node failures. Because the network nodes do not store any state needed for end-to-end communication, in case an area of the network fails, other routers can pick up the traffic and reroute it to the destination through another area of the network. Of course, in such faulty situations, packets may be lost or delayed or delivered out of order, but it is assumed that the end systems are responsible for compensating for such situations. This may include the need for the end systems to control IP network traffic, including end-to-end flow control and error detection. The IP network itself is dumb, and this allows it to scale better and be more robust. As stated in [RFC 1958], "The network's job is to transmit datagrams as efficiently and flexibly as possible. Everything else should be done at the fringes."

The version of the IP protocol that has been in use in the Internet for more than two decades is called IPv4, and is defined in [RFC 791]. It uses the popular 32-bit addresses (e.g., 169.254.31.25). A new version of the protocol, called IPv6, was developed in [RFC 2460]. IPv6 introduces a few new features and enlarges the address space (which was being exhausted) by defining 128-bit addresses. IPv6 has yet to find widespread adoption.

3.1.2 The Internet Paradigm

The Internet architectural principles and guidelines are described in [RFC 1958] and [RFC 3439]. From the above discussion, we have seen that the two key principles behind the Internet paradigm are:

1. The internetworking concept
2. The "dumb network" concept

Both of them are reflected in the following quote from [RFC 1958], "Architectural Principles of the Internet": "The goal is connectivity, the tool is the Internet Protocol, and the intelligence is end to end rather than hidden in the network."

End-to-end connectivity is a good thing, but what the end users are really interested in is applications (we, in this book, are also interested in a particular kind of Internet application: multimedia communication). So what does the Internet paradigm mean with regard to service creation?

First, application programs can be written on top of the IP layer and be independent of the underlying physical network. I can run the same program over a 100Base-T LAN (Local Area Network), over a dial-up connection, or over an ADSL (Asymmetric Digital Subscriber Line) access.[2] This is an important concept that is

[2]Obviously, different underlying physical networks may allow for different bandwidths, and this may have an effect on the user experience. However, from the functional perspective, the application does not need to bother about the physical network.

taken for granted (and therefore is somewhat underestimated), given that all existing operating systems have built-in IP support and offer drivers for very different physical networks, including at least Ethernet, dial-up, and ADSL physical networks.

Second, Internet applications work end to end. Application-level communication in the Internet is better achieved through the utilization of end-to-end protocols in such a way that the behavior of the underlying IP protocol is mirrored. This approach is better suited to deliver end-to-end functions. An example of such a function is security. Security can be better provided by using upper-layer end-to-end protocols. Information can be signed or encrypted by the endpoints, thus preventing the network from accessing the content.

Consequently, Internet applications are implemented at the network fringes. As an example, SIP is an application-layer end-to-end protocol. This end-to-end approach for designing communication applications provides great flexibility and reduces time to market because it reduces the dependency on the network.

Third, due to the way in which the Internet was conceived (as a service-agnostic network) at the beginning and how it has evolved over time, it so happens that access and service provision are decoupled in the Internet. Access providers and service providers do not necessarily have to be the same entity. As an example, one could obtain access through an ADSL provider and still get email service from Yahoo! This fact again fosters innovation and competitiveness because applications are not necessarily tied to the access provider.

Hence, the Internet can be considered a platform ideally suited for service creation.

All this discussion is particularly relevant in order to understand, in later chapters, the rationale behind SIP. This is defined as an end-to-end protocol, according to the Internet principles, in order to better deliver its end-to-end functions.

Notably, this implies quite a significant difference from other signaling protocols that are used today in circuit-switched networks, which are not end to end. In the traditional circuit-switched world, most of the intelligence is residing in the network, and access is tightly coupled to service provision. These aspects constrain the flexibility to deliver services in such networks. Much of the revolution currently taking place in the telecom industry has to do with abandoning the old signaling paradigms and embracing the Internet ideas that have proved to be the perfect ecosystem to boost application development.

3.2 TCP/IP Protocol Architecture

Internet Protocol architecture can be best described using a layered model. Any layer in such architecture is said to provide services to the layer just on top of it while obtaining services from the layer just below it. This idea provides a powerful abstraction for the development of communication software. Layers are independent—they provide a very definite set of functions, and can be replaced without affecting the rest of the layers, as long as the interfaces between them are maintained. The topmost layer represents the end user's view, whereas the layer at the bottom represents the hardware infrastructure that actually deals with the physical details of bits transmission.

The Internet layered model is typically referred to as the TCP/IP protocol suite, and is represented in Figure 3.4. The Internet layer sits on top of the data-link layers and physical layers, which are provided by the underlying network infrastructure (e.g., Ethernet, ATM, and so on). The transport layer uses the connectionless delivery service provided by the Internet layer, and offers specific transport services to the application layer. In the application layer, the end-to-end protocols that deliver the end-to-end functionality are implemented. Meanwhile, the applications that the end users "see" are implemented on top of the application layer, and use whatever application-layer protocol is needed to provide the requested functionality.

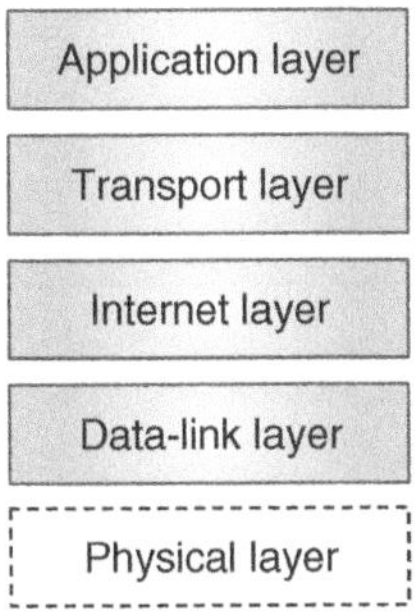

FIGURE 3.4

End-user services are therefore implemented on top of the application layer. For instance, an email application requires at least implementing a user interface through which the end user can submit emails and manage the emails that are in his or her mailbox (e.g., read, delete, and so on). A more complex email application might offer additional functionalities such as local folders and out-of-office announcements. Such an application would be built on top of the application layer, and would use the services of two protocols in such a layer: SMTP (Simple Mail Transfer Protocol, for submitting the emails) and IMAP4 (Internet Message Protocol version 4, for the management of the mailbox). Likewise, SMTP and IMAP4 are application-layer protocols that require the services of a transport-layer protocol such as TCP, which, in the same way, uses functionality provided by the IP protocol. This is shown Figure 3.5.

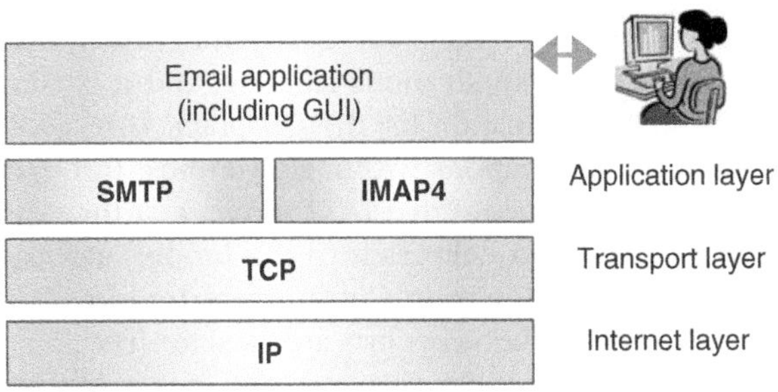

FIGURE 3.5

3.2.1 Application-Layer Protocols

As already stated, this layer comprises the end-to-end protocols that are required to implement the end-to-end functions. Some well-known protocols are sitting in this layer—for example, HTTP, SMTP, POP3, IMAP4, TELNET, FTP, and DNS.

SIP is also an application-layer protocol, and works together with other application-level protocols such as RTP (Real-time Transport Protocol) or SDP (Session Description Protocol).

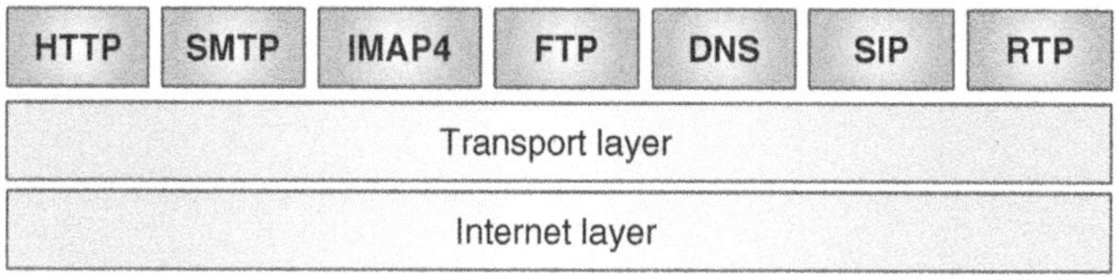

FIGURE 3.6

3.2.2 Transport-Layer Protocols

There are two widely used transport protocols in IP networks: TCP and UDP (User Datagram Protocol). In addition to these, another transport protocol, called SCTP (Stream Control Transmission Protocol), has been defined and is of special interest for signaling applications. We will now review the key functionality in these protocols.

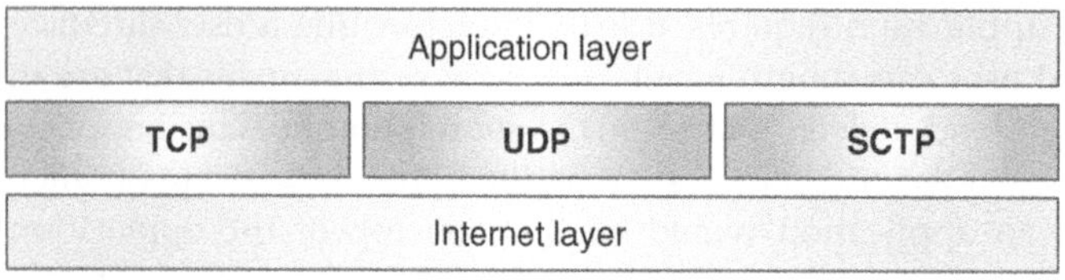

FIGURE 3.7

User Datagram Protocol

UDP [RFC 768] provides little functionality on top of the unreliable connectionless datagram-delivery service that the IP layer provides. UDP merely provides a multiplexing/demultiplexing function on top of IP. Communication in IP networks occurs between application programs in the hosts. In the destination host, identified by an IP address, there might be many applications running, and it is crucial to identify which one is the ultimate destination for the datagram. UDP adds the ability to distinguish among multiple destinations within a given host through the utilization of the destination port field. It is said that UDP software at the destination demultiplexes the received packet and delivers it to the proper application. Likewise, the sending application also adds a source port parameter to which replies should be addressed. Figure 3.8 shows the way ports are used in UDP.

UDP also adds an optional checksum parameter that just provides a way to guarantee that data has arrived intact.

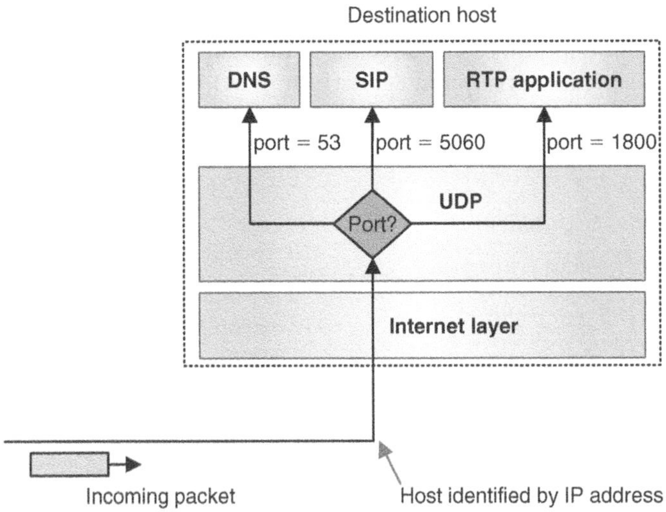

FIGURE 3.8

So, summarizing, the UDP transport layer does not ensure in any way that the datagrams have arrived at the destination. An application that uses UDP and needs this guarantee will have to implement the guarantee itself.

We will see in later sections that the service offered by UDP is extensively used in the context of real-time services.

Transmission Control Protocol

TCP [RFC 793] provides reliable transport of data streams. In order to accomplish such a function, it uses a fundamental technique known as "positive acknowledgment with retransmission." What this means is that the receiver host has to acknowledge the received packets. The sender host starts a timer after transmission of each packet, and, if a timeout occurs, retransmits the packet. At the receiver host, the TCP software delivers the packets to the destination application in sequence, exactly as they were sent, and also provides end-to-end flow control so as not to overload the receiver.

In order to provide these services, TCP uses the connection-oriented approach, which allows it to maintain the necessary context information in both sender and receiver host. An end-to-end TCP connection has to be established so that contexts can be initialized and data transmission can start. Similarly, once data transmission has finalized, the transport connection needs to be closed.

The TCP protocol also provides the multiplexing/de-multiplexing function and allows reaching a particular application in the destination host based on the destination port.

However, TCP takes the multiplexing concept further than UDP through the TCP connection concept. TCP can distinguish different flows for application processing even if they have the same destination port. The TCP server can de-multiplex different packets based on the connection in which they arrived, and can deliver them to the right application instance. A connection is identified by a pair of endpoints. An endpoint is defined as a pair of integers (host, port) where "host" is the host's IP address, and the "port" is a TCP port on that host. Figure 3.9 shows how the connection concept is used in TCP.

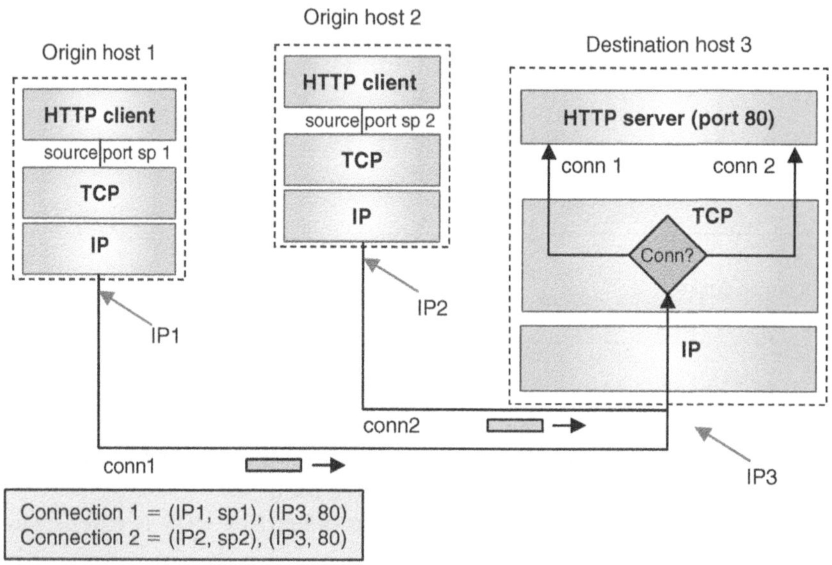

FIGURE 3.9

Stream Control Transmission Protocol

SCTP is yet another transport protocol that, like TCP, provides a reliable transport service. It assures in-sequence, error-free transmission. SCTP is also connection oriented, but, unlike TCP, has some specific features that are specially suited to the transport of signaling information:

- It is message oriented and supports framing of individual message boundaries (as opposed to TCP, which is byte oriented).
- It allows for multiple streams in the same transport connection. Each stream has independent sequence delivery (as opposed to TCP, which assumes a single stream of data).
- It supports multi-homing, or the ability for a single SCTP endpoint to support multiple IP addresses. This allows for greater survivability of the session in the presence of network failures.

SCTP is not yet as widespread as TCP or UDP. SCTP is specified in [RFC 2960], and a good introduction to it can be found in [RFC 3286].

SIP can use UDP, TCP, or SCTP in the transport layer. RTP, another important protocol for the delivery of multimedia services, always uses UDP as a transport.

3.3 Architecture for Internet Multimedia Communications

Multimedia communication is enabled in the Internet by a myriad of IP-based application-level protocols that work in concert. Among these, two types of protocols play a predominant role in all the architecture:

- The signaling protocols
- The media transport protocols

These two types of protocols form the core of multimedia communication systems; no multimedia communication architecture can exist without them. In addition to the signaling and media protocols, other protocols provide optional functionality that complements, extends, or facilitates the core communication functions under specific circumstances. Examples of these protocols are those related to provision of QoS (Quality of Service), policy control, conferencing, NAT (Network Address Translator) traversal, accounting, and so forth.

Figure 3.10 depicts the protocol architecture comprising both the core and the supporting protocols.

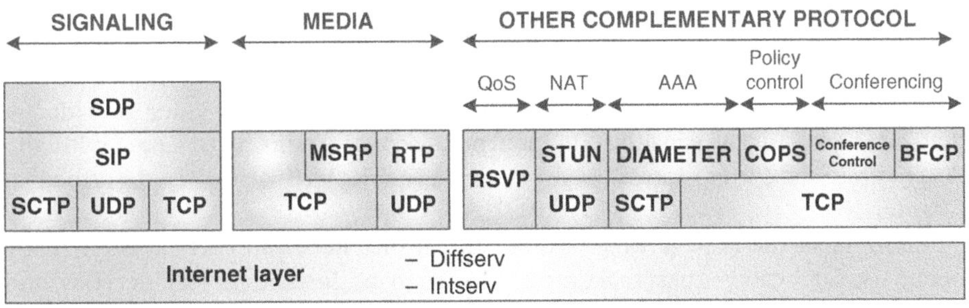

FIGURE 3.10

Furthermore, as we said in the introduction, the protocols used in multimedia communication scenarios can work together with the existing Internet protocols in other service domains, and so help users to achieve a total communication experience.

3.3.1 Core Protocols: Signaling

The core signaling protocol for multimedia communication is the Session Initiation Protocol. SIP works in concert with the Session Description Protocol. SIP deals with the session-management issues; SDP is responsible for session description. The SDP messages are transported in the body of SIP messages. This split between session management and session description is a powerful concept because it allows the two functions to evolve separately. For instance, new media types can be easily incorporated into the Internet multimedia framework by defining new session descriptors and not impacting at all the SIP functionality.

Likewise, new functionalities can be incorporated into SIP without the need to impact the way sessions are characterized.

SDP offers a generic mechanism to describe multimedia sessions. As such, it is not only used in communication scenarios. For instance, it is also used in the remit of streaming services, where it is conveyed by the RTSP (Real-time Streaming Protocol, [RFC2326]) in order to describe the characteristics of streaming sessions.

SDP was also traditionally used together with the Session Announcement Protocol (SAP, [RFC2974]) in the MBone (Multicast Backbone). SAP was used as a way to advertise the MBone multicast sessions among the potential participants. The multicast sessions were described by SDP content embedded in the SAP message.

SIP is detailed in Chapters 4, 6, and 7. SDP is examined in Chapter 9.

3.3.2 Core Protocols: Media

The core protocols used for media transport are:

- Real-time Transport Protocol (RTP).
- Message Session Relay Protocol (MSRP).
- Transmission Control Protocol (TCP).

RTP is typically used to carry pure real-time media—such as voice or video—that are highly delay sensitive. It incorporates a mechanism to cope with the delay variations (jitter) introduced by the network. RTP is further described in Chapter 10.

MSRP is, at the time of this writing, still an Internet Draft (I-D). It is currently being used to carry quasi-real-time traffic such as Instant Messaging (IM) and online gaming. MSRP is further described in Chapter 10.

TCP can also be used directly as a media transport protocol. Typical usages are for image sharing or file transfer in the middle of a voice or video conversation.

3.3.3 Complementary Protocols

There are other Internet protocols that can be used to enhance a multimedia communication system or that are needed to facilitate the operation of the core protocols. These complementary protocols encompass a number of aspects. Some examples are given next.

Quality of Service

In order to implement QoS in loaded IP networks, the IETF (Internet Engineering Task Force) has defined extensions to the traditional best-effort Internet service, such as Integrated Services (IntServ) or Differentiated Services (DiffServ). The provision of QoS sometimes implies the need to reserve resources in the IP routers. This can be done using the Resource Reservation Protocol (RSVP).

Chapter 21 is dedicated to examining the mechanisms and protocols that enable Quality of Service.

Policy Control

In scenarios where there is a requirement to implement QoS mechanisms, there is sometimes the need to enforce policy-based admission-control decisions. In such cases, the entity responsible for taking the policy decisions has to communicate them to the entity responsible for enforcing them. In order to enable such communication, protocols such as COPS (Common Open Policy Service) can be used.

Policy-control aspects are discussed in Chapter 21.

Authentication, Authorization, and Accounting (AAA)

In communication scenarios, service providers may want to charge for provision of the service and/or the utilization of the network resources. In those cases, it is crucial to have a mechanism that allows the service provider to request Authentication, Authorization, and Accounting from external servers. This can be done through the utilization of AAA protocols such as DIAMETER.

Conferencing

One of the most complex communication scenarios refers to the situation where many users participate in the same conversation (i.e., conference). In order to enable enhanced features in multiparty conversations, additional protocols are needed—for example, the Binary Floor Control Protocol (BFCP).

Conferencing is extensively discussed in Chapter 19.

NAT Traversal

Network Address Translators are frequently used in IP networks in order to separate private and public addressing realms. SIP and RTP are not NAT-friendly protocols, so their operation is severely disrupted in scenarios involving NAT devices.

The NAT traversal issue is one of the most critical aspects that SIP and RTP are faced with in real deployments. Many new procedures, mechanisms, and protocols have been defined to cope with that problem. One of the most relevant supporting protocols in this remit is the Simple Traversal Utilities for NAT (STUN).

NAT traversal is covered extensively in Chapter 22.

3.3.4 Internet Protocols in Other Service Domains

There are many other Internet protocols that are focused on delivering other types of services such as infotainment, streaming, or offline communications. Examples of such protocols are:

- *HTTP* (Hypertext Transfer Protocol): Defines the rules for transferring and conveying information on the web.
- *SMTP* (Simple Mail Transfer Protocol): Is used for email submission across the Internet.

- *IMAP4* (Internet Message Access Protocol): Allows clients to access and manage their email box.
- *RTSP* (Real-time Streaming Protocol): Allows a client to remotely control a streaming server. It offers VCR-like commands such as "play" or "rewind."

SIP has been designed in such a way that it can be smoothly integrated with Internet protocols used in other service domains. For instance, SIP addressing follows the URI (Universal Resource Identifier) format to address SIP resources. That is the same format that is used on the web and by email systems. This characteristic enables some interesting combined features (e.g., John might try to initiate a media session with Alice and, because Alice is not available, be redirected to her web page).

3.4 Summary

In this chapter, we have reviewed the TCP/IP basics and have presented the big picture for multimedia communications. In the next chapter, we will continue looking at the fundamentals of multimedia communications and will introduce SIP.

CHAPTER

SIP Overview

4

In this chapter, we will introduce SIP. First of all, we will define some key concepts in the SIP framework, such as sessions and addressing. Then the main functions of the protocol will be presented. After that, we will describe the different SIP entities in the SIP architecture. We will also show a first example of how the SIP entities are involved in a basic SIP call.

4.1 What is SIP?

The Session Initiation Protocol is an application-level signaling protocol defined by the IETF in [RFC 3261] for the creation and management of sessions over an IP network. The term "session" refers to the media plane aspect of the communication—that is, to the exchange of media (e.g., voice, video, and so on) among an association of participants.

Sessions can be described using the Session Description Protocol (SDP) defined in [RFC 4566]. In order to create sessions, SIP messages carry SDP session descriptions that allow participants to agree on a set of parameters needed for the multimedia communication, such as transport addresses or media types.

A key aspect here is that SIP, the signaling protocol, is independent of the session being established and of the mechanism used to describe it. SIP provides the way to distribute this information between potential participants in the session.

The Session Description Protocol defines a language to characterize the multimedia session. Some key pieces of information have to be present on a session description:

1. The types of media in the session
2. The available for each of the media types
3. The address (IP and port) where media packets should be sent.

In Chapter 9, we will dive in detail into the Session Description Protocol.

4.2 SIP Addressing

In the SIP architecture, users are usually identified using a SIP URI (Universal Resource Identifier). A SIP URI is a type of URI, therefore it complies with the general rules for URIs defined in [RFC 3986]. In general, SIP URIs identify communication resources. They contain enough information to initiate and maintain a communication session with the resource.

Example:

sip:john.smith@ocean.com

A SIP URI uses the "sip:" scheme, and is composed of two parts separated by the "@" sign. The two parts are:

- An optional user part, which identifies a particular resource at the host being addressed. In our previous example: john.smith.
- A host-port part, which identifies the source providing the resource. It may contain a Fully Qualified Domain Name (FQDN) or an IP address plus an optional port value. In our previous example: ocean.com.

Additionally, the SIP URI may contain a number of parameters that affect the request constructed from the URI. URI parameters are added after the host-port part, and are separated by semicolons.

SIP URIs may refer to SIP users and SIP servers. More specifically, a SIP URI may represent:

- *The public identity of a user*—that is to say, the global identifier that anyone could use in order to establish a multimedia communication with that user. For instance, the following SIP URI might represent John's public user identity:

  sip:john.smith@ocean.com

  That is the identity that John would advertise and include in his business cards.
- *A user at a specific host or location*. For example, the following SIP URI represents a user called Peter at a host whose FQDN is lab.computing.ocean.com:

  sip:peter.bower@lab.computing.ocean.com

  The next SIP URI refers to the same user at location 212.34.100.2:

  sip:peter.bower@212.34.100.2
- *A sip server*[1] SIP URIs can also be used to represent SIP servers, as in:

  sip:proxy1.ocean.com or
  sip:193.53.24.3
- *A group of users*. For instance, the URI

  sip:human-resources@ocean.com

  might represent the Human Resources Department in the company Ocean. Whenever someone tries to communicate with that resource, the server

[1]The role of SIP servers will be explained in later sections.

responsible for the URI would try all the people in the department until it finds someone who can accept the communication.

- *A service* A URI can also represent a service, as described in [RFC 3087]. For instance, the URI

  sip:dogs:conf@ocean.com

  might refer to a voice-conference service about dogs. Whoever communicates with that URI is joined into the conferencing system.

It is worth mentioning that there are URIs that point to logical identities (for example, sip:john.smith@ocean.com), whereas other URIs directly indicate locations (FQDNs or IP addresses)—for example, sip:peter.bower@212.34.100.2 or sip:proxy1.ocean.com.

SIP URIs that point to locations can be directly resolved to the corresponding IP address, port, and transport via DNS (Domain Name System)[2] queries. The "logical" SIP URIs, on the other hand, require that a Location Service is queried to resolve the "logical" SIP URI into a "location" SIP URI, which can then be resolved through DNS mechanisms. Location Services will be explained in Section 4.3.2, "Location of Users."

Other URIs can be used to identify communication resources—for example, the SIPS URI, which provides secure access to communication resources and implies the utilization of TLS (Transport Layer Security); or the TEL URI, which identifies a resource in the telephone network and is used in interworking scenarios between PSTN (Public Switched Telephone Network) and Internet. SIPS URIs are described in Chapter 14, and TEL URIs are tackled in Chapter 18.

SIP can also use generic URIs to identify resources. This is actually a powerful characteristic of SIP because it would allow the combination of other Internet services, such as email or web, with SIP communication services. For instance, Peter would use Alice's SIP URI in order to initiate a media session with her. Let us assume that she is unavailable. At that point, a SIP redirection might occur, which could convey, in the SIP signaling, her email address (mailto URI) or the HTTP (HyperText Transfer Protocol) URI of her web page. Peter's application might then send her an email or start the browser and go to her web page automatically. And all this would require only that Peter know her SIP URI. So SIP URIs have the capability of becoming the single identifier for users in the Internet irrespective of the communication method that will eventually be used.

4.3 SIP Functions

Let's now look more closely into the functions of SIP as a signaling protocol. SIP basically solves two key aspects in IP multimedia communications:

1. Session setup, modification, and termination
2. Location of users

[2]DNS is an Internet system that is used to associate several types of information (e.g., IP addresses) with meaningful high-level names (so-called domain names).

4.3.1 Session Setup, Termination, and Modification

As its name implies, one of the main functions of the Session Initiation Protocol is the initiation of multimedia sessions. By using SIP, Alice can signal her desire to engage in a multimedia session with John. Likewise, John can use SIP to signal his acceptance or rejection of the communication. During the session setup, session descriptors are exchanged so that both parties can agree on the crucial parameters for the session.

SIP can also be used to modify session parameters of the ongoing session—for instance, in order to add new media components into the session.

The last SIP function related to session management is session termination. Any of the session participants can use SIP to signal his or her desire to terminate the communication while effectively stopping media transmission and reception.

Let's look a bit more in detail into the specific SIP functions as part of the session establishment. For that purpose, let's use an example of a *multimedia call* between Alice and John. In the context of SIP, the term "IP multimedia call"—or "call," in short—is a generic term used to refer to a SIP-based IP real-time communication between peers.[3] Therefore, that is the meaning of call that we will use in the subsequent sections in the book.

It is John's birthday, and Alice wants to wish him a happy day. She wants to talk to him, but would also like to show him the nice cake she is preparing to celebrate the event. So what Alice wants is a multimedia (voice and video) communication with John. Therefore, Alice opens her multimedia-communication application on her PC, introduces the address of John, and presses the call button. John is currently in a work meeting, but he is armed with his IP Multimedia-enabled mobile phone.

In order to set up the exchange of multimedia data between Alice and John (i.e., the session), SIP needs to convey certain control (signaling) information:

- *First of all*, if Alice wants to communicate with John, she should signal her desire to communicate with him—in other words Alice should explicitly send John an invitation to participate in a communication. SIP will be responsible for carrying such an invitation from Alice to John.
- *Second*, it may take some time for John to respond to such an invitation. In the meantime, we need to give Alice some indication about how the call is progressing. In this case, SIP will convey the progress information back to Alice.
- *Third*, if John decides to answer, we need to communicate to Alice his willingness to take the communication. Again, SIP is used to convey to Alice the acceptance by John to take her call.
- *Fourth*, some parameters need to be negotiated between the two endpoints before actual delivery of the voice and video takes place. For example, the endpoints need to agree on which codecs for voice and video they will use so as to be sure that the voice samples encoded by the sender will be properly decoded in the receiver. The way SIP can enable this functionality is by distributing the session description between John and Alice.

---

[3] [RFC 3261] defines "call" as "an informal term that refers to some communication between peers, generally set up for the purposes of a multimedia conversation."

Once the session has been established, Alice and John start to talk to each other and see each other. At some point in time, Alice may decide that she wants to stop the video communication because she has already shown the cake to John. In such a situation, SIP will be used to modify the session parameters that were negotiated during the establishment phase. Alice's soft phone will use SIP to send a new session description to John. The new session description will not contain the video component. John agrees to eliminate the video component, and the communication proceeds just with voice.

When, later on in the conversation, John decides to terminate the session (because an important meeting with his boss is about to start), again SIP is used for that purpose.

In Figure 4.1, we can see an example of the call between Alice and John that highlights the concepts and definitions discussed in the previous sections.

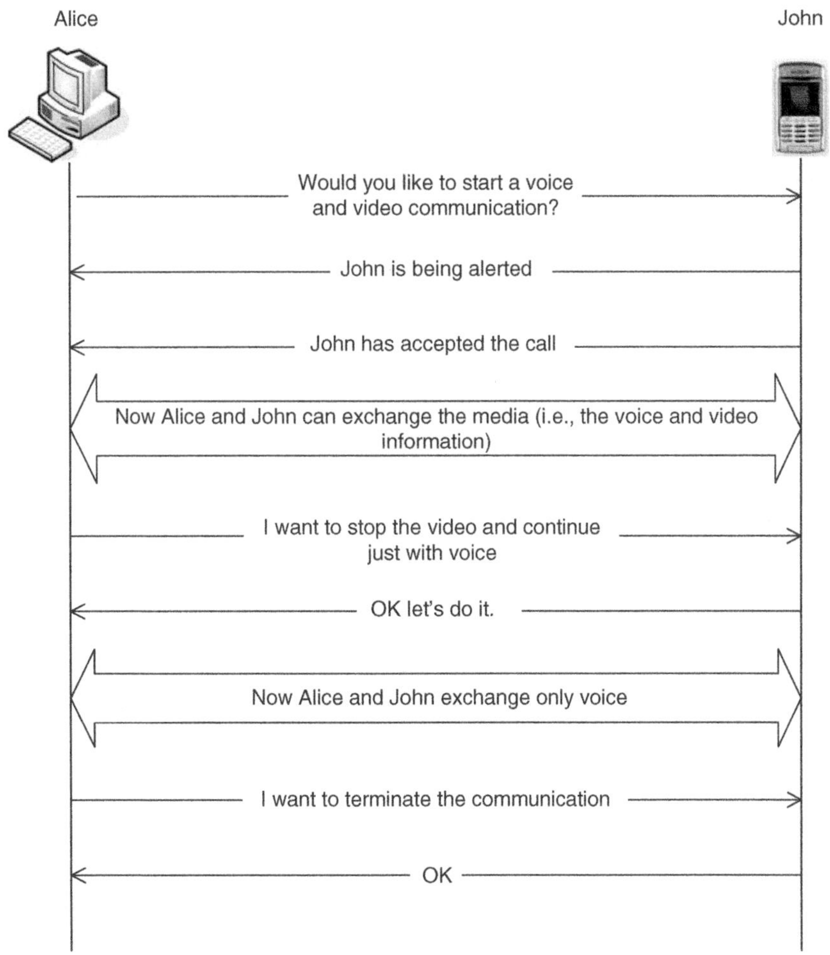

FIGURE 4.1

Note on the Usage of SIP in Multicast Conferences

SIP can also invite participants to already-existing sessions such as Internet multicast conferences. In this case, a multimedia conference may be taking place on the Internet—for instance, a rock concert is being multicast. At one point in time, Alice, who is listening to the conference (the concert), decides to invite John. She indicates the characterization of the session in her invitation, and once John has received the invitation, he can "tune" to the multicast conference.

This example above represents the scenario for SIP utilization that was very much in the minds of SIP designers when the first draft of SIP was produced back in 1996. However, SIP is used today predominantly in communication scenarios such as the ones that we described at the beginning of the section. Therefore, that will be the type of scenarios we will be focusing on throughout this book.

4.3.2 Location of Users

We have seen in the last section that the session-initiation request needs to be routed from Alice to John. In an IP network, routing of messages relies on the utilization of IP addresses. However, Alice does not know John's IP address—all she knows is John's public identity, expressed as a "logical" SIP URI: sip:john@ocean.com.

In fact, John might even want to use his application from different terminals: his PC at home, his IMS (Internet Multimedia Subsystem) mobile phone when traveling, or his laptop at work—and all these probably have different IP addresses.

So there is a need to derive John's location from his SIP public identity. What this highlights is the general problem of user mobility: users are identified by an abstract, "logical" SIP identity irrespective of their location, but in order to route messages to them, it is necessary to derive their "physical" location.

Therefore, what is needed is a system capable of tracking the IP address of the users, mapping it to their public identity, and storing that information in a table. In the process of establishing a new multimedia communication, it will be necessary to query the table containing the mapping in order to derive the right IP address to which the packets should be sent.

One of the main SIP functions is to enable user mobility. To that purpose, SIP defines the registration procedure.[4] Every SIP endpoint that wants to be able to receive multimedia calls has to previously be registered. That is to say, it has to communicate its present location (expressed as a "location" SIP URI), together with its public identity (expressed as a "logical" SIP URI), to its home SIP server (more specifically, to its registrar server), which will then maintain a table with the mapping.

---

[4]Registrations constitute a possible way to populate the Location Service, but not the only way. Arbitrary mapping functions can be configured at the discretion of the administrator.

The table might look like this:

ADDRESS OF RECORD	CONTACT ADDRESS
sip:alice@ocean.com	sip:alice@pcalice.home.ocean.com
...	...

Or like this:

ADDRESS OF RECORD	CONTACT ADDRESS
sip:alice@ocean.com	sip:alice@212.55.34.2
...	...

The table has two columns. The first one contains the public identities, so-called Addresses of Record (AORs). The second column contains the corresponding locations, so-called Contact Addresses. AORs are expressed as "logical" SIP URIs, and Contact Addresses are expressed as "location" SIP URIs.

The registration procedure is shown in Figure 4.2.

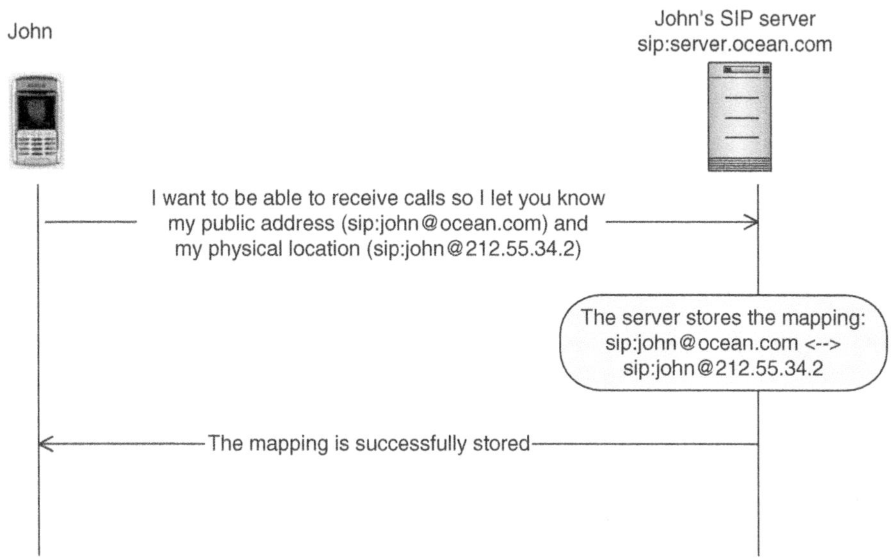

FIGURE 4.2

Whenever a call is made to a SIP endpoint, the call will be routed to the endpoint's associated SIP server, which will query that table and derive the SIP URI representing the location of the destination endpoint. Then it will make one or several DNS queries to finally determine what transport protocol, IP address, and port must be used to deliver the signaling message to John. DNS utilization in the remit of SIP is discussed in Chapter 6. Figure 4.3 shows an example of a call routed to John.

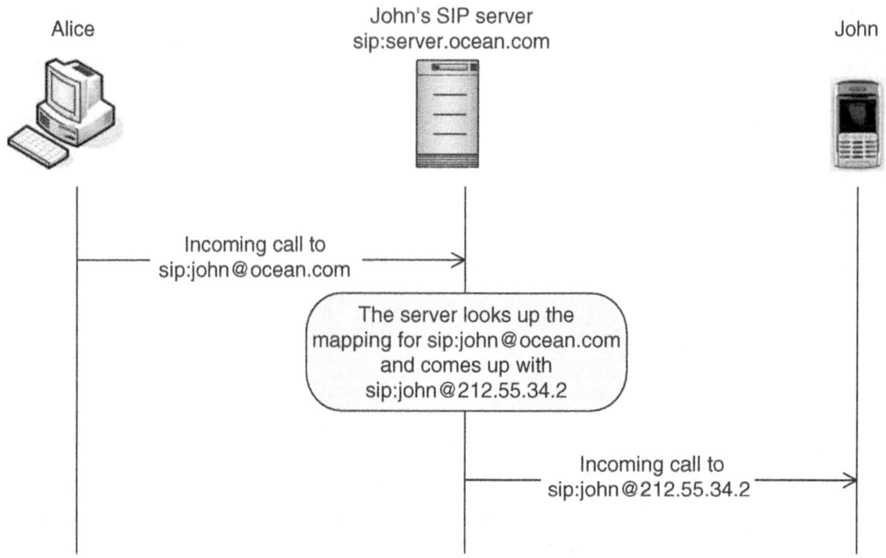

FIGURE 4.3

4.4 SIP Entities

The SIP specifications define a number of SIP elements as part of the SIP architecture:

- User Agents (UAs)
- Registrars
- Proxies
- Back-to-Back User Agents (B2BUAs)

4.4.1 User Agents

A SIP UA comprises two components: a User Agent Client (UAC) and a User Agent Server (UAS). The UAC is responsible for the generation of new SIP requests and the reception of the associated responses. The UAS is responsible for receiving SIP requests and generating the appropriate responses. This is shown in Figure 4.4.

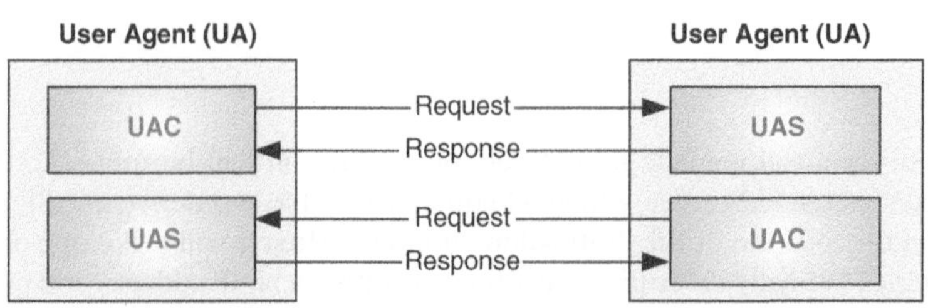

FIGURE 4.4

User Agents are typically located at the SIP endpoints, and the end user can interact with them through a user interface. If we look back to our previous example of a call between Alice and John, the multimedia application running on top of Alice's PC or John's mobile device includes a SIP User Agent. When Alice decides to call John, she typically makes use of a Graphical User Interface (GUI) where she can introduce John's SIP URI. Once John's address has been introduced, Alice would press a button in the GUI to signal her wish to initiate the call. The User Agent software will detect the button being pressed, and will generate the proper SIP request in order to initiate the call.

The multimedia application that both Alice and John are using does not just have to implement a user interface and handle the signaling. It also needs to handle the user plane traffic—that is, the voice and video (or other media) data. For that reason, the multimedia application needs to incorporate a voice and video tool or whatever tool is necessary in order to handle the desired media. The voice and video tool will have to include software or hardware components that implement the media coding and decoding (codecs).

So, summarizing, an end-user multimedia-communications application is typically made up of four types of components:

- A SIP UA, responsible for handling the signaling.
- A set of media tools, each of them specialized in a particular media. Different media components can be combined in the same call.
- A piece of service logic that typically maintains a state machine and forms the glue that makes the other component work together.
- A user interface through which the user gains access to the application.

This is represented in Figure 4.5. Here, we can clearly see how the SIP protocol itself is independent of the media session. SIP is not concerned with the type of

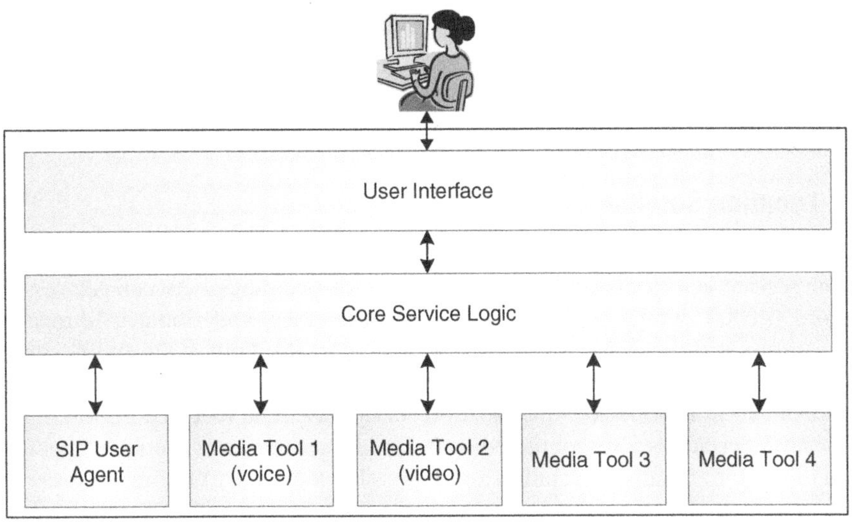

FIGURE 4.5

media session that needs to be established. It just distributes the descriptors for the session. For example, if we wanted to enhance our multimedia application to support whiteboarding (in addition to voice and video), we would need to add another component, the whiteboarding media tool, and integrate it with the user interface, but the SIP User Agent itself would remain unchanged.

The SIP UA is a critical part of any multimedia-communication application. SIP User Agents can be implemented in very different ways. A SIP UA can be, for instance, a software program running on top of a PC, or it can be implemented as part of a desktop phone, or it can run as an application on a mobile phone.

Software programs that implement a multimedia-communication application are typically called soft phones. The soft-phone concept is quite general, and does not necessarily imply the utilization of SIP as a signaling protocol. There are SIP soft phones, but also soft phones that use other signaling protocols such as H.323 (Packed-Based Multimedia Communications Systems), SCCP (Skinny Client Control Protocol), and so on.

We have said the SIP endpoints include a SIP UA. Additionally, there are situations in which SIP User Agents can also be included in network servers. Take the example of a SIP Voice Mail System (VMS). Such a system has to be able to receive SIP calls, accept them, play a greeting announcement, and record the message from the caller. Moreover, the VMS may also need to create outgoing calls to notify users of new messages and allow the users to directly listen to those messages. So the VMS has to implement a true multimedia-communication application that will include a SIP User Agent in order to handle the signaling and some media tools.

4.4.2 Registrar

A registrar is a server that accepts registration requests from the User Agents. The registration is the process by which a SIP UA communicates its current location along with its externally visible identifier to the registrar server. A SIP UA needs to be registered before it can receive multimedia calls. When the registrar accepts the registration request, it places the received information—that is, the mapping between user location and globally visible identifier—in a database called Location Service.

4.4.3 Location Service

The Location Service is not a SIP entity. As has been mentioned previously, a Location Service is a database that contains a list of mappings between Addresses of Record (AORs), which represent public SIP identities, and Contact Addresses (which represent the user location) for a specific domain. Both AORs and Contact Addresses are expressed as SIP URIs. When a registrar receives a registration request from a UA, it populates the Location Service with the received information. The Location Service is also contacted by proxy servers responsible for a specific domain in order to obtain information about possible locations of the called user.

The interface toward a Location Service is not SIP based. There is not a standardized mechanism to access a Location Service. Some SIP servers may use protocols such as LDAP (Lightweight Directory Access Protocol) or others. In many implementations, the Location Service and the SIP server are implemented on the same system, and the interface between them is internal.

ADDRESS OF RECORD	CONTACT ADDRESS
sip:alice@ocean.com	sip:alice@212.55.34.2
...	...

Figure 4.6 shows the registration procedure involving a SIP User Agent, a SIP registrar, and a Location Service.

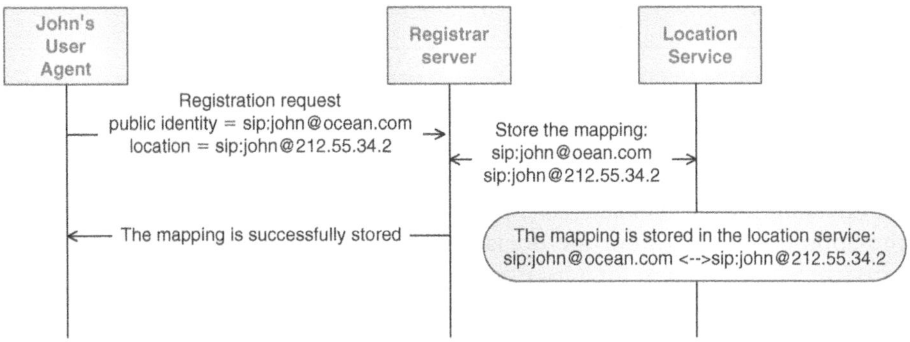

FIGURE 4.6

4.4.4 Proxy Servers

A proxy server is an intermediary entity that makes requests on behalf of other clients. It primarily plays the role of routing (SIP routing),[5] which means that its job is to ensure that a request is sent to another entity "closer" to the targeted user. Proxies are also useful for enforcing policy (for example, making sure a user is allowed to make a call). A proxy interprets and, if necessary, rewrites specific parts of a request message before forwarding it.

There may be a set of proxies between UAC and UAS that help to route requests. Two specific types of SIP proxies deserve our attention: outbound and inbound proxies.

Outbound Proxy

An outbound proxy (Figure 4.7) helps the UAs to route outgoing requests. UAs are usually configured to route all their requests to an outbound proxy, which will route the requests for them.

[5]Not to be confused with IP routing, which is the role of IP routers. SIP routing is at a higher level than IP routing (application level versus network level), and uses the SIP URI as the key field to determine the next hop, as opposed to the destination IP address used by IP routers.

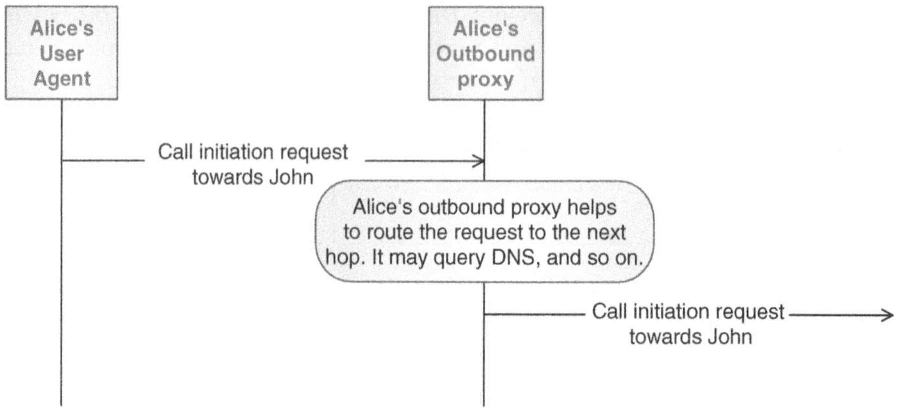

FIGURE 4.7

Inbound Proxy

An inbound proxy (Figure 4.8) is a proxy server that handles incoming requests for an administrative domain. So it basically helps to route incoming requests to the appropriate UA within the domain it is responsible for. When an inbound proxy receives a request for a user belonging to the domain for which that proxy is responsible, the proxy queries the Location Service, determines the contact address of the UA to which this request is directed, and forwards the request to that address.

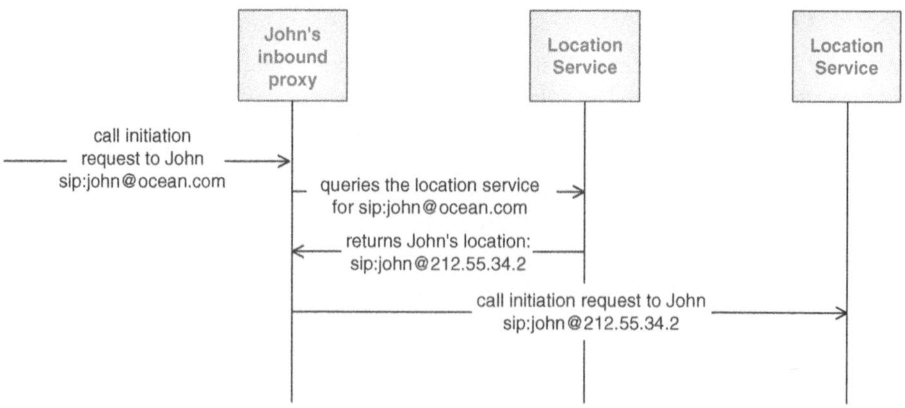

FIGURE 4.8

It is quite frequent that the call-initiation request, on its way from originator to recipient, traverses an outbound and an inbound proxy. This arrangement is commonly known as the SIP trapezoid, and is depicted in Figure 4.9.

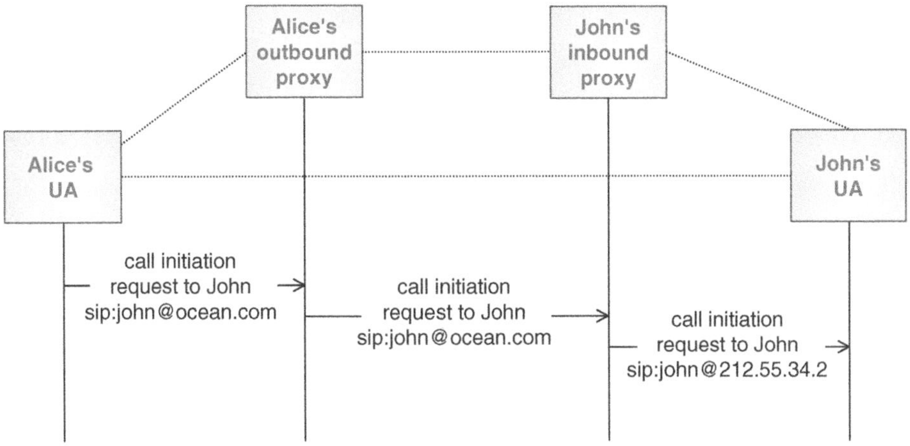

FIGURE 4.9

Inbound proxies and local outbound proxies may be implemented as part of the same system together with the registrar. In this case, they are referred to simply as SIP servers. This is shown in Figure 4.10.

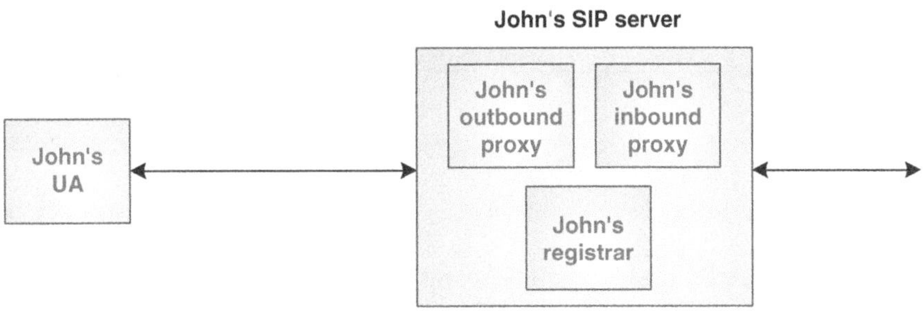

FIGURE 4.10

Forking

There are cases where a user identified by a logical identity (the Address of Record) may have registered several locations. For instance, he may have registered from different terminals with different IP addresses. When a call reaches his inbound proxy targeted to the AOR, the proxy will discover this situation and apply a specific algorithm to try and reach the user among the different locations. Typically, two approaches can be followed:

- Sequential search: The proxy tries each location, one after the other.
- Parallel search: The proxy tries all the locations simultaneously.

Figure 4.11 depicts a scenario for sequential search. Figure 4.12 shows parallel search.

Proxies are further discussed in Chapter 13.

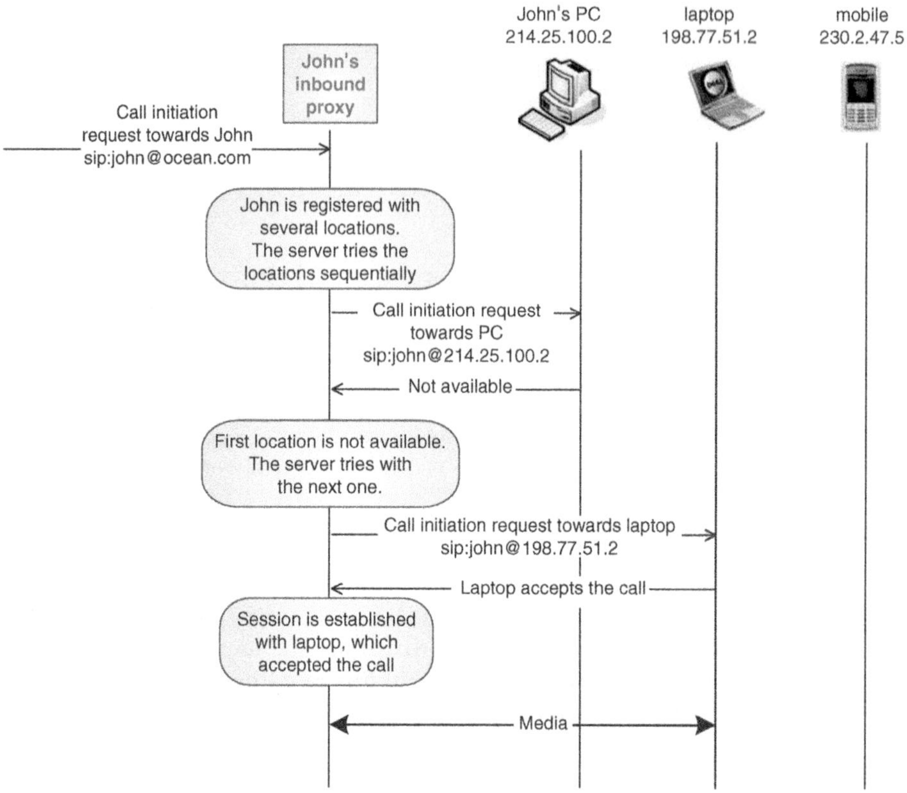

FIGURE 4.11

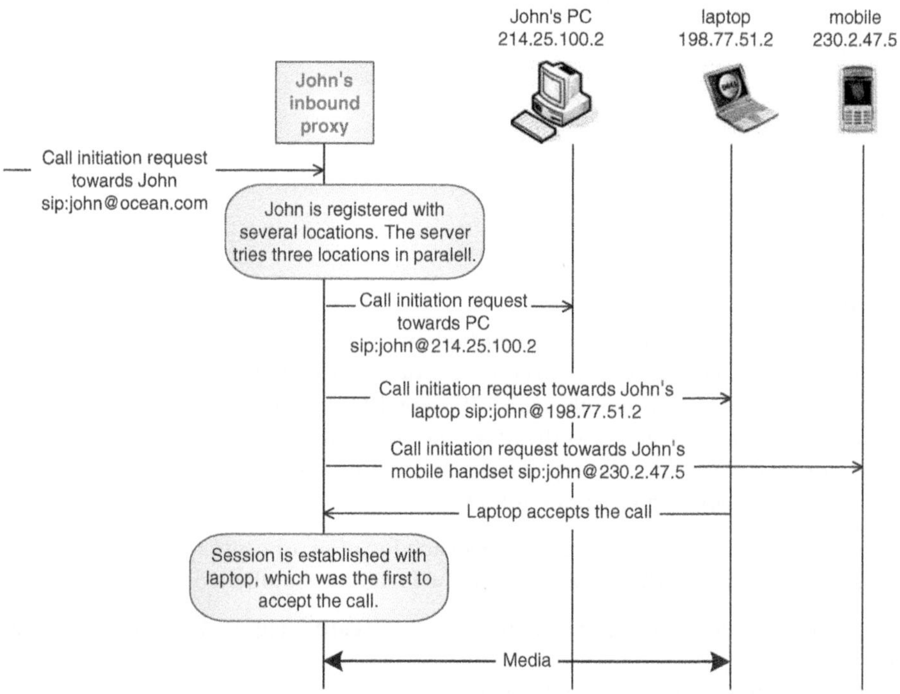

FIGURE 4.12

4.4.5 Redirect Servers

Redirect Servers (Figure 4.13) are User Agent Servers that receive requests from User Agent Clients and generate a specific type of responses to those. These responses always direct the UAC that generated the request to contact an alternate set of URIs.

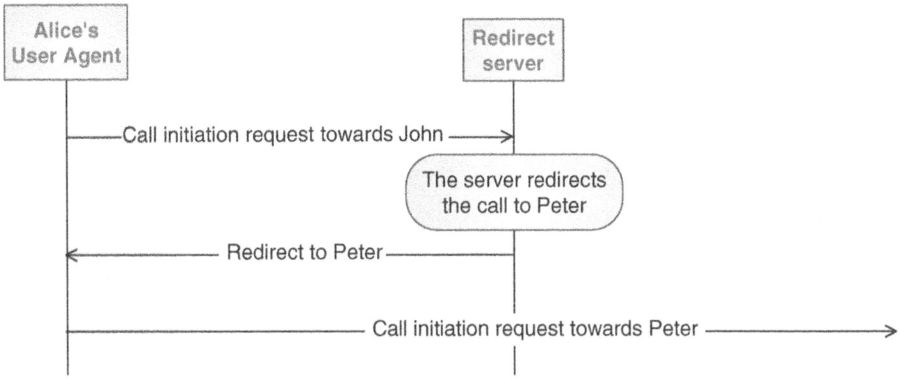

FIGURE 4.13

4.4.6 Back-to-Back User Agents

A B2BUA is a logical entity that acts as a User Agent to both ends of a SIP call. They are responsible for handling all SIP signaling between both ends of the call, from call establishment to termination. They remain in the call path for the complete duration of the call.

A B2BUA is logically made up of two UAs, which are linked through some kind of logic as shown in Figure 4.14.

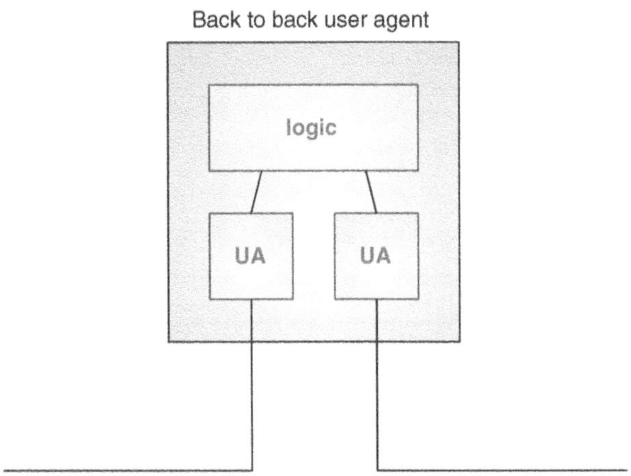

FIGURE 4.14

They are typically used as SIP application servers in order to provide enhanced functionality by manipulating signaling in the call or as network interworking entities.

B2BUAs can typically work in two modes: routing or initiating. In routing mode, they receive a session-initiation request, apply certain logic, and create a new call. This is shown in Figure 4.15.

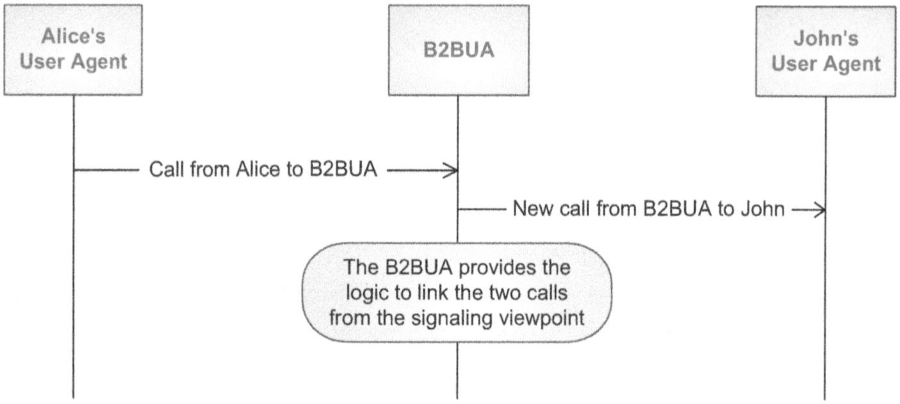

FIGURE 4.15

In initiating mode, they initiate two different calls and maintain the signaling linkage between them. Figure 4.16 depicts this case.

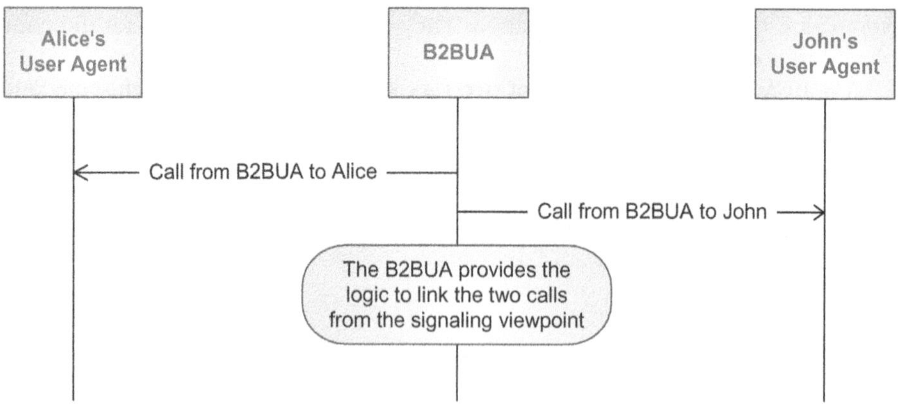

FIGURE 4.16

4.5 Summary

In this chapter, we introduced SIP at a high level. Its basic functions and architecture elements were presented. In order to complete our outlook on multimedia-communications fundamentals, we will, in the next chapter, show an overview of how Value-Added Services (VAS) can be built on top of the basic SIP functions.

CHAPTER

5 Multimedia-Service Creation Overview

One of the major benefits that SIP offers is its ability to be used by programmers as a tool for multimedia-service creation. In this chapter, we define what "SIP services" are. We also discuss the different approaches to provide SIP services, and analyze the tools available for SIP-service creation.

5.1 What are SIP Services?

As we saw in the Chapter 4, core SIP provides a basic functionality for the management of sessions and the location of users. Such functionality at the signaling level, together with other protocols at the media level, can enable a wide variety of multimedia scenarios.

Nevertheless, there are cases where users may want an enhanced functionality on top of the basic multimedia-session management. For instance, imagine that the called user wants incoming calls from specific users to be blocked, or a company wants all the incoming calls to a group number to be distributed among a group of agents. These are examples of services—that is, of enhanced functional-ity on top of the basic multimedia-session-management functions.

It is not always the end users who demand a specific enhanced treatment for their calls. For instance, in order to decide whether a call can continue or not, a service provider might want all originating calls from prepaid users to go through a service logic that checks if the user has enough credit in his or her account.

The previously described services can be easily implemented by having an extra service logic that implements a smart manipulation of the SIP signaling. This is yet another example of the benefits that the signaling concept offers in communication scenarios: it enables the delivery of services.

So far, we have mentioned just scenarios that involve signaling manipulation. However, even the simplest multimedia call requires some media-level handling at the endpoints, at least in order to capture and present the media and to receive and transmit the media packets over the network. Hence, even in the most basic case, there is a need for the applications at the endpoints to have direct access to the media-handling capabilities in the terminal.

In addition, there are other cases in which services are delivered to the users, and these services involve extra processing at the media level. Imagine, for instance, a conferencing service; in such a service, the media generated by different sources need to be mixed together before they are delivered to the destination. Such media mixing can be seen as an enhanced media function—that is, as a media service.

Enhanced manipulation of media is generally a very specialized task that is typically implemented by specific network elements called media servers. These elements typically offer a set of basic primitives that can be combined to deliver richer functionality. As it happens, in many cases, these primitives are accessible via SIP signaling. Thus, creation of multimedia services, be they pure signaling services or media services, in the end boils down to manipulating SIP signaling—that is, to creating SIP services.

5.2 SIP Services and SIP Entities

A SIP service is a piece of logic on top of a SIP entity that delivers an enhanced functionality. Depending on the requested functionality, SIP services may sit on top of a User Agent (UA), a proxy, or a Back-to-Back User Agent (B2BUA).

An example of a service sitting on top of a User Agent could be a simple wake-up call (Figure 5.1). This kind of service allows users to program when they want to receive a call that takes them out of bed in the morning. The machine that generates the call implements a simple logic on top of a UA. The simple logic consists of periodically polling a database that hosts the identity of users and the time when they want to be alerted. Once the application determines that a particular user needs to be alerted, it will use the call-initiation function that the underlying User Agent offers.

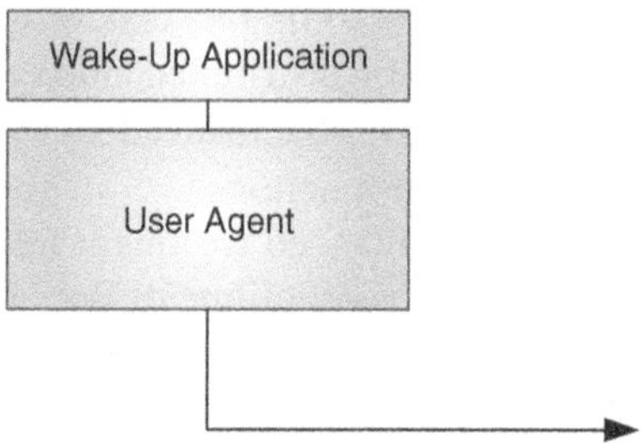

FIGURE 5.1

A voice-mail application is another example of service built on top of a UA (Figure 5.2). In this case, the application is able to receive calls and record or play a message.

SIP proxies can also host applications—for instance, a simple Call Forwarding on Busy (CFB) service (Figure 5.3). The service would receive an indication from the underlying proxy entity that the called user is busy, and it would then query a database to retrieve what the new address is to which the call needs to

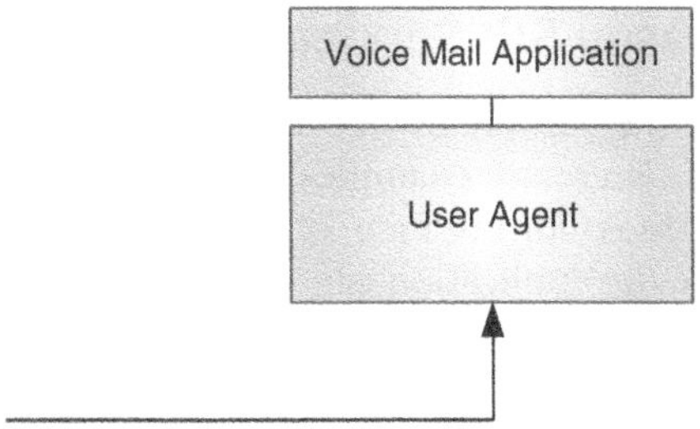

FIGURE 5.2

be diverted. Once obtained, the application would ask the underlying proxy to reroute the call to the new destination.

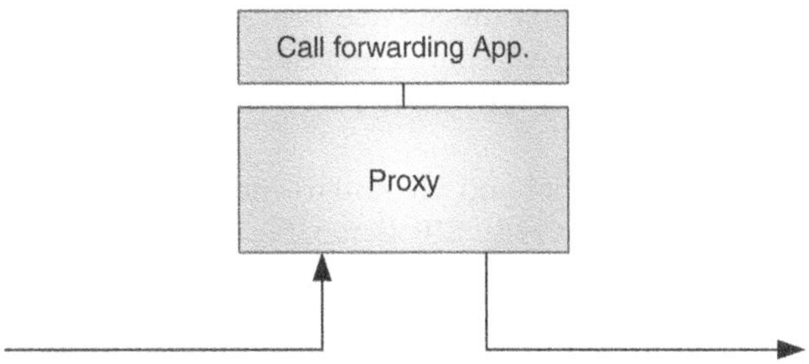

FIGURE 5.3

SIP services can also be hosted on B2BUAs. As a matter of fact, this is the most usual arrangement for providing services in the network by a service provider. That is because it is the approach that gives more flexibility to manipulate the SIP signaling among different endpoints. When a service requires complex signaling manipulation, B2BUAs are typically used. For instance a Click-to-Dial (CTD) service, where a user who is browsing on a web site that sells sports articles can click on a "customer care" link and have the server automatically establish a call between that user and the customer-care center (Figure 5.4).

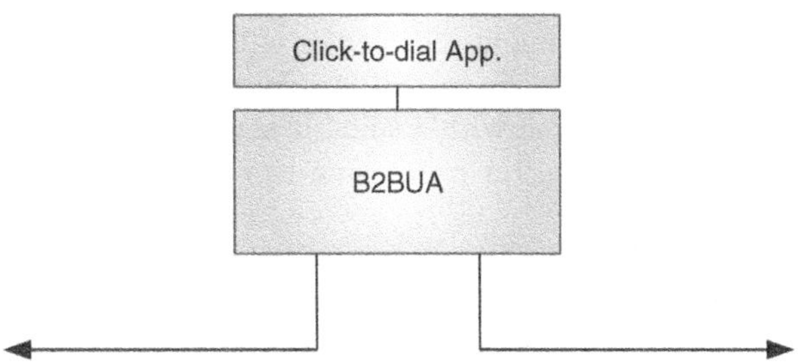

FIGURE 5.4

5.3 Terminal-Based or Network-Based SIP Services

Generally speaking, SIP services can sit on the SIP UA owned by the end user or they can be located in the network itself. There are examples of services that need to be implemented at the endpoints—think, for instance, of a gaming application. However, there are many cases where the application can be hosted either by the customer (in the terminal) or by the service provider (in the network). The discussion about where to place a particular service is not necessarily of a technical nature. For instance, in some cases, it is desirable to have a strong control on end users and on the services offered to them, which would call for a network-based approach. An enterprise SIP network infrastructure that offers PBX (Private Branch Exchange)-like services to the employees could represent an example of this type of scenario, as could a telecom operator's owned SIP network that keeps control on the services invoked by the users in order to charge them accordingly.

In other situations—for instance, in an Internet-wide deployment of multimedia services—the control relationship between the service provider and the end user might be weaker, and the user would have complete freedom to implement whatever services in the terminals, assuming only basic functionality in the network nodes.

As we discussed in Chapter 3, the Internet and SIP end-to-end approach very much advocate a decentralized model; however, SIP is flexible enough to also accommodate other scenarios that allow for having some intelligence in the network. These types of scenarios are very appealing to telecom operators because they can then offer their customers the benefits of being able to leverage Internet-based applications while still retaining the necessary control that allows them to continue making money out of new services. An example of this approach is exemplified by the IMS (Internet Multimedia Subsystem) network, which represents the paradigm for the application of SIP technology by telecom operators. The IMS will be looked at in Chapter 24.

In order to let the reader understand these concepts, we will next see an example of SIP service that can be implemented either in the end user's terminal or in the network. We will consider an Incoming Call Screening (ICS) service that blocks incoming calls to a particular user, say Alice, only when they come from specific users; for instance, Alice might want to block all incoming calls from John.

5.3.1 Option A: Implementation at Alice's Terminal

An application running on top of Alice's UA might receive the indication of a new incoming call, and check if the call originator is in a list for barring. If it is, the application would automatically reject the call with a suitable status code. If it is not, the application would allow the normal UA processing to continue. This is shown in Figure 5.5.

5.3.2 Option B: Implementation at Alice's SIP Inbound Proxy

In this case, when the call goes through Alice's inbound proxy, an application sitting on top of it checks the identity of the originator against a blacklist, and rejects the call if the calling party is on the list. This is shown in Figure 5.6.

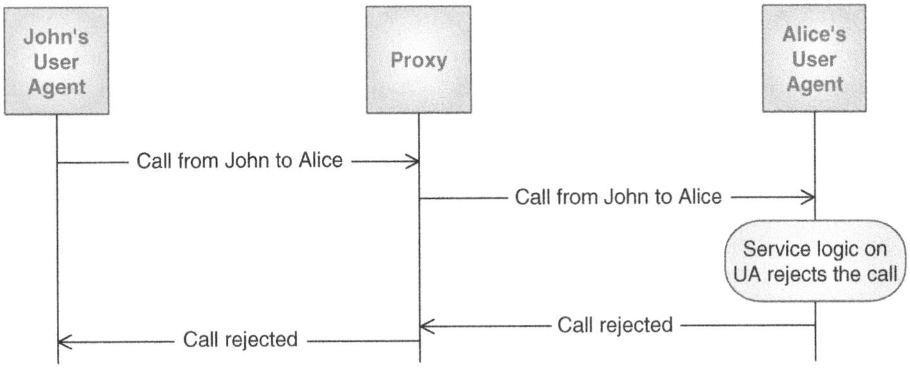

FIGURE 5.5

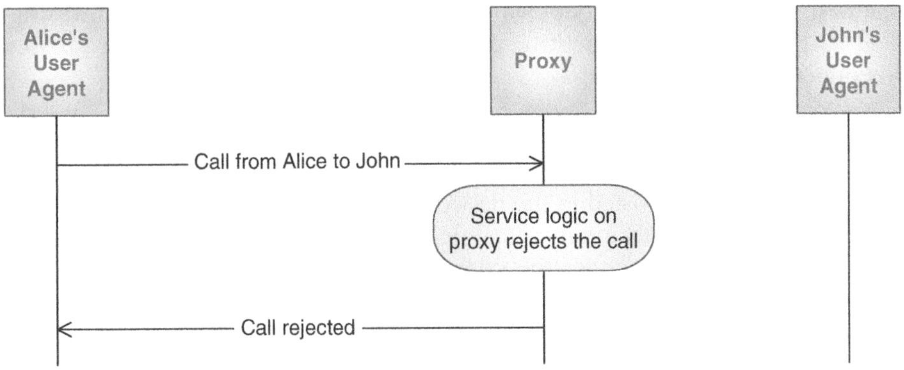

FIGURE 5.6

5.3.3 Aspects to Consider

When deciding whether to go for a network-based or a terminal-based approach, there are a number of aspects to consider:

1. *Control on Users*

Some service providers may want to have enough control on their customers and on the services that are delivered to them. In this case, services are better implemented as part of the network infrastructure. The service provider delivers services on behalf of the communicating users and can charge for them.

2. *Intelligence in the Terminals*

Although SIP terminals may have a huge amount of functionality that enables a lot of terminal-based services, there are basic and cheap terminals that support just the basic SIP functionality and cannot host applications on top. In order to deliver services to users with these terminals, a network-based approach is needed.

3. *Service Homogeneity*

In some cases, the potential users of a service may have very different types of SIP endpoints, with very different capabilities from each other. In order to offer all the users a homogeneous user experience, the best approach is to let the application be implemented in the network, once and the same for everyone.

4. *End-User Availability*

There are situations where a particular call-terminating handling mechanism needs to be applied. In those cases, if the service logic is implemented in the called terminal and the terminal is not available, the service logic cannot be executed. If, on the other hand, the service logic sits on the network, it can have enough intelligence to detect situations where the called user is unavailable, and can then apply alternative call-terminating actions such as forwarding to email.

The aspects just mentioned are particularly relevant in scenarios that involve private networks or telecom operators' networks. On the other hand, the model that best suits Internet-wide deployments is one where intelligence is fully distributed in the terminals, a model true to the freedom paradigm exemplified by the Net of nets.

5.3.4 Application Servers

An application that is hosted in the network typically resides in a SIP Application Server (AS). If the application requires specific media handling a media server can sometimes be deployed under the control of the AS. We will use the term SIP application server in its broadest sense to denote a network element that hosts a SIP application. As we saw in previous sections, such an element can be based on a SIP UA, proxy, or B2BUA, with B2BUAs the entities on which, most frequently, application servers are based.

5.4 SIP Programming Interfaces

In order to ease the development of SIP applications, programmers typically use Application Programming Interfaces (APIs) that encapsulate specific aspects of the SIP functionality so programmers can concentrate on the application service logic.

There are many ways to categorize the interfaces used for SIP programming. For instance, a first classification might split them into proprietary versus standard ones. SIP vendors may decide to expose the SIP functionality in their product by defining their own API that can be used only within the vendor's platform. On the other hand, a number of standardization bodies have defined a number of standard APIs for SIP-application development. The standard approach helps boost innovation and cost reduction by addressing a much larger community of developers as compared with the proprietary approach.

Another possible high-level categorization of SIP APIs might refer to the level of abstraction the interface provides. For instance, high-level APIs completely hide the SIP functionality, and offer developers an abstract programming model that is largely decoupled from the protocol and network concepts. On the other hand, low-level APIs give the programmer the capability to manipulate the SIP protocol objects at the lowest level: messages, headers, and so on.

The main advantage of low-level interfaces is the power and flexibility they offer in developing any SIP application. The main disadvantage refers to the fact that low-level programming is difficult, time-consuming, and requires the programmers to have a significant understanding of the underlying protocols.

On the other hand, high-level interfaces are easy to use, permit quick application development, and, "in theory," do not require programmers to have a huge understanding of network protocols. I have said "in theory" because, in the author's experience, in order to build quality SIP applications, the developer needs to fully understand how the protocol works, even if he or she is using a high-level API. The main drawback with high-level APIs is that, because they abstract a lot of underlying functionality, they do not provide the programmer with access to the full power of the SIP protocol—hence, complex applications cannot be developed using this type of interface.

Having access to an interface that encapsulates the functionality of the underlying protocol is not always enough. For instance, if our application is going to run in a network server, and therefore needs to handle many SIP messages concurrently in a robust, scalable, and performing way, then there is typically also the need to provide an additional piece of software that takes care of the nonfunctional aspects and provides the environment (in Java terminology, the container) where applications can be executed.

Next, we will list some examples of standardized technologies used in the context of SIP-application development. Some of them provide just the functional interface, whereas others represent a container for SIP applications as well.

5.4.1 Standard APIs

JAIN SIP

JAIN (Java APIs for Integrated Networks) SIP is a Java standard for a low-level SIP interface. It provides access to SIP at the lowest level—that is, at the SIP protocol level. Its programming constructs represent low-level concepts such as messages, headers, parameters, ports, and IP addresses. JAIN SIP is so low level that, as a matter of fact, it can be used to build SIP entities such as UAs, proxies, and B2BUA. It can also be used to develop applications, but the programmer is left with the burden of having to implement the core SIP entity logic first, and then the application on top—which can be time-consuming and not the best approach if time to market is crucial.

On the other hand, JAIN SIP, being so low level, gives access to the full power in the SIP protocol and enables the creation of SIP applications of any type.

JAIN SIP is just a functional API. In order to build an application running on a network server, it is also convenient for the programmer to have access to a piece of software (container) that facilitates handling the server-side and nonfunctional aspects. Another option would be for the programmer to build such a software layer on his or her own, which might be a gigantic task that would need to be repeated for every new application.

JAIN SIP is specified in [JSR 032] under the Java Community Process (JCP).[1]

JAIN SDP

SIP programming almost always implies manipulation of SDP (Session Description Protocol) content. JAIN SDP defines a Java interface to facilitate such task.

JAIN SDP corresponds to [JSR 141], but is not yet an approved standard.

SIP Servlets

The SIP servlets API represents an interface to a Java container for SIP applications, including the functional interface. The functional interface is a higher level than the one offered by JAIN SIP. The SIP servlets API is one of the most popular for creating server-side pure SIP applications. It can also be combined with the HTTP (HyperText Transfer Protocol) servlets interface, and offers the programmer a convenient way to develop applications that combine SIP and HTTP protocols.

The SIP servlets API is specified in [JSR 116]. A new version (1.1) is now being developed under [JSR 289].

SIMPLE Instant Messaging

[JSR 165] defines an interface for supporting SIP-based presence and Instant Messaging (IM) services. Presence and IM are covered in Chapter 16.

SIP API for J2ME

[JSR 180] defines a multipurpose SIP API for the Java 2 Platform, Micro Edition. It enables SIP applications to be executed in memory-limited terminals, specially targeted to mobile phones.

JAIN SLEE

JAIN SLEE is another Java standard ([JSR 22] and [JSR 240])—which, in this case, does not provide a functional API, but just the interface to a container for carrier-grade telecommunication applications. Thus, it must be combined with other functional APIs that provide the access to the protocol functionality—for example, JAIN SIP.

The JAIN SLEE container represents a horizontal software layer that can accommodate almost any type of network protocols, thus being the natural choice for building applications that require both legacy signaling protocols—such as IN (Intelligent Network)[2] protocols—as well as newer Internet-based protocols such as SIP.

---

[1]The Java Community Process is a formalized process that allows interested parties to be involved in the definition of future versions and features of the Java platform. New proposed specifications and technologies to be added to the Java platform are defined in Java Specification Requests (JSRs).

[2]IN represents a set of telecommunication standards providing the means to deliver enhanced applications on top of circuit-switched network equipment. Among other things, the standards define the interface between a Service Control Point (SCP: entity where the services are hosted) and an SSP (Service Switching Point) that sits on the voice switch.

IMS API

The IMS API is currently being developed under [JSR 281]. It is intended to be used by application developers who wish to build Java applications for terminals that use the IP Multimedia Subsystem. It is targeted at the Java Platform, Micro Edition (JME).

It offers the programmer access to the IMS enablers such as presence, Push-to-Talk (PTT), and XML (Extensible Markup Language). These and other IMS enablers will be described in Chapter 24.

OSA/PARLAY

OSA/Parlay APIs represent a family of standard interfaces that abstract the whole functionality in a telecommunication network (not just limited to SIP). As such, they cover very different aspects—for example, call control, user interaction, mobility, messaging, presence, and charging. A full list of the different OSA/Parlay APIs is defined in Table 5.1.

Table 5.1

OSA/Parlay API Name	3GPP Technical Specification
Generic Call Control	3GPP TS 29.998-04-2
Multipart Call Control	3GPP TS 29.998-04-3
Multimedia Call Control	3GPP TS 29.998-04-4
User Interaction	3GPP TS 29.998-05
Mobility	3GPP TS 29.998-06
Terminal Capabilities	3GPP TS 29.998-07
Data Session Control	3GPP TS 29.998-08
Generic Messaging	3GPP TS 29.998-09
Connectivity Manager	3GPP TS 29.998-10
Account Management	3GPP TS 29.998-11
Charging	3GPP TS 29.998-12
Policy Management	3GPP TS 29.998-13
Presence and Availability Management	3GPP TS 29.998-14
Multimedia Messaging Service	3GPP TS 29.998-15

These APIs are all service APIs rather than protocol APIs, and so they provide a significant level of abstraction over the network functionality. For instance, the OSA/Parlay call-control API allows programmers to develop applications that manage calls irrespective of whether they are traditional circuit-switched calls or SIP-based VoIP (Voice over Internet Protocol) calls.

OSA/Parlay standards are developed in a joint effort by both the Parlay Group [PARLAY] and the ETSI (European Telecommunications Standards Institute) and 3GPP (3rd Generation Partnership Project) in the OSA initiative.

PARLAY X

A number of factors have made the OSA/Parlay interfaces not as successful as many people had claimed they would be. On one hand, OSA/Parlay is based on CORBA (Common Object Request Broker Architecture),[3] and this has proved to hinder the operation of the API in an Internet environment. On the other hand, what many people see as the main problem in these interfaces is that they are neither high level nor low level. They stay in the intermediate ground. What this means is that programmers who need full control on the SIP signaling typically revert to low-level interfaces such as JAIN SIP or SIP servlets, whereas, for those programmers who desire a high level of abstraction, the OSA/Parlay APIs seem too complicated.

The Parlay-X APIs intend to resolve this situation by providing a very-high-level set of interfaces that are based on web services, and thus are suitable for Internet-wide operation.

Parlay-X interfaces are developed by the Parlay Group and adopted by 3GPP as part of the OSA initiative. The Parlay Group and 3GPP will work jointly in the future to further develop the specifications.

A full list of the different OSA Parlay-X Web Services APIs is defined in Table 5.2.

Table 5.2

OSA/Parlay X Web Services API Name	3GPP Technical Specification
Third Party Call	3GPP TS 29.199-02
Call Notification	3GPP TS 29.199-03
Short Messaging	3GPP TS 29.199-04
Multimedia Messaging Service	3GPP TS 29.199-05
Payment	3GPP TS 29.199-06
Account Management	3GPP TS 29.199-07
Terminal Status	3GPP TS 29.199-08
Terminal Location	3GPP TS 29.199-09
Call Handling	3GPP TS 29.199-10
Audio Call	3GPP TS 29.199-11
Multimedia Conference	3GPP TS 29.199-12
Address List Management	3GPP TS 29.199-13
Presence	3GPP TS 29.199-14

In addition to the standard interfaces mentioned so far, there are many proprietary interfaces (almost every vendor has its own).

[3]CORBA is a standard architecture for distributed objects that maximizes interoperability by allowing the objects to be written in different programming languages.

5.4.2 Open-Source Implementations

It is worth mentioning that there exist some open-source reference implementations for some of the previous APIs. Here are some examples:

- The NIST (National Institute of Standards and Technology)[4] reference implementation of the JAIN SIP API is quite popular, and is being successfully used nowadays in a number of commercial projects around the world. It can be downloaded from [JSIP].
- The Mobicents initiative represents the open-source approach for a JAIN SLEE implementation. It can be downloaded from [MOBICENTS].
- The Jiplet API is a nonstandard SIP servet-like API that uses JAIN SIP as the functional interface to the SIP protocol, and for which there exists an open-source implementation. It can be downloaded from [JIPLETS].

In addition to these, there are many open-source implementations of SIP entities—such as proxies, User Agents, and so on—that offer proprietary interfaces for building applications or extending the functionality in the product. For instance, the OpenSER [OPENSER] project offers an open-source implementation of a SIP server, and provides low-level, nonstandard APIs for SIP-application development.

5.5 Media-Programming APIs

In order to create applications that manipulate media, we can consider two main scenarios:

1. The programmer wants to develop a multimedia application that has direct access to the media capabilities in the underlying platform. An example of such a scenario could be a voice and video soft-phone application.
2. The programmer wants to develop an application that makes use of the existing media-handling capabilities present in an external platform, called a media server. An example of this scenario could be a conferencing application where the media mixer resides in a different platform than the controller of the conference.

In the first case, the programmer needs an API that exposes the media capabilities of the underlying platform. This can be a proprietary-platform API or a standard cross-platform API. An example of the latter could be the Java MMAPI (Mobile Media API) or JMF (Java Media Framework) interfaces.

In the second case, the programmer can leverage the fact that most media servers offer a control interface. Most frequently, such control interface is based on SIP; therefore, SIP APIs can be used for that purpose. In other cases, the control interface is based on protocols such as MEGACO (Media Gateway Control), for which specific protocol APIs need to be used. Yet another approach is to use

[4] NIST is a nonregulatory agency of the U.S. Department of Commerce's Technology Administration. Its mission is to promote U.S. innovation and industrial competitiveness.

protocol-agnostic APIs for media server control. There is currently work in progress to define such an API for Java under [JSR 309].

Next, we briefly describe two of the main Java APIs used for direct media manipulation: MMAPI and JMF.

5.5.1 Mobile Media API

MMAPI specifies a multimedia API for the Java Platform, Micro Edition. It is intended to be used in mobile terminals, and allows simple, easy access and control of basic audio and multimedia resources.

MMAPI is specified in [JSR 135].

5.5.2 Java Media Framework

JMF is a Java API that extends the Java Platform, Standard Edition, and enables audio, video, and other time-based media to be added to Java applications. It allows programmers to develop Java code to capture, present, store, and process time-based media.

JMF is specified in [JSR 908].

5.6 APIs Used in This Book

This book is about learning Internet multimedia applications. As such, it is very much focused on SIP as the fundamental protocol in the signaling layer. In order to let the reader better understand the SIP concepts, we have decided to include programming examples that use a protocol-level API—more specifically, JAIN SIP. From a learning perspective, we believe this is the best approach because it allows readers to take the SIP concepts learned in the theory and directly map them to software constructs by using a generic-purpose programming language. The JAIN SIP API very much resembles the internal layered architecture of the SIP protocol, and therefore is ideally suited to bring into practice the ideas that we will learn about SIP.

Moreover, given that the JAIN SIP reference implementation from NIST is freely downloadable form the web, this also proves to be a cost-effective approach for readers.

For the media part, we will use the JMF API, a Java-based API that is powerful yet very easy to use for building media applications. The reference implementation of the API from Sun Microsystems and IBM can also be freely downloaded from the web.

5.7 Summary

The signaling concept represents a powerful enabler for service creation in the IP communications space. SIP represents a very flexible tool for service creation.

Many different standards for APIs exist for SIP-service creation, each of them best suited for a particular scenario. Throughout this book, we will combine the theoretical explanations of the protocols with practical programming examples that help readers to better understand the theoretical concepts. With this chapter, the first part of this book (Fundamentals) is brought to an end. This part has been intended to give readers an overview of what they will find in the rest of the book, as well as to provide the key background information needed to proceed with the next part. The second part of this book (Core Protocols) dives in detail into the actual protocols used in multimedia applications, with a focus on SIP, SDP, RTP (Real-time Transport Protocol), and MSRP (Message Session Relay Protocol). In the next chapter, we start with SIP.

PART

II

Core Protocols

CHAPTER

SIP Protocol Operation

6

In this chapter, we present the way SIP operates. We will look at the basic types of SIP messages and scenarios where they are used. The SIP message format is also outlined, and we will describe the most important SIP headers. Then we will show how SIP routing works, and highlight the relevance of DNS in routing SIP messages. Last, we will describe a complete end-to-end call flow, including all the signaling messages involved in it.

6.1 SIP Mode of Operation

SIP operation is based on the exchange of SIP messages. Any exchange of messages in SIP is organized in requests and responses. A request, together with all the responses associated with it, is called a transaction. This transaction-oriented approach is taken from HTTP, on which SIP is based to some extent. In HTTP, when I want to connect to a web site, my browser sends an HTTP request, called GET, which includes the URL (Universal Resource Locator) of the web page that I want to see. The server at the web site receives the request, and generates a response that includes the content of the web page (i.e., the HTML code), which can then be visualized thanks to the browser.

SIP requests flow from a User Agent Client (UAC) to a User Agent Server (UAS); the responses flow the opposite way. This is depicted in Figure 6.1.

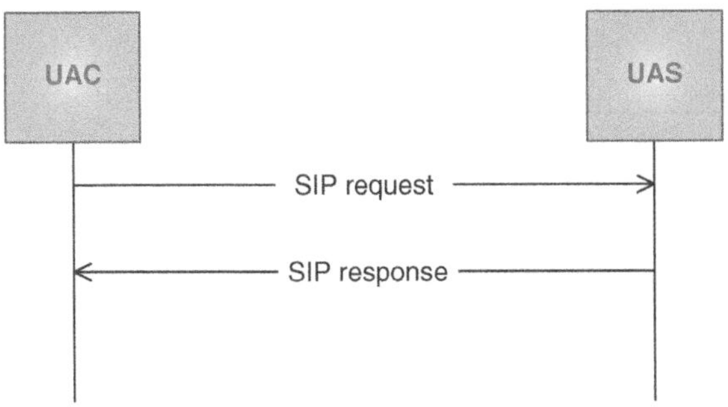

FIGURE 6.1

6.1.1 SIP Responses

Unlike HTTP, in SIP, there may be more than one response to a request. Any request must have at least one final response, and may also have a number of provisional responses. Responses include a numeric three-digit status code. The first digit defines the class of the response. If the first digit is 1, it indicates a provisional response. Otherwise, the response is final. [RFC 3261] allows six values for the first digit (Table 6.1).

For example, the status code 200 represents a successful outcome of the transaction.

Table 6.1

1xx	Provisional	Request received. Continuing to process the request.
2xx	Success	The action was successfully received, understood, and accepted.
3xx	Redirection	Further action needs to be taken in order to complete the request.
4xx	Client Error	The request contains bad syntax or cannot be fulfilled at this server.
5xx	Server Error	The server failed to fulfill an apparently valid request.
6xx	Global Failure	The request cannot be fulfilled at any server.

Figure 6.2 shows a SIP transaction consisting of a SIP request, two SIP provisional responses, and a final response.

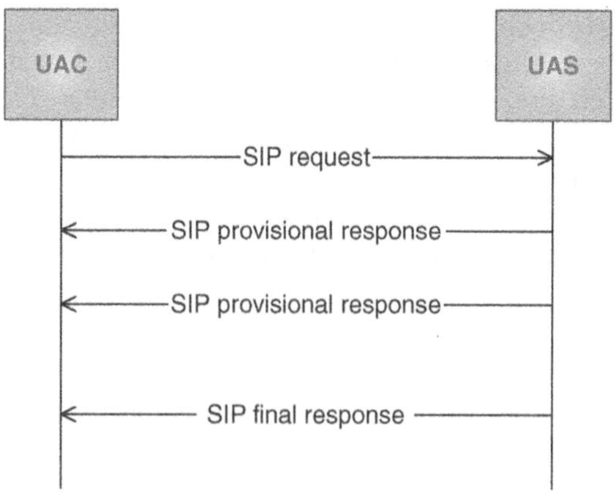

FIGURE 6.2

6.1.2 SIP Requests

[RFC 3261] defines six types of SIP requests, so-called methods:

- REGISTER
- INVITE

- ACK
- CANCEL
- BYE
- OPTIONS

SIP extensions documented in other RFCs may define additional methods. Let us now look at each of these methods separately.

REGISTER

This method is used by a User Agent in order to perform the registration procedure. As we saw in Chapter 4, the registration procedure occurs between a UAC and a registrar. It allows the UA to associate its public identity, the so-called Address of Record (AOR), to its current location, called Contact Address, from which the IP address can be easily obtained. The database that contains the list of bindings is called Location Service.

The UAC builds a REGISTER request, and includes the following information:

- The public identity, expressed as a SIP URI, that is to be registered (e.g., sip:john@sea.com). It is included in the To header field.
- The user location, expressed as a SIP URI (e.g., sip:john@1.2.3.4). It is included in the Contact header field.

The domain or address of the registrar server expressed as a SIP URI (e.g., sip:registrar.sea.com). It is included in the Request-URI element of the SIP message. The address or domain of the registrar may be preconfigured in the UA.

If the request is successful, the registrar will return a response with status code 200. The response will include a Contact header field that indicates the Contact Address stored in the Location Service.

Figure 6.3 shows the registration process. In this example, the Location Service is co-located with the registrar (as is usually the case).

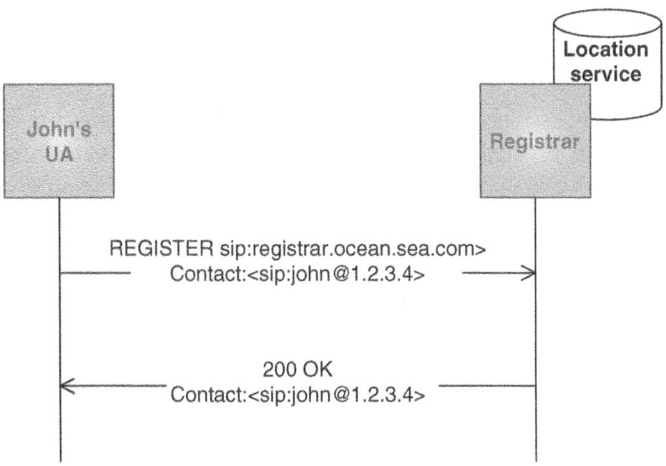

FIGURE 6.3

As a result of the registration procedure, a binding is created in the Location Service. The binding created in the Location Service is a soft state that expires if it is not refreshed. The UA may suggest in the REGISTER request the value of the desired expiry timer by using the Expires header field. However, it is up to the registrar to decide the final value and communicate it back to the UA in the Expires header field of the response.

The UA can refresh the binding before it expires by sending a new REGISTER request. Likewise, the UA can also explicitly request that the binding be removed by sending a REGISTER request with the Expires header field set to 0. For instance, a user that no longer wants to receive incoming calls can request that the binding be removed.

The usual case is that the UA initiating the REGISTER request is the one that is required to be registered. However, there are cases where a UA may want to perform a registration procedure on behalf of another UA. This is called third-party registration. The From header in a REGISTER request indicates the identity (i.e., AOR) of the originator of the request. This may be the same as the identity in the To header (first-party registration), or it may be different (third-party registration).

The information in the Location Service is used whenever a call is made to a SIP user. In those cases, the called user's associated SIP server will query the Location Service in order to derive the location of the destination endpoint needed to send him or her the session-invitation message.

INVITE

A UAC generates an INVITE method in order to initiate a session with a UAS. The request will contain the public identity, as a SIP URI, of the user to which the request is addressed in a field called Request-URI. The request can go directly from UAC to UAS, or may traverse one or more proxies, which can then assist in the routing of the request.

Once the UAS has received the request, it may generate some provisional response to inform about the progress of the call. For example, it might generate a response with status code 180, indicating that the called party is being alerted. If the called party accepts the call, his or her UA will generate a 200 OK final response.

Alternatively, a UAS might respond directly with a final 200 OK response to a session-initiation request. That is usually the case where the session is established with a machine such as a Voice Mail System (VMS) or other. In those cases there is no point in performing the alerting.

The INVITE transaction is also used to exchange and agree on some fundamental session parameters between the calling UA and the called UA. For instance, in a voice or video communication, the calling party and the called party need to agree on the codecs to use. They also need to inform each other about the address (IP address, port) where they expect to receive the RTP (Real-time Transport Protocol) packets. Several mechanisms can be used to describe the sessions; it is usual to use the Session Description Protocol (SDP) for that purpose.

For instance, if Alice wanted to set up a voice call to John, she would include the following parameters in the SDP session descriptor:

- Media types: voice
- Desired codecs for voice: AMR (Adaptive Multirate), PCM (Pulse-Code Modulation)
- IP address and port where she expects to receive the voice: 5.4.3.2: 40000

This indicates to John's UA that Alice wants to set up a voice communication using one of two codecs: Pulse Code Modulation or Adaptive Multirate. It also indicates the port in Alice's PC to which packets flowing from John should be sent. This session descriptor is called the "SDP offer." Please note that we have not described all the parameters in the SDP content, but only the most important ones; we are now focusing on letting the reader understand how the SIP methods work. In Chapter 9, SDP syntax and semantics will be described in detail.

In the 200 OK final response, John's UA will include another session descriptor that represents his answer to the SDP offer. Let us assume that John does not have a codec for AMR, so his SDP answer might look like:

- Media types: voice
- Desired codecs for voice: PCM
- IP address and port where she expects to receive the voice: 1.2.3.4: 80000

What this tells Alice is that John accepts the invitation, that he agrees to use a PCM codec, and that voice data should be sent to port 80000 in his PC at IP address 1.2.3.4.

Figure 6.4 shows an INVITE transaction that initiates a session between Alice and John.

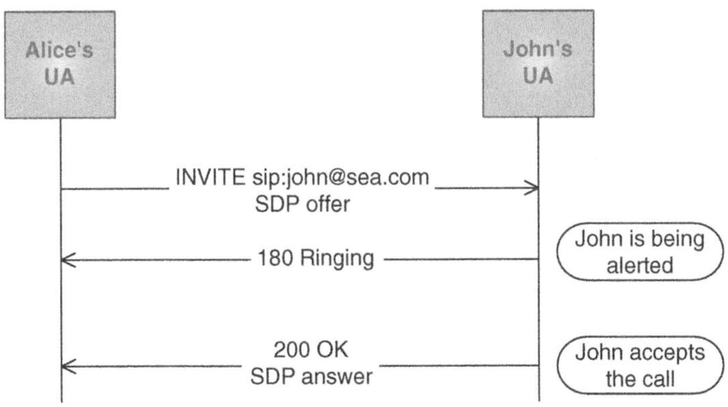

FIGURE 6.4

Another interesting aspect of the INVITE transaction is that it creates a peer-to-peer SIP relationship between Peter and Alice that is referred to as a dialog. The SIP dialog represents an information context in which to interpret SIP messages.

It basically facilitates sequencing of messages between the User Agents and proper routing of requests between both of them. Dialogs will be analyzed in Chapter 7.

Re-INVITE

An INVITE request can also be sent within an already-established dialog. In such case, it is normally referred to as a re-INVITE.[1] A re-INVITE is typically used in order to modify the parameters of the session. In our previous example, Alice and John set up a voice session. Let us imagine that, in the middle of the session, Alice decides to add a video component so that John is able to see the nice cake she is preparing. In that case, Alice would send a new INVITE (i.e., a re-INVITE) within the same dialog that established the session, except that now the SDP includes an additional video component. The SDP would contain, among others, the following information:

- Media types: voice and video
- Desired codecs for voice: AMR, PCM
- Desired codecs for video: H.261
- IP address and port where she expects to receive the voice: 5.4.3.2: 40000
- IP address and port where she expects to receive the video: 5.4.3.2: 40100

Figure 6.5 depicts this situation.

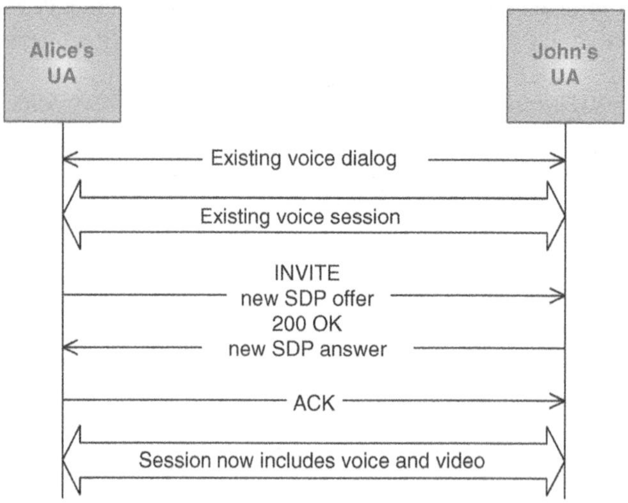

FIGURE 6.5

ACK

The INVITE transaction is the only transaction in SIP that uses a three-way handshake, as opposed to a two-way handshake used by the rest. So, after the final

[1] Even if called re-INVITE, it is actually a plain INVITE method, except that it is sent within an existing dialog (as opposed to the previous usage of the INVITE method in order to initiate a session).

response has been received by the UA, it will generate another request, called ACK, in order to acknowledge the reception of the final response. The reason for this different behavior will be explained in Chapter 7 when we look at the mechanisms that SIP uses in order to guarantee delivery of messages even when using unreliable transports such as UDP (User Datagram Protocol).

Figure 6.6 shows a complete INVITE transaction that initiates a session, including the ACK message.

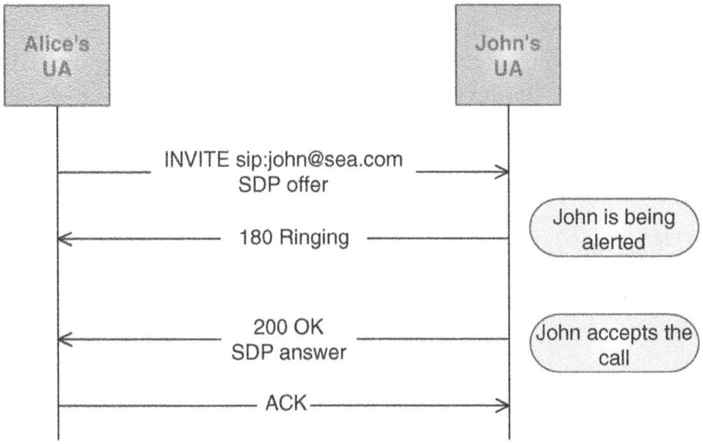

FIGURE 6.6

CANCEL

A UAC generates a CANCEL request (Figure 6.7) in order to cancel a pending request. The CANCEL request is part of a different transaction, but it refers to

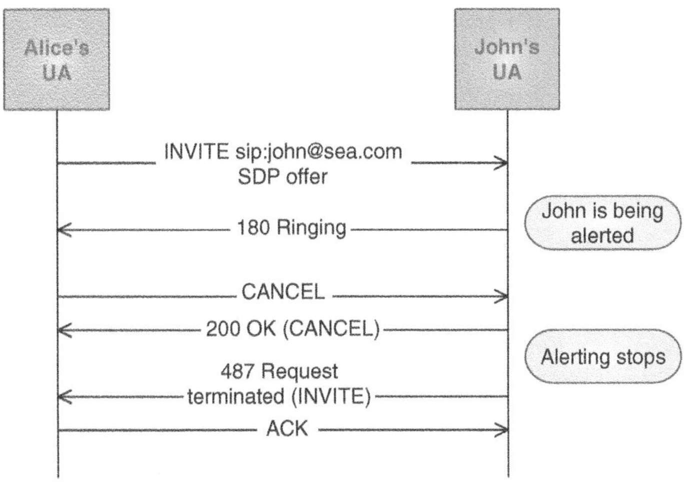

FIGURE 6.7

the original transaction. The reception of a CANCEL request causes the UAs to stop processing the pending transaction. When a CANCEL request is received for a transaction that is already completed, it has no effect.

For instance, let us consider that Alice calls John, so her UA generates an INVITE request. When the INVITE is received by John's UA, it sends back a 180 provisional response and starts alerting him. Nobody accepts the call for a while, and then Alice decides to hang up. She sends a CANCEL request to John, referring to the original INVITE. When the CANCEL request reaches John's UA, the UA stops ringing, and the transaction is canceled. John's UA generates a 200 OK response to the CANCEL transaction, but also a 487 "Request terminated" response to the original INVITE. Upon reception of the 487 response, Alice issues an ACK request to complete the three-way handshake.

BYE

The BYE request (Figure 6.8) is used to terminate a session. When a UAS receives a BYE request for an existing dialog, the UAS must terminate the session associated with that dialog (and therefore stop sending and listening for media).[2]

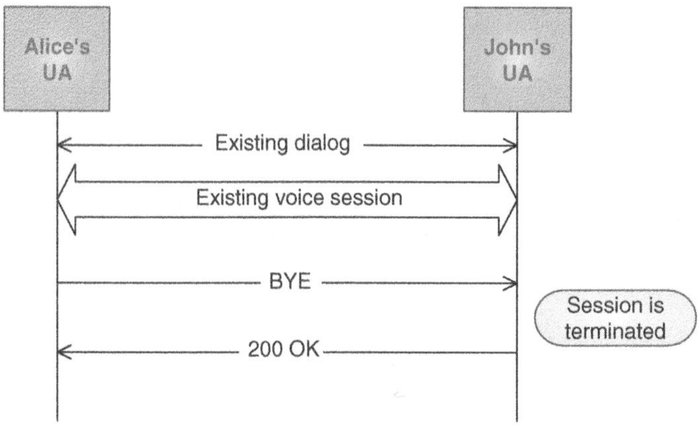

FIGURE 6.8

OPTIONS

The OPTIONS request (Figure 6.9) allows a UA to query a server about its capabilities. These capabilities include information about the supported methods, content types, extensions, codecs, and so on.

[2] Actually, there is a case where a UA can elect not to stop listening and sending media: multicast sessions. In this type of session, participation is possible even if the other participant in the dialog has terminated their involvement in the session.

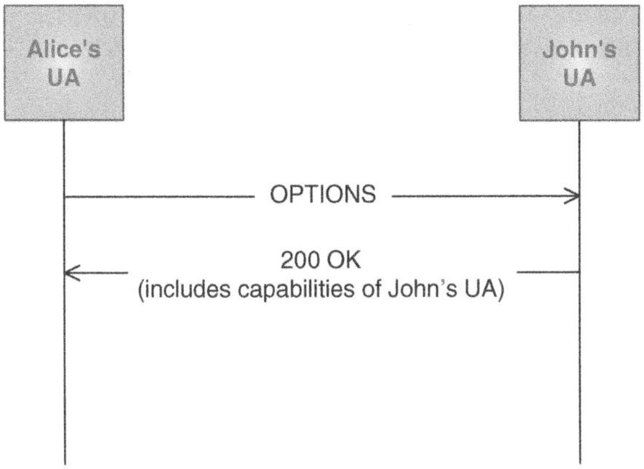

FIGURE 6.9

6.2 SIP Message Format

SIP is a text-based protocol. This means that the information exchanged within the protocol is encoded as strings of characters. SIP messages are divided into lines of characters. A line is a series of characters that is delimited with the two characters Carriage Return and Line Feed (CRLF).[3]

There are two types of SIP messages: requests and responses (Figure 6.10). Both of them consist of a start line, one or more header fields, an empty line indicating the end of the header fields, and an optional message body. Header fields are lines composed of a field name, followed by a colon (":"), followed by the field value, and terminated by CRLF. The body of a message is simply lines of characters.

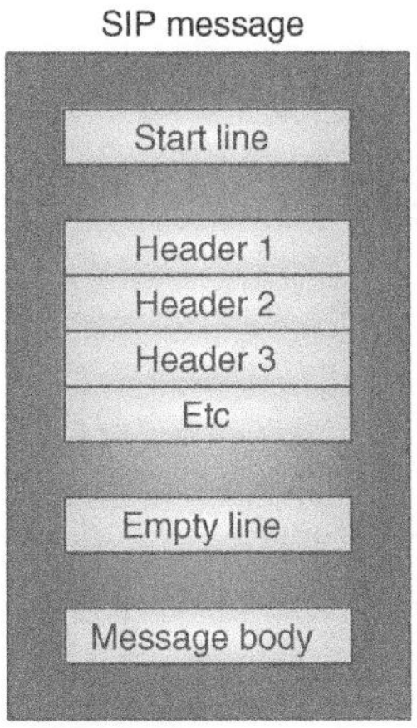

FIGURE 6.10

[3] That is, the Carriage Return (CR) character (ASCII [American Standard Code for Information Interchange] value 13), followed immediately by the Line Feed (LF) character (ASCII value 10).

As we saw in the last section, the message body can be used in some SIP messages to carry a session descriptor according to the Session Descriptor Protocol (SDP).

6.2.1 SIP Requests

In SIP requests, the start line is called a request line, and contains a method name, a Request-URI, and the protocol version, all them separated by a single space character.

Method <SP> Request-URI <SP> Protocol-version

The method name represents the type of the request (i.e., REGISTER, INVITE, and so on), and was explained in the last section. The Request-URI is typically a SIP URI, and indicates the user or service to which this request is being addressed. The protocol version is by default 2.0, which is the current version of the SIP specification. An example of a request line could be:

INVITE sip:john@ocean.com SIP 2.0

The Request-URI field is quite important because it is the primary key for routing the requests. Figure 6.11 shows the value of the Request-URI in the various hops from Alice to John in a typical SIP trapezoid architecture. We can see that, in steps 1 and 2, the Request-URI contains the SIP URI that represents John's public identity. However, when the request reaches John's inbound proxy, it queries the Location Service and retrieves John's location as a SIP URI with which it replaces the original value of the Request-URI. In all the chain, the Request-URI always identifies the destination of the request, and its value is changed by John's inbound proxy because it has more accurate information about the final destination (FQDN [Fully Qualified Domain Name] or IP address of the destination).

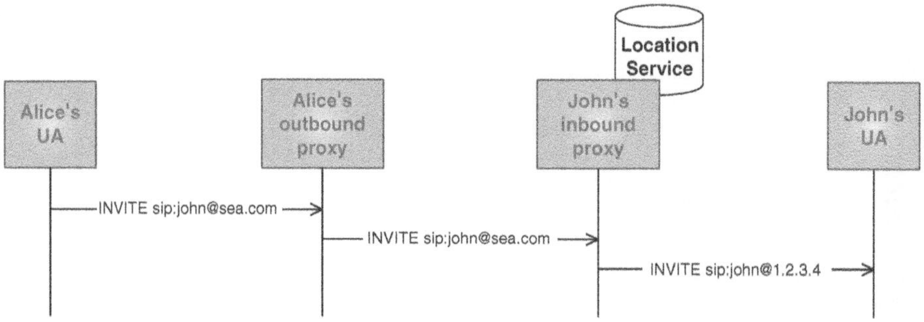

FIGURE 6.11

In Figure 6.12, John's inbound proxy implements a simple forwarding unconditional service such that, when it receives the request targeted at John, it automatically changes the value of the request-URI to the SIP URI of Mary (mary@mars.com), to whom John wants to forward all his incoming calls.

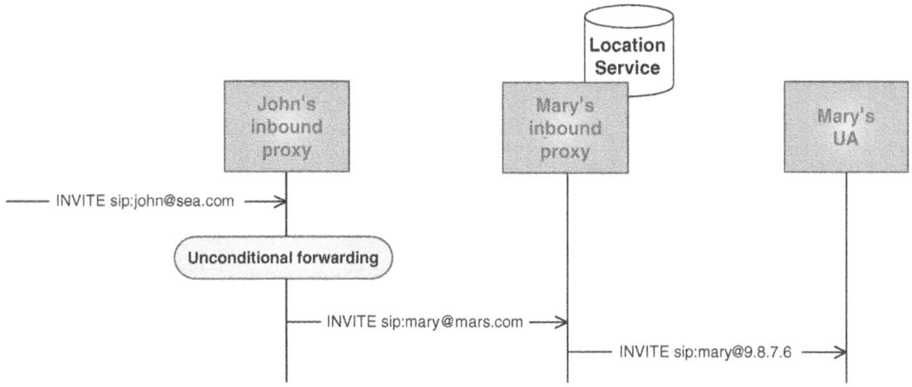

FIGURE 6.12

6.2.2 SIP Responses

In SIP responses, the start line is called a status line, and consists of the protocol version followed by a numeric status code and its associated reason phrase, with each element separated by a single space character.

Protocol-version <SP> Status-Code <SP> Reason-phrase

As was explained in the last section, the status code contains a three-digit numeric value that indicates the outcome of an attempt to understand and satisfy a request. The reason phrase is intended to give a short textual description of the status code, meaningful for the human user. An example of a status line could be:

SIP 2.0 180 Ringing

In Table 6.2, the status code values and reason phrases defined in RFC 3261 are presented.

Table 6.2

Status Code	Reason Phrase	Status Code	Reason Phrase
100	Trying	302	Moved Temporarily
180	Ringing	305	Use Proxy
181	Call Is Being Forwarded	380	Alternative Service
182	Queued	400	Bad Request
183	Session Progress	401	Unauthorized
200	OK	402	Payment Required
300	Multiple Choices	403	Forbidden
301	Moved Permanently	404	Not Found

(Continued)

Table 6.2 (*Cont.*)

Status Code	Reason Phrase	Status Code	Reason Phrase
405	Method Not Allowed	485	Ambiguous
406	Not Acceptable	486	Busy Here
407	Proxy Authentication Required	487	Request Terminated
408	Request Time-out	488	Not Acceptable Here
410	Gone	491	Request Pending
413	Request Entity Too Large	493	Undesirable
414	Request-URI Too Large	500	Internal Server Error
415	Unsupported Media Type	501	Not Implemented
416	Unsupported URI Scheme	502	Bad Gateway
420	Bad Extension	503	Service Unavailable
412	Extension Required	504	Server Time-out
423	Interval Too brief	505	SIP Version Not Supported
480	Temporarily Not Available	513	Message Too Large
481	Call Leg/Transaction Does Not Exist	600	Busy Everywhere
482	Loop Detected	603	Decline
483	Too Many Hops	604	Does Not Exist Anywhere
484	Address Incomplete	606	Not Acceptable

6.2.3 SIP Header Fields

Header fields come after the start line in requests and responses. They provide information about the request or response and about the body it contains. Each header field consists of a field name followed by a colon (:) and the field value.

field-name: *field-value*

The relative order of header fields with different field names is not significant. So, the following group of header fields:

Subject: *Meeting*
Route: *<sip:proxy1.ocean.com>*

is equivalent to:

Route: *<sip:proxy1.ocean.com>*
Subject: *Meeting*

If the entire field value for a header field is defined as a comma-separated list, then multiple header-field rows with the same field name may be present in a message. The relative order of header-field rows with the same field name is important. The following group of header fields:

Route: *<sip:proxy1.ocean.com>*
Route: *<sip:proxy2.ocean.com>*
Route: *<sip:proxy3.ocean.com>*

is equivalent to:

Route: *<sip:proxy1.ocean.com>*, *<sip:proxy2.ocean.com>*, *<sip:proxy3.ocean.com>*

Header fields may contain parameters. Parameters consist of a parameter name followed by a colon (:) and the parameter value. Parameters are separated from the header-field value by a semicolon.

field-name: *field-value;parameter-name=parameter-value*

Example:

From: *<sip:john@sea.com>;tag=1276879715*

There may be more than one parameter in a header field.

Next is a description of the most relevant SIP headers defined in the core SIP specification [RFC 3261].

From

The From header field indicates the logical identity of the initiator of the request (i.e., the user's Address of Record). This logical identity is typically expressed as a SIP URI. Because the From header field contains a logical identity, it is important that no IP addresses or FQDNs are present in it, but rather, an AOR. The From header field also contains a mandatory "tag" parameter. In our previous example, the From header field in the INVITE request generated by Alice might look like:

From: *<sip:alice@ocean.com>;tag=dei3i5h8sdshj88d*

The "tag" parameter is used for identification purposes. More specifically, it is used, together with the Call-ID header field and the "tag" parameter in the To header field, in order to identify a dialog.

The From header field may also contain an optional field called Display-name that would be added before the SIP URI. Display-name represents a name that identifies the initiator of the request and that might be displayed to the destination party.

From: *Alice Dawson <alice@ocean.com>;tag=dei3i5h8sdshj88d*

Usually the value that populates the From header field in requests generated by a particular UA is preprovisioned by the user or by the administrators of the user's local domain.

To

The To header field specifies the logical recipient of the request—that is, the Address of Record of the user or resource that is the target of this request. This logical identity is typically expressed as a SIP URI. Example:

sip:john@sea.com

The UAC sets the To header field, and no proxy in the path can change it. The proxies in the path might make rerouting decisions. For instance, they might, based on local policy, decide to forward a request to another destination; however, the To header is not changed. Therefore, the To header field really represents the original intended recipient of the request. This may or may not be the ultimate recipient of the request. Figure 6.13 depicts this idea in a call-forwarding scenario.

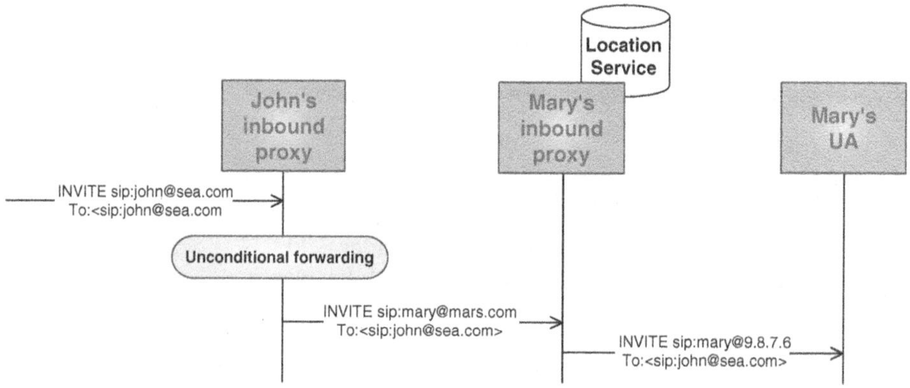

FIGURE 6.13

A UAC may learn how to populate the To header field for a particular request in a number of ways. Usually the user will suggest the To header field through a human interface, perhaps inputting the URI manually or selecting it from some sort of address book.

The optional "Display-name" is meant to be rendered by a human-user interface. Example:

sip:John Prescott <john@sea.com>

The "tag" parameter, together with the Call-ID header field and the "tag" parameter in the From header field, serves as a general mechanism for dialog identification.

Only requests within a dialog must contain a To tag.

Call-ID

The Call-ID header field acts as a unique identifier to group together a series of messages. It is generated by the UA as a combination of a random string and the UA's host name or IP address. The combination of the To tag, From tag, and Call-ID completely identifies a dialog. The Call-ID must be the same for all requests and responses sent within a dialog. Dialogs are explained in detail in Chapter 7.

The Call-ID is automatically generated by the UA, so no provisioning or human interface is required for the selection of the Call-ID header-field value for a request.

Example:

Call-ID: f81d4fae-7dec-11d0-a765-00a0c91e6bf6@pc.ocean.com

Via

SIP responses have to follow the same path as the corresponding requests, only in reverse order. In order to achieve this, the Via header field is used. The Via header field indicates the path taken by the request so far, and so expresses the path that should be followed in routing the responses.

The Via header field includes two fields:

- The *sent*-protocol field contains the transport protocol used to send the message.
- The *sent*-by field contains the client's host name or IP address, and possibly the port number at which it wishes to receive responses.

In addition, the Via header can contain one or more parameters such as "branch" or "received."

Here is an example of the Via header field:

Via: SIP/2.0/UDP 5.4.3.2.:5060; branch=z9hiueufewee

A UAC includes a Via header field in each request. It indicates the address where it expects to receive the responses. Every proxy in the path of the request adds its own Via header field so that responses traverse the same proxies as did the request. As the response makes its way back to the UAC, proxies delete the Via header field that they introduced in the request. Figure 6.14 shows this behavior.

Another function of the Via header field is to allow correlation of responses to requests in the same transaction. For this, the mandatory "branch" parameter is used. The "branch" parameter identifies the transaction. The UAC that creates the branch ID when sending a request has to assure its uniqueness across space and time for all requests sent by the UA. A CANCEL request contains the same "branch" parameter as the request it cancels.

The Via header field is also useful for detecting loops. Proxies are able to determine if a received request is looping just by looking at the Via header. The way this is done will be explained in Chapter 13, which deals with proxies.

Another important parameter in the Via header is the "received" parameter. When a server receives a request and the originating IP address as it appears in the IP layer does not correspond to the address in the topmost Via header, then the server adds a "received" parameter equal to the real IP address the request was sent from.

Let us consider that Alice has a multihomed UAC with two IP addresses: 5.4.3.2 and 5.4.3.1. *f*. She wants to set up a session with John, so first she sends an INVITE request to her outgoing proxy. The Via header in the request from UAC might look like:

Via: SIP/2.0/UDP 5.4.3.2:5060; branch=z9hG4bKl740ws

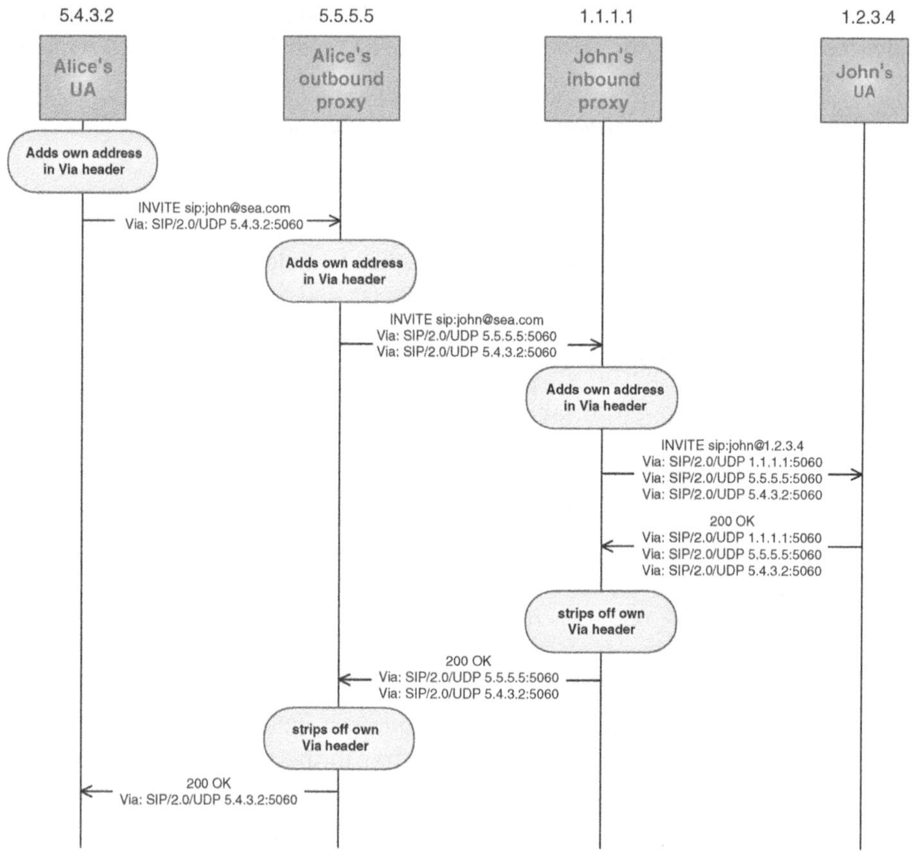

FIGURE 6.14

Let us also assume that the origin IP address at the IP layer is 5.4.3.1. Alice's proxy will detect such a situation, and add a "received" parameter to the Via header. Therefore, the Via headers that Alice's proxy (proxy.ocean.com) will include in the outgoing request toward John's proxy would be:

Via: SIP/2.0/UDP proxy.ocean.com:5060; branch=z9hG4bKos72hh
Via: SIP/2.0/UDP 5.4.3.2:5060; received=5.4.3.1; branch=z9hG4bKl740ws

Contact

The Contact header field is generated by a UA, and provides a SIP URI that can be used to contact that specific instance of the UA for subsequent requests. This means that new requests within a dialog might be routed directly to the peer UA using the Contact address. In this way, SIP proxies that do not need to be in the signaling path after routing the first INVITE would be off-loaded. In order for this direct routing to be possible, the Contact header field typically contains a "location" SIP URI rather than a logical identity.

Example:

Contact: <sip:alice@5.4.3.2>

In Figure 6.15, we can see the utilization of the Contact header in a dialog. The BYE request is routed directly between John and Alice, based on the SIP URI that Alice included in the Contact header field of the initial INVITE request.

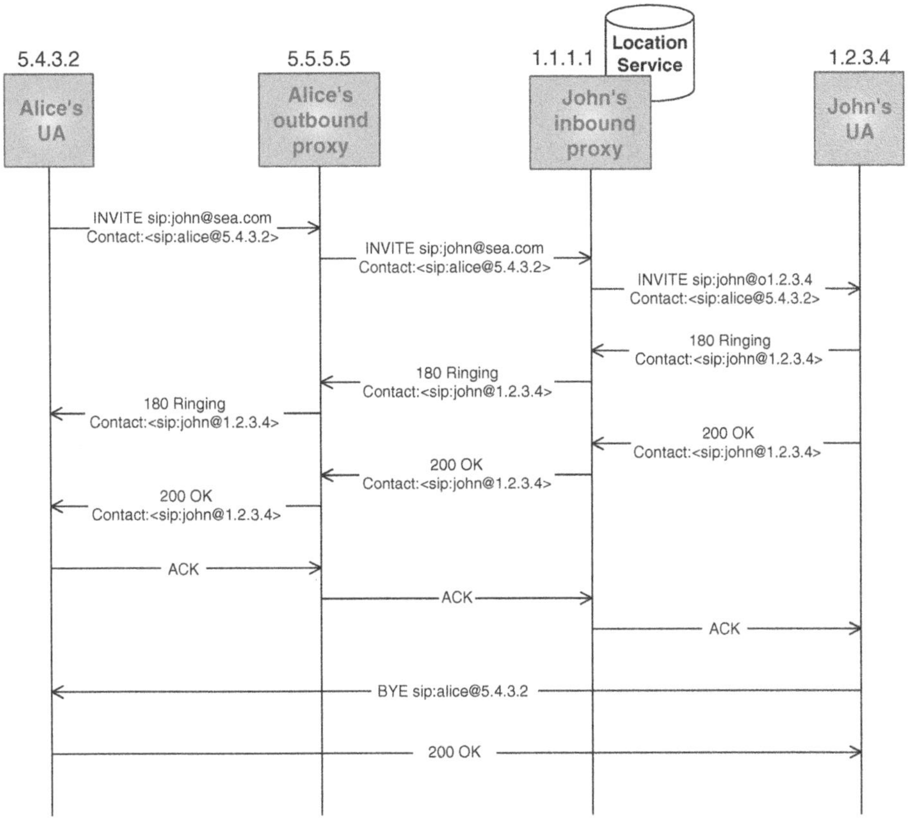

FIGURE 6.15

In a REGISTER request, the Contact header field represents the Contact Address that will be mapped to the Address of Record in the Location Service.

Record-Route and Route

Both the Record-Route and the Route header fields (Figure 6.16) contain a list of SIP URIs. Each list identifies a series of SIP proxies. Therefore, they are "location" SIP URIs that either contain an IP address or an FQDN from which it is easy (possibly through DNS queries) to determine IP address, port, and transport to use.

The Route header field is used by UAs and proxies to force routing of a request through the listed set of proxies. For instance, a UA might include the preconfigured SIP URI of the outgoing proxy as the first entry in the Route header of every new request, thus assuring that such requests would traverse the outgoing proxy.

The Record-Route header field is inserted in a request by a proxy so as to force future requests in the dialog to be routed through it. The UA will copy the

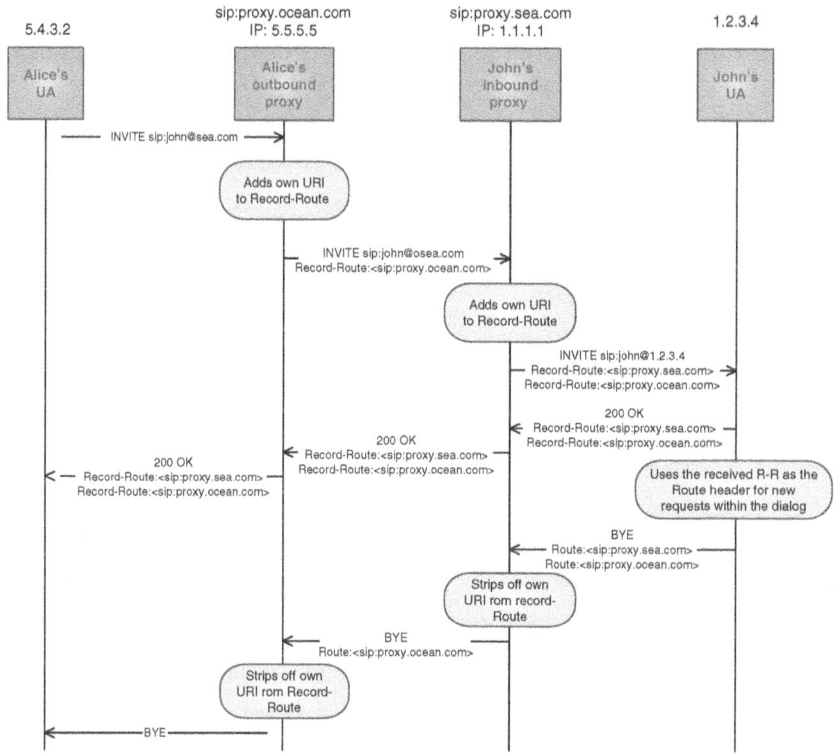

FIGURE 6.16

contents of the Record-Route header field in the received request into the Route header field of new requests generated within the dialog.

CSeq

The Command Sequence (CSeq) header field (Figure 6.17) consists of a sequence number and a method.

Example:

CSeq: 5 INVITE

The sequence number is used to order end-to-end requests within the same dialog. A UA generating requests within a dialog must increment by 1 the value of the sequence number in all subsequent end-to-end requests it sends. The peer UA keeps track of these values, and then can determine if a request within a dialog has arrived out of order.

The ACK and CANCEL requests do not cause the sequence number to be incremented because they are not always end-to-end requests, as will be explained in Chapter 13. The CANCEL request may, for instance, be created by a forking proxy. This situation occurs when a proxy starts two new transactions in order to make a parallel search. If a 200 OK is received in one of the transactions, the other transaction needs to be canceled. Thus, a CANCEL has to be sent by the

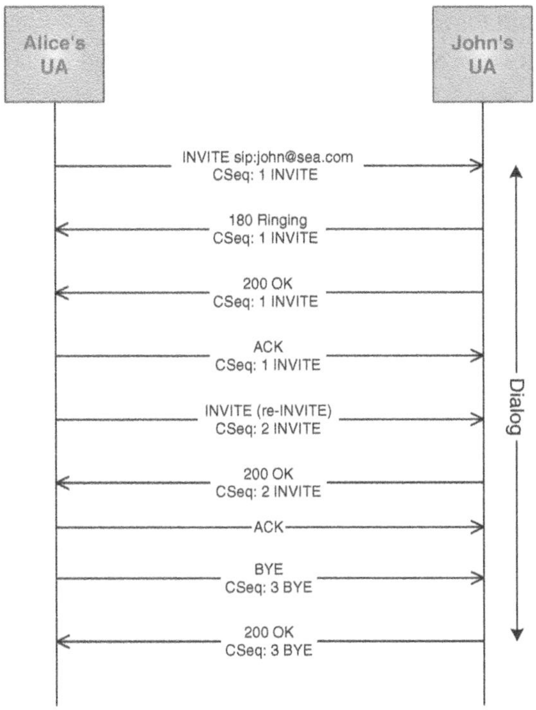

FIGURE 6.17

proxy. Likewise, when a proxy receives a 300-699 response to an INVITE, it has to generate an ACK for that transaction. Therefore, ACK and CANCEL requests never increment the sequence number. Otherwise, they might interfere with the sequence numbers generated by the UAs. More specifically, CANCEL requests will always contain a CSeq equal to that of the transaction that they want to cancel. An ACK request generated as a consequence of receiving a 300-699 response will also contain the same CSeq as the INVITE it acknowledges.

The Method field is used to help in the correlation of requests and responses pertaining to the same transaction. We said, when we discussed the Via header, that transactions are identified using the "branch" parameter in the Via header field. That is true; however, CANCEL transactions contain the same branch value as the transaction that they cancel. So, in order to distinguish a response for a CANCEL from a response to the INVITE, the Method field, which will be different in the two cases, is used.

Max-Forwards

SIP requests can traverse several proxies. In order to limit the number of proxies that a request can traverse on the way to its destination, SIP requests carry the Max-Forwards header field, which contains an integer that is decremented at each hop. When the value of the Max-Forwards header field reaches 0, the request is rejected.

Example:

Max-Forwards: 70

Content-Type, Content-Length, Content-Encoding, Content-Disposition

These SIP headers describe the message body, and thus will be presented in the next section.

6.2.4 SIP Message Body

SIP requests and responses may contain message bodies of different Internet media types (text, image, application, and so on.). The message body in a SIP message is usually an SDP session description, but it may consist of any object, such as a photo or image. It might also contain several parts by using the multipart MIME (Multipurpose Internet Mail Extensions)[4] type as defined by [RFC 2046]. For instance, an INVITE might carry an image object in addition to the session description. The image might be presented to the recipient of the call when he or she is being alerted.

The interpretation of the message body depends on the request method (for SIP requests) and on the request method and status code (for SIP responses).

Message bodies are transmitted end to end between UAs. Proxies must not add to, modify, or remove the message body.

In order to qualify the message body, a number of SIP headers are defined:

- Content-Type
- Content-Length
- Content-Encoding
- Content-Disposition

Content-Type

The Content-Type header field indicates the media type of the message body sent to the recipient. As we already saw, SIP messages can contain an SDP object in the message body. Figure 6.18 shows a SIP message containing an SDP object.

A SIP message body could also contain several parts, each of them pertaining to a different media type. This can be done by using a composite MIME type called multipart, as depicted in Figure 6.19.

Content-Length

The Content-Length header field indicates the size of the message body, in decimal number of octets, sent to the recipient.

Example:

Content-Length: 349

Content-Encoding

This header is used as a modifier to the media type. Its value indicates what additional encodings have been applied to the message body, and so lets the receiver know what decoding it has to apply in order to recover an object of the type

[4] As defined in [RFC 2045], [RFC 2046], and [RFC 2047], MIME is a set of Internet standards that define the format of Internet messages. It was originally conceived for the email service, but it is also extensively used to describe the payload of other protocol messages, such as HTTP or SIP. MIME objects are characterized by a type and a subtype. Examples of media types are text, image, application, and multipart.

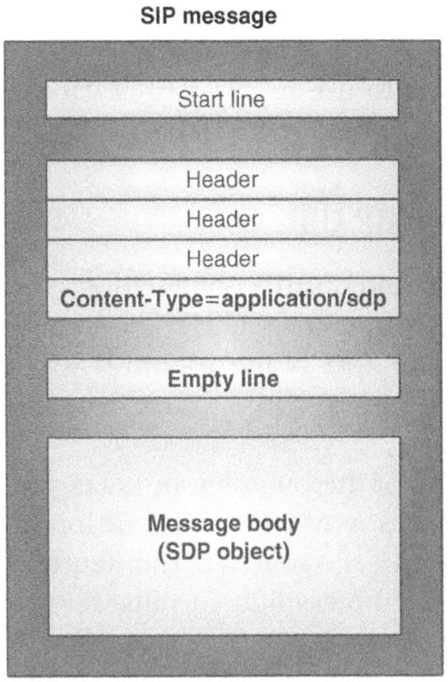

FIGURE 6.18

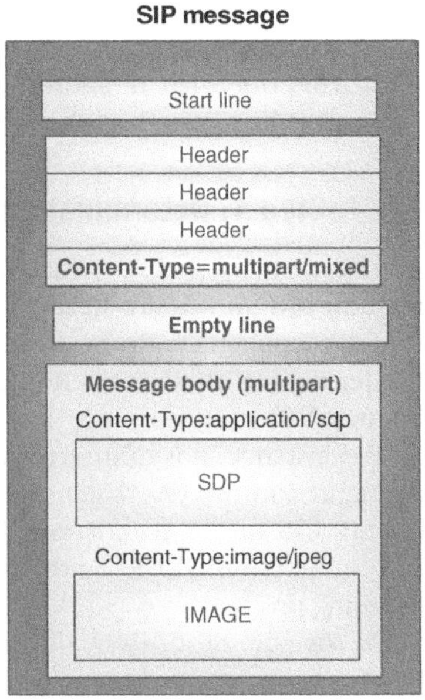

FIGURE 6.19

indicated by the Content-Type header field. It is used primarily for compressing the message body.

Example:

Content-Encoding: gzip

Content-Disposition

This header extends the MIME Content-Type, and thus provides more information about how the message body should be interpreted. Some possible values are:

- "render": Indicates that the message body should be displayed or rendered to the recipient.
- "alert": Indicates that the message body contains info, such as an audio clip, that should be rendered to the recipient for alerting.
- "icon": Indicates that the message body contains an image representing the caller, and that the image could be rendered by the recipient.

6.3 SIP Routing

SIP routing is the process by which a SIP node determines what is the next SIP entity (next hop) to which a SIP request needs to be forwarded. The process comprises two steps:

1. Determine the SIP URI of the next hop. This determination is typically based on some message header fields (e.g., the Request-URI) and local configuration or service logic. The Request-URI field is the primary key

to routing SIP requests because it represents the *final destination* of the request.

2. Find out what IP address, port, and transport to use in order to reach the next hop, based on the SIP URI of the next hop (obtained in step 1).

6.3.1 Step 1: Determination of the Next-Hop SIP URI

In the case of a UA, based on the user input and local configuration, the Request-URI and Route header of the outgoing message are set. If the outgoing message contains a Route header, the next-hop SIP URI is the topmost Route header field. If there is no Route header, the next-hop SIP URI is taken from the Request-URI.

For instance, it is quite frequent that the SIP URI of the outgoing proxy is preconfigured in the UA. When the user wants to send a new SIP request, it inputs the SIP URI of the destination. The software in the User Agent sets the Request-URI to the inputted URI, and the Route header to the preconfigured value for the outgoing proxy.

In the case of a proxy, the next-hop SIP URI is taken from the topmost Route header if it exists. If there is no Route header field, then the Request-URI is used. Two cases may exist:

1. The proxy is not authoritative for the domain in the Request-URI. In this case, the next-hop SIP URI is the Request-URI itself.
2. The proxy is authoritative for the domain in the Request-URI.

In this case, the corresponding Location Service for the domain is queried, and the Contact Address in the form of a SIP URI is retrieved, which is taken as the next-hop SIP URI.

The previously described routing approach is referred to as "loose routing," and the proxies that implement it are typically called loose routers. This is the way routing has to be implemented according to the SIP specification [RFC 3261].

Strict Routing

The old SIP specification RFC 2543, now obsolete, defined another approach to SIP routing, commonly referred to as "strict routing." In this mode, the Request-URI always represents the SIP URI of the next hop. A SIP entity that wants to send a request to <sip:john@sea.com> and that wants the request to traverse a predefined set of proxies should then set the Request-URI to the URI of the first proxy to be traversed. The Route header would then contain the remaining proxies plus the final destination, so that the last value can be retrieved by the last proxy in order to route to the final destination. Every proxy in the path would get the topmost Route header-field value and place it in the Request-URI in order to route the request to the next hop.

In order to understand the difference between loose and strict routing, let us consider a scenario where the originator of the request wants to send a request to sip:john@sea.com, and it wants it to force the request through two predetermined proxies (proxy 1, proxy 2).

Figure 6.20 shows this scenario in a "loose-routing," approach, whereas Figure 6.21 represents the same scenario in a "strict-routing" approach.

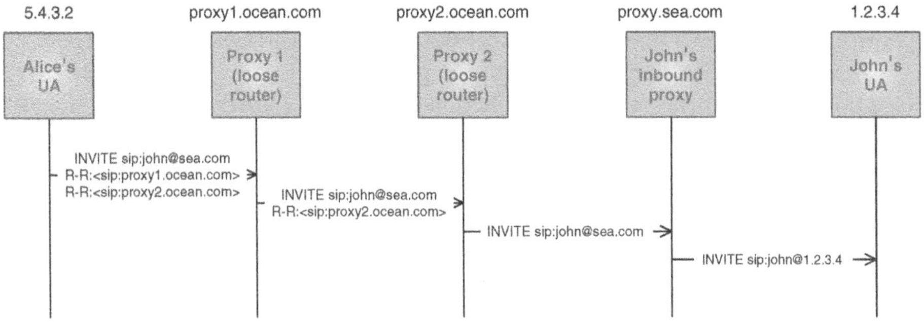

FIGURE 6.20

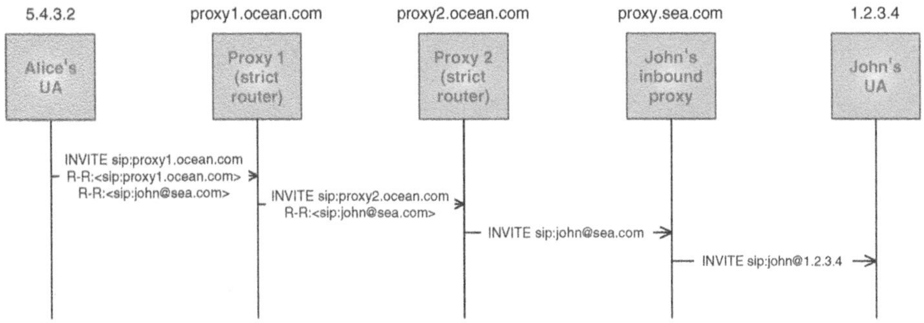

FIGURE 6.21

The strict-routing approach is a legacy one, so we will not consider it anymore in this book. The reason we have presented this approach is for the reader to be aware of it because there are still some implementations in the market that use it.

The URI parameter "lr" is used to indicate that the element responsible for this resource implements loose routing. If it is not present, strict routing is assumed.

6.3.2 Step 2: Determination of IP address, Port, and Transport

We have seen in previous sections that the key to SIP routing is a SIP URI (obtained from the Request-URI or the Route header field, depending on the situation). But a SIP URI does not, in most cases, contain the information needed at IP and transport level to route the request in an IP network. Thus, when routing SIP requests, there is a need to determine, based on a SIP URI, the IP address, the port, and the transport address of the next hop to contact. The Domain Name System is used for that purpose. SIP entities implement an algorithm based on DNS queries in order to derive these parameters from the SIP URI.

In general, any SIP element that wishes to send a request may need to perform DNS processing. For example, we saw in the previous section that, in a SIP trapezoid architecture, Alice's outgoing proxy needed to query the DNS to determine, based on the SIP URI present in the Request-URI, which IP address, destination port, and transport to use in the next hop.

The selection of the transport protocol to use is particularly relevant because we saw that SIP can run on a variety of protocols (UDP, TCP [Transmission Control Protocol], SCTP [Stream Control Transmission Protocol], and so on).

The procedure to determine all these parameters is fully specified in [RFC 3263]. Figure 6.22 represents a simplified view of such a procedure. The entry to this algorithm is the TARGET defined as the host-port part of the SIP URI.

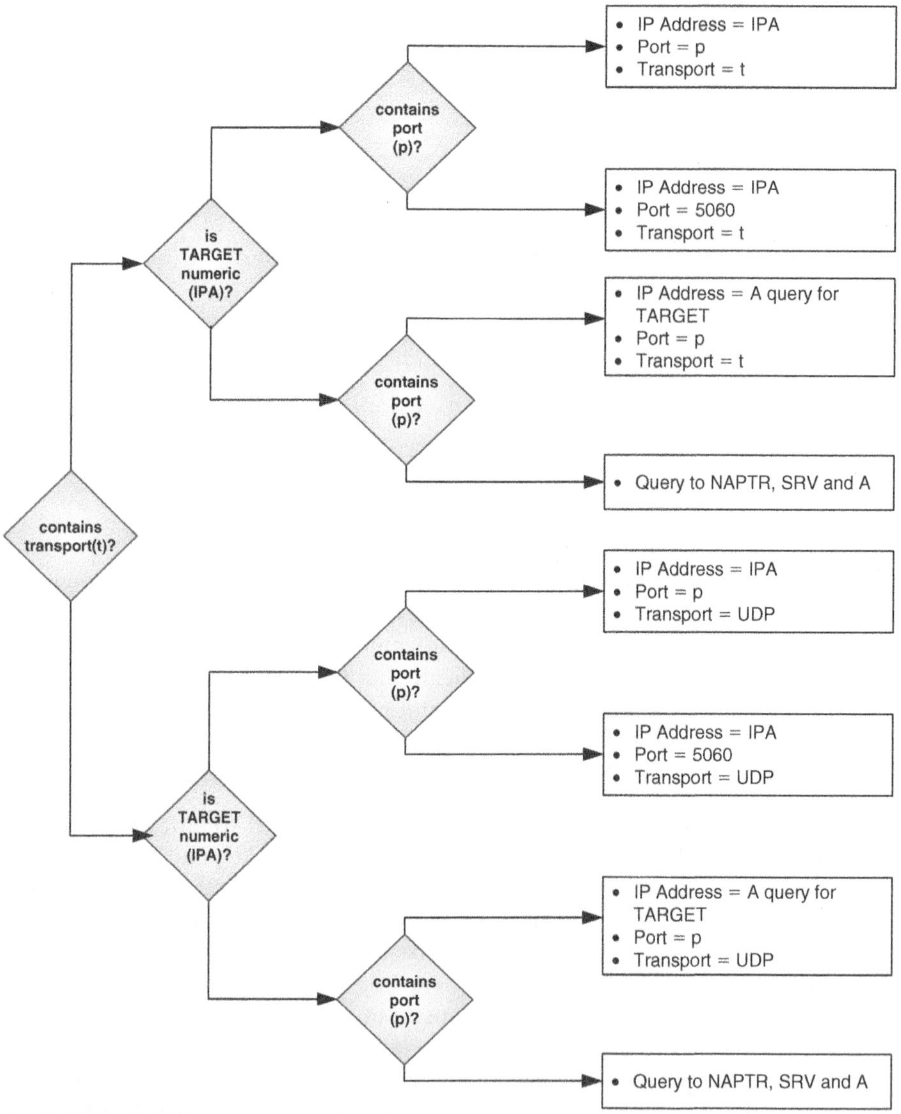

FIGURE 6.22

In some cases, the procedure implies querying DNS for different types of Resource Records (RRs)—for example, NAPTR RR (Naming Authority Pointer Resource Record), SRV RR (Service Resource Record), and A RR (Address Resource Record). The NAPTR RR is used in order to determine the port from the TARGET. The result from the NAPTR is fed into the SRV in order to obtain the port and FQDN of the next hop. Finally, an A query is sometimes needed to derive the IP address from the FQDN.

Let us consider a couple of examples to illustrate how the algorithm works.

Example 1: SIP URI is <sip:john@sea.com>

In this case, the SIP URI does not contain explicit information about the transport protocol—neither the port nor the IP address. This is the most complex case, and requires that the SIP element perform three chained DNS queries.

In this example, the TARGET is the domain "sea.com."

The SIP entity would perform a first NAPTR query for the domain "sea.com" in order to retrieve the transport to use. Let us assume that the NAPTR records shown in Table 6.3 are returned.

Table 6.3

Address Type	RR Type	Order	Pref.	Flags	Service	Reg exp	Replacement
IN	NAPTR	20	50	"s"	"SIP+D2T"	""	_sip._tcp.sea.com
IN	NAPTR	30	50	"s"	"SIP+D2U"	""	_sip._udp.sea.com

The "Service" parameter returned indicates that the server supports both UDP (SIP+D2U) and TCP (SIP+D2U). The SIP element chooses TCP, and thus performs an SRV lookup of "_sip_tcp_sea.com," which might return the results shown in Table 6.4.

Table 6.4

Address Type	RR Type	Priority	Weight	Port	Target
IN	NAPTR	0	1	5060	proxy.sea.com

This indicates that port 5060 should be used, and that the domain of the next hop is "proxy.sea.com."

At this point, an A (IPv4) or AAAA (IPv6) query would be done in order to resolve the domain name "proxy.sea.com" into an IP address (e.g., 1.1.1.1).

This process is represented in Figure 6.23.

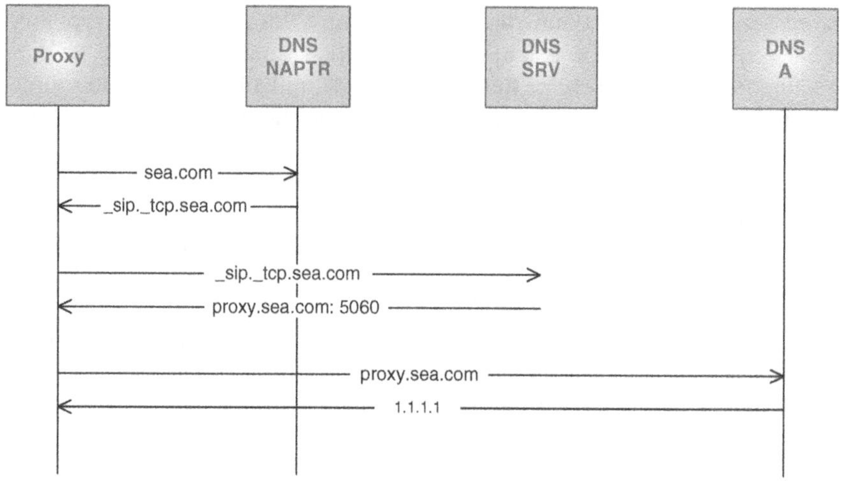

FIGURE 6.23

Example 2: SIP URI is <sip:john@1.1.1.1>

In this case, the SIP URI contains an explicit reference to the destination IP address, but does not say anything about the port or transport. In this situation, and according to the algorithm represented in Figure 6.22, the request must be sent toward port 5060 (the default port for SIP) using UDP transport. [RFC 3261] defines that both UDP and TCP are mandatory transports in any SIP node. However, the legacy SIP specification RFC 2543 mandated only UDP; therefore, for backward-compatibility purposes, UDP is considered as the default in this case.

6.3.3 SIP Routing Scenarios

We have in previous sections understood the rules and algorithms applied in SIP routing. Now we will apply these mechanisms to two well-known SIP scenarios: the direct-mode scenario and the proxy-assisted-mode scenario.

Continuing with our previous examples, let us assume it is Alice who wants to establish a multimedia session with John.

Direct-Mode Scenario

In the direct mode, the UA initiating the session (in our case, Alice's UA) knows beforehand the IP address of the target UA (John's UA). So, in this case, Alice might introduce the following SIP URI to indicate the destination of the call:

sip:john@1.2.3.4

Alice's UA would generate an INVITE request, and introduce this SIP URI in the Request-URI field (and also in the To header field). At the same time, it would derive the destination IP address from the SIP URI, which is straightforward, and select the default destination port (5060) and the default transport (UDP). At this point, John's UA can send the message directly to Alice. There is no need for any proxy in between the two UAs. Figure 6.24 describes this scenario.

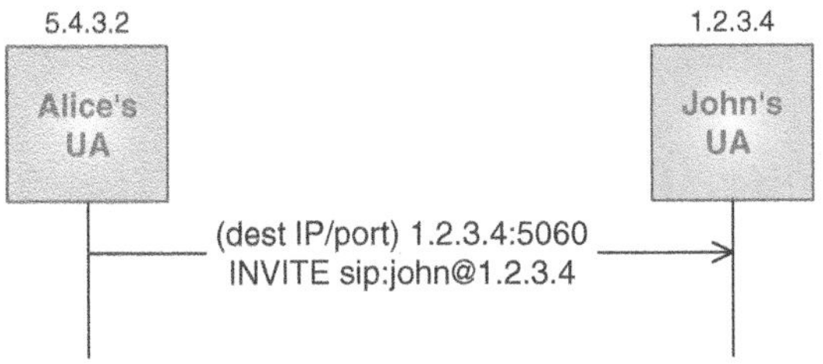

FIGURE 6.24

Regarding the routing of responses, these are sent back to the originator of the request thanks to the Via header field—which the originator includes in the request, and which contains its own IP address.

Proxy-Assisted-Mode Scenarios

In the proxy-assisted mode, Alice does not know the IP address of John's UA. All she knows is his SIP public identity in the form of a SIP URI:

sip:john@sea.com

As opposed to the SIP URI in the previous examples, this SIP URI does not indicate a location; it represents a "logical" identity. So, in this case, there is a need to query a Location Service and retrieve a "location" SIP URI from which the parameters needed to route the call (IP address, port, and transport) can be easily derived.

Obviously, the Location Service needs to have been previously populated with the Address of Record-to-Contact Address mapping that we saw in previous sections. That is typically done through the registration procedure.

Typically, John would be subscribed to a SIP service provider (in this case, called "Sea"). This company deploys a registrar, a proxy, and a Location Service. John registers with the registrar and Location Service. The proxy is an inbound proxy that responds for the domain sea.com and has the capability to query the Location Service. That proxy, proxy.sea.com, could also act as an outbound proxy for calls originated by John.

In this scenario, Alice would introduce John's SIP URI (sip:john@sea.com), and his UA would place it in the Request-URI of the INVITE message (and also in the To header field). Alice's UA would need to route the request to the authoritative proxy for the domain sea.com—that is, it must send the request to John's inbound proxy. For that, Alice's UA needs to determine the address, port, and transport to use, for which it has to perform some DNS queries. Then the UA sends the message directly to the obtained IP address and port, using the obtained transport type. John's inbound proxy receives the INVITE request and examines the domain (sea.com) in the Request-URI. It recognizes the domain as its own, for which it handles a Location Service. So proxy.sea.com queries the Location Service for the public identity sip:john@sea.com, and obtains a "location" URI sip:john@1.2.3.4.

The proxy changes the SIP URI after the location query, and sends the message to the IP address in the new SIP URI.

This scenario is depicted in Figure 6.25.

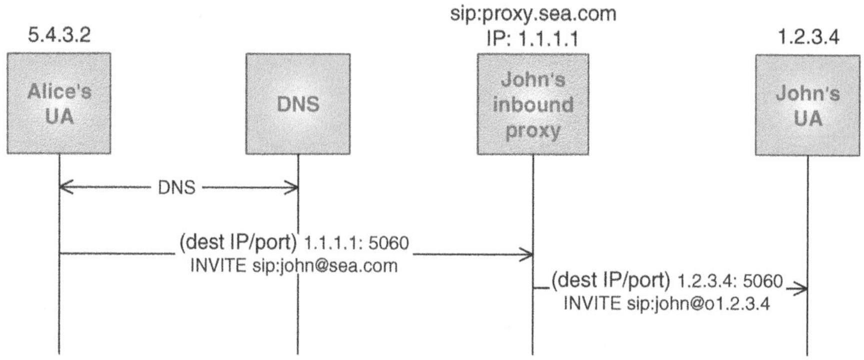

FIGURE 6.25

In the previous scenario, it has been Alice's UA that directly makes all the necessary DNS queries. Although this is definitely a possible scenario, it is more frequent to delegate those queries to an outbound proxy. This proxy—let us call it proxy.ocean.com—is deployed by Alice's SIP provider ("Ocean"), and might also act as inbound proxy for incoming calls to Alice. In this new scenario, we have the familiar *SIP trapezoid*, which is the most usual architecture for SIP. This scenario is equivalent to the previous one, except that the DNS queries for the domain ocean.com are now performed by the outgoing proxy, and Alice's UA has to make sure that all outgoing calls are sent to that proxy. This is usually achieved through configuration (static or dynamic) of Alice's UA. When Alice initiates a session, her UA reads the "Outbound proxy" configuration parameter and puts it as the first entry in the Route header field (John's address would go into the Request-URI) so the message would be routed first to proxy.ocean.com.

The SIP trapezoid scenario is depicted in Figure 6.26.

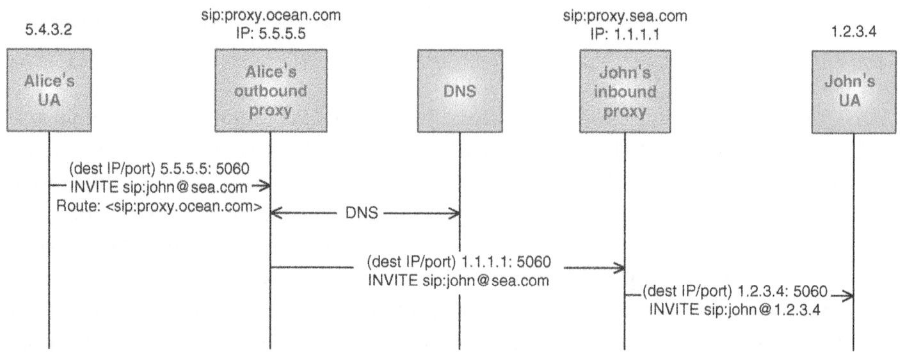

FIGURE 6.26

In a real SIP scenario, there might be even more than two proxies in the path. Those proxies could help in routing the call, and may need to make DNS queries.

Once the dialog has been established, subsequent requests within the dialog might need to traverse all the proxies or could just skip them. This depends on whether the proxies, during the dialog setup, decided to be included in the path of subsequent messages. Proxies signal that situation by including their SIP URI in the Record-Route header field of the INVITE message. New requests within the dialog can nevertheless be routed directly to the peer UA without the need to again query a Location Service, thanks to the fact that UAs include in the INVITE request a header field called Contact header, which represents a SIP URI that can be used to directly reach the UA.

The reader may wonder what the use is of having the proxies remain in the path after the call has already been routed. Actually, proxies may have some (limited) service logic. Let us imagine, for example, that a SIP provider wants to charge calls initiated by its subscribers. The provider somehow needs to generate a record indicating the duration of each call, together with the identity of the caller and the callee. A proxy that record-routes would be able to generate these records because it knows when the call starts and also when the call is released, and therefore it can measure the call duration.

In all the previous scenarios, responses follow the same path as requests—that is, they traverse the same proxies. This can be achieved thanks to the Via header field, which was explained in previous sections.

6.4 SIP Detailed Call Flows

As a summary of the concepts learned in this chapter, we present here a simple example of a SIP registration and a SIP call. For each step in the call flow, we show the content of the SIP message, except for the SDP, which will be described in detail in Chapter 9.

6.4.1 SIP Registration

This example shows John's UA registering with his registrar server and Location Service. It is depicted in Figure 6.27.

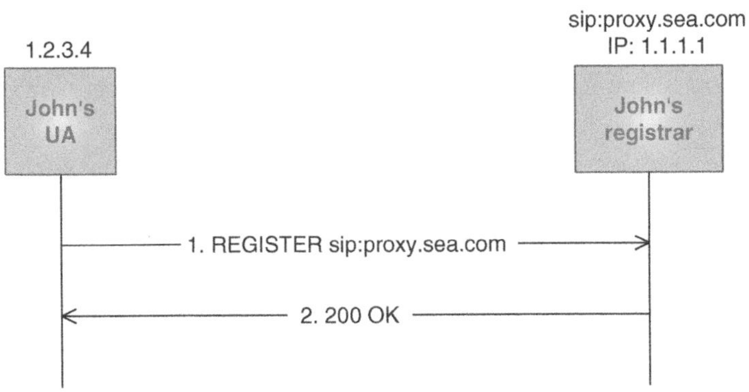

FIGURE 6.27

Step 1

John's soft phone may have two pieces of preconfigured information:

- The SIP URI of his SIP registrar: <sip:proxy.sea.com>[5]
- His public identity (AOR): <sip:john@sea.com>

When John turns on his soft phone, it will automatically generate a REGISTER request such that:

- The From header field is set to the identity of the originator of the request, that is:

  <sip:john@sea.com>.

- The To header field is set to the identity that is to be registered, that is:

  <sip:john@sea.com>.

- The Request-URI header field is set to the registrar's SIP URI:

  <sip:proxy.sea.com>.

- The Contact header field is set to a SIP URI indicating the location of John's UA:

  <sip:john@1.2.3.4>.

Given that there is no Route header, the next-hop SIP URI is contained in the Request-URI. Following DNS procedures (not shown), it will be resolved into an IP address, port, and transport for forwarding the message.

```
REGISTER sip:proxy.sea.com SIP/2.0
Via: SIP/2.0/UDP 1.2.3.4:5060;branch=z9hG4bKjjf9d45
Max-Forwards: 70
To: <sip:john@sea.com>
From: <sip:john@sea.com>;tag=635529
Call-ID: 99183245223553@43je8ew9236
CSeq: 540 REGISTER
Contact: <sip:john@1.2.3.4>
Expires: 6300
Content-Length: 0
```

Step 2

The registrar creates a binding between John's AOR and his location SIP URI, and returns a 200 OK message that indicates to John that the request was successfully performed.

```
SIP/2.0 200 OK
Via: SIP/2.0/UDP 1.2.3.4:5060;branch=z9hG4bKjjf9d45
To:<sip:john@sea.com>;tag=546229
From: <sip:john@sea.com>;tag=635529
Call-ID: 99183245223553@43je8ew9236
CSeq: 540 REGISTER
Contact: <sip:john@1.2.3.4>
```

[5] We are assuming that John's registrar and inbound proxy are co-located in proxy.sea.com.

```
Expires: 6300
Content-Length: 0
```

6.4.2 SIP Call

This example includes the session establishment, conversation phase, session modification, and session termination between Alice and John. We assume a SIP trapezoid architecture—that is, signaling traverses an outbound proxy that acts on behalf of Alice, and an inbound proxy acting on behalf of John, while the media is directly carried between the endpoints. These proxies facilitate the session establishment by helping to route the requests.

In this example, Alice is using a soft phone running on her PC, and John is using a multimedia-enabled mobile phone. Both of them include a SIP User Agent plus the needed functionality to handle voice and video media. As a prerequisite for this example, John's soft phone is registered.

Figure 6.28 shows the message exchange for the call between the involved entities. Please note that, for simplicity reasons, the 100 (Trying) provisional responses, typically generated by proxies, are not shown in this example.The usage of the 100 (Trying) provisional response will be further explained in chapter 13, dedicated to SIP proxies.

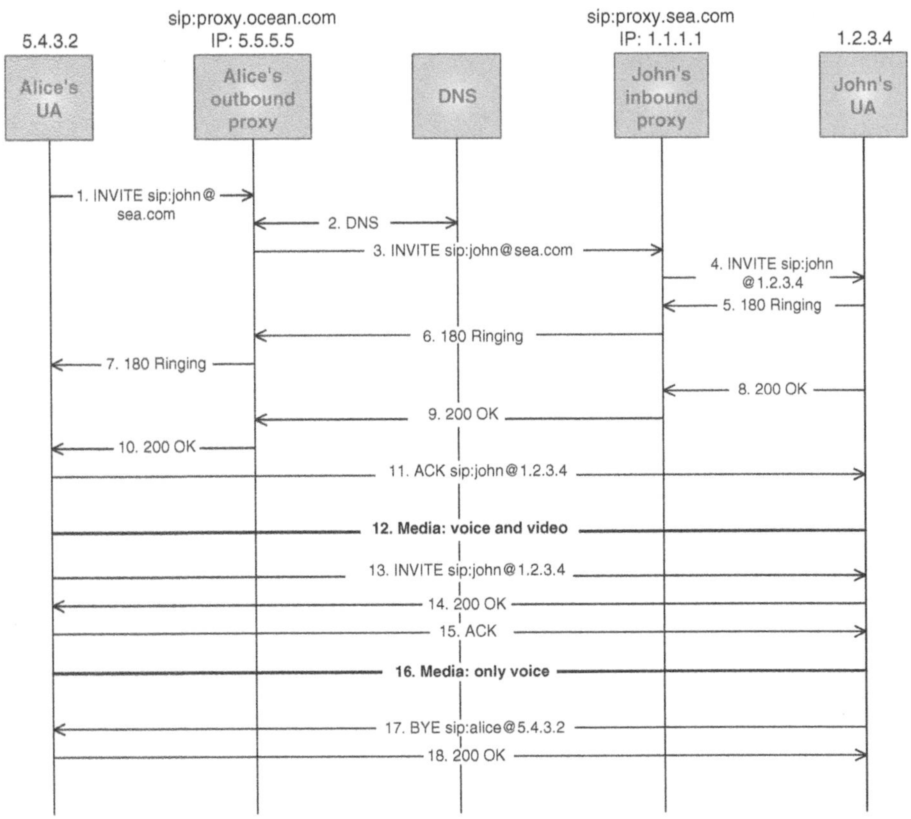

FIGURE 6.28

Step 1

Alice's soft phone may have two pieces of preconfigured information:

- The SIP URI of her outgoing proxy:

  <sip:proxy.ocean.com>

- Her public identity (AOR):

  <sip:alice@ocean.com>

In order to set up a voice and video session with John, Alice needs to do three things:

1. Introduce John's identity:

   sip:john@sea.com.

2. Introduce the desired media (voice and video) and codecs. The available codecs for each media may already be preconfigured.
3. Press the "Call" button.

When Alice presses the "Call" button, her UA generates an INVITE message such that:

- The From header is set to her identity:

  <sip:alice@ocean.com>

- The To and Request-URI headers are set to John's identity:

  <sip:john@sea.com>

- The Route header is set to:

  <sip:proxy.ocean.com>

- The SDP offer in the message body includes voice and video with the corresponding codecs.

Then the message is sent to the IP address of proxy.ocean.com, which would be obtained through a DNS A query (not shown in the diagram). By default, it uses UDP as a transport and destination port 5060.

```
INVITE sip:john@sea.com SIP/2.0
Via: SIP/2.0/UDP 5.4.3.2;branch=z9hG4bKyw76s8a
Max-Forwards: 70
To: <sip:john@sea.com>
From: <sip:alice@ocean.com>;tag=5462622185
Call-ID: 384g2hs17wv3l4
CSeq: 50 INVITE
Contact: <sip:alice@5.4.3.2>
Content-Type: application/sdp
Content-Length: 180
```

(Alice's SDP is not shown. It indicates voice and video media components.)

Step 2

Alice's outbound proxy receives the request, looks into the destination address (sip:john@sea.com), and determines that it is not responsible for that domain. Thus, the next hop's SIP URI is sip:john@sea.com. At this point, and following the algorithm shown in Figure 6.22, the outgoing proxy will perform a number of DNS queries (NAPTR, SRV, and A) in order to retrieve the IP address, port, and transport to be used. The DNS determines that the next hop is proxy.sea.com (John's inbound proxy), whose IP address is 1.1.1.1, and which has to be contacted using TCP and destination port 5060.

Step 3

Alice's outbound proxy opens a TCP connection against proxy.sea.com (if there was not already a connection open), and sends the INVITE request. We will assume that Alice's outbound proxy does not need to be in the path of new requests generated within the dialog, so it does not add a Record-Route header.

```
INVITE sip:john@sea.com SIP/2.0
Via: SIP/2.0/UDP proxy.ocean.com;branch=z9hG4bK6feww3ty2
Via: SIP/2.0/UDP 5.4.3.2;branch=z9hG4bKyw76s8a
Max-Forwards: 69
To: <sip:john@sea.com>
From: <sip:alice@ocean.com>;tag=5462622185
Call-ID: 384g2hs17wv3l4
CSeq: 50 INVITE
Contact: <sip:alice@5.4.3.2>
Content-Type: application/sdp
Content-Length: 180
```

(Alice's SDP is not shown. It indicates voice and video media components.)

Step 4

John's inbound proxy receives the message, looks at the destination address (sip: john@sea.com), and extracts the domain part ("sea.com"). The proxy realizes that sea.com is the domain for which it is responsible, hence it queries the Location Service for John's address of record, sip: john@sea.com. As a result, the proxy obtains John's contact address as a SIP URI: <sip:john@1.2.3.4>. The proxy will then apply the algorithm in Figure 6.22 to determine the port and transport to use, which will be 5060 and UDP (the default ones), and then forwards the request message to John's phone.

We will assume that John's inbound proxy does not need to be in the path of new requests generated within the dialog, so it does not add a Record-Route header.

```
INVITE sip:john@1.2.3.4 SIP/2.0
Via: SIP/2.0/UDP proxy.sea.com;branch=z9hG4bK58jt4257h
Via: SIP/2.0/UDP proxy.ocean.com;branch=z9hG4bK6feww3ty2;
  received=5.5.5.5
```

```
Via: SIP/2.0/UDP 5.4.3.2;branch=z9hG4bKyw76s8a
Max-Forwards: 68
To: <sip:john@sea.com>
From: <sip:alice@ocean.com>;tag=5462622185
Call-ID: 384g2hs17wv3l4
CSeq: 50 INVITE
Contact: <sip:alice@5.4.3.2>
Content-Type: application/sdp
Content-Length: 180
```

(Alice's SDP is not shown. It indicates voice and video media components.)

Step 5

John's phone receives the message and alerts him to the incoming call from Alice so that he can decide whether to answer the call. While John decides if he takes the call or not, Alice should be informed that John is being alerted. Therefore, John's phone automatically generates a 180 Ringing response message, which is routed back to proxy.sea.com based on the value in the received Via header.

```
SIP/2.0 180 Ringing
Via: SIP/2.0/UDP proxy.sea.com;branch=z9hG4bK58jt4257h ;received=1.1.1.1
Via: SIP/2.0/UDP proxy.ocean.com;branch=z9hG4bK6feww3ty2;
  received=5.5.5.5
Via: SIP/2.0/UDP 5.4.3.2;branch=z9hG4bKyw76s8a
To:<sip:john@sea.com>;tag=43rg573
From:<sip:alice@ocean.com>;tag=5462622185
Call-ID: 384g2hs17wv3l4
Contact: <sip:john@1.2.3.4>
CSeq: 50 INVITE
Content-Length: 0
```

Step 6

Proxy.sea.com strips off the topmost value of the Via header, and sends back the response to the address indicated in the topmost Via header, which corresponds to proxy.ocean.com.

```
SIP/2.0 180 Ringing
Via: SIP/2.0/UDP proxy.ocean.com;branch=z9hG4bK6feww3ty2;
  received=5.5.5.5
Via: SIP/2.0/UDP 5.4.3.2;branch=z9hG4bKyw76s8a
To:<sip:john@sea.com>;tag=43rg573
From: <sip:alice@ocean.com>;tag=5462622185
Call-ID: 384g2hs17wv3l4
Contact:<sip:john@1.2.3.4>
CSeq: 50 INVITE
Content-Length: 0
```

Step 7

Proxy.ocean.com strips off the topmost value of the Via header, and sends back the response to the address indicated in the topmost Via header, which corresponds to Alice's UA.

```
SIP/2.0 180 Ringing
Via: SIP/2.0/UDP 5.4.3.2;branch=z9hG4bKyw76s8a
To:<sip:john@sea.com>;tag=43rg573
From:<sip:alice@ocean.com>;tag=5462622185
Call-ID: 384g2hs17wv3l4
Contact: <sip:john@1.2.3.4>
CSeq: 50 INVITE
Content-Length: 0
```

Step 8

John accepts the call, so his UA generates a 200 OK response, which is routed to proxy.sea.com in the same way as the 180 provisional response (i.e., based on the Via header). The 200 OK response includes the SDP answer that indicates that John accepts a voice and video session with the offered codecs.

```
SIP/2.0 200 OK
Via: SIP/2.0/UDP proxy.sea.com;branch=z9hG4bK58jt4257h ;received=1.1.1.1
Via: SIP/2.0/UDP proxy.ocean.com;branch=z9hG4bK6feww3ty2;
  received=5.5.5.5
Via: SIP/2.0/UDP 5.4.3.2;branch=z9hG4bKyw76s8a
To:<sip:john@sea.com>;tag=43rg573
From:<sip:alice@ocean.com>;tag-5462622185
Call-ID: 384g2hs17wv3l4
CSeq: 50 INVITE
Contact: <sip:john@1.2.3.4>
Content-Type: application/sdp
Content-Length: 168
```

(John's SDP is not shown. It accepts voice and video media components.)

Step 9

Proxy.sea.com receives the 200 OK response, and routes it back to proxy.ocean.com in the same way as the 180 provisional response (i.e., based on the Via header).

```
SIP/2.0 200 OK
Via: SIP/2.0/UDP proxy.ocean.com;branch=z9hG4bK6feww3ty2;
  received=5.5.5.5
Via: SIP/2.0/UDP 5.4.3.2;branch=z9hG4bKyw76s8a
To:<sip:john@sea.com>;tag=43rg573
From:<sip:alice@ocean.com>;tag=5462622185
```

```
Call-ID: 384g2hs17wv3l4
CSeq: 50 INVITE
Contact: <sip:john@1.2.3.4>
Content-Type: application/sdp
Content-Length: 168
```

(John's SDP is not shown. It accepts voice and video media components.)

Step 10

Proxy.ocean.com receives the 200 OK response, and routes it back to Alice's UA in the same way as the180 provisional response (i.e., based on the Via header).

```
SIP/2.0 200 OK
Via: SIP/2.0/UDP 5.4.3.2;branch=z9hG4bKyw76s8a
To:<sip:john@sea.com>;tag=43rg573
From:<sip:alice@ocean.com>;tag=5462622185
Call-ID: 384g2hs17wv3l4
CSeq: 50 INVITE
Contact: <sip:john@1.2.3.4>
Content-Type: application/sdp
Content-Length: 168
```

(John's SDP is not shown. It accepts voice and video media components.)

Step 11

Given that the proxies in the path did not record-route, Alice's UA generates and sends an ACK request directly to John's UA, based on John's contact address received in the Contact header of the 200 OK response.

```
ACK sip:john@1.2.3.4 SIP/2.0
Via: SIP/2.0/UDP 5.4.3.2;branch=z9hG4bKnashds9
Max-Forwards: 70
To: <sip:john@sea.com>;tag=43rg573
From: <sip:alice@ocean.com>;tag=5462622185
Call-ID: 384g2hs17wv3l4
CSeq: 50 ACK
Content-Length: 0
```

Step 12

The media is established, and John and Alice can talk to each other and see each other.

Step 13

Alice wants to remove the video component in the session, so she sends a new INVITE request with a new SDP that includes only audio.[6] The request goes directly to John by using his contact URI (sip:john@1.2.3.4).

---

[6] As we will see in the next chapter, to be more precise, it includes a video component, but with a corresponding port set to 0, meaning that the video component is to be removed.

```
INVITE sip:john@1.2.3.4 SIP/2.0
Via: SIP/2.0/UDP 5.4.3.2;branch=z9hG4bK34du7i8
Max-Forwards: 70
To:<sip:john@sea.com>;tag=43rg573
From:<sip:alice@ocean.com>;tag=5462622185
Call-ID: 384g2hs17wv3l4
CSeq: 51 INVITE
Contact: <sip:alice@5.4.3.2>
Content-Type: application/sdp
Content-Length: 172
```

(Alice's SDP is not shown. Port in the video component is set to 0.)

Step 14

John's UA accepts the session modification and sends back a 200 OK, including a new SDP answer that includes only audio.

```
SIP/2.0 200 OK
Via: SIP/2.0/UDP 5.4.3.2;branch=z9hG4bK34du7i8
To:<sip:john@sea.com>;tag=43rg573
From:<sip:alice@ocean.com>;tag=5462622185
Call-ID: 384g2hs17wv3l4
CSeq: 51 INVITE
Contact:<sip:john@1.2.3.4>
Content-Length: 160
```

(John's SDP is not shown. Port in the video component is set to 0.)

Step 15

Alice's UA sends an ACK message.

Step 16

John and Alice can still talk to each other, but they no longer see each other.

Step 17

John now wants to terminate the session, so he sends a BYE request directly to Alice's contact URI (sip:alice@5.4.3.2), which was obtained by Alice's UA from the Contact header field in the initial INVITE.

```
BYE sip:alice@5.4.3.2 SIP/2.0
Via: SIP/2.0/UDP 1.2.3.4;branch=z9hG4bK64gf2d58
Max-Forwards: 70
From:<sip:john@sea.com>;tag=43rg573
To:<sip:alice@ocean.com>;tag=5462622185
Call-ID: 384g2hs17wv3l4
```

```
CSeq: 220 BYE
Contact:<sip:john@1.2.3.4>
Content-Length: 0
```

Step 18

Alice responds with a 200 OK, and the session is terminated.

```
SIP/2.0 200 O.0
Via: SIP/2.0/UDP 1.2.3.4;branch=z9hG4bK64gf2d58
From:<sip:john@sea.com>;tag=43rg573
To:<sip:alice@ocean.com>;tag=5462622185
Call-ID: 384g2hs17wv3l4
Contact:<sip:alice@5.4.3.2>
CSeq: 220 BYE
Content-Length: 0
```

6.5 Summary

In this chapter, we have analyzed the operation of the SIP protocol. We have focused on an external view of the protocol—that is, we have considered the SIP entities as black boxes that interact with each other through the protocol. In the next chapter, we will concentrate on the internal view—that is, on how the SIP functionality can be internally organized in different layers within the SIP entities. This will allow us to dive a bit more into the lower levels of the protocol, those that cope with the transport and the transactions aspects. The next chapter will give us enough insight on the operation of a SIP stack, which will prove to be very useful for the programming practices of subsequent chapters.

CHAPTER

SIP Protocol Structure

7

In Chapter 4, we looked at the functionality that SIP (Session Initiation Protocol) provides from the end user's point of view. In Chapter 6, we learned a bit more about the network perspective: SIP messages and how they are exchanged between the SIP entities. In this chapter, we take a closer look into the internals of the protocol itself, how its functionality is internally organized and achieved. From that perspective, we will see a model that splits the protocol functionality into several layers. The interest of this approach, apart from giving us a deeper insight into the way SIP works, lies in the fact that many SIP software implementations use a similar layered approach in order to implement the SIP functions. Most specifically, that is the case of the JAIN SIP API (Application Programming Interface), which we will be looking at in the next chapter. So a good understanding, especially of the transaction layer, is crucial to fully understand how JAIN SIP applications work. Last, we will look into the SIP dialog concept. The SIP dialog is a crucial concept for building User Agents (UAs)and advanced SIP applications on top of UAs or Back-to-Back User Agents (B2BUAs).

7.1 Protocol Structure Overview

7.1.1 The Layered Approach

[RFC 3261] structures the SIP functionality in several layers. This means that SIP protocol behavior is described, in this specification, as a set of fairly independent processing stages with only a loose coupling between each stage. These processing stages can be seen as layers that obtain services from the layer below and provide services to the layer above. This is very much in the same way as different protocol layers in the TCP/IP suite also communicate to each other in order to achieve the complete functionality for end users. This layered approach for SIP in [RFC 3261] does not dictate how SIP implementations should be made; however, many SIP implementations follow this model to some extent, and offer APIs for some of the layers. That is the case of the JSIP API, which offers mainly an interface for a SIP transaction layer. We will start using the JSIP interface in the next chapter once the concepts in this chapter are clearly understood.

7.1.2 About the Terminology

Because the layers described in this section are internal layers within SIP, which is itself sitting at the application layer in the TCP/IP model, I will refer to them as sublayers. I think this helps to better understand where SIP stands in the context of the TCP/IP suite, and also avoids confusions between the SIP transport layer (called "SIP transport sublayer" in this book) and the TCP/IP transport layer (called simply "transport layer" in this book). As we will see, the SIP transport *sublayer* is a layer within SIP, and therefore pertains to the application layer, whereas the transport layer (e.g., UDP, TCP) is a full TCP/IP layer on its own. These two layers are contiguous layers, and therefore need to communicate to each other.

7.1.3 SIP Protocol Sublayers

Next is a top-down list of the SIP sublayers. Higher layers are closer to the actual SIP application and the end-user view, whereas lower layers are closer to the next layer down in the TCP/IP protocol suite.

- *SIP core sublayer*: This is the sublayer where the service logic specific to each SIP entity is implemented. It may have five different components, called cores, corresponding to the different SIP entities: UAC (User Agent Client), UAS (User Agent Server), registrar, stateful proxy, and stateless proxy.
- *SIP transaction sublayer*: This is the sublayer where the transaction processing is implemented. It contains a service logic that is common to many SIP entities. It comprises two components: a client side called client transaction, and a server side called server transaction.
- *SIP transport sublayer*: This is the sublayer responsible for actual transmission and reception of the SIP messages. It has two components: a client side called client transport, and a server side called server transport.
- *SIP syntax and encoding function*: Rather than a sublayer, this represents a function that needs to be invoked in order to encode/decode the SIP messages when they are sent/received through the TCP/IP socket interface.[1] For the purpose of the following discussion, we will consider this function to be a part of the SIP transport sublayer.

Figure 7.1 shows the SIP layer, with its sublayers, in the context of the rest of the TCP/IP protocol suite.

7.1.4 What Layers Do the SIP Entities Implement?

In order for the reader to realize how the different sublayers are used by the different SIP entities, in this section we depict the internal sublayers within each of the SIP entities.

[1] The socket API is a popular programming interface to the transport and internetwork layer in the TCP/IP suite.

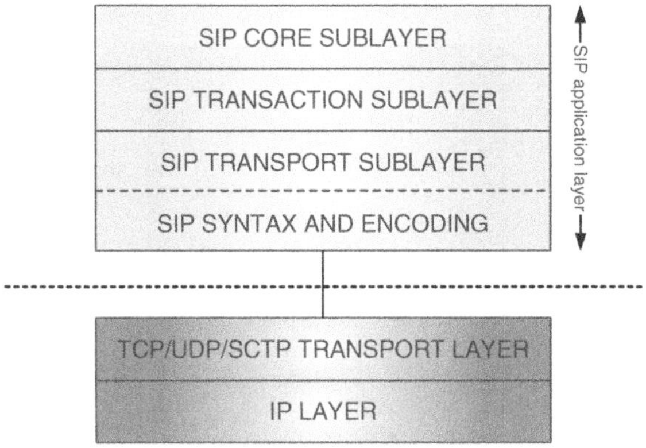

FIGURE 7.1

SIP User Agent

A SIP UA (Figure 7.2) implements the UAC-core, UAS-core, transaction, and transport sublayers.

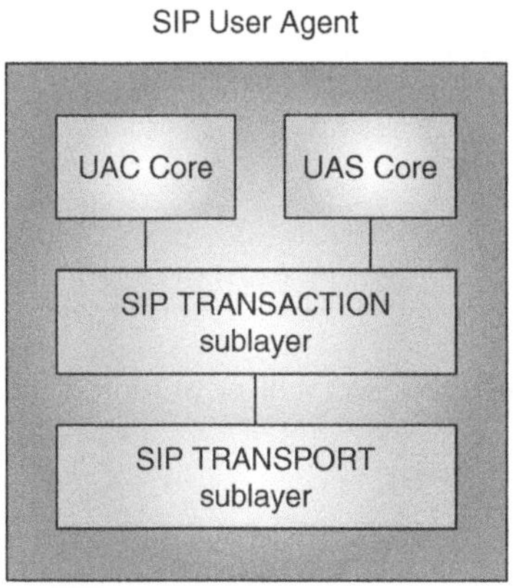

FIGURE 7.2

Registrar

A registrar (Figure 7.3) implements the registrar-core, transaction, and transport sublayers.

Stateful Proxy

A stateful proxy (Figure 7.4) implements the stateful-proxy-core, transaction, and transport sublayers. Proxies will be studied in Chapter 13.

Stateless Proxy

A stateless proxy (Figure 7.5) implements the stateless-proxy-core and transport sublayers. It has no transaction sublayer. Proxies will be studied in Chapter 13.

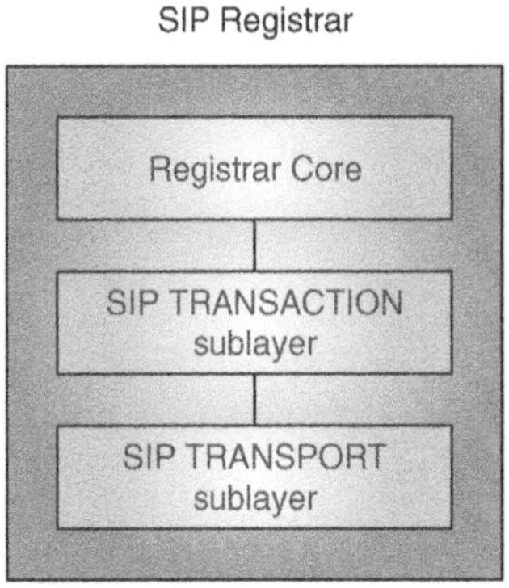

FIGURE 7.3

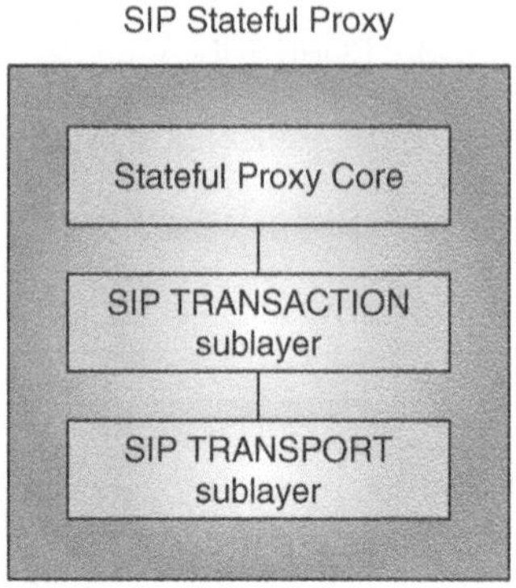

FIGURE 7.4

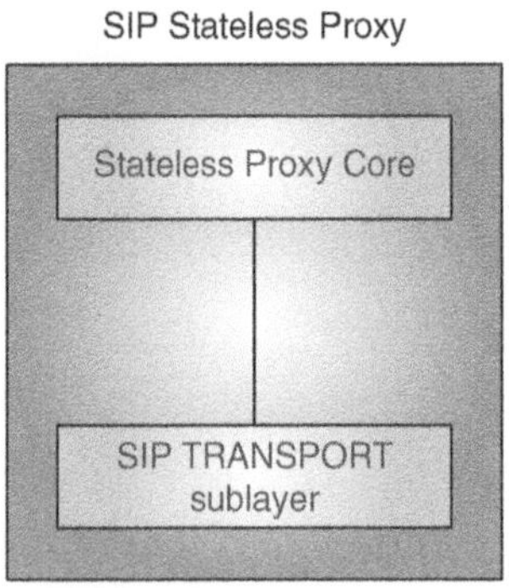

FIGURE 7.5

Now that the SIP protocol layers have been outlined, we will now look a bit more in detail into each of them.

7.2 SIP Core Sublayer

This is the highest layer. It is the layer where the specific functionalities of SIP entities are implemented. Different SIP entities have different service logics in this layer, although they might share the logic in the other layers. These service logics are called SIP cores. So, all the SIP entities contain a core that distinguishes them from each other. The SIP core sublayer contains a number of SIP cores, one for each SIP entity: UAC, UAS, stateless proxy, stateful proxy, and registrar. Actually, a registrar is a type of UAS, but, given its relevance, it is given a special name and considered as a separate core. It is important to bear in mind that these SIP entities are logical elements, not physical ones. A physical implementation might act as different SIP entities. Usually SIP registrars and proxies are bundled together in the same box, typically referred to as a SIP server.

The SIP cores implemented in this layer can be split into two types: transaction users and transport users.

7.2.1 SIP Transaction Users

A SIP core is said to be a transaction user if it makes use of the transaction sublayer below. In order to send a request, a transaction user creates a client transaction instance in the transaction sublayer below, and passes to it the request, along with the destination IP address, port, and transport to which to send the request. Likewise, incoming responses are received from the same client transaction instance.

The following cores are transaction users: UAC core, UAS core, stateful-proxy core, registrar core.

7.2.2 SIP Transport Users

A transport user is said to be an entity that uses the SIP transport sublayer. In that sense, the transaction sublayer is a transport user. There is only one SIP core that is not a transaction user but a transport user, meaning that it directly communicates with the transport sublayer, bypassing the transaction sublayer, in order to implement its functionality. Such a core is the stateless-proxy core. Proxies, both stateless and stateful, will be examined in Chapter 13.

Figure 7.6 shows the transport users and the transaction users and their relationship with the rest of the SIP sublayer components.

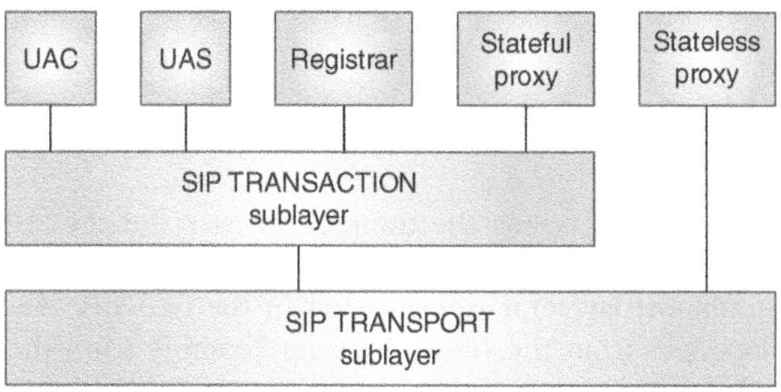

FIGURE 7.6

7.3 SIP Transaction Sublayer

SIP, as an application-layer protocol, makes use of transport-layer protocols such as UDP or TCP to send and receive requests and responses. We saw in Chapter 3 that TCP provides a reliable transport service. Therefore, when SIP uses TCP as the transport, it knows that the messages will be reliably delivered to the destination. On the other hand, SIP can also use UDP as a transport, and this protocol does not offer a reliable message-delivery service. Therefore, SIP, when forwarding a message to the UDP layer for transmission, does not have the guarantee that the message will reach the destination. In order to cope with this limitation when using UDP, SIP implements, as part of the application layer, a service logic that guarantees reliable delivery of messages. This logic basically utilizes retransmissions of messages upon expiration of timers in order to guarantee reliability in message delivery. This piece of service logic resides mainly in the transaction sublayer. Actually, this is its main function, though this layer also offers other functions, as we will see in the next sections. The transaction sublayer is utilized by the transaction user irrespective of the used network transport protocol (TCP/UDP/SCTP [Stream Control Transmission Protocol]), but its full functionality is exploited mainly when SIP uses UDP.

The mechanism that is used in order to implement this reliability at the application layer revolves around the transaction concept. As we said in the previous chapter, any SIP message is either a request or a response. A SIP transaction consists of a single request and any response to that request, which include zero or more provisional responses and one or more final responses. The transaction sublayer assures reliable message delivery within each transaction. It contains the logic needed to handle transactions and retransmit messages. Figure 7.7 shows a SIP transaction composed of a request and the corresponding response.

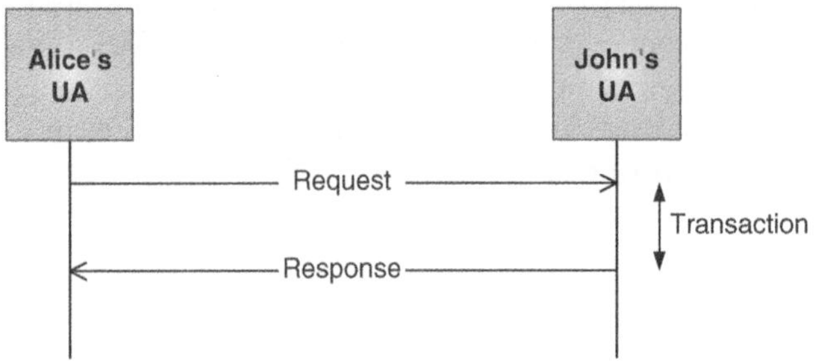

FIGURE 7.7

The transaction sublayer is located between the transaction user and the SIP transport sublayer. On one hand, it receives messages from the transaction user and passes them to the SIP transport layer for transmission in the network. On the other hand, it receives messages from the transport layer (coming from the network) and passes them to the transaction user. This is depicted in Figure 7.8.

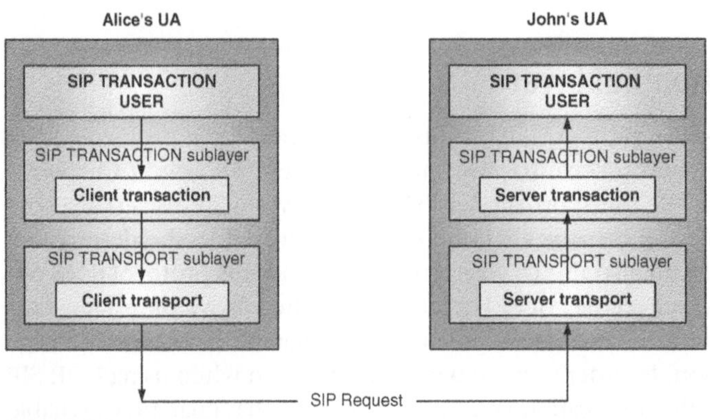

FIGURE 7.8

7.3.1 Client Transaction and Server Transaction

Transactions have a client side and a server side. The client side is known as a client transaction, and the server side as a server transaction. The client transaction sends the requests and receives the responses, whereas the server transaction receives the requests and sends back the responses.

Client and server transactions provide their functionality through the maintenance of a state machine. The state machines are different depending on the type of transaction: INVITE or non-INVITE transaction. The state machines for the client transactions in the different cases are shown in Figures 7.9, 7.10. The state machines for the server transactions are shown in Figures 7.11, and 7.12. These are included for information, but will not be explained in detail in this book. Readers are referred to RFC 3261 for a detailed explanation of the state machines.

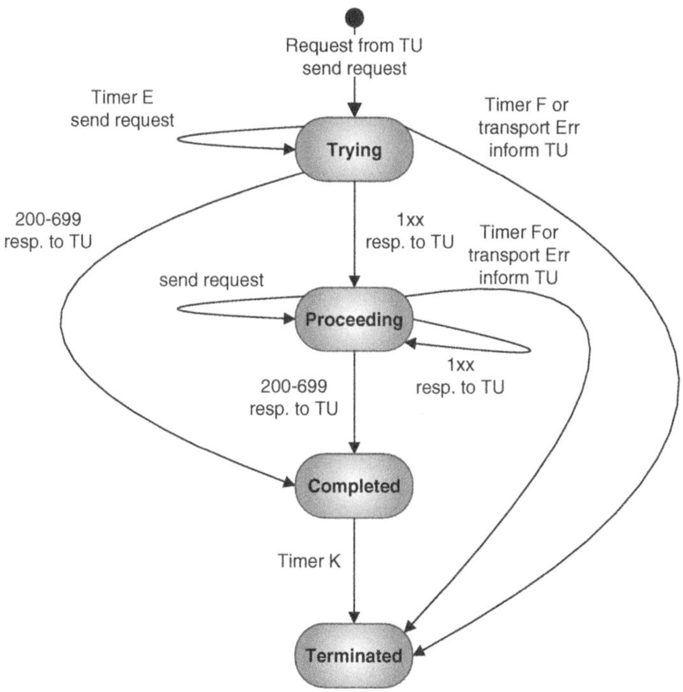

FIGURE 7.9

The client and server transactions are logical functions that are embedded in any number of elements. Specifically, they exist within User Agents and stateful-proxy servers.

7.3.2 Transaction-Layer Functions

The transaction layer is not a mere relay of messages between software layers. It offers two main services to the transaction user.

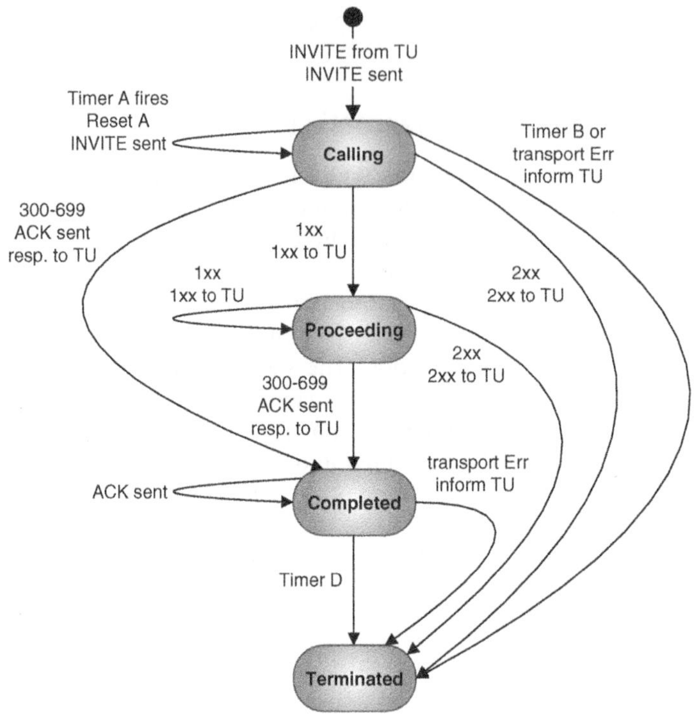

FIGURE 7.10

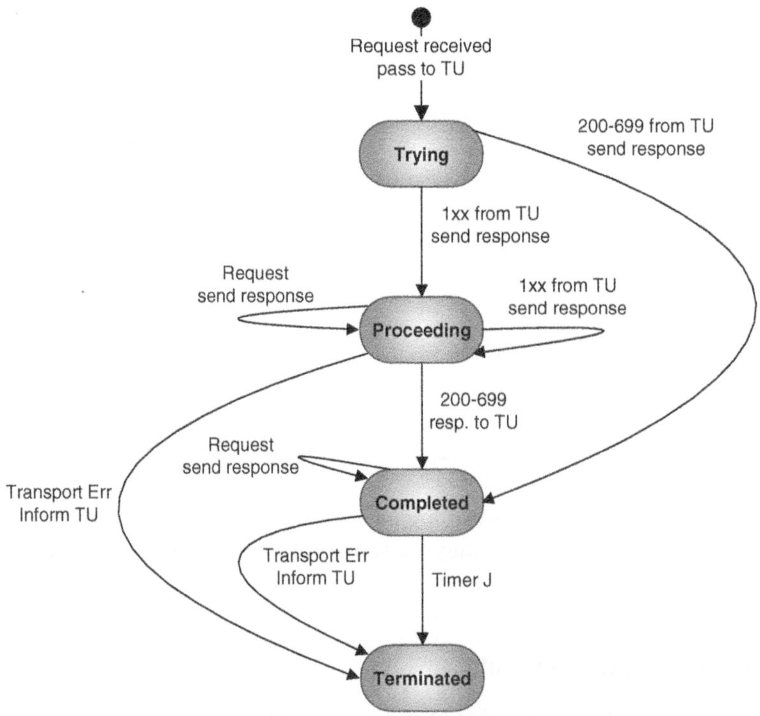

FIGURE 7.11

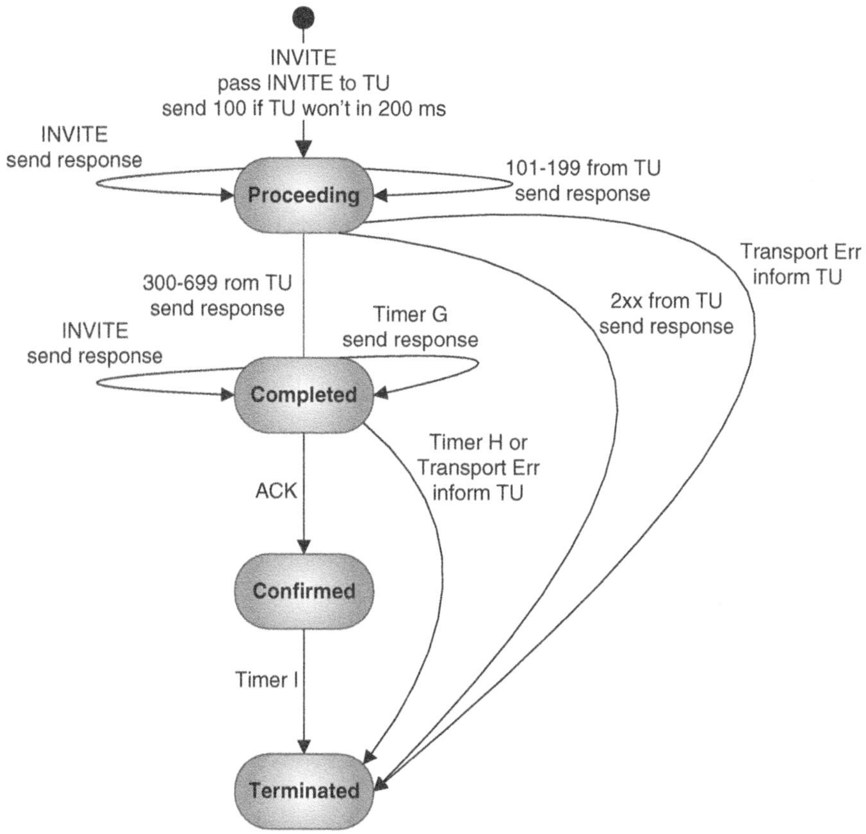

FIGURE 7.12

Request/Response Correlation

The first one is the correlation of messages pertaining to the same transaction. This is particularly useful for SIP entities, such as proxies, that need to handle a lot of transactions simultaneously, and therefore need to know to which transaction a particular incoming message corresponds in order to apply the proper service logic. A response belongs to the same transaction as a request if the two following conditions are met:

- Both request and response have the same value as the "branch" parameter in the top Via header field.
- Both request and response have the same value as the "method" parameter in the Cseq header field.[2]

[2] The method is needed because a CANCEL request constitutes a different transaction, but shares the same value as the "branch" parameter of the request that it cancels.

Reliable Delivery

The second function, as was already mentioned, is the reliable transmission of SIP messages within the transaction. This aspect is particularly useful when using non-reliable transports such as UDP. In such cases, the transaction layer implements the retransmission mechanisms necessary to assure reliable delivery. The transaction layer also filters out the retransmission in the receiving end so that the SIP core layer is not bothered by them. All in all, the transaction layer frees the transaction user from the need of implementing the necessary mechanisms in order to guarantee reliable delivery of messages in those cases where a nonreliable transport protocol, such as UDP, is used.

The transaction sublayer provides reliability in a hop-by-hop fashion—that is, between peer-transaction sublayer elements. In case the signaling transmission path goes through various proxies, transactions provide reliability in each hop, not in an end-to-end way. This is shown in Figure 7.13.

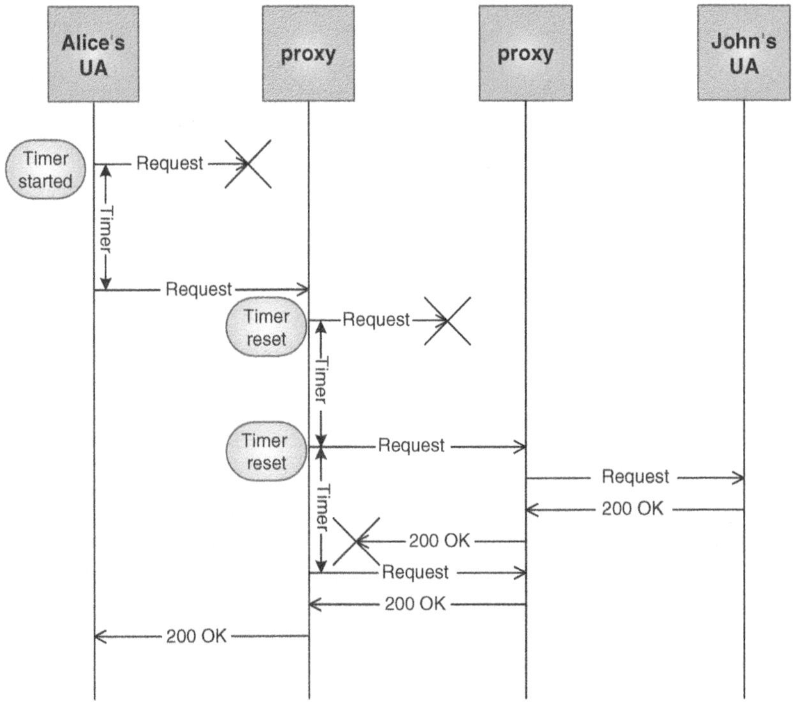

FIGURE 7.13

The way reliable delivery is implemented by the transaction sublayer depends on the type of transaction. We consider the split between non-INVITE transactions and INVITE transactions.

Non-INVITE transactions

Non-INVITE transactions implement a two-way handshake. For unreliable transports, requests are retransmitted by the client transaction at specified intervals.

On the other hand, the server transaction will retransmit responses if a new request arrives. Once a final response has been sent by the server transaction, it will still wait for some time (timer J) to see if it receives a new retransmission of the request, which would indicate that the response was not transmitted successfully. After timer J expires, the server transaction is terminated. This behavior is reflected in the transaction-state machines shown in Figures 7.9 and 7.11.

In Figure 7.14, a generic non-INVITE transaction between Alice and John is shown. We assume that the transport is UDP and that some messages are lost, so that we can see the retransmissions in action.

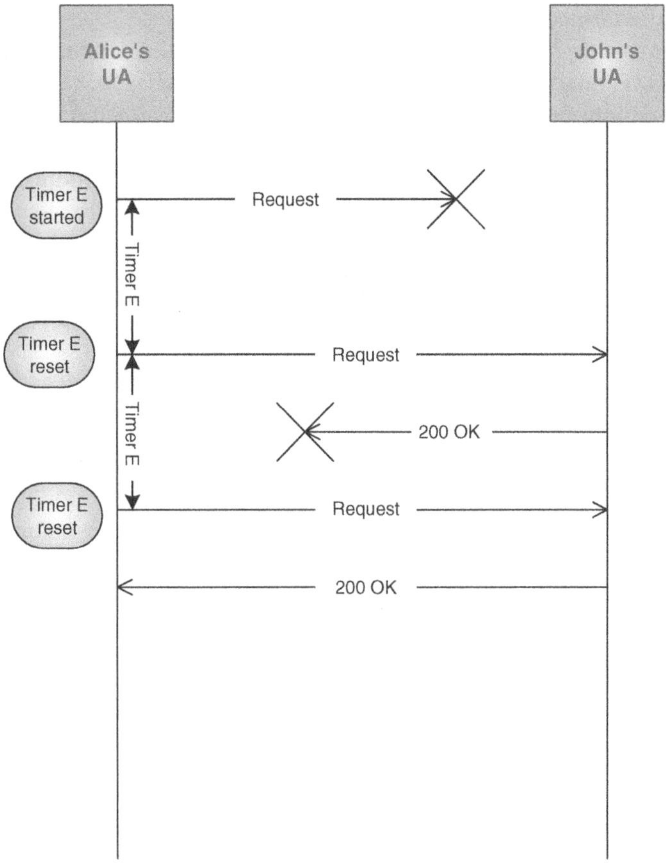

FIGURE 7.14

INVITE transactions

Non-INVITE transactions are expected to complete rapidly. For instance, when a REGISTER request reaches a registrar, the registrar will populate the Location Service and immediately send a response. On the other hand, when Alice sends an INVITE request to John, he needs to press a button in order to accept Alice's incoming call, and that might take some time. INVITE transactions normally require human input to complete, and therefore they typically have an extended duration. The long delays expected for sending a response argue for a three-way handshake, as opposed to the two-way handshake in non-INVITE transactions. In the next paragraphs, we explain the reason for this.

As soon as a request is sent, the client transaction will retransmit the request at specified intervals until a provisional response is received (provisional responses do not normally need human input to be generated). At that point, retransmissions are stopped; there is no point in continuing with the retransmissions because the UAC is just waiting for the UAS to accept the call, which may take some time. This is as opposed to what happens in non-INVITE transactions, where the client transaction does not stop sending retransmissions until a final response is received.

So, if the client transaction for the INVITE requests stops sending retransmissions after the first provisional response is received, how can the server transaction be sure, after sending back a final response, that the response has been received by the client transaction? In order to solve this issue, the INVITE transaction departs slightly from the simple request/response model and introduces a three-way handshake. In this model, after receiving a final response, the client transaction should send an ACK message so that the server transaction can be sure that the final response was successfully delivered. After sending the final response, the server transaction will retransmit it at the occurrence of either of these two events: a new INVITE is received, or a timer, called timer G, expires. Once a final response has been sent by the server transaction, it will still wait for some time (timer H) to receive the ACK. If timer H fires, it implies that no ACK was received, and thus the server transaction is terminated and an error condition reported to the transaction user.

This way of dealing with final responses and ACK messages is, though, applied only for final responses with status codes from 300 to 699—that is, in failure scenarios. Why is this so, and what happens with the 2xx responses? In order to answer this question, we have to remember that the transaction layer offers reliable delivery only in a hop-by-hop approach. What this means is that a transaction-aware SIP entity assures that messages are received by the next transaction-aware SIP entity. It is the next transaction-aware entity (for instance, a SIP stateful proxy) that takes responsibility for delivering the message to the next entity. And this process is repeated in every hop until the message gets to the target UA. The 2xx responses are considered too important to use this hop-by-hop reliability mechanism. This type of response typically triggers additional procedures in the UA media layer, so it is crucial to have an end-to-end-reliability approach when handling them. What this means is that retransmission of 2xx messages and generation of ACK messages is considered a function of the SIP core layer, and not of the transaction sublayer. A corollary of all this is that the ACK message, when sent as a result of the reception of 2xx responses, is not part of the INVITE transaction, whereas if the received response had status code between 300 and 699, the subsequent ACK would be part of the INVITE transaction.

This behavior is reflected in the state machines for INVITE transactions shown in Figures 7.10 and 7.12.

7.3.3 Example

We will now look at a practical example in order to illustrate the behavior of client and server transactions. We will show the most complex case of an INVITE transaction—first in a direct scenario (without proxies), and then in the typical SIP trapezoid architecture. In the following examples, the transport protocol is considered to be UDP so as to highlight the transaction-layer functions related to providing reliability in the message exchange.

Direct Call

Let us assume that Alice wants to set up a voice call with John, and her UA is able to determine the IP address and port to use in order to set up the call directly to John. Figure 7.15 shows the example.

1. Alice will produce some input (i.e., press a button), and the UAC core will generate an INVITE, create a new client transaction, and pass the message to it.
2. The client transaction will pass the message to the SIP transport sublayer for transmission, and start Timer A.
3. The network happens to be congested at that moment, and so an IP router in the path discards the UDP datagram.
4. Timer A expires, and the client transaction passes the INVITE request again to the client transport. The client transaction resets timer A.
5. The client transport sends the request, and, in this case, the INVITE reaches John's UA.
6. The SIP transport sublayer receives the request and passes it to the UAS core.
7. The UAS core creates a new server transaction, alerts John by locally generating a ringing tone, creates a 180 provisional response, and forwards the response to the recently created server transaction.
8. The server transaction passes the response to the transport sublayer for transmission.
9. The 180 Ringing response reaches Alice's UA.
10. The transport sublayer passes the message to the appropriate client transaction.
11. The client transaction stops timer A and passes the message to the UAC core. The UAC core generates a local ringing tone to let Alice know that John is being alerted.
12. John accepts the call. The UAS core generates a 200 OK response, starts a timer, and passes the message to the server transaction.[3]

[3] Because the server transaction will be destroyed as soon as the UAS core receives this final response, it is necessary to periodically pass the response directly to the transport sublayer until the ACK arrives, hence the timer that is started at this step.

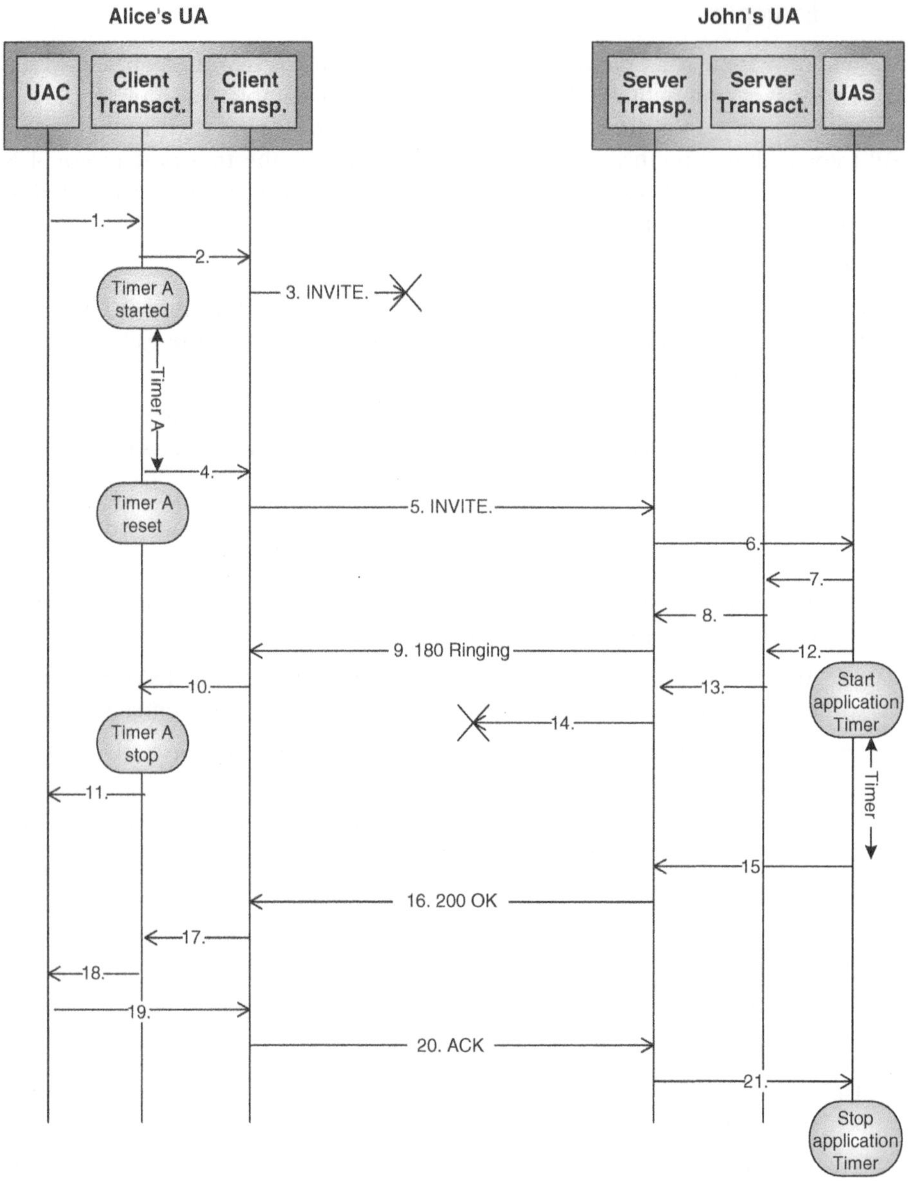

FIGURE 7.15

13. The server transaction passes the response to the transport sublayer and is automatically terminated.
14. The transport sublayer transmits the response, but a new congestion situation in a router in the path cause the message to be dropped.
15. The timer in step 12 fires, and causes the UAS core to pass the message again for transmission, this time directly to the transport sublayer because the transaction is now terminated.

16. The 200 OK is now received by the transport layer in Alice's UA.
17. The transport layer in Alice's UA passes the 200 OK response to the client transaction.
18. The client transaction forwards the message to the UAC core and is destroyed.
19. The UAC core will generate an ACK request and pass it directly to the transport sublayer for transmission.
20. ACK message reaches the transport sublayer in John's UA.
21. The message is passed to the UAS core, which stops the timer.

SIP Trapezoid

In this case, for simplicity reasons, we will not show the SIP transport sublayers. Figure 7.16 shows the call flow.

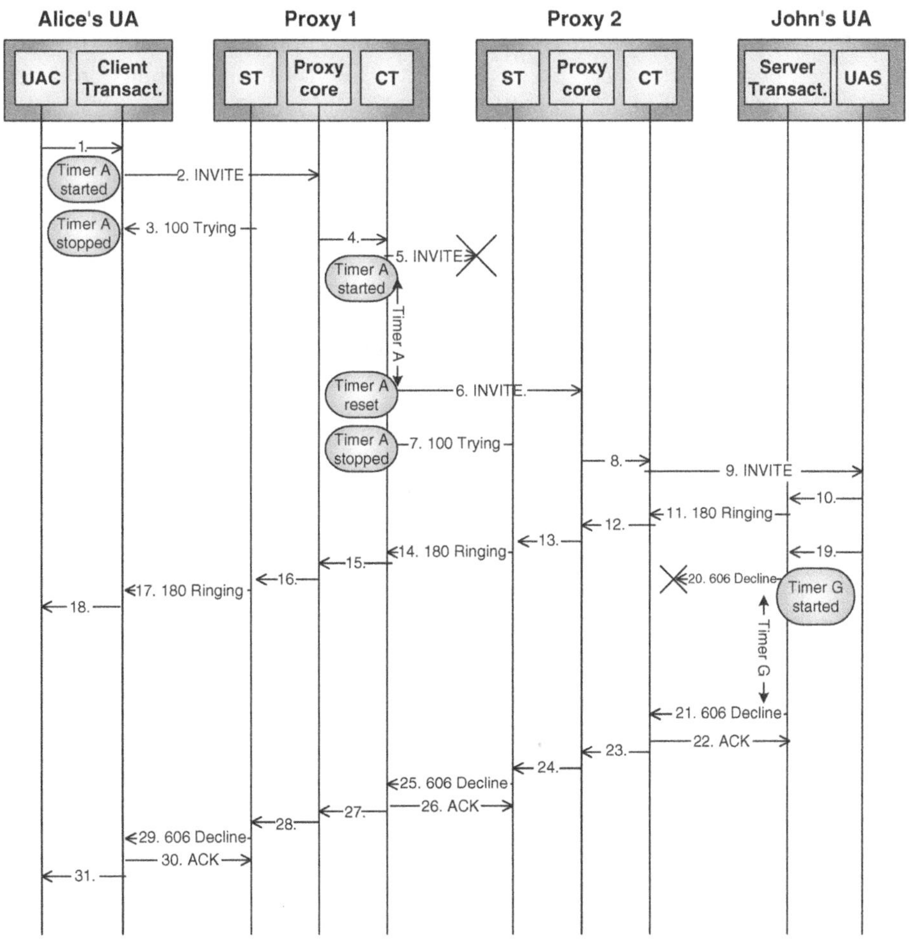

FIGURE 7.16

1. Alice's UAC core generates an INVITE request and passes it to client transaction.
2. Client transaction in UAC sends the message and starts timer A.
3. Message is received by proxy 1's core. Proxy 1's core creates a new server transaction. The server transaction creates a 100 Trying response and forwards it back to the UAC. The client transaction in Alice's UA receives the message and stops timer A.
4. The proxy core processes the request, creates a new client transaction, and passes the message to it.
5. The client transaction sends the INVITE and starts timer A. The message is lost on the way.
6. Timer A in proxy 1 fires, and the proxy sends the INVITE again. In this case, the message gets to the next proxy—proxy 2—and to the proxy core layer.
7. The proxy core creates a new server transaction and sends a 100 Trying response back to the previous proxy. The 100 Trying response reaches the client transaction in proxy 1, which consumes the message and stops timer A.
8. The proxy core processes the request, creates a new client transaction, and passes the message to it.
9. The client transaction sends the INVITE and starts timer A. The message gets to the UAS core in John's UA.
10. The UAS core creates a new server transaction, starts alerting John (i.e., generates a ringing tone), and sends back a 180 Ringing response.

11–18. The 180 Ringing response reaches Alice's UAC.

19. John decides to reject the call, and his UA generates a 603 Decline final response.
20. The server transaction sends back the response to the client transaction in proxy 2. It starts timer G. The response is discarded by a router in the path.
21. Timer G fires in the server transaction of John's UA. The server transaction sends the response again. This time, it reaches the server client transaction in proxy 2.
22. Client transaction in proxy 2 generates an ACK and sends it to Alice's UAS. ACK reaches John's UA. Timer I is set. When it fires, the server transaction is terminated.
23. Client transaction in proxy 2 passes the response to proxy core.
24. Proxy core passes the response to the client transaction.

25. The client transaction sends the response backward to the server transaction in proxy 1.

26–31. Response reaches UAC through proxy 1, and ACKs are generated by either proxy 1 or UAC.

7.4 SIP Transport Sublayer

The SIP transport sublayer is responsible for the actual transmission/reception of requests and responses over/from network transports. So, the SIP transport sublayer:

- Determines the transport connection over which requests and responses need to be sent or received.
- Instructs the transport layer to create transport connections.
- Instructs the transport layer to listen for incoming messages.
- Instructs the transport layer to send or receive SIP messages.
- Forwards received responses from the transport layer to the appropriate transport user (either a client transaction or the UA core).
- Is responsible for framing SIP messages.
- Handles transport-layer errors.

The network transport-layer functionality is normally exposed by the socket API implemented by the operating system. In those cases, it would be the SIP transport sublayer, the one responsible for managing the socket API (creating sockets, sending and receiving data through them, and so on). Any upper layer that uses the SIP transport sublayer is called the transport user.

The SIP transport sublayer is split into client transport and server transport. Let us look more in detail at the functions of each.

7.4.1 Client Transport

The client transport is responsible for receiving requests from the transport user and transmitting them over the network. It is also responsible for receiving responses from the network and forwarding them to the appropriate transport user.

Sending Requests

The user of the transport layer passes to the client transport the request, an IP address, port, and transport. Before the request is sent, the client transport inserts an address (IP address, port) into the "sent-by" field in the Via header. This address is used to help the server route responses back to the client (see the section "Sending Responses"), and typically corresponds to the IP address of the host where the client transaction is located, and to the port used as source port for sending the request. If the port is absent, the default value depends on the transport. It is 5060 for UDP, TCP, and SCTP; 5061 for TLS (Transport Layer Security).[4]

[4]In Chapter 14, "Securing Multimedia Communications," we will explain TLS utilization in the remit of SIP.

The behavior of the client transaction depends on the value of the transport passed by the transport user.

- If the requested transport is reliable (TCP or SCTP), and the request is destined to an IP address, port, and transport to which an existing connection is open, the client transport would use that connection to send the request. If there is no match, the client would create a new connection and send the request over the new connection. The client transport must be prepared to receive the responses to the request over the used connection. In addition, the client must also be prepared to receive incoming connections on the port contained in the Via header.
- If the requested transport is not reliable (UDP), then the client transport will directly send the message to the indicated address. The client transport must be prepared to receive responses on the port contained in the Via header.

Receiving Responses

When receiving a response, the client transport will try to match it to an existing client transaction. If there is a match, the client transport passes the response to the appropriate client transaction. If there is no match, the client transport passes the response directly to the SIP core.

7.4.2 Server Transport

The server transport is responsible for receiving requests from the network and forwarding them to the transport user.

Receiving Requests

A transport server is typically listening on port 5060 for UDP, TCP, and SCTP (5061 for TLS), or any other port on which it knows that requests may be received. When the transport server receives a request, it will check what is the real IP address from which the request was received. If that address is different from the one contained in the "sent-by" field of the Via header, then the server transport will add a "received" parameter into the Via header, set to the value of the originator's IP address.

Next, the server transport will pass the request to a server transaction (if the request can be matched to an existing server transaction) or to the SIP core.

Sending Responses

The way to send the response depends on what transport was used in the request.

If the request was sent over a reliable transport protocol, such as TCP or SCTP, the response must be sent on the existing connection over which the request was received. If such a connection does not exist anymore, a new connection should be opened to the IP address in the "received" parameter and the port in the Via header.

If the request was sent over UDP, the response will be sent to the IP address in the "received" parameter and the port in the Via header. If no "received" parameter exists, the response will use the IP address in the "sent-by" field of the Via header instead.

Example

In order to illustrate some of the concepts related to the behavior of the SIP transport sublayer, let us look at how a simple registration procedure would work from the transport perspective.

Let us assume that John receives SIP services from a SIP provider called "Sea." This provider offers a registrar service identified by the following SIP URI (Universal Resource Identifier):

sip: registrar.sea.com

The provider also offers a DNS (Domain Name System) service that maps that URI into the actual address (1.1.1.1), port (5060), and transport (TCP) on which the registrar expects to receive requests.

The SIP provider communicates to John, as part of the subscription information, the SIP URI of the registrar and the IP addresses of the DNS service. John configures his User Agent with all this data.

When John starts up his UA, the UAC core component will look into the preconfigured SIP URI for the registrar, and will resolve it to an IP address, port, and transport—in this case: 1.1.1.1, 5060, and TCP. After that, the following steps will take place:

1. The UAC core builds a REGISTER request, creates a client transaction, and forwards the request to it, together with the IP address, port, and transport.
2. The client transaction receives the request, creates the necessary state, and executes its functions, after which it passes the request—together with the IP address, port, and transport—to the client transport.
3. Given that the requested transport is TCP, the client transport will check if there is an existing TCP connection that links with the requested IP address and port. Given that the UA was just started, we will assume that there exists no valid TCP connection, so the client transport will establish a new TCP connection to IP 1.1.1.1 and port 5060, and send the request over it. Before sending the message, the client transport adds its IP address into the Via header of the request.

   The client transport will listen for responses to the request on the newly created connection.
4. The registrar is listening for new connections on port 5060. It accepts the new connection from John and receives the request on that connection. The server transport will check the Via header. Given that the IP address in the Via header corresponds to the same IP address from which the request was received, it does not add a "received" parameter.
5. The server transport finds no match for the request to an existing transaction, and therefore passes the request to the UAS core, which will create a new server transaction.

6. The UAC core will update the bindings in the Location Service, generate a successful 200 OK response, and pass it to the recently created server transaction.
7. The server transaction will execute its functions and pass the response to the server transport. The server transport will check that the request corresponding to the actual response was sent over a TCP connection, so it will send the response back to the UAC over the same TCP connection.[5]
8. The client transport will receive the response over the original connection, find a match for the corresponding client transaction, and pass the response to the client transaction.
9. The client transaction passes the response to the UAC core, which notifies John that the UA is now registered.

7.5 SIP Syntax and Encoding Function

This function represents the actual encoding of the SIP messages for transmission on the wire. The data passed by the SIP transport sublayer to the socket API for transmission over the TCP/IP suite needs to comply with the SIP syntax and encoding rules.

Encoding rules for SIP are specified using Augmented Backus-Naur Form (ABNF) grammar [RFC 4234].

7.6 SIP Dialogs

When a SIP UA sends an INVITE request to another UA, and the latter responds with a 200 OK response, a peer-to-peer relationship is created between the two UAs—a relationship that will persist for the duration of the call. This peer-to-peer relationship is called a SIP dialog, and it represents a context in which to interpret SIP messages. In [RFC 3261], the INVITE request is the only one that can create dialogs, but other methods defined in SIP extensions may also set up dialogs (e.g., the SUBSCRIBE method, which we will see in Chapter 15).

So, what is the use of dialogs?

First of all, UAs need to be able to ascertain what messages pertain to a particular dialog. Let us imagine that there are several dialogs established against the same UAS. At a certain point in time, the UAS core receives a BYE request to terminate one of those dialogs. In order to know what dialog needs to be terminated, the UAS needs to identify to which dialog the BYE request belongs.

Second, once a dialog has been established, new requests can be sent by any of the participating User Agents. In order to route these new mid-dialog requests, the UA uses some information that it stored during the dialog-initiation phase.

[5]This requires the server transport to maintain an association between server transactions and transport connections.

This information context will be used to facilitate proper routing and sequencing of new messages generated within that dialog. Furthermore, this context information might vary during the dialog, and it is important to keep it updated.

Third, in some cases, there are end-user applications built on top of the UA core that may need to store states associated with each dialog. For instance, we might consider a voice-mail application built on top of a UAS. The users can set up a session toward this UAS. Once the session has been established, the users can interact with the application by dialing DTMF (Dual-Tone Multi-Frequency) in order to decide what actions they want to execute: listen to stored voice messages, delete messages, change the welcome message, and so on. Typically, Voice Mail Systems (VMSs) implement a call-flow logic that requires maintaining some state associated to each user so that the application can know in every moment where in the call flow a particular user is. In other words, the application needs to maintain the state associated with the dialog.

The three examples above highlight the need for UAs to be able to:

- Unambiguously identify dialogs.
- Store the state associated with each dialog, and use it to generate future in-dialog requests.

7.6.1 Identification of Dialogs

Dialogs are identified at each UA (local and remote) with a dialog ID. The dialog ID consists of a call-identifier value, a local tag, and a remote tag. The Call-ID is the same in both User Agents, and the local tag in a UA is identical to the remote tag in its peer. Figure 7.17 shows the parameters at each UA that make up the dialog ID.

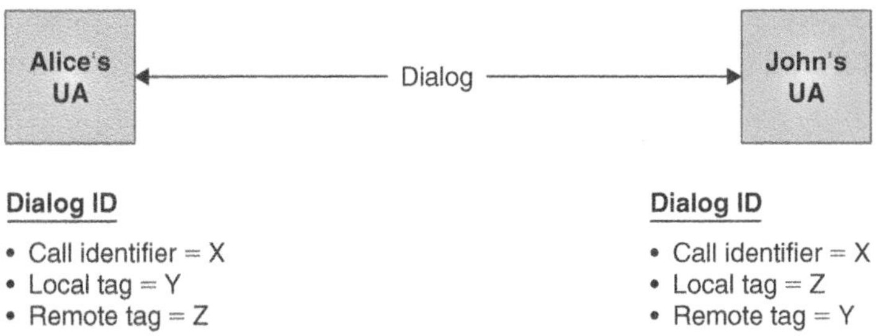

FIGURE 7.17

Dialog identification is carried in the signaling, and so, by looking at the content of a SIP message, the UAS can learn to which dialog the message pertains. Let us see how.

If UA1 is the one that initiates the dialog, then it generates a Call-ID header and a tag in the From header, and includes them in the outgoing request. When UA2 receives the request, it generates a tag in the To header, and stores the following dialog ID:

- *Call identifier* = Call-ID in the incoming request
- *Local tag* = tag generated for the To header
- *Remote tag* = tag present in From header of the request

After that, UA2 sends back the response. When UA1 receives the response, it stores the following dialog ID:

- *Call identifier* = Call-ID in the outgoing request
- *Local tag* = Tag present in From header of the request
- *Remote tag* = Tag present in To header of the response

Figure 7.18 shows how the dialog ID is created.

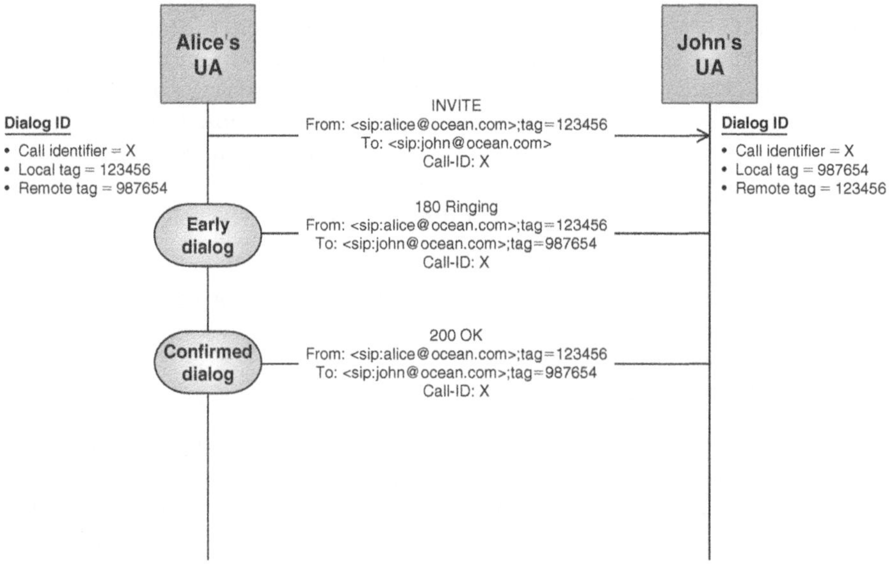

FIGURE 7.18

For new requests within the dialog, the rule to fill in Call-ID, From tag, and To tag is:

- *Call-ID* = Call identifier
- *From tag* = Local tag
- *To tag* = Remote tag

Therefore, once the dialog ID has been created in each UA, whenever a new mid-dialog request comes, the UAS can determine—out of the value of Call-ID, From tag, and To tag—the value of the dialog ID to which that request pertains.

7.6.2 Dialog Information

A UA stores some information for each dialog. This information is used for routing and sequencing of subsequent requests within the dialog.

The pieces of state information are:

- Dialog ID—Used to identify the dialog.
- Local sequence number—Used to order requests from the User Agent to its peer.

- Remote sequence number—Used to order requests from its peer to the User Agent.
- Local URI—The address of the local party.
- Remote URI—The address of the remote party.
- Remote target—The address from the Contact header field of the request or response.
- "Secure" Boolean—Determines if the dialog is secure (i.e., use the sips: scheme).
- Route set—An ordered list of URIs. The route set is the list of servers that need to be traversed to send a request to the peer.

7.6.3 How Dialogs Work

A dialog is created through the generation of 2xx or 1xx responses to an INVITE request. A dialog established by a nonfinal response to a request is in the "early" state, and it is called an early dialog. Once a dialog is created, the UAC and UAS fill in the pieces of dialog-state information. When either of the UAs generates a new request within the dialog, they use the stored state to construct the new messages following some rules. The main rules for request creation within a dialog are explained next. We will assume for this discussion that it is UA1 that originates the dialog-initiating INVITE request.

1. If UA1 generates a new request, the URIs in From and To headers must be equal to the URIs in From and To headers in the dialog-creating INVITE.

2. If UA2 generates a new request, the URIs in From and To headers must be exchanged with respect to the URIs in From and To headers in the dialog-creating INVITE.

3. Request-URI in new mid-dialog requests must be set to the value of the remote target. UA1's remote target is the Contact header-field value in the response to the initial INVITE, whereas UA2's remote target is the Contact header-field value in the initial INVITE request.

4. Route header is set to the value of the route set. UA1's route set equals the value of the Record-Route header received in the response to the INVITE, but in reverse order. UA2's route set contains the value of the Record-Route header received in the initial INVITE request.

5. Cseq header field in new requests must be equal to the stored local sequence number increased by 1.

Rules 1 and 2 just define how the URIs in the From and To header fields are configured. Rules 3 and 4 determine how new requests are routed, either directly to the Contact Address of the peer, if the Route set is empty, or according to the route-set values that were filled in based on the values that the proxies traversed by the initial INVITE set in the Record-Route header field. Rule 5 is meant to help in the sequencing of messages so that if a UA receives a mid-dialog request with a Cseq header field value lower than the remote sequence number, it will reject the request with a 500 (Server Internal Error) response.

7.7 Summary

At this point in the book, we hope that the reader has a good understanding of SIP operation and of the way it works internally. Armed with this knowledge, we can now start looking at how to program on top of a SIP implementation and build SIP-enabled communication applications. This will be the topic of the next chapter.

CHAPTER

Practice with SIP

8

In this chapter, we start putting into practice some of the SIP concepts learned so far. We will show some very simple programming examples that illustrate how SIP works. As was stated in previous chapters, the purpose of this book is not to teach the reader how to program commercial SIP applications. This book's goal is to enable the reader to understand SIP-based multimedia communication. We believe that letting readers "play" with practical programming examples using a protocol-level API may help them to consolidate the learning about SIP. In order to understand the next examples, only a basic understanding of the Java language is required. Actually, we believe that the complexity of managing low-level SIP APIs such as JAIN SIP or SIP servlets does not stem from the complexity of the Java aspects, but rather, from the complexity of the underlying protocol. During the past few chapters, the reader has, we hope, obtained a sound understanding of what SIP is and how it works—so this chapter should be easy to follow, even for people with little programming experience. We invite even those readers without programming experience to have a look at the code snippets and identify the SIP concepts interleaved between the Java artifacts.

The chapter begins by reviewing the concepts around the Java Event model. Then we describe the general architecture of the JAIN SIP API and highlight its main interfaces and classes. We will then construct very simple programming examples to illustrate basic SIP concepts. First, we will show you how to set up the JAIN SIP environment; then we will learn how to build SIP messages. After that, we will learn how to use the SIP transport sublayer in order to send and receive messages statelessly. The next step will be to use the transaction sublayer, and last we will practice with the SIP dialog concept.

After this chapter has been completed, the reader should have the necessary tools to start thinking of building more-complex applications.

8.1 What Is JAIN SIP?

JAIN SIP is a Java API specification for the Session Initiation Protocol. It is developed for the J2SE environment, and provides application developers with a standardized interface for SIP services that are functionally compatible with the RFC 3261 specification. More specifically, JAIN SIP API mainly provides the application developer with an interface to:

- Build and parse SIP messages.
- Use the transaction sublayer (i.e., send/receive messages statefully).
- Use the transport sublayer (i.e., send/receive messages statelessly).

In addition to that, the interface also provides access to SIP dialog functionality. The dialog functionality eases the task of writing applications that need to handle SIP dialogs. For example, SIP User Agents or SIP Back-to-Back User Agents are classical applications that require extensive management of SIP dialogs.

The JAIN SIP API can be seen as an interface to an implementation of SIP. In the industry jargon, a protocol implementation is commonly referred to as a SIP stack.[1] A SIP stack may consist just of Java code, or it may be written in other languages—in which case there is still the need for some Java wrapper classes that implement the JAIN SIP interfaces on one hand, and connect to the non-Java code on the other.[2] The application programmer does not need to bother with how the underlying protocol implementation is done. He or she will just "see" the Java interface in any case. Moreover if he or she is dissatisfied with the vendor that provides the protocol implementation, the application programmer could even replace it without the need to rewrite his or her application.

JAIN SIP is a protocol API—that is to say, it is a low-level API. An interesting aspect about a protocol API is that there are no limitations as to the type of SIP applications that may be developed using the interface. For instance, we could develop a SIP UA, a proxy, a B2BUA, and so forth. On the other hand, when using a protocol-level API, the programmer has to basically implement all the SIP core sublayer logic by himself or herself. Therefore, the JAIN SIP API is very good for helping us to better understand how the SIP protocol works, but we would recommend that readers use a higher-level interface if they want to build a quick-to-market and complex application.

Figure 8.1 shows the layering model for the SIP protocol that we learned in Chapter 7, and highlights how it maps to the functionality provided by JAIN SIP. The JAIN SIP API offers access to the functionality in the transport, transaction, and dialog sublayer, plus only partial access to the SIP core sublayer. Most of the functionality in the SIP core sublayer has to be implemented by programmers themselves in applications sitting on top of JAIN SIP.

---

[1] On one hand, the industry uses the term *SIP stack* in order to refer to SIP implementation. On the other hand, the JAIN SIP specification defines an interface called `SipStack`, which actually represents a management interface to SIP implementation (or SIP stack). So the same term is used to refer to two different aspects. The context and the fact that the Java interface name is written without embedded blank spaces should permit the reader to distinguish when we are referring to one case or the other.

[2] In order to access non-Java functionality from a Java class, the so-called JNI (Java Native Interface) is used.

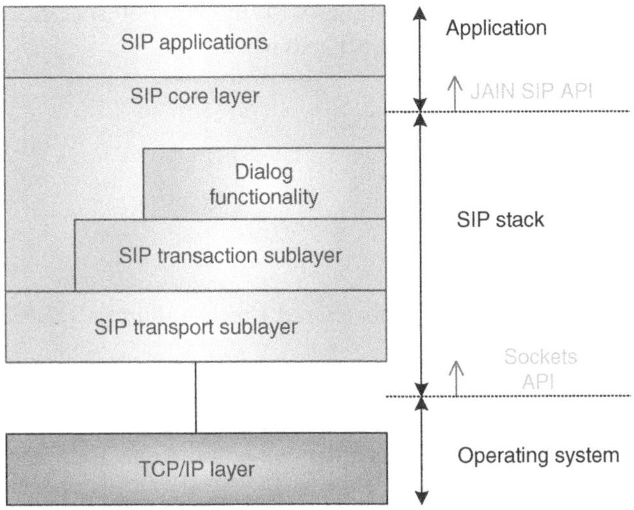

FIGURE 8.1

8.1.1 JAIN SIP Versions

To date, there have been three versions of the JAIN SIP API. The first one (1.0) was based on SIP spec RFC 2543. As we already know, that SIP specification was replaced by RFC 3261. So, a newer version (1.1) of the JAIN SIP API, which had compliancy for RFC 3261, was developed. The latest JAIN SIP version is 1.2. It incorporates some enhancements to the 1.1 specification, and it is the one that we will use in this book. Table 8.1 shows some of the main differences between the three JAIN SIP specifications.

Table 8.1

JAIN SIP 1.0	JAIN SIP 1.1	JAIN SIP 1.2
Supports RFC 2543	Supports RFC 3261 and some SIP extensions	Supports RFC 3261 plus additional extensions
No transaction interface	Transaction interface defined	Transaction interface enhanced
No explicit dialog support	Dialog object is added	Dialog support is enhanced
No possibility to configure the protocol implementation	Added SipStack properties to configure the protocol implementation	SipStack properties are extended

Version 1.2 of the JAIN SIP specification complies with the base SIP specification defined in RFC 3261 and with the following SIP extensions:

- INFO method [RFC 2976]
- Reliability of provisional responses [RFC 3262]
- Event Notification Framework [RFC 3265],
- UPDATE method [RFC 3311]
- Reason header [RFC 3326]
- MESSAGE method [RFC 3428]
- REFER method [RFC 3515]
- Distributing Authoritative Name Servers via Shared Unicast Addresses [RFC 3258]
- PUBLISH method [RFC3903]

We have not yet looked at SIP extensions. These and other SIP extensions will be explained in the third part of this book. In this chapter, we will use only the basic SIP functionality that JAIN SIP provides.

8.2 JAIN SIP Architecture

The JAIN SIP architecture is based on a number of patterns:

- Peer-provider pattern
- Factory pattern
- Event-listener pattern

The main interfaces and classes in the JAIN SIP API are shown in the following UML class diagram in Figure 8.2.

8.2.1 The Peer-Provider Pattern

A peer is a platform-specific implementation of a Java API. In the case of JAIN SIP, the peer corresponds to a particular vendor's SIP protocol stack—that is, the actual software that implements SIP. We have represented it with some pieces of machinery to illustrate this fact.

A provider provides functions using the platform-specific capabilities of the peer with which it is associated. In the case of JAIN SIP, the provider allows applications to send and receive SIP messages. It is represented by a Java interface called `SipProvider`.

In addition to `SipProvider`, there are other two interfaces that also provide access to some aspects of the underlying SIP implementation:

- the `SipStack` interface
- the `ListeningPoint` interface

The `SipStack` interface allows programmers to manage and configure the underlying SIP stack. For instance, it includes methods to start or stop the SIP stack. The SIP stack configuration is specified through a set of `SipStack` Java properties that define aspects such as stack name, outbound proxy, automatic dialog support,

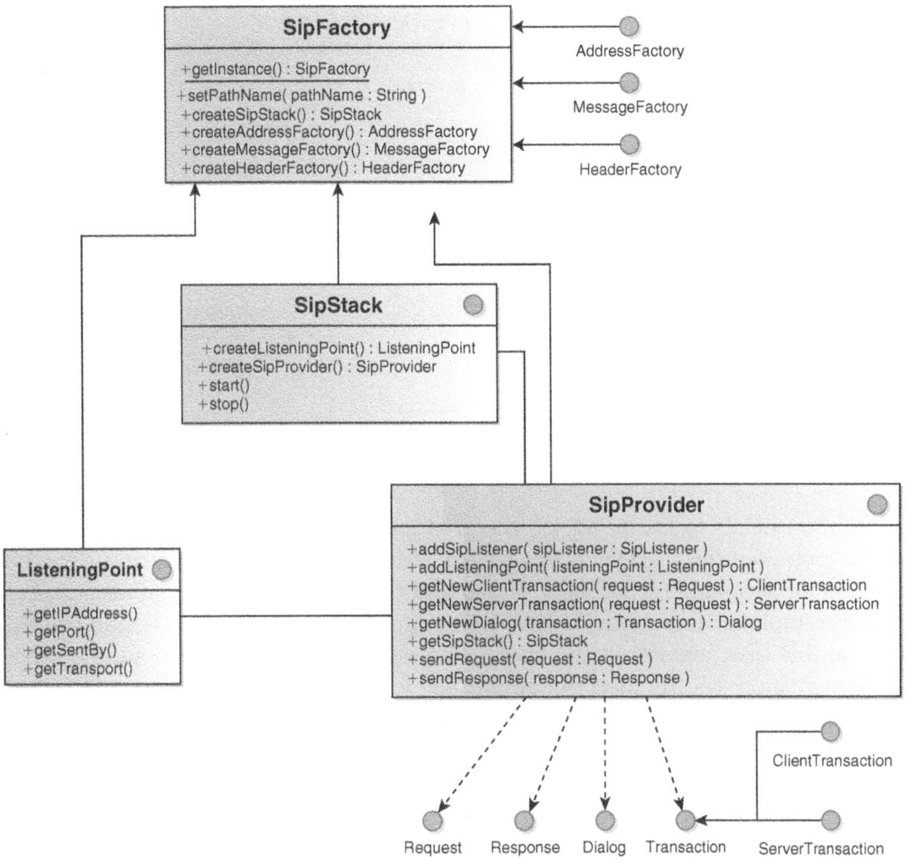

FIGURE 8.2

and so on. The `SipStack` interface also contains operations to create instances of `SipProvider` and `ListeningPoint`.

The other interface to the SIP stack functionality is the `ListeningPoint`. A `ListeningPoint` is a Java representation of the socket that a `SipProvider` messaging entity uses to send and receive messages. The underlying SIP stack may use several sockets for communicating with the network. The `ListeningPoint` interface allows the application to set and get the transport parameters (IP, port, transport) corresponding to a particular `ListeningPoint` instance (i.e., socket).

Therefore, the main three interfaces toward a SIP stack are the `SipProvider`, the `SipStack`, and the `ListeningPoint`, each of them exposing different aspects of the underlying implementation. This is shown in Figure 8.3.

8.2.2 The Factory Pattern

The application developer that wants to build a SIP application needs to gain access to the peer—that is, to the underlying SIP software machinery. In other words, the

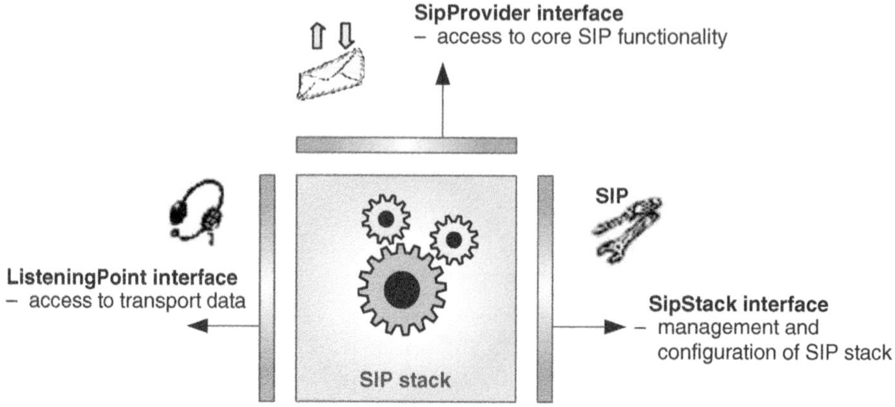

FIGURE 8.3

application needs to create SIP objects that encapsulate the SIP functionality. The application does this via a factory. A factory is an intermediary that encapsulates the method for accessing the SIP peer, and allows the application to obtain instances of the peer implementation classes. This is a common Object-Orientated design pattern that, in this case, maximizes the decoupling between the application and the peer implementation. For instance, our application is shielded from changes in the names of the implementation classes because it will always obtain the instances from the factory in the same way. One advantage of this decoupling is that the application will work transparently with different peer implementations. This is shown in Figure 8.4.

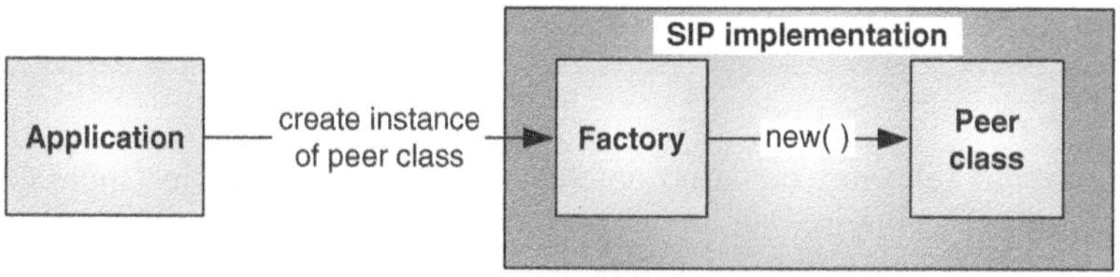

FIGURE 8.4

The factory class in JAIN SIP is called `SipFactory`. The factory is a singleton class—that is, there is only a single instance of it in the entire system. The application will get the instance of the factory and then invoke its methods, which create instances of the implementation classes.

Not all the JAIN SIP peer objects are obtained through the `SipFactory`. There are other objects that are obtained through the following factories also provided by JAIN SIP:

- the `MessageFactory`
- the `AddressFactory`
- the `HeaderFactory`

These factories allow the developer to create Java objects that represent SIP messages, SIP addresses, and SIP headers, respectively.

The programmer can get an instance of these factories by invoking factory-creation methods on the `SipFactory`.

8.2.3 The Event-Listener Pattern

This pattern represents occurrences of interest as events. Each occurrence is represented by a Java object. The mechanism for processing events is defined by an event-listener interface that includes a "processEvent" operation for each type of event. When the SIP stack receives SIP messages (requests and responses) from the network, the `SipProvider` passes them as events on to the event listener, which is called `SipListener` in the JAIN SIP case. This situation is depicted in Figure 8.5.

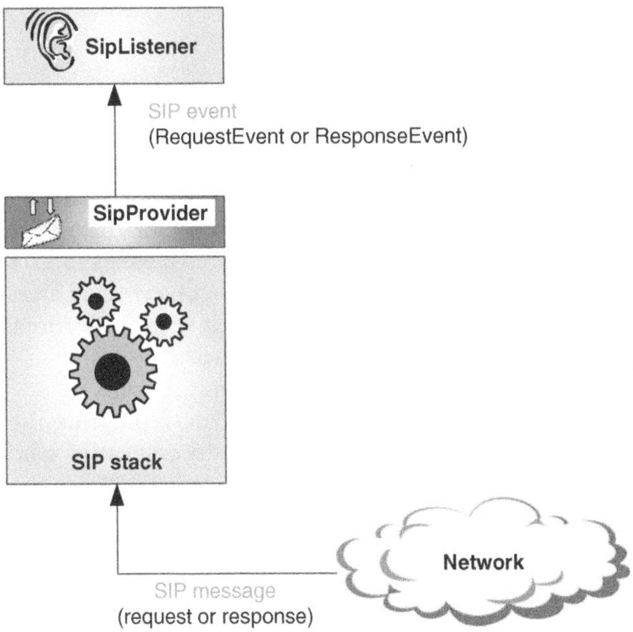

FIGURE 8.5

The application developer is responsible for implementing the methods in the `SipListener` interface. These methods contain the code that processes the events fired by the `SipProvider`. The application on top of the JAIN SIP API will include an object that implements the `SipListener` interface. A `SipListener` has to register with the `SipProvider` for the reception of SIP events. Once registered, as soon as SIP messages arrive at the SIP stack, the SIP provider will invoke the corresponding "processEvent" method in `SipListener`.

The SIP events represent incoming messages from the network to the SIP stack. There are two types of events (Figure 8.6):

- RequestEvent: Represents a SIP request received from the network.
- ResponseEvent: Represents a SIP response received from the network.

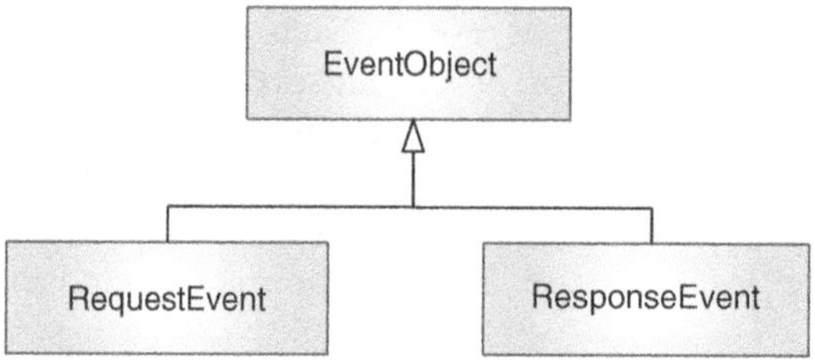

FIGURE 8.6

8.3 The SipStack, SipProvider and ListeningPoint

Let us now look a bit more in detail at the way these classes and interfaces are used. As we said, first of all, the application needs to get a reference to an instance of the SipFactory. We will use the static getInstance() method for that. Then we need to get an instance of SipStack, by invoking the createSipStack() method on the SipFactory. This method takes a Properties object as an argument that contains the configuration for the SIP implementation (e.g, stack name, retransmission behavior, etc.). Table 8.2 shows the methods in SipFactory.

The next step is to create a ListeningPoint by invoking createListeningpoint() on the SipStack instance. The ListeningPoint represents the IP address, port, and transport that a SipProvider messaging entity will use to send and receive SIP messages, so in the creation method, the application will need to pass the "port" and "transport" parameters. Once the ListeningPoint is created, the application will create a SipProvider messaging entity by calling createSipProvider() on the SipStack instance. It uses the ListeningPoint previously created as an argument for the creation method. Table 8.3 shows the main methods in the SipStack interface, and Figure 8.7 is a sequence diagram that shows the creation of the relevant objects.

As we have said before, the SipProvider interface is absolutely key in JAIN SIP because it provides the application with a window to the operation of SIP. This interface hides the implementation of all the messaging functionality in SIP, including the transport and transaction sublayer. So this is the interface that we will use to send messages statelessly and to create transactions over which the application can send messages statefully. In addition to that, the SipProvider is also responsible for delivering the events to the SipListener as soon as they occur (a SIP message is received from the network or a timer fires). Furthermore,

Table 8.2

	SipFactory Methods	Description
AddressFactory	**createAddressFactory()**	Creates an instance of the AddressFactory implementation.
HeaderFactory	**createHeaderFactory()**	Creates an instance of the HeaderFactory implementation.
MessageFactory	**createMessageFactory()**	Creates an instance of the MessageFactory implementation.
SipStack	**createSipStack (Properties properties)**	Creates an instance of a SipStack implementation based on the configuration properties object passed to this method.
SipFactory	**getInstance()**	Returns an instance of a SipFactory.
String	**getPathName()**	Returns the current path-name of the SipFactory.
Void	**resetFactory()**	Resets the SipFactory's references to the objects it has created.
Void	**setPathName (String pathname)**	Sets the pathname that identifies the location of a particular vendor's implementation of this specification.

Table 8.3

	SipStack Methods	Description
ListeningPoint	**createListeningPoint (String ipAddress, int port, String transport)**	Creates a ListeningPoint at a given IP address, port, and transport.
SipProvider	**createSipProvider (ListeningPoint listeningPoint)**	Creates a new peer SipProvider on the specified ListeningPoint.
Void	**start()**	Initiates the stack processing.
Void	**stop()**	Initiates the stack shutdown.

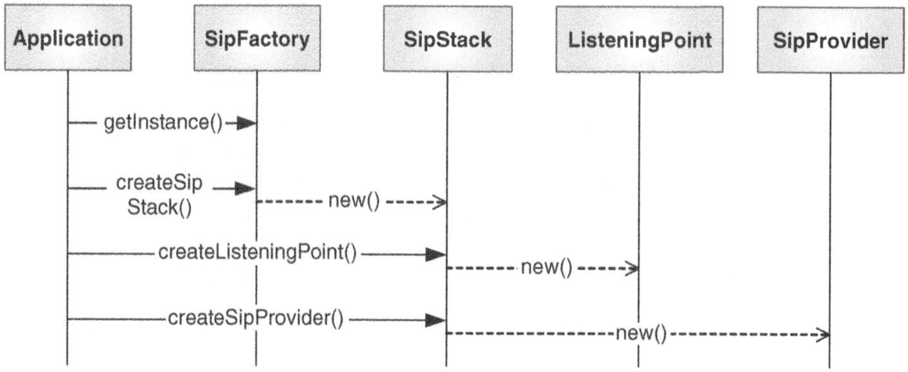

FIGURE 8.7

Table 8.4

	SipProvider Methods	Description
`Void`	**`addSipListener (SipListener sipListener)`**	Registers the `SipListener` object to the SipProvider.
`ClientTransaction`	**`getNewClientTransaction (Request request)`**	Creates a new `ClientTransaction` in order to send messages statefully.
`ServerTransaction`	**`getNewServerTransaction (Response response)`**	Creates a new `ServerTransaction`.
`Void`	**`sendRequest (Request request)`**	Sends a SIP request statelessly.
`Void`	**`sendResponse (Response response)`**	Sends a SIP response statelessly.

the SIP provider also implements the SIP dialog functionality, and allows the application to obtain access to SIP dialogs. This fact particularly contributes to easing the development of SIP UAs or applications on top of them, because this type of application relies heavily on the dialog concept. Table 8.4 summarizes the main methods in the `SipProvider` interface.

8.4 The SipListener

So far, we have created the `SipProvider` so we would have the capability to send messages for transmission into the network. Now we need to enable my application to receive events as well. For that, we need to create a class that implements the `SipListener` interface and then registers the listener with the provider. For that, it will use a method called `addSiplistener()` invoked over the `SipProvider` (Figure 8.8). The methods in the `SipListener` interface are shown in Table 8.5.

The meaning of these methods is quite straightforward. When a SIP request is received from the network, the `SipProvider` invokes the `processRequest()` method on the `SipListener` and passes the received request as an argument. The same applies for the `processResponse()` method relative to SIP responses. The remaining methods inform the `SipListener` about events occurring in the `SipStack`, such as time-outs and so on. All events that are used as arguments for these methods (`RequestEvent`, `ResponseEvent`, and so on.) derive from the Java `EventObject` class, whereas the `SipListener` interface derives from the `EventListener` interface.

Table 8.5

	SipListener Methods
Void	**processRequest(RequestEvent requestEvent)**
Void	**processResponse(ResponseEvent responseEvent)**
Void	**processTimeOut(TimeoutEvent timeoutEvent)**
Void	**processTransactionTerminated (TransactionTerminatedEvent transactionTerminatedEvent)**
Void	**processDialogTerminated(DialogTerminatedEvent dialogTerminatedEvent)**
Void	**processIOException(IOExceptionEvent ioexceptionEvent)**

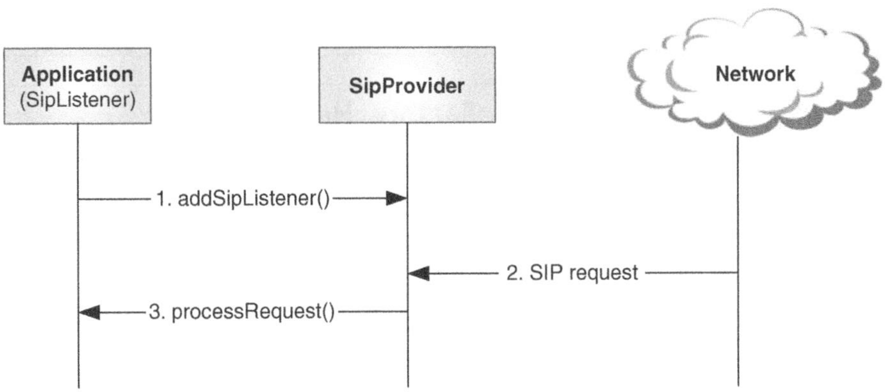

FIGURE 8.8

It is important to highlight that, in JAIN SIP terminology, SIP messages that are sent by the application are simply called messages, whereas SIP messages received by the application are referred to as events.[3] This is shown in Figure 8.9,

[3] This is because the upward path (network to application) is represented as an event stream received via the listener, and the downward path is triggered by "downcalls" (method calls) on the provider object. The pattern is different in each direction.

which also shows the different levels (transport, transaction, dialog) that an application can use to send messages to or receive events from the SipProvider.

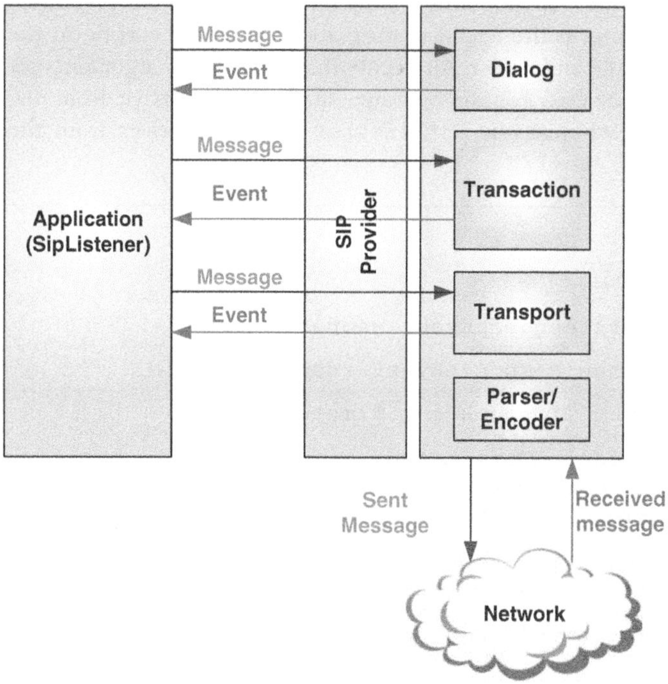

FIGURE 8.9

8.5 Other Factories: MessageFactory, HeaderFactory, AddressFactory

In addition to `SipFactory`, the JAIN SIP API also defines three other factories: `MessageFactory`, `HeaderFactory` and `AddressFactory` (Figure 8.10). The application can invoke methods on these factories in order to create Java objects that implement useful functionality for the manipulation of SIP messages, headers, and addresses.

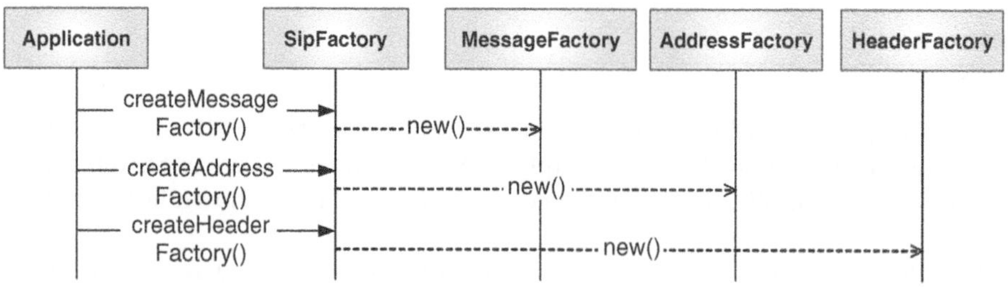

FIGURE 8.10

8.5.1 MessageFactory

The MessageFactory allows the application to create Request and Response objects that represent SIP request and response messages. In Table 8.6, we can see the two main methods in MessageFactory: createRequest() and createResponse(). Input arguments to the methods are not shown here; they are used to specify the different elements of a SIP message (start line, headers, and so on).

Table 8.6

	MessageFactory Methods	Description
Request	**createRequest()**	Creates a Request object.
Response	**createResponse()**	Creates a Response object.

The Request and Response interfaces provide access to SIP requests and responses. These interfaces extend the Message interface, as is shown in Figure 8.11.

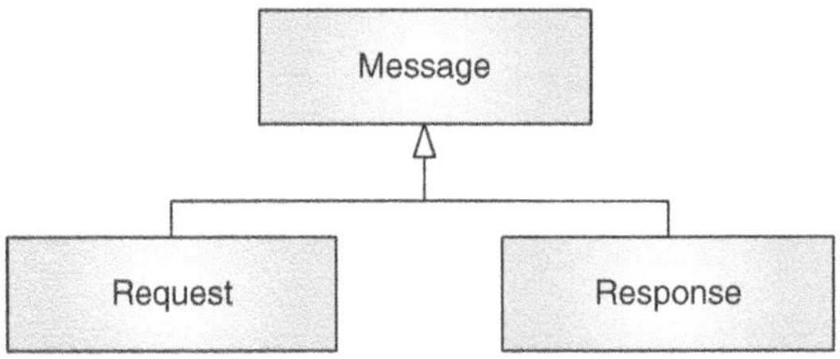

FIGURE 8.11

The Message interface provides mainly:

- Generic accessor functions to headers
- Convenience header accessor methods for the body content type, language, disposition, and length
- Accessor methods to the body content itself

The methods in the Message interface that we will more frequently use during this book are shown in Table 8.7.

The Request interface adds some methods to manipulate the request line, whereas the Response interface adds some others to manipulate the response line. These are shown in Tables 8.8 and 8.9.

8.5.2 HeaderFactory

The HeaderFactory allows the application to create instances of peer classes that implement interfaces for the manipulation of SIP headers. All of these interfaces are derived from the Header interface (Figure 8.12). Table 8.10 contains a list of the methods in HeaderFactory that we will most often use during this book.

Table 8.7

	Message Methods	Description
Void	**addHeader (Header header)**	Adds a new header to the message.
Void	**setHeader (Header header)**	Sets the new header to replace existing headers of that type in the message.
Void	**removeHeader (String headerName)**	Removes the header of the supplied name from the message.
Void	**removeFirst(String headerName)**	Removes the first header from a list of headers.

Table 8.8

	Request Methods	Description
String	**getMethod()**	Gets the method of the SIP request.
URI	**getRequestURI()**	Gets the request-URI.
Void	**setMethod(String method)**	Sets the method of the SIP request.
Void	**setRequestURI(URI requestURI)**	Sets the request-URI.

Table 8.9

	Response Methods	Description
String	**getReasonPhrase()**	Gets the reason phrase of the response.
Int	**getStatusCode()**	Gets the status code.
Void	**setReasonPhrase (String reasonPhrase)**	Sets the reason phrase of the response.
Void	**setStatusCode (int code)**	Sets the status code.

Table 8.10

	HeaderFactory Methods
ContactHeader	**createContactHeader (Address address)**
ViaHeader	**createViaHeader (Address address)**
ToHeader	**createToHeader (Address address, String tag)**
FromHeader	**createFromHeader (Address address, String tag)**
CallIDHeader	**createCallIDHeader (String callID)**
MaxForwardsHeader	**createMaxForwardsHeader (int maxForwardsheader)**
CSeqHeader	**createCSeqHeader(int cseq, String method)**

In addition to the header interfaces, there is another relevant interface called `Parameters`, which allows manipulation of the SIP parameters in the SIP headers. The interfaces for those headers that may have parameters extend the `Parameters` interface (in addition to the header interface).

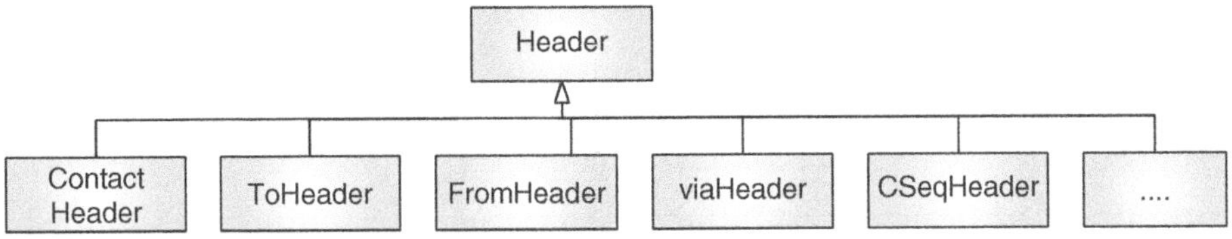

FIGURE 8.12

8.5.3 AddressFactory

The `AddressFactory` interface allows the application to create Java objects that implement addresses of various kinds. More specifically, it allows us to create objects that implement the following interfaces:

- Address
- URI
- SipURI
- TelURL

Table 8.11 shows some of the creation methods in `AddressFactory` that we will use throughout the book.

Table 8.11

	AddressFactory Methods
`Address`	**`createAddress (String address)`**
`URI`	**`createURI (String uri)`**
`SipURI`	**`createSipURI (String user, String host)`**
`TelURL`	**`createTelURL (String phoneNumber)`**

An `Address` object is used to represent a SIP user's address. It comprises two elements: a display name and a URI. The display name of an address is optional, but, if included, can be displayed to an end user. The URI is the user's address.

A URI object represents a generic Uniform Resource Identifier. It is the base interface for any type of URI. The URI interface has two subinterfaces: `SipURI` and `TelURL`.

A `SipURI` object represents a SIP URI, and the `TelURL` object represents a TEL URL. Figure 8.13 is a diagram that shows the relationships between the different interfaces. Both the `SipURI` and `TelURL` interfaces also extend the `Parameters` interface.

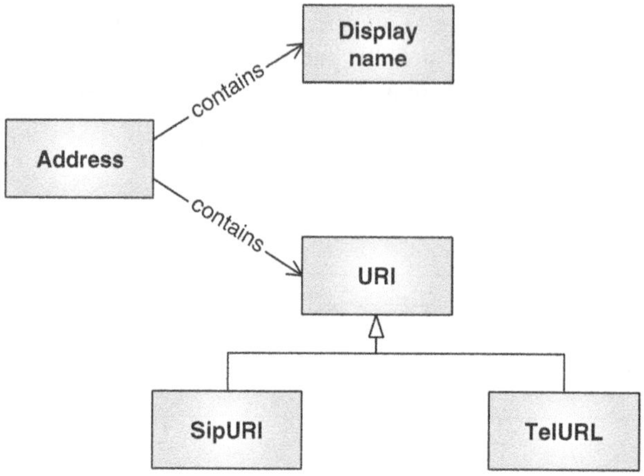

FIGURE 8.13

8.6 Programs and Practice

8.6.1 Structure of the Applications

For the practices in this chapter—except for Example 1, which is not a full application—we will use a simple architecture. The SIP application will consist of just two classes. The first one, called `ExampleGUI`, will contain the user interface. The second one, called `ExampleListener`, will be the core class where events will be processed.

`ExampleListener` will implement the `SipListener` interface in order to receive events from the underlying SIP implementation (3). These events will be passed to `ExampleListener` in `processRequest()` or `processResponse()` calls invoked by the `SipProvider` onto `ExampleListener`.

`ExampleListener` will also receive calls (2) from the `ExampleGUI` class representing events generated in the user interface (1). For example, when a user presses a button to initiate a call, `ExampleGUI` will invoke the custom `userInput()` method onto `ExampleListener`. The `userInput()` method may have an input parameter that indicates the type of GUI event that has been generated (e.g., user pressed "Yes" button or "No" button) so that `ExampleListener` can apply the appropriate service logic.

`ExampleListener` class will also generate SIP messages (4) toward the `SipProvider`, and it may also produce outputs to the user interface by invoking the display method (5) on `ExampleGUI` in order to display the received or sent SIP message (for tracing purposes).

Figure 8.14 illustrates this architecture.

In this architecture, we will not use Java events for the communication between `ExampleGUI` and `ExampleListener` but rather, direct method calls because it results in a simpler code. The `ExampleListener` class implements a simple state machine that receives events from the `SipProvider` and calls from

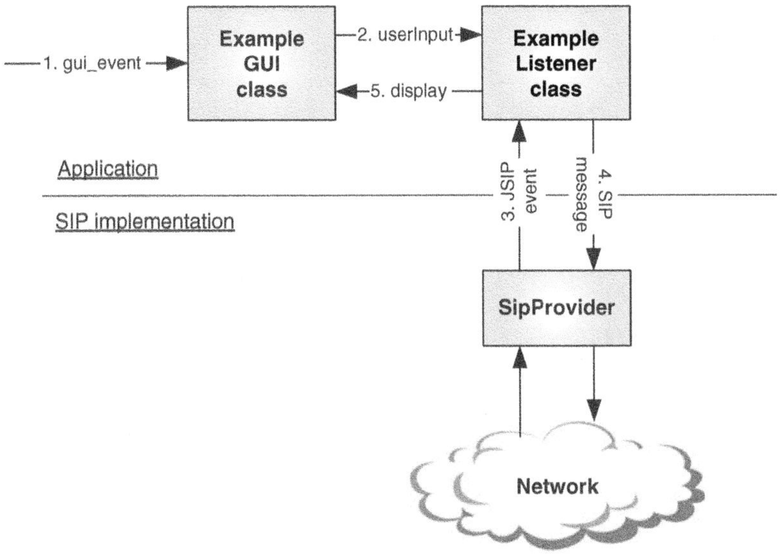

FIGURE 8.14

the `ExampleGUI`, processes them and generates the appropriate output to the network or/and to the GUI.

We will focus on the `ExampleListener` class, which is the one that contains the actual SIP-related code. The reader may actually implement the `ExampleGUI` class as he or she prefers, using whatever graphical tool at hand to design the interface. GUI design is not the focus of this book.

Figure 8.15 shows the template that all our examples in this chapter will use in order to implement the `ExampleListener` class.

The program starts by importing the JAIN SIP packages plus other Java packages (e.g., `java.net`, `java.util`) that we may use in our class:

```
import javax.sip.*;
import javax.sip.message.*;
import javax.sip.header.*;
import javax.sip.address.*;
import java.net.*;
import java.util.*;
```

After the import section, there comes the name of the class. We can observe that `ExampleListener` implements the `SipListener` interface. Next comes the declaration section and the constructor. The constructor will be identical in all the examples in this chapter.

Next are the `SipListener` methods that process the events coming from the `SipProvider`. And, at the end of the class code, we will have the `userInput()` method that `ExampleGUI` will invoke on `ExampleListener` in order to communicate actions happening in the user interface. For example, if, when the user

```
// IMPORT PACKAGES

import javax.sip.*;
import javax.sip.message.*;
import javax.sip.header.*;
import javax.sip.address.*;

public class exampleListener implements SipListener {
// DECLARATIONS

    private SipFactory mySipFactory;
    ...

// CONSTRUCTOR

    public exampleListener() {

    }

// SIP LISTENER METHODS

    public void processRequest(RequestEvent requestReceivedEvent) {
    }
    public void processResponse(ResponseEvent responseReceivedEvent) {
    }

// METHOD CALL INVOKED FROM GUI

    public void userInput(int type, ....) {
    }

}
```

SIP environment initialization

Processing of network events

Processing of GUI events

FIGURE 8.15

presses a button, there is a need to send a SIP message to the network, the code needed to send a SIP message would be included in the `userInput()` method.

All the examples shown in this chapter simply allow the reader practice with the API. Neither the clients nor the servers built here are full User Agent Clients (UAC) or User Agent Servers (UAS).

The full code, including GUI and listener, for all the examples can be downloaded from the book's web page (see Appendix A).

8.6.2 JAIN SIP Initialization

When the application is started, the GUI is loaded. At that point, the user has to fill in some configuration parameters (listening port, and so on), and then press the "On" button. This GUI event causes `ExampleGUI` to create an instance of `ExampleListener`. The constructor method for `ExampleListener` contains the code needed for the JAIN SIP environment initialization. Once the system has been initialized, `ExampleListener` is ready to receive events from the `SipProvider` or from the user interface.

We will now see the code, contained in the constructor method, that is needed in order to set up the JAIN SIP environment and create instances of the fundamental classes.

We will consider two arguments in the constructor method. The first one is the port that we will be using. This will be introduced through the GUI, and communicated to the `ExampleListener` through the constructor method. The port will always refer to a UDP port because we will in all examples use UDP as the network transport. The second argument contains a reference to `ExampleGUI` so that `ExampleListener` can instruct the GUI to generate appropriate output when necessary by invoking the `display()` method on such a reference. So, the signature of the constructor methods would look like:

```
public ExampleListener (int port, ExampleGUI GUI) {
```

In the code of the constructor. we will create the main JAIN SIP objects. The first thing is to get an instance of `SipFactory`:

```
mySipFactory=SipFactory.getInstance();
```

The next step is to create the `SipStack`. Before invoking the creation method for `SipStack`, we need to set the pathname that identifies the location of a particular vendor's implementation of the JAIN SIP implementation. The pathname must be the reverse domain name assigned to the vendor that provides the implementation. In our case, we will be using the open-source JAIN SIP implementation from NIST. Its pathname must commence with "gov.nist":

```
mySipFactory.setPathName("gov.nist");
```

We will also need to get an instance of the remaining factories:

```
myMessageFactory=mySipFactory.createMessageFactory();
myHeaderFactory=mySipFactory.createHeaderFactory();
myAddressFactory=mySipFactory.createAddressFactory();
```

For the creation of the `SipStack`, we need first to create and configure the `Properties` object that we will pass as an argument to the creation method. The `Properties` class is imported from the `java.util` package. For the examples, we will use all the default values of the `SipStack` properties but one: the `SipStack` name.

```
Properties myProperties=new Properties();
myProperties.setProperty("javax.sip.STACK_NAME," "myStack");
mySipStack=MySipFactory.createSipStack(myProperties);
```

Then we create the `ListeningPoint`. In order to create the `ListeningPoint`, we need to pass as an argument the IP address, port, and transport. We already said that we will use UDP as the transport for our examples. On the other hand, it is the user who configures the port in the GUI, and then it is communicated to `ExampleListener` as an argument in the constructor method. So the only thing we don't know is the IP address. There is a very simple way to programmatically determine the IP address of our computer. It consists of using the `InetAddress` class from the `java.net` package.

```
myIP=InetAddress.getLocalHost().getHostAddress();
```

So now we can create the `ListeningPoint`:

```
myListeningPoint=mySipStack.createListeningPoint(myIP,port,
"udp");
```

The next step is to create the SipProvider, passing the recently created `ListeningPoint` as an argument. We are telling the SIP implementation to create a SIP messaging entity (the SipProvider) that listens at the specified `ListeningPoint`:

```
mySipProvider=mySipStack.createSipProvider(myListeningPoint);
```

Last, we register the SipListener with the SipProvider:

```
mySipProvider.addSipListener(this);
```

A sequence diagram for the JAIN SIP initialization process is depicted in Figure 9.16. For simplicity, method arguments are not shown.

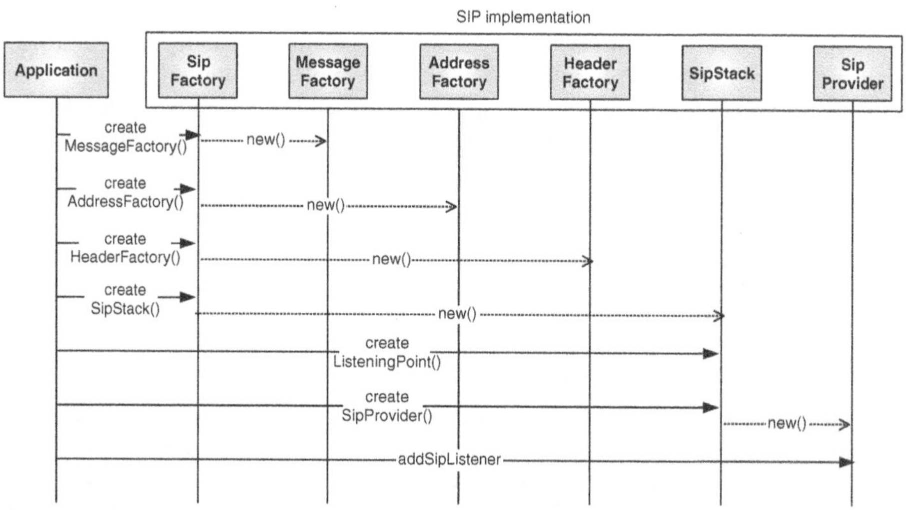

FIGURE 8.16

The main JAIN SIP entities are now created. Let us now look at the particular examples.

8.6.3 How to Test the Examples

We will show four different examples in this chapter. But for the first one, which is aimed at just showing how to build a SIP message, the rest of the examples imply an exchange of SIP messages between two communicating applications. Readers have two options in order to test those examples.

Option 1

If the reader has at his or her disposal two computers connected to a local area network or to the Internet, he/she can start one instance of our example applications in each machine. One application will initiate requests, and the other will respond to them. This approach has an interesting benefit: we can also run a network sniffer in either of the two machines, and we will be able to see all the SIP traffic generated and received by our application. The drawback comes from the fact that, for our examples, the application that initiates the requests needs to know the IP address of the other machine. Although this might be a practical way of running the examples if the reader has a couple of computers connected to a switch at home, it may be cumbersome to run it in an Internet environment, given that we would need to find an alternative way of communicating the IP addresses between the two machines before SIP communication can start. In Chapter 13, we will build some network infrastructure (a registrar) that will be used to locate the users so we will no longer need to know the IP address of the other party, but just his or her logical identity.

All in all, we recommend that readers follow the second option in order to run the examples.

Option 2

In this option, just one PC is needed (Figure 8.17). We will run two instances of our application on the same PC. As before, one application will act as client, and the other as server. The trick here is that we will use the local loop address of the TCP/IP stack (127.0.0.1) to avoid the need to have a physical network. Although the TCP/IP stack sees an IP packet destined to the local loop address, it knows the packet does not need to go out through the network interface, but rather, must be delivered to an application on the same machine. The only precaution we need to have in order for this scenario to work is that the two instances of our applications need to listen in two different ports.

A minor drawback of this option is that not all the sniffers in the market allow us to trace traffic on the local loop. In order to overcome such an issue, we will build a very simple sniffer functionality in our application so that whenever a SIP message is generated or received by it, the SipListener can pass it as a String to `ExampleGUI` using the `display()` method. `ExampleGUI` will display the message in a window of our application.

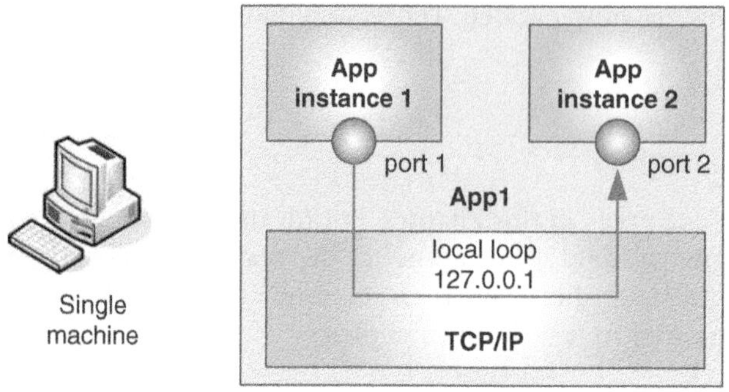

FIGURE 8.17

8.6.4 Example 1: Building SIP Messages

In this first example, we do not yet intend to send or receive SIP messages. We will just learn how to use the interfaces provided by the `MessageFactory`, `HeaderFactory`, and AddressFactory in order to build a SIP message. This first example is not a full Java application yet; it just intends to show the Java code needed for building a SIP message.

Let us imagine we want to build the following REGISTER message:

```
REGISTER sip:registrar.ocean.com SIP/2.0
Via: SIP/2.0/UDP peterpc.ocean.com:5060;branch=z9hG4bKnashds7
Max-Forwards: 70
To: Bob <sip:peter@ocean.com>
From: Bob <sip:peter@ocean.com>;tag=456248
Call-ID: 843817637684230@998sdasdh09
CSeq: 1826 REGISTER
Contact: <sip:peter@169.254.153.60>
Content-Length: 0
```

The first thing we will do is create the addresses that we will need for this example. There are three SIP URIs in different fields of this message:

- The registrar's SIP URI: sip:registrar.ocean.com
- Peter's Address of Record: sip:peter@ocean.com
- Peter's Contact Address: sip:peter@169.254.153.60

```
Address destAddress=myAddressFactory.createAddress("sip:
  registrar.ocean.com");
Address addressOfRecord=myAddressFactory.createAddress("sip:
  peter@ocean.com");
Address contactAddress= myAddressFactory.createAddress("sip:
  peter@169.254.153.60");
```

The destination address will have to be converted to a URI object before we can pass it to the `createRequest()` method, so:

```
javax.sip.address.URI myRequestURI=destAddress.getURI();
```

Next, we create the headers:

```
ArrayList viaHeaders=new ArrayList();
ViaHeader myViaHeader=myHeaderFactory.createViaHeader("peterpc.
  ocean.com"
,5060,udp,"z9hG4bKnashds7");
viaHeaders.add(myViaHeader);
MaxForwardsHeader myMaxForwardsHeader =
   myHeaderFactory.CreateMaxForwardsHeader(70);
ToHeader myToHeader= myHeaderFactory.createToHeader
  (addressOfRecord,null);
FromHeader myFromHeader=myHeaderFactory.createFromHeader(address
  OfRecord,
"456248");
CallIDHeader myCallIDHeader=
  myHeaderFactory.createCallIDHeader("843817637684230@
  998sdasdh09");
CseqHeader myCSeqHeader=
  myHeaderFactory.createCSeqHeader(1826,"REGISTER");
```

Then we create the message introducing the main headers as arguments to the `createRequest()` method in `MessageFactory`:

```
Request myRequest=myMessageFactory.createRequest(myRequestURI,
"REGISTER," myCallIDHeader myCSeqHeader, myFromHeader
,myToHeader, viaHeaders, myMaxForwardsHeader);
```

And last, we add to the message those headers that were not introduced as arguments to the `createRequest()` method:

```
ContactHeader myContactHeader=
HeaderFactory.createContactHeader(contactAddress);
myRequest.addHeader(myContactHeader);
```

The `Request` object (myRequest) now contains all the info in the SIP message that we wanted to build. The next line of code prints the message on the screen:

```
System.out.println(myRequest);
```

8.6.5 Example 2: Using the Transport Sublayer

In this example, we will build a simple application that is able to send and receive SIP messages statelessly. We have chosen to send a SIP REGISTER message. There will be two instances of the application. One instance will act as a client, sending the REGISTER, and the other one will act as a server, receiving the REGISTER.

User Interface

The program will present a simple GUI that includes the following elements:

- A text field where the user can input the local port (where the application is bound). In the server instance, this port represents the listening port where incoming messages from the network are received. In the client instance, this port represents the value of the UDP Source Port field in outgoing packets.
- A text field where the user introduces his or her *own Address -of -Record*. It is introduced only in the client instance.
- A text field where the user introduces the *SIP URI of the server* instance. It is introduced only in the client instance.
- An "*On*" *button* for initializing the SIP environment.
- A "Send" button for sending the messages.
- A *text screen*, where the user can visualize the sent and received messages.

Figure 8.18 shows a possible layout for the GUI.

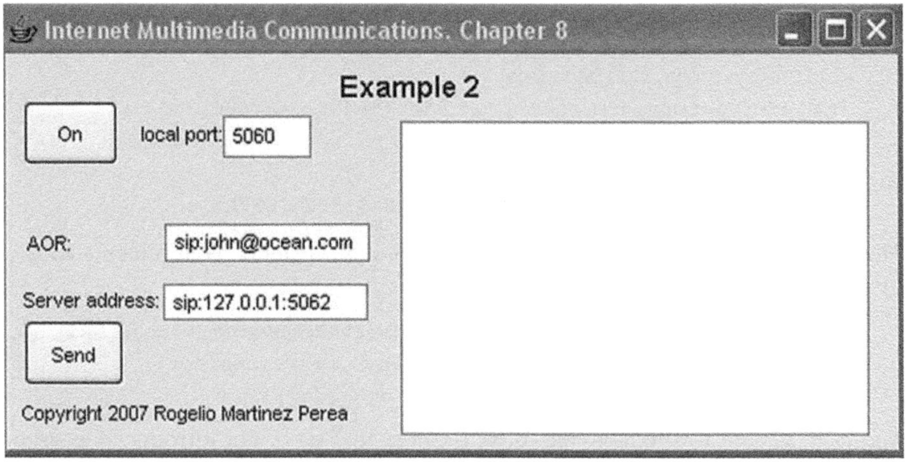

FIGURE 8.18

Architecture

The application follows the general architecture for the practices that we described in previous sections. It consist of two classes: `Example2GUI` and `Example2Listener`. In addition to the SipListener methods, `Example2 Listener` will implement a method called `userInput()` that will be invoked by `Example2GUI` when the user presses the "Send" button. The signature for the `userInput()` method is:

```
void userInput(String destination, String aor)
```

where "destination" is a String representing the SIP URI of the recipient of the request, and "aor" is a String representing the Address of Record of the user initiating the request. These two parameters are inputted in the GUI by the user, and conveyed as arguments in the `userInput()` method.

Likewise, Example2GUI will implement a method called "display." This method will contain a String as argument that represents the SIP message sent or received so that it can be displayed in the GUI.

Figure 8.19 shows the method calls between the two classes.

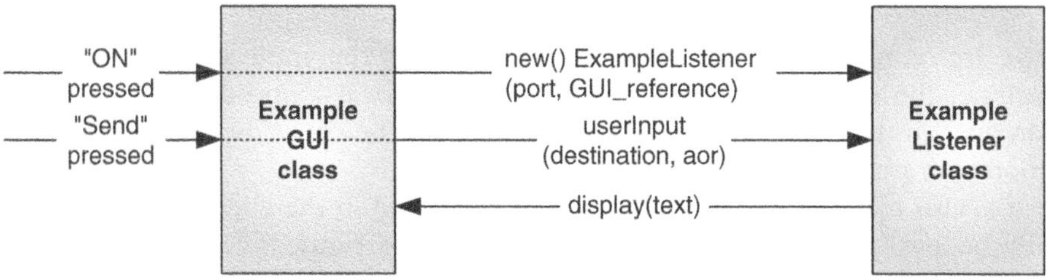

FIGURE 8.19

Initialization

The way the application works is quite simple. As soon as the program is started and the frame is loaded, the user should configure the local (own) port. After doing so, the user will press the "On" button, causing Example2GUI to create an instance of Example2Listener. The constructor method of Example2Listener will set up the JAIN SIP environment on the port introduced by the user. If the initialization has been successful, we will see a message in the GUI that shows the own IP address and port to which our application is successfully bound (Figure 8.20). The port was introduced in the GUI, whereas the IP address is directly obtained by the program:

```
String myIP=InetAddress.getLocalHost().getHostAddress();
```

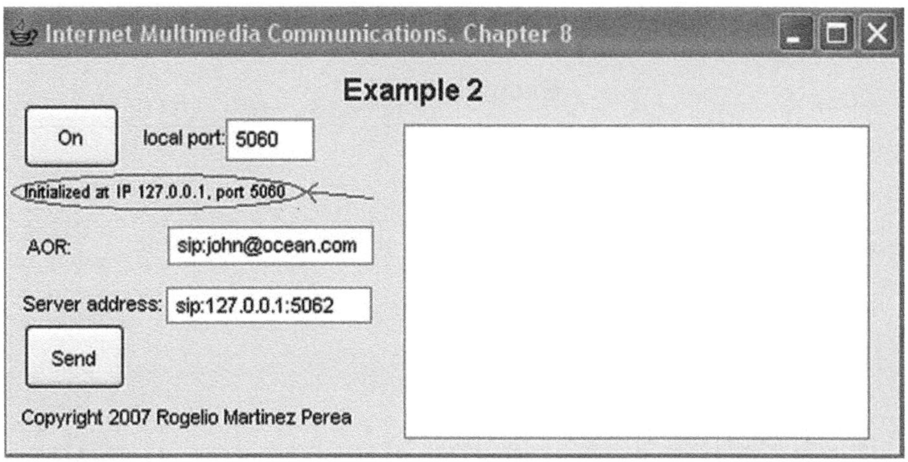

FIGURE 8.20

Creating and Sending the Request

Once both application instances (client and server) are initialized, the user will fill in his or her own Address of Record and the server address in the GUI for the client instance.

The server address will be of the form:

sip:<destination IP address>:<destination port>

If we are running the client and server instances of the application in the same machine, the destination IP address will be the local loop address: 127.0.0.1. Moreover, in that case, we need to make sure that the client own port and destination port are different!

It is also crucial that the destination port entered in the client GUI coincides with the local port configured in the server instance. Figure 8.21 shows the GUIs for the client and server instances.

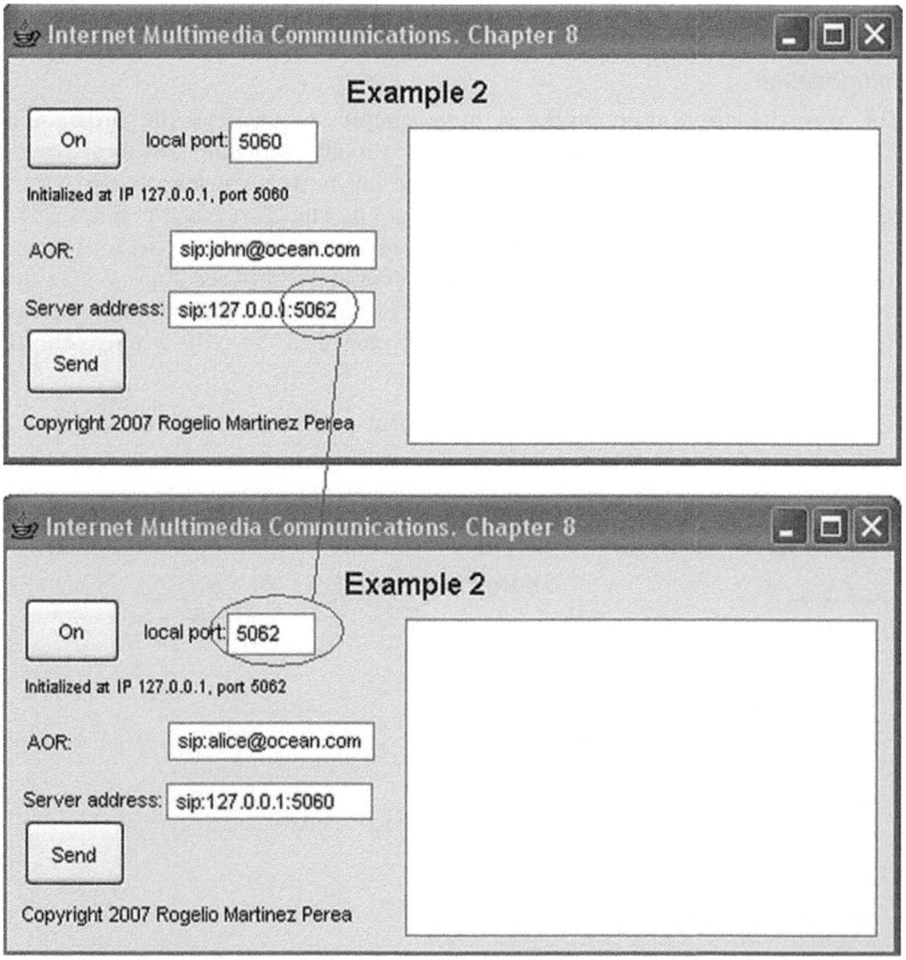

FIGURE 8.21

The user will then press the "Send" button. At that point, `Example2GUI` will call the method `userInput()` in `Example2Listener`, including the parameters introduced by the user. The code in the `userInput()` method will first build the REGISTER message.

In order to create the request, we follow a similar procedure as in Example 1. Instead of inputting the CallID value into the header-creation method, we will ask the SIP implementation to generate a CallID value for us:

```
CallIdHeader myCallIdHeader=mySipProvider.getNewCallId();
```

Next, we have to send the created message statelessly. For that, we just need to invoke the `sendRequest()` method on the `SipProvider`. This will cause the `SipProvider` to pass the message to the transport sublayer, bypassing the transaction sublayer, and therefore sending the message statelessly:

```
mySipProvider.sendRequest(myRequest);
```

After this, we will then invoke the `display()` method on the `Example2GUI` object, whose reference we obtained as an argument in the constructor method. By invoking `display()`, the sent message can be presented to the user:

```
myGUI.display(">>> "+ myRequest.toString());
```

Figure 8.22 shows a sequence diagram that represents the actions needed for creating and sending the message.

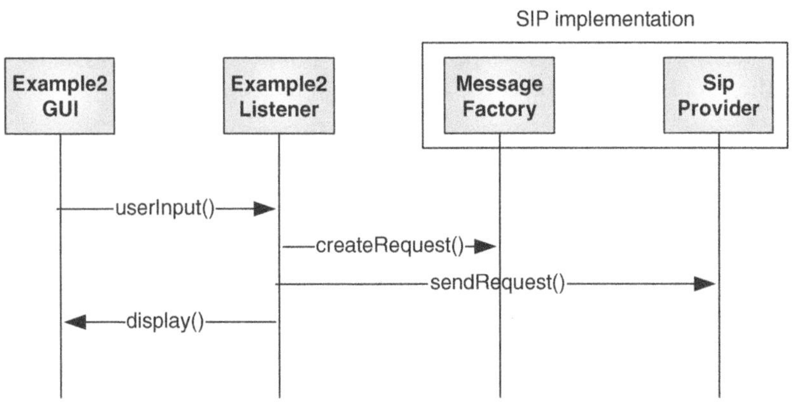

FIGURE 8.22

Receiving the Request

When the server instance receives the message, its SipProvider will invoke the `processRequest()` method on `Example2Listener`. The code in the `processRequest()` method will first obtain the `Request` object from the `RequestEvent`:

```
Request myRequest=requestReceivedEvent.getRequest();
```

Then we just convert the Request object into a string and send it to the GUI to be displayed by invoking the `display()` method on `Example2GUI` so that we can see the actual received message:

```
Request myRequest=requestReceivedEvent.getRequest();
myGUI.display("<<< "+myRequest.toString());
```

Figure 8.23 shows a sequence diagram that represents the actions taken at reception of a message.

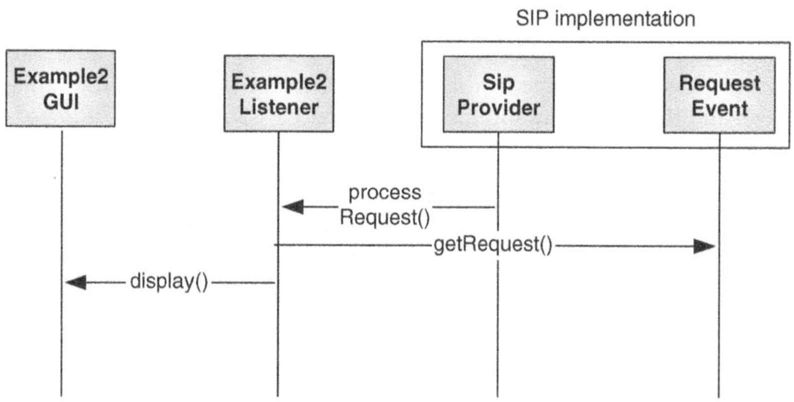

FIGURE 8.23

In Figure 8.24, we can see a snapshot of the running client and server. The tracing facility embedded in the application (i.e., the display method) allows us to see all the details of the transmitted and received messages.

8.6.6 Example 3: Using the Transaction Sublayer

We will now repeat the example in the previous section, but, in this case, sending the REGISTER message statefully instead of statelessly. That is to say, we will use the transaction sublayer. The program is then equivalent to the previous one, except for the following points:

- The methods `userInput()` and `processRequest()` have been modified so as to send and receive the messages statefully.
- When the server receives the request, it generates a 200 OK response. This will also allow us to understand how responses are constructed and managed.

Next is the code in class `Example3Listener`.

Let us try to understand the new code for handling messages statefully.

Creating the Request

In order to create the request, we follow the same procedure as in Example 2. The only difference in this case is that, rather than inputting the branch id value into

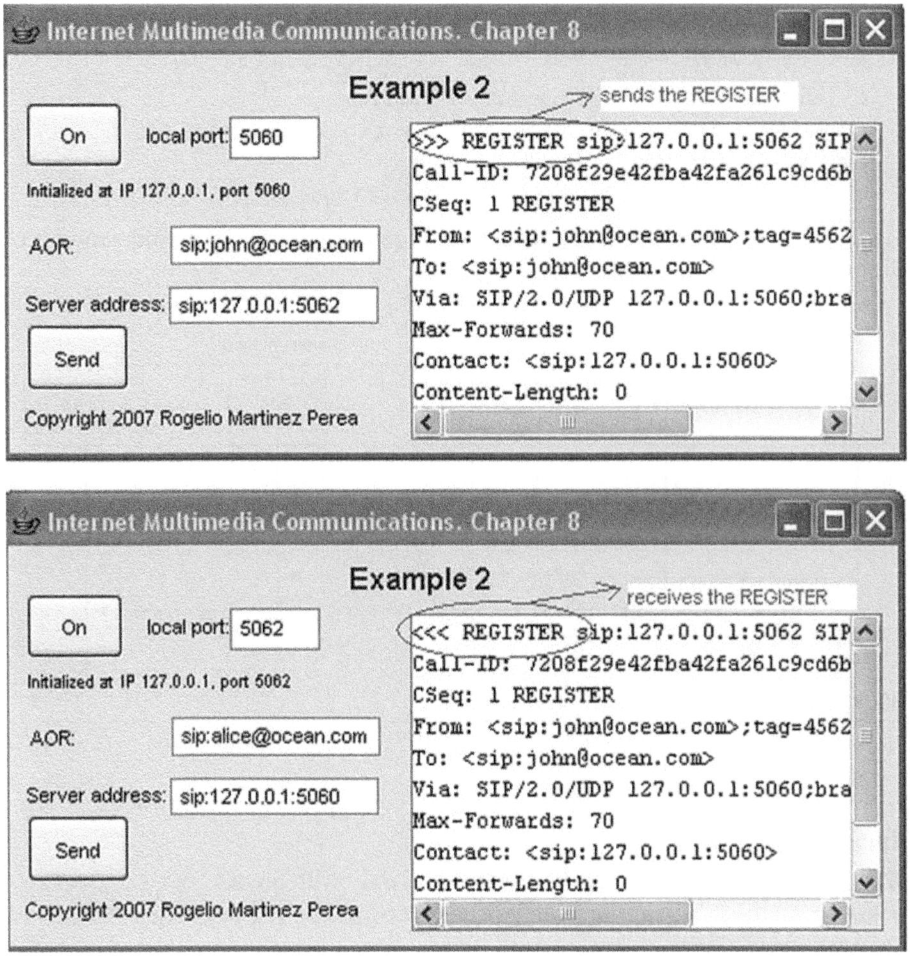

FIGURE 8.24

the via header-creation method, we will ask the SIP implementation to generate a branch id value for us. In order to do so, we will set the branch id argument as null:

```
ViasHeader myViaHeader=HeaderFactory.createViaHeader(myIP,myP
  ort,"udp,"null);
```

Sending a Request

In order to send a request statefully, we first need to create a client transaction using `SipProvider's` method `getNewClientTransaction()`. Then we can send the request using the `sendRequest()` method on the `ClientTransaction` interface.

After sending the message, the display method will be executed so as to visualize the sent message on the GUI:

```
ClientTransaction myClientTransaction=
  mySipProvider.getNewClientTransaction(myRequest);
myClientTransaction.sendRequest();
gui.display(">>> "+ myRequest.toString());
```

Figure 8.25 depicts a sequence diagram comprising the creation and sending of the request.

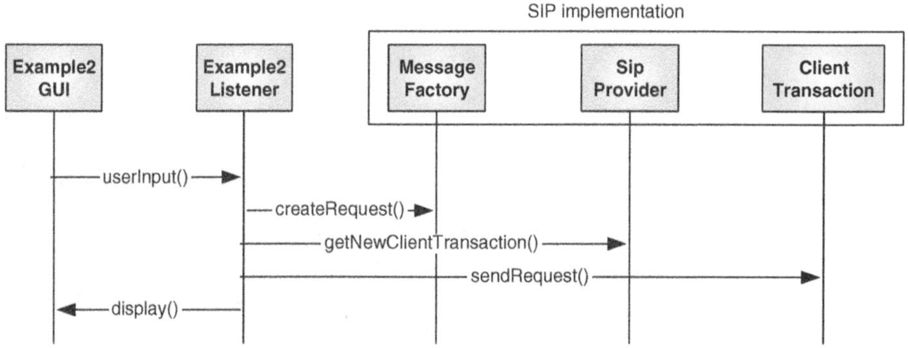

FIGURE 8.25

Receiving a Request

When a request is received, the `SipProvider` will invoke the `processRequest()` method. The application will also convert the request into a string, and display it in the GUI:

```
Request myRequest=requestReceivedEvent.getRequest();
myGUI.display("<<< "+myRequest.toString());
```

Sending a Response

In order to send a response statefully, the application has to obtain a new server transaction associated to the request just received. This is done by invoking the `getNewServerTransaction()` method on the `SipProvider`.

Then we need to create the response through the `createResponse()` method on the `MessageFactory`. Next, we just send it by invoking the `sendResponse()` method on the `ServerTransaction`:

```
ServerTransaction myServerTransaction=
  mySipProvider.getNewServerTransaction(myRequest);
Response myResponse=myMessageFactory.createResponse(200,
  myRequest);
myServerTransaction.sendResponse(myResponse);
myGUI.display(">>> "+myResponse.toString());
```

Figure 8.26 depicts a sequence diagram comprising the reception of the request and sending of the response.

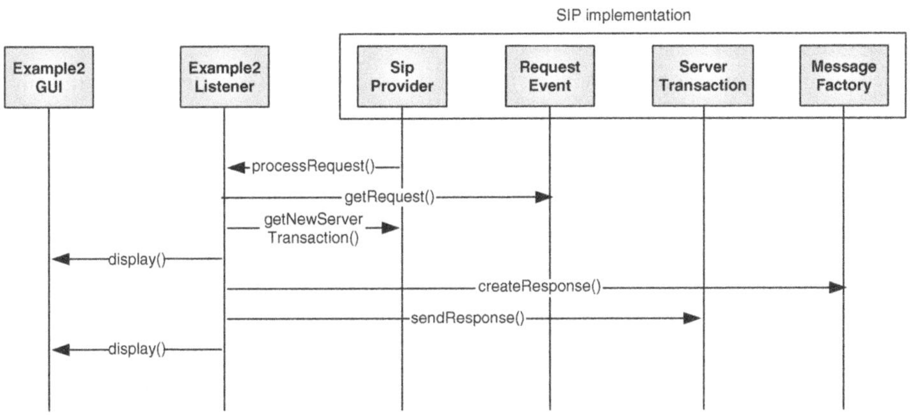

FIGURE 8.26

Receiving a Response

When a response is received, the SipProvider will invoke the `process-Response()` method. We will obtain the `Response` object by invoking `get-Response()` on the `ResponseEvent`. Then we will just convert the `Response` object into a string and send it to the GUI to be displayed:

```
Response myResponse=responseReceivedEvent.getResponse();
myGUI.display("<<< "+myesponse.toString());
```

Figure 8.27 depicts a sequence diagram for the reception of the response at the client.

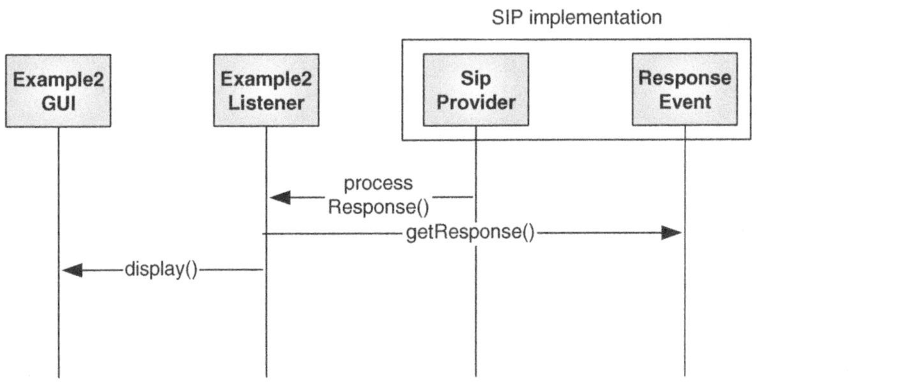

FIGURE 8.27

8.6.7 Example 4: Creating a Dialog

In this example, we will play with the `Dialog` interface. The dialog functionality that we learned in Chapter 7 is encapsulated in the JAIN SIP `Dialog` interface.

The `Dialog` interface eases the task of writing applications that manage dialogs. In this example, we will also build a client and a server. The client will initiate the dialog by sending an INVITE.[4] As soon as the server receives the INVITE, it generates a 180 Ringing response. When the user accepts the invitation, the server will generate a 200 OK response.

The program structure will be similar to the one in the previous example. There will be some differences, though:

- There will be two buttons in the GUI. One is used in the client to initiate the dialog; it is called "Initiate." The other one is called "Accept," and it is used in the server in order to accept the invitation.
- Pressing either of the two buttons will cause `Example4GUI` to invoke the `userInput()` method on `Example4Listener`. In order to distinguish between the two buttons, we have added a new argument in `userInput()` called "type," which takes value 0 when the "Initiate" button is pressed, and value 1 when the user presses the "Accept" button.
- There is a new `showStatus()` method that `Example4Listener` will invoke on `Example4GUI`. This method allows us to present additional information on the GUI in a separate label. We will use it in order to convey dialog status information to be displayed.
- In order to display dialog status information, we will need to obtain the Dialog object in different situations.

Figure 8.28 shows a possible layout for the GUI.

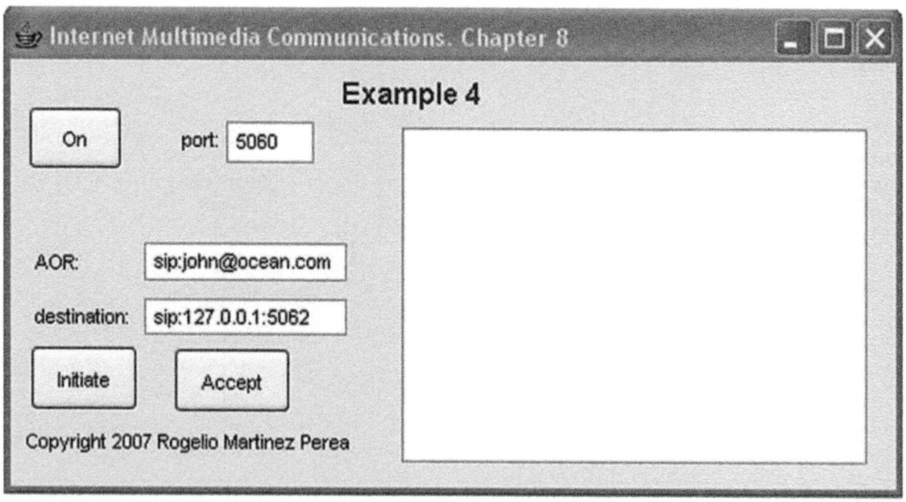

FIGURE 8.28

[4]Let us remember that the only method that is able to create a dialog in RFC 3261 is the INVITE method.

Creating the INVITE Request

The creation of the INVITE request is similar to the creation of the REGISTER in previous examples. The main difference is obviously the name of the method, and the fact that the To header contains the address of the recipient.

Sending the INVITE Request

This is done exactly in the same way as in Example 3. The dialog-creating request, in this case the INVITE, is not yet part of any dialog, so we will just create a new client transaction and send the message through it:

```
ClientTransaction myClientTransaction=
  mySipProvider.getNewClientTransaction(myRequest);
myClientTransaction.sendRequest();
```

Receiving the INVITE Request

This scenario is resolved in the same way as in Example 3. When a request is received, the `SipProvider` will invoke the `processRequest()` method:

```
Request myRequest=requestReceivedEvent.getRequest();
```

Sending a Provisional Response

Just after receiving the INVITE request, the application will send back a 180 Ringing provisional response. Before sending the response, we will include a tag in the To header, as well as add a contact header to the message. Once the message has been sent, we obtain the Dialog object and show the dialog's status on the GUI:

```
ServerTransaction myServerTransaction=
  mySipProvider.getNewServerTransaction(myRequest);
Response myResponse=myMessageFactory.createResponse(180, myRequest);
ToHeader responseToHeader=(ToHeader) myResponse.getHeader("To");
ResponseToHeader.setTag("454326");
Address contactAddress =
  myAddressFactory.createAddress("sip:"+myIP+":"+myPort);
myContactHeader=myHeaderFactory.createContactHeader(contactAddress);
myResponse.addHeader(myContactHeader);
myServerTransaction.sendResponse(myResponse);
myDialog= myServerTransaction.getDialog();
myGUI.showStatus("Dialog status: "+myDialog.getState().toString());
```

Sending a 200 OK Response

When the called user presses the "Accept" button, the application needs to create a 200 OK response and send it back to the calling user. So, within the code for the `userInput()` method, for the case where type = 1 (ACCEPT), we will first need to invoke the `createResponse()` method on `MessageFactory`. For that, we pass as an argument the originally received request. In addition to that, we also obtain the Dialog object, which represents SIP dialog that has just been created:

```
Request originalRequest=myServerTransaction.getRequest();
Response myResponse =myMessageFactory.createResponse(200,
  originalRequest);
ToHeader responseToHeader=(ToHeader) myResponse.getHeader("To");
ResponseToHeader.setTag("454326");
myServerTransaction.sendResponse(myResponse);
myDialog= myServerTransaction.getDialog();
myGUI.showStatus("Dialog status: "+myDialog.getState().toString());
```

Receiving a 180 Provisional Response

When a response is received, the SipProvider will invoke the process Response() method, and we will get the Response object from the Response Event. We also get the client transaction and the dialog corresponding to the request, and show the dialog state:

```
Response myResponse=responseReceivedEvent.getResponse();
myClientTransaction=responseReceivedEvent.getClientTransaction();
myDialog= myClientTransaction.getDialog();
myGUI.showStatus("Dialog status: "+myDialog.getState().toString());
```

Receiving a 200 OK Response

When a response is received, the SipProvider will invoke the processResponse() method, and we will get the Response object from the ResponseEvent. We also get the client transaction and the dialog corresponding to the request. It is crucial that we obtain the Dialog because we need it in order to generate the ACK in the next step:

```
Response myResponse=responseReceivedEvent.getResponse();
myClientTransaction=responseReceivedEvent.getClientTransaction();
myDialog= myClientTransaction.getDialog();
myGUI.showStatus("Dialog status: "+myDialog.getState().toString());
```

Sending the ACK

In order to send the ACK, we first need to build it. JAIN SIP offers a method called createAck() to build an ACK message from the Dialog that we obtained in the last step. We need to include as an argument to the method the sequence number of the original INVITE request that created the dialog. Once created, the Dialog interface again offers a method to send the ACK:

```
Request ackRequest=myDialog.createAck(1);
ackRequest.addHeader(myContactHeader);
myDialog.sendAck(ackRequest);
```

Receiving the ACK

When a request is received, the `SipProvider` will invoke the `processRequest()` method, and we will get the `Request` object from the `RequestEvent`:

```
Request myRequest=requestReceivedEvent.getRequest();
```

In Figure 8.29, we can see a snapshot of the running client and server.

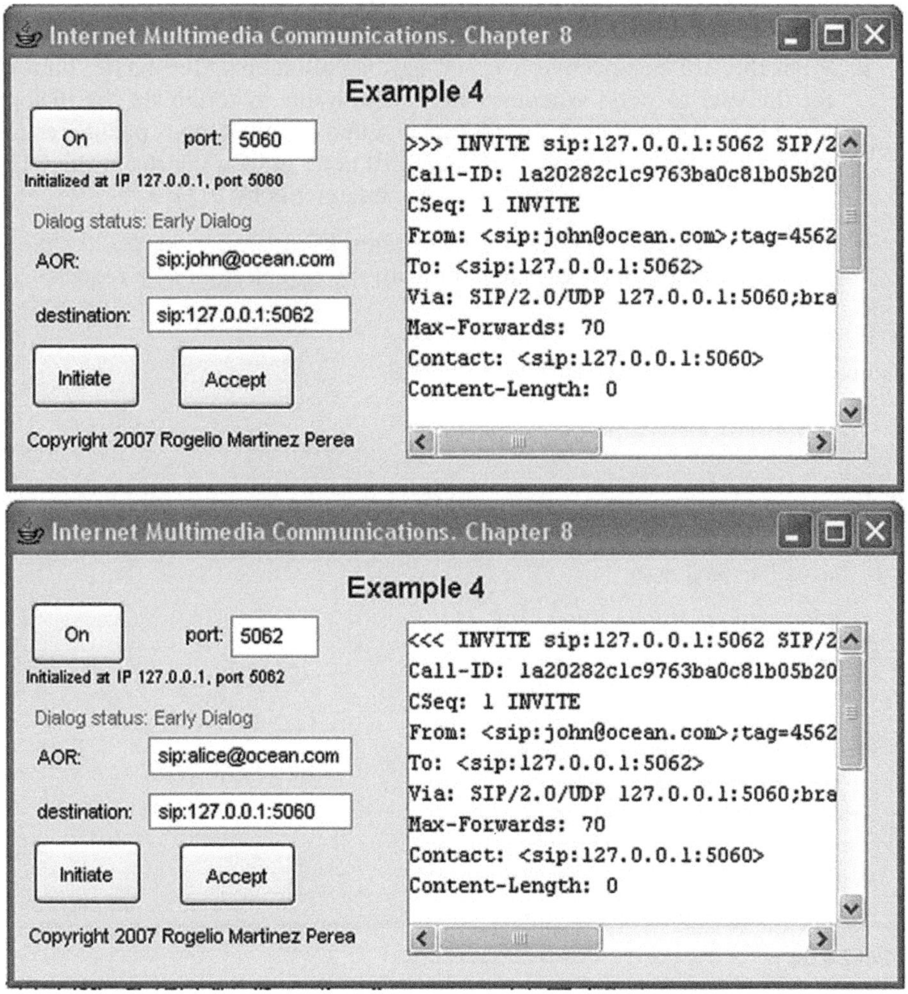

FIGURE 8.29

Initiating a dialog without offering the user the capability of terminating it is not of much use to the user. In the next example (Example 5), we will extend Example 4 to incorporate also the possibility for terminating dialogs.

8.6.8 Example 5: Terminating a Dialog

- We will now extend the previous example with the capability for the user to be able to terminate the dialog by sending a BYE message, which is a mid-dialog request.[5] This example will show how we can use the `Dialog` interface to construct and send any new requests within the dialog. So this is applicable to the BYE request, but also to any other mid-dialog requests (e.g., re-INVITE, and so on).

The new aspects as compared with Example 4 are:

- From the GUI perspective, we will have an additional "Terminate" button for the user to press whenever he or she wants to terminate the dialog. Therefore, we will have an additional value for the "type" parameter in the `userInput()` method, and additional code in it to construct the BYE request. The new value of the "type" parameter will be 2.
- We will need extra code in the `processRequest()` and `processResponse()` methods in order to cope with the reception of BYE requests or responses.

Figure 8.30 shows a possible layout for the GUI.

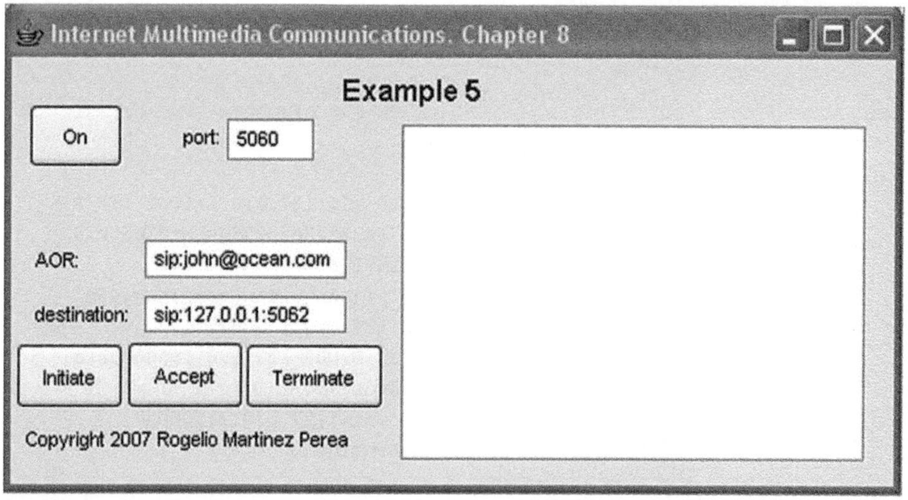

FIGURE 8.30

[5]Strictly speaking, the BYE method is used to terminate a session (not a dialog); however, the dialog created when establishing that session is also terminated. Given that in these academic exercises, we are not yet playing with the media plane (so there is no effective media session established), the practical effect of the BYE request is to terminate the dialog.

Sending a BYE Request

Sending a mid-dialog request is a very easy process by using the `Dialog` interface. A `Dialog` object stores all the state needed by a SIP dialog that will be used for constructing new requests.

First, we invoke the `createRequest()` method on the `Dialog`. The new mid-dialog request needs to be sent statefully, so we will also create a new client transaction that will be used to send the request. Finally, we send the request by invoking the `sendRequest()` method on the `Dialog` object; we pass the client transaction as an argument:

```
Request myRequest= myDialog.createRequest("BYE");
myClientTransaction= mySipProvider.getNewClientTransaction
  (myRequest);
myDialog.sendRequest(myClientTransaction);
myGUI.showStatus("Dialog status: "+myDialog.getState().toString());
```

Figure 8.31 shows a sequence diagram that includes the creation and sending of a mid-dialog request.

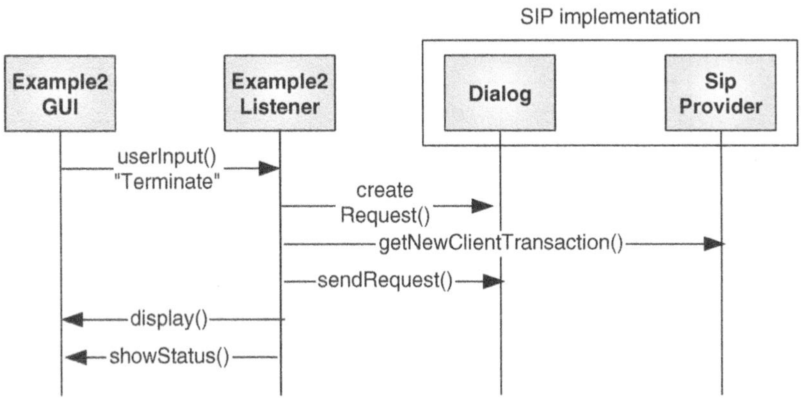

FIGURE 8.31

Receiving the BYE Request

When a request is received, the `SipProvider` will invoke the `processRequest()` method. The application then must obtain the server transaction. In order to obtain server transactions for requests outside of a dialog, we have so far used the `getNewServerTransaction()` method. However, for requests within a dialog, such as a BYE request, the server transaction is included in the received `RequestEvent`, so we can easily obtain it by:

```
Request myRequest=requestReceivedEvent.getRequest();
myServerTransaction=requestReceivedEvent.getServerTransaction();
```

Sending the 200 OK Response to BYE

After receiving the BYE request, the application will create a 200 OK response, and send it using the obtained server transaction for the BYE request. The response will be created based on the request message that created this transaction and that was previously stored:

```
Response myResponse=myMessageFactory.createResponse(200, myRequest);
myServerTransaction.sendResponse(myResponse);
myDialog=myServerTransaction.getDialog();
myGUI.showStatus("Dialog status: "+myDialog.getState().toString());
```

Figure 8.32 shows a sequence diagram that includes the reception of a mid-dialog request and the sending of a 200 OK response to it.

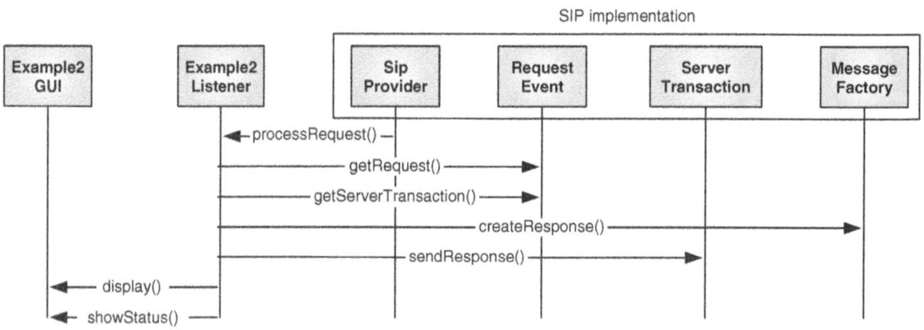

FIGURE 8.32

Receiving the 200 OK Response to BYE

When a response is received, the `SipProvider` will invoke the `processResponse()` method, and we will get the `Response` object from the `ResponseEvent`:

```
Response myResponse=responseReceivedEvent.getResponse();
```

In Figure 8.33, we can see a snapshot of the running client and server.

8.7 Summary

In this chapter, we have introduced the main concepts around the JAIN SIP interface, and we have built some very simple applications that allow us to experiment with the SIP signaling. But IP communications is not just signaling—there is media as well, and there is also the need to describe the media. In the next chapters, we will learn how to programmatically access the media layer so as to be able to code, decode, send, and receive media packets. We will also learn how

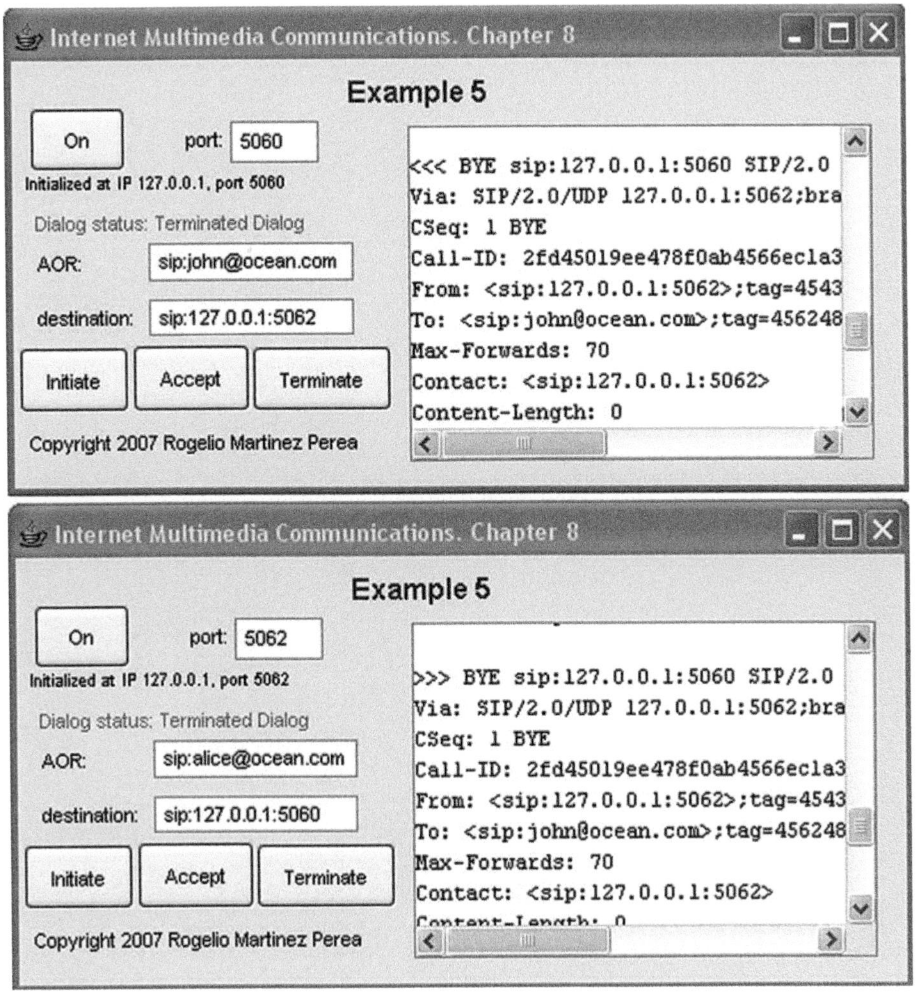

FIGURE 8.33

to build applications that use the Real-time Transport Protocol, as well as learn to program the Session Description Protocol. Armed with these three ingredients (signaling, media, and session description), we will be able, in Chapter 12, to tackle the design and implementation of a simple SIP soft phone.

CHAPTER

Session Description

9

In this chapter, we will look at how multimedia sessions can be described. First we will explain the need for describing sessions and list some examples of scenarios in which sessions need to be described. Then we will focus on the Session Description Protocol, which defines the syntax for describing multimedia sessions. After that, the SDP offer/answer model will be explained. It describes a procedure for the exchange of session descriptions between communicating parties that is crucial for enabling IP multimedia communication services. We will also show how SDP is used in some particular IP communication scenarios.

Once the theory has been presented, we will also include an SDP programming section that shows the reader how to programmatically build and parse session descriptions. As part of this section, we will build a simple Java component that will be reused in our soft-phone project in Chapter 12.

9.1 The Purpose of Session Description

[RFC 4566] defines a multimedia session as "a set of multimedia senders and receivers and the data streams flowing from senders to receivers." This is not a very specific definition, which highlights the fact that a multimedia session can be many different things. Examples of sessions[1] are:

- a voice over IP call
- a multicast conference in the Internet
- the exchange of a series of related instant messages between two parties
- an online game
- a video-on-demand streaming session
- the online transfer of an image as a TCP data stream between two communicating parties

[1] Strictly speaking a session qualifies as multimedia only if it includes more than one media. For instance, following such a terminology, a VoIP call would be a one-medium session, whereas an audio/video conference could be considered a true multimedia session. This requirement is very much relaxed in practice, and many people refer to multimedia sessions even if there is just one medium included.

These scenarios represent examples of IP multimedia communication or streaming services, and, in all of them, the session concept is used. In all of them, there is a need to describe the characteristics of the session and then to convey that information to the participants of the session. Such a description of the session would include parameters such as media types, transport addresses, start time and duration of the session, and so on, the knowledge of which is crucial for the participants in the session. Let's take, for instance, the example of a multicast conference in the Internet. In order for a user to be able to participate, he or she needs to know:

- in what multicast address they need to listen (that is, what "channel" they need to tune)
- what media types and codecs the conference will use (otherwise, he or she will be unable to decode the media information correctly)
- at what time the conference will start
- etc.

These, and others, are parameters that characterize the conference and that need to be conveyed among the participants before the conference starts.

Also, in peer-to-peer real-time communication scenarios, there is a need to exchange session descriptions. Take, for instance, a two-party voice call. Before the actual voice transmission can start, the participants need to learn what IP addresses and ports they need to send the media packets to. Moreover, they also need to agree on what voice codec to use for transmission and reception, and so forth.

These examples highlight:

1. The need to find a common format for describing sessions.
2. The need to find a mechanism (protocol) for delivering those session descriptions among the participants.

The SDP specification covers the first point as it defines a general-purpose format for describing multimedia sessions. SDP is used in a variety of scenarios such as streaming services, real-time communication services, or Internet multicast conferences.

The second need is covered by different protocols depending on the particular service. For instance, we have seen that, for real-time communications, SIP is the protocol used to carry session descriptions, so, in those cases, SDP is included as content in the SIP message. In the streaming cases, the SDP content is embedded in RTSP (Real Time Streaming Protocol) messages exchanged between client and server, whereas, in Internet multicast conferences, it is included in Session Announcement Protocol (SAP) [RFC 2974] messages in order to announce a multicast conference to potential participants.

In the case of multicast sessions, other alternative ways of conveying session descriptions may include use of email or the web so that applications for participating in a session could be automatically launched from the WWW client or email reader in a standard manner.

In the rest of this chapter (and the book!), we will focus on the utilization of SDP just in the remit of real-time IP communication services. In those cases, SDP is typically carried by SIP.

9.2 The Session Description Protocol (SDP)

9.2.1 Origins of SDP

SDP was originally conceived to describe multicast sessions on the MBone. In those scenarios, the SDP session descriptor was distributed among the potential participants using the Session Announcement Protocol [RFC 2974]. The SDP included, among other things, information about the multicast address for the media and the set of codecs used in the session.

SDP is used in many scenarios, including streaming, IP communications, and others. In order to apply SDP to IP communication scenarios, it is necessary to extend its semantics. For example, in a multicast conference, it is necessary only to convey a single multicast address for a particular media stream, whereas, in the case of a two-party communication, two unicast addresses are needed.

Moreover, there is also the need to define the operational details of how to use SDP in communication scenarios. In the case of multicast conferences, the codecs to be used for the session are simply indicated in the SDP sent to the participants, whereas, in the case of IP communications, the parties need to agree on the set of codecs to use; therefore, some negotiation needs to occur.

In the next sections, we will see the SDP syntax and semantics that are applicable to IP communication services, as well as a limited negotiation framework defined by [RFC 3264].

9.2.2 SDP Overview

SDP is specified in [RFC 4566]. As has already been mentioned, SDP does not define a true protocol, but rather, a language for representing the key parameters that characterize a multimedia session.

SDP is text based. An SDP message consists of a set of lines of text of the form:

<type>=<value>

where <type> is a single character, and <value> is a structured text whose format depends on <type>. An example of SDP message is shown next.

```
v=0
o=alice 2890844526 2890842807 IN IP4 1.2.3.4
s=
c=IN IP4 1.2.3.4
t=0 0
m=audio 49170 RTP/AVP 0
a=sendrecv
```

An SDP message contains three levels of information:

- *Session-level description*: contains lines that describe characteristics of the whole session.
- *Time description*: contains lines indicating time-related aspects of the session.

- *Media description*: contains lines that characterize the different media present in the session.

Tables 9.1, 9.2, and 9.3, taken from [RFC 4566], show the different types of lines for each level, indicating whether the field is required (R) or optional (O).

Table 9.1 Session-Level Description SDP Lines

Field	Description	R/O
v	Protocol version	R
o	Originator and session identifier	R
s	Session name	R
i	Session information	O
u	URI of description	O
e	Email address	O
p	Phone number	O
c	Connection information[a]	O
b	Bandwidth information	O
z	Time zone adjustments	O
k	Encryption key	O
a	Session attribute	O

[a] *Not required if included in all media.*

Table 9.2 Time-Level Description SDP Lines

Field	Description	R/O
t	Time the session is active	R
r	Repeat time	O

Table 9.3 Media-Level Description SDP Lines

Field	Description	R/O
m	Media name and transport addr.	R
i	Media title	R
c	Connection information[a]	R
b	Bandwidth information	O
k	Encryption key	O
a	Attribute line	O

[a] *Optional if included at session level.*

Next we will focus on those lines that are mandatory or of relevance for real-time communication services. We will explain the meaning of the different parameters in the remit of this kind of services.

9.2.3 Protocol Version (v-line)

The "v=" line gives the version of the Session Description Protocol.

It is set to 0 for the current version of the spec [RFC 4566].

Example:

```
v=0
```

9.2.4 Origin (o-line)

The "o=" line identifies the originator of the session, and contains the following parameters:

- *username*: Name of the originator. In our case of IP communication scenarios, the id of the user is already conveyed in the From header in the SIP signaling, so this parameter is not necessary and we may set it to "-."
- *session id*: A numeric string that has to be unique for this session in conjunction with the address. A way to assure uniqueness is to use NTP (Network Time Protocol) [RFC 1305] timestamp values.
- *session version*: A version number for the session description data. Again it is recommended to use NTP timestamp values.
- *network type*: It is set to "IN" for Internet.
- *address type*: It may be IP4 or IP6.
- *unicast address*: The sender's IP address.

An example would be:

```
o=alice 2890844526 2890842807 IN IP4 1.2.3.4
```

9.2.5 Session Name (s-line)

The "s=" line conveys the subject of the session. This makes sense for multicast uses of SDP. In the case of unicast (as is the case in IP communication services), a session has no meaningful name, so the s-line will be set to just a blank space "s=."

Example:

```
s=
```

9.2.6 Connection Information (c-line)

The "c=" line contains information about the connection address. That is the address at which the SDP sender expects to receive the incoming media packets.

Example:

```
c=IN IP4 1.2.3.4
```

where IN indicates that the following address is an Internet address, and IP4 indicates the version of the IP protocol.

The c-line can be present at session level—that is, valid for all the sessions—or be present in the m-line, implying it is valid for a particular media, in which case it overrides the session-level value.

9.2.7 Time Line (t-line)

The "t=" line conveys the time of the session. This is again meaningful for multicast sessions where the potential receivers need to know beforehand when the session will start, following very much a similar approach to what occurs in TV broadcasting. In the case of unicast sessions, it is set to "0 0."

Example:

```
t=0 0
```

9.2.8 Media and Transport (m-line)

The "m=" line includes information about a particular media.

A session description may contain several m-lines, implying the session may contain several media. Each m-line indicates:

- The type of media: voice, video, message, image, and so on.
- The port where the sender expects to receive media packets.
- The protocol to use for media transport: RTP, UDP, TCP, MSRP/TCP, and so on.
- The media format.

The interpretation of the media format depends on the actual media transport protocol. When RTP/AVP is used, the media format represents the RTP payload type number (see Chapter 10). The RTP payload number can be static or dynamic. If it is static, there exists a well-known id number associated to it, so there is no need to include further information about the payload type in the SDP. However, if it is dynamic, there is no fixed association, so the next line in the SDP should include more information that characterizes the format.

Dynamic payload types are assigned numbers between 96 and 127.

Next follows an example of an m-line with a static payload type (0), which indicates a PCM μ-law[2] encoding for audio.

```
m=audio 40000 RTP/AVP 0
```

The next example shows an m-line with a dynamic type (96).

```
m=audio 49230 RTP/AVP 96
a=rtpmap:96 L8/8000
```

Note that in this last case, there is an additional a-line, which is used to describe the type of encoding (L8) and the clock rate dynamically assigned to payload type 96.

9.2.9 Bandwidth (b-line)

The optional "b=" line denotes the proposed bandwidth to be used by the session or media.

[2]Pulse Code Modulation (PCM) is a scheme for digitally representing an analog signal. The magnitude of the signal is sampled regularly at uniform intervals and the samples are converted into a digital code. PCM μ-law is a variant used in North America and Japan, whereas PCM A-law is a variant used in Europe and the rest of the world.

A b-line contains two elements:

1. The bandwidth figure itself expressed, by default, in kilobits per second.
2. An alphanumeric modifier that gives the meaning to the bandwidth figure.

The values of the modifier more frequently used in IP communications are:

- *AS*: Is typically used to specify the total bandwidth (in kilobits per second) allocated for a single media stream from a single site (source).
- *RS*: Indicates the requested RTCP bandwidth (in bits per second) allocated to active data senders.
- *RR*: Indicates the requested RTCP bandwidth (in bits per second) allocated to receivers.

The use of the modifier values RS and RR is not defined in the base SDP specification [RFC 4566], but on [RFC 3556].

The following SDP session description offers an audio communication, and requests a total bandwidth of 64 kilobits per second. For RTCP senders, the requested bandwidth is 800 bps; for RTCP receivers, it is 2400 bps.

```
v=0
o=alice 2890844526 2890842807 IN IP4 1.2.3.4
s=
c=IN IP4 1.2.3.4
t=0 0
m=audio 49170 RTP/AVP 0
b=AS:64
b=RS:800
b=RR:2400
```

9.2.10 Attributes (a-line)

Attributes are the primary means for extending SDP. They may be defined to be used as "session-level" attributes, "media-level" attributes, or both.

Some important attributes in the case of IP communication services are:

- *rtmap*: In the case of RTP/AVP transport, it is used to map the payload type in an m-line with some parameters characterizing the payload type, such as the encoding name, clock rate, or encoding parameters. For example, the following a-line maps the dynamic payload type 96 to an L8 encoding at a 8000 Hz sampling rate:

  ```
  a=rtpmap:96 L8/8000
  ```

- *sendrec*: Indicates that the sender of the media description wants to send and receive media.
- *recvonly*: Indicates that the sender of the media description wants only to receive media.

- *sendonly*: Indicates that the sender of the media description wants only to send media.
- *inactive*: Indicates that the sender of the media description does not want to send or receive media.

Next follow some examples of SDP session descriptions for different types of media.

9.3 Example IP Communication Sessions Described with SDP

SDP can be used to describe many different types of sessions. Now we will see five possible uses of SDP to describe different types of IP communication sessions. All of these communication sessions can be established via SIP.

9.3.1 Voice and Video

This corresponds to the most classical use of SDP to describe a session composed of "pure" real-time media components such as audio and video transported over RTP. We can see that the SDP message indicates that the RTP audio/video profile should be used (see Chapter 10 for the definition of the audio/video profile). It also includes a media line for audio with PCM codec (payload type=0), and a media line for video with the H.261 codec (payload type=31).

```
v=0
o=alice 2890844526 2890844526 IN IP4 host.ocean.com
s=-
c=IN IP4 host.ocean.com
t=0 0
m=audio 49170 RTP/AVP 0
a=rtpmap:0 PCMU/8000
m=video 51372 RTP/AVP 31
a=rtpmap:31 H261/90000
```

9.3.2 Telephony Tones

In PSTN (Public Switched Telephony Network) scenarios, it is common to use telephony tones. An example of this is the so-called DTMF (Dual-Tone Multi-Frequency) tones, which are standard signals that are generated by pressing a ordinary telephone's touch keys. These are typically used in scenarios involving interactive voice response (IVR) machines that prompt the user to introduce some information (e.g., "If you want information in English, press 1; if you want information in Spanish, press 2").

Multimedia applications in the Internet may need to send or receive these types of signals, especially in (but not limited to) scenarios that involve interworking with the PSTN.[3] DTMF and telephony tones are considered a particular type

[3] Interworking with the PSTN is further described in Chapter 18.

of audio media carried over RTP that is separately described using SDP. By using SDP, endpoints in an Internet multimedia communication can signal whether they support or not the generation of telephony tones in case those need to be generated during the conversation.

Next follows an example of SDP that offers support for DTMF (only the relevant lines are shown).

```
m=audio 42000 RTP/AVP 100
a=rtpmap:100 telephone-event/8000
```

Transport of telephony tones over RTP is described in [RFC 4733] and [RFC 4734].

9.3.3 Real-time Text

"Real-time text over IP" sessions can be conveyed using RTP with a specific payload type. An example of SDP for a text session might be:

```
v=0
o=alice 2890844526 2890844526 IN IP4 host.ocean.com
s=-
c=IN IP4 host.ocean.com
t=0 0
m=text 49170 RTP/AVP 98
a=rtpmap:98 t140/1000
```

As we can see, the dynamic payload type 98 is mapped to the T.140 protocol, which is used for describing the content of a text session (see Chapter 10).

9.3.4 Instant Messages (MSRP)

Another type of media that can be described by SDP is the exchange of related instant messages between two parties. Such an exchange is also considered to be a media session. This scenario is called session-based instant messaging, and the media transport protocol in this case is the Message Session Relay Protocol (MSRP). At the time of writing, there is not yet an RFC for MSRP. It is specified in an Internet draft [draft-ietf-simple-message-sessions]. Therefore, it is considered work in progress. The status of the draft is quite advanced, and it is expected that very soon it will become a standards track RFC.

In order to describe an MSRP session using SDP, two new mandatory media-level attributes are defined:

- *path*: This attribute always accompanies an MSRP media line. It indicates the MSRP URI of the user agent that sent this session description. An MSRP URI represents the end user address where he or she expects to receive incoming instant messages. An MSRP URI has the form:

  msrp://host:port/session_id;transport

- *accept-types*: This is also a mandatory attribute that accompanies an m-line. It indicates the media types that are acceptable to the endpoint. It may indicate wrapper types (e.g., message/cpim) or simple types (e.g., text/plain).

In addition to these new attributes, the connection and media line in an SDP message describing an MSRP session have the following requirements:

c-line

- The address in this line must coincide with the IP address or FQDN indicated in the path attribute.

m-line

- The protocol parameter is "tcp/msrp."
- The media field must be "message." In order to further qualify the media type, the accept-types attribute is used.
- The port parameter must match the port value used in the MSRP URI in the path attribute.

A curious reader might wonder why some values such as port or FQDN are duplicated in the SDP description. The reason is that actually the c-line and m-line are not used by MSRP devices; however, they need to be there and provide meaningful information for backward compatibility reasons.

Next follows an example of SDP describing an MSRP session:

```
v=0
o=-2890844526 2890844527 IN IP4 alice.ocean.com
s=-
c=IN IP4 alice.ocean.com
t=0 0
m=message 8341 TCP/MSRP *
a=accept-types: message/cpim text/plain text/html
a=path:msrp://alice.ocean.com:8341/7hr38r3ew;tcp
```

9.3.5 TCP Content

The media described by SDP can also represent media that is conveyed as a data stream using the TCP protocol between two communicating parties. The protocol identifier in this case has the value "TCP." It indicates just the transport protocol, so the m-line must further qualify the application-layer protocol using a format identifier. Furthermore, two new attributes must be defined to describe how and when the TCP connection setup procedure is performed:

- *setup*: This attributes indicates which of the endpoints should initiate the TCP connection establishment. It can have the following values:
  - "active": The endpoint offers to initiate the connection.
  - "passive": The endpoint offers to receive an incoming connection.
  - "actpass": The endpoint is willing to accept an incoming connection or to initiate an outgoing connection.
  - "holdconn": The endpoint does not want the connection to be established for the time being.

- *connection*: This attribute indicates if a new connection needs to be established or the already existing one should be reused.[4] It can have the following values, which are straightforward: "new" or "existing."

In the following example, we can see an example of SDP for this type of session. In this case, the media type is "image." The transport protocol is TCP, and the format indicates a T.38 fax application. The setup attribute is active, so the sender is willing to initiate the TCP connection and the connection attribute is new, which means that a new TCP connection needs to be established.

```
v=0
o=alice 2890844526 2890844526 IN IP4 host.ocean.com
s=-
c=IN IP4 host.ocean.com
t=0 0
m=image 34772 TCP t38
a=setup:active
a=connection:new
```

The SDP usage to describe TCP media transport is defined in [RFC 4145].

9.4 The Offer/Answer Model with SDP

As we said before, the use of SDP in communication scenarios also requires defining a limited negotiation framework so that the communicating parties can agree on the session characteristics, such as which media streams are in the session, the codecs, and so forth. Such negotiation framework is called the offer/answer model, and is defined in [RFC 3264].

The way it works is quite simple. A party wanting to communicate indicates the desired session description from his or her point of view. That is called the SDP offer. The offer contains, among others:

- the set of media streams that the offerer wants to use.
- the desired characteristics of the media streams as qualified by the format parameter and the media-line attributes.
- the IP addresses and ports where the offerer wants to receive the media.
- the additional parameters, if needed, that further qualify the media transport.

The other party receives the offer, and replies with an SDP answer. It contains the following pieces of information:

- whether a media stream is accepted or not.[5]
- the media streams characteristics that will be used for the session.
- the IP addresses and ports that the answerer wants to use in order to receive media.

[4] A TCP connection may already exist if the SDP is sent to modify parameters in an existing session.

[5] The way to indicate that a media stream is not accepted is by setting the port value in the m-line for that media to zero.

The offerer receives the answer, and, at this point, if the answer accepts at least one media, both parties have found an overlap in their respective desired session descriptions, and communication can start.

In addition to the media types and their characteristics, the parameters that can be negotiated using the offer/answer model differ slightly depending on the type of session being established. We will now see three examples of offer/answer model utilization for three different cases of IP communication.

In case of media types that are conveyed using RTP, we have seen that the offer/answer model enables the negotiation of the type of codecs. For other types of media, the offer/answer model allows us to negotiate other parameters.

9.4.1 Voice/Video

Let us assume that John wants to set up a communication with Alice that includes a bidirectional audio stream and two bidirectional video streams, using H.261 (payload type 31) and MPEG (payload type 32). Therefore, his SDP offer will look like:

```
v=0
o=john 2890844526 2890844526 IN IP4 host.sea.com
s=
c=IN IP4 host.sea.com
t=0 0
m=audio 48450 RTP/AVP 0
a=rtpmap:0 PCMU/8000
m=video 52792 RTP/AVP 31
a=rtpmap:31 H261/90000
m=video 53630 RTP/AVP 32
a=rtpmap:32 MPV/90000
```

Alice does not want to receive or send the first video stream, so she returns the SDP below as the answer:

```
v=0
o=alice 2890844730 2890844730 IN IP4 host.alice.com
s=
c=IN IP4 host.alice.com
t=0 0
m=audio 48950 RTP/AVP 0
a=rtpmap:0 PCMU/8000
m=video 0 RTP/AVP 31
m=video 53700 RTP/AVP 32
a=rtpmap:32 MPV/90000
```

We can notice that in the answer, the port for the first media stream is set to 0, indicating that Alice does not want to communicate using that particular media. Alice, on the other hand, accepts both the audio and the second video stream, so the communication will start including these two media.

As we can seen from this example, in the case of media types that are conveyed using RTP, the offer/answer model enables the negotiation of the type of codecs.

Putting a Media Stream on Hold

Let us assume in our previous example that, once the call is established, John decides to put the audio stream on hold. In our example, media is flowing in both directions, which is the default value if no specific direction attribute is present in the SDP (sendrecv, sendonly, recvonly, or inactive). Therefore, in order to put the call on hold, John just needs to send a reINVITE to Alice that includes an SDP with the attribute sendonly for the audio stream. If, later on, he wants to retrieve the call, he needs to just send a new reINVITE and change the SDP attribute to sendrecv or simply not add any attribute.

9.4.2 MSRP

Let us consider now that John wants to set up an instant messaging session with Alice. John intends to send messages containing text, and also he wants to send an image. This means that he will offer two media types to Alice:

- text/plain
- image/jpeg

John also includes his MSRP address in the path attribute. His SDP offer would be:

```
v=0
o=john 2890844526 2890844527 IN IP4 host.sea.com
s=-
c=IN IP4 host.sea.com
t=0 0
m=message 6554 TCP/MSRP *
a=accept-types: text/plain image/jpeg
a=path:msrp://host.sea.com:6554/5u42ihy542;tcp
```

Alice does not support the jpeg format, so she answers with the following SDP, in which she also includes her MSRP address in the path attribute:

```
v=0
o=alice 2890844530 2890844532 IN IP4 host.ocean.com
s=-
c=IN IP4 host.ocean.com
t=0 0
m=message 8651 TCP/MSRP *
a=accept-types: text/plain
a=path:msrp:// host.ocean.com:8651/6tejdtw5eyde;tcp
```

At this point, John would set up a TCP connection to the address and port specified by the MSRP URI sent by Alice—that is, host.ocean.com:8651. Once the TCP connection is established, the exchange of just text messages might start.

9.4.3 TCP Content

When using TCP-based transport, it is possible to negotiate how and when the connection setup procedure is performed based on the exchanged values of the "connection" and "setup" attributes.

For instance, the offerer might set setup attribute to passive, and, if the answerer responds with active, it means that the answerer will be the one responsible for initiating the TCP connection. This scenario is seen in the following exchange of SDP messages between John and Alice for a T.38 fax session:

Offer

```
m=image 52887 TCP t38
c=IN IP4 1.2.3.4
a=setup:passive
a=connection:new
```

Answer

```
m=image 55330 TCP t38
c=IN IP4 4.3.2.1
a=setup:active
a=connection:new
```

In another scenario, John might offer to either initiate an outgoing connection or accept an incoming one by setting the setup attribute to actpass. If Alice responds with a value of passive, that would mean that John is responsible for initiating the connection.

Offer

```
m=image 52887 TCP t38
c=IN IP4 1.2.3.4
a=setup:actpass
a=connection:new
```

Answer

```
m=image 55330 TCP t38
c=IN IP4 4.3.2.1
a=setup:passive
a=connection:new
```

The connection attribute can also be negotiated. For instance, while already on a session, John might initiate a new SDP exchange. In the offer, he proposes to use the existing TCP connection. Alice responds that she wants a new connection to be created; therefore, a new connection will be established, in this case by Alice, if we look at the values of the exchanged setup attributes.

Offer

```
m=image 52887 TCP t38
c=IN IP4 1.2.3.4
```

```
a=setup:passive
a=connection:existing
```

Answer

```
m=image 55330 TCP t38
c=IN IP4 4.3.2.1
a=setup:active
a=connection:new
```

9.5 SDP Programming

As we have seen, IP communication applications that use SIP will in many cases need to describe sessions using SDP and transport, such a description as part of the SIP message payload. From the developer's perspective, there is a need then to be able to encode and parse SDP content. There are a number of different ways to do this. One possible way to accomplish this is by using an implementation of the JAIN SDP API. JAIN SDP is part of the Java network API family to which JAIN SIP also belongs. Therefore, and given that we are using JAIN SIP as the API that allows us to illustrate the SIP concepts throughout the book, it seems appropriate to embrace JAIN SDP for our discussion on SDP programming. Actually, we will use JAIN SIP in combination with JAIN SDP for the soft-phone project that we will describe in Chapter 12.

9.5.1 JAIN SDP Overview

JAIN SDP is a very simple API that just allows us to encode and decode SDP content. Like the JAIN SIP API, it is also based on the factory pattern. It defines a factory class called `SdpFactory`, and a number of interfaces that represent the key concepts in SDP. By invoking creation methods on `SdpFactory`, the programmer can obtain objects that implement those key interfaces in the API.

As already stated, JAIN SDP provides a number of interface classes that represent the key concepts in the Session Description Protocol. These interfaces fall into two categories. On one hand, there is the `SessionDescription` interface, which models the SDP message itself; on the other, there are a myriad of interfaces, each of them representing one or more lines in the SDP message.

Table 9.4 shows some of the main interfaces in the API and their mapping to the SDP concepts that they represent. Table 9.5 shows the methods needed to create them from the `SdpFactory`.

It is worth noting that in order to create a `MediaDescription`, we need to pass a vector of integer values for the media formats to the `createMediaDescription()` method so as to reflect the fact that more than one media format may be included in the same m-line.

So far, we have seen how to create `SessionDescription` objects as well as objects representing the different lines in an SDP message. We will now see how to actually encode and parse SDP messages.

Table 9.4

Interface Name	SDP Concept
SessionDescription	SDP message
Version	v-line (protocol version)
Origin	o-line (originator and session identifier)
SessionName	s-line (session name)
Connection	c-line (connection information)
Time	t-line (time the session is active)
Media	m-line (media name and transport address)
MediaDescription	m-line and related a-lines (media name, transport address, and associated attributes)

Table 9.5

	SdpFactory Creation Methods	Description
SessionDescription	**createSession Description** ()	Creates an empty SessionDescription to which we can then add the different lines.
SessionDescription	**createSession Description** (String s)	Creates a SessionDescription out of a String that represents the received SDP message. Once created, we can invoke "getter" methods to parse the message and obtain the different lines.
Version	**createVersion** (int value)	Creates a v-line.
Origin	**createOrigin** (String userName, long sessionId, long sessionVersion, String networkType, String addrType, String address)	Creates an o-line.
SessionName	**createSessionName** (String name)	Creates an s-line.

(Continued)

Table 9.5 *(Cont.)*

	SdpFactory Creation Methods	Description
Connection	**createConnection** (String netType, String addrType, String addr)	Creates a c-line.
Time	**createTime** ()	Creates a "t=0 0" line.
MediaDescription	**createMedia Description** (String media, int port, int numPorts, String transport, int[] staticRtpAvpTypes)	Creates an m-line. Once createdn we can add related a-lines by invoking setAttribute() on the MediaDescription object.

9.5.2 Encoding SDP Messages

To encode an SDP message, the following steps need to be followed:

1. Obtain an instance of the singleton SdpFactory class:

```
SdpFactory mySdpFactory=SdpFactory.getInstance();
```

2. Create an empty SessionDescription object:

```
SessionDescription mySessionDescription=mySdpFactory.
createSessionDescription();
```

3. Create the lines I will want to include in the SDP message (e.g., a "v=0" line):

```
Version myVersion=mySdpFactory.createVersion(0);
```

4. Add those lines to the SessionDescription by invoking the appropriate "setter" method:

```
mySessionDescription.setVersion(myVersion);
```

There are setter methods for all the lines in an SDP message. Table 9.6 shows the main ones.

After these steps have been completed, we have SessionDescription object representing our SDP message. In order to include it into a SIP message, we would need to convert it into a String and pass it as an argument of the JAIN SIP setContent() method.

An important aspect to highlight is that in order to include the m-lines in the message, rather than invoking several times a "setter" method to include a MediaDescription, the JAIN SDP API offers only a setMediaDescriptions() method to which we need to pass a Java vector containing all the

Table 9.6

	SessionDescription Setter Methods	Description
Void	**setVersion** (Version v)	Sets the v-line.
Void	**setOrigin** (Origin o)	Sets the o-line.
Void	**setSessionName** (SessionName s)	Sets the s-line.
Void	**setConnection** (Connection c)	Sets the c-line.
Void	**setTimeDescriptions** (Vector v)	Sets the t-lines. The argument is a `Vector` of `Time` objects.
Void	**setMediaDescriptions** (Vector v)	Sets the m- and related lines. The argument is a `Vector` of `MediaDescription` objects.

`MediaDescriptions` that we want to add to the message. A similar approach is followed for the `Time` object.

For instance, if we wanted to add the following lines to an SDP message:

m=audio 3401 RTP/AVP 0
m=audio 3550 video RTP/AVP 31

Our code should look like:

```
int[] mf1=new int[1];
mf1[0]=0;
int[] mf2=new int[1];
mf2[0]=31;
MediaDescription media1 = mySdpFactory.
  createMediaDescription("audio," 3401, 1,
  "RTP/AVP," mf1);
MediaDescription media2 = mySdpFactory.
  createMediaDescription("video," 3550, 1,
  "RTP/AVP," mf2);
Vector myMediaDescriptionVector=new Vector();
myMediaDescriptionVector.add(media1);
myMediaDescriptionVector.add(media2);
mySdp.setMediaDescriptions(myMediaDescriptionVector)
```

9.5.3 Parsing SDP Messages

To parse an SDP message, the following steps need to be followed:

1. Obtain an instance of the singleton `SdpFactory` class:

```
SdpFactory mySdpFactory=SdpFactory.getInstance();
```

2. Create a `SessionDescription` object from the received String representing the SDP message:

```
SessionDescription receivedSessionDescription=
  mySdpFactory.createSessionDescription(receivedSdp);
```

3. Obtain the desired lines from the session description (e.g., the v-line):

```
Version receivedVersion = receivedSessionDescription.
  getVersion();
```

There are getter methods for all the lines in an SDP message. Table 9.7 shows the main ones.

Table 9.7

	SessionDescription Setter Methods	Description
`Version`	**`getVersion`** `()`	Gets the v-line.
`Origin`	**`getOrigin`** `()`	Gets the o-line.
`SessionName`	**`getSessionName`** `()`	Gets the s-line.
`Connection`	**`getConnection`** `()`	Gets the c-line.
`Vector`	**`getTimeDescriptions`** `(boolean b)`	Gets the t-lines as a `Vector` of `Time` objects.
`Vector`	**`getMediaDescriptions`** `(boolean b)`	Gets the m- and related lines as a `Vector` of `MediaDescription` objects.

9.5.4 SDP Practice

In order to put into practice the JAIN SDP concepts learned so far, we will now create a simple component that will ease the task of creating and parsing SDP content. This component will be used by the soft-phone application that we will build in Chapter 12. Such application is built only for training purposes and has a limited scope. With regard to SDP handling in our soft-phone application, we take the following assumptions; some of them will help in keeping the code as simple as possible while still allowing us to show the fundamental concepts:

- The soft phone will support audio and video.
- The soft phone will support two media codecs for audio: GSM and G723.
- The soft phone will support two media codecs for video: JPEG and H263.
- The end user will select in the GUI the type of media that he or she desires for their communications:
  - audio only
  - audio and video
- The end user will select in the GUI which codec (only one) he or she desires to use for each media.

- The first media line will be audio, and the second one (if it exists) will be video. This assumption simplifies the SDP parsing.
- The SDP offer will contain only one proposed codec per media.
- The recipient will always accept the voice media, but may not accept the video component, depending on GUI configuration.
- All the payload formats will be static, therefore there is no need to include or read a-lines associated to the m-lines.

Under all the previous assumptions, our soft-phone application will need only to include or get five pieces of information in or from the SDP message:

- IP address
- voice port
- audio format
- video port
- video format

The SDP component that we will build now will simplify the task of setting or getting these pieces of information from an SDP message. The component is a Java class called `SdpManager`. We will also use another Java class called `SdpInfo` that is a data structure that holds the value of the five parameters we are interested in.

The `SdpInfo` class is shown next.

```
public class SdpInfo {
   String IpAddress="";
   int aport=0;
   int aformat=0;
   int vport=0;
   int vformat=0;
   public SdpInfo() {}
   public void setIPAddress(String IP) {IpAddress=IP;}
   public void setAudioPort(int AP) {aport=AP;}
   public void setAudioFormat(int VF) {aformat=AF;}
   public void setVideoPort(int VP) {vport=VP;}
   public void setVideoFormat(int VF) {vformat=VF;}
   public String getIpAddress() {return IpAddress;}
   public int getAudioPort() {return aport;}
   public int getAudioFormat() {return aformat;}
   public int getVideoPort() {return vport;}
   public int getVideoFormat() {return vformat;}
}
```

The `SdpManager` class offers two methods:

1. `byte[] createSdp(SdpInfo sdpinfo)`
2. `SdpInfo getSdp(byte [] sdpcontent)`

The first one receives as input an `SdpInfo` object, and creates as output a byte array representing the SDP content.

The second one gets an SDP message as a byte array, and produces an `SdpInfo` object with the key info we are interested in.

The constructor method for `SdpManager` just obtains the instance of `SdpFactory` that will be used in the two main methods.

```
mySdpFactory = SdpFactory.getInstance();
```

The code for the `createSdp()` method is shown next. It is quite straightforward.

```
Version myVersion = mySdpFactory.createVersion(0);
long ss=mySdpFactory.getNtpTime(new Date());
Origin myOrigin = mySdpFactory.createOrigin("-
   ",ss,ss,"IN","IP4",sdpinfo.getIpAddress());
SessionName mySessionName = mySdpFactory.createSessionName("-");
Connection myConnection = mySdpFactory.createConnection("IN,""IP4,"
   sdpinfo.getIpAddress());
//Time description lines
Time myTime=mySdpFactory.createTime();
Vector myTimeVector=new Vector();
myTimeVector.add(myTime);
//Media description lines
int[] aaf=new int[1];
aaf[0]=sdpinfo.getAudioFormat();
MediaDescription myAudioDescription=mySdpFactory.
  createMediaDescription("audio",
   sdpinfo.getAudioport(), 1, "RTP/AVP",aaf);
Vector myMediaDescriptionVector=new Vector();
myMediaDescriptionVector.add(myAudioDescription);
if (sdpinfo.getVideoPort()!=-1) {
   int[] avf=new int[1];
   avf[0]=sdpinfo.getVideoFormat();
   MediaDescription myVideoDescription =
      mySdpFactory.createMediaDescription("video" sdpinfo.
        getVideoPort(), 1,
      "RTP/AVP",
   avf);
   myMediaDescriptionVector.add(myVideoDescription);
}
SessionDescription mySdp = mySdpFactory.createSessionDescription();
mySdp.setVersion(myVersion);
mySdp.setOrigin(myOrigin);
mySdp.setSessionName(mySessionName);
mySdp.setConnection(myConnection);
mySdp.setTimeDescriptions(myTimeVector);
mySdp.setMediaDescriptions(myMediaDescriptionVector);
mySdpContent=mySdp.toString().getBytes();
return mySdpContent;
```

It is worth mentioning that we have followed the recommendation in [RFC 4566] to create the session id based on NTP timestamps. The JAIN SDP API offers a convenience method to create NTP timestamps from a Java Date object:

```
static long getNtpTime(Date d)
```

The third parameter in the o-line—that is, the version of the session information—has been initialized to the same value as the session id.

Next we show the code for the `getSdp()` method:

```
String s = new String(content);
SessionDescription recSdp = mySdpFactory.createSessionDescription(s);
String myPeerIp=recSdp.getConnection().getAddress();
String myPeerName=recSdp.getOrigin().getUsername();
Vector recMediaDescriptionVector=recSdp.
  getMediaDescriptions(false);
//We assume first media line is audio
MediaDescription myAudioDescription = (MediaDescription)
recMediaDescriptionVector.elementAt(0);
Media myAudio = myAudioDescription.getMedia();
int myAudioPort = myAudio.getMediaPort();
Vector audioFormats=myAudio.getMediaFormats(false);
Integer myAudioMediaFormat = (Integer) audioFormats.elementAt(0);
int myVideoPort =-1;
Integer myVideoMediaFormat = new Integer(-1);
//We assume second media line, if it exists, is video
if (recMediaDescriptionVector.capacity()>1) {
   MediaDescription myVideoDescription =
      (MediaDescription) recMediaDescriptionVector.elementAt(1);
   Media myVideo = myVideoDescription.getMedia();
   myVideoPort = myVideo.getMediaPort();
   Vector videoFormats = myVideo.getMediaFormats(false);
   myVideoMediaFormat = (Integer) videoFormats.elementAt(0);
}
mySdpInfo=new SdpInfo();
mySdpInfo.setIpAddress(myPeerIp);
mySdpInfo.setAudioPort(myAudioPort);
mySdpInfo.setAudioFormat(myAudioMediaFormat.intValue());
mySdpInfo.setVideoPort(myVideoPort);
mySdpInfo.setVideoFormat(myVideoMediaFormat.intValue());
return mySdpInfo;
```

It is worth highlighting that the port and the media format parameters are obtained through a `Media` object, not directly through the `MediaDescription` object. So, in order to get these parameters, we had to:

1. obtain the `MediaDescription` from the `SessionDescription`

2. obtain the `Media` object from the `MediaDescription`
3. obtain the desired parameters from the `Media` object

9.6 Summary

In this chapter, we have analyzed the way to describe multimedia sessions using the Session Description Protocol. In the next chapter, we will examine the protocols used to convey the media that is described by SDP. Thus, we will look at RTP, MSRP, TCP, and the different applications that they can support. Once we have covered the media protocols, we will be in a position to look at how a complete multimedia application works, and build one ourselves in Chapter 12!

CHAPTER

The Media Plane

10

We have already seen that IP multimedia communications comprise two planes: the signaling plane and the media plane. We dealt with the signaling plane in the chapters dedicated to SIP. Now we will look into the media plane. First we will introduce general concepts related to the media plane, and then we will examine two concrete examples of protocols used in the media plane for IP multimedia services: RTP and MSRP.

10.1 Overview of the Media Plane

As has been stated many times already, SIP plays the part of the signaling protocol in IP multimedia communication services. A key aspect is that SIP is used to control multimedia communications irrespective of the actual nature of the session; voice, video, messaging, a game, and so on. This works perfectly well because SIP, in order to deliver its functions, does not need to care about the nature of the session. There is still, at specific moments, such as session creation, the need to exchange session descriptions, which are actually dependent on the nature of the session. This is done using SDP, and the SDP content is carried in SIP messages. So SIP does not need to know about session specifics.

In the media plane, what is needed is a protocol that takes care of the media transport. Someone might think that, as occurs in the signaling plane, there might also be a protocol in the media plane suitable for all the types of media sessions. However, that is not the case. The types of sessions that can be established using SIP are so different that it is impractical to use a single media transport protocol fitting all of them. Let us recall that in a multimedia session, we may have strict real-time media (e.g., voice, video), quasi-real-time media (e.g., instant messaging, a game, whiteboard), or even other types of media (e.g., an image, a file).

All these types of media are quite different in nature, and introduce different requirements for the protocol used to transport them. For instance, in a voice communication, timely delivery is crucial, therefore packet retransmission schemes to cope with transmission errors are not applicable there. If a packet is received that contains an error, it is just discarded, and the receiver builds a sample by interpolating between the adjacent sample values.

On the other hand, in instant messaging, the delay requirements are not so strict, and therefore we can cope with a retransmission mechanism to recover from errors and so always present the original, error-free message to the recipient.

A packet network such as the Internet typically impacts packet transmission in three ways:

- It introduces delay.
- It may lose packets.
- It may deliver packets out of sequence.

Depending on the media type, these aspects may be more or less important, and thus the requirements for the transport protocol are different. For instance, as we said before, delay has quite harmful effects for voice transmission, but may be not so critical in a chess game. On the other hand, for a chess game, the loss of a few packets (e.g., representing a checkmate move) might be very negative, whereas, in the case of voice, it may be not so relevant.

The number of media transport protocols for IP communications may be very large and dependent on the specific application. This is, by the way, an area that is constantly evolving, and we may see new protocol proposals arising in the next months to cover specific types of applications. The most common media transport protocols for IP communications are listed next. SIP can be used to set up media sessions carried by all these protocols:

- *Real-time Transport Protocol (RTP)*: It is an Internet standard (STD 64, RFC 3550) for the transport of strict real-time data such as voice or video. Virtually all the voice and video over IP deployments nowadays use RTP as the media transport protocol. RTP can also be used for transport of real-time Text over IP (ToIP).[1]
- *Message Session Relay Protocol (MSRP)*: It is work in progress in the IETF, and covers the transport of messages related to a session. There are already a number of commercial products that implement the MSRP draft for utilization in instant messaging. Additionally, MSRP is also being used for image sharing between mobile devices. The main terminal vendors already support MSRP (version 19 of the draft), thanks to successful interoperability meetings since Q1 2007. See [GSMA_MSRP].
- *Transmission Control Protocol (TCP)*: Session media can also be transported by TCP for certain applications (e.g., online file transfer). The media session would be negotiated via an SDP exchange, and the session created using SIP. Such a use of TCP is specified in [RFC 4145] and [RFC 4572].
- *T.38 fax transmission over UDP*: The ITU T.38 recommendation describes the media transport for sending fax messages over IP networks (FOIP) in real-time.[2] [RFC 3362] defines the "image/t38" media type intended to indicate a T.38 media stream in SDP.

---

[1] Reader should be aware that the acronym ToIP is sometimes used to mean Telephony over IP. Whether we are referring to Text over IP or Telephony over IP should be clear by the context.

[2] T.38 (real-time FOIP) is not to be confused with T.37, which defines a store and forward mechanism for sending faxes over IP using email as transport (SMTP and TIFF attachments).

Next we will examine with a bit more detail the first two media protocols: RTP and MSRP.

10.2 Real-time Transport Protocol (RTP)

10.2.1 Motivation

Let us consider that we want to exchange strict real-time media such as voice or video in the Internet. We saw that IP networks produce some undesirable effects when carrying traffic. In order to understand what the requirements are for a protocol capable of conveying real-time media, we next analyze how these effects impact real-time traffic.

End-to-End Delay and Packet Loss

End-to-end delay is caused by the processing delay at each endpoint (operating system, codecs, and so on), plus the delay caused by the IP network itself (queuing and processing time in routers, transmission delay, and so on). The end-to-end delay may have a negative impact in the interactivity requirements of IP multimedia communication services in general. More specifically, for real-time media such as voice or video, interactivity requirements result in very little tolerance to delay. Imagine a conversation between John and Alice. John starts talking; when he stops, he waits for Alice's answer. If the end-to-end delay is large, John may think he was not heard. He will repeat what he said, only to be interrupted by the delayed response from Alice. John and Alice will stop talking, and then commence again simultaneously. In this situation, it is very difficult to maintain the interactivity in the conversation in a natural way.

Table 10.1 shows a qualitative estimation of voice interactivity depending on the one-way delay.

Table 10.1

One-Way Delay	Interactivity
Less than 100 ms	Good
Between 100 and 250 ms	Acceptable
Between 250 and 400 ms	Bad
More than 400 ms	No interactivity

Another aspect of transmission in an IP network is packet loss. This is typically produced by congested routers dropping packets. The common approach to recover a packet that was lost by the network is to ask for a retransmission. This implies an extra delay, which, in the case of real-time communications, is unacceptable.

Therefore, the delay requirement for real-time media transport imposes that no end-to-end packet retransmission scheme is used. This requirement rules out the possibility of using TCP as transport protocol for this type of media. At this point of the discussion, we might think that UDP is a good candidate because it does not include retransmissions, implies little overhead on top of the IP protocol, and its checksum and multiplexing services may come handy.

UDP is certainly a possibility to directly transport real-time media, but let us look at other requirements to understand why additional functionalities in addition to the ones offered by UDP are needed.

Out-of-Sequence Delivery

This is another undesirable effect of IP networks. It is due to the fact that IP packets from a source to a destination may go thorough different network paths. If there is a congested router in the path of a packet, it is possible that subsequent packets that traverse different routers might arrive first to the destination.

It is important, in IP communication scenarios, that packets are fed in order to the application, hence there is the need for the receiver to reorder the packets. Some transport-level protocols such as TCP already include services for achieving in-sequence delivery. However, we already saw that TCP is not an option for real-time media. We could always define some protocol on top of UDP that includes a monotonically increasing sequence number in each packet in the session, and have the receiver reorder the packets. As we will see, this is one of the functions of RTP.

Jitter

We already discussed the negative impact of end-to-end delay in the interactivity of a conversation. Actually, delay in an IP network is not constant for all the packets in a session. The time it takes a router to process a packet depends on its congestion situation, and this may vary during the session. The variation in delay is called jitter. So the overall delay introduced by an IP network can be described as composed by a fixed component (L) and a variable component (or jitter, J) that accounts for the delay that is produced in routers due to their congestion state.

$$D = L + J$$

Although a big overall delay can cause loss of interactivity, jitter may cause loss of intelligibility. Let us consider, for instance, a voice communication between John and Alice. While John speaks, his voice signal is sampled at a constant rate, coded, packetized, and sent over the network. At the receiver side, the samples are recovered and then sent to the soundcard at a constant rate so that the original voice signal can be fully reconstructed. If a voice sample arrives a bit late after its playback time, then it is useless and needs to be discarded. If jitter is too big, too many samples will have to be discarded, and the voice signal will be unintelligible. That is why jitter is a big issue for real-time communications.

There is, however, a way to reduce the adverse impact of jitter. It relies on using buffers at the receiver. When a packet arrives and the audio content is decoded, instead of playing the voice sample immediately, it is stored in a buffer. After some time (order of milliseconds), the buffer content is sent to the soundcard. By doing this, we have introduced some additional artificial delay, but this has allowed us to compensate for the jitter. The voice samples will now be present in the buffer when they need to be sent to the soundcard even if they arrived with variable delays. This idea is shown in Figure 10.1. In the top diagram, we can see that packet number 3 arrives late, and thus it has to be discarded. In the bottom diagram, a buffer to compensate for the jitter is introduced; we can see that packet 3 is now on time for the playback.

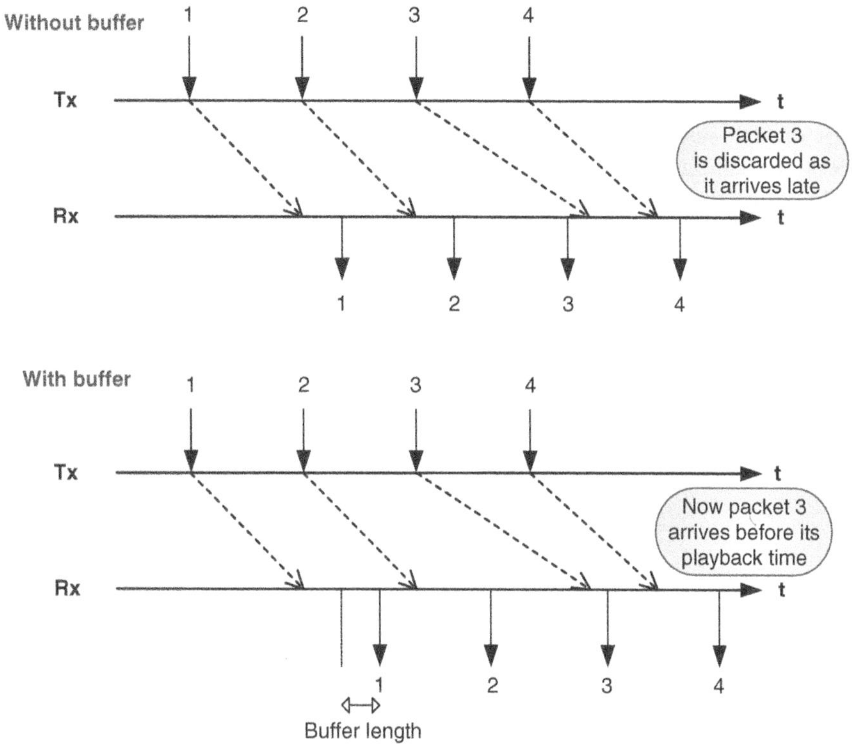

FIGURE 10.1

The bigger the buffer is, the more effective we can be at neutralizing the jitter. However, the buffer implies extra delay, and we saw that overall delay can severely impact the interactivity of the conversation. Therefore, in IP communication services, there is an upper limit to the length of the buffer so as not to impact interactivity. In streaming services, in which media flow is only unidirectional, there is not such an issue with the interactivity; therefore, receivers can accommodate big buffers to better handle jitter. The additional introduced delay is, in these cases, not a big issue. For instance, in a live streaming scenario, if we are watching a soccer match and we see a goal being scored a couple of seconds after it really happened, it does not really happen.

In order to be able to fight against jitter, it is crucial that the receiver can recover the time information of the received signal so as to know at what precise moment it needs to be played. This requirement calls for transporting the timing information associated with each voice packet. In other words, we need a protocol that includes a header to transport such timing information. As we will see, RTP also complies with this requirement.

10.2.2 RTP Overview

RTP is an IETF standard protocol (STD 64, RFC 3550) that provides end-to-end delivery services for data with real-time characteristics, such as voice and video. Among these, it includes sequence numbering and timestamping, which, as we saw previously, are crucial functionalities for transporting real-time media.

RTP defines the concept of RTP session. An RTP session is identified by a transport address, and includes just one type of media. This is different from the concept of SDP session, which included all the media flowing from senders to receivers. Actually, an SDP session may encompass several RTP sessions. One single SDP multimedia session might, for instance, include a voice RTP session plus a video RTP session.[3]

RTP typically runs on top of UDP (Figure 10.2). An RTP packet consists of a header and the payload data. The payload data contains the actual coded voice or video, whereas the header includes information needed to deliver the services that the protocol provides.

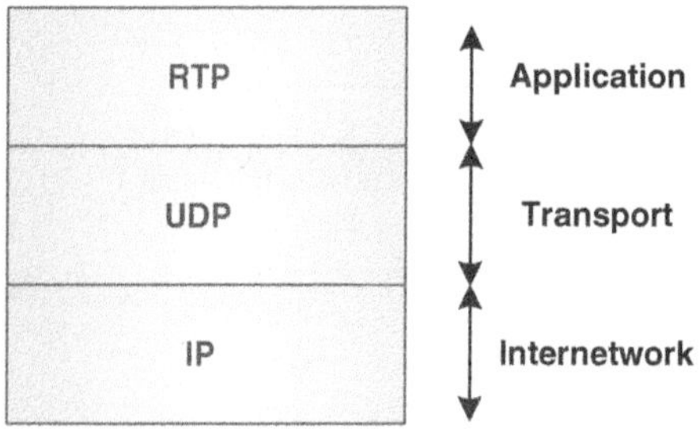

FIGURE 10.2

In Figure 10.3, we can see the RTP header. As we already discussed, the sequence number allows the receiver to reconstruct the packet's sender sequence,

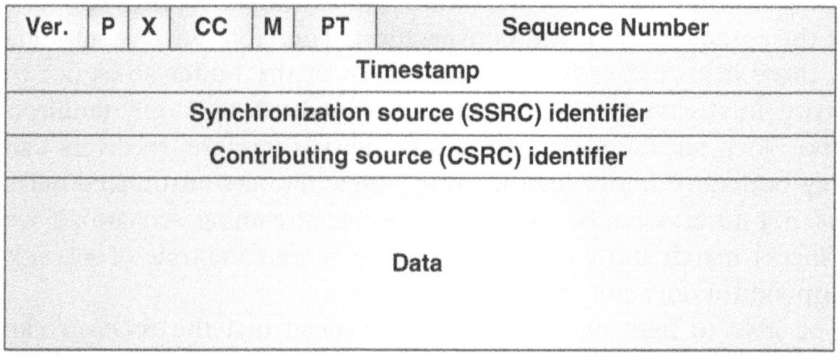

FIGURE 10.3

[3] Throughout this book, a "session" is, by default, an SDP session. If we want to refer to an RTP session, we will explicitly say "RTP session."

whereas the timestamp information allows it to reconstruct the timing produced by the source and remove jitter.

Other interesting headers are:

- Payload type (PT): identifies format of the payload—that is, the codec.
- Synchronization source (SSRC): identifies the source of the IP packets.

RTP was originally conceived to be used in the remit of multicast conferences in the Internet. In this kind of conference, every participant sends real-time data (e.g., voice) to a multicast address, and this data is received by the rest of the participants. In this kind of environment, it is important to be able to identify each of the senders that are transmitting in the same RTP session. That is achieved by the SSRC field. This is of little use in unicast IP multimedia communications, where we already have powerful signaling means to identify media senders.

The payload type field is also quite interesting for multicast conferences because it allows the receivers to be notified about a change in the codec. However, in unicast IP communications, codec changes are communicated using a signaling protocol (SIP).

RTP offers quite generic functionality. Applications that use it may be quite different. An interesting aspect about RTP is that it allows applications to tailor it to their needs. For instance, an application might include modifications or additions to existing headers. Therefore, in order to use RTP with a particular application—for instance, voice or video—we need to have the information about how RTP is tailored to that particular application. That is defined in two companion documents per application. One is the profile specification, and the other is the payload format specification.

Profile Specification

The profile specification defines what aspects of RTP are defined by a particular application (e.g., voice). Examples of possible aspects are the RTP data header, payload types, RTP header extensions, and so forth.

Payload Format Specification

In the RTP header, the payload type (PT) is a field that identifies the payload format. This payload format must be specified elsewhere, in a payload format specification document. The specification includes aspects such as the clock rate or the number of channels.

10.2.3 RTCP

RTP comes together with a lightweight control protocol called Real-time Transport Control Protocol (RTCP). Its primary function is to provide feedback on the quality of the media distribution. For instance, it can report number of lost packets or measured jitter. It is useful in order to diagnose problems or even trigger a codec change. This feedback information is conveyed in particular types of RTCP packets called SR (Sender Report) and RR (Receiver Report). All participants in an RTP session send RTCP reports. Senders send "sender reports," and receivers send "receiver reports." An endpoint that both transmits and receives RTP media would send both types of reports.

RTCP is also used to carry a persistent identifier of the RTP source that can be correlated with the SSRC (SSRC identification is not persistent because it changes among sessions). This identifier is called CNAME, and is carried in yet another type of RTCP packet called SDES (Source DEScription). This is a function not really interesting for unicast IP multimedia communications because this type of information is already conveyed in the signaling. Let us remember that RTP was originally conceived to be used in multicast scenarios in which this kind of information makes sense (because these do not use an additional signaling protocol).

10.2.4 Application Examples

Audio/Video

One of the most interesting applications to be run on top of RTP is audio and video transmission. Such an application has a corresponding profile called the Audio Video Profile (AVP) and a payload format specification. Both of them are defined in a combined document, [RFC 3551]. This RFC includes a definition of several possible payload types for audio and video. Some of the most frequent ones are depicted in Table 10.2.

Table 10.2

PT	Encoding Name	Media Type	Clock Rate (Hz)	Channels C
0	PCMU[a]	Audio	8.000	1
3	GSM	Audio	8.000	1
4	G723	Audio	8.000	1
8	PCMA[b]	Audio	8.000	1
26	JPEG	Video	Variable	-
31	H261	Video	90.000	-
34	H263	Video	90.000	-
96–127	Dynamic	Audio/Video	-	-

[a] *refers to Pulse Code Modulation μ-law*
[b] *refers to Pulse Code Modulation A-law*

Payload types can be static or dynamic. Static payload types are defined with a fixed identification number. By looking at Table 10.2, we can know, for instance, that a payload type=3 in an RTP header indicates that the payload contains one channel of voice data with GSM encoding and sampled at 8000 Hz.

Dynamic payload types do not have a number statically assigned. The assignment is done in a dynamic way, typically via signaling (for instance, using SDP, as we saw in the previous chapter). Identification numbers between 96 and 127 are allocated to dynamic payload types.

Telephony Tones

DTMF (Dual-Tone Multi-Frequency) tones and telephony signals can also be carried over RTP using a particular payload format defined in [RFC 4733] and [RFC 4734]. The payload format is called "telephone-event." It does not have a static payload type number; the payload type is established dynamically in the SDP exchange.

The "telephony-event" payload type is considered to be just another audio codec by the endpoints.

Real-time Text

Another application that can be conveyed on RTP is real-time Text over IP (ToIP). This refers to real-time transmission of text in a character-by-character fashion for use in conversational services. It can be considered as a text equivalent to voice-based conversational services. Conversational text is defined in [ITU F.700].

Real-time ToIP has special relevance in the context of communication services for deaf, hard of hearing, or speech-impaired individuals.[4] However, it can also be used by mainstream users. For instance, imagine that John and Alice are engaged in a voice over IP conversation. John is at his mobile phone; he is moving, and enters into a very noisy environment that makes voice communication impractical. He might add a new real-time text media to the conversation while he remains in that environment so that John and Alice can still communicate in real-time with text.

Text conversation session contents are specified in ITU-T Recommendation T.140. [RFC 4103] defines how to transport those contents on RTP. It defines the "text/t140" RTP payload type.

Real-time ToIP sessions can be established with SIP.

10.3 Messaging Service Relay Protocol (MSRP)

As we saw in Chapter 9, a series of related instant messages between two or more parties can be viewed as a media session. Such a media session can be negotiated using the SDP offer/response model. The SDP session descriptors for the messaging session would be carried by SIP. SIP is, in fact, not concerned with the nature of the media session; from SIP's point of view, all media sessions (voice, video, messaging, and so on) are treated in the same way.

The utilization of SIP and SDP to signal messaging sessions allows an enhanced degree of integration with other media types, and a more complete communication experience. For instance, John might want to communicate with Alice. Because he does not know whether Alice has her phone or her IM client with her, he will offer an SDP that contains both messaging and voice. The SDP will be embedded in a SIP INVITE message sent to Alice's address-of-record: sip:alice@ocean.com.

[4] Generic user requirements for SIP in support of deaf, hard of hearing, and speech-impaired individuals are defined in [RFC 2251].

Alice accepts the invitation at her IM client, and the messaging session can start. This is shown in Figure 10.4.

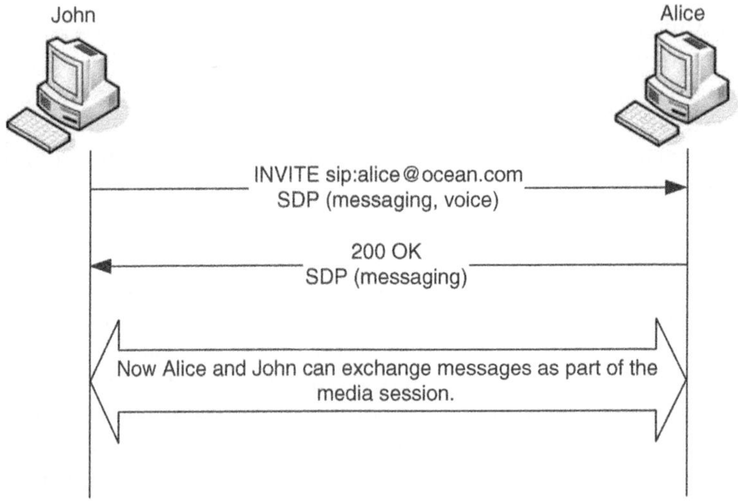

FIGURE 10.4

The media transport protocol used for transmitting a series of related instant messages is called Messaging Service Relay Protocol (MSRP). At the time of writing, the MSRP specification is not yet an RFC. It is covered in just two Internet drafts:

- [draft-ietf-simple-message-sessions]: This covers the core protocol.
- [draft-ietf-simple-msrp-relays]: This covers the extensions needed for relays support.

Therefore the MSRP specification is still work in progress, though these drafts are about to be published as RFCs.[5]

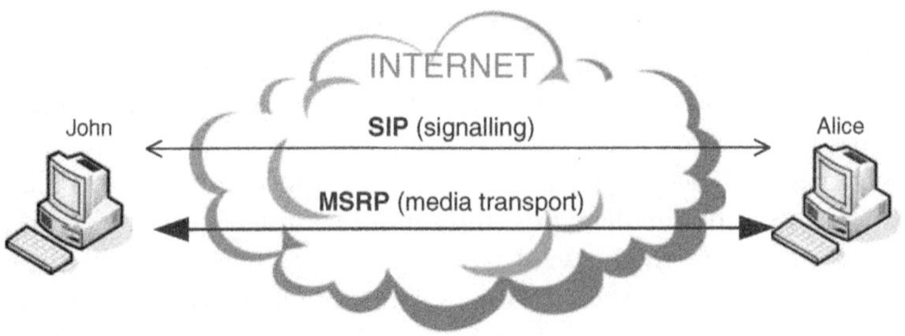

FIGURE 10.5

[5] The status of these Internet drafts at the time of writing is "RFC Editor's Queue," which is the status just previous to RFC publication.

This type of instant messaging service where there exists a conversational exchange of messages with a definite beginning and end is called "session-mode" messaging—as opposed to "page-mode" messaging, which refers to just the transmission of individual instant messages.

In this section, we will look at the MSRP protocol, which represents the media plane component in "session-mode" messaging communication systems. Page-mode messaging can be implemented without the need of a media plane, but just having the signaling plane carry the individual messages. Page-mode messaging will be analyzed in Chapter 16.

The main drawback of carrying messages over the signaling plane appears when messages are big (photos, videos, and so on). The SIP signaling network was not designed to carry large messages, so this type of traffic might impose a severe degradation in its performance. By using MSRP, the user messages are moved to the media plane using a protocol specifically designed for media transport, and thus relieving the SIP network.

10.3.1 Main Features

MSRP is a text-based, connection-oriented protocol for the transmission of instant messages in the context of a session. It sits on top of TCP, and allows the exchange of arbitrary MIME content. Next is a brief description of its main features.

Message Chunking

Instant messages sent using MSRP can be divided into different chunks for transmission. Moreover, a long chunk may be interrupted in mid-transmission, and the remaining content sent in subsequent chunks. This feature is useful in order to ensure fair access to shared transport connections. Each chunk contains a Byte-Range header field that indicates the overall position of the chunk inside the complete instant message.

Message Framing

In order to provide the previous feature, MSRP uses a boundary-based framing mechanism. A unique identifier is used to mark the beginning and the end of each message. The identifier at the end of the message indicates whether there are more chunks to come or whether this chunk was the last one in the message.

MSRP Addressing

MSRP clients are identified by an MSRP URI. The MSRP URIs of the parties (clients) involved in a communication are included in SDP session descriptions that are exchanged using SIP at session creation. In this way, each party can know the address (MSRP URI) of its peer so that message transmission in the media plane can take place.

An MSRP URI is used for two purposes:

- Identify the IP address (or FQDN) and port against which the media plane TCP connection needs to be established. Once established, the instant messages will be sent over that connection.

- Identify the MSRP session. Each MSRP URI contains a unique session identifier that allows endpoints to identify the session and correlate it with a specific transport connection.

An example of MSRP URI would be:

msrp://host.ocean.com:8564/tfg3gy3i;tcp

FQDN port session id protocol

MSRP relays are also identified by MSRP URIs.

Reporting

MSRP includes support for a very flexible mechanism for reporting on the outcome of message delivery. An MSRP client can specify what the desired reporting mechanism for the messages in a session is. These mechanisms range from no report at all (neither positive nor negative) to reporting absolutely every success or failure situation during message delivery. The way this is implemented will be explained in the next section.

10.3.2 MSRP Nodes

MSRP defines two types of nodes: MSRP clients and MSRP relays.

An MSRP client is the initial sender or final target of messages and delivery status. MSRP clients constitute the endpoints of the MSRP protocol. See Figure 10.6.

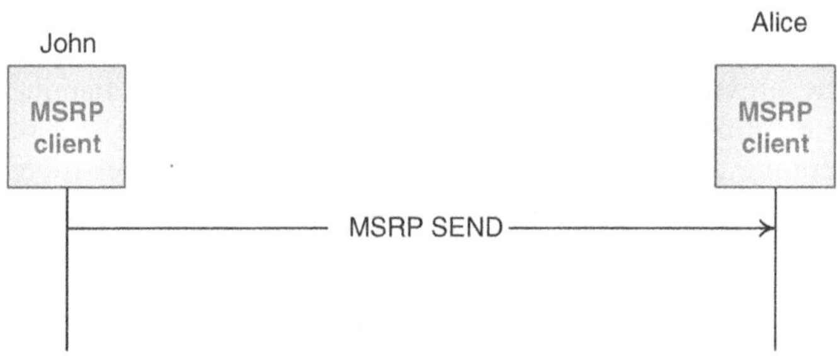

FIGURE 10.6

Between sender and receiver, an MSRP session may go through one or more MSRP relays. MSRP relays are intermediary MSRP entities that forward the messages and delivery status. This is shown in Figure 10.7. Relays are typically used for policy enforcement and firewall/NAT traversal.

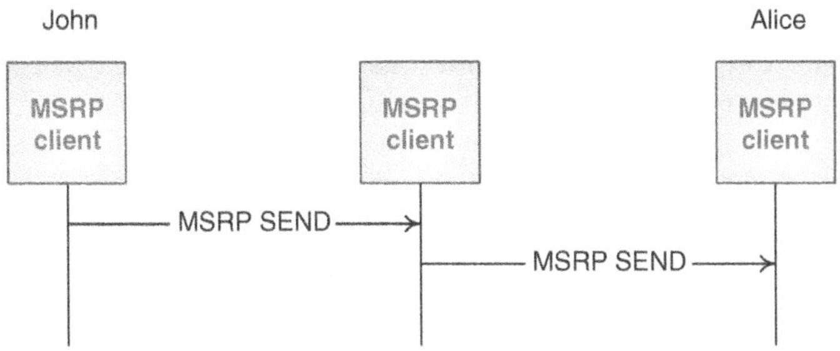

FIGURE 10.7

10.3.3 MSRP Message Format

MSRP is organized as requests and responses. There are three types of requests—that is, methods:

- SEND
- REPORT
- AUTH

Unlike what happens with SIP, not every MSRP request has an associated response; more specifically, REPORT requests do not have an associated response, and SEND requests may or may not have a corresponding response, depending on the value of specific header fields in the request.

The SEND request is used in order to deliver a complete instant message or a chunk (a portion of a complete message). It includes a request start line, followed by some headers, the instant message content itself, and an end line. See Figure 10.8.

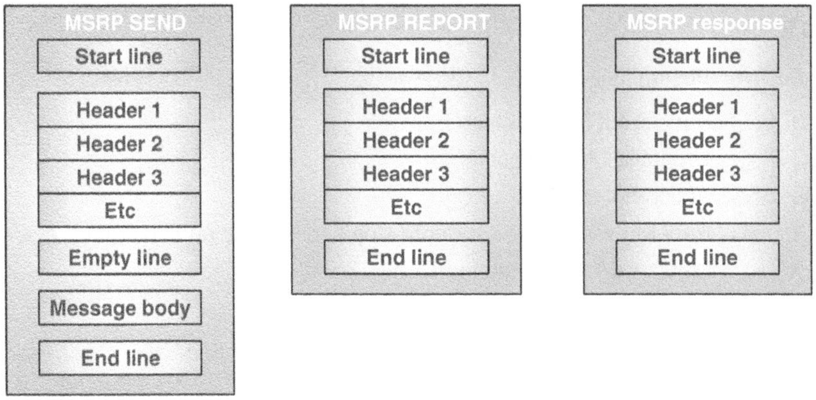

FIGURE 10.8

The REPORT request is used to confirm the delivery of a complete message. Alternatively, it may be used to confirm the delivery of a chunk or group of chunks received so far.

A REPORT request contains a request start line, some headers, and an end line, but no content, as shown in Figure 10.8.

AUTH requests are sent from clients to relays in order to obtain from them an MSRP URI or list of URIs. Clients can then provide this list of URIs to their peers so as to force incoming messages through the relays whose URI is in the list.

Irrespective of the method, the start line in MSRP requests always contains the name of the protocol, a transaction id, and the name of the method (SEND, REPORT, or AUTH). An example of start line might be:

MSRP dhe63iy3 SEND

The end line contains a string of seven hyphens, followed by the transaction id plus a character that indicates whether this is the last chunk ("$") or if there are more chunks to come ("+").

Example

- This end line indicates that the message is the last chunk:------- dhe63iy3$
- This end line indicates that there are more chunks to come:----- dhe63iy3+

The transaction id has two purposes:

- It is used as a mechanism to frame the MSRP messages (it is a random string that appears both in the start line and in the end line).
- It is used to correlate requests and responses.

MSRP responses contain a response start line, some headers, and the end line, as shown in Figure 10.8. The start line in responses contains the name of the protocol, transaction id, and a status code. Table 10.3 shows the possible values for the status codes.

Table 10.3

Status Code	Description
200	Successful transaction
403	Unintelligible request
408	Action not allowed
413	Receiver wishes the sender to stop sending the particular message
415	Media type not understood
423	Requested parameter out of bounds
481	Indicated session does not exist
501	Request method not understood
506	Request arrived on session already bound to another new connection

MSRP Header Fields

The MSRP Internet draft currently defines just a reduced set of headers, which are described next.

From-Path

The From-Path header field indicates the MSRP URI of the originator of the request or response.

To-Path

The To-Path header field indicates the MSRP URI of the destination of the request or response. Both From-Path and To-Path must be present in all requests and responses.

Message-ID

The Message-ID header field provides a unique identifier for the unit of content that the sender wishes to convey to the recipient. For instance, let us assume that John wants to send an image to Alice. The image file may be split into several chunks that are conveyed in different SEND request; however, all the SEND requests carry the same Message-ID header field value. The Message-ID is also used by to correlate status reports with the original message.

Success-Report and Failure-Report

These two header fields may be present in SEND requests, and are used to determine the reporting scheme that should be used for the messages in the session.

As we will see in the next sections, MSRP supports the concept of relays. In the path from originator to recipient, there may be several relays. When it comes to message acknowledgment, there appear two concepts:

- *Hop-by-hop acknowledgment*: This may be done by each hop when receiving the message. It is implemented by sending MSRP responses to requests. Responses contain the "transaction status"
- *End-to-end acknowledgment*: This may done by the final recipient of the message when it is processed. It is implemented by sending a REPORT request. REPORT requests contain the "delivery status"

This is illustrated in Figure 10.9.

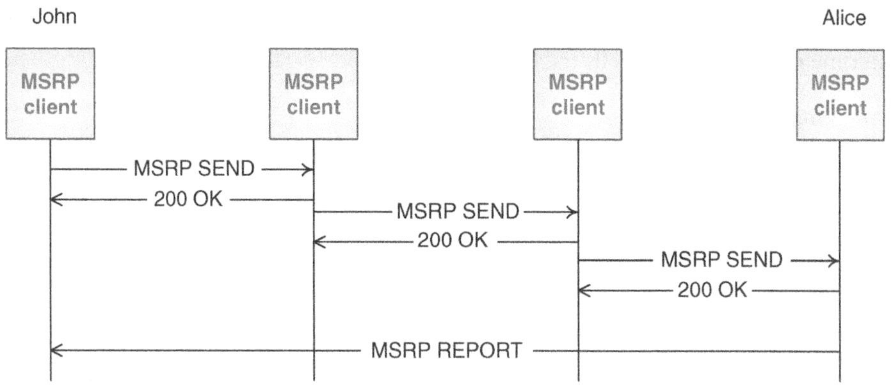

FIGURE 10.9

The way acknowledgments work can be configured by setting the appropriate values to the Success-Report and Failure-Report header fields. For instance, if John wanted to have both positive and negative acknowledgments for the delivery of a message to Alice, he would set both header field values to "yes." If, on the other hand, John does not want to receive any acknowledgment whatsoever, he would set both header fields to "no."

Table 10.4 summarizes the behavior related to reporting based on the possible combinations of values for these two headers. For each possible combination, it is indicated which type of acknowledgments are generated (end-to-end or hop-by-hop) and whether positive, negative, or both.

Table 10.4

Success-Report	Failure-Report	Hop-by-Hop Acknowledgments	End-to-End Acknowledgments
Yes	Yes	Positive and negative	Positive and negative
No	Yes	Positive and negative	Only negative
Yes	No	None	Only positive
No	No	None	None
Yes	Partial	None[a]	Positive and negative
No	Partial	None[b]	Only negative

[a] Or negative, if the recipient is unable to process the response.
[b] Or negative, if the recipient is unable to correlate the response.

If no Success-Report header field value is present in the SEND request, it is treated identically to one with a value of "no."

If no Failure-Report header field value is present in the SEND request, it is treated identically to one with a value of "yes."

Status

This header field is present in responses and REPORT requests, and indicates the outcome of the message delivery.

Byte-Range

The Byte-Range header field may be present in both SEND and REPORT requests. When present in SEND requests, it identifies the specific chunk of a message being carried by the request. When present in a REPORT, it identifies the specific chunk of a message that is being acknowledged.

10.3.4 MSRP Mode of Operation

The protocol operation is quite simple. First we will consider a situation where there are no MSRP relays.

Operation without Relays

Let us assume that John wants to set up a messaging session with Alice. As part of the messaging session, John wants to send Alice text messages, but also some jpeg photos. Therefore, John will generate a SIP INVITE message that contains the description for the messaging session, including two media types: text and jpeg. The SDP offer will also contain John's MSRP URI.

Alice will answer the INVITE with a 200 OK response in which she includes an SDP answer. The SDP answer accepts both media types, and also includes her MSRP URI. When John receives the 200 OK, his MSRP client establishes a TCP connection against the IP address and port resolved from Alice's MSRP URI. Once the TCP connection has been set up, John immediately send the initial MSRP SEND request. This request may or may not already include message content, but it is necessary in order for the recipient to have the assurance that the TCP connection has been established by the party who actually received the SDP. The recipient makes this check by comparing the session id in the MSRP URI in the To-Path of the MSRP SEND request with the session id present in the SDP answer.

Once the initial message has been sent, both John and Alice can exchange messages using the established TCP connection in a conversational fashion. When both parties finish their messaging conversation, one of them—for instance, John—sends a SIP BYE request and closes the session. (See Figure 10.10 in next page)

We saw in the last section (Table 10.4) that, by setting specific values in the Success-Report and Failure-Report header fields, a client can specify whether responses or REPORT requests need to be sent back to the client or not. As an example, we will show two possible scenarios:

1. The client sets Success-Report=yes and Failure-Report=yes. The message contains several chunks, and the delivery is successful. Figure 10.11 depicts this situation. The recipient generates a response per chunk, and also a REPORT for the complete message.[6]
2. The client sets Success-Report=no and Failure-Report=no. The message contains just one chunk, and the delivery is successful. No response or REPORT request is generated. Figure 10.12 shows this scenario. This example may reflect situations where system messages such as "the system is going down in 5 minutes" are sent to many people, and we do not want to flood the sender with responses.

Operation with MSRP Relays

Let us now tackle the protocol operation when there are MSRP relays in the media path. Let us assume that John wishes to start an instant messaging session with Alice. We will consider that there are two relays in the path:

- relay 1, which acts on John's behalf
- relay 2, which acts on Alice's behalf

[6] The recipient might as well have generated several REPORT requests acknowledging each chunk or the group of chunks received so far.

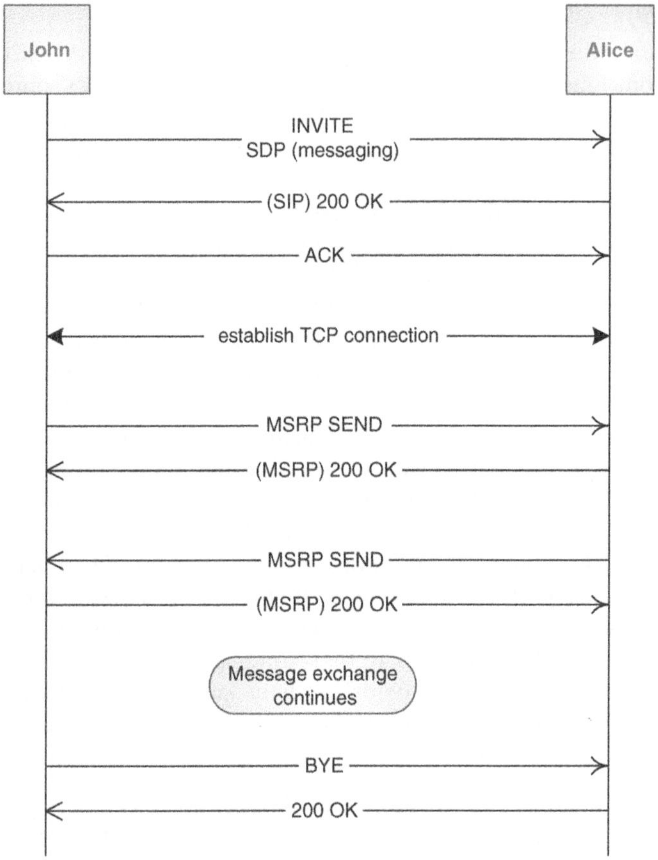

FIGURE 10.10

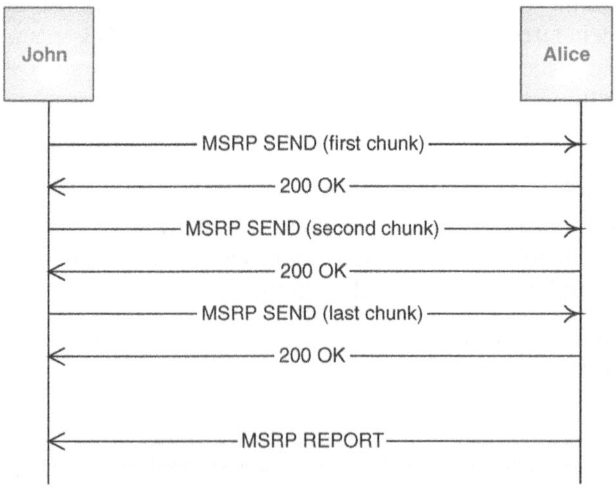

FIGURE 10.11

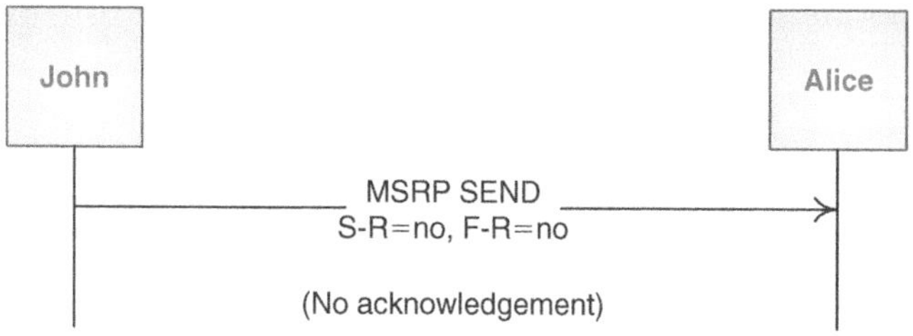

FIGURE 10.12

MSRP relays are also identified by MSRP URIs, in the same way as clients. For the purpose of this discussion, the MSRP URIs of the four entities involved will be denoted:

- msrpA: MSRP URI of John
- msrp1: MSRP URI of relay 1
- msrp2: MSRP URI of relay 2
- msrpB: MSRP URI of Alice

Figure 10.13 shows the message flow for the scenario with relays that is described next.

In order to use a relay, the MSRP client first opens a TLS[7] connection against it. As part of the TLS procedures, the MSRP client authenticates the MSRP relay. Then the MSRP client sends an AUTH request to the relay. This request is rejected with a challenge for client authentication. The MSRP generates a new AUTH including the credentials. If the request is authenticated, the relay responds with a MSRP 200 OK that includes the MSRP URI of the relay (msrp1) in the Use-Path header field.[8]

At that point, the client generates an SDP offer whose path attribute contains two MSRP URIs: msrp1 and msrpA.

Then the SIP session establishment process takes place. The SDP offer is typically sent in the SIP INVITE request, and the SDP answer received in the SIP 200 OK response.

Once having received the SDP answer, the client reads the MSRP URIs included in the path attribute (msrp2,msrpB), and elaborates a new list of MSRP URI by merging the URI received from relay A in the Use-Path header field of the AUTH response and the set of URIs received in the SDP answer.

list= msrp1,msrp2,msrpB

Then the MSRP client builds an MSRP SEND request setting the To-Path header field value to the previous list, and setting the From-Path header field value to his own MSRP URI. We said in the previous section that the To-Path and From-Path header field contain the recipient and originator, respectively, of the MSRP request/response. In order to support the operation with MSRP relays, these two headers can actually contain lists of MSRP URIs.

[7] TLS (Transport Layer Security) is discussed in Chapter 13, dedicated to security.

[8] This header field is present only in AUTH requests.

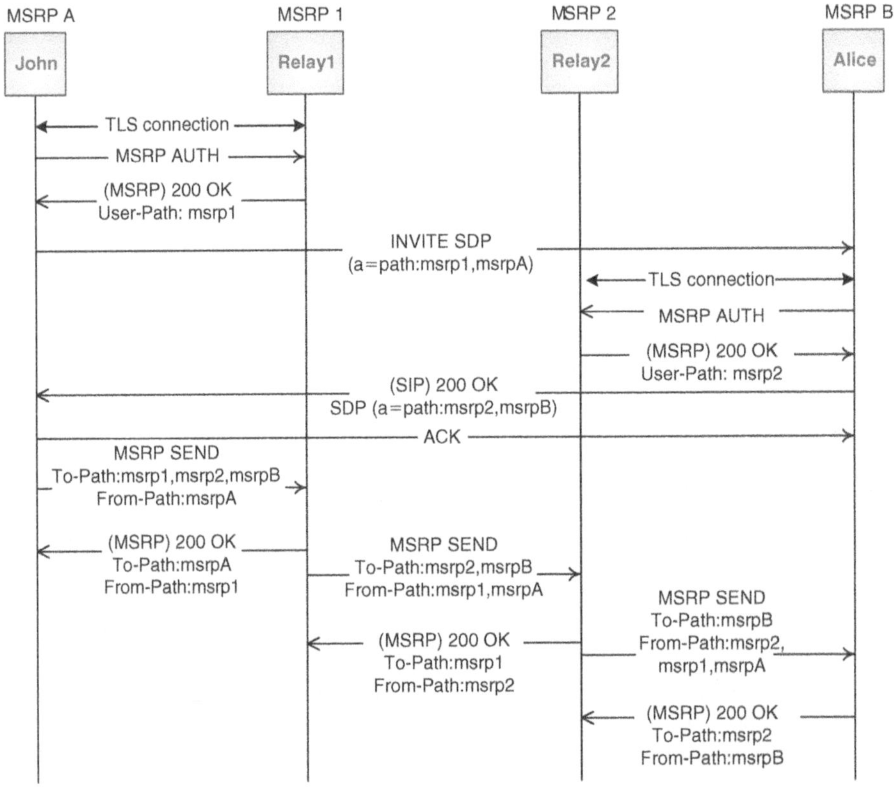

FIGURE 10.13

The list of URIs in the To-Path header field identifies the MSRP entities that need to be visited by the MSRP requests and responses in order to reach the final target. The rightmost MSRP URI in the To-Path header identifies the final target; the leftmost MSRP URI is the next hop to deliver the request or response.

The list of URIs in the From-Path header field indicates how to get back to the original sender of a request or response. The leftmost MSRP URI in the list identifies the last visited MSRP node; the rightmost URI is the originator of the message.

When a relay forwards a request, it removes its address from the To-Path header, and inserts it as the first URI in the From-Path header.

When an MSRP entity receives a request for which it needs to send a response, the MSRP entity copies the list of URIs in the From-Path header of the request into the To-Path header of the response, and sets the From-Path header of the response to its own URI.

In Figure 10.13, we can see how the From-Path and To-Path headers are modified as the SEND message progresses through the different relays.

Reporting

We saw in the previous section the effect that the Success-Report and Failure-Report header fields have on MSRP reporting mechanisms when no relay was involved. The behavior expressed in Table 10.4 is valid also for a situation with relays. We just need to take into account that:

- Relays may generate hop-by-hop acknowledgments (i.e., MSRP responses) depending on the values of Success-Report and Failure-Report header fields.
- If the values in these headers indicate the need for hop-by-hop acknowledgments, the relay will start a transaction timer when forwarding the SEND request to the next hop.
- REPORT requests are generated by the endpoints, not by relays. An exception to this is those situations where the relay receives a negative response for a SEND request or the transaction timer expires. In those cases, the relay will generate a negative REPORT request and send it directly to the originator of the original message.

Now we will see some examples that illustrate how reporting works in the presence of relays.

1. The client sets Success-Report=yes and Failure-Report=yes. The message contains just one chunk, and the delivery is successful. This situation is shown in Figure 10.14. There are hop-by-hop acknowledgments, and also and end-to-end confirmation (REPORT) that the message was delivered.

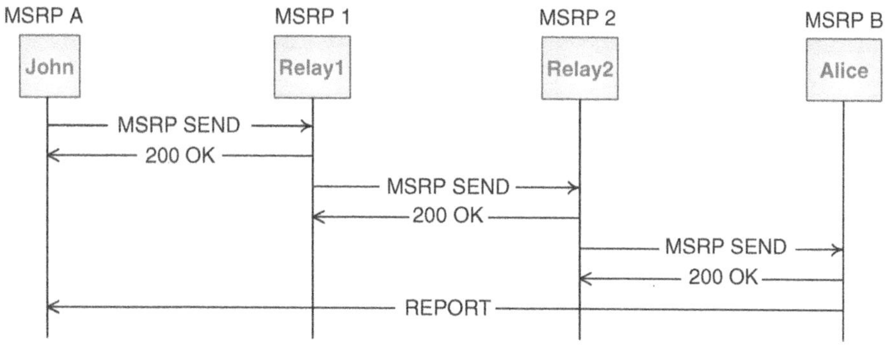

FIGURE 10.14

2. The client sets Success-Report=yes and Failure-Report=no. The message contains just one chunk, and the delivery is successful. This situation is shown in Figure 10.15. According to Table 10.4, there are no hop-by-hop acknowledgments, but there exists the end-to-end REPORT request.
3. The client sets Success-Report=yes and Failure-Report=yes. The message contains just one chunk, and the delivery fails in the last hop. The transaction timer expires in relay 2, and it sends back a negative REPORT request to the originator. Figure 10.16 shows this scenario.

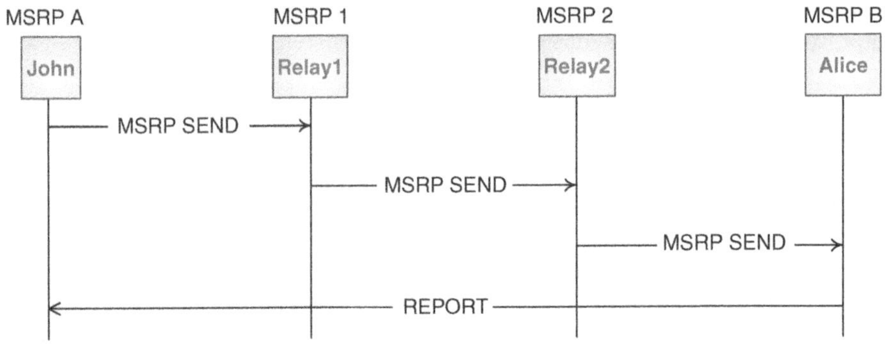

FIGURE 10.15

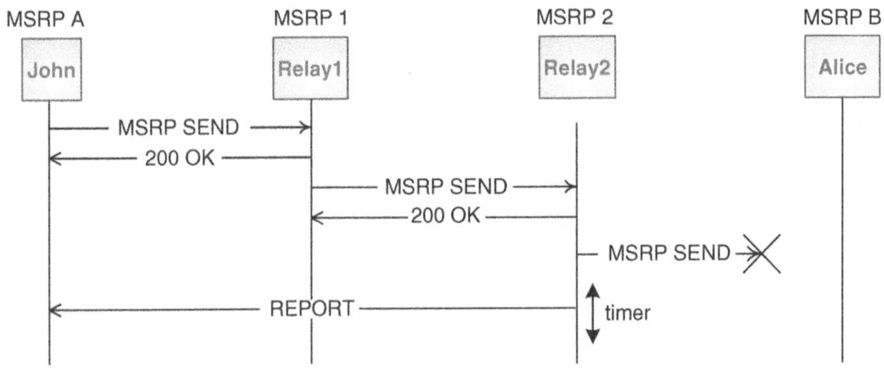

FIGURE 10.16

10.3.5 Detailed MSRP Example

In order to illustrate the concepts learned so far, we will now show the protocol traces of a simple messaging scenario. The scenario does not include any proxies; it is just a simple call between John and Alice with two exchanged messages: "How are you?" and "Fine, thank you." We will include just the most relevant header fields.

(SIP/SDP session establishment)

John to Alice:

```
INVITE sip:alice@ocean.com SIP/2.0
To: <sip:alice@ocean.com
From: sip:john@sea.com>;tag=9317
Call-ID: gd3y8r37z3
Content-Type: application/sdp
c=IN IP4 sea.com
m=message 7881 TCP/MSRP *
```

```
a=accept-types:text/plain
a=path:msrp://host.sea.com: 7881/geiuf4oi3yr;tcp
```

Alice to John:

```
SIP/2.0 200 OK
To: <sip:alice@ocean.com>;tag=3y44
From: <sip:john@sea.com>;tag=9317
Call-ID: gd3y8r37z3
Content-Type: application/sdp
c=IN IP4 ocean.com
m=message 11644 TCP/MSRP *
a=accept-types:text/plain
a=path:msrp://host.ocean.com:11644/p33deirfwy2;tcp
```

John to Alice:

```
ACK sip:alice@biloxi SIP/2.0
To: <sip:alice@ocean.com>;tag=3y44
From: <sip:john@sea.com>;tag=9317
Call-ID: gd3y8r37z3
```

(Message exchange)

John to Alice:

```
MSRP j4l34uud7 SEND
To-Path: msrp://ocean.com:12763/p33deirfwy2;tcp
From-Path: msrp://sea.com:7654/geiuf4oi3yr;tcp
Message-ID: 85749983
Byte-Range: 1-19/19
Content-Type: text/plain
Hello, how are you?
-------j4l34uud7$
```

Alice to John:

```
MSRP j4l34uud7 200 OK
To-Path: msrp://sea.com:7654/geiuf4oi3yr;tcp
From-Path: msrp://ocean.com:12763/p33deirfwy2;tcp
Byte-Range: 1-19/19
-------j4l34uud7$
```

Alice to John:

```
MSRP fy4u4uu3i SEND
To-Path: msrp://sea.com:7654/geiuf4oi3yr;tcp
From-Path: msrp://ocean.com:12763/p33deirfwy2;tcp
Message-ID: 83678263
Byte-Range: 1-17/17
Content-Type: text/plain
```

```
I am fine, thanks
-------j4l34uud7$
```

John to Alice:

```
MSRP j4l34uud7 200 OK
To-Path: msrp://ocean.com:12763/p33deirfwy2;tcp
From-Path: msrp://sea.com:7654/geiuf4oi3yr;tcp
Byte-Range: 1-17/17
-------j4l34uud7$
```

10.4 Summary

We have so far described with some detail two protocols that are used at the media level. In the next chapter, we will put into practice some of the concepts learned by building an RTP sender and receiver.

CHAPTER

Media Plane Programming 11

In order to show how media programming can be done, we introduce in this chapter the Java Media Framework (JMF), a simple yet powerful tool for handling media in Java applications. This is by no means the only media tool available to programmers, not even Java programmers. Furthermore, high-performing applications may require lower-level APIs than the one provided by JMF. For instance, another option to develop voice application could be to use the lower-level Java Sound API.

We do not intend to make a thorough coverage of the JMF API; actually, that would take a complete separate book by itself. Our sole interest is just to focus on some of the key functionalities offered by the API, and let the reader gain an understanding of its scope of applicability and potential. Again, we will be focusing just on the functional aspects, so the code in this chapter is not valid for commercial purposes.

Additionally, we will build a simple program that is able to:

- capture media and transmit it over the network
- receive media over the network and render it to the user

We will use this simple program for the media part of our soft-phone application in later chapters.

11.1 Overview

The Java Media Framework (JMF) is an application programming interface (API) for handling time-based media in Java applications. It allows programmers to develop Java code to capture, present, store, and process time-based media. Moreover, it can be extended to support additional media types and perform custom processing.

Additionally, JMF defines an optional RTP API to enable the transmission and reception of RTP streams. The JMF reference implementation from Sun and IBM that we will be using throughout the book fully supports the JMF RTP API.

Figure 11.1 shows the fundamental data-processing model offered by the JMF API.

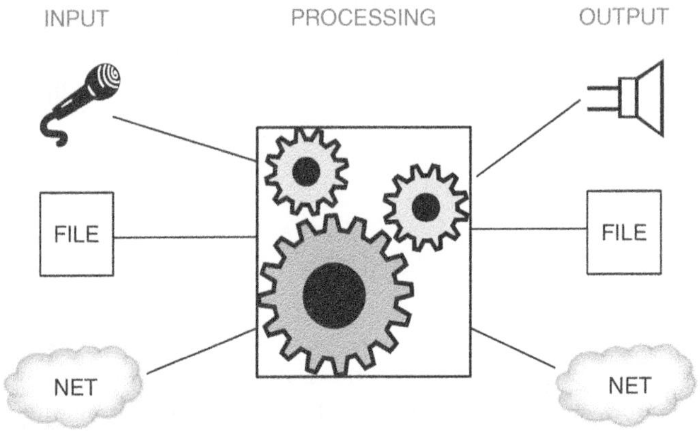

FIGURE 11.1

The model considers three stages in a data-processing flow: input, processing, and output.

- The input stage is meant to acquire the media data. The media data can be obtained from different sources.
  - From capture device (e.g., from microphone or camera)
  - From file (e.g., music.wav)
  - From the network (e.g., from received RTP stream)
- The processing stage takes the data obtained at the input stage and applies some processing to it, such as:
  - Multiplexing/demultiplexing
  - Encoding/decoding
  - Packetizing/depacketizing
- The output stage is responsible for sending the media data to the destination. Possible destinations are:
  - A presentation device (e.g., soundcard and loudspeakers)
  - A file
  - The network (e.g., transmit the media data as an RTP stream)

JMF allows programmers to configure media-processing scenarios that combine different input, output, and processing options. It offers a high-level API to manage the data capture, presentation, and processing of time-based media. Additionally, it also offers a low-level API, called the JMF plug-in API, that supports the seamless integration of custom processing components and extensions. This is shown in Figure 11.2.

We will be focusing on the JMF high-level API. This API does not give the programmer real-time access to the low-level media-processing functions, but rather, allows him or her to configure and manipulate a set of high-level objects that

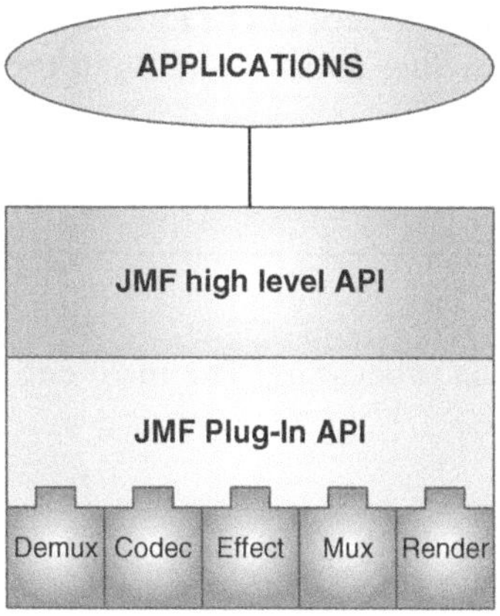

FIGURE 11.2

encapsulate the main media functions such as players, processors, data sinks, and so on, and thus to build the desired media-handling scenario in a Java application.

11.1.1 Media streams

Time-based media takes the form of a media stream. The aim of the input stage is to obtain a media stream. The processing stage also results in a new media stream, which can then be fed into the output stage for presentation and so forth.

In order to obtain a media stream at the input stage, we can programmatically specify its location and the protocol used to access it. In order to represent the location and the protocol, sometimes a URL or a media locator[1] format is used. For example:

- A media stream obtained from a local file could be identified by a "file://" URL.
- A media stream obtained from a file in a web server might be identified by an "http://" URL.
- A media stream obtained from the network could be represented by an "rtp://" media locator.
- A media stream captured from the soundcard could be represented by a "dsound://" media locator.

Media streams can also contain multiple channels of data called tracks. For example, a media stream might contain both an audio track and a video track. A media stream that contains multiple tracks is said to be multiplexed. The process of extracting the individual tracks is called demultiplexing.

[1]A media locator provides a way to identify the location of a media stream when a URL cannot be used. It has a similar format as a URL, though it supports non-IETF standardized schemes. For instance, there is no such a thing as an IETF-standard RTP URL, but we can model media obtained from the network via RTP with a RTP media locator. The media locator is represented by the MediaLocator class. The MediaLocator class is closely related to the URL class. URLs can be obtained from MediaLocators, and MediaLocators can be constructed from URLs.

A track is identified by a media type (e.g., audio or video) and a format that defines how the data for the track is structured, including information about the sample rate, bits per sample, and number of channels.

Tables 11.3 and 11.4 show some of the formats that can be used with JMF.

11.2 JMF Entities

The JMF API defines several entities that model media processing. The main entities are:

- Managers
- Data source
- Player
- Processor
- Data sink
- Session manager

11.2.1 Managers

In order for an application to obtain instances of objects that represent the main JMF entities (such as datasources, players, processors and datasinks), the application uses intermediary objects called managers. JMF uses four managers:

- `Manager`
- `CaptureDeviceManager`
- `PackageManager`
- `PlugInManager`

Throughout this book, we will use the first two types of managers:

- The `Manager` class handles the construction of `Player`, `Processor`, `DataSource`, and `DataSink` objects. Table 11.1 shows some of the main methods of the `Manager` class.

Table 11.1

	Manager Methods	Description
`DataSource`	**`createDatasource`** `(MediaLocator ml)`	Creates a `DataSource` for the specified media.
`Player`	**`createPlayer`** `(DataSource ds)`	Creates a `Player` for the `DataSource`.
`Processor`	**`createProcessor`** `(DataSource ds)`	Creates a `Processor` for the `DataSource`.
`DataSink`	**`createDataSink`** `(DataSource ds, MediaLocator ml)`	Create a `DataSink` for the specified input `DataSource` and destination `MediaLocator`.

- The `CaptureDeviceManager` class maintains a registry of available capture devices. An application can use its `getDeviceList()` method, passing a `Format` object as argument in order to obtain a list of `CaptureDeviceInfo` objects. The list represents a set of devices capable of capturing media in the desired format. Table 11.2 shows some of the main methods of the `CaptureDeviceManager` class.

Table 11.2

	CaptureDeviceManager Methods	Description
`vector`	**`getDeviceList`** `(Format format)`	Gets a list of `CaptureDeviceInfo` objects that correspond to devices that can capture data in the specified format.
`boolean`	**`addDevice`** `(CaptureDeviceInfo di)`	Adds a `CaptureDeviceInfo` object for a new capture device to the list of devices maintained by the `CaptureDeviceManager`.
`boolean`	**`removeDevice`** `(CaptureDeviceInfo di)`	Removes a `CaptureDeviceInfo` object from the list of devices maintained by the `CaptureDeviceManager`.

11.2.2 Data Source

A data source is an entity that encapsulates a media stream. During the media-handling process, different data sources may represent the underlying media streams at different stages of the process, as shown in Figure 11.3, where the data source is represented as a circle.

FIGURE 11.3

A data source is modeled by the `DataSource` abstract class. At the input phase of the media-processing model, a `DataSource` object can be obtained from a URL or media locator. In the following example, a `DataSource` is obtained from a file:

```
MediaLocator ml=new MediaLocator("file://c:\\music.wav");
DataSource ds= Manager.createDataSource(ml);
```

A `DataSource` can also be obtained as the output of a processing stage.

The Format Class

The JMF API defines the `Format` class that represents a media format. It is extended by the `AudioFormat` and `VideoFormat` classes.

For instance, in order to create an `AudioFormat` object, we would specify the following parameters:

- type of encoding (e.g., LINEAR, GSM, G723, etc.)
- sample rate
- number of bits per sample
- number of channels

The following line of code creates an `AudioFormat` object that represents a GSM media format with sampling rate of 8,000 samples per second, 8 bits per sample, and just one channel:

```
AudioFormat af=new AudioFormat(AudioFormat.GSM,8000,8,1);
```

Table 11.3 shows some of the supported audio formats in JMF; the first column indicates the JMF name for the format. When the string "_RTP" is appended to a format name, it refers to the packetized version of the format. As such, "GSM" refers to the actual format used in European 2G mobile systems, whereas "GSM_RTP" refers to the packetized GSM format suitable to be conveyed using RTP.

The same consideration applies for video formats. Table 11.4 shows some JMF-supported video formats; the first column indicates the JMF name for the format.

Table 11.3

JMF Audio Format	Description
ULAW	ITU-T G.711 standard that uses logarithmic PCM-encoded samples for voice, sampled at 8,000 samples/second. Used in North America and Japan.
ALAW	ITU-T G.711 standard that uses logarithmic PCM-encoded samples for voice, sampled at 8,000 samples/second. Used in Europe and rest of the world.
ULAW_RTP	Packetized version of ULAW.
G723	ITU-T G.723 standard wideband speech codec. Superseded by G.726.

(Continued)

Table 11.3 *(Cont.)*

JMF Audio Format	Description
G723_RTP	Packetized version of G.723.
GSM	ETSI GSM standard linear predictive coding (LPC) full rate (FR) codec.
GSM_RTP	Packetized version of GSM codec.
LINEAR	PCM encoded voice samples.
MPEG	Corresponds to the MovingPicture Expert Group (MPEG) standard MPEG-1 for voice.
MPEG_RTP	Packetized version of MPEG.
MPEGLAYER3	Corresponds to the Moving Picture Expert Group (MPEG) standard MPEG-1 layer 3 (the popular MP3).

Table 11.4

JMF Video Format	Description
H261	ITU-T H.261 video coding standard that operates at video rates between 40kbps and 2Mbps.
H261_RTP	Packetized version of H.261.
H263	ITU-T H.263 video coding standard that operates at low bitrates. It is more advanced than H.261 and provides a suitable replacement.
H263_RTP	Packetized version of H.263.
MPEG	Corresponds to the Moving Picture Expert Group (MPEG) standard MPEG-1 for video.
MPEG_RTP	Packetized version of MPEG.
YUV	Refers to a video format that embraces the Y(luminance), U (chrominance), B(chrominance) color model.

11.2.3 Player

A player is an entity responsible for processing and rendering a media stream. It is modeled by the `Player` interface. The media stream is conveyed to the `Player` as a `DataSource`. For instance, the following line of code creates a `Player` for the `DataSource` ds:

```
Player p=Manager.createPlayer(ds);
```

In Figure 11.4 a Player is shown in the last stage of the media-handling process.

In order to start a player, we can invoke the `start()` method:

```
p.start();
```

FIGURE 11.4

A player can be either at the Started or Stopped state. When we instruct the player to start, it will go through different preparation states as it obtains the necessary resources. The methods that can be invoked on a `Player` depend on its state. The JMF implementation can inform the application about the transitions between the different states using a Java Event model. More specifically, our application can implement the `ControllerListener` interface and can receive notifications of changes of state. This allows programmers to build highly responsive systems.

Figure 11.5 shows the different states a `Player` can go through. Table 11.5 contains a brief description of each state.

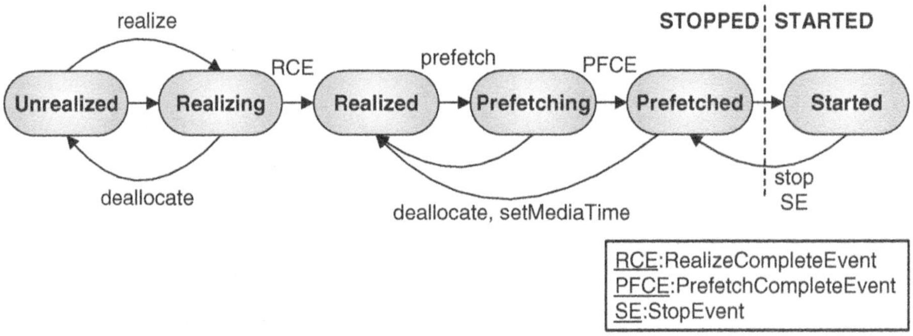

FIGURE 11.5

Table 11.5

State	Description
Unrealized	The Player has been instantiated, but does not yet know anything about its media.
Realizing	The Player is in the process of determining its resource requirements.
Realized	The Player knows what resources it needs and information about the type of media it is to present.
Prefetching	The Player is preparing to present its media.
Prefetched	The Player is ready to be started.
Started	The Player's clock starts running.

The `Player` interface extends the `Controller` interface, from which it obtains methods, such as `realize()` or `prefetch()`, that explicitly attempt to move the `Player` to the Realized state or the Prefetched state, respectively (via the Realizing state and the Prefetching states).

11.2.4 Processor

A processor is a specialized type of player that provides control over media stream processing. It is modeled through the `Processor` interface that extends the Player interface. A `Processor` typically receives an input `DataSource` and produces an output `DataSource`. This is shown in Figure 11.6. The `Processor` can multiplex, demultiplex, encode, decode, and apply effect filters over a media stream. A `Processor` can also render a media stream to a presentation device.

The following code would create a Processor object for the `DataSource` ds:

```
Processor p=Manager.createProcessor(ds);
```

FIGURE 11.6

A `Processor` has two additional preparation states (as compare with a `Player`), Configuring and Configured, which occur before the `Processor` enters the Realizing state. In order to cause the `Processor` to enter the Configuring state, the `configure()` method can be invoked on it. In order to start a `Processor`, the `start()` method can be invoked.

Figure 11.7 shows the different states a `Player` can go through.

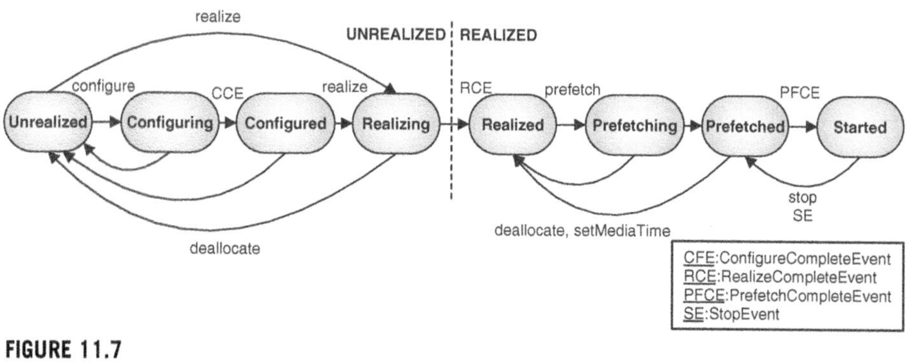

FIGURE 11.7

11.2.5 Data Sinks

A data sink gets a media stream as input, and renders the data to some destination (typically different from a presentation device). In that way, data sinks can be used to write data to a file or to send data over a network. This is shown in Figure 11.8 where we can see a DataSink in the last stage of the media-handling process.

A data sink is represented by the `DataSink` interface.

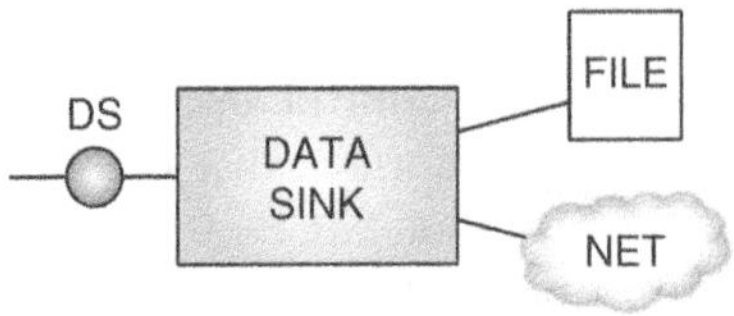

FIGURE 11.8

The following line of code would create a `DataSink` for the specified input `DataSource` and destination `MediaLocator`:

```
DataSink dsink=Manager.createDataSink(ds,ml);
```

In order to start transferring data to the destination, two steps are needed:

- First we need to call `open()` on the `DataSink` in order to open a connection to the output destination identified by the `MediaLocator`.
- Next we need to invoke `start()` to actually initiate the data transfer:

```
dsink.open();
dsink.start();
```

11.2.6 SessionManager

In scenarios that involve sending or receiving RTP sessions over or from the network, a `SessionManager` may be used instead of a `DataSink` (see Figure 11.9). A `SessionManager` offers an enhanced degree of control over RTP sessions compared to a `DataSink` (which offers almost no degree of control).

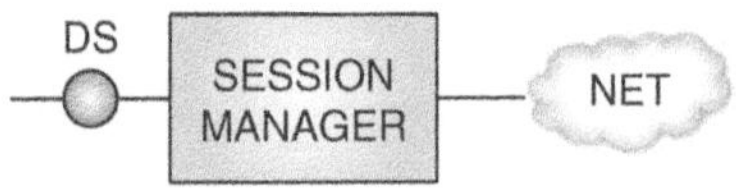

FIGURE 11.9

The `SessionManager` represents an entity that is used to manage and coordinate an RTP session. It keeps track of the participants in the media session and keeps track of the media being transmitted. It also handles the RTCP control channel. Thus, it offers methods to:

- start and close an RTP session
- create RTP streams to be sent
- add and remove peers
- obtain session statistics
- etc.

RTP Streams

A key concept when working with a `SessionManager` is the `RTPStream` class, which represents an RTP stream. There are two types of RTP streams:

- `ReceiveStream`: represents an incoming RTP stream.
- `SendStream`: represents an outgoing RTP stream.

We will see in the next sections how these classes are used in order to transmit and receive RTP streams.

Listeners

A `SessionManager` can send session-related events to objects that implement specific listener interfaces. Four types of listener are defined for the `SessionManager`:

- `SessionListener`: Receives notifications of changes in the state of the session.
- `SendStreamListener`: Receives notifications of changes in the state of the stream that is being transmitted.
- `ReceiveStreamListener`: Receives notifications of changes in the state of the stream that is being received.
- `RemoteListener`: Receives notifications of control messages from a remote participant.

In our practices, we will be using just the `ReceiveStreamListener`. It offers an `update()` method, which is invoked as soon as the first RTP packets in the session are received. The `SessionManager` passes a `ReceiveStreamEvent` object as an argument to the `update()` method. The `ReceiveStreamEvent` represents an event occurring at the receiving side (in this case, the particular type of event we are interested in is `NewReceivedStream`, which extends `ReceiveStreamEvent`). It is possible to obtain a reference to the `ReceiveStream` from the `ReceivedStreamEvent`. Then we can convert the `ReceiveStream` into a `DataSource` and further process it in our application. In the next section, we will see all this in action.

SessionManager Operation

In order to use a `SessionManager`, first we have to create an instance of it. That is achieved by directly using the `new()` method for the implementation class. In our case, we will be using the `RTPSessionMgr` class provided by the IBM and Sun implementation, therefore we would include the following code to our application:

```
RTPSessionMgr sm=new() RTPSessionMgr;
```

Next we would need to initialize the `SessionManager` by calling its `initSession()` method and passing some configuration parameters such as the local session addresses and so forth. The local session address represents the source address (IP and port) that will be used in outgoing RTP and RTCP packets:

```
sm.initSession(localAddress,.......);
```

Then we would call the `startSession()` method, which starts the session, causing RTCP reports to be generated and callbacks to be made through the `SessionListener` interface.

There are several flavors of the `startSession` method. Some of them are more oriented to multicast scenarios, whereas others are targeted at bidirectional unicast scenarios. We will look at one of the latter because it fits better for our purpose of building a peer-to-peer communication application.

In the unicast version of the `startSession` method, we need to pass as parameters, among others, the destination session address where the application will send outgoing packets, and the receiver session address where the application expects to receive the incoming packets. The destination session address represents the destination address (IP and port) for RTP packets and RTCP packets:

```
sm.startSession(receiver address,......,destination address,....);
```

Calling `startSession()` over the `SessionManager` does not start transmission of the media stream. If we wanted to start transmission of a concrete media stream represented by a `DataSource` object, ds, we would need to first create a `SendStream` object from the `DataSource`. The second argument in the creation method represents the index of the stream in the `DataSource` that we want to use to create the RTP stream. In our case, we just set it to 1, which means the first stream in the `DataSource`:

```
SendStream ss=sm.createSendStream(ds,1);
```

And then we could start actual transmission of the stream:

```
ss.start();
```

In order to receive a media stream, as soon as this is detected by the `SessionManager`, it would fire a `ReceivedStreamEvent` event to our listener, which would then obtain a reference to the `ReceivedStream`:

```
ReceiveStream rs= event.getReceiveStream();
```

And next we would obtain a `DataSource` from the `ReceiveStream`;

```
DataSource ds=rs.getDataSource();
```

Session Addresses

The `startSession()` and `initSession()` methods that we saw in the previous section require that we pass a session address as an argument. JMF defines the `SessionAddress` class that encapsulates a session address. It comprises four pieces of information:

- IP address for RTP
- Port for RTP
- IP address for RTCP
- Port for RTCP

The IP addresses are passed to the constructor method as `java.net.InetAddress` objects, whereas the port argument is an integer value (`int`).

Example:

```
InetAddress addr=InetAddress.getByName("1.2.3.4");
SessionAddress sa=new SessionAddress(addr, 50000, addr, 50001);
```

11.3 JMF Operation

Now that we have described the main pieces, let us now see how the API is used in order to implement the following operations:

- capture live media
- capture media file
- present media
- send media to file
- process media
- receive media from network
- send media over network

11.3.1 Capture Live Media

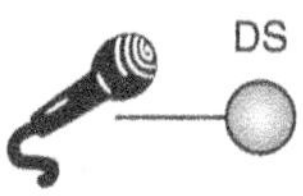

FIGURE 11.10

Let us say we want to obtain a media stream from a capture device such as a microphone or a camera. In JMF terms, what we want is the `DataSource` corresponding to the live media. We can use the `Manager` to create the `DataSource`. JMF provides two ways to obtain the `DataSource` from a capture device:

1. If we know the media locator of the capture device, we can directly obtain the `DataSource` from it. In the following example, "dsound://8000" represents an audio card that samples voice at 8,000 Hz:

   ```
   MediaLocator ml=new MediaLocator("dsound://8000");
   DataSource ds= Manager.createDataSource(ml);
   ```

2. Obtain the `CaptureDeviceInfo` corresponding to a capture device that supports a specified format. As we saw in previous sections, we can invoke the method `getDeviceList` on the `CaptureDeviceManager`, passing the specification of the desired format. Once we have the `CaptureDeviceInfo`, we can obtain a media locator from it:

   ```
   AudioFormat df=new AudioFormat(AudioFormat.LINEAR,8000,8,1);
   Vector devices=CaptureDeviceManager.getDeviceList(df);
   ```

```
CaptureDeviceInfo di=(CaptureDeviceInfo) devices.elementAt(0);
DataSource ds=Manager.createDataSource(di.getLocator());
```

In a commercial application, we would need to cope with the situations where there are no devices that support the specified `AudioFormat`. In our examples, we will always be using a linear format with voice sampled at 8,000 Hz and with 8 bits per sample. Such a format is supported by virtually all the soundcards in the market, therefore we will not worry about those situations in our examples.

11.3.2 Capture Media File

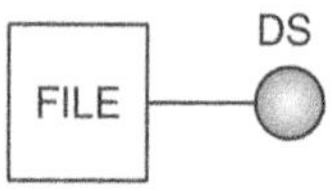

FIGURE 11.11

Capturing a media stream from a file is equal to obtaining a `DataSource` that represents that stream. The best way to do that is through a URL that represents the local file. For instance, in order to obtain the media stream from the file music.wav, we could do the following:

```
MediaLocator ml=new MediaLocator("file://c:\\music.wav");
DataSource ds=Manager.createDataSource(ml);
```

If the media stream were stored in a remote file in a web server, we could obtain it by using an HTTP URL.

11.3.3 Present Media

FIGURE 11.12

Let us assume that we already have a `DataSource` that represents a media stream that we want to render to a presentation device. The most common way to do so is by using a `Player`. The following example represents the simplest way to play the media stream contained in `DataSource ds`:

```
Player player = Manager.createPlayer(ds);
player.start();
```

The `start()` method attempts to transition the `Player` to the Started state as soon as possible. Therefore, it automatically tries to move the `Player` to the

Realized state, then to the `Prefetched` state, and finally to the Started state. Applications that want to determine with more accuracy when the `Player` is started may want to retain the control of moving the `Player` from one state to the other. One way to do that is by implementing the `ControllerListener` interface and explicitly invoking the `realize()` and `prefetch()` methods when appropriate. For our simple examples, we will always directly use the `start()` method.

11.3.4 Send Media to File

FIGURE 11.13

In order to send a media stream to a file, we need two pieces of information:

- a `DataSource` object representing the media stream
- a URL representing the location of the file

The simplest way to send media to a file is to create a `DataSink` object that points to the file URL, and pass the input `DataSource` in the creation method. Once created, we just open and start the data sink. In our example, `ds` represents the `DataSource` object:

```
MediaLocator ml=new MediaLocator("file://c:\\oo.wav");
DataSink sink=Manager.createDataSink(ds,ml);
sink.open();
sink.start();
```

It is important to note that, in this case, the `DataSource` ds represents the input media stream to the `DataSink`, whereas the `MediaLocator` ml is used to determine the file acting as sink for the media.

11.3.5 Process Media

FIGURE 11.14

In order to be able to process the media stream, we need an input `DataSource` and a `Processor` object.

The first step is to create the `Processor` from the input `DataSource iDS`:

```
Processor p=Manager.createProcessor(iDS);
```

Instead of directly starting the `Processor` (as we did with the `Player` in previous examples), we need to explicitly control the transition of the `Processor` through the different states. The reason for that is that we need to set up the processing rules in the `Processor`, and for that, the `Processor` needs to have reached the Configured state. Therefore, the next step would be to instruct the `Processor` to transit to the Configured state:

```
p.configure();
```

The `configure` method is asynchronous, therefore we need to wait until the Configured state is reached in order to set up the processing rules. This may be achieved in different ways. For the purpose of our simple example, which focuses on functionality and not on performance, a possible option would be to create a loop that checks the state:

```
while (p.getState()!=Processor.Configured) {
  Thread.sleep(20);
}
```

Using the loop approach is not recommended for commercial code. A commercial product might want to implement the `ControllerListener` interface and set the rules when a transition event to Configured is fired. Another possible option is to use the `StateHelper` class included in the JMF package.

Next we set the processing rules by defining which is the desired format of the first and only track in the input media stream. To do so, first we create an `AudioFormat` object that represents the desired GSM format with a sampling rate of 8,000 samples per second and 4 bits to represent each sample. The last argument represent the number of audio channels; in our case, just one:

```
AudioFormat af=new AudioFormat(AudioFormat.GSM,8000,4,1);
```

Then we get a `TrackControl` object that allows us to invoke the `setFormat()` method:

```
TrackControl track[]= p.getTrackControls();
track[0].setFormat(af);
```

Once the output format is defined in the `Processor`, we move it to the Realized state and wait for the `Processor` to become Realized:

```
p.realize();
while (p.getState() != Processor.Realized) {
  Thread.sleep(20);
}
```

Then we obtain the output `DataSource` and invoke `start()` on the `Processor`:

```
DataSource oDS = p.getDataOutput();
p.start();
```

If we wanted to send the output media stream over the network, we should have asked the `Processor` to not only encode the input stream, but also to perform packetization. The way to indicate to the `Processor` that the stream needs to be packetized for sending it in an RTP session is just to append "_RTP" to the desired media format that is passed as a parameter to the `setFormat()` method:

```
AudioFormat af=new AudioFormat(AudioFormat.GSM_RTP,8000,4,1);
```

11.3.6 Receive and Send Media from/over the Network

The JMF RTP API offers two ways to receive and send RTP media from the network. The first way uses just RTP media locators, whereas the second one implies using a `SessionManager`. Using media locators is the simplest form, and is good enough if we want to send just one media stream. If we want to send several media streams, or if more control over the session is desired, then using the `SessionManager` becomes a must.

In any event, in the receiving case, the goal is to obtain a `DataSource` object that represents the RTP media stream received over the network. We will call the received `DataSource rDS`. In the sending case, the goal is to transmit a stream represented by a `DataSource`. We will call the transmitted `DataSource tDS`.

We will see here the two approaches.

Approach 1: Media Locators

For the receiving case, let us imagine that the IP address and port where our receiver application is expecting the media is 1.2.3.4:40000. In the simplest approach, we just create a `DataSource` from an RTP media locator:

```
MediaLocator ml=new MediaLocator("rtp://1.2.3.4:40000/audio/1");
DataSource rDS=Manager.createDataSource(ml);
```

The last "1" in the RTP media locator represents the time to live (TTL) in RTP packets.

For the sending case, in its simplest form, in order to send a media stream over the network using RTP, we just need to create a `DataSink` object and pass two arguments to it:

- The `DataSource` object that represents the media stream that we want to send over the network.
- A RTP media locator that identifies the destination of the stream. Let us assume that the address of the destination is 5.4.3.2:50000:

```
MediaLocator ml=new MediaLocator("rtp://5.4.3.2:50000/audio/1");
DataSink sink=Manager.createDataSink(tDS,ml);
```

Once the data sink has been created, we just need to open and start it:

```
sink.open();
sink.start();
```

The sending scenario is depicted in Figure 11.15.

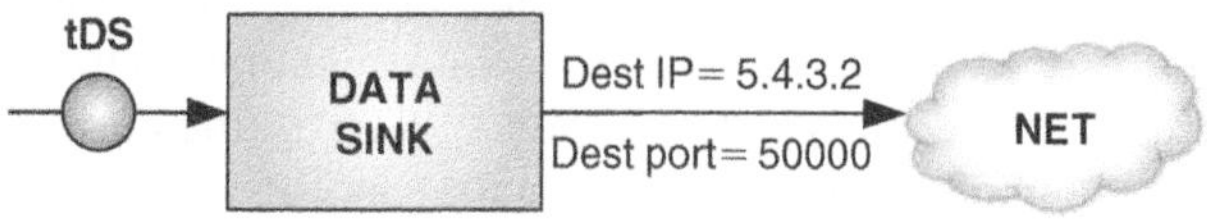

FIGURE 11.15

Approach 2: SessionManager

Another approach to receive and send media from/over the network consists of using a `SessionManager`.

In order to receive incoming streams, our application would implement the `ReceiveStreamListener` interface. As soon as the incoming session is detected (i.e., the first RTP packets are received), the `SessionManager` will post a `NewReceiveStreamEvent`. From that event, we will get the `ReceiveStream`, and from the `ReceiveStream`, it is possible to obtain a `DataSource (rDS)`.

On the other hand, let us assume that we want to transmit via RTP the stream represented by a `DataSource (tDS)`. First we need to obtain a reference to a `SendStream` object from the `DataSource` object. Then we would simply call the `start()` method on the `SendStream` object in order to start transmitting. Figure 11.16 shows the JMF entities involved in this scenario.

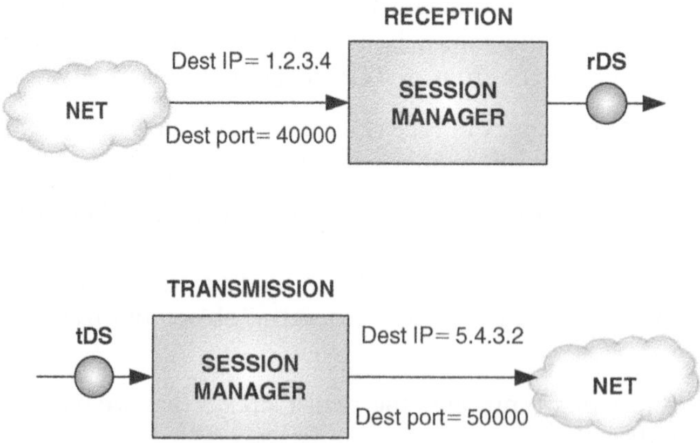

FIGURE 11.16

Let us see step-by-step how this works.

First we need to create an object that implements the `SessionManager` interface. In the reference implementation from Sun and IBM that we are using, the class that implements the `SessionManager` interface is called `RTPSessionMgr`. Thus, we would use the following line of code to create the `SessionManager`:

```
RTPSessionMgr sm = new RTPSessionMgr();
```

In order to receive the `ReceiveStreamEvents`, our class needs to implement the `ReceiveStreamListener` interface. We also need to register our interest in receiving events from the `SessionManager`. That is achieved by invoking the method `addReceiveStreamListener()` on the `SessionManager`:

```
sm.addReceiveStreamListener(this);
```

Then we need to initialize and start the session in the `SessionManager`. We need to pass some configuration parameters as arguments to the `initSession()` and `startSession()` methods on the `SessionManager`.

In the `initSession()` method, we need to pass the following parameters:

- A `SessionAddress` object that encapsulates the IP address and port that we would use as origin address and port in outgoing packets.[2] We will assume at this point that we are using a computer with just one IP address, and that we are not concerned with the source port in outgoing packets. Thus, we will let the `SessionManager` choose the values itself by passing an empty `SessionAddress` to the `initSession()` method.

- A `SourceDescription` object that describes the source user description as used in SDES RTCP packets. As we explained in Chapter 10, the SDES is not relevant in peer-to-peer communications, so we will set it to null.

- An integer value that represents the fraction of the session bandwidth that the `SessionManager` must use when sending out RTCP reports. We will set it to 0.05, which is a reasonable value in most cases.

- An integer value that represents the fraction of the previous value that the `SessionManager` must use to send out RTCP sender reports from the local participant. We will set it to 0.25, which is a reasonable value in most cases.

In the `startSession()` method, we need to pass the following parameters:

- A receiver `SessionAddress` object that encapsulates the IP address and port where our application expects to receive both RTP and RTCP packets. This parameter is crucial. In a communication scenario, we would obtain this information from the received SDP. In our example, the IP address for both RTP and RTCP is "1.2.3.4." The port for RTP is 40000, and the RTCP port is 40001.[3]

---

[2] Even if we were not sending RTP packets, there will always be RTCP packets being sent, so this parameter is necessary.

[3] [RFC 3550] states that RTP should use an even destination port number and that the corresponding RTCP stream should use the next higher (odd) destination port number.

- A sender SessionAddress object that encapsulates the IP address and port that our application will use as source address when sending packets.
- A destination SessionAddress object that encapsulates the IP address and port that our application will use in order to send outgoing packets. In our example, the remote destination IP address for both RTP and RTCP is "5.4.3.2." The remote destination port for RTP is 50000, and the RTCP port is 50001.
- An EncryptionInfo object that encapsulates the encryption parameters for the session. We are not using encryption here, so we will set it to null.

With all the previous considerations, the necessary code would be:

```
InetAddress localIP = InetAddress.getByName("1.2.3.4");
InetAddress remIP = InetAddress.getByName("5.4.3.2");
SessionAddress senderAddr = new SessionAddress();
SessionAddress localAddr = new SessionAddress(localIP,
  40000,localIP,40001);
SessionAddress remAddr=new SessionAddress(remIP,50000,remIP,
  50001);
sm.initSession(senderAddr, null, 0.05, 0.25);
sm.startSession(localAddr,localAddr,remoteAddr, null);
```

Now that a bidirectional unicast media session has been created, we need to actually receive and send data.

In order to receive data, we need to provide the method that will be invoked when a ReceivedStreamEvent is fired. The method is called update(). We first check if the received event corresponds to the detection of a new received stream. If that is the case, we obtain the ReceiveStream. From it, we obtain the DataSource object, which was our target:

```
public class MyReceiveStreamListener implements
 ReceiveStreamListener {
  public void update(ReceiveStreamEvent event) {
    if (event instanceof NewReceiveStreamEvent){
     rs=event.getReceiveStream();
     DataSource rDS=rs.getDataSource();
    }
  }
}
```

In order to send data, once the session manager is started, we just need to create a SendStream from our DataSource and invoke the start method on the SendStream objects:

```
ss = tManager.createSendStream(tDS, 1);
ss.start();
```

In the next sections, we will create a practical component that puts all these ideas together.

11.4 Putting It All Together: The VoiceTool

We have in the previous section seen how to implement different steps in the JMF media-processing model. Now we will build an end-to-end scenario that combines some of the individual steps seen previously. In particular, we are interested in developing a `VoiceTool` component that can later be used by the soft-phone application that we will build in Chapter 12.

The `VoiceTool` Java class contains the necessary methods to start and stop transmission and reception of voice. It uses a single session manager, `myVoiceSessionManager`, for both reception and transmission, which is defined as a member of the class. `VoiceTool` implements the `ReceiveStreamListener` interface. Next we see the class definition and data fields:

```
public class VoiceTool implements ReceiveStreamListener {
private RTPSessionMgr myVoiceSessionManager=null;
private Processor myProcessor=null;
private SendStream ss=null;
private ReceiveStream rs=null;
private Player player=null;
private AudioFormat af=null;
private DataSource oDS=null;
```

`VoiceTool` offers three methods:

- `int startMedia (String peerIP, int peerPort, int recvPort, int fmt)`: This method creates the RTP unicast session between the local host at `recvPort`, and the remote host, `peerIP`, at `peerPort`. Then it starts voice transmission and reception. The last argument, `fmt`, indicates the audio format used for transmission. For simplicity, we will consider only two possible video formats (GSM_RTP and G723_RTP). This method will return an integer value of 1 if it was executed successfully, or a negative value if an error was encountered.
- `void stopMedia()`: This method is used to stop voice transmission and reception.
- `void update(ReceiveStreamEvent event)`: This is a method from the `ReceiveStreamListener` interface that `VoiceTool` implements.

Let us now explain the code in the methods step-by-step.

startMedia(String peerIP, int peerPort, int recvPort, int fmt)

First we obtain the `DataSource` for the captured media:

```
AudioFormat df=new AudioFormat(AudioFormat.LINEAR,8000,8,1);
Vector devices=CaptureDeviceManager.getDeviceList(df);
CaptureDeviceInfo di=(CaptureDeviceInfo) devices.elementAt(0);
DataSource iDS=Manager.createDataSource(di.getLocator());
```

Then we create a `Processor` and set up the processing rules:

```
myProcessor = Manager.createProcessor(daso);
myProcessor.configure();
while (myProcessor.getState()!=Processor.Configured) {
   Thread.sleep(20);
}
myProcessor.setContentDescriptor(new ContentDescriptor
  (ContentDescriptor.RAW_RTP));
TrackControl track[]=myProcessor.getTrackControls();
switch (fmt) {
   case 3: af=new AudioFormat(AudioFormat.GSM_RTP,8000,4,1);
   case 4: af=new AudioFormat(AudioFormat.G723_RTP,8000,4,1);
}
track[0].setFormat(af);
myProcessor.realize();
while (myProcessor.getState() != Processor.Realized) {
   Thread.sleep(20)
}
```

Next we obtain the output `DataSource`:

```
oDS = myProcessor.getDataOutput();
```

Then we create a `SessionManager` object and invoke `initSession()` and `startSession()` on it. Additionally, we also register our interest in receiving `ReceiveStreamEvents`:

```
myVoiceSessionManager = new RTPSessionMgr();
// Next line we register our interest in receiving
// ReceiveStreamEvents
myVoiceSessionManager.addReceiveStreamListener(this);
SessionAddress senderAddr = new SessionAddress();
myVoiceSessionManager.initSession(senderAddr, null,
  0.05,0.25);
InetAddress destAddr = InetAddress.getByName(peerIP);
SessionAddress localAddr = new SessionAddress (InetAddress.
  getLocalHost(),recvPort,InetAddress.getLocalHost(),recvPort+1);
SessionAddress remoteAddr = new SessionAddress(destAddr,
  peerPort, destAddr, peerPort + 1);
myVoiceSessionManager.startSession(localAddr , localAddr ,
  remoteAddr,null);
```

Next we obtain a `SendStream` from the `Datasource` obtained as output of the processor:

```
ss = myVoiceSessionManager.createSendStream(oDS, 1);
```

We then start capture and transmission:

```
ss.start();
myProcessor.start();
```

update(ReceiveStreamEvent event)

The `VoiceTool` class implements the `update()` method in the `ReceiveStreamListener` interface. The code for the method is shown next. As soon as a new received stream is detected, we obtain the `DataSource` from it, and create a `Player` passing the obtained `DataSource` as argument:

```
public void update(ReceiveStreamEvent event) {
  if (event instanceof NewReceiveStreamEvent){
    rs=event.getReceiveStream();
    DataSource rDS=rs.getDataSource();
    try{
      player = Manager.createPlayer(rDS);
      player.start();
    }catch (Exception ex){
      ex.printStackTrace();
    }
  }
}
```

Figure 11.17 shows the main JMF entities involved in the previous scenarios for sending and receiving.

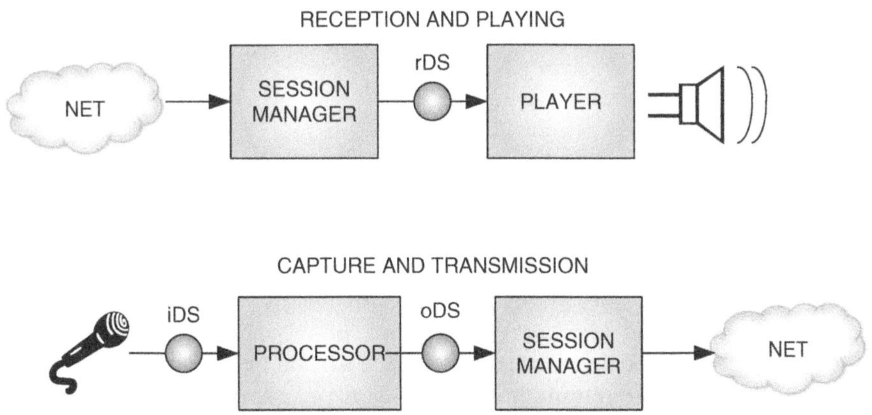

FIGURE 11.17

stopMedia()

First we need to stop and close the `Player`:

```
player.stop();
player.deallocate();
player.close();
```

Next we stop transmission:

```
ss.stop();
```

Then we stop capture and processing:

```
myProcessor.stop();
myProcessor.deallocate();
myProcessor.close();
```

And finally, we close the RTP session and free the used source ports:

```
myVoiceSessionManager.closeSession();
myVoiceSessionManager.dispose();
```

11.5 Putting It All Together: The VideoTool

Based on the previous example, we can easily develop a tool valid for video transmission and reception. Such a tool will also be used in our audio/video soft-phone project in the following chapters.

The `VideoTool` Java class contains the necessary methods to start and stop transmission and reception of video. It uses a single session manager, `myVideoSessionManager`, for both reception and transmission, which is defined as a member of the class. `VideoTool` implements the `ReceiveStreamListener` interface. Next we see the class definition and data fields:

```
public class VideoTool implements ReceiveStreamListener {
private RTPSessionMgr myVideoSessionManager=null;
private Processor myProcessor=null;
private SendStream ss=null;
private ReceiveStream rs=null;
private Player player=null;
private VideoFormat vf=null;
private DataSource oDS=null;
private VideoFrame vframe;
```

`VideoTool` offers three methods:

- `int startMedia (String peerIP,int peerPort,int recvPort, int fmt)`: This method creates the RTP unicast session between the local host at `recvPort` and the remote host, `peerIP`, at `peerPort`. Then it starts video transmission and reception. The last argument, `fmt`, indicates the video format used for transmission. For simplicity, we will consider only two possible video formats (JPEG_RTP and H263_RTP). This method will return an integer value of 1 if it was executed successfully, or a negative value if an error was encountered.
- `void stopMedia()`: This method is used to stop video transmission and reception.

- `void update(ReceiveStreamEvent event)`: This is a method from the `ReceiveStreamListener` interface that `VideoTool` implements.

In the `VoiceTool` example, the capture device was a standard microphone. In this case, for the video, we will use a webcam connected to our computer via USB. Such webcams are commonplace in the market today, and can typically be obtained for around $30. Not all the webcams in the market work fine with JMF. In order to work with JMF, readers using MS Windows should have a webcam that supports WDM (Windows Driver Model) or VFW (Video for Windows) interfaces. Most webcams in the market today comply with this requirement.

Let us now explain the code step-by-step.

startMedia()

First we obtain the `DataSource` for the captured media. In this case, we will get the `DataSource` directly from a media locator, as was explained in previous sections. Thus, we need to learn the media locator for our webcam. A simple way to determine this is through the utilization of the JMStudio, which is an application that is included in the JMF package that can be downloaded from the Sun site. This application includes several features to test the capture, presentation, transmission, and reception of media in our computer. It also includes a JMF Registry Editor that allows us to browse through all the different media components in the system, including capture devices.

In order to determine the media locator for our camera connected via USB, we need to follow these steps:

1. Start the JMStudio (Figure 11.18).

FIGURE 11.18

2. Go to File, Preferences menu (Figure 11.19).
3. We will see the main window of the JMF Registry Editor. We click on the Capture Devices tab. Once there, we click on the Detect Capture Devices button. It may take some seconds to detect the new camera. When it is ready, the description of the webcam capture device, including its media

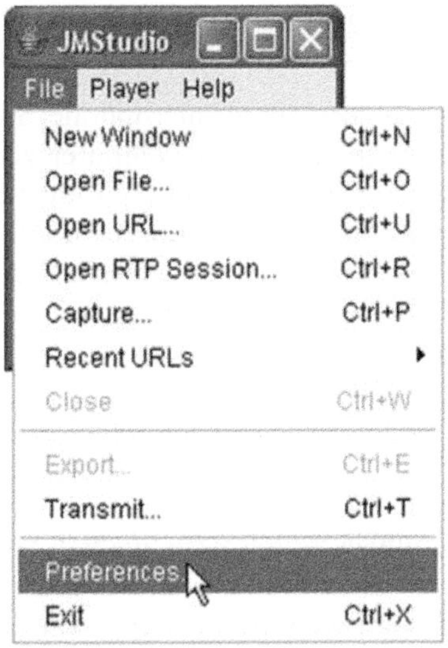

FIGURE 11.19

locator, will appear on the right pane on the window. In this case, we see that the media locator is "vfw://0." This is shown in Figure 11.20.

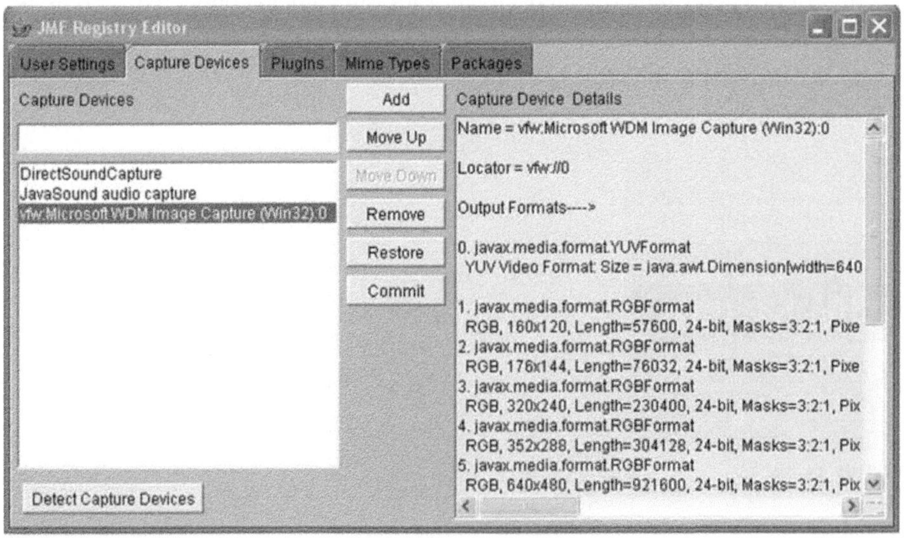

FIGURE 11.20

So now we can proceed to obtain the `DataSource`:

```
MediaLocator ml=new MediaLocator("vfw://0")
DataSource iDS=Manager.createDataSource(ml);
```

Then we create a `Processor` and set up the processing rules:

```
myProcessor = Manager.createProcessor(daso);
myProcessor.configure();
while (myProcessor.getState()!=Processor.Configured) {
   Thread.sleep(20);
}
myProcessor.setContentDescriptor(new ContentDescriptor
  (ContentDescriptor.RAW_RTP));
TrackControl track[] = myProcessor.getTrackControls();
switch (fmt) {
   case 26: vf=new VideoFormat(VideoFormat.JPEG_RTP);
   case 34: vf=new VideoFormat(VideoFormat.H263_RTP);
}
```

At this point, we want to check if the chosen format (`vf`) is supported by the `Processor`. The way to do that is to go through the list of all supported formats and see if we find a match for `vf`. We will use the `getSupportedFormats()` method in the `TrackControl` interface. The list that is obtained in this manner will contain only the supported video formats that can be sent over RTP, given that we already set the `ContentDescriptor` in the `Processor` to "RAW_RTP."

If the format is not supported, the method stops execution and returns −1.

```
boolean match=false;
format mySupportedFormats[]=track[0].getSupportedFormats();
for (int j=0;j< mySupportedFormats.length;j++) {
   if (vf.matches(mySupportedFormats[j])) match=true;
}
if (match==false) return -1;
```

If the format is supported, the method continues with the next steps. We set the output format and obtain the output `DataSource`:

```
track[0].setFormat(af);
myProcessor.realize();
while (myProcessor.getState() != Processor.Realized) {
   Thread.sleep(20)
}
oDS = myProcessor.getDataOutput();
```

Then we create a `SessionManager` object and invoke `initSession()` and `startSession()` on it. Additionally, we also register our interest in receiving `ReceiveStreamEvents`:

```
myVideoSessionManager = new RTPSessionMgr();
// Next line we register our interest in receiving
// ReceiveStreamEvents
myVideoSessionManager.addReceiveStreamListener(this);
```

```
SessionAddress senderAddr = new SessionAddress();
myVideoSessionManager.initSession(senderAddr, null, 0.05,
  0.25);
InetAddress destAddr = InetAddress.getByName(peerIP);
SessionAddress localAddr = new SessionAddress(InetAddress.
  getLocalHost(), recvPort,InetAddress.getLocalHost(),
  recvPort + 1);
SessionAddress remoteAddr = new SessionAddress(destAddr,
  peerPort,destAddr, peerPort + 1);
myVideoSessionManager.startSession(localAddr , localAddr ,
  remoteAddr,null);
```

Next we obtain a `SendStream` from the `Datasource` obtained as output of the processor:

```
ss = myVideoSessionManager.createSendStream(oDS, 1);
```

We then start capture and transmission:

```
ss.start();
myProcessor.start();
```

update()

The `update()` method here is similar to the one in the voice case. The difference resides in the code needed to present the received video. For presenting the video, we need to obtain a visual component of the `Player` through the `getVisualComponent()` method. Then we create a video frame and add the visual component on it. The `VideoFrame` is a simple external class that extends `JFrame` and includes a panel called `JPanel1`.

The complete code for the `update()` method is:

```
public void update(ReceiveStreamEvent event) {
if (event instanceof NewReceiveStreamEvent){
  rs=event.getReceiveStream();
  DataSource rDS=rs.getDataSource();
try{
  player = Manager.createRealizedPlayer(rDS);
  Component comp=player.getVisualComponent();
  Dimension d=comp.getSize();
  vframe=new VideoFrame();
  vframe.jPanel1.add(comp);
  vframe.setSize(d);
  vframe.pack();
  vframe.setVisible(true);
  player.start();
}catch (Exception ex){
```

```
      ex.printStackTrace();
   }
   }
   }
```

The code for the `VideoFrame` class is:

```
public class VideoFrame extends JFrame {
   JPanel jPanel1=new JPanel();
   FlowLayout f1=new FlowLayout();
   FlowLayout f2=new FlowLayout();
   Public VideoFrame() {
      try{
         this.setTitle("Remote video");
         jbInit();
      }
      }catch (Exception ex){
         ex.printStackTrace();
      }
   }
   void jbInit() throws Exception {
      this.getContentPane().setLayout(f1);
      jPanel1.setLayout(flowLayout2);
      this.getContentPane().add(jPanel1,null);
   }
}
```

stopMedia()

It is almost identical to the voice case, but for the fact that when video reception stops, we need to close the frame in the GUI that we used to present the media:

```
public void stopMedia() {
   try{
      player.stop();
      player.deallocate();
      player.close();
      ss.stop();
      myProcessor.stop();
      myProcessor.deallocate();
      myProcessor.close();
      // close the video frame
      vframe.dispose();
      myVideoSessionManager.closeSession("terminated");
      myVideoSessionManager.dispose();
      }catch(Exception ex) {
```

```
            ex.printStackTrace();
        }
    }
```

11.6 Putting It All Together: The TonesTool

In the next chapter, we will build a soft-phone application. There are cases where a soft-phone application needs to play tones to the user. This typically happens in two situations:

- When an incoming call is received, the soft-phone generates an alerting signal to let the called user know a call is being received.
- When a user places a call, he or she may receive an indication that the remote party is being alerted. Such indication is commonly expressed as a ringing tone that is played to the caller.

In this section, we will build a simple component that allows playing an alerting signal or a ringing tone based on two prestored files to which the soft-phone application is supposed to have access:

- alertsignal.wav
- ringtone.wav

The example is quite straightforward; we will build a class called `TonesTool` that offers three methods:

- `void prepareTone (String filename)`
- `void playTone ()`
- `void stopTone()`

In order to build a responsive system, we have separated the preparation phase from the actual playing phase. In the preparation phase, we just create a `DataSource` object for the file to be played. This is a quite time-consuming process, and thus we should not do it in realtime when just the tone or signal needs to be played. One possible moment to invoke the `prepareTone()` method is when the soft-phone is started.

The code is straightforward.

prepareTone(String filename)

```
try{
  MediaLocator ml=new MediaLocator(filename);
  dsource=Manager.createDataSource(ml);
  player=Manager.createPlayer(dsource);
  player.addControllerListener(this);
  }catch(Exception ex){
    ex.printStackTrace();
  }
```

playTone()

```
try{
   end=false;
   player.start();
   }catch(Exception ex){
      ex.printStackTrace();
   }
```

stopTone()

```
end=true;
   notify();
   player.stop();
   }catch(Exception ex){
      ex.printStackTrace();
   }
```

There is one aspect that deserves more attention: how to play a recurrent signal. The wave files contain only a single instance of the tone or signal. Thus, we need to play it again and again. In order to create this effect, we will use the `controllerListener` interface, which allows a `Player` to post events to an object that implements such an interface. The method in the interface that we will use is called `controllerUpdate()`.

When `controllerUpdate()` is invoked, we just check if the posted event is an `EndOfMediaEvent`, which would mean that the file is finished and we need to play it again. Before invoking `start()` on the player again, we check the value of the class variable end. It is a Boolean variable that we use to control if playing needs to continue.

controllerUpdate(ControllerEvent cEvent)

```
if (cEvent instanceof EndOfMediaEvent){
   if (!finAlert) {
      player.start();
   }
}
```

11.7 Using the Components. Example 6

The three components that we developed—`VoiceTool`, `VideoTool`, and `TonesTool`—will be used by the soft-phone application that we will build in the next chapter. Still, it should be easy for readers to build a simple Java program to test these components.

For instance, in order to test the `VoiceTool` class, we could build a very simple GUI with two buttons. When a user presses the `StartMedia` button, the

GUI reads the input parameters, creates an instance of `VoiceTool`, and invokes the `startMedia()` method:

```
VoiceTool myVoiceTool=new VoiceTool();
MyVoiceTool.startMedia(destIP,destPort,recvPort,format)
```

Likewise, when the user presses the `StopMedia` button, the `stopMedia` method in `VoiceTool` is called:

```
MyVoiceTool.startMedia(destIP,destPort,recvPort,format)
```

Next we show, in Figure 11.21, what the GUI might look like.

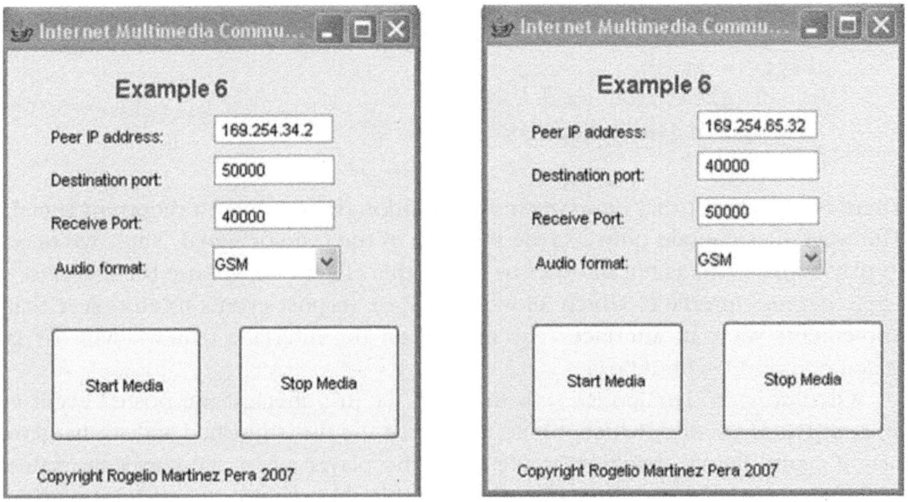

FIGURE 11.21

In order to make this example work, we should run one instance of it in each computer. The value of the destination port in computer A should be equal to the value of the receive port in computer B, and vice versa.

11.8 Summary

In this chapter, we learned how to develop simple programs that manipulate media streams. So far, we have learned how to program SIP, SDP, and media—that is, the three key ingredients that make up a multimedia application. Thus, in the next chapter, we will put these three ingredients together and cook a SIP-based voice and video soft-phone!

CHAPTER

The SIP Soft-Phone

12

As a summary of the theoretical and practical concepts learned so far, in this chapter we will build a simplified soft-phone application. We will first establish the scope of the application and its architecture. Then we will look at what the user interface looks like and what the relevant configuration parameters in the soft-phone are. The core of the soft-phone application implements a finite state machine that is analyzed in detail. Last, some ideas are given about possible further developments on the prototype soft-phone.

12.1 Scope

Building a full-fledged soft-phone application is a complex task. Actually, we would need a complete separate book in order to explain in detail how that could be done. That is not the purpose of this book. As we have stated in previous chapters, this book is about learning SIP-based multimedia communications, and, in order to accomplish this objective more effectively, we use simple programming examples. In the preceding chapters, we built some very simple examples that have allowed us to experiment with different aspects of SIP: transactions, dialogs, and so forth. We also learned how to encode and parse SDP objects, and we practiced with the media plane and the Real-Time Transport Protocol (RTP). Now is the moment to tie all these examples together in a single application that represents the summary of what we have learned. Such an application is a very simple, and limited in scope, soft-phone. The application is limited in scope for several reasons:

- It does not implement all the functionality of a SIP UA. However, it implements the functionality that is needed for a basic example of peer-to-peer voice/video call.
- We have deliberately omitted the bulk of error checking and recovery. This allows us to focus on the protocol details that otherwise would be lost among the numerous lines of code. So the code is not fully robust, and it will work just as long as it is fed with consistent user input.

- It supports only the direct-routing model, so the simplified UA that we have implemented does not need to register with a registrar. In later chapters, we will enhance it so that it can work with an external SIP server.
- It supports only two codecs for voice (GSM and G723), and two codecs for video (JPEG and H263). The caller decides what media to use: only audio or audio/video. The caller also selects just one codec for each media. The SDP negotiation is purposely very limited; it allows the called party just to accept or reject the video component, if it is present in the offer, based on the soft-phone configuration.

All in all, and in spite of the limitations, the application will be capable of setting up and releasing voice/video over IP calls, and, most importantly, it will contain the necessary elements to show the reader how a SIP soft-phone can be built and, in general, how SIP applications work.

12.2 Architecture

In Chapter 3, we described how a multimedia communications application might look from a very high-level point of view. It was made up of four main components:

- The user interface
- The multimedia application core logic
- A SIP UA
- A number of media tools

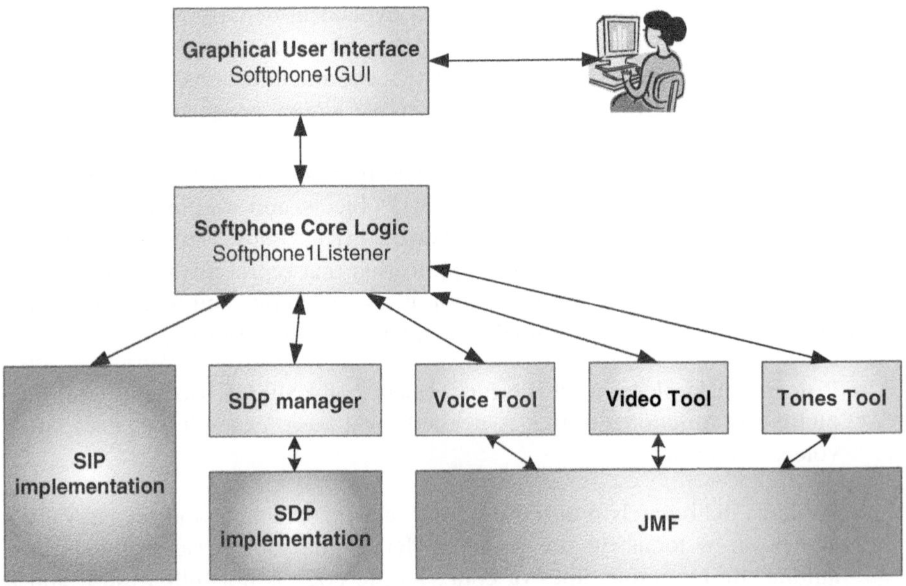

FIGURE 12.1

Our soft-phone application will have an architecture that is aligned with that generic model. The differences are that, in our example, we will have only three media tools—one for voice, another one for video, and another one for the telephony signals (tones)—and we will have a separate component to deal with the SDP parsing and coding. In Figure 12.1, the soft-phone's high-level architecture is presented.

The light boxes represent application components, and the dark boxes refer to components in the underlying JAIN SIP, JAIN SDP, or JMF implementation provided by third parties. Table 12.1 summarizes the third-party components that our application is using.

Table 12.1

Component	Version	Provider	Comments
SIP stack	1.2	NIST	Reference implementation is public domain.
SDP stack	0.x (under public review)	NIST	Reference implementation is public domain.
JMF stack	2.1.1.e	IBM and Sun	Freely downloadable under Binary Code License agreement.

12.2.1 Components

The application is running on top of the Java Virtual Machine (JVM), and comprises the following components:

- *User interface*: It is implemented by the `Softphone1GUI` class, and shows the graphical user interface that allows the user to interact with the soft-phone.
- *Soft-phone application core logic*: It represents the core logic in our application, and is implemented by the `Softphone1Listener` class. It consists of a finite state machine that receives events from `Softphone1GUI` and from the SIP stack, and coordinates the execution of all the other components.
- *SIP implementation*: In our case, it is the SIP stack from NIST, which offers a JAIN SIP 1.2 standard interface.
- *SDP manager*: It is a custom wrapper software layer that abstracts and simplifies the functionality in the JAIN SDP API for the purposes of our soft-phone application. It was built in Chapter 9.
- *SDP implementation*: It is the SDP stack from NIST, which implements the JAIN SDP interface.
- *VoiceTool*: This custom component, which we created in Chapter 11, offers a simple API for capturing/presenting the voice media streams and transmitting/receiving them over the network. It uses the services of the Java Media Framework (JMF). It supports two audio formats: GSM and G723.

- *VideoTool*: This custom component, which we created in Chapter 11, offers a simple API for capturing/presenting the video media streams and transmitting/receiving them over the network. It uses the services of the Java Media Framework (JMF). It supports two video formats: JPEG and H263.
- *TonesTool*: This custom component, which we created in Chapter 11, offers a simple API for playing tones.
- *The JMF implementation*: We will be using the JMF 2.1.1.e reference implementation from IBM and Sun. This piece of software implements the JMF Presentation API and the JMF RTP API.

12.2.2 Interfaces

Next we describe the interfaces between the different components.

Interface between Softphone1GUI and Softphone1Listener

This interface is used for three purposes:

- to let `Softphone1GUI` communicate the user interface events (e.g., user presses a button) to `Softphone1Listener`
- to let `Softphone1GUI` communicate the softphone configuration to `Softphone1Listener`
- to let `Softphone1Listener` instruct `Softphone1GUI` to render status information on the screen

For the first purpose, the custom `userInput()` method is used:

```
void userInput(int type, String destination)
```

It has two arguments:

- *type*: It is an integer value that represents the type of GUI action that has occurred.
  - type=0: user presses "Yes" button.
  - type=1: user presses "No" button.
  - type=2: user presses "Off" button.
- *destination*: It is a String that represents the destination address input by the user. It makes sense only when type=0; in other cases, its value will be ignored by `Softphone1Listener`.

For the second purpose, we use two methods invoked on `Softphone1 Listener`:

```
Sphone1Listener(Configuration conf,Sphone1GUI GUI)
void updateConfiguration(Configuration conf)
```

- the `Softphone1Listener()` constructor method that is invoked when the user presses the "On" button and triggers the creation of a new instance of `Softphone1Listener`.
- The `updateConfiguration()` method that is invoked whenever the user presses the "Apply Configuration" button in the configuration area, typically after the user changes some configuration parameters. This method causes `Softphone1Listener` to update the class variables that store the soft-phone configuration parameters.

Both methods include a `Configuration` object that encapsulates the soft-phone configuration. The `Configuration` class is described in Section 12.5, "Implementation Aspects." Additionally, the `Softphone1Listener` constructor method also includes as an argument a reference to the `Softphone1GUI` object so that, later on, `Softphone1Listener` can invoke the methods described next for the "third purpose."

For the third purpose, we use a method invoked on `Softphone1GUI`:

```
void showStatus(String text)
```

The `showStatus()` method is used to display status information (represented by the text argument) on the soft-phone user interface, such as phone is ringing, call is established, and so on.

This interface is shown in Figure 12.2.

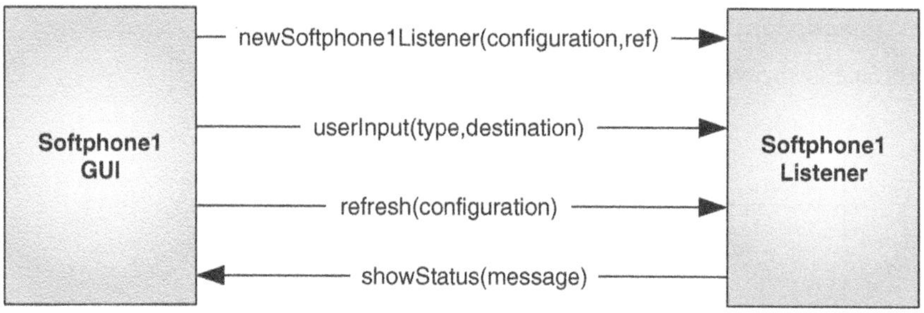

FIGURE 12.2

Interface between Softphone1Listener and the SIP Implementation

This interface complies with the JAIN SIP 1.2 specification.

Interface between Softphone1Listener and the SDPManager

This interface offers two methods:

```
byte[] createSdp(SdpInfo sdpinfo)
SdpInfo getSdp(byte[] content)
```

- `createSDP()`: Creates an SDP message based on the key relevant parameters for the application.
- `getSDP()`: Obtains the relevant SDP parameter for the application from a SDP message.

This interface is shown in Figure 12.3.

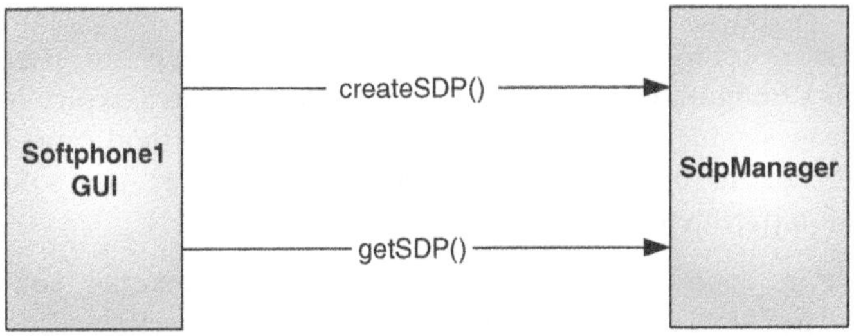

FIGURE 12.3

Interface between SDPManager and the SDP Implementation

This interface complies with the JAIN SDP specification.

Interface between Softphone1Listener and the VoiceTool

This interface is used for `Softphone1Listener` to instruct `VoiceTool` to start/stop transmission or reception of voice streams.

The following methods are used that were explained in Chapter 11:

- `int startMedia(String peerIP,int peerPort,int recvPort, int fmt)`
- `void stopMedia()`

This interface is shown in Figure 12.4.

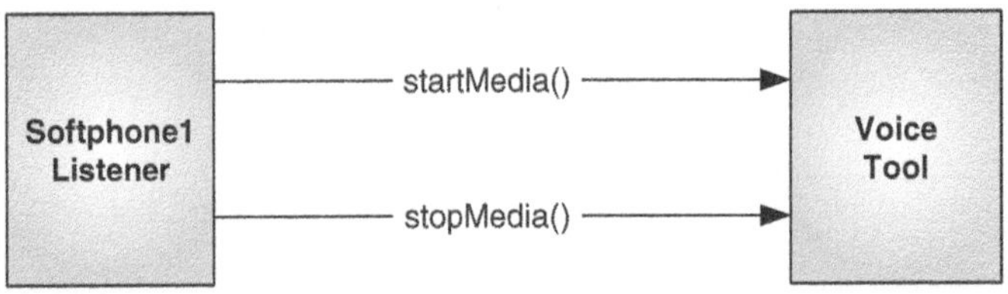

FIGURE 12.4

Interface between Softphone1Listener and the VideoTool

This interface is used by `Softphone1Listener` to instruct VideoTool to start/stop transmission or reception of voice streams.

For this purpose, the following methods are used that were explained in Chapter 11:

- `int startMedia (String peerIP,int peerPort,int recvPort, int fmt)`
- `void stopMedia()`

This interface is shown in Figure 12.5.

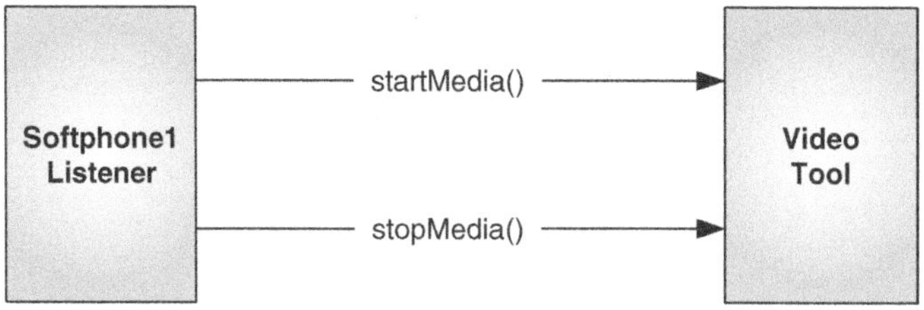

FIGURE 12.5

Interface between Softphone1Listener and the TonesTool

This interface is used for `Softphone1Listener` to instruct `TonesTool` to play a ringing tone or an alerting signal during the call-establishment phase if needed.

The following methods are used that were explained in Chapter 11:

- `void prepareTone (String filename)`
- `void playTone ()`
- `void stopTone()`

As a summary of the architecture topic, Figure 12.6 shows the different components in our application and the interfaces between them.

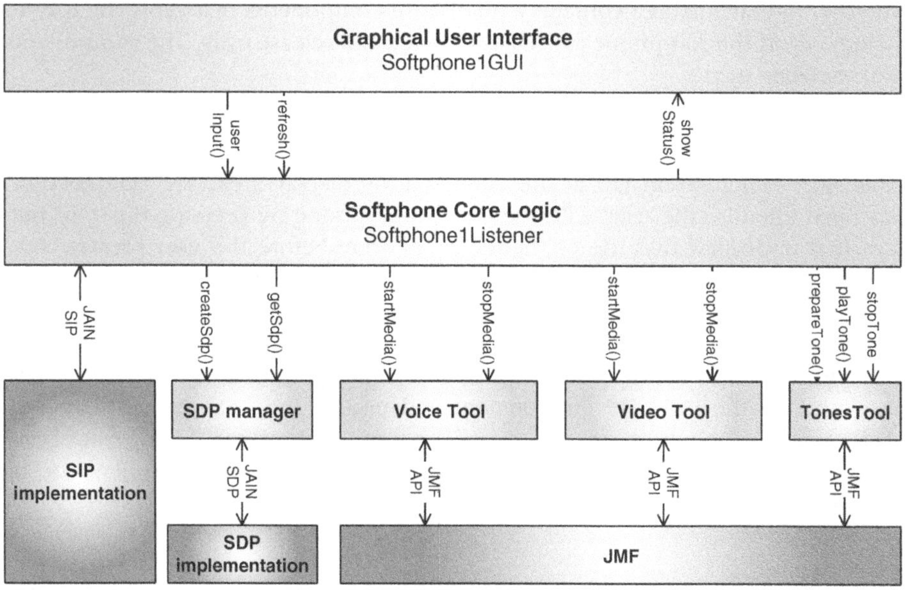

FIGURE 12.6

12.3 User Interface and Configuration

Our soft-phone offers a very simple graphical interface. It consists of two differentiated areas: the user interaction area and the configuration/display area. This is depicted in Figure 12.7.

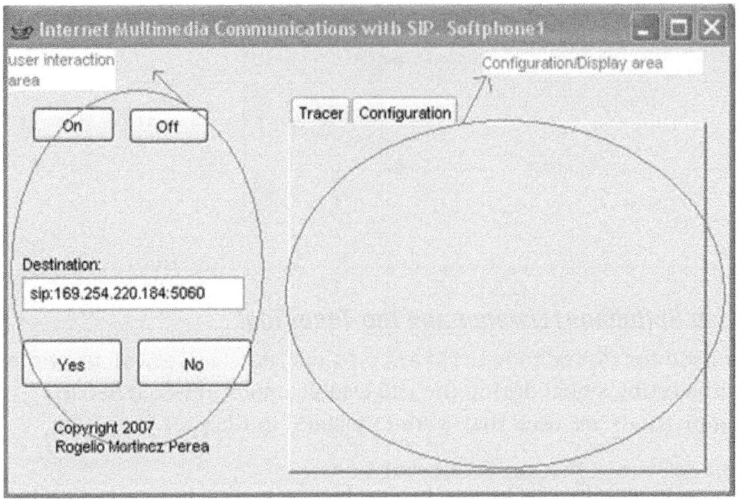

FIGURE 12.7

12.3.1 User Interaction Area

The user interaction area contains a number of components that allow the user to switch on/off the soft-phone as well as to place and release calls. The components are described next.

"On" Button

Once the configuration tab in the configuration/display area (see next section) has been filled in, the user will "switch on" the phone by pressing the "On" button. It is important that the configuration is done before the user presses "On," otherwise the SIP initialization will fail.

Pressing the "On" button will cause `Softphone1GUI` to invoke the constructor method for `SipListener`. This method will retrieve the machine's IP address and show it in the GUI (in the configuration tab). The execution of this method will also initialize the JAIN SIP environment and update the `Softphone1Listener` class variables that store the configuration parameters. The soft-phone automatically enters into the IDLE state, and is therefore ready to generate or receive calls.

"Off" Button

If the user presses the "Off" button, the `close()` method is invoked on `Softphone11Listener`. This method contains the code necessary to shut down the SIP environment. If there is an ongoing call and the user wants to switch off the phone, given that our soft-phone does not include all the code for error checking and recovery, we recommend users to first release the call by pressing the "No" button before pressing the "Off" button.

Info Label

Below the "On" and "Off" buttons, there is an information panel that will appear as soon as the phone is started ("On" button pressed). This panel will give us information on the call state: idle, alerting, ringing, established. `Phone1Listener` will call the `showInfo()` method on the `Softphone1GUI` in order to write specific text on the Info label.

Destination Text Field

This text field must be filled in by the user; it represents the identity of the desired recipient of the call. Because we are using direct routing in this example, the address will have the format:

sip:IPaddress:port or
sip:userinfo@ IPaddress:port

"Yes" Button

This button is used in two scenarios:

- to initiate a new call
- to accept an incoming call

Pressing the "Yes" button will cause `Softphone1GUI` to invoke the `userInput()` method with type=YES on `Softphone1Listener`.

"No" Button

It is used in the following scenarios:

- to reject an incoming call
- to cancel an already-initiated but not-yet-established call
- to release an already-established call

Pressing the "No" button will cause `Softphone1GUI` to invoke the `userInput()` method with type=NO on `Softphone1Listener`.

12.3.2 Configuration/Display Area

The configuration/display area is located at the rightmost part of the GUI. It consists of a `JTabbedPane` with two tabs. The first tab is the tracer display, where the signaling messages sent or received by the soft-phone will be shown in realtime. This is depicted in Figure 12.8.

The other tab contains the configuration area (shown in Figure 12.9), which is itself divided into two parts. The topmost half is the user configuration area. It includes a number of configuration parameters related to the user or to the UA. These parameters need to be filled in before the soft-phone is started (i.e., before

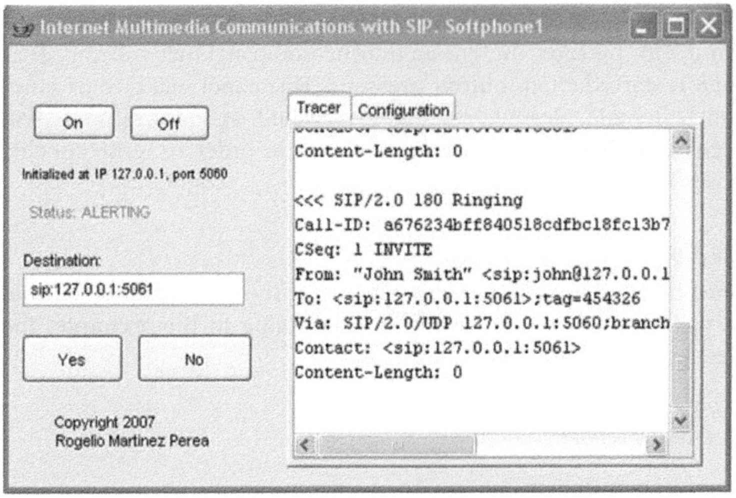

FIGURE 12.8

"On" is pressed). Once the phone has been started, these parameters cannot be changed. These parameters are:

- *SIP UDP port*: That is the port that our application will use to send and receive the SIP messages.[1] The default value for SIP is 5060.
- *User identity*: Given that, in this example, we are using the direct-routing mode (no proxies), the user identity contains the IP address of the machine where the soft-phone is running. This is automatically filled in by the application when the user presses the "On" button. The user will just need to enter the userinfo part of the identity.

The bottom most half of the configuration tab contains media-related parameters. These can be changed at any time. In order for the changes to take effect, we need to press the button "Apply media configuration." The changes will be effective from the next placed or received call. These parameters are:

- *User name*: It represents the name that will appear in the display-name field of the From header for outgoing calls from this soft-phone.
- *Voice RTP port*: This is the port where our application expects to receive the voice RTP packets.[2] This port will appear in the voice media line in SDP offers sent by the soft-phone.
- *Video RTP port*: This is the port where our application expects to receive the video RTP packets. This is the port that will appear in the video media line in SDP offers sent by the soft-phone.

[1] It is a UDP port because our soft-phone application will use only UDP as transport for the SIP signaling.

[2] Following the recommendation in [RFC 3550], the port for RTCP packets that we will be using is RTP port +1, so there is no need to explicitly specify it.

- *Media*: Two options are possible—audio only or audio plus video. The value of this configuration parameter has two effects:
  - When our soft-phone originates a call, the SDP offer will contain just audio or audio/video, depending on the configuration parameter.
  - When our soft-phone receives a call containing audio and video, it will reject the video component if the media configuration parameter is set to audio only.
- *Voice codecs*: Two options are given—GSM or G723. It is either one or the other. The soft-phone will include only one codec in the SDP offer.
- *Video codecs*: Two options are given—JPEG or H263. It is either one or the other. The soft-phone will include only one codec in the SDP offer.

The configuration tab of our soft-phone is shown in Figure 12.9.

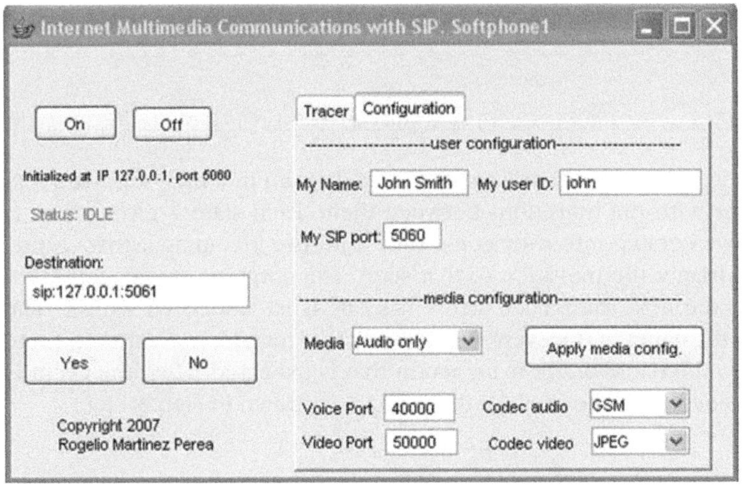

FIGURE 12.9

12.4 State Model

The class `Softphone1Listener` is the core component in the system. It receives network events from the `SipProvider`, and method calls from the GUI.[3] It can invoke methods on the `SipProvider`, the GUI, the `SdpManager`, or the media tools. It is the central intelligence point where the soft-phone logic is implemented. This is depicted in Figure 12.10.

The way `Softphone1Listener` implements the core logic is through a finite state machine. It defines a number of states and the events (implemented as Java events or method calls) that cause a transition from one state to another.

[3]As was explained in previous sections, there is also a scenario in which `Softphone1Listener` receives a method call from the `VideoTool` when a video component in detected.

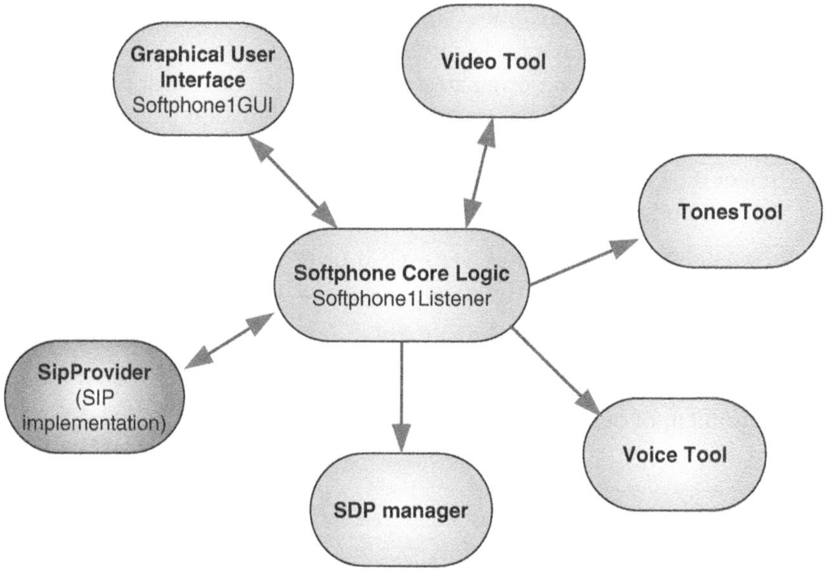

FIGURE 12.10

In order to show the state model, we will use a diagram in which states are represented together with the transitions between them. Each state is given a name, and shows arrows coming into it or going out of it. The incoming arrows represent events that trigger the transition to that state. The outgoing arrows represent the transition to the next state. Each arrow has one label associated with it. The label represents the name of the event that triggers that transition. Next to it, there is, in some cases, the name of the main action that is executed when the event is triggered. This general scheme used for the diagram is shown in Figure 12.11.

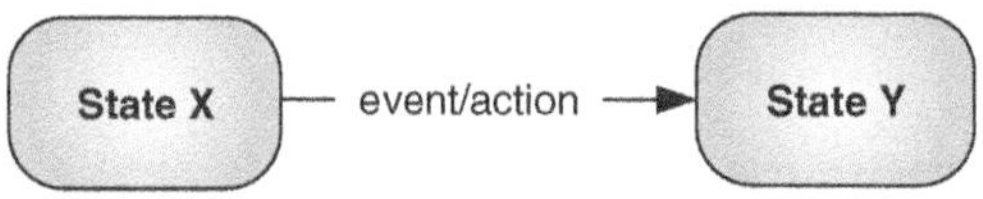

FIGURE 12.11

Figure 12.12 shows the soft-phone state model. As we said at the beginning of this chapter, this application is very simplified. This is also reflected in the simplicity of the state model that we are using.

Next is a description of the different states and the events and actions associated with them. For each state, we highlight which are the events that cause the soft-phone to reach that state (incoming events), and which are the events that cause the soft-phone to leave that state (outgoing events).

12.4.1 IDLE State

This is the state the soft-phone enters when it is switched on ("On" button is pressed). It represents absence of active calls. The phone is ready to originate or

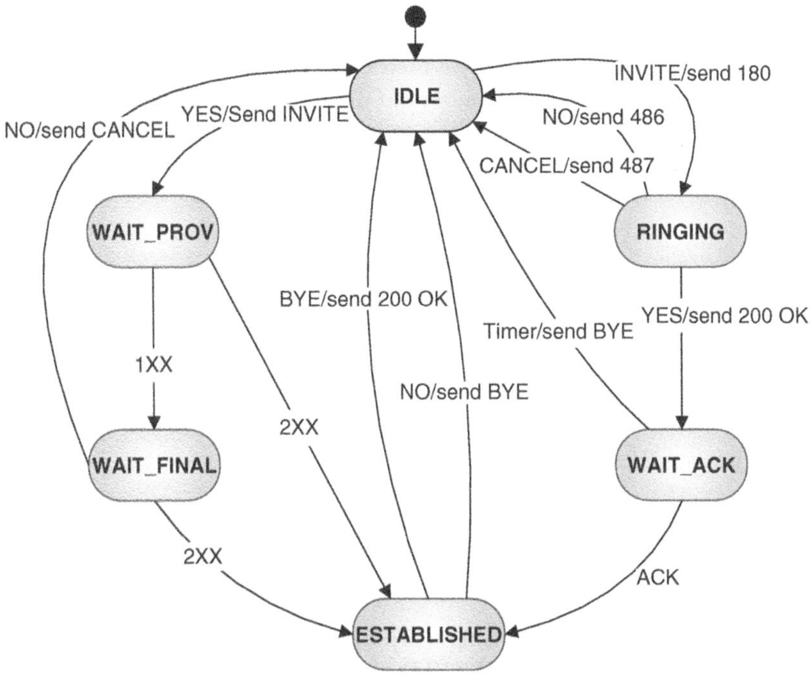

FIGURE 12.12

receive calls. Whenever calls are completed, the phone comes back to the IDLE state.

Incoming Events

- The calling user presses "No" when the call is proceeding, causing a CANCEL to be issued. Please note that this implies that there may be a residual pending CANCEL transaction for a small amount of time while in IDLE state. This fact does not interfere with the correct working of the soft-phone.[4]
- The called user presses "No" in order to reject an incoming call.
- Timer for the ACK expires, which causes the application to release the session.
- The calling or called user initiates a call release (user presses "No," resulting in the sending of a BYE) or receives a call release (receive a BYE). Please note that this implies that there may be a residual pending CANCEL transaction for a small amount of time while in IDLE state. This fact does not interfere with the correct working of the soft-phone.

[4]Another approach to deal with this situation might be to define a new state before reaching IDLE, which is left only if 200 OK to CANCEL is received. This would mean that in faulty transmission situations, it might take some time for the user to be able to initiate a new call. For the sake of this leaning exercise, we will not define such a state.

Outgoing Events

- The user presses the "Yes" button, which causes the phone to send out an INVITE message. The soft-phone moves to the WAIT_PROV state.
- An INVITE request is received, which causes the soft-phone to send back a 180 Ringing provisional response. The soft-phone moves to the RINGING state.

12.4.2 WAIT_PROV State (in Originator)

This state is entered when the phone sends an INVITE, and is not left until it receives a provisional or final response.

Incoming Events

- The user presses "Yes" when in IDLE state.

Outgoing Events

- A provisional response is received, in which case a transition to the WAIT_FINAL state occurs.
- A final response is received, causing the phone to send an ACK request. The soft-phone transits to the ESTABLISHED state, and it will start transmitting and receiving media.
- The user presses the "No" button, and a CANCEL request is generated. The soft-phone goes to IDLE.

12.4.3 WAIT_FINAL State (in Originator)

In this state, a provisional response to an INVITE has been received, and the phone is waiting for the final response.

Incoming Events

- A provisional response is received. The soft-phone state does not change.

Outgoing Events

- A final response is received, which causes the phone to send back an ACK request. The soft-phone transits to the ESTABLISHED state, and it will start transmitting and receiving media.
- The user presses the "No" button, and a CANCEL request is generated. The soft-phone goes to IDLE.

12.4.4 ESTABLISHED State (in Both Originator and Recipient)

This state represents the situation where the call is active and the session fully established between the two peers.

Incoming Events

- A final response is received, causing an ACK message to be sent.
- An ACK request is received.

Outgoing Events

- The calling or the called user initiates a session release or receives a request to release the session. The soft-phone moves to IDLE.

12.4.5 RINGING State (in Recipient)

This is the state produced when a call has been received and a 180 provisional response has been generated, but the call has not yet been accepted.

Incoming Events

- An INVITE is received, and a provisional response is generated.

Outgoing Events

- The called user accepts the call and generates a 200 OK. The soft-phone transits to WAIT_ACK.
- The called user rejects the call and generates a 486 final response. The soft-phone moves back to IDLE.
- A CANCEL request is received for the ongoing transaction. The transaction is terminated with a 487 response. The soft-phone moves back to IDLE.

12.4.6 WAIT_ACK State (in Recipient)

This state represents the situation where a call has been accepted, but the ACK message has not yet been received.

Incoming events

- The called user accepts the call and generates a 200 OK.

Outgoing events

- An ACK request is received. The soft-phone moves to ESTABLISHED.
- The ACK timer expires, which causes a BYE to be sent and a transition to IDLE state.

12.5 Implementation Aspects

The implementation of the state model described in the previous section is straightforward because it mainly reuses the code that we already described in previous chapters. There are, though, some new implementation aspects, not tackled so far, which we will highlight next.

12.5.1 Soft-phone Configuration

The soft-phone configuration is entered by the user in the configuration area of the user interface. At phone start-up, or whenever the user presses the "Apply Configuration" button, the configuration parameters are conveyed, as a `Configuration` object to `Softphone1Listener` in the `userInput()` or `update-Configuration()` methods.

The `Configuration` class is just a data structure to hold the parameters entered by the user:

```
public class Configuration {
   int sipPort=5060;
   String name="";
   String userID="";
   int audioPort=40000;
   int videoPort=50000;
   int audioCodec=3;
   int videoCodec=26;
   public Configuration() {}
   public void setSipPort(int sp) { sipPort=sp;}
   public void setName(String nm) {name=nm;}
   public void setUserID(String UID) {userID=UID;}
   public void setAudioPort(int AP) {audioPort=AP;}
   public void setVideoPort(int VP) {videoPort=VP;}
   public void setAudioCodec(int AC) {audioCodec=AC;}
   public void setVideoCodec(int VC) {videoCodec=VC;}

   public int getSipPort() {return sipPort;}
   public String getName() {return name;}
   public String getUserID() {return userID;}
   public int getAudioPort() {return audioPort;}
   public int getVideoPort() {return videoPort;}
   public int getAudioCodec () {return audioCodec;}
   public int getVideoCodec () {return videoCodec;}
}
```

A situation where the media configured by the user is "Audio only" is represented by giving the `videoPort` field in the `Configuration` object a value of −1.

On the other hand, the configuration parameters are stored in `Softphone1 Listener` in the following class variables:

```
private int myPort; // this represents the SIP UDP port
private int myAudioPort;
private int myVideoPort;
private int myAudioCodec;
private int myVideoCodec;
```

Again, if `myVideoPort=-1`, it means that the user has configured "Audio only" media.

12.5.2 Treatment of CANCEL Requests

When the calling user presses the "No" button while in the WAIT_FINAL state, his or her soft-phone generates a CANCEL request. JAIN SIP offers the `createCancel()` method in order to create a CANCEL request from the original client transaction that the user wants to cancel. Once the CANCEL has been created, we will need to get a new client transaction through which we will send the CANCEL request:

```
Request myCancelRequest = myaClientTransaction.createCancel();
ClientTransaction myCancelClientTransaction =
  mySipProvider.getNewClientTransaction(myCancelRequest);
myCancelClientTransaction.sendRequest();
```

The called user will receive the CANCEL request while in the RINGING state. At that point, his or her phone must terminate the INVITE transaction with a 487 (Request terminated) response, after which it must respond to the CANCEL transaction itself with a 200 OK:

```
ServerTransaction myCancelServerTransaction=
  requestReceivedEvent.getServerTransaction();
Request originalRequest=myServerTransaction.getRequest();
Response myResponse=
  myMessageFactory.createResponse(487,originalRequest);
myServerTransaction.sendResponse(myResponse);
Response myCancelResponse=
  myMessageFactory.createResponse(200,myRequest);
myCancelServerTransaction.sendResponse(myCancelResponse);
```

12.5.3 Tag Calculation and Management

Tags in the From and the To header, together with the CallID, are used to identify a SIP dialog. The tag in the From header is set by the calling UA, and provides only half of the dialog identification. The other half is set by the recipient of the request by including a tag in the To header of provisional and successful final responses.[5] RFC 3261 states that UAs need to compute the tag in such a way that it is globally unique and cryptographically with at least 32 bits of randomness. The actual algorithm for generating a tag is implementation-specific.

In previous examples, we always used the same tags in the From and To header. Readers may want to enhance their soft-phone implementation by generating truly random tags. A possible option is to use the `SecureRandom` class provided in the

---

[5] The tag in the To header, set by the recipient, helps the originating UA to disambiguate the multiple dialogs established from a single request in those cases where there is a forking proxy between calling and called parties.

standard java. security package. This class provides a cryptographically strong pseudo-random number generator. The following code generates a set of random bytes.

```
numBytes == 4; //adequate for the From/To tag;
byte[] rand = new byte[numBytes];
SecureRandom random = SecureRandom.getInstance("SHA1PRNG");
random.nextBytes(bytes);
```

In order to use it in the From or To header we would need to convert the byte array into a string that is safe to use in SIP headers. We could, for instance, use Base64 encoding. There are a number of open source Base64 encoders that readers may use.

12.5.4 Error Conditions and Timeouts

As we said at the beginning of this chapter, our soft-phone application is very simplified. This is also reflected in the simplicity of the state model that we are using. This call model is not catering for all the possible error conditions and timeout situations. More specifically, this state model does not respond to timeout events in the transaction layer. This means that when timers in the transaction layer expire, the transaction is terminated, but the application takes no specific action.

12.5.5 Retransmissions

The state model also reflects the situation that the application is not taking care of any message retransmission whatsoever. As was explained in Chapter 7, the transaction sublayer takes care of retransmissions at that level. End-to-end retransmissions of INVITE, 200 OK, and ACK are handled by the JAIN SIP dialog implementation as corresponds to the fact that the SipStack property RETRANSMISSON_FILTER is set to ON.[6] Regarding the INVITE transaction, there is, though, one aspect not specifically addressed by the JAIN SIP spec that the application therefore needs to implement. This refers to the situation when a UAS keeps sending retransmissions of the 200 OK response to an INVITE, but it does not receive any ACK. RFC 3261 states that the UAS core (in our case, it will be the dialog object) keeps retransmitting the 200 OK responses for 64*T1[7] seconds, after which, if no ACK was received, the UAS needs to terminate the session by sending a BYE. This particular behavior is implemented in the state model by the explicit consideration of state WAIT_ACK and its associated timer.

The following code shows how this timeout situation is implemented in our application.

---

[6] RETRANSMISSION_FILTER has a default value of ON. Let us recall that in this application, we are using all default values of SipStack properties. The only exception is the SipStack name.

[7] T1 represents the round-trip delay (RTT) and is typically assumed to be 500 ms.

First we create a class in the declaration section of `Softphone1Listener` that extends the abstract class `TimerTask`. In its `run()` method, we include all the code that needs to be executed when the timer expires:

```
class MyTimerClass extends TimerTask {
   Softphone1Listener myListener;
   public void MyTimerTask (Softphone1Listener myListener){
      this.myListener=myListener;
   }
   public void run() {
      Request myBye=myListener.myDialog.createRequest("BYE");
      myBye.addHeader(myListener.myContactHeader);
      myListener.myClientTransaction=
      myListener.mySipProvider.getNewClientTransaction(myBye);
      myListener.myDialog.sendRequest(myListener.myClientTransaction);
   }
}
```

In addition to defining this class, we also need to start the timer when a transition occurs from the RINGING state to the WAIT_ACK state. That is, we need to add the following code if the YES button is pressed when in the RINGING state:

```
new Timer().schedule(new MyTimerTask(this),60000);
```

12.5.6 Call Management and Transactions

Another important assumption in the soft-phone implementation is the fact that it will not support more than one simultaneous call. During the process of call management, there will be one main transaction (either INVITE or BYE) that refers to the existing call. There may also be a parallel CANCEL transaction in case the user has tried to abort the call before it is established. In those cases where the user releases a call and immediately initiates another one, it may happen, if transport conditions are not good, that the new INVITE transaction starts before the BYE transaction is terminated (200 OK received). The soft-phone implementation will not be aware of those situations—it will just let the transaction sublayer decide when the transaction needs to be finalized. From the application point of view, the only transaction to worry about is the new one.

So we will define the following object variables at class level to refer to the main transaction at every moment in time:

- `myClientTransaction`: It represents the main non-CANCEL client transaction at any moment in time.
- `myServerTransaction`: It represents the main non-CANCEL server transaction at any moment in time.

We will also use the following variables to represent the parallel CANCEL transaction, if one exists:

- `myCancelClientTransaction`
- `myCancelServerTransaction`

12.5.7 Reception of 486 Busy Here and Generation of ACK

Another aspect in our soft-phone application that is different from the practices done so far in the book is the reception of 4XX responses, such as the 486 (Busy Here) response that the soft-phone will receive if the called party is busy or rejects the incoming call. When such a response is received, the underlying client transaction implementation will automatically generate an ACK request, therefore our application does not need to bother with that aspect.

12.5.8 SDP Handling and Media Tool Utilization

[RFC 3264] describes the SDP offer/answer model. Among other things, it describes possible options to activate the media reception and transmission at the different steps in the model. The approach that we will be taking is based on the following considerations:

1. The calling party sends the SDP offer.
2. The called party receives the offer and generates an answer. As soon as the SDP answer is sent, the answerer commences media transmission and starts listening on the receive ports specified in the SDP answer.
3. When the offerer receives the SDP answer, it starts listening on the receive ports that were specified in the SDP offer; and commences media transmission.

This is depicted in Figure 12.13.

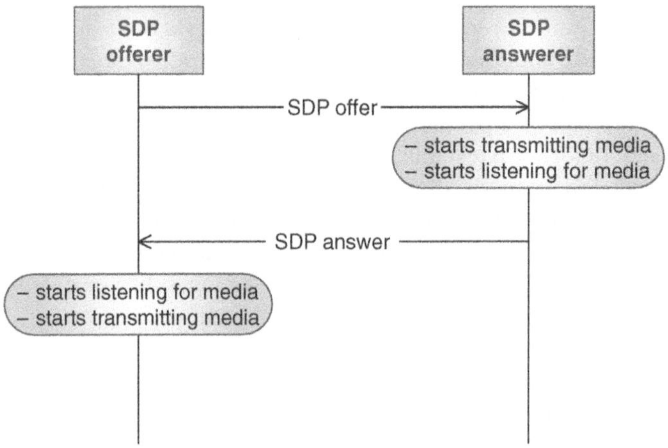

FIGURE 12.13

Additionally, we make some assumptions[8] as to the way the SDP is configured and manipulated by the soft-phone. These assumptions allow us to simplify the code and to focus on the fundamental concepts. Next we describe in detail the different aspects of SDP and media handling. At each step, we will highlight the assumptions that we have made.

[8] See the last section in Chapter 9 to see the list of assumptions regarding SDP handling.

In order to manipulate the SDP, we will use the `SdpManager` class, which was introduced in Chapter 9. Likewise, in order to handle the media, the classes `VoiceTool` and `VideoTool`, which were described in Chapter 11, will be utilized.

In any case, in order not to complicate the soft-phone implementation, we do not include code for the cases where the execution of `startMedia()` fails. It is left as an exercise to the reader to add the necessary code that causes the soft-phone to move to IDLE if these methods fail.

Sending the SDP Offer

In order to build the SDP offer, our soft-phone will check the media configuration parameters. If the configured media is audio only, then the SDP will contain only an audio m-line. If, on the other hand, it is audio and video, the SDP will contain an audio m-line and a video m-line.

The offered codecs are also taken from the configuration parameters: `myAudioCodec` and `myVideoCodec`. These were introduced by the user in the soft-phone configuration area, and conveyed to `Softphone1Listener` in a `Configuration` object. The SDP will contain only one codec per media.

The ports for audio and video are taken from the configuration parameters: `myAudioPort` and `myVideoPort`. These were introduced by the user in the soft-phone configuration area:

```
offerInfo=new SdpInfo();
offerInfo.setIpAddress(myIP);
offerInfo.setAudioPort(myAudioPort);
offerInfo.setAudioFormat(myAudioCodec);
offerInfo.setVideoPort(myVideoPort);
offerInfo.setVideoFormat=(myVideoCodec);
ContentTypeHeader contentTypeHeader=
  myHeaderFactory.createContentTypeHeader("application,""sdp");
byte[] content=mySdpManager.createSdp(offerInfo);
myRequest.setContent(content,contentTypeHeader);
```

If the video component is not desired, `vPort` and `vformat` are set to −1, causing the `SdpManager` to not include the video m1000-line in the SDP.

Receiving the SDP Offer

When an INVITE is received that contains an SDP offer, the UA will get the SDP content and obtain the relevant parameters (ports and codecs):

```
byte[] cont=(byte[]) myRequest.getContent();
offerInfo=mySdpManager.getSdp(cont);
```

Next we build the SDP answer with the following parameters:

- The audio port in the answer is the configured port for audio (`myAudioPort`).
- The audio format in the answer is the same as the audio format in the offer.
- If the offer does not contain a video m-line, then the answer will not contain it either (`vport=-1`).

- If the offer contains video, but the recipient UA wants only audio (configured `myVideoPort=-1`), then the video component is rejected (`vport=0`):
-

```
answerInfo.setIpAddress(myIP);
answerInfo.setAudioPort(myAudioPort);
answerInfo.setAudioFormat(offerInfo.getAudioFormat());
if (offerInfo.getVideoPort()==-1) {
  answerInfo.setVideoPort(-1);
}
else if (myVideoPort==-1) {
  answerInfo.setVideoPort(0);
  answerInfo.setVideoFormat(offerInfo.getVideoFormat());
}
else {
  answerInfo.setVideoPort(myVideoPort);
  answerInfo.setVideoFormat(offerInfo.getVideoFormat());
}
```

Sending the SDP Answer

When the called party accepts the call, he or she issues a 200 OK that contains the SDP answer previously calculated. It will also start listening for media and will start transmitting media:

```
ContentTypeHeader contentTypeHeader=
myHeaderFactory.createContentTypeHeader("application,""sdp");
byte[] content=mySdpManager.createSdp(answerInfo);
myResponse.setContent(content,contentTypeHeader);
myVoiceTool.startMedia(offerInfo.getIpAddress(),offerInfo.
  getAudioPort(),answerInfo.
   getAudioPort(),offerInfo.getAudioFormat());
if (answerInfo.getVideoPort()>0) {
   myVideoTool.startMedia(offerInfo.getIpAddress(),offer
     Info.getVideoPort(),
      answerInfo.getVideoPort(),offerInfo.getVideoFormat());
}
```

Receiving the SDP Answer

When the calling party receives the 200 OK, it will start listening on the receive ports for the offered media. It will also extract the SDP answer and will start transmission of media toward the address present in the answer:

```
byte[] cont=(byte[]) myResponse.getContent();
answerInfo=mySdpManager.getSdp(cont);
myVoiceTool.startMedia(answerInfo.getIpAddress(),answerInfo.
  getAudioPort(),offerInfo
   .getAudioPort(),answerInfo.getAudioFormat());
```

```
if (answerInfo.getVideoPort()>0) {
   myVideoTool.startMedia(answerInfo.getIpAddress(),answer
     Info.getVideoPort(),
      offerInfo.getVideoPort(), answerInfo.getVideoFormat());
}
```

12.5.9 Session Termination

We also need, in our soft-phone implementation, to stop media transmission and reception as soon as a BYE request is sent or received.

If the soft-phone is in established state and it receives a BYE request, then we need to add the following code:

```
myVoiceTool.stopMedia();
if (answerInfo.getVideoPort()>0) {
   myVideoTool.stopMedia();
}
```

Likewise, when the soft-phone is in established state and the user presses "No," the soft-phone will send a BYE request. In addition to that, we need to stop the media session. So we must again include the same code as before:

```
myVoiceTool.stopMedia();
if (answerInfo.getVideoPort()>0) {
   myVideoTool.stopMedia();
}
```

12.5.10 Playing Tones and Signals

Our soft-phone will need to play an alerting signal when an INVITE is received, or play a ringing tone when it receives a 180 Ringing provisional answer. For that purpose, we will use the `TonesTool` class, which we built in Chapter 11.

As soon as the soft-phone is started, we will create two instances of `TonesTool`: one for the alerting signal, and the other for the ringing tone. Additionally, we will prepare the `DataSource` objects by calling the `prepare-Tone()` method, passing as an argument a string that represents the location of the file containing the audio tone.

Thus, in the `Softphone1Listener's` constructor method, we will include:

```
myAlertTool=new TonesTool();
myRingTool=new TonesTool();
myAlertTool.prepareTone("file://c:\\alert.wav");
myRingTool.prepareTone("file://c:\\ring.wav");
```

The alert.wav and ring.wav files MUST be present in the c:\\ root directory, otherwise the program execution will fail.

The alerting signal will be played by the called party,s soft-phone when an INVITE is received in IDLE state:

```
myAlertTool.playTone();
```

In order to stop the alerting signal, we will include the following code:

```
myAlertTool.stopTone();
```

in the following situations:

- Called party accepts an incoming call by pressing "Yes" in RINGING state.
- Called party rejects an incoming call by pressing "No" in RINGING state.
- Called party receives a CANCEL request when in RINGING state.

The ringing signal will be played by the calling party's soft-phone when a 180 provisional response is received in either the WAIT_PROV or WAIT_FINAL states:

```
myRingTool.playTone();
```

In order to stop the ringing signal, we will include the following code:

```
myRingTool.stopTone();
```

in the following situations:

- A 200 OK is received in the WAIT_PROV or WAIT_FINAL states.
- The calling party presses "No" when in WAIT_FINAL state.
- The calling party receives a 603 response message because the call is declined by the called party.

12.5.11 Running the Code

The full code for the application can be downloaded from the book's web page (see Appendix A).

Figure 12.14 shows a snapshot of two communicating user agents. In this case, both user agents are running in the same machine, but with different ports. Although this is an approach that allows us to look at the signaling exchanges, it does not allow us to experience the media side. For a full-fledged, end-to-end scenario also including the media, two PCs are needed, one for each user agent.

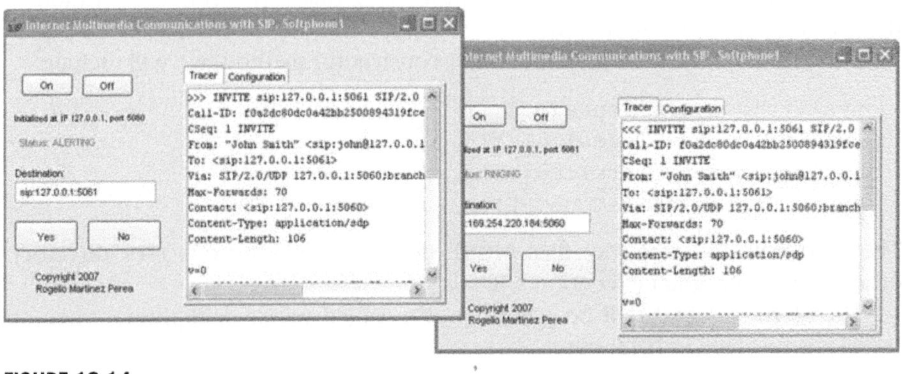

FIGURE 12.14

12.6 Summary

In this chapter, we have put into practice the concepts learned so far about SIP, SDP, and RTP. The soft-phone that we built was not registered with a registrar server, and thus we needed to know the called party's IP address beforehand. That is not a practical scenario. In a real scenario, there are SIP servers that at least handle the user location and routing aspects. Our target is to build a realistic scenario, so, in the next chapter, we will examine in detail the SIP proxy behavior, and build a proxy and a registrar that can work in conjunction with our soft-phone.

CHAPTER

13 SIP Proxies

In Chapter 4, we presented the different SIP entities. SIP proxies were briefly described there. In the present chapter, we will explain a bit more in detail how SIP proxies work. The chapter starts by defining what a SIP proxy is, and by explaining its crucial role in the routing of SIP messages in the SIP architecture.

Then we classify the mode of behavior of SIP proxies into stateless and stateful. A detailed explanation of the proxy behavior is then presented. This is particularly useful for the last part of this chapter, in which we will show some practical examples of how a very much simplified SIP proxy might be implemented using JAIN SIP.

13.1 What Is a SIP Proxy?

SIP proxies are defined in the base SIP spec [RFC 3261]. A SIP proxy server is an intermediary entity that helps route SIP requests to UASs, and SIP responses to UACs. There may be several SIP proxies between a UAC and a UAS. Responses traverse the same set of proxies as the requests, but in reverse order. This is shown in Figure 13.1.

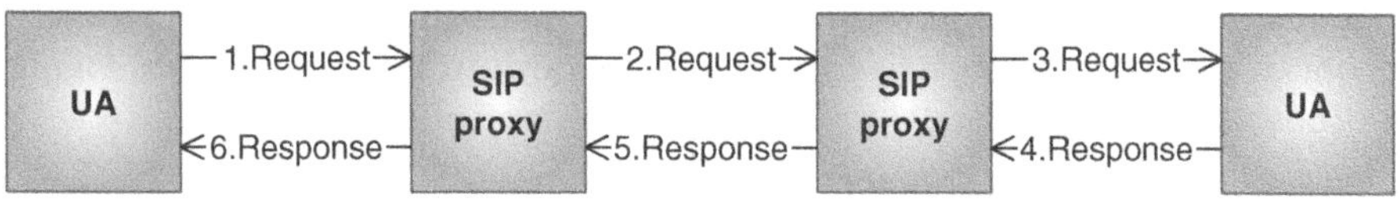

FIGURE 13.1

13.1.1 Sip Routing

SIP proxies typically make routing decisions by changing the Request-URI. In a simplified model, a proxy receives a request, modifies the Request-URI according to some rules, and then forwards the request to the new destination URI.

SIP proxies may modify specific header fields in a request before forwarding it.

An important case of proxy utilization is an inbound proxy. An inbound proxy, as was explained in Chapter 4, is the entity that receives requests addressed for a particular domain, queries a location service, replaces the Request-URI with the contact address retrieved from the location service, and forwards the call to the UAS. This scenario is shown in Figure 13.2. Proxies can also help UACs to route outgoing requests, in which case they are referred to as outbound proxies.

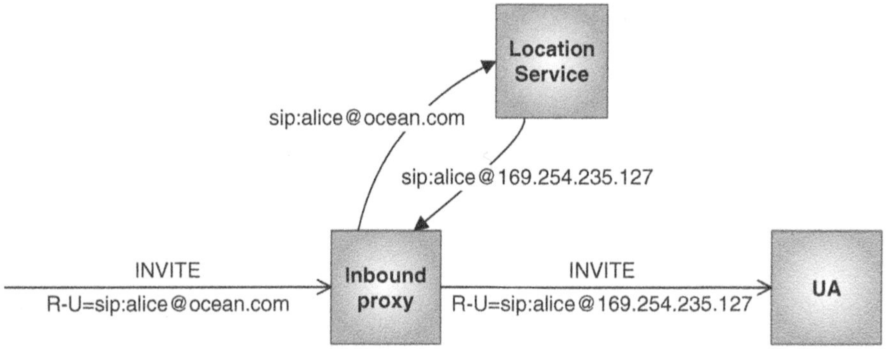

FIGURE 13.2

Outbound and inbound proxies are typically implemented together in the same piece of equipment alongside the registrar for the corresponding domain. Such an aggregated entity is sometimes informally referred to as the SIP server for the particular domain.

Proxies are not limited to outbound or inbound types. In the path from UAC to UAS, an arbitrary number of proxies may be traversed, as is shown in Figure 13.3.

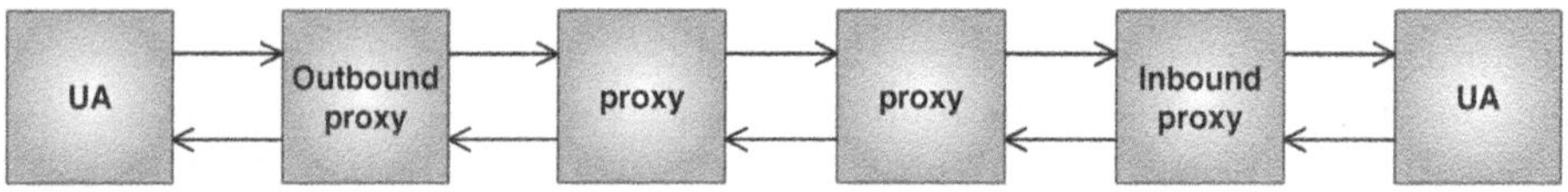

FIGURE 13.3

In addition to making routing decisions, proxies may also implement a limited amount of service logic, such as call barring, call forwarding, and so forth. Figure 13.4 shows an example of call-forwarding service implemented by a SIP proxy.

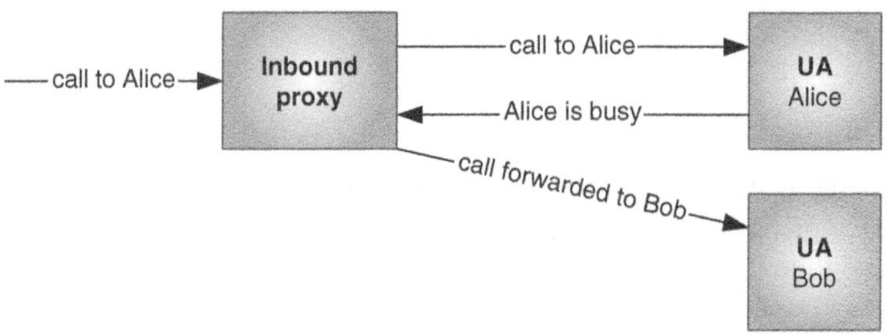

FIGURE 13.4

More-complex service logic requires that B2BUAs are used. For instance, SIP applications that require SIP dialog manipulation (e.g., terminate a confirmed dialog, generate new dialogs, change parameters of the session, initiate calls from the application server, and so on) cannot be implemented using a SIP proxy; they require B2BUA functionality. Let us imagine, for example, that we want to offer a prepaid service. Such a service must monitor the call for its complete duration, and check, in realtime, if there is enough credit for it. Once the call has started, if the user runs out of credit, the prepaid server would need to terminate the session—that is, it should send a BYE request. A proxy cannot generate new requests within a confirmed dialog, so this would need to be implemented with a B2BUA.

Proxies are devoted mainly to routing, whereas the main role of B2BUAs is to deliver network-based services.

13.1.2 Proxy Types

We have already classified proxies into inbound and outbound according to the functions they fulfill. Another classification of SIP proxies is based on the amount of state information that the proxy stores and uses to perform its functions. Following such a categorization, SIP proxies can be split into transaction stateful and transaction stateless proxies. This categorization refers, in fact, to the roles that a proxy can perform, rather than to proxies themselves. So the same proxy may play a stateful role in some cases (e.g., when dealing with some particular requests), but behave like a stateless proxy in other situations.

13.2 Transaction Stateful Proxies

A transaction stateful proxy, also called stateful proxy in short, has a server transaction associated with one or more client transactions. The service logic that maintains the association between server transaction and client transactions is called the proxy core.

In a very simple scenario, a request is received through the server transaction, processed by the proxy core (which might change the Request-URI), and then forwarded through a client transaction. Likewise, responses would be received by the client transaction, passed to the proxy core, and sent back through the server transaction. This is shown in Figure 13.5.

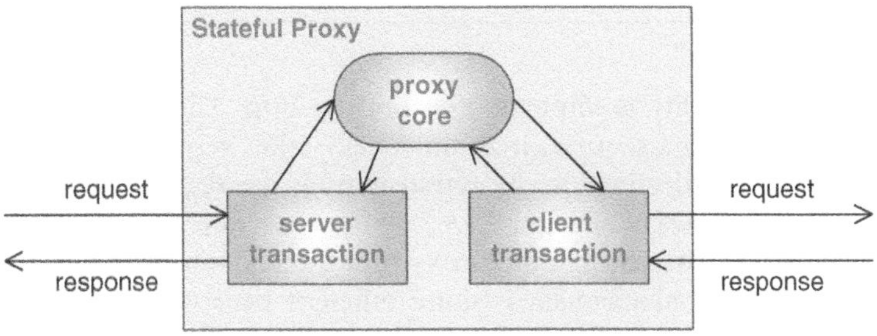

FIGURE 13.5

Therefore, stateful proxies keep information about the requests that they handle. This state information has two components. The first is the information stored in the server and client transaction, which is needed for the proper behavior of SIP transactions (retransmissions). The second is the state needed by the proxy core to perform its function. For instance, the proxy core needs to maintain an association between server and client transactions.

13.2.1 Treatment of Transactions

The approach taken by [RFC 3261] in order to relay messages in stateful proxies is based on considering that reliability is dealt with in a hop-by-hop fashion, whereas the request/response exchanges take place end to end. This end-to-end behavior of requests and responses is represented in Figure 13.6. The reader may notice that the 100 (Trying) provisional response does not follow the end-to-end approach. It represents an exception to the rule: it is sent by the SIP proxy as soon as it receives the INVITE request to quench requests retransmissions rapidly in order to avoid network congestion.

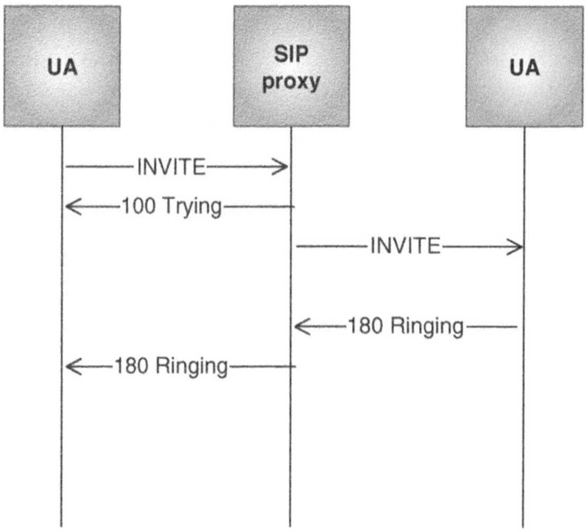

FIGURE 13.6

On the other hand, reliability is implemented hop by hop. This means that when a stateful proxy receives a request, it automatically takes responsibility for delivering that request to the destination, by retransmitting the request if necessary, and so forth. This is shown in Figure 13.7. where we see that the first request in the second hop is lost, causing the proxy (not the UA) to retransmit it.

This hop-by-hop reliability mechanism is quite efficient because retransmissions are implemented just in the hop where they are needed. Let us just think

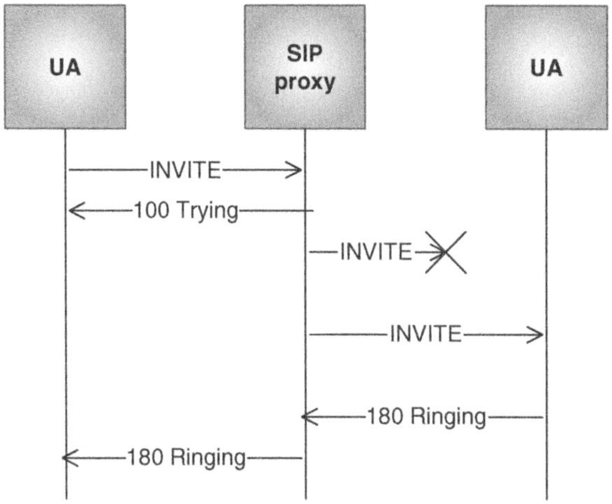

FIGURE 13.7

that we might encounter scenarios with a number of hops in which all of them but one are based on reliable transport (such as TCP). In such kinds of scenarios, SIP retransmissions take place only in the hop that uses UDP.

This kind of behavior—end-to-end request/response and hop-by-hop reliability—is applied to all SIP transactions, with some quite important exceptions. We describe these exceptions next:

1. As we already mentioned, a SIP proxy sends back a 100 (Trying) provisional response as soon as it receives an INVITE request. This is done in order to quench retransmissions rapidly and so avoid network congestion.

2. If the INVITE transaction is answered with a 200 OK, it is quite important that the reliability mechanism used to assure delivery of the response is end to end rather than hop by hop. This has to do with the fact that a successful INVITE transaction generates, in both endpoints, state that needs to be fully synchronized. Therefore, when a server transaction sends a 200 OK, it terminates. Likewise, when a client transaction receives a 200 OK, it also immediately terminates. This implies that the retransmission of 200 OK messages is made end to end by the SIP core layer. Moreover, the ACK request is sent statelessly and treated statelessly by the proxy. These ideas are shown in Figure 13.8.

3. If the INVITE transaction is answered with a non-2XX final response, the stateful proxy must generate the ACK for that response, being the ACK part of the original INVITE transaction. What this means is that 4XX, 5XX, or 6XX responses to INVITE are always treated hop by hop rather than end to end. This is shown in Figure 13.9.

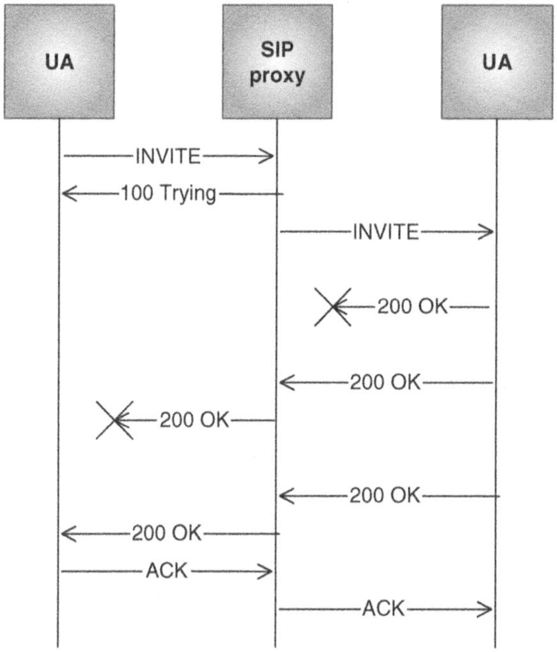

FIGURE 13.8

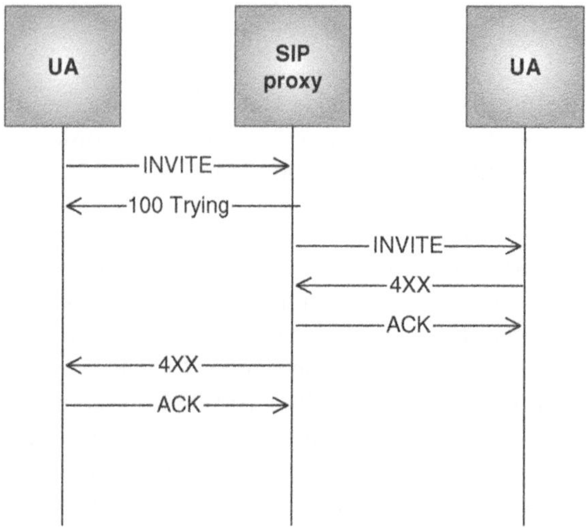

FIGURE 13.9

4. The CANCEL transaction is by nature a hop-by-hop request. It has significance only between a client transaction and its adjacent server transaction. When receiving a CANCEL request, the stateful proxy will generate new CANCEL requests in the outgoing branches that it created when the INVITE was received. This behavior is depicted in Figure 13.10.

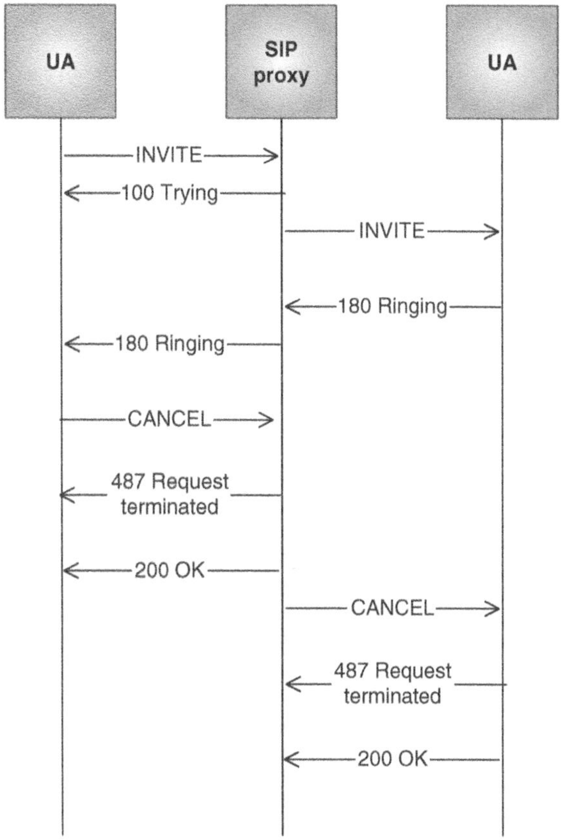

FIGURE 13.10

13.2.2 Call Stateful Proxies

Call stateful proxies are transaction stateful proxies that keep track of calls traversing them. Such proxies record-route (see Chapter 6), so as to be in the signaling path of all the messages within a dialog, and also maintain information related to the call. These proxies may be used, for instance, to generate records that include both the start time and finish time of the call for charging purposes. It is important that record-routing is used carefully (as stated in Chapter 6) because it increases processing required by a proxy.

13.3 Stateful Proxy Behavior

In this section, we summarize the behavior of a stateful proxy at a high level. We will make extensive use of the concepts around SIP routing learned in Chapter 6 (e.g., role of Via, Route, and Record-Route header, and so on). Therefore, the reader is advised to review these concepts before going through this section.

13.3.1 Treatment of Requests

Whenever the stateful proxy receives a request for which there is not already a server transaction, it creates a new server transaction and then processes the request in the proxy core. The main steps in the request processing are described next. These steps are valid for any request except for CANCEL and ACK requests. Processing of CANCEL and ACK requests is described in separate sections.

1. The first thing the proxy core does is to validate the request. It checks a number of aspects:
   - The syntax is correct
   - The scheme in the Request-URI is understood
   - Max-Forwards header field is not zero (a zero value would indicate that this request has gone through too many hops)
   - Loop detection
   - Others

2. Requests that reach the proxy may have a Route header field whose first value indicates this proxy. This situation may occur because a previous proxy or UAC may have put that value in the Route header so as to force the requests to traverse the proxy. In such a case, the proxy should delete that value because it has already been used and is no longer useful.

3. The next step is to determine the new target(s) of the request—that is, the new Request-URI. This step is the essence of the proxy role. Two situations may occur:
   - If our proxy is not responsible for the domain that appears in the Request-URI, then the Request-URI is not modified.
   - If our proxy is responsible for the domain that appears in the Request-URI, then a location service is accessed in order to determine the new Request-URI.

4. The next step is to decrement the Max-Forwards header-field value by 1 in order to reflect the fact that the request has just traversed another proxy.

5. If the received request initiates a dialog, and the proxy wishes to remain in the path of future requests within that dialog, the proxy then inserts a new Record-Route header value that indicates its address.

6. If local policy[1] in the proxy mandates that the request needs to traverse a specific set of other proxies, our proxy could push new Route header-field values into the request that point to these other proxies.

[1]A service provider might want, based on user subscription information, to force all the requests to go through a number of proxies or B2BUAs that apply specific services. An example could be a prepaid service. If the calling user is a prepaid user, the user's outgoing proxy might force the request to traverse a B2BUA where the prepaid application resides. The IMS, which is an example of SIP-based multimedia network applied to the telecommunications environment, does use this feature of SIP proxies in order to apply services residing in external application servers. In the IMS terminology, this is referred to as service control, and will be discussed in Chapter 24.

7. The next step is to determine the IP address, port, and address for the next hop. This is done according to [RFC 3263], as was explained in Chapter 6.
8. Then the proxy inserts a new Via header-field value, creates a new client transaction, and forwards the request through it.
9. The last step consists of starting a timer (called Timer C) in order to handle the case where an INVITE request never generates a final response.[2] The proxy updates the timer as soon as it receives a provisional response.

If the proxy determines more than one target for the requests, then steps 5 to 9 are repeated for each target. The proxy may handle the new branches sequentially or in parallel. This type of proxy processing such that the proxy can create more than one new branch is known as forking. Figure 13.11 shows a typical scenario with a forking proxy. When the INVITE request is received by the proxy, the proxy forwards the request in parallel to UA2 and UA3. When UA2 responds, the proxy sends back the 200 OK to UA1, and cancels the INVITE transaction toward UA3.

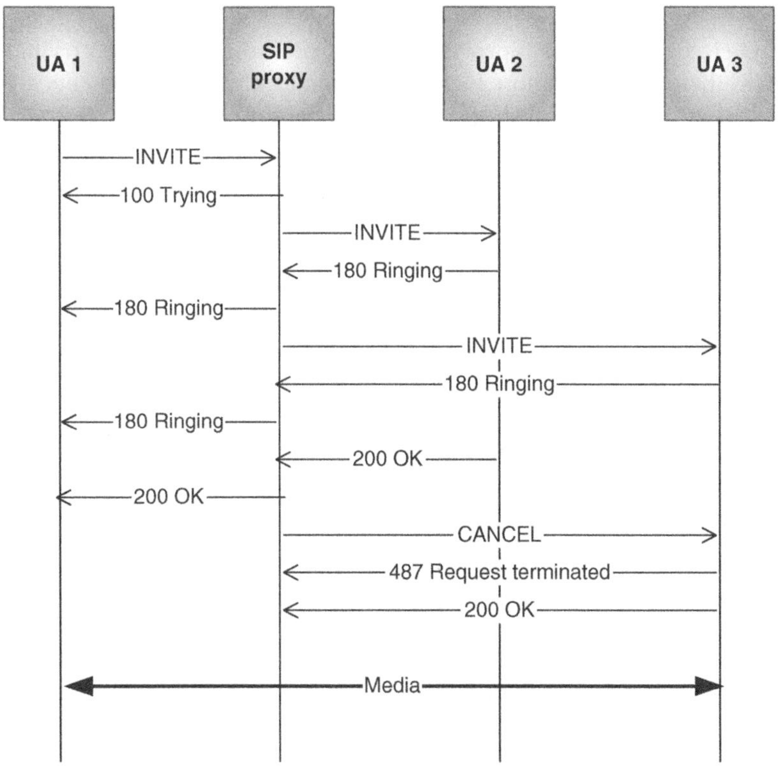

FIGURE 13.11

[2]If the timer fires, the proxy may decide to either reset it or terminate the client transaction.

For each new branch that is generated, the proxy core creates a response context that maintains information about that request and that links the client transaction used to send the new request with the server transaction on which the original request was received. This context will be used later on, for instance, to route back the received responses.

13.3.2 Treatment of Responses

Whenever the stateful proxy receives a response, the client transaction passes it to the proxy core, which processes it. The main steps in the response processing are described next.

1. The proxy core receives a response through a specific client transaction. The first thing the proxy core does is to find the response context, and so determine which server transaction is linked to that client transaction.
2. Update Timer C for provisional responses.
3. The next step is to remove the topmost Via header-field value in the response. Such a value has already been used by the element that sent the response in order to route it to our proxy, so it is no longer useful.
4. If the received response is a provisional response other than 100 (Trying) or a 2XX, then the proxy must forward it immediately. If all the clients are terminated and yet no final response has been sent on the server transaction, the proxy then has to pick up the best response among all the received ones and send it through the server transaction.
5. In order to forward a response, the server transaction that is indicated in the response context is used.
6. Once a final response has been forwarded through the server transaction, the proxy must cancel all those other branches on which a final response has not yet been received. It does so by generating CANCEL requests in each of those branches.

13.3.3 Receiving a CANCEL Request

As stated before, CANCEL requests have a particular processing, and this processing is described next.

When the stateful proxy receives a CANCEL request, it creates a new server transaction, and then the proxy core searches its existing response contexts associated with the server transaction the CANCEL request refers to. When a match is found, the proxy sends back a 200 (OK) response to the CANCEL request, and generates new CANCEL requests for any pending transactions in the response context.

13.3.4 Receiving an ACK Request

ACK requests also have a particular treatment by proxies. Two situations may occur:

- The proxy receives an ACK request that matches an existing server transaction. Such a request is processed by the server transaction and is not passed to the proxy core.

- The proxy receives an ACK request that does not match any existing server transaction. This would mean that this request was generated by a UAC after receiving a 2XX response to the original INVITE. In such a situation, the proxy core does not create any new server transaction, but just forwards the request statelessly according to the rules described in the next section.

13.4 Transaction Stateless Proxies

A transaction stateless proxy, or stateless proxy in short, is not transaction aware. It just receives requests directly from the server transport, processes them based on the information contained in the message, and forwards them directly to the client transport. Likewise, it receives responses from the server transport and sends them back through a client transport. This behavior is depicted in Figure 13.12.

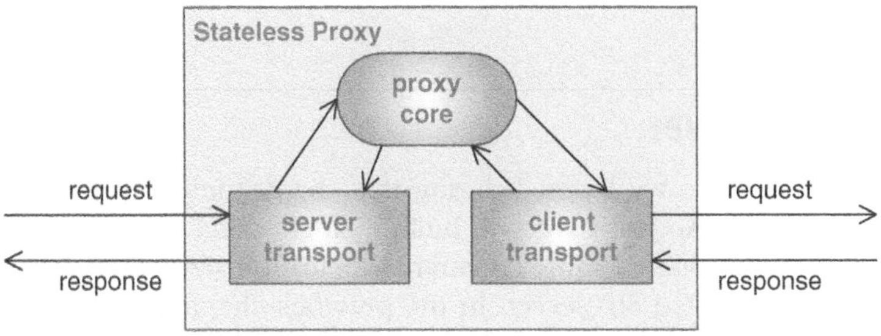

FIGURE 13.12

A stateless proxy does not keep any state. It discards information about a message once the message has been forwarded. The selection of the appropriate server and client transport is done based on the information in the message itself, not on stored state.

13.5 Stateless Proxy Behavior

A stateless proxy does not have a notion of a transaction. It stores no information, so it does not keep any response context. A stateless proxy routes requests and responses based only on the parameters present in the received message. Given that stateless proxies are not aware of the transactions, they do not generate any retransmissions on their own. A stateless proxy is just a simple message forwarder.

Apart from these quite important aspects (related to the nonexistence of the transaction sublayer) that differentiate stateless from stateful proxies, the stateless proxy core behavior is quite similar to its stateful counterpart. Next we describe the main aspects in which a stateless proxy core behavior is different from the behavior of a stateful proxy core, described in previous sections.

- Stateless proxies can forward requests to only one single destination. In other words, they cannot fork requests. The reason for this is that forking requests requires keeping state, which the stateless proxy is not allowed to do.
- Original requests and their retransmissions are undistinguishable by the stateless proxy. They must be processed exactly in the same way so that the output generated by the proxy is identical.
- Received requests do not cause the proxy core to generate a server transaction. In order to forward requests, these are sent directly to the transport sublayer.
- Stateless proxies do not perform special processing for CANCEL requests. They treat all types of requests in the same way.
- Response processing, as described in Section 13.3.2, "Treatment of Responses," does not apply to a stateless proxy. In order to forward responses, a stateless proxy uses just the Via header in order to determine the next hop in the backward direction.

13.6 Practice: SIP Server

We will now put the concepts we learned during this chapter into practice by building a simple SIP proxy. Actually, we will build a single piece of code that acts as a simple proxy, but also as a simple registrar and location service. In other words, we will build a simplified SIP server. In the previous chapter, we built a soft-phone able to set up peer-to-peer sessions without the need of any proxy. This forced us to know beforehand the address of the party we wanted to communicate with. That is an unrealistic scenario. We will use the SIP server in this chapter in order to create a more realistic end-to-end scenario composed by two communicating soft-phones and a SIP server that acts as the home server for both of them. Both soft-phones will register against our SIP server, and the soft-phones will be able to call each other by using their logical names without the need to know their actual IP address. In order to test this scenario, we will also need to extend the code of our previous soft-phones so that now they can also register toward our SIP server.

13.6.1 Scope

Our SIP server application itself is quite simple. It encompasses a very simple SIP proxy, SIP registrar, and location service. Next are some considerations about the scope of our application:

- The SIP proxy is a simple routing engine. It does not implement forking. An incoming request maps to one (and only one) outgoing request.
- The SIP proxy implements routing by querying an internal location service that is implemented by a class variable. That is, the location information is not persistent.

- The SIP proxy can be configured to record-route or not.
- The SIP registrar is a quite simple one. It just receives REGISTER requests and updates the location service accordingly.
- The SIP registrar accepts only one contact address for each address of record. It does not store or check the expiration time of the records in the location service. It always includes in responses to REGISTER the same Expires header that was received in the original request.

13.6.2 Architecture

The application follows the architecture of previous SIP practices, which separates the user interface (`SipproxyGUI.class`) from the listener (`SipproxyListener.class`). This is shown in Figure 13.13.

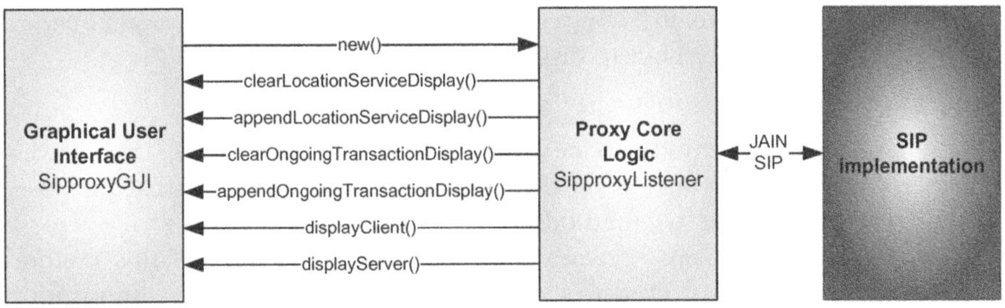

FIGURE 13.13

The main class implements the `SipListener` interface, and is focused mainly on processing the requests and responses received from the network. There is also the need for a very simplified GUI as a form of management console that allows us to set up the main configuration parameters for the proxy, such as home domain and port. The management console is also used for displaying information about the ongoing client and server transaction handled by the proxy, as well as the content of the location service (mapping between addresses of record and contact addresses).

There are two main interfaces in this architecture:

1. Interface between `SipproxyListener` and the SIP implementation (JAIN SIP)
2. Interface between `SipproxyGUI` and `SipproxyListener`

The JAIN SIP interface between the listener and the SIP implementation is used, as always, so that the listener class can receive network events and trigger actions toward the network. The main function of a proxy is to receive a message from the network, process it, and then send it back to the network, having changed some routing parameter. So this interface reflects most of the activity a proxy does.

The interface between the management console and the listener is used mainly for two purposes:

- Configuration of the proxy at start-up.
- Displaying proxy internal data in the management console, such as the list of ongoing transactions or the actual content of the location service database.

Let us look in detail to see exactly what this interface that we will be using looks like.

From `SipproxyGUI` to `SipproxyListener`:

- At proxy start-up (i.e., when the proxy administrator presses the "On" button), `SipproxyGUI` will create an instance of `SipproxyListener`, passing the following parameters as arguments to the constructor method:
  - SIP server home domain, passed as a Java string.
  - SIP server listening port, passed as a Java integer.
  - Record-Route configuration. A Boolean value indicates whether the proxy is required to record-route or not.
  - A reference to the `SipproxyGUI` object so that `SipproxyListener` can invoke methods to display information.

From `SipproxyListener` to `SipproxyGUI`:

- Whenever the location service data changes, the `SipproxyListener` displays updated information on the management console. For that purpose, the listener will use two methods on `SipproxyGUI`:
  - `clearLocationServiceDisplay()`: The invocation of this method causes the GUI class to clear the text area that displays the location service information.
  - `appendLocationServiceDisplay(String newEntry)`: The invocation of this method updates the display of the location service information with a new entry.

- Whenever the list of ongoing transactions changes, the `SipproxyListener` displays updated information on the management console. For that purpose, the listener will use two methods on `SipproxyGUI`:
  - `clearOngoingTransactionsDisplay()`: The invocation of this method causes the GUI class to clear the text area that displays the ongoing transactions information.
  - `appendOngoingTransactionsDisplay(String newEntry)`: The invocation of this method updates the display of ongoing transactions information with a new entry.

- Whenever a SIP message is received or sent by the proxy, the `SipproxyListener` displays the messages on the management console. For that purpose, the listener will use two methods on `SipproxyGUI`:
  - `displayClient(String text)`: The invocation of this method causes the GUI class to show the message sent or received by the client transaction on the management console.
  - `displayServer(String text)`: The invocation of this method causes the GUI class to show the message sent or received by the server transaction on the management console.

13.6.3 Management Console (GUI)

The user interface of our SIP server is shown in Figure 13.14. It is quite simple. As has already been mentioned, it is used for two purposes:

1. Configure the SIP server.
2. Display real-time information about its internal data.

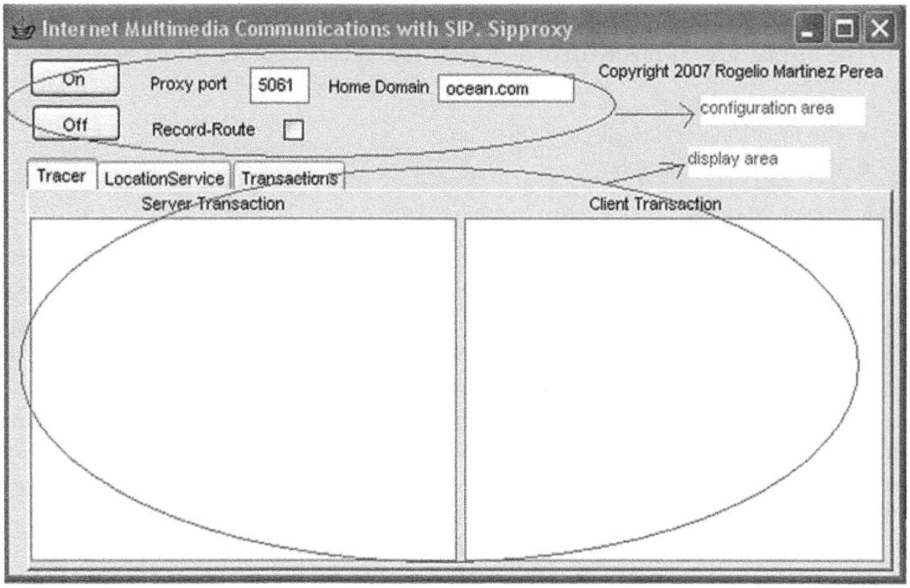

FIGURE 13.14

Its GUI has two parts: a configuration area and a display area.

The configuration area includes the following components:

"On" Button

When the "On" button is pressed, the proxy is started up. The `SipproxyGUI` creates a new instance of `SipproxyListener`. The constructor method for the latter initializes the JAIN SIP environment, configures the proxy, and starts listening for incoming requests from the network. The proxy is then ready to execute its function.

"Off" Button

The "Off" button switches the proxy off. It shuts down the SIP environment.

Home Domain Text Box

This box has to be configured before the proxy is started up (i.e., before pressing the "On" button) because it contains a key parameter for the proxy configuration. It represents the domain that the SIP server is responsible for. The SIP server will receive registrations for users that pertain to such a domain, as well as terminating/originating calls to/from users in that domain.

Port Text Box

It contains the UDP port the SIP server will be listening on. It also needs to be configured before the proxy is started up because the port is a crucial configuration parameter.

Record-Route Check Box

It is used to configure the behavior of the proxy. If the box is checked, the proxy will record-route.

The display area is made up of a `JTabbedPane` that contains three tabs:

- the tracer display
- the location service display
- the transaction display

The Tracer Display

It contains two text areas. The one on the left shows in realtime the signaling messages processed by the proxy's server transaction—that is, the requests received by the proxy and its corresponding responses. The one on the right shows the signaling messages processed by the proxy's client transaction—that is, the requests sent by the proxy and its corresponding responses.

It is important to note that, because the tracer is showing just the messages handled by the listener class, messages generated by the transaction layer do not appear in the display. That is to say, 100 Trying responses generated by the proxy or message retransmissions at the transaction layer would not be reflected in the tracer display.

In Figure 13.15. we can see the tracer display in action.

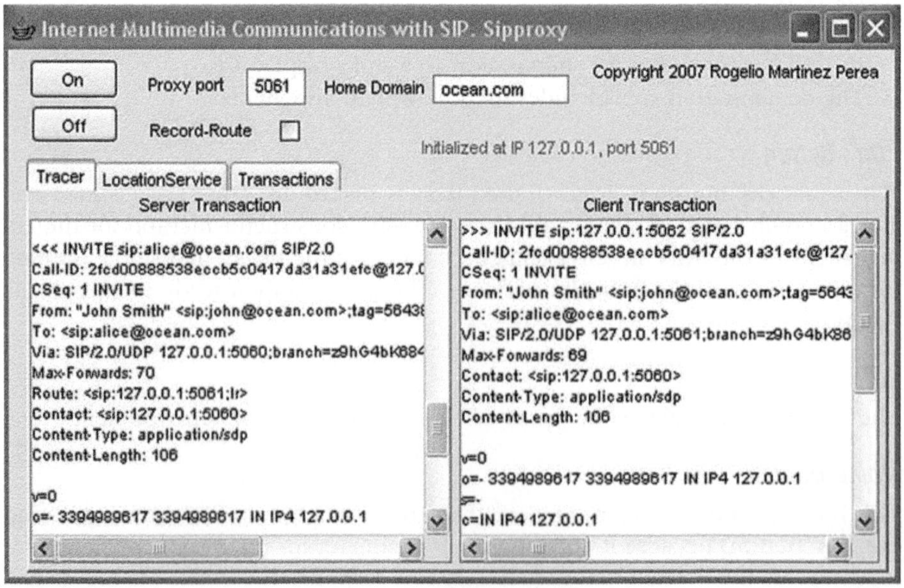

FIGURE 13.15

The Location Service Display

It contains a text area that shows the address of record to contact address mapping for the registered users. It is updated in realtime as new registrations are received from User Agents.

In Figure 13.16. we see the content of the location service. John and Alice are registered with the local host IP address, but with different ports: 5060 and 5062, respectively.

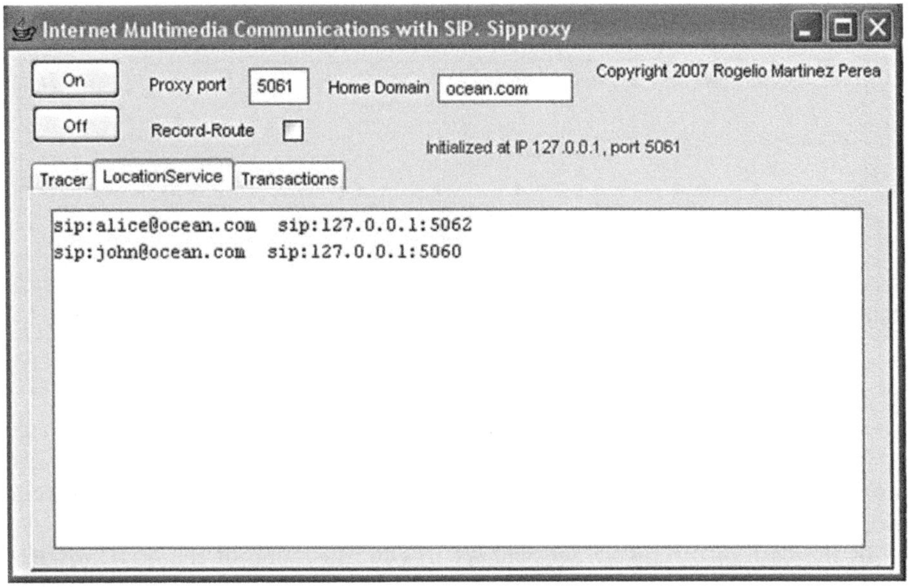

FIGURE 13.16

The Transaction Display

It includes a text area that lists, in real-time, the transactions being handled by the proxy. It shows only the transactions for which the standard proxy treatment is applied. Those cases that call for specific treatment—such as CANCEL transactions or ACK messages—are not shown in this box, though they are fully handled by our proxy. The fundamental purpose of this component is to show the existence of peer server and client transactions in the proxy as they are created or destroyed.

Figure 13.17 shows a snapshot of the transaction display. In this case, the proxy is handling just one transaction: corresponding to an INVITE request between John and Alice.

13.6.4 JAIN SIP Initialization

JAIN SIP initialization is included in the code for the `SipproxyListener` constructor method. The way to implement the JAIN SIP initialization in the proxy

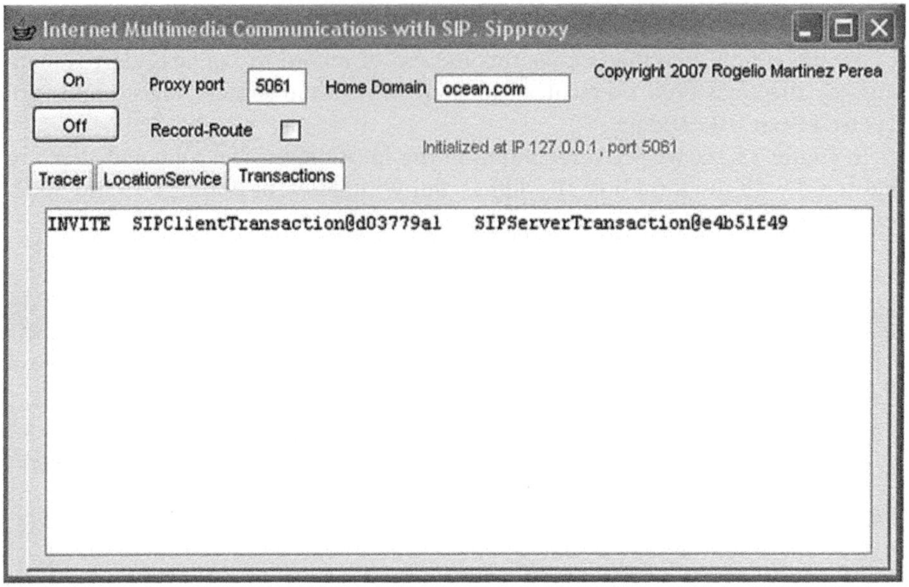

FIGURE 13.17

case is identical to the soft-phone case that we saw in the previous chapter. There is, however, one difference that relates to the configuration of the `SipStack` properties. In the soft-phone case, we used all the default values for the different properties, except for the StackName.

In the case of the proxy, we will set to OFF the value of the AUTOMATIC_DIALOG_SUPPORT property, whose default value is ON. This property determines if the underlying implementation automatically generates and handles dialog objects. This is quite useful if we want to implement dialog-aware SIP applications such as User Agents. If, on the other hand, our application does not need to be aware of dialogs, there is no need to impose this additional overhead on the implementation. For those cases, the recommended value is OFF. That is the case of our SIP proxy application:

```
myProperties.setProperty("javax.sip.AUTOMATIC_DIALOG_SUPPORT,"
  "OFF");
```

13.6.5 Proxying Requests

The main function of a proxy is routing of requests and responses. Treatment of requests in a proxy is, as we saw earlier in this chapter, dependent on the actual request method. A SIP proxy must at least differentiate between:

- CANCEL requests
- ACK requests
- Non-ACK, non-CANCEL requests (including INVITE, and so on)

Therefore, as soon as a request is received by the proxy core, the proxy must determine the method of this request:

```
Request myRequest=requestReceivedEvent.getRequest();
ServerTransaction myServerTransaction =
   requestReceivedEvent.getServerTransaction();
String method=myRequest.getMethod();
myGUI.displayServer("<<< "+myRequest.toString());
if (myServerTransaction==null) {
   myServerTransaction=mySipProvider.getNewServerTransaction
     (myRequest);
   }
```

Let us recall that the last line is necessary to cope with those cases where the `requestReceivedEvent` does not already include a server transaction.

Non-ACK, Non-CANCEL Requests

In order to process this type of request (e.g., INVITE requests), the proxy follows the steps that we already explained in this chapter.

The first step is request validation. Our simple proxy will not implement any request validation.

The next step is to check the topmost received `RouteHeader` and delete it if it coincides with our proxy address:

```
RouteHeader receivedRouteHeader =
   (RouteHeader) myRequest.getHeader(RouteHeader.NAME);
SipURI receivedRouteHeaderSipURI=(SipURI)
   receivedRouteHeader.getAddress().getURI();
String receivedRouteHeaderDomain=receivedRouteHeaderSipURI.
  getHost();
Request newRequest = (Request) myRequest.clone();
if (receivedRouteHeaderDomain.equals(myIP)) {
   newRequest.removeFirst(RouteHeader.NAME);
}
```

The reader will have observed that we have created a copy of the request using the `clone()` method. The changes on the request as a result of the proxy processing will be reflected on this copy (for instance, deleting the topmost `RouteHeader`).

Next comes the essence of the proxy role, which is to determine the new target for the request. It will check the domain in the Request-URI. If the domain corresponds with the domain this proxy is responsible for, the proxy will query the location service using the received Request-URI as the key and retrieving the new Request-URI:

```
SipURI receivedRequestURI=(SipURI)myRequest.getRequestURI();
String receivedRequestURIDomain=receivedRequestURI.getHost();
```

```
if (receivedRequestURIDomain.equals(myDomain) {
   URI newRequestURI= (URI) locationService.get(receivedRequestURI);
   newRequest.setRequestURI(newRequestURI);
}
```

The location service is implemented by a simple `HashMap` object, where the key elements are the addresses of record and where the values correspond to the contact addresses. This is shown in Table 13.1. The `HashMap` object is populated during the registration phase as we will see later.

Table 13.1

Key	Value
address of record	contact address

Next the proxy should decrement the Max-Forwards header:

```
MaxForwardsHeader newMaxForwardsHeader=(MaxForwardsHeader)
newRequest.getHeader(MaxForwardsHeader.NAME);
newMaxForwardsHeader.decrementMaxForwards();
```

The following step is to include a Record-Route header if the proxy is configured to record-route:

```
if (recordRoute) {
   Address proxyAddress = myAddressFactory.createAddress(mySipURI);
   RecordRouteHeader recordRouteHeader =
      myHeaderFactory.createRecordRouteHeader(proxyAddress);
   newRequest.addHeader(recordRouteHeader);
}
```

The recordRoute Boolean variable defines the proxy behavior and is set up at proxy start-up.

The next step in proxy processing is Route header modification. Our proxy does not define any local routing policy, so it will not further modify the Route header.

Next the proxy needs to add the Via header and send the new request statefully:

```
ViaHeader vH = myHeaderFactory.createViaHeader(myIP,
  myPort,"udp," null);
newRequest.addFirst(vH);
ClientTransaction myClientTransaction=
   mySipProvider.getNewClientTransaction(newRequest);
String bid=myClientTransaction.getBranchId();
myClientTransaction.sendRequest();
myGUI.displayClient(">>> "+newRequest.toString());
```

Figure 13.18 includes a simplified sequence diagram that corresponds to the relay of an INVITE request targeted to a user that is registered in the domain the proxy is responsible for ("ocean.com"). The diagram does not show all the processing stages, just the main ones.

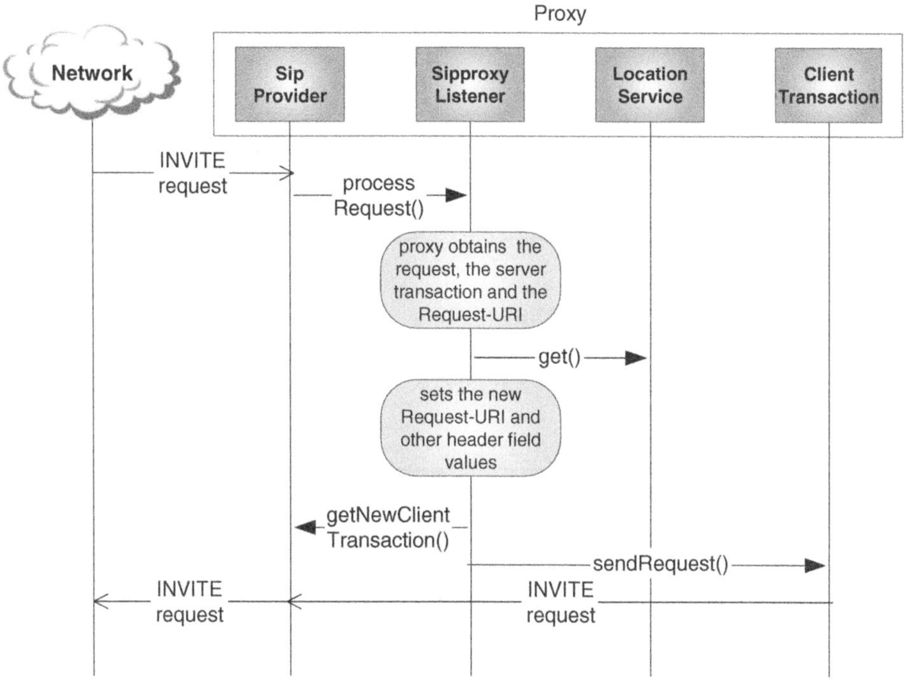

FIGURE 13.18

The last step for proxy processing for non-CANCEL and non-ACK requests is to generate the necessary proxy context information associated with this transaction. This context information is later used in two situations:

1. In order to route responses back. When a response is received through a client transaction, the proxy needs to determine which is the associated server transaction, and send the response through it.
2. In order to handle the received CANCEL requests. When a CANCEL request is received, the proxy first identifies the server transaction the CANCEL refers to. After that, the context information is used to determine which is the associated client transaction. A new CANCEL is then generated by the proxy for that transaction.

Therefore, the context information needs to hold sufficient information in order to implement these scenarios. At least it must contain the mapping between server and client transaction. We have created an `ArrayList` in `SipproxyListener` called `transactionContext`, which keeps all the context information. The `ArrayList` is composed of `Context` objects. The `Context` class is a new class that we have created. It represents the state stored by the proxy for each non-CANCEL, non-ACK transaction that it handles. The members of the `Context` class are shown in Table 13.2.

Table 13.2

	Context Fields	Description
`ServerTransaction`	`serverTrans`	Server transaction on which the original request was received.
`ClientTransaction`	`clientTrans`	Client transaction used by the proxy to relay the received request.
`String`	`Method`	Method of the received request.
`Request`	`requestIn`	Actual received `Request` object.
`Request`	`requestOut`	`Request` object that is sent out after proxy processing.

As we said, the last proxy processing step for non-CANCEL, non-ACK requests is to populate the `transactionContext` object:

```
Context ctxt=new Context();
ctxt.clientTrans=myClientTransaction;
ctxt.serverTrans=myServerTransaction;
ctxt.method=method;
ctxt.requestIn=myRequest;
ctxt.requestOut=newRequest;
transactionContext.add(ctxt);
```

And to update the displayed info in the management console:

```
myGUI.appendOngoingTransactionDisplay(ctxt.method+ " " +
   ctxt.clientTrans.toString().substring(25) +" "+
   ctxt.serverTrans.toString().substring(25)+"\n");
```

ACK Requests

Two cases can be distinguished.

1. The ACK request matches an existing transaction. This occurs if the ACK is generated by the UAC when it receives a non-2XX final response. In those cases, the ACK is part of the INVITE transaction, and is processed just by the server transaction in the proxy. The ACK is not passed to our proxy application.

2. The ACK request does not match an existing transaction. This occurs if the ACK is generated by the UAC when it receives a 2XX response. In those cases, the ACK is NOT part of the INVITE transaction, and is passed to our proxy application for processing.

Therefore, we just need to provide code to cope with case 2. The ACK requests, in this case, are handled in the same way as non-CANCEL, non-ACK requests, except for the following aspects:

- ACK requests are forwarded statelessly:

  ```
  mySipProvider.sendRequest(newRequest);
  ```

- ACK requests do not generate context information. Therefore, the `transactionContext` object must not be updated.

CANCEL Requests

If the request is a CANCEL request, the proxy must explore the `transactionContext` object in order to retrieve the context information associated with the server transaction that is to be canceled. In order to find this information, the branch id in the CANCEL request is compared against the branch id of the server transactions stored in the `transactionContext ArrayList`. Once the corresponding element in the `ArrayList` is found, its data is used to generate and send a 487 (Request Terminated) response through the original server transaction, and a new CANCEL request that cancels the client transaction associated with the original server transaction. Likewise, a 200 OK response to the CANCEL request is sent back to the originator:

```
Iterator iter = transactionContext.iterator();
while (iter.hasNext()) {
   Context con=(Context) iter.next();
   if (con.serverTrans.getBranchId().equals(myServerTransaction.
     getBranchId())) {
      Request originalRequest = (Request) con.requestIn;
      Response originalTransactionResponse =
         myMessageFactory.createResponse(487, originalRequest);
      Response cancelResponse = myMessageFactory.createResponse(200,
         myRequest);
      Request newCancelRequest = con.clientTrans.createCancel();
      con.serverTrans.sendResponse(originalTransactionResponse);
      myGUI.displayServer(">>>" + originalTransactionResponse.
        toString());
      myServerTransaction.sendResponse(cancelResponse);
      myGUI.displayServer(">>>" + cancelResponse.toString());
      ClientTransaction cancelClientTransaction =
         mySipProvider.getNewClientTransaction(newCancelRequest);
      cancelClientTransaction.sendRequest();
      myGUI.displayClient(">>>" + newCancelRequest.toString());
   }
}
```

13.6.6 Proxying Responses

The response processing is quite simple. First we receive the response:

```
Response myResponse=responseReceivedEvent.getResponse();
ClientTransaction myClientTransaction=
   responseReceivedEvent.getClientTransaction();
myGUI.displayClient("<<< " + myResponse.toString());
```

Then we check if the response is a 100 (Trying) or 487 (Request Terminated). We also check if the response corresponds to a CANCEL transaction. In all these cases, the proxy must not relay the response backward:

```
int statusCode=myResponse.getStatusCode();
CSeqHeader originalCSeq=
   (CSeqHeader) myClientTransaction.getRequest().
    getHeader(CSeqHeader.NAME);
String method=originalCSeq.getMethod();
if ( (statusCode == 100)||(statusCode==487) ) return;
if ( method.equals("CANCEL") ) return;
```

If the response does not match any of the previous conditions, normal response treatment continues. First we will clone the response and strip off the topmost `ViaHeader`:

```
Response newResponse = (Response) myResponse.clone();
newResponse.removeFirst(ViaHeader.NAME);
```

Then we search the `transactionContext` for a `Context` object whose client transaction maps the one on which this response was received.

If a match is found, the response is sent back through the corresponding server transaction. If no match is found, the response is sent back statelessly:

```
Iterator iter = transactionContext.iterator();
while (iter.hasNext()) {
   Context con=(Context) iter.next();
   if (con.clientTrans.equals(myClientTransaction)) {
      con.serverTrans.sendResponse(newResponse);
      myGUI.displayServer(">>> "+ newResponse.toString());
   break;
   }
}
} else {
   Response newResponse = (Response) myResponse.clone();
   newResponse.removeFirst(ViaHeader.NAME);
   mySipProvider.sendResponse(newResponse);
   myGUI.displayServer(">>> "+ newResponse.toString());
   }
```

13.6.7 Terminated Transactions

Whenever a transaction is terminated, the JAIN SIP implementation fires a `TransactionTerminatedEvent` on to the SIP listener. We can use such a procedure in order to update the `transactionContext` object so that terminated transactions are deleted.

So we will include the following code in the `processTransactionTerminated` method in `SipproxyListener`:

```
public void processTransactionTerminated(TransactionTerminatedEvent
        transactionTerminatedEvent) {
   if (transactionTerminatedEvent.isServerTransaction()) {
      ServerTransaction st = transactionTerminatedEvent.
        getServerTransaction();
      Iterator iter = transactionContext.iterator();
      myGUI.jTextArea3.setText("");
      while(iter.hasNext()) {
         Context con=(Context) iter.next();
         if (con.serverTrans.equals(st)) {
            iter.remove();
         }
         else myGUI.appendOngoingTransactionsDisplay(con.method+"  "+
            con.clientTrans.toString().substring(25)+
            "  "+con.serverTrans.toString().substring(25)+"\n");
      }
   }
}
```

13.6.8 Handling Registrations

Processing of REGISTER requests is quite straightforward. First we will check if the Expires header contains a zero value, indicating a deregistration. If that is the case, the corresponding entry in the location service is deleted by using the `remove()` method in the `locationService HashMap`. Otherwise the location service is updated using the `put()` method:

```
ToHeader registerToHeader = (ToHeader) myRequest.getHeader
  (ToHeader.NAME);
URI addressOfRecord = registerToHeader.getAddress().getURI();
ContactHeader registerContactHeader =
   (ContactHeader) myRequest.getHeader(ContactHeader.NAME);
URI contactAddress = registerContactHeader.getAddress().getURI();
ExpiresHeader expH=(ExpiresHeader) myRequest.
  getHeader(ExpiresHeader.NAME);
int exp=expH.getExpires();
if (exp==0) locationService.remove(addressOfRecord);
else locationService.put(addressOfRecord, contactAddress);
```

Then a new 200 OK response is generated and sent back to the UAC. The received Contact header and Expires header are copied in the response:

```
Response registerOK=myMessageFactory.createResponse(200,myRequest);
registerOK.addHeader(registerContactHeader);
registerOK.addHeader(expH);
myServerTransaction.sendResponse(registerOK);
myGUI.displayServer(">>>"+registerOK.toString());
```

13.6.9 The Enhanced Client

In order to take advantage of our brand-new SIP server, we need to slightly modify the soft-phone that we built in Chapter 12 so that it can now register against the SIP server.

Our new soft-phone application will be named Softphone2.

Softphone2GUI

The new user interface is almost identical to the one in Softphone1. The differences are described next:

- There is a new text box that allows the user to configure the IP address of the home SIP server. This is a crucial configuration parameter that will be passed to the `Softphone2Listener` constructor method. It represents the address where registrations need to be sent, as well as the address of the outbound proxy to use for outgoing calls. The new `Softphone2Listener` constructor method has the following signature:

  ```
  public Softphone2Listener(int port,String name,String
    ID,Softphone2GUI GUI, String sipserver)
  ```

  The `sipserver` argument is stored in the `myServer` class variable of `Softphone2Listener`.
- The ID box is now renamed Public ID, and it must now contain the full public ID of the user—that is, both userinfo and domain fields in the following

  format: userinfo@domain

In Figure 13.19. we can see Softphone2's GUI.

Softphone2Listener

The main difference from `Softphone1Listener` is the fact that the new softphone needs to register against a SIP server. This leads us to add a couple of new states to our soft-phone application. Those states are:

- UNREGISTERED: It represents the state the application enters when the registration process is not successful.
- REGISTERING: It represents the state the application enters when the REGISTER message has been sent out, but a response has not yet been received from the server.

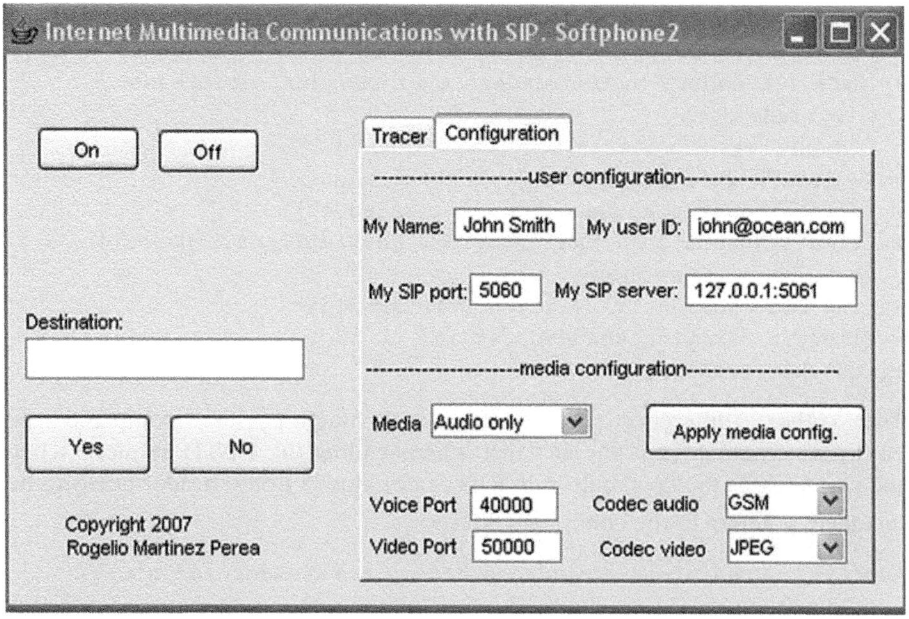

FIGURE 13.19

Also, the IDLE state is redefined to mean that the soft-phone is actually registered.

In the constructor method, `Softphone2Listener` we will now include the generation and sending of the REGISTER command:

```
Address registrarAddress=myAddressFactory.createAddress("sip:"
  +myServer);
Address registerToAddress = fromAddress;
Address registerFromAddress=fromAddress;
ToHeader myToHeader = myHeaderFactory.createToHeader(registerTo
  Address, null);
FromHeader myFromHeader = myHeaderFactory.createFromHeader
  (registerFromAddress,
   "647554");
myViaHeader = myHeaderFactory.createViaHeader(myIP,
  myPort,"udp," null);
ArrayList myViaHeaders = new ArrayList();
myViaHeaders.add(myViaHeader);
MaxForwardsHeader myMaxForwardsHeader = myHeaderFactory.
  createMaxForwardsHeader(70);
CSeqHeader myCSeqHeader = myHeaderFactory.createCSeqHeader(1,
  "REGISTER");
ExpiresHeader myExpiresHeader=myHeaderFactory.
  createExpiresHeader(60000);
CallIdHeader myCallIDHeader = mySipProvider.getNewCallId();
SipURI myRequestURI = (SipURI) registrarAddress.getURI();
```

```
Request myRegisterRequest = myMessageFactory.createRequest(my
  RequestURI,"REGISTER,"
   myCallIDHeader, myCSeqHeader, myFromHeader, myToHeader,
     myViaHeaders,
   myMaxForwardsHeader);
myRegisterRequest.addHeader(myContactHeader);
myRegisterRequest.addHeader(myExpiresHeader);
myClientTransaction = mySipProvider.getNewClientTransaction
  (myRegisterRequest);
String bid=myClientTransaction.getBranchId();
myClientTransaction.sendRequest();
status=REGISTERING;
```

The other difference in `Softphone2Listener` as compared to `Softphone1Listener` is the fact that when sending the INVITE request (when the user presses the "Yes" button in IDLE state), now a Route header needs to be included, pointing to the configured SIP server:

```
Address routeAddress=myAddressFactory.createAddress("sip:"+
  myServer+";lr");
myRouteHeader= myHeaderFactory.createRouteHeader(routeAddress);
myRequest.addFirst(myRouteHeader);
```

13.6.10 Putting It All Together

Now we have already available all the pieces to run a realistic end-to-end SIP communication example, including two soft-phones and a SIP server.

Starting the SIP Server

First we need to start the proxy. For that purpose, we will first fill in the necessary configuration parameters in the proxy GUI. We just need to enter:

- the home domain
- the UDP port
- the desired Record-Route behavior

Once done, we just need to press the "On" button. The proxy will take the desired configuration and start listening for incoming requests.

Starting the Soft-phones

Then we need to start the soft-phones. First we need to configure them through the GUI. The parameters we need to enter are:

- the UDP port
- the user's name
- the user's public ID in userinfo@domain format
- the IP address of the home SIP server

Once done, we press the "On" button, and the soft-phone automatically registers against the SIP server. The soft-phone state is displayed in the GUI.

Making Calls

As soon as the soft-phones are registered, we will see the IDLE status displayed in their GUIs. We can also check the successful registration by examining the location service database in the proxy GUI. It must contain the soft-phones' addresses of record and contact addresses.

At this point, we can initiate calls. For that, we just need to enter the desired destination in SIP URI format (e.g., sip:alice@ocean.com) and press the "Yes" button. The way to use Softphone2 is at this point identical to the way we used Softphone1 in Chapter 12. Users will just be unaware that their signaling is traversing a SIP proxy.

The proxy management console in Figure 13.20 shows an end-to-end scenario including two running soft-phones and the proxy. In order to make Figure 13.20 simple, we have run the three elements in the same machine, but with different ports:

- John: 5060
- Alice: 5062
- Proxy: 5061

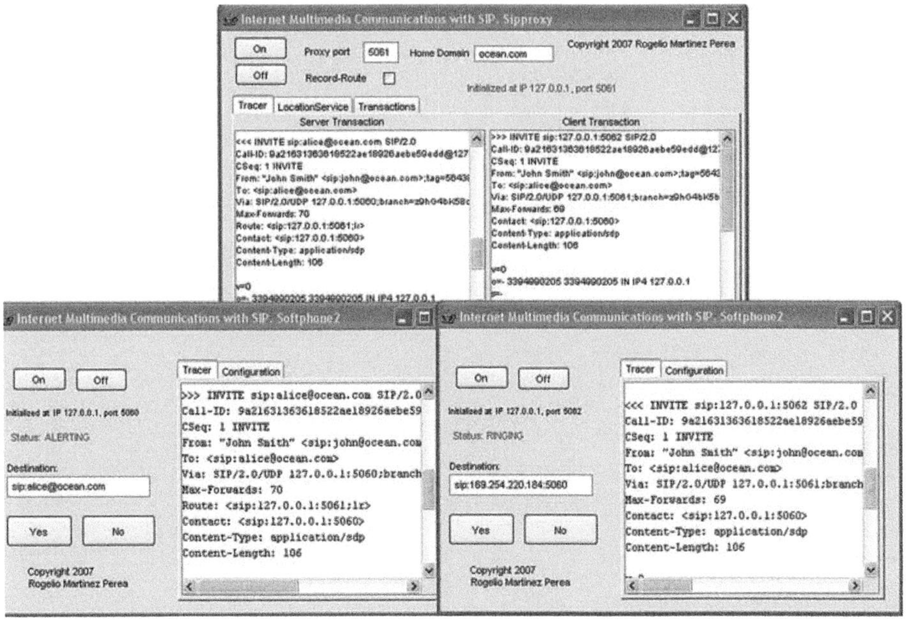

FIGURE 13.20

This setup allows us to see all the signaling flowing between the elements in a convenient way; however, it is not valid for establishing the media because John and Alice cannot capture and present media simultaneously on the same hardware (soundcard, webcam). For a full-fledged scenario, including the media plane, at least two different hosts are needed. The proxy and the first soft-phone could run on one host, and the second soft-phone would run in the other host.

13.7 Summary

At this point, we have covered all the basic aspects in SIP, SDP, and RTP and we have even built an end-to-end realistic scenario including User Agents and SIP servers. In order to finalize our discussion on the core protocols, we just need to look at the very important security topic. We will do so in the next chapter, after which the second part of the book will have been completed.

CHAPTER

Securing Multimedia Communications

14

Information transfers over the open Internet are subject to all kinds of security threats; multimedia communications are no exception. Securing multimedia communications includes two aspects: securing the signaling plane (i.e., SIP), and securing the media plane (e.g., RTP, MSRP, TCP, and so on). Security in SIP signaling is decoupled from security in the media plane; for example, any media associated to a session can be encrypted end to end independently of any SIP signaling. In this chapter, we will review the fundamental approaches for securing each of the planes.

Security in SIP is a topic that deserves particular attention. There are several aspects in SIP that make it a difficult protocol to secure—for instance, its use of intermediaries or its expected usage between elements with no trust at all. For that reason, there is not a single mechanism that solves all the issues. Rather, SIP uses a combination of different security mechanisms depending on the scenario. Furthermore, most of these mechanisms already exist in other remits of the Internet, and are just reused or adapted to secure SIP.

We will begin this chapter by reviewing the basic encryption concepts, such as digital certificates, public keys, and so forth. This will help us to better understand the subsequent sections. Next we will start tackling SIP security. First we will enumerate the most common security threats for SIP deployments, and describe what the fundamental security services required for SIP are. Then the main security mechanisms used in SIP are presented, and some examples are shown that explain how these mechanisms are used in practical scenarios. Then, in the last section of the chapter, we will review existing techniques to secure the media plane.

The security topic in general is a complex subject that relies on complicated algorithms and abstract mathematical concepts. A thorough discussion of these topics would require an entire book. That is not our purpose here. Our aim in this chapter is just to let the reader obtain a high-level and basic understanding of what mechanisms are at hand to secure multimedia communications, which he or she may then use in practical deployments.

14.1 Review of Basic Encryption Concepts

Encryption and its related technologies are the cornerstones of security in IP networks. We will now review some of the most important concepts and techniques used in this remit.

- Cryptography
- Symmetric ciphers
- Asymmetric ciphers
- Hash functions
- Digital signatures
- Certificates
- Cipher suites

14.1.1 Cryptography

Cryptography is the art of protecting information by transforming it into an unreadable format using some sort of reversible algorithm. In cryptography, such a process is referred to as *encryption*. The information used as input to the encryption algorithm is referred to as *plaintext*, and the result of applying the algorithm to the plaintext is called *ciphertext*. Given that the algorithm is reversible, encrypted messages can also be *decrypted* in order to derive the original version from the ciphered text. The algorithm that is used is referred to as a *cipher*.

Using just an algorithm to encode data is not practical because once the algorithm is known, all the messages can be decrypted. Therefore, in practice, cryptographic algorithms use keys to control how the plaintext is converted into ciphertext. In order to decrypt the message, two things are needed: the algorithm and the key.

Ciphers can be broadly categorized into symmetric and asymmetric ciphers. Symmetric ciphers use the same key for encryption and decryption, whereas asymmetric ciphers use a pair of keys—one to encrypt, and one to decrypt.

14.1.2 Symmetric Ciphers

Given that symmetric ciphers use the same key to encrypt and decrypt, both parties have to have a copy of the key. If a third party gets hold of the key, they could decrypt all the messages encrypted with it. Once both parties have a copy of the key stored in a secure place, this is not a big problem. The issue with symmetric ciphers is how to exchange the key securely. This is again not a big issue if I know the other party and we can find a secure way to exchange the keys—for instance, I might invite him to my house so that he can give me the key there. However, this is not a realistic scenario. In practice, I may want to communicate with people I don't know, or even with servers that I cannot invite home! So, how to exchange the keys securely? In the next section, we will see how to use the asymmetric ciphers for the distribution of symmetric keys.

On the other hand, symmetric ciphers have the advantage of being very fast. This is very important for real-time communications, so these ciphers are the most widely used today.

In Figure 14.1, we see an example of symmetric ciphers. John wants to send a message to Alice. He encrypts the message with the symmetric key and sends the message to Alice. When Alice receives the message, she uses the key to decipher the message.

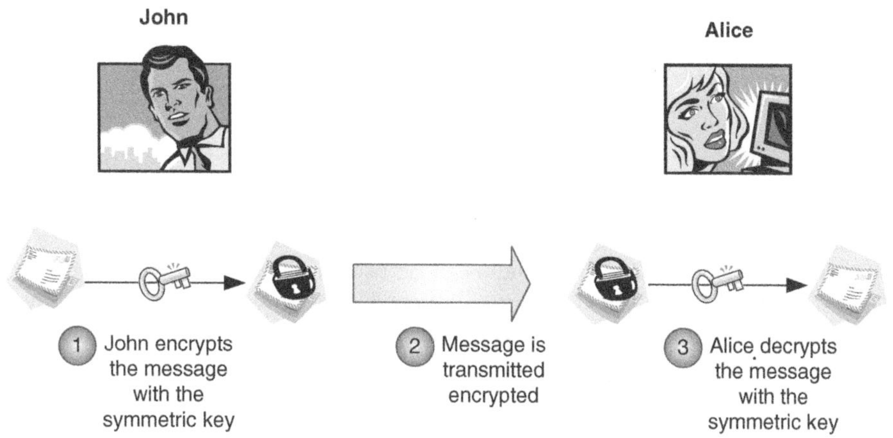

FIGURE 14.1

14.1.3 Asymmetric Ciphers

This type of cipher uses a matched pair of keys. One is the public key, and the other one is the private key. The private key has to be kept secret, whereas the public key can be known by everyone. The public key is derived from the private key, using a mathematical algorithm that confers on them two interesting properties:

- It is virtually impossible to deduce the private key if you know the public key.
- A message encrypted with the public key can be decrypted only with the private one. It also works the other way round: a message encrypted with the private key can be decrypted only with the public key.

In Figure 14.2, we can see how asymmetric ciphers work. John wants to send a message to Alice. He just needs to know Alice's public key. John then encrypts the message with Alice's public key and sends the message. Alice receives the message, and decrypts it using her private key. She is the only one that can decrypt the message because the private key is required for that.

Asymmetric ciphers have opposed properties to symmetric ciphers. On one hand, they show the advantage that the public key can be exchanged in a nonsecure way, whereas the private key does not need to be exchanged by the communicating parties. On the other hand, asymmetric ciphers take considerably

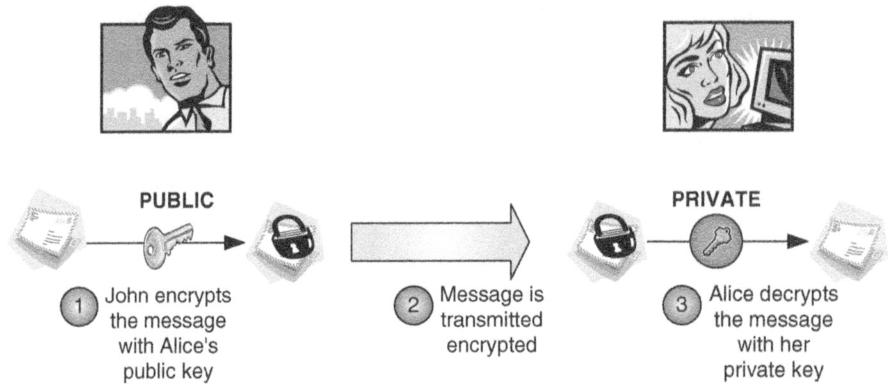

FIGURE 14.2

more computing power than their symmetric counterparts, so it is not feasible to use them to encrypt all the data transmitted in a communication.

Asymmetric and symmetric ciphers can be used in combination in order to get the best of both worlds. Data encryption is best done with symmetric ciphers, given that these are faster and simpler. Asymmetric ciphers can still be used to provide a secure exchange of the symmetric keys. Let us see how this works (Figure 14.3).

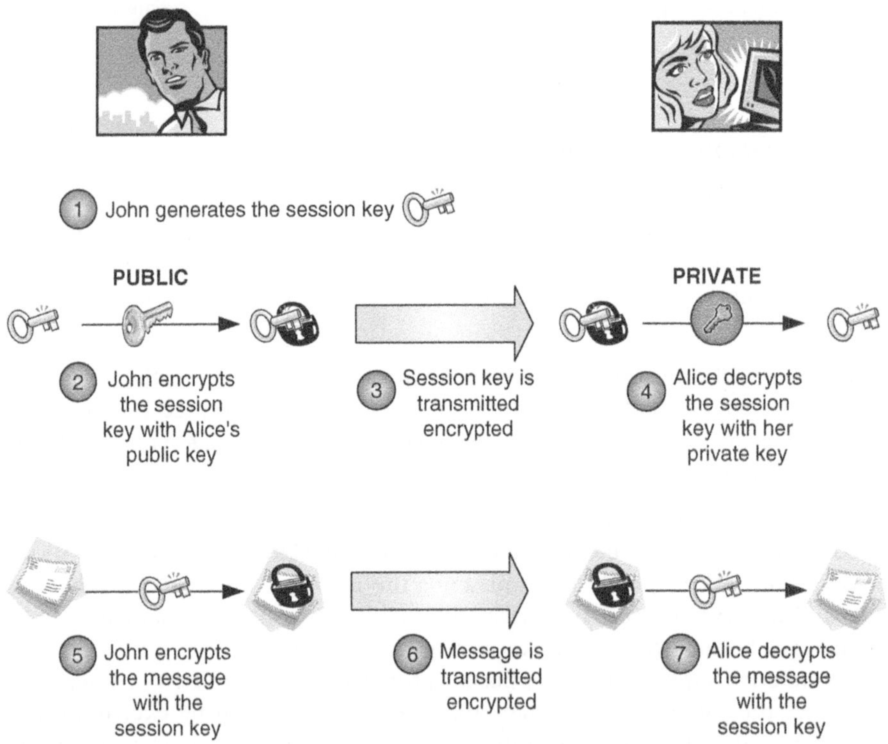

FIGURE 14.3

John needs to send some information to Alice. They want to use a symmetric cipher, so they need to know the symmetric key, called the session key. First, John generates the session key randomly. Then he needs to share it with Alice. In order to do so in a secure way, John ciphers the session key with Alice's public key and sends it to Alice. She decrypts the session key using her private key. At this point, they both know the session key. Now John gets the information message, encrypts it with the session key, and sends it to Alice. She decrypts the message using the session key previously exchanged.

14.1.4 Hash Functions

Hash functions are typically used to assure message integrity—that is, to make sure that the received messages were not tampered with during transmission. This is usually achieved by deriving a hash value for the message and transmitting it along with the message. Hash values are calculated by applying a mathematical function, called the hash function, to the message. Hash functions take a long string (i.e., the message) of any length as input, and produce a fixed-length string as output. Hash functions need to be collision resistant—that is, it should be hard to find two messages with the same hash value.

Let us assume that John wants to send a message to Alice. He wants to assure that no third party will be able to modify the message during its transmission. Therefore, he applies a hash function to the message and obtains a hash value, also called a message digest (because it can be considered a "digested" version of the message). Then he sends both the message and the hash value to Alice. Alice calculates the hash value of the message, and checks that it coincides with the received hash value, meaning that the message was not tampered with.

Adding a message hash value can be used to verify that the message has not been tampered with, but it does not preclude nonauthorized parties from reading the message itself. In order to provide confidentiality in addition to integrity, the message should be also encrypted.

Other related algorithms are MAC (message authentication code) algorithms. A MAC is basically a message digest that has been calculated using a key. MAC functions are similar to hash functions, though they possess different security requirements.

14.1.5 Digital Signatures

Digital signatures are the electronic counterpart to written signatures. They provide message authentication and integrity. In order to sign a message, John applies the hash function to it and generates the message digest. Then he uses his private key to encrypt the message digest. He sends the signed message to Alice, who applies John's public key to obtain the transmitted message digest. She then computes the message digest from the received message. If both message digests coincide, the message is authenticated and has not been tampered with.

This procedure is illustrated in Figure 14.4.

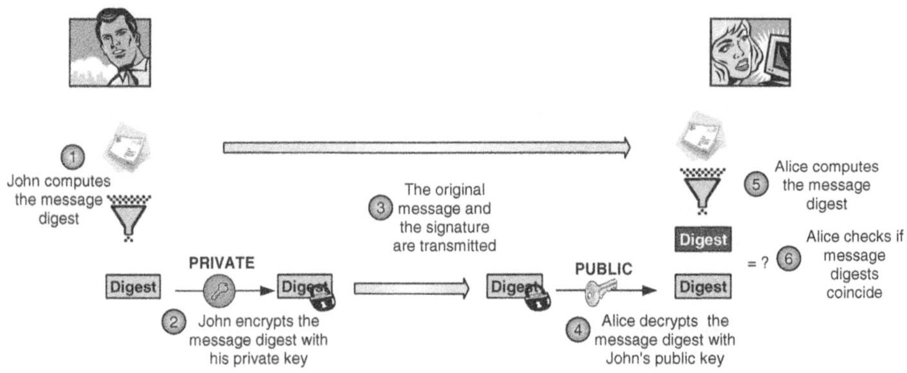

FIGURE 14.4

14.1.6 Digital Certificates

As we have seen, public keys may need to be exchanged by communicating parties. Digital certificates are used to vouch that a public key corresponds to a specific party. They contain, among other things, a subject, which represents the party being vouched for and the associated public key. These pieces of information are then signed by a Certificate Authority (CA) that certifies such a binding and is trusted by the parties.

Let us imagine that John wants to communicate securely with the server sip:server.ocean.com. First of all, he may need to know the server's public key in order to be able to encrypt the information he will send to it (or at least to encrypt the session key). So, before the actual communication can start, the server will send a certificate containing its public key to John. The certificate is signed by a CA. The first thing that John will check is if he trusts the CA. If he does, he uses the CA's public key (which he is supposed to know) to decrypt the certificate. Once decrypted, he knows the public key corresponding to the party identified in the subject (sip:server.ocean.com).

The term PKI (Public Key Infrastructure) is used to denote the framework that allows us to bind public keys with respective user identities by means of a Certificate Authority (CA).

14.1.7 Cipher Suites

Cipher suites are collections of algorithms that support the necessary functions for the secure transmission of data. They include algorithms for:

- Key exchange
- Encryption
- Hash and MAC functions

Key-exchange algorithms permit the secure exchange of symmetric keys. They use asymmetric keys to facilitate the exchange of a shared secret. From the shared secret, it is then possible to derive the symmetric key. Rather than directly exchanging the encrypted symmetric key, as we saw in Figure 14.3, what is shared is a value. That shared value is then used to generate the symmetric key. This approach further enhances security. The main key-exchange algorithms are DH, RSA, and ECC.[1]

Data encryption during communications is done using symmetric keys exchanged using the previous algorithms. Some of the most popular encryption algorithms are TripleDES, AES, IDEA, and RC4.[2]

The most widely used algorithms for message digest are SHA-1 and MD5.[3]

Now that we have reviewed the basic encryption technology concepts, we will, in the next section, start tackling security in the signaling plane.

14.2 Attacks and Threat Models in SIP

SIP is frequently used to support IP communications in the most hostile of all environments: the Internet. In such an environment, attackers can potentially read and/or modify any packet on the network. Let us see what the most common forms of attacks are.

14.2.1 Registration Hijacking

This attack occurs when an attacker registers on a user's behalf. This would cause all the traffic destined to the affected user to be directed toward the attacker's device. This kind of threat demonstrates the need for authentication in the registration process.

14.2.2 Tearing Down and Modification of Sessions

An attacker might forge messages within an established session. It might forge a BYE request to force the termination of the session, or it might issue a re-INVITE message to modify session parameters (for instance, it could modify the session descriptions to redirect media to a specific point in a kind of wiretapping attack).

This type of attack illustrates the need to:

- Preclude attackers from reading SIP messages so that they are not able to forge a request.
- Assure that requests within a dialog come from the same sender that initiated the session.

14.2.3 Impersonating a Server

An attacker might impersonate a server and create a forged response. This forged response might redirect the originator to inappropriate or insecure resources, or might simply stop requests from succeeding.

---

[1] DH (Diffie-Hellman), RSA (Rivest, Shamir, and Adelman), ECC (Elliptic Curve Cryptography).

[2] TripleDES (Triple Data Encryption Standard), AES (Advanced Encryption Standard), IDEA (International Data Encryption Algorithm), RC4 (Rivest's Cipher 4)

[3] SHA-1 (Secure Hash Algorithm), MD5 (Message Digest).

This type of attack demonstrates the need for UAs to authenticate the servers to which they send requests.

14.2.4 Tampering with Message Bodies

An attacker in the middle of a SIP message exchange might want to modify the content carried in a SIP message. For instance, in some cases, session-encryption keys for a media session are carried in the SIP message body. An attacker might want to have access to them so as to be able to decrypt the media session. Attackers might also want to modify the SDP in the SIP message body so as to redirect the session to a wiretapping device and so on.

For these reasons, UAs may require end-to-end security for SIP message bodies.

In addition to the message body, there are some SIP headers that are meaningful just end to end. These headers are not needed by proxies, so UAs might also want to secure them.

14.2.5 Denial of Service

DOS attacks are targeted at causing a particular network element, such as a UA or proxy, to become unavailable by flooding it with requests. Attackers might even want to leverage network elements such as forking proxies in order to amplify the effect of their DOS attack.

14.3 Security Services for SIP

In order to prevent the above-described attacks, the main security services required by the SIP protocol are:

- *Authentication*: It is the process to assure that the user or entity I am communicating with is who it claims to be. Both user and network authentication are needed in SIP.
- *Integrity*: This is needed in order to assure that SIP messages were not modified or tampered with by a third party.
- *Confidentiality*: It is required in order to prevent third parties from obtaining sensitive information that is carried in the SIP message. Confidentiality is usually achieved through encryption.

14.4 Security Mechanisms for SIP

In this section, we will learn different mechanisms that are commonly used in order to provide SIP with the required security services of authentication, confidentiality, and integrity. These mechanisms make use of some of the encryption techniques reviewed in previous sections.

As we already said, rather than defining new security mechanisms for SIP, [RFC 3261] fosters the reuse, wherever possible, of existing mechanisms derived from the HTTP and SMTP space. More specifically, in order to secure SIP, the following technologies can be used, depending on the requested security service:

- Network-layer security
- Transport-layer security
- SIPS URI scheme
- HTTP authentication
- S/MIME

14.4.1 Network-Layer Security (IPsec)

IPsec is a suite of network-layer protocols, developed by the IETF, to support secure exchange of packets at the IP layer. The services IPsec offers include:

- Data-origin authentication
- Data confidentiality
- Data-integrity protection

IPsec can operate in two modes: transport mode and tunnel mode. In transport mode, it offers protection for upper-layer protocols (UDP, TCP, and so on). Tunnel mode offers protection also for IP headers, and is typically used to create tunnels between security gateways.

IPsec can use public-key techniques (certificates) or a preshared secret, stored in the security gateways or hosts. In order to implement the key exchange, IPsec uses the IKE (Internet Key Exchange) protocol based on the Diffie-Hellman algorithm. IKE is specified in [RFC 4306].

Two typical SIP scenarios in which IPsec may be used are:

1. *Securing communication between two SIP nodes or two SIP networks.* In this case, the security gateways or hosts need to have a preshared secret or have access to a public-key infrastructure. Figures 14.5 and 14.6 show these scenarios.

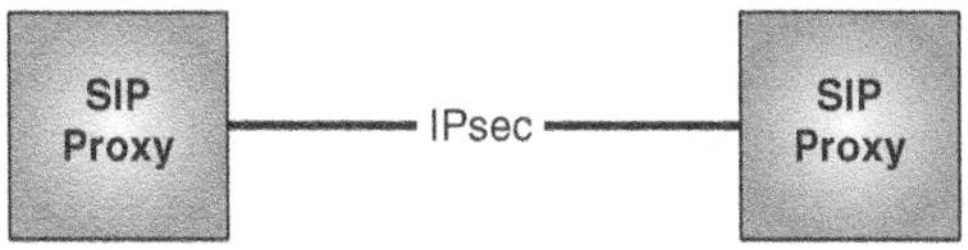

FIGURE 14.5

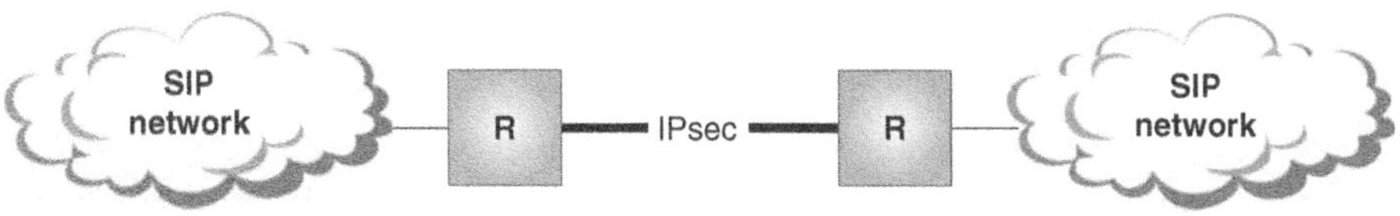

FIGURE 14.6

2. *Securing communication between UA and SIP network.* User Agents that have a preshared keying relationship with their outbound proxy server are

good candidates for this scenario. This is the technique used in the 3GPP IMS (Internet Multimedia Subsystem). In that case, the user has the secret key stored in a smart card,[4] and the authentication and key agreement is done through the Authentication and Key Agreement (AKA) protocol. The AKA protocol will be described in Chapter 24, which is fully dedicated to the IMS.

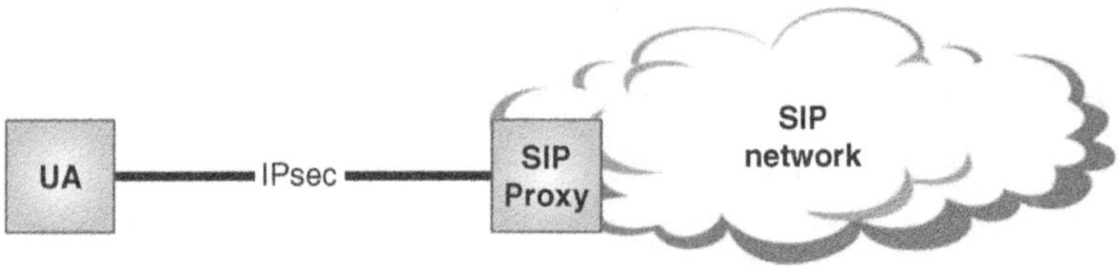

FIGURE 14.7

The IPsec architecture is defined in [RFC 4301]. IPsec uses a couple of protocols in order to provide packet-level security for IP. These are AH (Authentication Header) [RFC 4302] and ESP (Encapsulating Security Payload) [RFC 4303]. The cryptographic algorithms to be used in both of them are defined in [RFC 4835], and include HMAC-SHA1 for integrity protection, and TripleDES and AES for confidentiality.

14.4.2 Transport Layer Security (TLS)

TLS provides transport-layer security over connection-oriented protocols such as TCP. Applications can use it transparently to secure communications between each other.

TLS provides confidentiality, data integrity, and authentication over a connection between two endpoints. TLS can provide mutual authentication (both endpoints are sure of whom they are talking to) through the utilization of certificates. However, deploying certificates in the clients is not always possible or convenient, so, in most cases, only the server is authenticated via TLS. In those cases, alternative mechanisms for user authentication are needed—such as SIP digest, which we will look at in following sections.

TLS involves three basic phases:

- Negotiation of encryption and data-integrity algorithms
- Key exchange and authentication using public-key techniques
- Traffic encryption using symmetric ciphers

TLS provides support for a large number of cipher suites. It may use RSA or Diffie-Hellman, among others, for key exchange. Algorithms such as IDEA or TripleDES

[4] In 3GPP terminology, the smart card is called UICC (Universal Integrated Circuit Card). An application called ISIM (IP Multimedia Services Identity Module) runs on top of the UICC, and is responsible for storing the preshared secret.

may be used for symmetric encryption, and MD5 or SHA-1 may be used for hash functions.

When used in a SIP application, the TLS_RSA_WITH_AES_128_CBC_SHA cipher suite must be supported. This cipher suite for TLS is proposed in [RFC 3268].

Two typical SIP scenarios in which TLS may be used are:

1. *Securing communications between two adjacent SIP nodes*. Two SIP proxies in a peering relationship can have two permanent TLS connections (one for each direction of the traffic). Both SIP entities in this case should possess certificates, and therefore mutual authentication could occur. Figure 14.8 shows this scenario.

FIGURE 14.8

2. *Securing communication between UA and SIP network*. In this case, the first-hop proxy server possesses a certificate, and the UA authenticates the server by inspecting it. TLS offers in this case data integrity, confidentiality, and server authentication. For client authentication, other mechanisms may be used, such as SIP digest. Figure 14.9 shows this scenario.

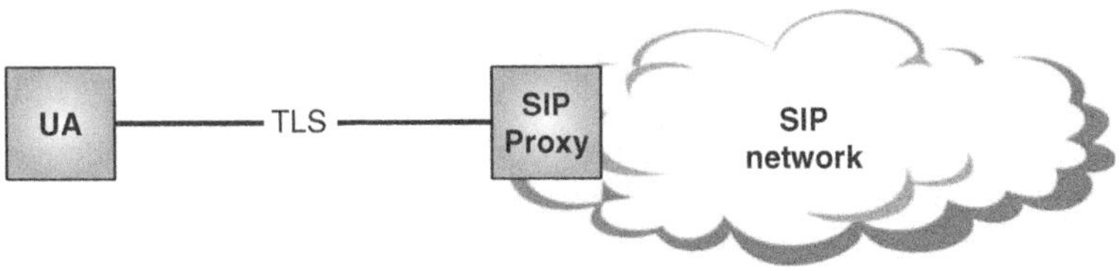

FIGURE 14.9

[RFC 4346] contains the TLS core specification, and it is extended by [RFC 4366], [RFC 4680], and [RFC 4681].

14.4.3 SIPS URI Scheme

In addition to the SIP URI format, [RFC 3261] also defines a secure URI, called SIPS URI. The format for a SIPS URI is the same as the SIP URI, except that the scheme is "sips" instead of sip. An example could be:

sips: alice@ocean.com

A SIPS URI identifies a resource that needs to be reached securely with TLS. A SIPS URI may be used as an address of record for a particular user, or it may identify a SIP server. When used as an address of record, a SIP request toward the SIPS URI is guaranteed to use a TLS transport from the originator up to the domain of the recipient. Once in the domain of the recipient, the request will be delivered securely, but the specific security mechanisms will depend on the policy of the domain of the recipient. When used to identify a server, the SIPS URI indicates that a TLS transport will be used to reach the particular server.

14.4.4 HTTP Authentication

The SIP specification [RFC 3261] provides a mechanism for authentication that is based on HTTP Digest Access Authentication [RFC 2617].[5] It allows UAs or proxy servers to check if the initiator of the request is really who he or she claims to be. The authentication mechanism is based on verifying that parties to a communication know a shared secret (i.e., the password). The way this is done is through a challenge-response mechanism. When the server receives the request, it may challenge the client by sending them a "question" in the form of a data string (referred to as the *nonce* value). The client then needs to determine the response to the question. A valid response is the result of applying a specified algorithm (typically MD5) to the username, password, the given nonce value, the SIP method, and the Request-URI. Once the client has determined the response, it will send it to the server. The server also calculates the response by itself, using the shared secret stored in it. When the server receives the response from the client, it compares the client's response with its own calculated response. If both responses match, the server concludes that the client knows the password, and thus it is authenticated.

In order to implement the challenge-response mechanism, the HTTP specification introduced two headers (WWW-Authenticate and Authorization) that are also used in SIP. When a server first receives an authenticated request, it may challenge the client by sending back a 401 (Unauthorized) response. The server includes in this response the WWW-Authenticate header, which actually contains the challenge generated by the server. The client, when receiving the response, may want to resend the request, only this time it adds an Authorization header that includes the calculated response to the challenge.

Next is a description of the main fields in these two headers.

WWW-Authenticate Header

The WWW-Authenticate header contains the challenge generated by the server, and is made up of an authentication scheme followed by some authentication parameters.

[5] HTTP also defines another, simpler authentication scheme called Basic Access Authentication (in addition to the Digest Access Authentication). The Basic Authentication mechanism relies on the password being sent in clear from client to server—therefore, it is not considered secure, and its applicability to SIP has been deprecated in RFC 3261.

For SIP, the authentication scheme will always be Digest.[6] The main authentication parameters are listed next, together with an explanation of their meaning in the SIP remit:

nonce: A server specified data string that should be generated every time a 401 response is made.

realm: In SIP, this parameter identifies the protection domain. It is meant for UAs to know which username and password they have to use. A username/password combination is connected to a particular protection domain (i.e., realm). When a 401 response is received, UAs may display the realm parameter received in the WWW-Authenticate header so that users can introduce the right user/password combination. Alternatively, the association between username/password and realm may be preconfigured in the UA.

qop-options: Quality of protection options. It may have two values: "auth," which indicates authentication, or "auth-int," which indicates authentication with integrity protection.[7] The response to the challenge is calculated in a different way depending on the value of this parameter.

opaque: A string of data, specified by the server, that should be returned by the client unchanged in the Authorization header. It may be used to transport authentication session state information.

Authorization Header

The WWW-Authorization header contains the credentials supplied by the user, and is made up of an authentication scheme followed by some authentication parameters.

For SIP, the authentication scheme will always be Digest.[8] The main authentication parameters are listed next, together with an explanation of their meaning in the SIP remit:

response: A string of 32 hexadecimal digits proving that the user knows the password.
username: The user name in the specified realm.
realm: Identifies the realm for which credentials are supplied.
nonce: Same value as in the WWW-Authenticate header.
digest-uri: The URI from Request-URI. It is replicated here because proxies are allowed to change the Request-URI.
qop: Indicates the quality of protection that the client has applied to the message.
opaque: Same value as in the WWW-Authenticate header.

Figure 14.10 shows an example of an authenticated registration sequence flow.

---

[6] The Basic Authentication scheme has been deprecated for its use in SIP.

[7] The Digest Authentication has a limited support for integrity protection. Readers are referred to [RFC 2617].

[8] The Basic Authentication scheme has been deprecated for its use in SIP.

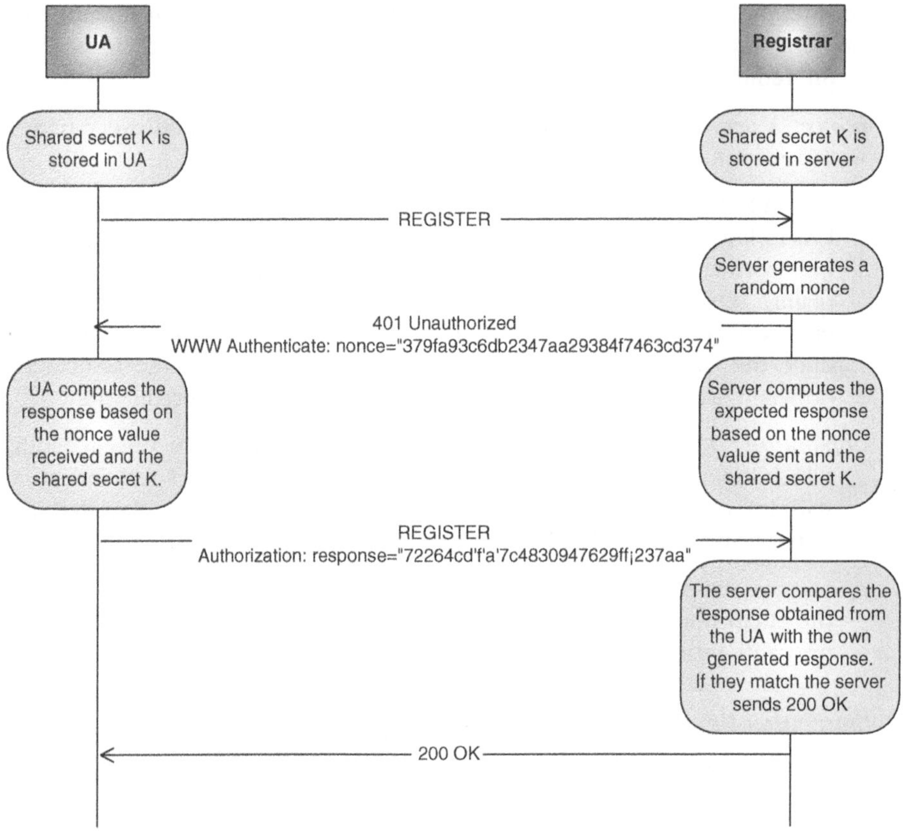

FIGURE 14.10

14.4.5 S/MIME

As we said in Chapter 6, SIP messages may carry MIME bodies. The MIME standard includes a mechanism for securing MIME contents. It is called S/MIME, and provides mutual authentication, confidentiality, and data integrity end to end. Security for MIME contents is defined in [RFC 3851] and [RFC 3850].

S/MIME strongly relies on public-key mechanisms. Each of the communicating UAs must have a certificate. The identity of the holder of these certificates corresponds to the user's address of record. Whenever a UA wants to send a secure MIME body inside a SIP message, it must sign the body with the UA's private identity, and then encrypt the body with the public key of the recipient. When the recipient receives the message, it uses its private key to decrypt the message, and then checks if the signature is correct by using the public key of the sender. In this way, authentication, confidentiality, and integrity are achieved.

One drawback associated with this approach comes from the fact that some SIP intermediaries such as SIP B2BUAs may need to view and/or modify the message body in SIP messages. Using S/MIME in this case would prevent those kinds of SIP entities from working.

S/MIME can also be used in tunnel mode, and this would allow for securing not just the message body, but also the SIP headers. The encrypted original body and SIP headers would be included in the body of a new SIP message and sent to the destination.

14.5 Best Practices on SIP Security

We have so far described all the available mechanisms to secure SIP. Now we will try to draw some conclusions and recommendations regarding how to best use these different techniques.

First of all, in order to achieve confidentiality and integrity of signaling, the best approach is to have full encryption of the SIP messages. However, SIP proxies need to read and even modify some signaling fields in the SIP messages, therefore these should not be encrypted end to end. The recommended approach, then, is to use hop-by-hop security using lower-layer mechanisms such as TLS or IPsec. With such an approach, we obtain hop-by-hop message confidentiality and integrity. Moreover, it allows endpoints to verify the identity of the proxy servers to whom they send requests.

Another important aspect is SIP authentication in order for a UA or proxy server to be able to verify the identity asserted by a SIP endpoint. SIP digest authentication is the recommended approach.

Last, if end-to-end mutual authentication and encryption of SIP message bodies is required, S/MIME can be used.

Next is a practical example in which some of these security concepts are illustrated. It shows the typical SIP trapezoid architecture composed by two UAs belonging to John and Alice, and two proxies belonging to different domains: "sea.com" and "ocean.com." In this example, we will use TLS with HTTP authentication, which is one of the most common arrangements for SIP security.

14.5.1 Example

When John's and Alice's UAs are started, they will initiate the registration procedure. As readers may recall, the SIP registration procedure's main purpose is to create a binding between the address of record and the contact address in the location service. It is crucial that the communication between the user and the registrar for the purpose of the registration procedure is secured so as to avoid the registration hijacking attack that we saw in previous sections.

Therefore, first of all, in order to execute the registration procedure, John and Alice would establish a TLS connection with their respective registrar servers. We will assume that the registrar, location service, and inbound and outbound proxies for John are collocated in server proxy.sea.com, and that the registrar, location service, and inbound and outbound proxies for Alice are collocated in server proxy.ocean.com. Next the TLS handshake takes place, as part of which the registrar offers its certificate to the UA, which verifies it. The subject of the certificates must correspond with their respective registrar domain ("sea.com" or "ocean.com").

Then the UA and server exchange the cryptographic keys and negotiate the encryption and data-integrity algorithms to be used. Once all this is done, the UA can start to communicate securely with the registrar; the only security aspect not yet achieved at this point is authentication of the UA.

Next the UA would build the REGISTER request addressed to the registrar (the registrar's URI in the Request-URI should correspond to the certificate subject received from the registrar), and send it over the TLS connection. This request would then be rejected by the registrar with a 401 (Unauthorized) response, indicating that the UA needs to provide its credentials. The 401 response will include the authentication challenge in the WWW-Authenticate header field. The UA will then respond with a new REGISTER that includes an Authorization header field that contains the UA's credentials. The registrar will check at this point the authenticity of the credentials. If the check is passed, the user is authenticated, and the location service is correspondingly updated. Additionally, the UA may leave the TLS connection open for future outgoing or incoming requests (note that registrar and proxy are collocated in our example).

This process is shown in Figure 14.11.

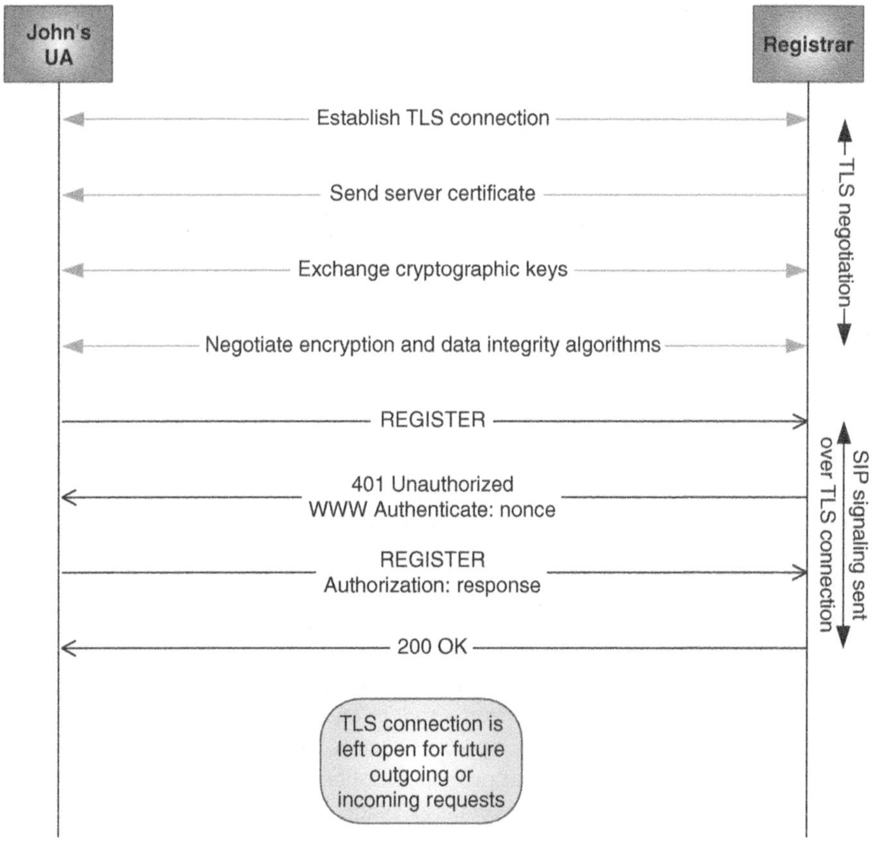

FIGURE 14.11

Let us now assume that John calls Alice. His UA will send the INVITE to his outbound proxy, and it will reuse the TLS connection that is open. Proxy.sea.com will then analyze the domain in the Request-URI, and determine that the call needs to be routed to proxy.ocean.com. Then proxy.sea.com will check if there is already an existing open TLS connection with proxy.ocean.com. If there is, it may be reused. Otherwise proxy.sea.com opens a new TLS connection to proxy.ocean.com. Both proxies possess certificates that are exchanged during the process of establishing the TLS connection, therefore allowing them to achieve mutual authentication. Once the TLS connection is established, the INVITE is sent to proxy.ocean.com. This proxy recognizes, by looking at the Request-URI, that this request is destined to its own domain. Therefore, it queries the location service and determines where the INVITE needs to be sent. Given that there is an open TLS connection to Alice, proxy.ocean.com sends the INVITE through that connection. This scenario is shown in Figure 14.12 (not all the call-setup process is shown—just the INVITE requests, enough to illustrate the security mechanisms with TLS).

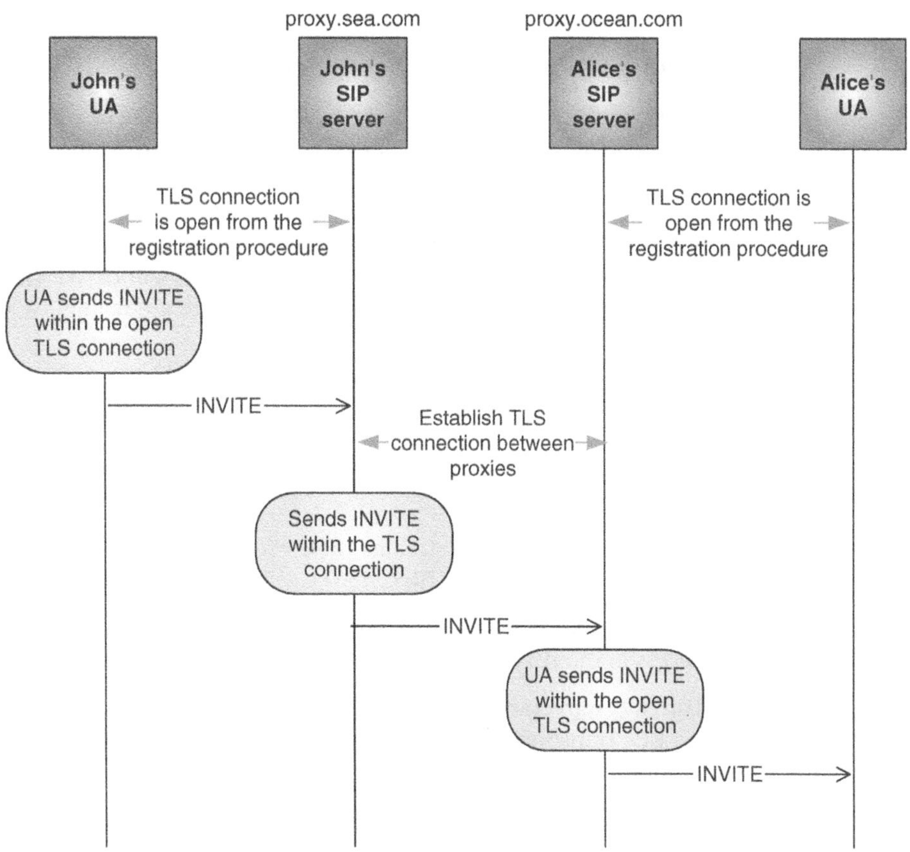

FIGURE 14.12

The scenario depicted here is quite a common one, and shows the concepts related to hop-by-hop security and SIP digest authentication at the registration.

14.6 Securing the Media Plane

In many scenarios, securing the media plane is critical. For instance, let us assume that John and Alice are engaged in a multimedia communication that comprises both voice (RTP) and instant messaging (MSRP) media. They may want to prevent other parties from hearing what they say or reading the messages that they exchange. Moreover, they would also like to be sure that the exchanged instant messages have not been manipulated by any other party in the path from origin to destination. This is just one example of a possible security service needed in the media path. A number of techniques have been defined in order to provide confidentiality, integrity, and authentication in the media path. In this section, we will briefly review these techniques. We will focus on the three main media-transport protocols: RTP, MSRP, and TCP.[9]

14.6.1 Securing the Real-time Transport Protocol

In order to secure RTP traffic, the Secure Real-time Transport Protocol (SRTP) [RFC 3711] is commonly used. [RFC 3711] defines a profile for RTP that provides encryption, message authentication, and integrity to the RTP and RTCP traffic. This profile is an extension to the RTP Audio/Video profile [RFC 3551].

For SRTP to work, there is a need to use a key-exchange protocol in order to exchange a master key. From that master key, the two endpoints will derive the session key with which the session data can be encrypted. There are mainly two ways to exchange the master keys:

1. handshake in signaling channel (SIP/SDP)
2. handshake in media plane

For the first case (handshake in signaling path), two approaches have been defined:

- SDP Security descriptions for media streams [RFC 4568]
- Key Management extensions for SDP [RFC 4567]

For the second case (handshake in media path), several approaches also exist that are still work in progress in the IETF:

- ZRTP: Media Path Key Agreement for secure RTP [draft-zimmermann-avt-zrtp]
- EKT: Encrypted Key Transport [draft-mcgrew-srtp-ekt]

---

[9] RTP sits on UDP, whereas MSRP uses TCP. Additionally, let us recall from Chapter 10 that, in some particular scenarios, TCP may also be used directly for media transport without the need of an additional application-level media-transport protocol.

Another approach for securing the media plane, instead of using SRTP, is to use IPsec. However, SRTP has the advantage that it is more bandwidth efficient. This aspect is particularly critical in voice and video scenarios.

Next we briefly describe some of the main approaches for key exchange used in conjunction with SRTP.

SDP Security Descriptions

This approach defines the new SDP "crypto" attribute that contains a cryptographic key and other parameters that serve to configure security for the media stream. [RFC 4568] defines how to use this attribute for SRTP media.

Next we can see an example of SDP that uses this approach to describe the security parameters of an SRTP audio session:

```
v=0
o= john 2890844526 2890844527 IN IP4 1.2.3.4
s= -
c=IN IP4 1.2.3.4
t=0 0
m=audio 45140 RTP/SAVP 0
a=crypto:1 AES_CM_128_HMAC_SHA1_32
   inline:NzB4d1BINUAvLEw6UzF3WSJ+PSdFcGdUJShpX1Zjl2^20l1:32
```

The crypto attribute identifies the cryptographic suite to be used. In this case, the SDP message proposes the AES_CM_128_HMAC_SHA1_32 suite. Next the "inline:" keyword appears, followed by the keying material (master keys, and so on).

It is important to mention that for this approach to work, the SDP contents need to be secured. In order to secure the signaling plane, we can use some of the methods seen in previous sections.

Key-Management Extensions for SDP

[RFC 4567] describes a more general solution in the form of a framework that allows us to integrate existing or future key-exchange protocols and to negotiate their parameters by using SDP. It provides end-to-end security establishment of the media irrespective of the security at the signaling plane. Thus, as opposed to the previous approach, it does not require that the signaling plane is secured.

One of the most frequent key-exchange protocols used in this approach is Multimedia Internet KEYing (MIKEY), described in [RFC 3830] and [RFC 4738]. However, the framework is generic enough in order to accommodate other protocols.

MIKEY is a key-management protocol specially designed for real-time multimedia applications. As such, it is typically considered the best choice in order to support the Secure Real-time Transport Protocol (SRTP).[10]

[10] In previous sections, we already saw other key-management protocols such as IKE, which is used in the context of IPsec.

Next we show an example of SDP offer that proposes three key-management protocols in order to secure an audio stream with SRTP:

- MIKEY
- and two fictitious protocols (kmp1 and kmp2):

```
v=0
o= john 2890844526 2890844527 IN IP4 1.2.3.4
s= -
c=IN IP4 1.2.3.4
t=0 0
a=key-mgmt:mikey AQAFgM0XflABAAAAAAAAAAAAAAsAyO
a=key-mgmt:kmp1 727gkdOshsuiSDF9sdhsdKnD/dhsoSJokdo7eWD
a=key-mgmt:kmp2 DFsnuiSDSh9sdh Kksd/dhsoddo7eOok727gWsJD
m=audio 45140 RTP/SAVP 0
```

ZRTP

ZRTP is being developed by the IETF; it is an extension to Secure Real-time Transport Protocol (SRTP) that describes an in-band method of Diffie-Hellman key agreement for SRTP. It is still work in progress in [draft-zimmermann-avt-zrtp].

EKT

Encrypted Key Transport (EKT) is an SRTP extension that can be used to securely distribute the SRTP master key and other information for each SRTP source. It uses secure RTCP in order to convey that information. It is still work in progress in [draft-mcgrew-srtp-ekt].

Other Approaches for Securing the RTP Traffic

A myriad of other approaches are currently under investigation in order to secure the RTP traffic. For instance, it has been suggested to use Datagram Transport Layer Security protocol (DTLS), instead of SRTP in order to secure the RTP traffic [draft-fischl-sipping-media-dtls]. Datagram Transport Layer Security is defined in [RFC 4347].

Another example approach relies on DTLS just to support the in-band key negotiation while using SRTP for securing the traffic negotiation [draft-ietf-avt-dtls-srtp].

14.6.2 Securing TCP-Based Media Transport

A possible way to secure a connection-oriented media transport is to use TLS. TLS provides the main security services required for securing media: authentication, confidentiality, and integrity. However, TLS relies on the endpoints having valid digital certificates. Obtaining certificates signed by a Certificate Authority (CA) for the communicating endpoints is, most of the time, difficult to achieve. For example, most hosts have dynamic IP addresses or host names assigned via

DHCP. It would be impractical to obtain a certificate from a CA valid for just the duration of the DHCP lease.

An approach to overcome this problem might consist of using self-signed certificates by the endpoints. However self-signed certificates cannot be trusted unless there is a previous relationship between the communicating endpoints. Such prior relationship could be achieved by including a hash value of the certificate in an SDP attribute. Such hash value is called a fingerprint.

Such an approach is defined by [RFC 4572], which specifies how to establish secure connection-oriented media-transport sessions over the Transport Layer Security (TLS) protocol using the Session Description Protocol (SDP). It defines a new SDP protocol identifier, TCP/TLS. It also defines the syntax and semantics for an SDP "fingerprint" attribute that identifies the certificate that will be presented for the TLS session. [RFC 4572] is considered an extension to [RFC 4145], which introduced the TCP-based media transport (see Chapter 9).

The way this approach works is quite simple:

1. First, as part of the SDP exchange, the communicating parties will present a certificate fingerprint to each other. It is carried in the SDP "fingerprint" attribute.
2. Once the session has been established, the endpoints will exchange their certificates as part of the TLS handshake. Then they will check if the fingerprint matches the certificate. If it does, it can be assured that the author of the SDP coincides with the originator of the TLS connection.
3. From this point onward, normal TLS operation will guarantee confidentiality and integrity of the media session.

It is important to highlight that, for this process to work, the integrity of the SDP needs to be assured. This can be done using any of the mechanisms discussed in previous sections for securing the signaling plane.

Next we can see an example of the SDP needed to establish a TLS media stream. In this case, it is a [ITU T.38] fax session established securely. Readers will observe that the protocol identifier is TCP/TLS. Also, the SDP includes the fingerprint attribute that contains the name of the hash function used, SHA-1 in this case, and the hash value itself:

```
v=0
o= john 2890844526 2890844527 IN IP4 1.2.3.4
s= -
c=IN IP4 1.2.3.4
t=0 0
m=image 51221 TCP/TLS t38
a=setup:passive
a=connection:new
a=fingerprint:SHA-1 \75:D6:C9:61:2E:12:78:3A:78:56:0A:83:2A:BB:88:
   C5:11:4A:61:CB
```

14.6.3 Securing the Message Service Relay Protocol

In order to secure the MSRP media, TLS can be used by following the approach depicted in the previous section as defined in [RFC 4572]. An example of SDP describing an MSRP session over TLS could be:

```
v=0
o= john 2890844526 2890844527 IN IP4 1.2.3.4
s= -
c=IN IP4 1.2.3.4
t=0 0
m=message 51221 TCP/TLS/MSRP *
a=accept-types: message/cpim text/plain text/html
a=path:msrp://1.2.3.4:8341/7hr38r3ew;tcp
a=fingerprint:SHA-1 \75:D6:C9:61:2E:12:78:3A:78:56:0A:83:2A:BB:88:
   C5:11:4A:61:CB
```

Another approach might consist of using media relays. MSRP clients can then establish TLS connections to relays, which are likely to have a certificate. This would be a similar approach to the one described in previous sections to secure SIP traffic.

When TLS is not used, another approach to secure the media traffic is to have MSRP carry S/MIME protected messages.

14.7 Summary

Securing multimedia communications is crucial, especially when these take place over the Internet. As we have seen, this is not a simple process; it implies the utilization of additional protocols and algorithms. When designing multimedia communication solutions, it is important that we first understand the security requirements. Once the requirements are clear, we should then know what tools can be used in order to comply with them. In this chapter, we saw different possible approaches for providing confidentiality, integrity, and authentication in multimedia communications. Armed with this information, solution designers should then be able to select products that support the mechanisms needed to comply with their requirements.

Solutions that cover all the security aspects may be too complex. In some cases, it may be necessary to reach a compromise between fulfillment of all security requirements and maintaining the simplicity of the overall solution.

By the end of this chapter, we have already covered the most relevant aspects of the core communication protocols. So here we close the second part of this book. The third part of the book is dedicated to more-advanced topics involving the utilization of SIP extensions. In the next chapter, we will start by defining the way SIP can be extended, and reviewing some of the most important general-purpose extensions to the SIP protocol.

PART

III

Advanced Topics

CHAPTER

Extending SIP

15

So far, we have seen what the core capabilities of SIP are. These capabilities need to be present in any SIP-compliant implementation. Therefore, any SIP UA can always assume that the UA it is communicating with (or trying to communicate with) will always support the core SIP.

In some cases, new applications appear for which it makes a lot of sense to use SIP, but that requires some kind of extension to the protocol. Foreseeing these situations, the core SIP specification defined built-in mechanisms to allow protocol extension while not disrupting the core SIP behavior.

In this chapter, we will first describe what these mechanisms are. Then we will present some of the general-purpose SIP extensions. In subsequent chapters, we will introduce additional extensions that are needed for new applications or for SIP to work in specific environments.

15.1 Defining New Extensions

The SIP core protocol can be extended in order to support new applications or solve known problems. The design of a new extension needs to follow a specific set of guidelines as specified in [RFC 4485]. These guidelines intend to assure that new extensions fit into the scope of the protocol and that they conform to the general SIP architecture model.

As we have seen, SIP is a protocol for initiating, modifying, and terminating multimedia communication sessions; therefore, if someone would propose an extension to the protocol for using it as a way to remotely control, say, a refrigerator,[1] such an extension would not fit within SIP's scope.

Also, new extensions must not break the SIP key architectural principles—such as the fact that SIP is independent of the session it establishes, that it is transactional, and so forth. Therefore, a new extension that forces SIP to be aware of

[1] Funny as it may seem, using SIP for the control of networked appliances such as home devices was actually proposed sometime ago (draft-tsang-appliances-reqs), but was discarded and never became an RFC.

the type of session being established, or a new method that is not transactional, would not be accepted as a valid SIP extension.

15.2 SIP Architectural Principles

[RFC 4485] summarizes the primary architectural assumptions that underlie SIP. New SIP extensions should comply with these principles:

- *Session independence*: SIP is independent of the session it establishes. SIP operation should not depend on the characteristics of the media.
- *SIP and session independence*: The set of routers traversed by SIP messages is unrelated to the set of routers traversed by the media packets.
- *Multiprovider and multihop*: SIP assumes that its messages will traverse the Internet—that is, it works through multiple networks administered by different service providers. SIP messages may traverse many hops (proxies).
- *Transactional*: SIP messages follow the request/response model.
- *Proxies can ignore bodies*: This allows proxies to scale well.
- *Proxies don't need to understand the method*: This is one of the key aspects to assure extensibility of the protocol. Proxies just pass the new method on.
- *INVITE requests carry full state*: New applications should not require data to be collected from multiple INVITEs within the same session. Each INVITE within the session carries all the necessary information.
- *Generality over efficiency*: General-purpose components are preferred even if slightly less efficient.
- *The Request-URI is the primary key for forwarding*: New extensions should not change the semantics of the Request-URI.
- *Heterogeneity is the norm*: New extensions should not assume universal support for such extension. The SIP environment is quite heterogeneous, and SIP devices that support the new extension will have to live together with other SIP devices that do not support it.

15.3 Extensibility and Compatibility

SIP is an extensible protocol. It can be extended by adding new headers, methods, parameters, or bodies. [RFC 3427] defines the change process for the SIP protocol.

SIP was designed in such a way that extending the protocol would not mean a huge impact on existing systems. For instance, proxies do not need to understand the SIP method apart from the three special ones (INVITE, CANCEL, and ACK). This means that the addition of new methods would have no impact on proxies.

The same applies to content types because proxies are not supposed to care about the SIP body.

Still, in the SIP architecture, there are other entities apart from proxies. Moreover, the protocol can also be extended by adding new headers; therefore, when adding new features into the protocol, there appears the generic issue of compatibility and protocol interoperability. How can the entities that support the new extensions live with the "older" ones that do not support these extensions? SIP was designed with the following rule in mind: "Be strict when sending; be loose when receiving." This rule makes SIP forward compatible as much as possible. For instance, RFC 3261 states that if a SIP UA receives a header field that it does not understand, the UA should ignore it. However, this does not solve the problem in all cases. Let us see why.

Let us consider, for instance, the case of a request that contains an already-existing method (e.g., INVITE), but with a new header field. Two cases may arise:

1. The extension is backward compatible—that is, a request containing the new header can be processed reasonably by a proxy or UA without understanding the new header.
2. The extension is not backward compatible, which occurs when the request cannot be processed reasonably without understanding the semantics of the new header.

Fortunately, SIP has built-in mechanisms in order to minimize possible interoperability breaks that might arise in the second case. We will see now what these mechanisms are for all the possible cases of SIP extensions: new headers, new methods, and new content types.

15.3.1 Extending SIP with New Headers

When adding new header fields or header-field parameters that are not backward compatible into the protocol, there are mainly two possible ways to handle the possible interoperability break:

1. *The first approach* consists of having the UA use the new header only when the UA knows beforehand that the header will be supported by the other involved SIP entities. This approach can be implemented in two different scenarios: from client to server, and from server to client.
   a. *From client to server*: A client, before sending a request with a new header, might want to send an OPTIONS request to learn about the support of such a header in the server (see Chapter 6). It will not include a header in subsequent requests if the header is not supported by the server. This is shown in Figure 15.1.
   b. *From server to client*: A client declares in the SIP request what extensions it supports. In that way, the server is prevented from including in the response a new header that the client does not understand.

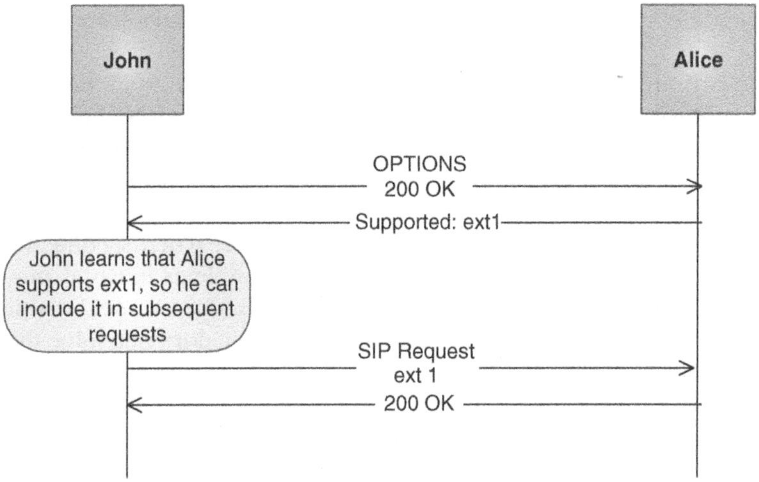

FIGURE 15.1

A UAC would implement this behavior by including a Supported header in the outgoing request. The Supported header would list all the extensions that the client supports. When the request gets to the server, several situations may occur:

- The server might see that a specific extension is supported by the client, and then might answer, including such an extension in the response. This is shown in Figure 15.2.

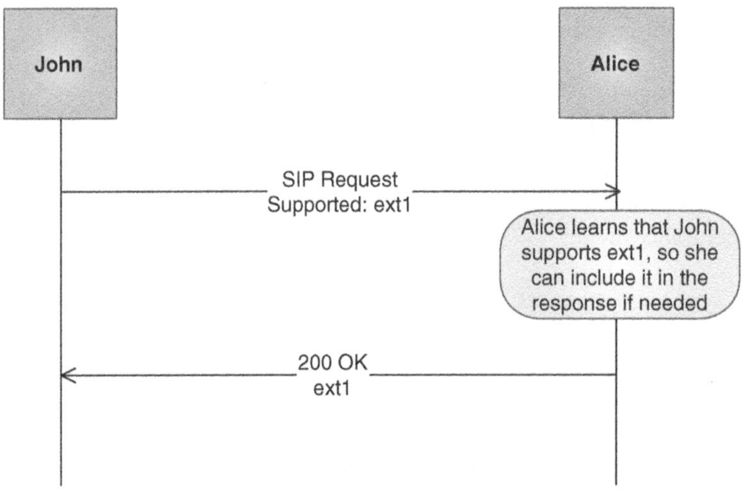

FIGURE 15.2

- Another possibility is that the server intends to respond using an extension, but sees that it is not supported by the client, and then falls back to baseline SIP. This is depicted in Figure 15.3.

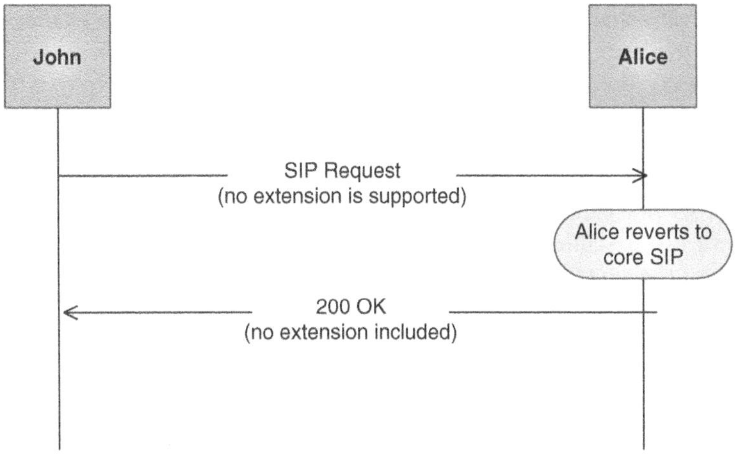

FIGURE 15.3

- A third situation would happen if the server is unable to respond without using an extension that the client does not support. In this case, the server would answer with a 421 (Extension required), including a Require header that lists the extensions required by the server. Figure 15.4 shows this situation. This behavior is not recommended because it will generally break interoperability.

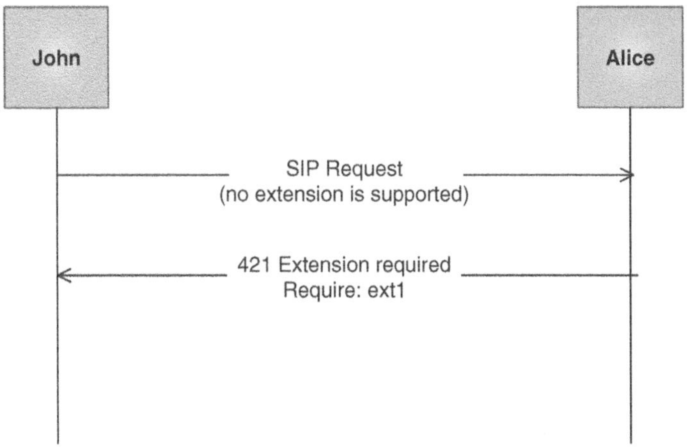

FIGURE 15.4

2. *In the second approach,* a client would straightforwardly send the request including the new extension, but it would state that the server is not to process the request if it does not understand the new header.

The way to implement this is by using two headers: Require and Proxy-Require, defined in the base SIP specification. A UAC will include the Require and/or Proxy-Require headers in outgoing requests if it wants to indicate to the UAS or to a proxy, respectively, that the extensions listed as parameters in those headers must be supported by them.

If the UAS or proxy does not support the extensions, the UAS or proxy will send back a 420 (Bad Extension) response. In the 420 response, the server or proxy will include an Unsupported header field indicating which extensions that were required are actually not supported. At this point, the UAC has two options: to assume that the service cannot be delivered because there is an interoperability problem, or to revert to baseline SIP and issue the request again.

As an example of the previous discussion, let us consider an example of extension negotiation between John and Alice.

John's UA supports the extensions ext1, ext2, ext3, and ext4. He wants to use ext1 in the session, so he includes it in the Require header field. The Supported header field would include ext1, ext2, ext3, and ext4. He sends the initial INVITE to Alice. Alice's UA supports ext1, ext3, and ext4, and she wants to use ext3 in the response as well. So, at this point, Alice's UA knows that:

- It must use ext1 in the response because it was required by John's UA.
- It may use ext3 in the response because it is supported by John's UA.

So Alice sends a response that uses extensions ext1 and ext3, and includes a Supported header stating that she supports ext1, ext3, and ext4. This will give John additional information as to the extensions that he can use in subsequent requests to Alice.

This is shown in Figure 15.5.

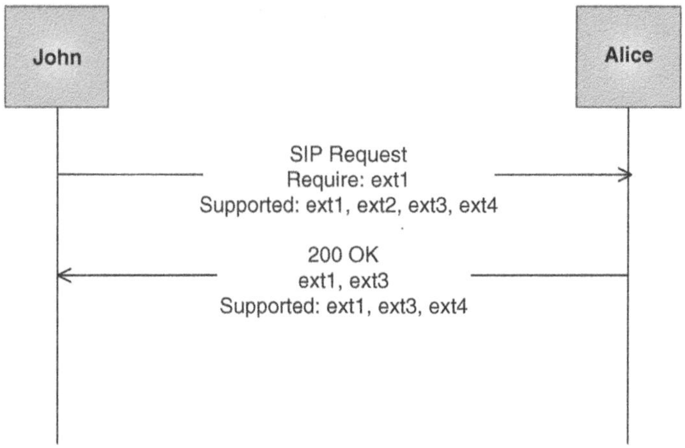

FIGURE 15.5

Option Tags

In the previous examples, we have needed to refer to SIP extension in the Require, Proxy-Require, or Supported header fields. This is done by using option tags, which are unique identifiers used to designate new extensions in SIP.

P-Headers

A specific type of SIP extensions is referred to as a "private" extension. Private headers include the "P-" prefix. These are extensions that are "either not ready for standards track, but might be understood for that role after some running code, or are private or proprietary in nature, because a characteristic motivating them is usage that is known not to fit the Internet architecture for SIP" [RFC 3427].

P-headers are typically defined for SIP usage in non-Internet, controlled-network scenarios such as those occurring in telecom operators' networks. When we deal with IMS in Chapter 24, we will see various examples of P-headers.

15.3.2 Extending SIP with New Methods

In order to handle the possible interoperability break caused by the introduction of new methods, the only approach is to use the new method only if the client knows beforehand that it will be understood by the server. There are two possible ways to achieve this:

1. Use the OPTIONS request before sending a new method. The response to the OPTIONS request will indicate in the Allow header which methods are supported by the server.
2. Indicate in the outgoing requests what new methods are supported by the UAC. This would be implemented by having the client include an Allow header field that lists the methods supported by the client. The UAS would also include an Allow header in the response. At this point, both UAC and UAS would know what are the methods allowed by each other, and therefore they would avoid sending not-allowed methods in new requests.

15.3.3 Extending SIP with New Content Types

In order to handle this scenario, there are two possible approaches:

1. A UA uses a specific body only if it knows that the body will be supported by the peer UA. There are two ways to discover this:
    a. Use the OPTIONS request before sending a message including a new content type. The response to the OPTIONS request will indicate in the Accept, Accept-Encoding, and Accept-Language whether the content type, encoding, and language are supported by the server.
    b. Indicate in the outgoing requests and responses what new content types are supported by the UA. This would be implemented by having both UAC and UAS include an Accept header that lists the content types supported by them.
2. In addition to the previous approach, the UA, when including a new content type in the SIP body, may include a Content-Disposition header with a parameter that indicates that support for the new content is optional.

We have seen what the mechanisms are in SIP to handle new extensions. Let us now review some of the most common ones.

15.4 Reliability of Provisional Responses

15.4.1 Motivation

We saw in previous chapters that SIP defines two types of responses: final and provisional. Final responses convey the result of the request processing, whereas provisional responses, sent within an INVITE transaction, just provide information about the progress of the session establishment.

We also saw that core SIP [RFC 3261] includes mechanisms in order to assure the reliability of final responses. However, the core SIP spec does not include any mechanism to deliver provisional responses reliably. This is shown in Figure 15.6, where a 180 provisional response is lost and no corrective action is taken by the UAS.

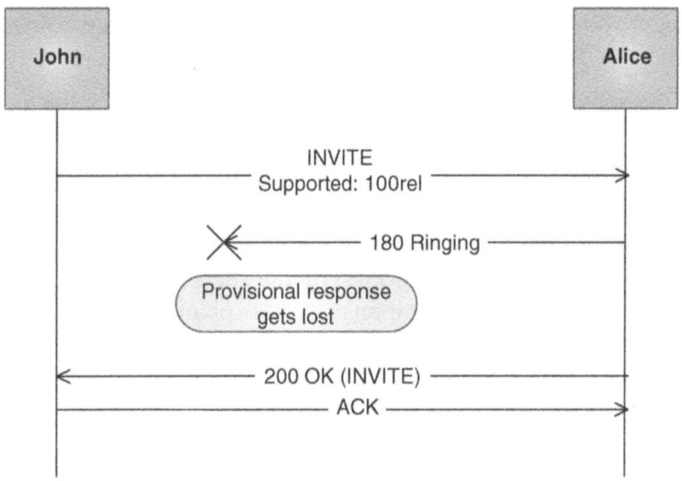

FIGURE 15.6

There are cases, though, where it would also be important to assure the delivery of a provisional response. For instance, imagine an application that applies a particular action (e.g., playing an announcement) when the call is being forwarded or queued. Such an application may require that the 181 (Call Is Being Forwarded) or 182 (Queued) provisional responses are delivered reliably because they signal the condition for playing the announcement.

Another case where a provisional response would need to be sent reliably occurs when the provisional response contains an SDP answer as a result of an SDP offer sent in an INVITE request. Effectively, the core SIP specification states that "if the initial SDP offer is in an INVITE, the SDP answer must be in a reliable non-failure message." If the SDP answer is carried in the 200 OK response, there is no problem because this message is delivered reliably by core SIP—but if we wanted to carry an SDP in a provisional response, core SIP does not include mechanisms to deliver the response reliably.

An example of a scenario where SDP may need to be sent in a provisional response is an early-media scenario. In early-media scenarios, the media is established before the call has been accepted (i.e., before 200 OK is sent). These scenarios are typical in the PSTN, where it is common to play announcements to the caller before the call is answered. In this case, early media would flow from called to caller. In other scenarios, it is also necessary to let early media flow from caller to called. An example of these could be the toll-free routing services that prompt the user for the telephone number before routing the call. In this case, the caller would typically need to send DTMF tones before the call has been answered.

Early-media scenarios in SIP are typically implemented by having the called party send back a 183 (Session progress) provisional response that includes an SDP. If the early media needs to flow from caller to called, the SDP would contain the address where media needs to be sent by the caller. If the early media needs only to flow from called to caller (e.g., an early announcement), then the SDP would indicate to the caller the address where RTCP reports need to be sent.

Another scenario where SDP needs to be sent in a provisional response is a SIP call establishment with QoS preconditions. This scenario will be explained in Chapter 21, and it also requires that provisional responses are delivered reliably.

In order to cope with the general issue of assuring reliability in provisional response, the IETF has defined an extension to the SIP protocol. This extension is specified in [RFC 3262], and introduces a new SIP method (PRACK) and an option tag for this extension (100rel).

15.4.2 How It Works

Let us imagine, for instance, that John makes a call to his voice-mail system in order to listen to his stored messages. In a typical setup, the voice mail first plays a welcome announcement and then accepts the call (i.e., sends 200 OK). Once the call is accepted, the voice mail starts playing the stored messages. In this case, the welcome announcement is a form of early media. Let us see how this works in detail.

John's UA would generate an INVITE request that includes a Supported header with the option tag 100rel. When receiving the INVITE, the voice mail sends back a 183 (Session progress) provisional response containing the SDP answer. This response needs to be sent back reliably, so the voice mail includes in the response a Require header that contains the option tag 100rel.[2] The response also contains a new header field called RSeq, which will also be present in the subsequent PRACK. RSeq allows the voice mail to know what provisional response the PRACK is acknowledging.

When John's UA receives the 183 response, it generates a PRACK request that contains the received RSeq header field. When the PRACK request reaches the voice mail, the voice mail is sure that the 183 response was delivered to the UAC. The voice mail sends a 200 OK response to the PRACK. The voice mail plays the welcome announcement, and when the announcement is done, the voice mail

[2]The voice mail knows that it can require John's UA to use PRACK because John signaled in the request that this extension is supported.

sends a 200 OK final response to the INVITE (i.e., answers the call) and starts playing the stored messages. This is shown in Figure 15.7, where we are assuming that the first 183 response was lost.

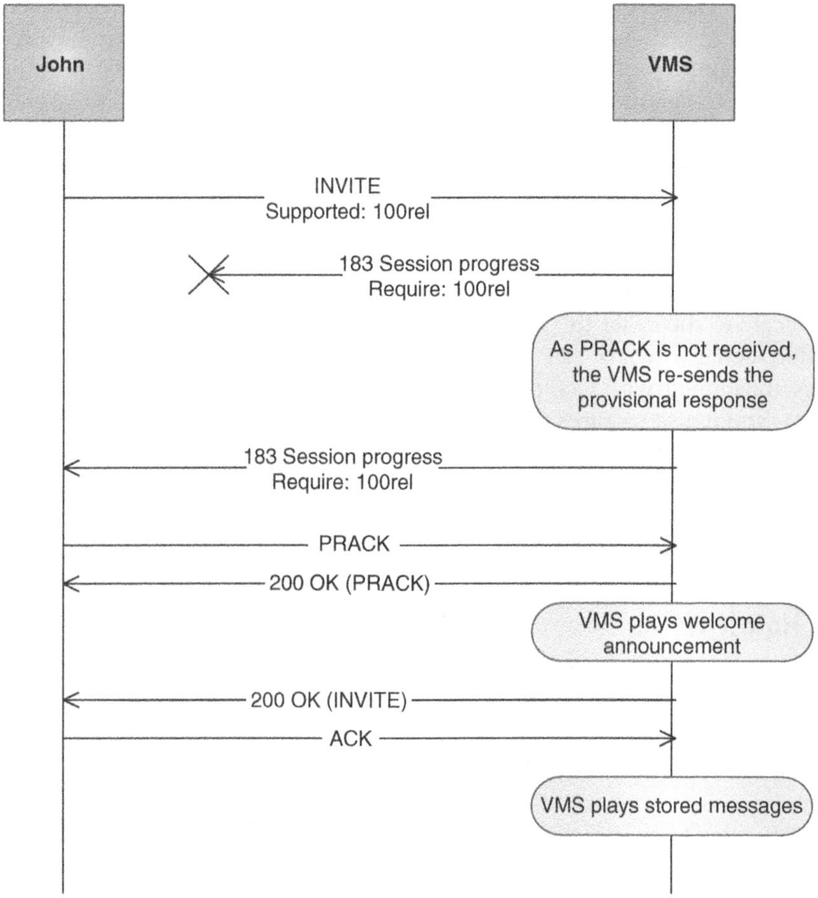

FIGURE 15.7

Readers may wonder what is the use of the 200 OK response to the PRACK request. The 183 response is already acknowledged with the PRACK request, so why generate another message? This has to do with our discussion at the beginning of the chapter. New SIP extensions have to comply with the SIP architectural principles. One such principle is the Transactional principle, which states that new messages added to SIP should comply with the request-response model. This is important because many of the rules of operation in SIP are based on general processing of requests and responses. This includes reliability mechanisms, routing mechanisms, and state maintenance rules. For instance, if we add a new method such as PRACK, we also need to consider that it will need to have its corresponding response. By doing this, for instance, we assure that proxies do not need to be modified to handle the PRACK. Proxies are prepared to handle all new methods in the same way, provided they follow the request-response mechanism.

In this case, the solution is less efficient (one more message), but it is more general, and therefore allows us to benefit from underlying SIP rules of operation and to leverage its extensible design.

15.5 UPDATE

15.5.1 Motivation

Following up on the previous example, let us imagine that while John is listening to the voice-mail welcome announcement, he wants to put the call on hold. We saw in Chapter 9 that, in order to put the call on hold, the UAC should send a re-INVITE request with the SDP sendonly attribute. Because the re-INVITE request modifies the dialog state, RFC 3261 forbids a UAC to send a re-INVITE request if the previous INVITE transaction is not completed.

Therefore, there is no way in RFC 3261 to put a stream of early media on hold because the dialog initiating INVITE request has not yet been completed.

In order to solve this type of issue and others, a new SIP extension [RFC 3311] has been defined. This extension introduces the UPDATE method, which allows us to update parameters in the session while it does not change the dialog state (unlike INVITE, which can be used to update parameters in the session, but does modify the dialog state).

The UPDATE method is very useful whenever we want to update session parameters within an early dialog.

15.5.2 How It Works

Following up on our previous example, let us assume that John makes a call to the voice mail. When he is listening to the welcome announcement, he receives a new call from Alice, so he decides to take the new one and put on hold the call to the voice mail. Let us see how this works.

John sends an initial INVITE that includes an Allow header field listing the UPDATE method. When receiving the INVITE, the voice mail, if it is capable of receiving the UPDATE method, would include an Allow header field listing the UPDATE method in the provisional 183 response. When John's UA receives that response, it knows that it can use the UPDATE method toward the voice mail if John desires to update some session parameters.

The voice mail starts playing the welcome announcement, but then John receives another call, and he decides to take the new call and put the call to the voice mail on hold. In order to put the call on hold, he issues an UPDATE request with the SDP sendonly attribute. When the voice mail receives the request, it acknowledges the request by sending a 200 OK. Some seconds later, John wants to retrieve the call, so he sends a new UPDATE with the SDP sendrecv attribute. He then resumes the communication with the voice mail.

This example is shown in Figure 15.8.

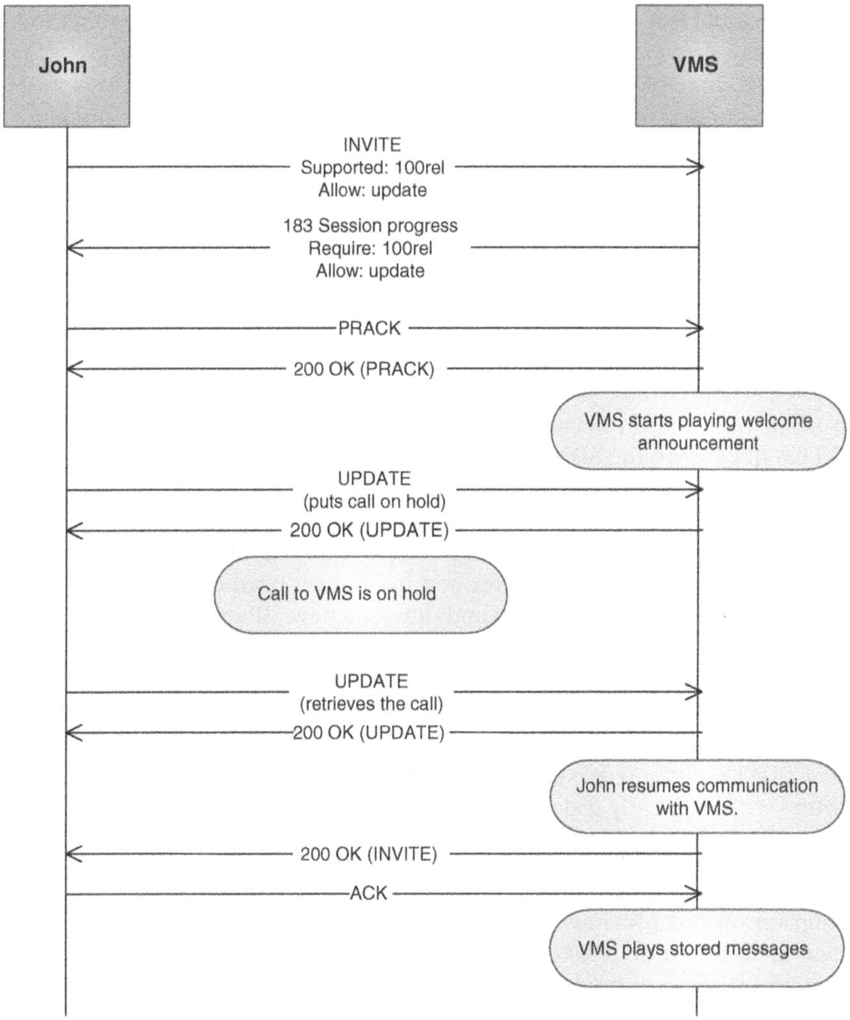

FIGURE 15.8

15.6 SIP-specific Event Notification

15.6.1 Motivation

In communication systems, there is sometimes the need for end users or applications to receive a notification of an event related to the state of some communication resource. For instance, if John calls Alice, and he gets a busy signal because Alice is already engaged in another conversation, he might then want to be notified as soon as Alice becomes free, so that he can call her again. In another scenario, John might be interested to know when new messages arrive to his voice mail.

The core SIP specification defines how to set up, modify, and release communication sessions. Core SIP does not include any mechanism to allow UAs or applications to be notified of communication-related events.

[RFC 3265] defines a new SIP extension that provides a framework for asynchronous event notification in the context of SIP-based communication systems. It is important to understand that this framework is not intended to be a general-purpose infrastructure for all classes of event subscription and notification. On the contrary, it is SIP specific, and focused on complementing the key communications functionalities enabled by the core SIP. Therefore, this extension is considered to fit into SIP's solution space.

15.6.2 How It Works

The extension provides a framework that allows SIP nodes to request notification from remote nodes indicating that certain events have occurred. User Agents can, in the remit of this framework, play the following roles:

- *Subscriber*: The User Agent that subscribes to specific events and receives notifications when these events occur.
- *Notifier*: The User Agent that receives the subscription requests and generates the notifications toward the subscriber

The extension also defines two new SIP methods:

- SUBSCRIBE: This request is sent by a subscriber in order to subscribe to an event or class of events. It may include a body that contains a filter for the class of events being requested. The SUBSCRIBE request creates a SIP dialog.[3]
- NOTIFY: This request is sent by the notifier in order to inform the subscriber about the occurrence of an event. The request includes a body that contains the description of the state of the monitored resource.

The operation of event subscription and notification is quite simple. A UA (subscriber) interested in being informed about the state information of a communication resource sends a SUBSCRIBE message to the UA (notifier) responsible for that communication resource. In the SUBSCRIBE request, the subscriber includes a new header field, called Event, that indicates the event or class of events that it is subscribing to. If the notifier accepts the subscription, it responds to the SUBSCRIBE request with a 200 OK. Then the notifier immediately constructs and sends to the subscriber a NOTIFY request including the state information required. From then on, until the subscription is terminated, the notifier will send new NOTIFY requests whenever a change in the requested state information is produced.

[3] In [RFC 3261], the only dialog-creating request was the INVITE request. [RFC 3265] defines a new method, called SUBSCRIBE, that can also create a SIP dialog. Some people are confused by this because they tend to associate "dialog" with "session," although these are completely different concepts, as was explained in previous chapters. A SUBSCRIBE request does not initiate any session.

In the SUBSCRIBE request, the subscriber includes an Expires header field that indicates the duration for the subscription. The subscription is refreshed whenever a new SUBSCRIBE message is received on the same SIP dialog. A subscription is terminated either because the subscriber sends a SUBSCRIBE request with an Expires header field set to "0" or because the subscription timer expires.

In Figure 15.9, we see the basic operation for the event subscribe and notification.

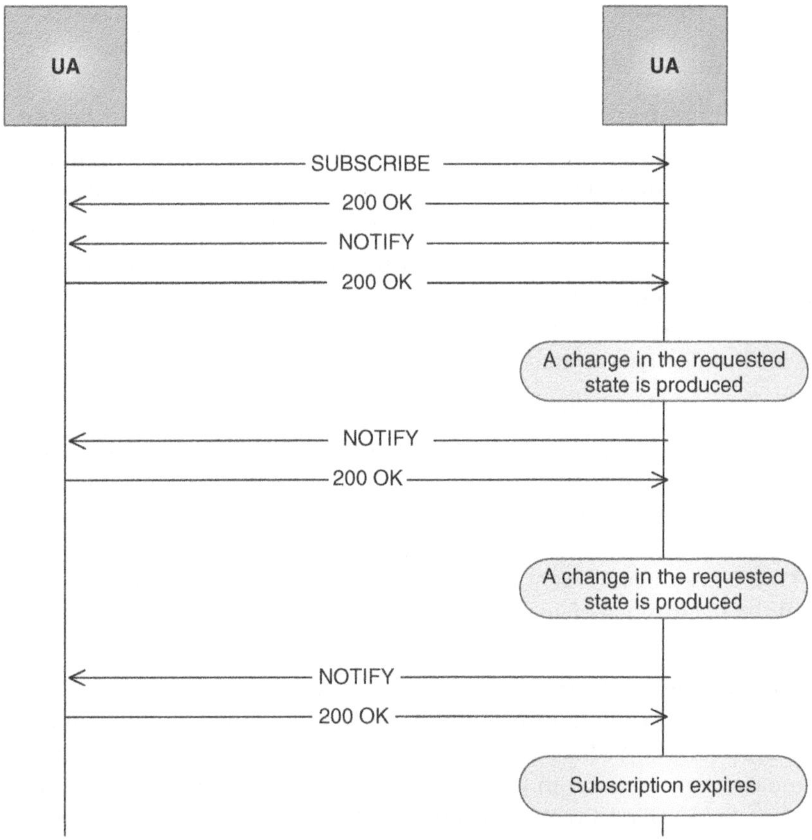

FIGURE 15.9

The operation of the SUBSCRIBE and NOTIFY methods is detailed in RFC 3265. However, this RFC does not describe an extension that may be used directly; it needs to be extended by other documents, referred to as an event package. Event packages provide more information on the syntax and semantics of the state information for a particular class of events, as well as additional information about the operation of subscribers and notifiers specific to that particular class of events. There are separate

RFCs that define event packages for different types of events. For instance:

[RFC 3515]: event package for the REFER method[4]
[RFC 3680]: event package for SIP-registration events
[RFC 3842]: event package for voice-mail notification events
[RFC 4235]: event package for SIP-dialog events
[RFC 4354]: event package for SIP Push to talk over Cellular (PoC) events
[RFC 4575]: event package for SIP-conferencing events[5]
[RFC 4730]: event package for media server events[6]

User agents indicate support for the SIP notification framework and specific event packages by adding an Allow-Events header field in all methods that initiate dialogs and in the responses to these methods. The Allow-Events headers field contains a list of tokens indicating the event packages supported by the User Agent. For instance:

Allow-Events: reginfo, conference

Such a header field indicates that the UA supports the event packages for registration events and conferencing events.

15.6.3 Event Packages

The RFCs for event packages contain, among other things, the following information related to a particular class of events:

- *Event package name*: It identifies the event package. The Event header field in a SUBSCRIBE request will contain the name of the event package being subscribed. Furthermore, a UA wanting to indicate support for a particular event package will include the name of the UA in the Allow-Event header field of dialog-initiating requests and their responses.
- *SUBSCRIBE bodies*: SUBSCRIBE requests may contain bodies that represent a filter to be applied to the subscription.
- *NOTIFY bodies*: NOTIFY requests contain bodies that include the state information for the class of events. The state information may be expressed as an XML document, as plain text, or other.
- *Additional processing of SUBSCRIBE and NOTIFY requests*: Includes details on how to perform the authentication and authorization, detailed information about what events shall cause a NOTIFY to be sent, and so forth.
- Others

By way of example, we will look a bit more in detail at some of these event packages.

[4] The REFER method will be examined in Chapter 17.
[5] SIP conferencing will be analyzed in Chapter 19.
[6] Media servers will be explained in Chapter 19.

15.6.4 Event Package for SIP Registrations

In some cases, a SIP entity may be interested to be informed about the registration status of a User Agent. Consider, for instance, a "welcome news" application such as the sort that is quite typical in mobile networks. When users turn on their phone in a foreign country, they receive a welcome message that provides them with general information about the country.

In a SIP environment, such a service might be implemented by having an application server subscribe to the registration state of the user. When the user turns on the phone, the phone will generate a registration toward the REGISTRAR. The REGISTRAR would then send a NOTIFY request to the "welcome" application server, which might then take the action to send the welcome message to the user. The welcome message might be sent as a SIP page-mode instant message, as we will see Chapter 16.

In Figure 15.10, we can see the message flow for this example.

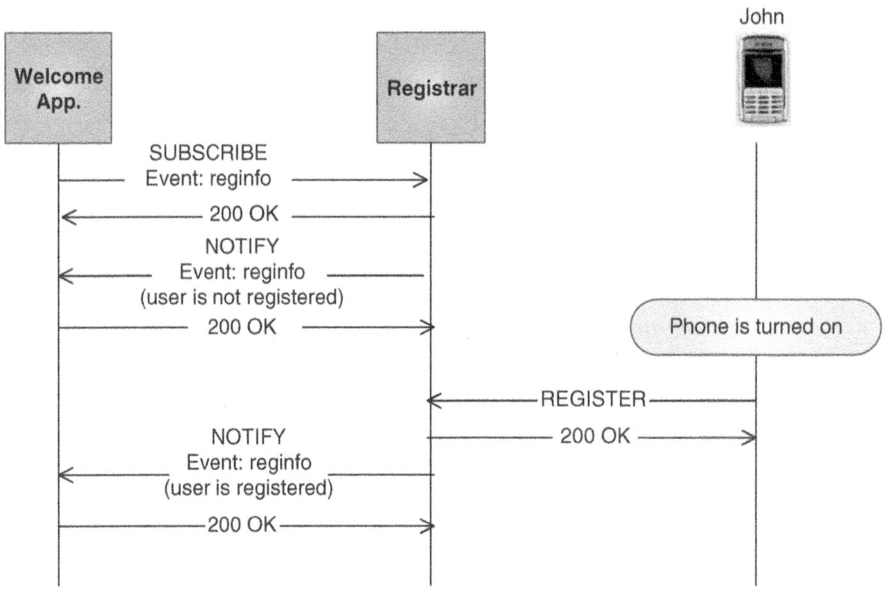

FIGURE 15.10

The name for the registration event package is "reginfo." The state information contained in the body of NOTIFY messages is expressed as an XML document.

The first NOTIFY request contains a body that indicates that John is not yet registered:

```
<?xml version="1.0"?>
<reginfo xmlns="urn:ietf:params:xml:ns:reginfo"
        version="0" state="full">
  <registration aor="sip:john@sea.com" id="a7" state="init"/>
</reginfo>
```

The body in the second NOTIFY request reflects the fact that John has registered:

```
<?xml version="1.0"?>
<reginfo xmlns="urn:ietf:params:xml:ns:reginfo"
      version="1" state="partial">
 <registration aor="sip:john@sea.com" id="a7" state="active">
  <contact id="76" state="active" event="registered"
      duration-registered="0">
   <uri>sip:john@pc3.sea.com</uri>
  </contact>
 </registration>
</reginfo>
```

15.6.5 Event Package for SIP Dialogs

Another interesting event package allows a User Agent to receive notifications of dialog-related events occurring in other User Agents. These events include dialog initiation, termination, and so forth. The name of the event package is "dialog."

Let us consider the following scenario: John calls Alice, but she is actually engaged in another call. John gets a busy signal. John wants to know when Alice becomes free again, so he sends a SUBSCRIBE request to Alice. The Event header field in the SUBSCRIBE is:

Event: dialog

Alice's UA responds with a 200 OK, and generates an initial NOTIFY request that indicates that Alice is busy. Later on, Alice becomes free, and her UA sends another NOTIFY request, indicating this change in the dialog state. John receives the NOTIFY, and immediately calls Alice again. Now she is free and takes the call.

This call flow is shown in Figure 15.11.

The SIP event package for dialogs is expressed in XML format. As an example, the first NOTIFY in our previous example might look like:

```
<?xml version="1.0"?>
<dialog-info xmlns="urn:ietf:params:xml:ns:dialog-info" version="1" state="full"
      entity="sip:alice@ocean.com">
 <dialog id="rv7ew84js" call-id="gs8j44l3d8fdj4" local-tag="8493948539"
      remote-tag="iw32p" direction="initiator">
  <state>confirmed</state>
 </dialog>
</dialog-info>
```

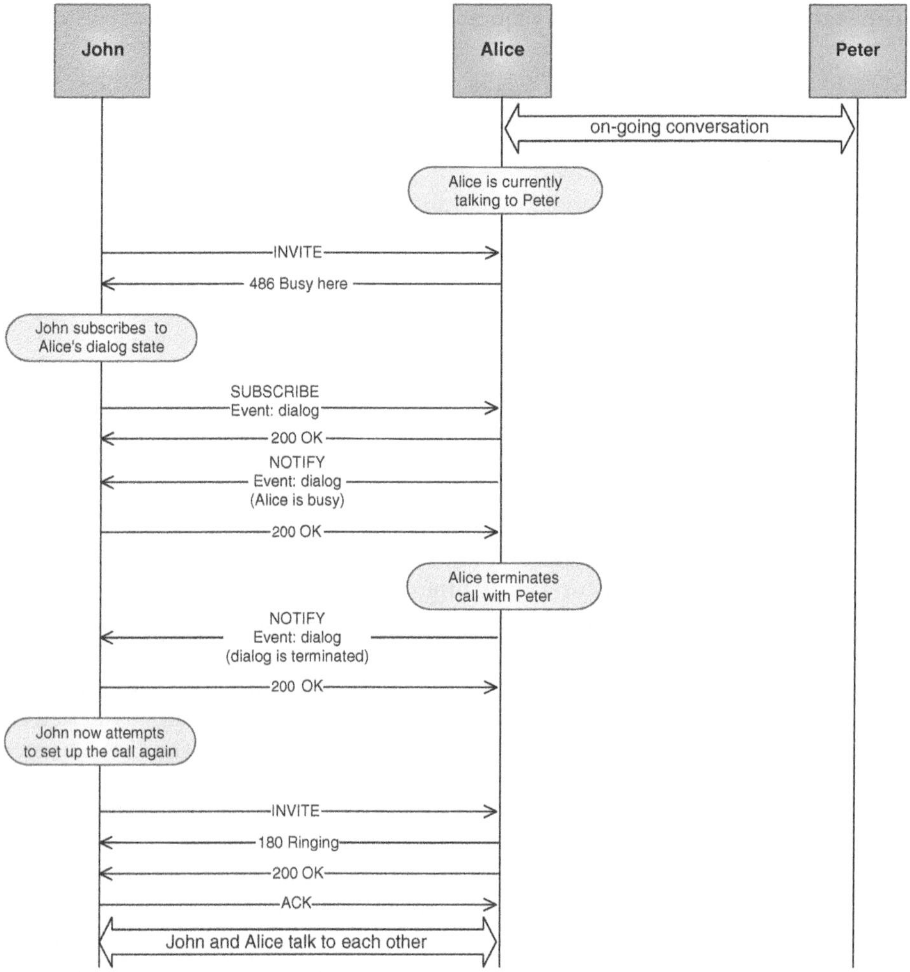

FIGURE 15.11

The body of the second NOTIFY indicates that the dialog is terminated:

```
<?xml version="1.0"?>
<dialog-info xmlns="urn:ietf:params:xml:ns:dialog-info"
      version="2" state="partial" entity="sip:alice@ocean.com">
  <dialog id=" rv7ew84js " call-id="gs8j44l3d8fdj4"
      local-tag="8493948539" remote-tag="iw32p" direction="initiator">
    <state reason="remote-bye">terminated</state>
  </dialog>
</dialog-info>
```

15.7 History-Info

15.7.1 Motivation

SIP proxies and B2BUAs may change the Request-URI of a request, therefore changing the target of the request. Such a process is called retargeting. In the process of retargeting, old routing information can be lost. There are cases where, in order to apply a service, it is necessary to know how the call arrived at a particular application—that is, it is necessary to know how the Request-URI was modified in the different processes of retargeting that the call went through. In other words, there is a need to know the "request history" of the call. This request history information would allow an application to know how and why the application arrived at the application/user.

Let us think, for instance, of a simple call-forwarding application implemented in a proxy. John calls Alice, but Alice is busy, so her inbound proxy forwards the call to the voice mail. In order to do so, the proxy removes the original Request-URI, alice@pacific.com, and sets it to vms.pacific.com. Therefore, the information about the original destination of the call is lost. The call then reaches the voice mail. The voice mail should access Alice's mailbox, but the Request-URI no longer points at Alice, so the voice-mail system does not know what mailbox to access.

This problem would be resolved if the information about the original recipient or destination of the call were maintained when retargeting the request in the proxy.

[RFC 4244] defines a SIP extension that allows us to capture the request history information of a call. It is based on a new header field called History-Info, which is updated every time retargeting occurs.

15.7.2 How It Works

The mechanism is quite simple. A UAC that desires to receive the History-Info in responses includes a Supported header with the option tag "histinfo" in outgoing requests. Additionally, the UAC originating the request can also add a History-Info header with a value equal to that of the Request-URI. As a result, intermediaries and the UAS can know what the original Request-URI was.

Whenever retargeting occurs, the SIP entity implementing the retargeting may, provided that this entity supports History-Info and based on local policy, add the new target to the History-Info header field.

Finally, the UAS will copy the received History-Info into the response it sends back to the UAC.

A SIP request or response may contain a list of History-Info header fields. Each header field must contain at least two elements:

- The new Request-URI in the retargeted request
- An index, which reflects the chronological order of the information.

In addition, each header field may also contain a Reason parameter that indicates the Reason for the retargeting, and a Privacy parameter that indicates if a specific History-Info header may be forwarded.[7]

Figure 15.12 depicts the previously described scenario with the voice mail.

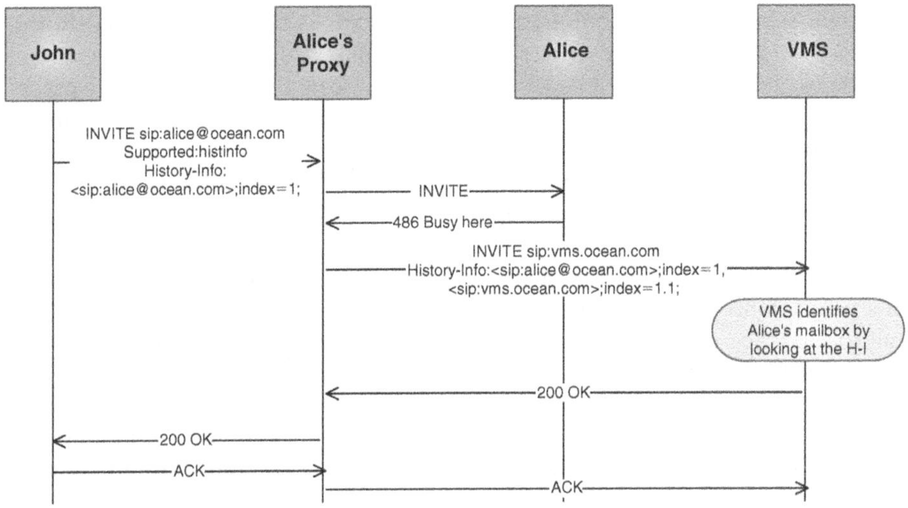

FIGURE 15.12

15.8 Globally Routable User Agent URIs (GRUUs)

15.8.1 Motivation

We have seen in previous chapters that a user is identified, for SIP purposes, by the address-of-record (AOR), which typically has the form of a SIP URI (e.g., sip:john@sea.com). The AOR identifies the user, but the user may have more than one device (PC, laptop, mobile, and so on), all of them corresponding to the same user, the same AOR. When the UA in a device is turned on, it registers its contact address for the AOR. If, say, three User Agents, one in each device (PC, laptop, and mobile), are registered, the registrar would show an AOR connected to three different contact addresses. This situation is depicted in Figure 15.13.

The situation just described is perfectly supported by the core SIP specification. In order to determine how calls destined to the AOR are terminated, different approaches might be followed. For instance, each contact address might have a different priority assigned to it so that the authoritative proxy tries some devices before others. It is also possible that all contact addresses have the same priority, thus forcing the proxy to perform parallel ringing. This scenario is shown in Figure 15.14.

[7] The decision to forward or not a particular History-Info header field may depend on the value of the Privacy header, on local policy, and on whether the request is being forwarded to a Request-URI associated with a domain for which the processing entity is responsible.

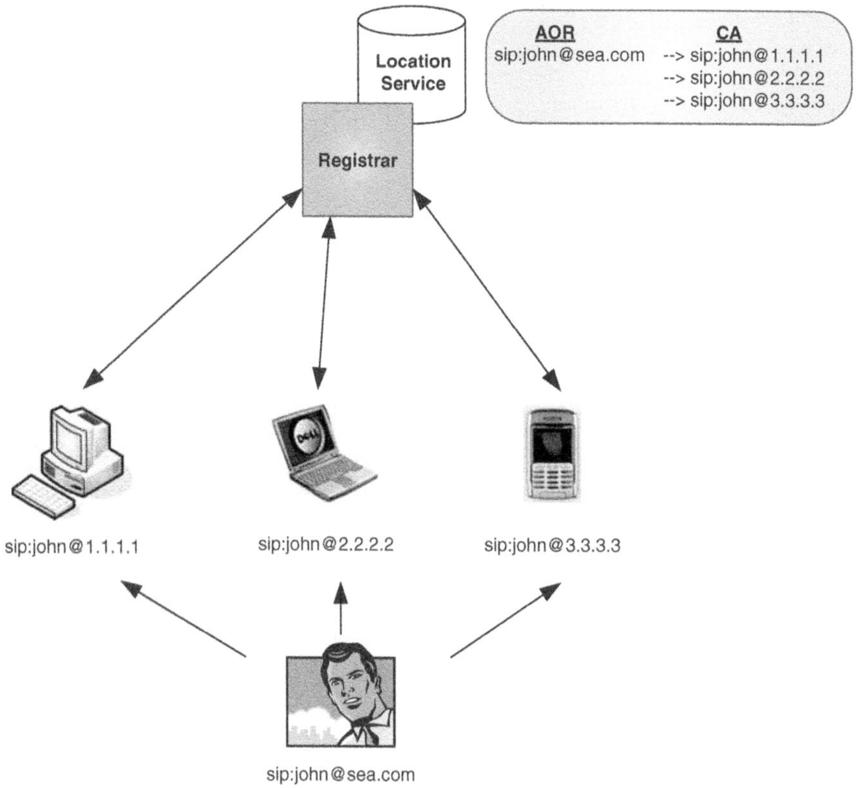

FIGURE 15.13

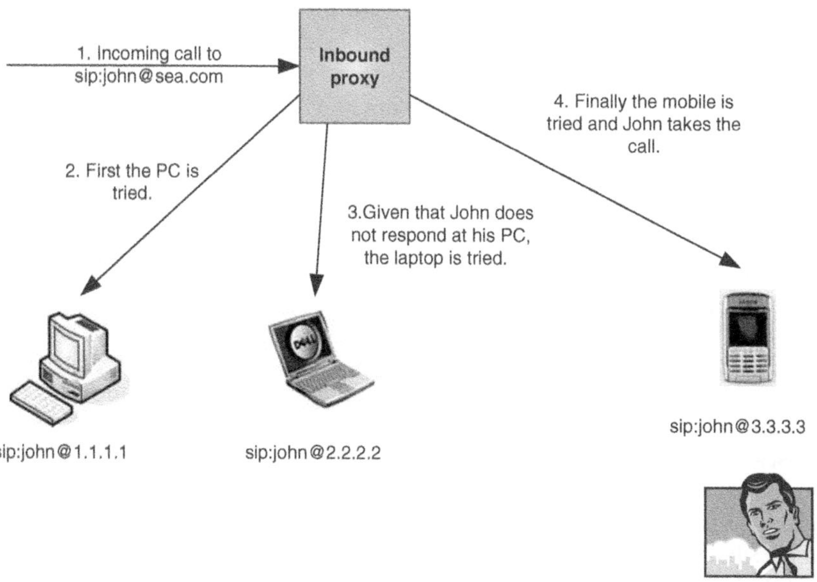

FIGURE 15.14

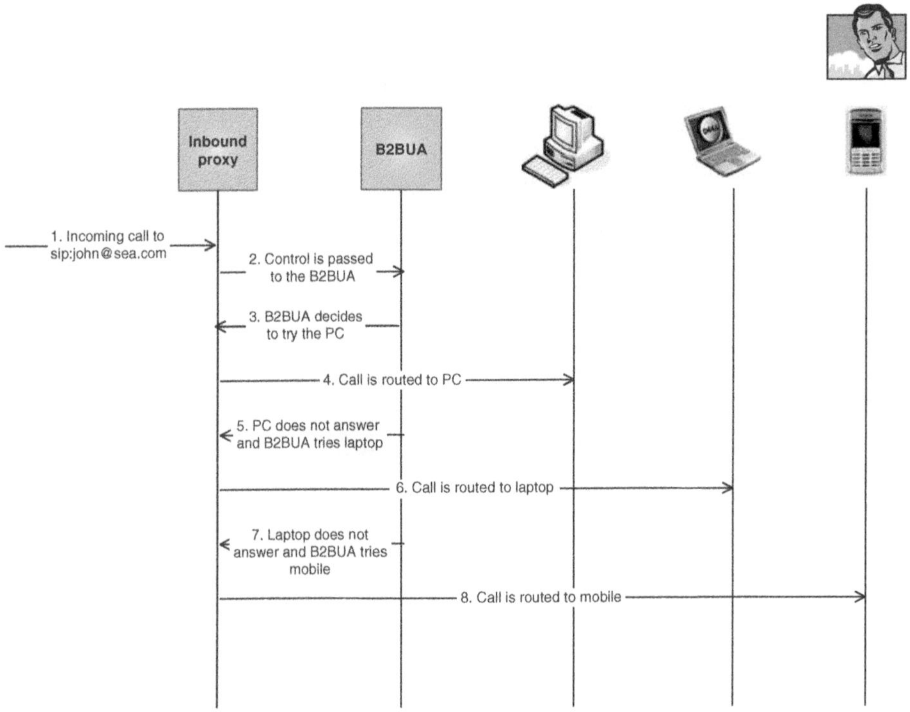

FIGURE 15.15

The usual case, though, is that the call termination logic for these kinds of scenarios is handled by an application server in the form of a B2BUA that can take into consideration a number of factors (not just the priority in the contact header), such as presence, time of day, subscriber data, and so forth. This type of service is commonly known as multidevice service. Figure 15.15 shows an arrangement where a B2BUA controls the termination of calls destined to the multidevice user.

The question that is raised here is: How can the proxy or the application server force the routing to specific instances of the same AOR—that is, to a specific device?

In the case of the proxy, the answer is clear. The authoritative proxy uses the bound contact address to perform the routing; each device has a different contact address, so the proxy just needs to select the appropriate contact address corresponding to the device that is to be reached and put it into the Request-URI of the outgoing request.

The same solution might be applied in the case of the application server; however, this might pose a problem because contact addresses typically contain IP addresses that may not be routable if there are NAT devices or firewalls in between. When the NAT is placed between the proxy and the UA, there are solutions to address the NAT traversal problem, as we will see in Chapter 22. However, it is not possible to assure that contact addresses are routable from any point of the Internet.

We have just depicted a particular scenario, but there are several other use cases[8] that justify the need for a globally routable identifier for a UA instance that can be used by arbitrary external clients. As of the time of writing, there is work in progress in the IETF [draft-ietf-sip-gruu] to specify a SIP extension that defines such an identifier, called GRUU.

Even if it is still an Internet draft, we have purposely included it in this chapter alongside other extensions published in official RFC documents because we believe the GRUU concept has considerable relevance.

15.8.2 How It Works

From a high-level point of view, it is quite easy to understand how the GRUU extension is used.

First of all, when a UA that performs a registration procedure supports the GRUU extension, it indicates so by including the "gruu" option tag in the Supported header field. In addition, the UA provides, as part of the address in the Contact header field, an instance ID value in the new "+sip.instance" parameter.

When the registrar receives such a REGISTER request, if the request supports the GRUU extension, the registrar will construct a GRUU. Then the registrar associates the GRUU with the corresponding instance ID and contact address. It also communicates the GRUU back to the UA in a specific parameter (pub-gruu) in the Contact header field of the 200OK response.

The GRUU generated by the registrar is a SIP URI that includes a "gr" parameter with a value chosen by the registrar that identifies the particular UA instance. For example, a GRUU for John might look like:

sip:john@sea.com;gr=yd72394b9374d3

The easiest way for the registrar to construct a public[9] GRUU is to take the address of record, and place the actual value of the instance ID into the contents of the "gr" URI parameter.

Figure 15.16 shows a registration process when GRUU is supported.

Once a UA is registered, if an incoming request destined for the GRUU reaches the authoritative proxy, it will query the location service and retrieve the contact address associated to the specific UA instance that the GRUU refers to. It will then forward the request to that contact address.

User Agents that have obtained a GRUU will indicate its value in the Contact header field of any non-REGISTER request that they generate. This

---

[8] Actually, the example that is commonly shown to illustrate the need for the GRUU is the blind-transfer application. Readers can find the explanation on that use case in [draft-ietf-sip-gruu]. In the text, I have preferred to use the multidevice example, which also presents a practical scenario where there is a need for the GRUU.

[9] There are two types of GRUUs: public and temporary. Both of them must be constructed by the registrar and returned to the UA in the REGISTER response. In this high-level introduction to the GRUU concept, we are referring just to public GRUUs. Our aim is that readers can get just an overall understanding of this SIP extension. For a clear explanation on the differences between public and temporary GRUUs, readers are referred to [draft-ietf-sip-gruu].

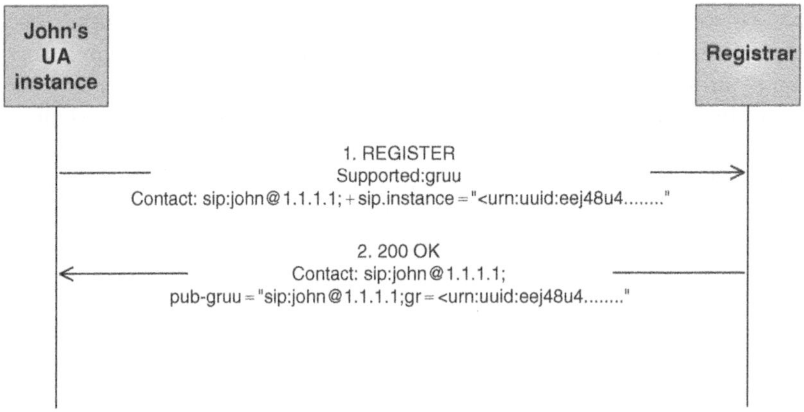

FIGURE 15.16

would allow other SIP entities to learn about the GRUU of the UA instance so as to use it in subsequent requests that need to be targeted to that particular instance. Another approach for external SIP entities (such as application servers) to learn about the GRUU of a particular UA instance could be to use an extension to the SIP-registration event package that includes the GRUU value [draft-ietf-sipping-gruu-reg-event]).

15.9 Summary

In this chapter, we presented the way SIP can be extended, and we also introduced some important general-purpose extensions. There are many other SIP extensions that are used in specific scenarios. In the next chapters, we will look into specific areas of applicability of the SIP protocol. While doing so, we will also highlight what new SIP extensions are needed in those specific areas. We will start in the next chapter by examining the presence and instant messaging services together with the SIP extensions needed to implement them.

CHAPTER

Presence and Instant Messaging 16

In this chapter, we will present a very popular IP-based communications service called instant messaging and the presence service traditionally associated with it. Again we will see that SIP can play an important role in order to deliver these services.

We will start the chapter by describing these services and setting the scene with regard to the standardization activities around them. Then we will focus on the presence service, explaining the abstract presence model and how it is materialized with SIP. We will also touch upon the presence data format and other topics such as resource lists and the utilization of the XCAP protocol.

Then we will present the instant messaging service and the two different modalities for its SIP-based implementation. Last we will review the main functions of an IM server.

16.1 Overview of Presence and Instant Messaging

16.1.1 Presence and Online Communications

We said in Chapter 1 that the email service is an example of an offline IP communication service. The sending of the email is decoupled from its reception by a store and forward mechanism, and therefore sender and recipient do not necessarily need to be "connected" simultaneously for communication to happen.

Hence, when John sends an email to Alice, he does not necessarily need to know beforehand if she is currently connected. He just sends the email and forgets about it. Supposedly, Alice will read the email at some time that may be one minute, one day, or one month after John sent it, and then she may or not want to respond to him.

As opposed to email, the popular instant messaging service offered by Yahoo!, Microsoft, Jabber, and others is an online IP communications service. Communication happens immediately between originator and recipient, and both of them need to be connected simultaneously. In such a kind of scenario, when John intends to engage in a communication with Alice, he may want to know beforehand if Alice is connected or not. The submission of an instant message, as opposed to what happened with email, will fail if Alice is not connected. Likewise, Alice might be connected but currently in a meeting, unable to engage in a communication. That is also something that John might want to know in advance. In other words, John might be interested in knowing Alice's presence.

This is the reason why instant messaging and presence were somehow coupled together from the beginning, and this is also the reason why several standardization efforts considered them together. Actually, the presence concept is not exclusively associated with instant messaging. Rather, it can be associated with online communications in general. We saw that SIP plays a key role in online communication scenarios, and we will see during this chapter that it also plays an important role in order to enable the presence service.

A popular example of implementation of presence and instant messaging (together with other communication means) is the so-called "communicator applications." This type of application typically offers a user interface that represents a buddy list. Associated with each name in the buddy list, there is a label or an icon indicating that buddy's presence information (available, unavailable, busy, in a meeting, and so on). If John wants to communicate with Alice, who is one of his buddies, he will check her presence by looking at the buddy list in his communicator application. If it shows that Laura is available, he can then click in her name entry and select a communication service such as instant messaging, voice, or other. If he selects voice, for instance, the application automatically launches a call to Alice. If he selects instant messaging, a box appears in the screen where he can write a message that is immediately sent to Alice. Yahoo! and Microsoft, among others, offer this type of communicator application.

16.1.2 Presence and Instant Messaging Standards

Instant messaging became popular in the mid-1990s with services such as ICQ (pronounced: "I seek you") and AIM (AOL Instant Messenger). Others—such as IBM, Yahoo!, and MSN—soon followed, but all of them used proprietary protocols, so typically users needed to have a different client for each different service, and the different services were not interoperable. So were things when the IMPP (Instant Message and Presence Protocol) Working Group within IETF tried to define a common architecture for Internet-scale deployment of presence and instant messaging. The IETF defined an abstract model for presence and instant messaging, but there was eventually no agreement as to what transport protocol to use. Therefore, new, different Working Groups were created in order to deal with each of the different protocols. Still, the IMPP WG, in an attempt to facilitate the interworking between the different systems, defined a common profile and a data format, both for presence and instant messaging, with which the different implementations should comply.

One of the new Working Groups was called SIMPLE, and it attempted to define a way to implement presence and instant messaging using SIP.[1] Sometime later,

[1] The other proposed protocols were IMXP (Instant Messaging eXtensible Protocol), which leverages ideas from email, and PRIM (PResence and Instant Messaging), aimed at minimally satisfying the IMPP model. Both of them were discontinued soon after.

another IETF WG was chartered to standardize the open-source Jabber Extensible Messaging and Presence Protocol (XMPP). XMPP, which is not SIP based, is used by a significant number of people in the Internet.

Later on, in 2002, the Open Mobile Alliance (OMA)—a forum formed by systems manufacturers, mobile operators, and software vendors—was created with the mission to provide interoperable service enablers for the mobile-phone industry. They proposed yet another approach in order to implement presence and instant messaging in a mobile environment that is typically referred to as IMPS (Instant Message and Presence Service).[2]

In recent years, a lot of commercial products have started to incorporate SIP/SIMPLE. Examples are Microsoft, with their communications solution for enterprises called Microsoft Office Live Communication Server; IBM; Avaya; Nortel; and others.

Moreover, SIP/SIMPLE has also been adopted in the remit of 3GPP and IMS.[3] Actually, the Open Mobile Alliance (OMA) has also defined a SIMPLE-based presence enabler meant to work in an IMS environment. SIP-based implementations for instant messaging and presence are increasingly gaining acceptance. One of the key advantages of using SIP for instant messaging and presence is that it allows us to easily combine them with other communications services such as voice, video, gaming, whiteboarding, and others, and so provide a total communication experience to end users.

16.2 The Presence Model

Presence is defined as the willingness and ability of a user to communicate with other users on the network. For instance, John's presence information might tell us that he is not connected (in a SIP environment, this equals "not registered"), or that he is connected but he is in a meeting and cannot accept communications, and so forth. Moreover, an extended presence concept might even give information about the user's mood, location, communication capabilities (depending on the device through the user he or she is currently connected), and so on.

The IMPP Working Group defined an abstract model meant to provide a means for describing instant messaging and presence systems [RFC 2778]. The IMPP also defined a minimum set of requirements for an instant messaging and presence protocol [RFC 2779]. The presence model is quite simple. It defines three different entities:

- the presentity
- the watcher
- the presence service

The presentity is the entity that provides presence information. For instance, John may want to provide his presence information (online, busy, and so on) to his buddies. The presentity is an abstract concept that represents John for the presence

[2] Or IMPS enabler, to be more specific.
[3] The 3GPP IMS is described in Chapter 24.

service. The watcher is the entity that receives presence information. For instance Alice, a buddy of John's, might be interested in "watching" his presence information. The presence service receives presence information from the presentities and distributes it among the watchers. This is represented in Figure 16.1.

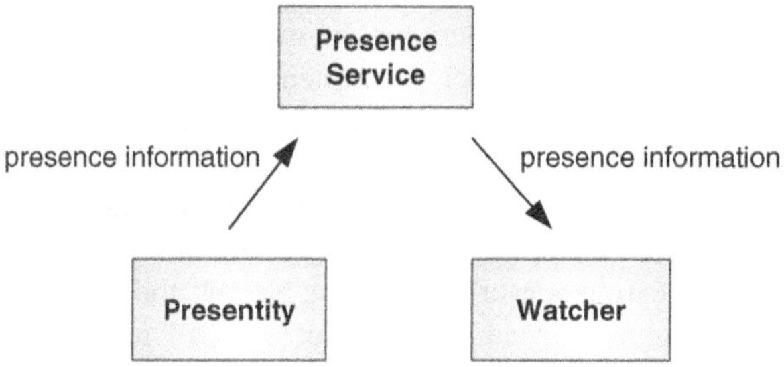

FIGURE 16.1

There are two types of watchers, called subscribers and fetchers. A subscriber requests notification from the presence service of changes in the presentity's presence information. A fetcher, on the other hand, simply requests the current value of the presentity's presence information. Moreover, a special type of fetcher that requests information on a regular basis is called a poller. This is shown in Figure 16.2.

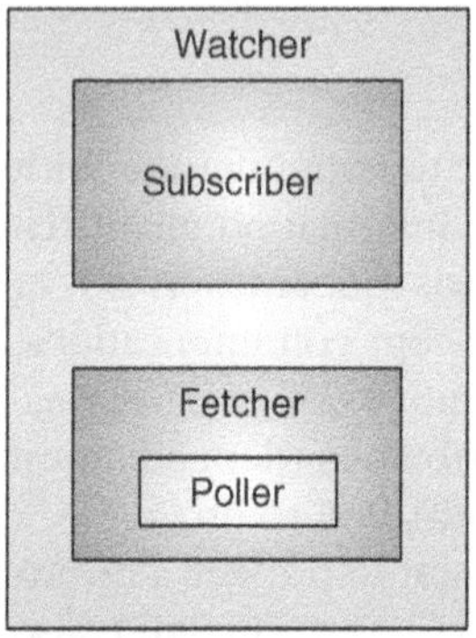

FIGURE 16.2

So far, we have seen the basic model for presence. In addition to this basic model, the IMPP Working Group has also defined:

- *A common profile for presence (CPP)*: That is, a set of operations and parameters involved in the provision of the presence service. For instance, it defines the abstract "subscribe" operation, which allows a watcher to subscribe to the presence information of a particular presentity, or the abstract "notify" operation, which allows the presence service to inform the watcher about a change in the presentity's presence information [RFC 3859].
- *A presence information data format (PIDF)*: That is, a common XML format to represent the presence information [RFC 3863].

These two specifications allow for interoperability between CPP-compliant systems even if these systems use different transport protocols. In the next section, we will see an implementation of a CPP-compliant presence system using the SIP protocol. In subsequent sections, we will discuss the way to represent presence information.

16.3 Presence with SIP

The presence model depicted in the previous section can be implemented using the SIP protocol. More specifically, it can be implemented using the SIP event notification framework that we saw in Chapter 15, together with a newly defined "presence" event package. Additionally, a new SIP extension for event state publication is also needed. [RFC 3856] defines the "presence" event package, whereas [RFC 3903] defines a generic mechanism for publication of event state information that can again be applied for presence by using the presence event package. The resulting architecture can be seen as composed of three entities:

- The Presence User Agent (PUA)
- The Presence Agent (PA)
- The watcher application

The PUA manipulates presence information for a presentity. It can publish presence information.

The PA is a SIP UA with the following functions:

- Process the published presence information.
- Authenticate subscribe requests.
- Authorize subscribe request.
- Process subscribe requests.
- Generate notifications of changes in presence state.

The watcher application is a SIP UA that can subscribe to presence information and receive notifications about the change of state of a presentity's presence information.

16.3.1 Publication of Presence Information

A PUA may publish presence information by sending a SIP PUBLISH message to the Presence Agent (PA). The PUBLISH request contains, among others, three interesting pieces of information:

- The Request-URI, which identifies the resource whose event state is to be published, and contains enough information to route the request to the PA.
- The Event header, which indicates the type of the published event—in this case, the type is "presence."
- The body, which contains a presence document, which, in turn, describes the state of the presentity.

When the PUBLISH request is successful, the PA generates and assigns an entity-tag and returns it in the new SIP-ETag header field of the 2XX response. If, later on, the PUA wants to refresh the presence information, it will include such entity-tag value in the SIP-If-Match header of the new PUBLISH request so as to refer to the info that needs to be refreshed. This is shown in Figure 16.3.

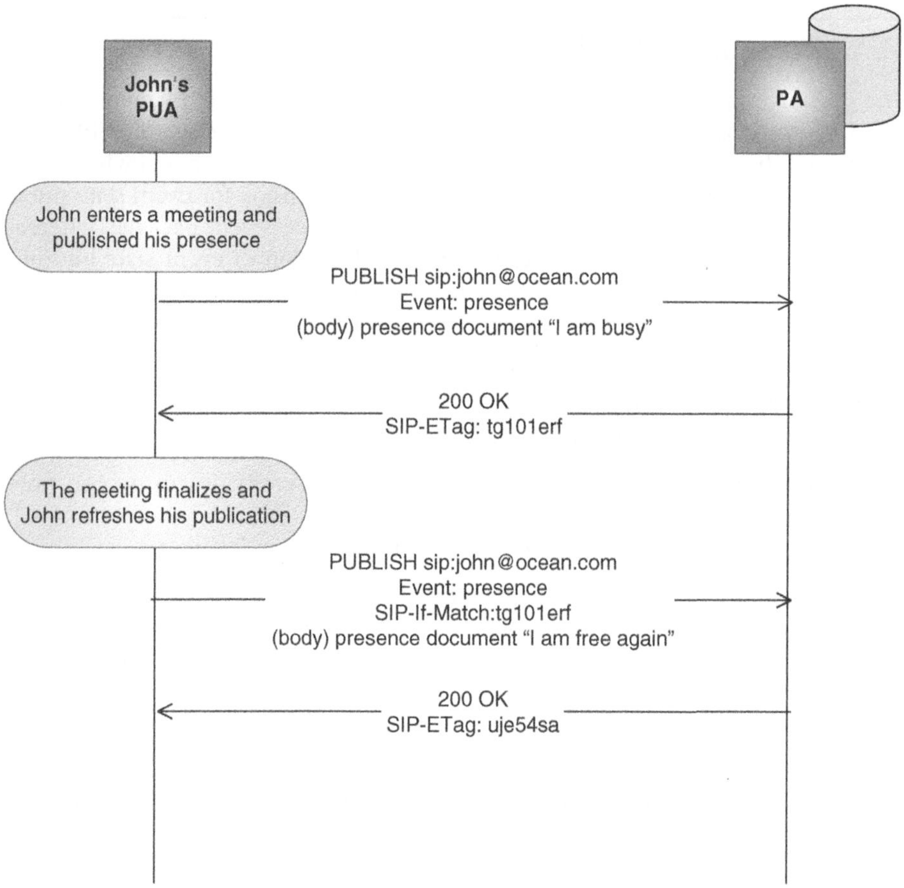

FIGURE 16.3

16.3.2 Subscribing to Presence Information

A watcher application subscribes to a presentity's presence information by generating a SUBSCRIBE message with "presence" event type, and by setting the Request-URI to indicate the resource whose presence is requested. Additionally, the body of the SUBSCRIBE may contain a filter document. This filter can request that only certain presence events generate notifications, or can ask for a restriction on the set of data returned in NOTIFY requests. [RFC 4660] contains a functional description of event notification filtering.

SUBSCRIBE requests have to be authenticated and authorized by the PA. Authentication might be achieved using HTTP digest as specified in RFC 3261.

The authorization may be provided by access lists in the form of XML documents that can be modified by the user.

Figure 16.4 depicts Alice subscribing to John's presence information.

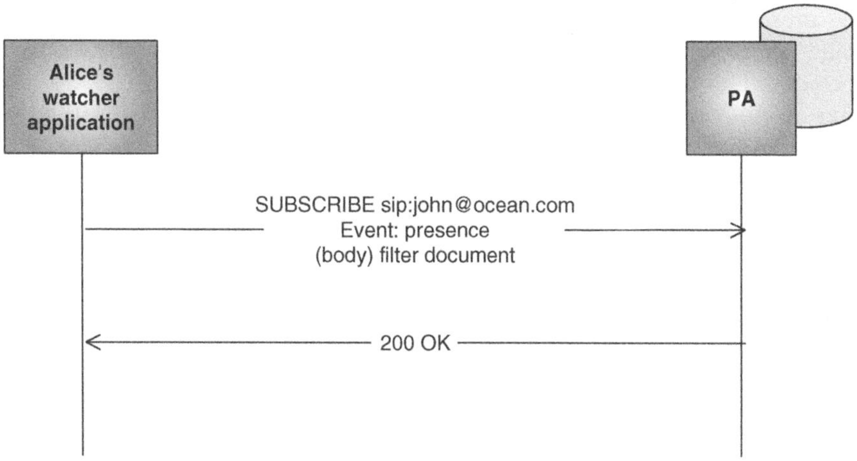

FIGURE 16.4

16.3.3 Generation of Notifications

A PA can notify watchers about a change of the presentity's state by sending a SIP NOTIFY message to the watcher (see Figure 16.5). The body of the NOTIFY message contains a presence document.

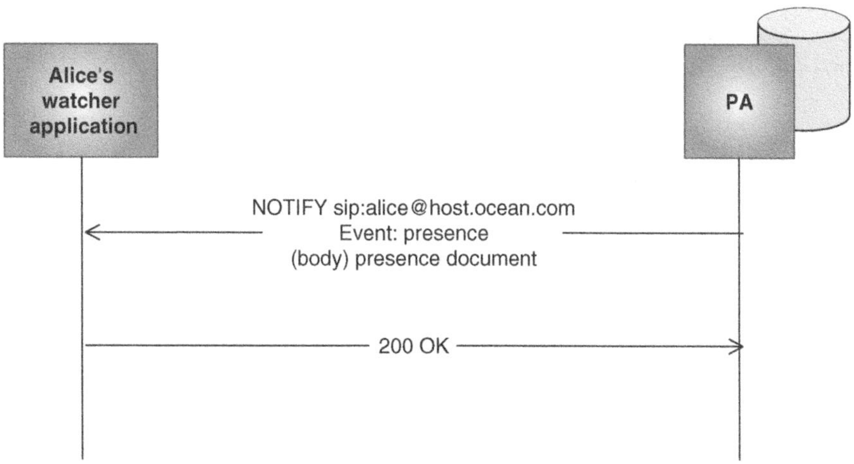

FIGURE 16.5

16.3.4 Example

Let us now see an end-to-end example. Let us assume that presence information from Alice is managed by a presence server that implements a Presence Agent. The presence server has access to a database where presence information is stored.

John wants to be informed about Alice's presence information. Therefore, he, acting as a watcher, sends a SUBSCRIBE to Alice's presence server.

The presence server responds with a 200 OK, and generates a first NOTIFY message. The NOTIFY includes a presence document that describes Alice's current presence information.

Later on, Alice enters a meeting, and therefore her PUA sends a PUBLISH message to her PA to indicate that her presence has changed and that she is now in a meeting.

As soon as the PA receives the PUBLISH, it generates a new NOTIFY message toward John to inform him that Alice is now in a meeting. This is shown in Figure 16.6.

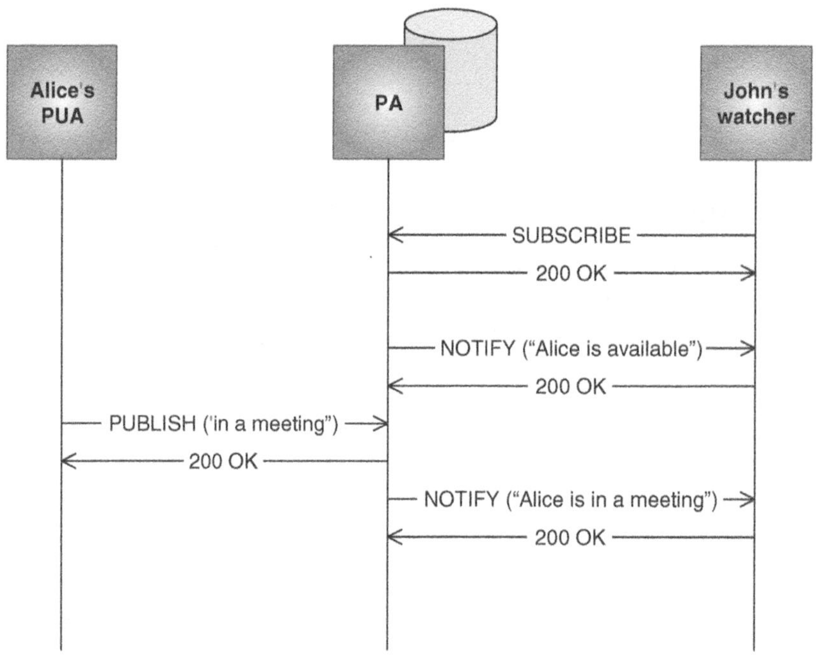

FIGURE 16.6

16.4 Presence Information

[RFC 3863] defines an XML-based format to describe the presence information called PIDF (Presence Information Data Format). The presence information always refers to a presentity, which is identified by a presence (pres) URI. This will be described in the next section. The presence information itself consists of one or more presence tuples. Next is a description of the PIDF content:

- Presentity URI
- List of presence tuples:
  - *Identifier*: Token to identify this tuple within the presence information.
  - *Status*: The status may contain the value OPEN (i.e., available for communication), CLOSED (i.e., not available for communication), or other values that may or may not be registered (for instance, "busy" or "meeting").
  - *Communication address (optional)*: It consists of a communication means (instant messaging, telephony) and a contact address (an IM URI, a SIP URI, a telephone number and so on).
  - *Priority (optional)*: A numerical value specifying the priority of this communication address.
  - *Timestamp (optional)*: Refers to the timestamp of the change of this tuple.
  - *Human readable comment (optional)*: Free text memo about this tuple.
- Presentity human readable comment (optimal): Free text memo about the presentity.

Next is a simple example of a presence document for Alice:

```
<?xml version="1.0" encoding="UTF-8"?>
<presence xmlns="urn:ietf:params:xml:ns:pidf "entity="pres:alice@ocean.com">
  <tuple id="js92t4">
    <status>
      <basic>open</basic>
    </status>
    <contact priority="0.9">sip:alice@ocean.com</contact>
  </tuple>
</presence>
```

The basic PIDF that we have just presented has been extended over time in order to include other pieces of information. For instance, [RFC 4480] defines Rich Presence extensions to the PIDF, referred to as RPID. These extensions provide additional information about the presentity—such as what the person is doing, the person's mood, the time zone the person is located in, an icon reflecting the presentity's status, and so on. For instance, the new <activities> element is used to indicate what the person is doing. This element can take a lot of possible values—for example, away, busy, lunch, holiday, and so forth. Likewise, possible values for the new <mood> element include happy, sad, worried, angry, and so on.

Next is an example that indicates that Alice is not available because she is on vacation and happy:

```
<?xml version="1.0" encoding="UTF-8"?><presence xmlns="urn:ietf:params:xml:ns:
pidf" xmlns:rpid="urn:ietf:params:xml:ns:pidf:rpid" entity="pres:alice@ocean.com">
  <tuple id="hy7691">
    <status>
      <basic>closed</basic>
    </status>
    <rpid:activities><rpid:holiday/></rpid:activities>
    <rpid:mood><rpid:happy/></rpid:mood>
    <contact priority="1.0">mailto:secretary@ocean.com</contact>
  </tuple>
</presence>
```

Additionally, [RFC 4482] adds new elements that provide contact information about a presentity and its contacts, including references to address book entries and icons. Likewise, [RFC 4481] extends the PIDF by defining a way to indicate status information for past and future events.

16.5 Address Resolution

The Common Profile for Presence [RFC 3859] defines a URI scheme "PRES" for presentities and watchers. An example of pres URI might be:

pres:john@ocean.com

The pres URI represents a protocol agnostic way to identify a presentity or a watcher, and therefore it is an identifier suitable for achieving interoperability between different presence service implementations.

In order to route a request to a presence server, it is necessary to determine the server address. That is done by performing a lookup for SRVs for the target domain, the presence service, and the desired protocol. For instance, if the presence server is SIP based, in order to resolve the previous pres URI, a DNS SRV record lookup would need to be performed for:

_pres._sip.ocean.com

It would give back the FQDN of the presence server, which would be resolved to an IP address through a DNS A record query for IPv4 (or DNS AAAA record query for IPv6). Address resolution for presence and instant messaging is defined in [RFC 3861].

16.6 Resource Lists

In some scenarios, a subscriber is interested in the presence information related to a list of resources. Instead of sending a SUBSCRIBE request for each resource, which would generate substantial message traffic, [RFC 4662] specifies a mechanism for requesting and conveying notifications for list of resources. The list of resources is identified by a URI (PRES or SIP URI), and it represents a list of zero or more URIs. The notifier for the list is called a Resource List Server (RLS), and the document that describes the list members and their state is called an RLMI (Resource List Meta-Information). The RLS may have direct information about some of the resources in the list. If it does not, the RLS could subscribe to any nonlocal resources specified by the list resource. This is referred to as back-end subscription, and it might be a SIP subscription or any other type of subscription.

Figure 16.7 shows an example of how this works. In this example, John has a list of buddies comprising Alice, Robert, and Peter; this buddy list is maintained in RLS1. The Resource List Server RLS1 is authoritative for the presence information of Alice and Robert, but does not have information about Peter. The authoritative server for Peter's presence information is PA1.

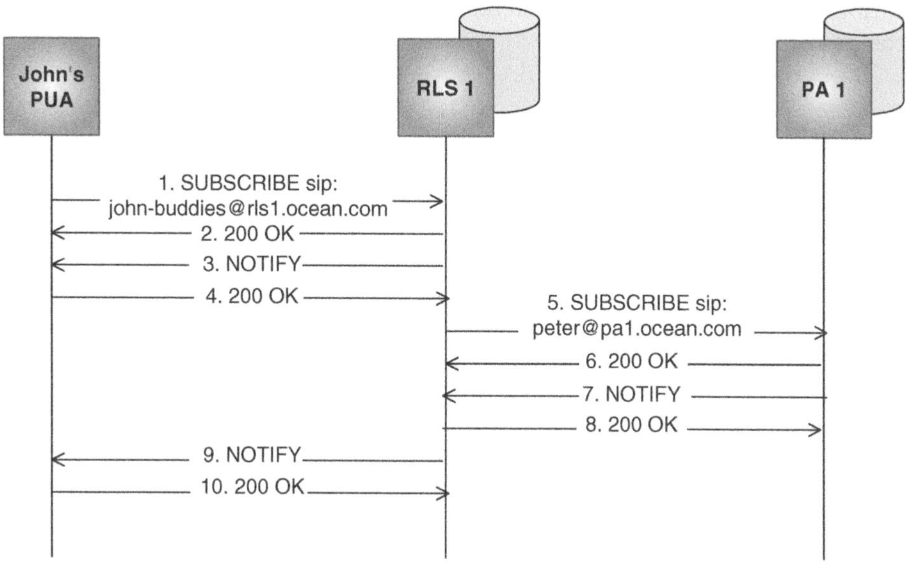

FIGURE 16.7

John subscribes (1) to the resource list identified by the SIP URI:

sip:john-buddies@rls1.ocean.com

RLS1 responds with a NOTIFY (3) whose body contains an RLMI document that describes the entire buddy list as well as the presence information for Alice and Robert. Peter's presence appears empty at this stage because RLS1 is not authoritative for his presence.

Then RLS1 subscribes to PA1 for Peter's presence information. Once it has Peter's presence, RLS1 sends a notification to John indicating just Peter's presence. Alternatively, RLS1 might send a full notification including the presence information of all the buddies.

16.7 XCAP

In communication scenarios, there are many situations where there is a need for network servers to access per-user information in the process of servicing a request. Moreover, in many cases, the end users themselves must be capable of writing, reading, and manipulating this information. Examples of this type of information are access control lists in Voice over IP application servers, presence authorization lists, resource lists, and so on.

For those cases where this information is based on XML, the IETF has defined an HTTP-based protocol called XCAP (XML Configuration Access Protocol), which allows a client to manage this per-user data.

XCAP resources are accessed using HTTP methods (GET to read, PUT to create or modify, DELETE to remove). The key to XCAP operation is that the protocol defines an algorithm for constructing a URI that can be used to reference a component within an XML document. A component can be any element or attribute within the XML document. Thus, XCAP offers a direct access to components.

XCAP is specified in [RFC 4825].

16.8 Instant Messaging

Instant messaging is a type of online communication based on the exchange of messages. These messages are usually short, though there is not a requirement for that. An important characteristic is that instant messages are meant to be used in a conversational mode, in such a way that participants can maintain an interactive conversation.

In the same way that occurred with presence, in order to achieve interoperability between instant messaging services based on different protocols, the IETF has defined a Common Profile for Instant Messaging (CPIM) in [RFC 3860], and an associated instant messages format in [RFC 3862]. All CPIM-compliant implementations must adhere to those specifications.

Likewise, a protocol agnostic URI scheme for instant messaging has also been defined: the IM URI. In order to resolve IM URIs into actual IP addresses, the same procedures as for PRES URIs are followed that were described in previous sections. The difference is that the Service Label for the SRV query is, in this case, "_im."

Instant messaging can be implemented using SIP. There are mainly two ways to do this: session mode and page mode.

Session-mode instant messaging splits the signaling from the media and creates a signaling relationship among the participants that helps to relate all the exchanged message content. SIP is used as the signaling protocol, whereas MSRP is used as the media protocol. MSRP is explained in Chapter 10.

Page-mode messaging is based on submitting the complete instant message in the body of the new SIP MESSAGE request [RFC 3428]. As opposed to session-based mode, in page mode, each message is sent as an independent unit. The body of a SIP MESSAGE request contains a MIME object that represents the instant message itself. The body can be of any MIME type including "text/plain," which is used for sending text messages, and "message/cpim," for CPIM-compliant messages.

In Figures 16.8 and 16.9, we show these two different models for instant messaging.

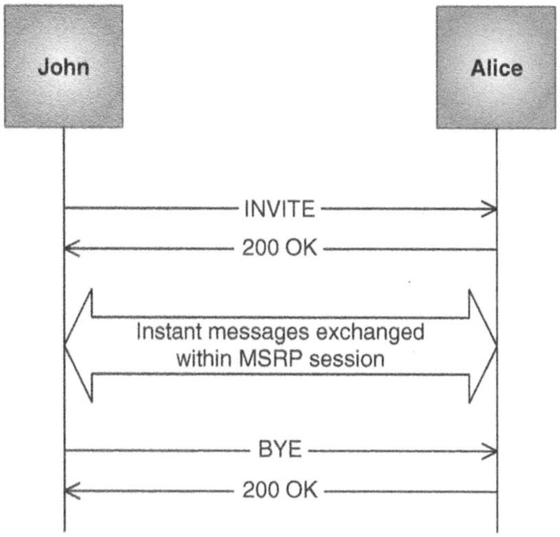

FIGURE 16.8

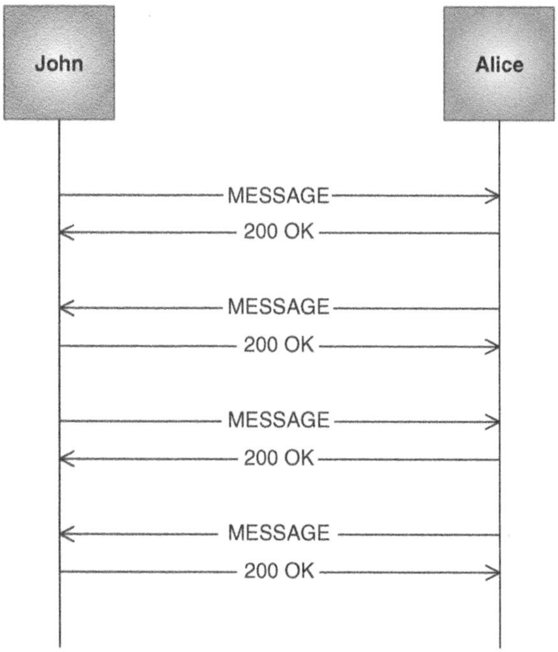

FIGURE 16.9

16.8.1 Content Indirection

SIP is a signaling protocol that was not designed to carry media in its messages. However, we have just seen that SIP MESSAGE requests do carry media. This does not pose any challenge as long as the media content is small. However, SIP MESSAGE bodies that contain large media content (e.g., a photo, a clip) may hamper the performance of a SIP network. In those cases, it is recommended to use the session-based approach with MSRP. Alternatively, another, simpler mechanism might be used by those clients that do not support MSRP: the content indirection mechanism. With this approach, a client wanting to send a message would first post the media content to a server using HTTP, and then it would send a SIP MESSAGE request containing a reference, in the form of a URI, to that content. When the recipient receives the SIP MESSAGE, it starts an HTTP GET operation to retrieve it. This is shown in Figure 16.10.

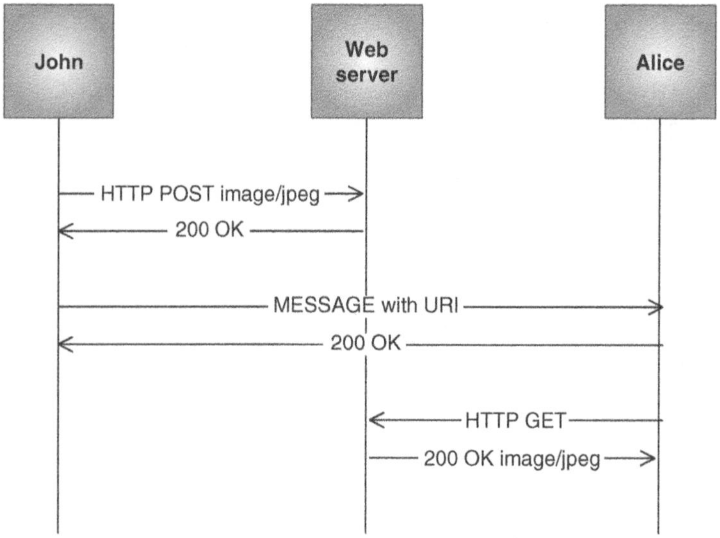

FIGURE 16.10

[RFC 4483] defines the previous mechanism for content indirection in SIP. It is a generic mechanism that can be used with any SIP request, not just MESSAGE. For instance, it might also be used in NOTIFY messages in order to refer to a large PIDF document.

16.9 IM Servers

Though instant messages can be directly sent peer to peer, without the intervention of an application server, there are cases where an application server (so-called IM server in this case) may prove useful. The typical functions that such an AS might perform are:

- Policy enforcement for incoming and outgoing instant messages
- Chat applications
- Interworking with other instant messaging systems such as OMA IMPS or XMPP
- Interworking with legacy offline messaging systems such as email, SMS, or MMS
- Deferred delivery (as an optional feature)
- Others

Figure 16.11 shows an example of SIP/SIMPLE interworking with SMS.

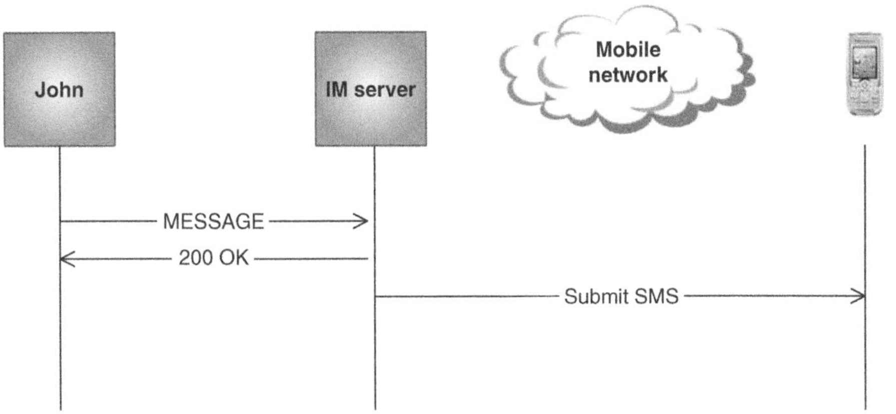

FIGURE 16.11

16.10 Practice: Softphone3

In order to illustrate some of the concepts learned in this chapter, we will now build a new version of our soft-phone, the third version! The Softphone3 application offers all the features of Softphone2, plus the capability to send and receive page-mode instant messages. The exchange of instant messages can occur between soft-phones that are either in IDLE or ESTABLISHED mode. When in ESTABLISHED mode, the MESSAGE requests are sent within the already-existing dialog.

Let us now see what are the new additions needed in both `Softphone2GUI` and `Softphone2Listener` classes in order to implement these features.

16.10.1 Softphone3GUI

The new GUI is shown in Figure 16.12. It adds three new elements as compared with the GUI in Softphone2. These elements are:

- A text field where the user can introduce the message he/she desires to send.
- A text area where both the sent and received messages are displayed.

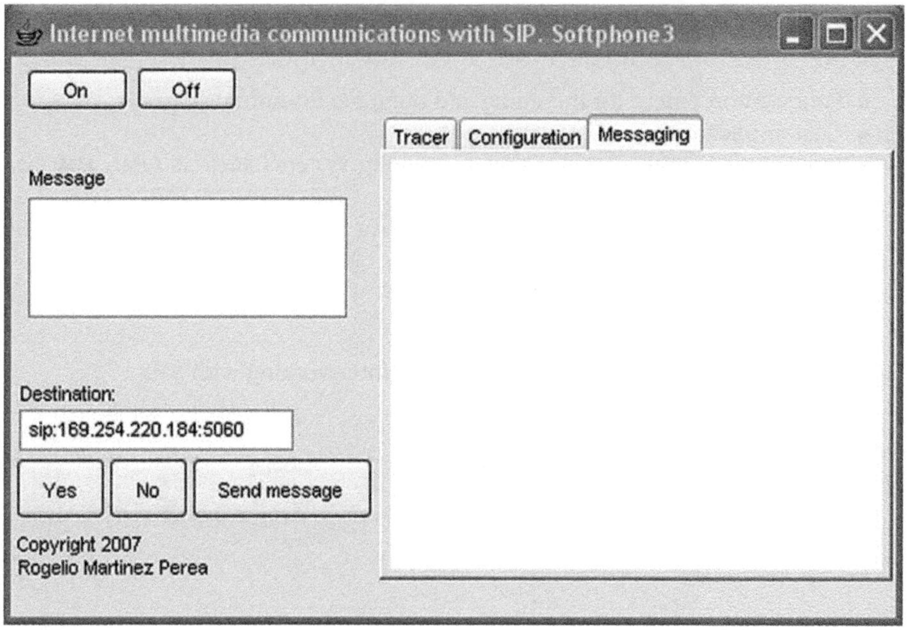

FIGURE 16.12

- A "Send Message" button used in order to send the instant message. Pressing this button will cause `Softphone3GUI` to invoke the `userInput()` method on `Softphone3Listener` with a new type value of 2. Additionally, a new argument is added to the `userInput()` method to convey the message to be sent. The new signature for the `userInput()` method is:

```
public void userInput(int type, String destination, String
  message)
```

`Softphone3GUI` will also include an additional method:

```
public void displayMessage(String text)
```

which is invoked by `Softphone3listener` with the purpose of displaying incoming or outgoing instant messages.

16.10.2 Softphone3Listener

New code is added into this class in order to implement the sending and receiving of instant messages. Two methods in this class need to be updated:

- `userInput()`: in order to enable the sending of messages
- `processRequest()`: in order to enable the reception of messages

Sending Instant Messages

In the `userInput()` method, we will need to add the following code when status is IDLE in order to send the instant message:

```
Address toAddress = myAddressFactory.createAddress(destination);
ToHeader myToHeader = myHeaderFactory.createToHeader(toAddress,
  null);
FromHeader myFromHeader = myHeaderFactory.createFromHeader(fromAd
  dress, "685354");
ViaHeader myViaHeader = myHeaderFactory.createViaHeader(myIP,
  myPort,"udp," null);
ArrayList myViaHeaders = new ArrayList();
myViaHeaders.add(myViaHeader);
MaxForwardsHeader myMaxForwardsHeader = myHeaderFactory.
  createMaxForwardsHeader(70);
CSeqHeader myCSeqHeader = myHeaderFactory.createCSeqHeader
  (1L,"MESSAGE");
CallIdHeader myCallIDHeader = mySipProvider.getNewCallId();
javax.sip.address.URI myRequestURI = toAddress.getURI();
Request myRequest = myMessageFactory.createRequest(myRequestURI,
  "MESSAGE,"
   myCallIDHeader, myCSeqHeader, myFromHeader, myToHeader,
   myViaHeaders, myMaxForwardsHeader);
myRequest.addFirst(myRouteHeader);
myRequest.addHeader(myContactHeader);
ContentTypeHeader myContentTypeHeader =
   myHeaderFactory.createContentTypeHeader("text,""plain");
byte[] contents = message.getBytes();
myRequest.setContent(contents,myContentTypeHeader);
myClientTransaction = mySipProvider.getNewClientTransaction
  (myRequest);
String bid=myClientTransaction.getBranchId();
myClientTransaction.sendRequest();
SipURI fromURI=(SipURI) fromAddress.getURI();
String name=fromURI.getUser();
myGUI.displayMessage(name+ ": "+message);
```

It is almost identical to the code needed in order to send the INVITE. The only differences are:

- The method name is MESSAGE.
- The content type is text/plain.
- The content represents the instant message itself rather than a session descriptor.
- The soft-phone status is not changed.

Likewise, when the status is ESTABLISHED, we need to add the following code in order to send an instant message:

```
Request myMessage = myDialog.createRequest("MESSAGE");
myMessage.addHeader(myContactHeader);
ContentTypeHeader myContentTypeHeader =
  myHeaderFactory.createContentTypeHeader("text,""plain");
byte[] contents = message.getBytes();
myMessage.setContent(contents,myContentTypeHeader);
myClientTransaction= mySipProvider.getNewClientTransaction
  (myMessage);
myDialog.sendRequest(myClientTransaction);
SipURI fromURI=(SipURI) fromAddress.getURI();
String name=fromURI.getUser();
myGUI.displayMessage(name+ ": "+message);
```

The code is again equivalent to that in the INVITE case, except for the aspects we described earlier.

Receiving Instant Messages

In the `processRequest()` method, we will need to add the following code in order to receive an instant message while in IDLE mode:

```
Response myResponse=myMessageFactory.createResponse(200,
  myRequest);
myResponse.addHeader(myContactHeader);
ToHeader myToHeader = (ToHeader) myResponse.getHeader("To");
FromHeader myFromHeader = (FromHeader) myRequest.
  getHeader("From");
javax.sip.address.Address messageFromAddress=myFromHeader.
  getAddress();
SipURI fromURI=(SipURI) messageFromAddress.getURI();
String name=fromURI.getUser();
byte[] myByteContent=myRequest.getRawContent();
String myContent=new String(myByteContent);
myToHeader.setTag("454326");
myServerTransaction.sendResponse(myResponse);
myGUI.displayMessage(name+ ": "+myContent);
```

This code is similar as the one used in the INVITE case, but for the fact that a 200 OK response is generated rather than a 180 (Ringing).

Likewise, when the status is ESTABLISHED, the code needed to receive an instant message is:

```
Response myResponse=myMessageFactory.createResponse(200,
  myRequest);
myResponse.addHeader(myContactHeader);
FromHeader myFromHeader = (FromHeader) myRequest.
  getHeader("From");
```

```
javax.sip.address.Address messageFromAddress=myFromHeader.
  getAddress();
SipURI fromURI=(SipURI) messageFromAddress.getURI();
String name=fromURI.getUser();
byte[] myByteContent=myRequest.getRawContent();
String myContent=new String(myByteContent);
myServerTransaction.sendResponse(myResponse);
myGUI.displayMessage(name+ ": "+myContent);
```

Figure 16.13 shows a snapshot of the two running soft-phones that are exchanging instant messages with each other.

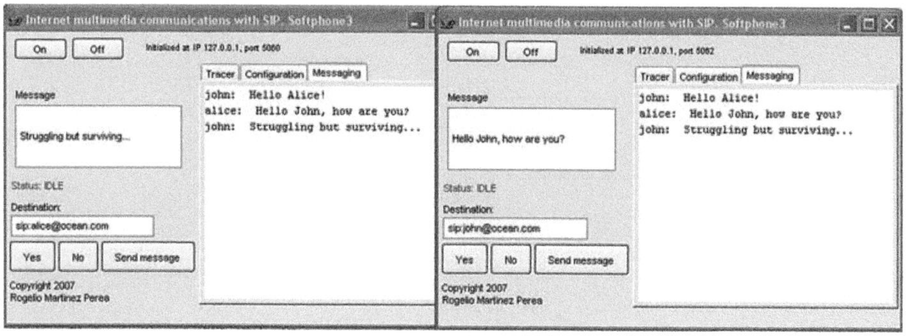

FIGURE 16.13

16.11 Summary

In this chapter, we examined the presence and instant messaging services, which account for an important percentage of the scenarios where SIP is used. In the next chapter, we will look at the call control services, typically associated with voice and video media, which also find widespread utilization.

CHAPTER

Call Control

17

Since the inception of the core SIP, numerous SIP extensions have been defined that provide new tools and capabilities to manipulate SIP calls and dialogs. The combination of these tools allows us to build many SIP-based services. In this chapter, we will look at some of these extensions. We start by explaining what we mean by "call control" in the remit of SIP, and then we will see different approaches to implement call control and the tools that are available.

17.1 What Is Call Control?

In the remit of SIP, we will use the term call control to refer to the manipulation of SIP session dialogs or SIP conference media policy in order to cause participants in a conversation to perceive specific media relationships. All the participants that have access to all the media sent in the conversation are called the "conversation space."

The conference media policy manipulation aspects will be looked at in the next chapter, fully dedicated to SIP conferencing. In this chapter, we will focus on the dialog-manipulation aspects of call control.

Many SIP services require the capability to move participants into and out of the conversation space. For instance, let us imagine that John is talking to Alice; their conversation space is formed by the two of them. At some point, Alice decides to transfer the call to Peter. What this means is that Peter has to be moved into the conversation space and Alice has to be moved out. Once the transfer is fulfilled, the new conversation space is formed by Peter and John. This is an example of a call control service, but there are many others. Examples of SIP call control services are shown in [draft-ietf-sipping-services-examples].

What is needed is a way to manipulate SIP dialogs in order to cause changes in the conversation space. To cause these changes, we will use SIP signaling. There are different approaches for this manipulation of SIP dialogs. Each of the approaches will use a number of call control primitives to achieve the change in the conversation space.

A possible approach is to use *Third Party Call Control (3PCC)*. This approach relies only on the three basic primitives that are part of the core SIP specification:

- Create a new dialog (INVITE).
- Modify a dialog (re-INVITE).
- Destroy a dialog (BYE).

3PCC represents a centralized approach where there exists a central controller (implemented as a B2BUA) that is capable, by issuing these primitives, of manipulating the SIP dialogs between two or more other parties in the appropriate way in order to deliver a specific service. User Agents in this approach need to support just the basic SIP functionality. This approach is shown in Figure 17.1.

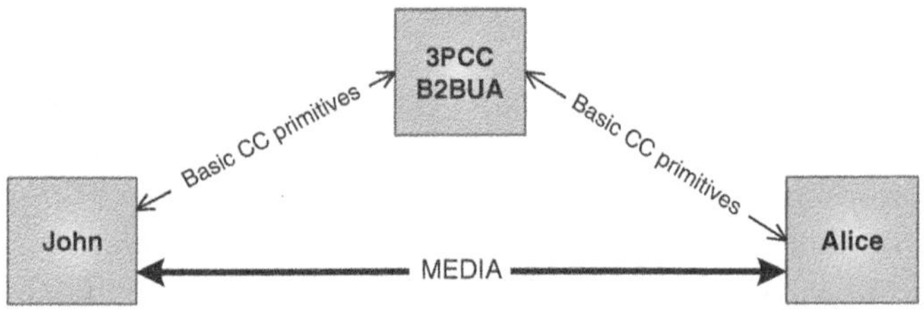

FIGURE 17.1

Another approach to call control is *the peer-to-peer approach*.[1] It does not require the intervention of a central controller, but does have a need for support of additional call control primitives in the User Agents. Some of these primitives are:

- Replace an existing dialog.
- Join a new dialog with an existing dialog.
- Ask another UA to send a request on your behalf.

These primitives are not included in the core SIP spec. but have been included in several SIP extensions that we will examine throughout this chapter. The peer-to-peer call control approach is shown in Figure 17.2.[2]

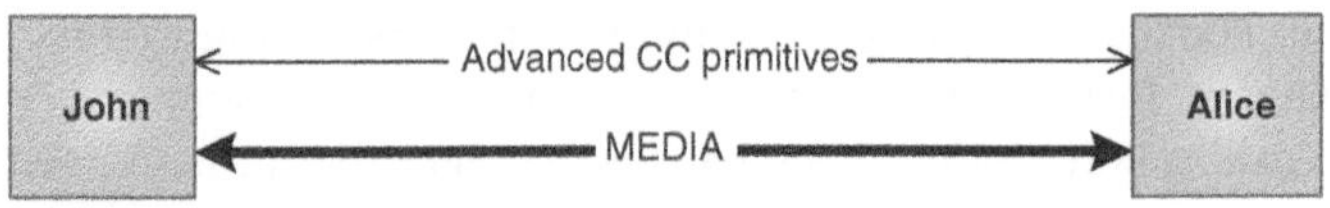

FIGURE 17.2

[1] The peer-to-peer approach to call control as described in the present chapter simply refers to the fact that the conversation space is modified without the need of a central call control entity. The call control functionality is implemented at the endpoints. This terminology should not be confused with the new term "Peer-to-peer SIP," which refers to a different framework for the utilization of SIP where there is not a need for location management (registrars) in the network.

[2] The fact that in the peer-to-peer call control approach, there is no central controller (B2BUA) does not preclude that there may exist one or several SIP proxies in the path between the SIP endpoints.

In addition to these two approaches to call control, there is a recent proposal [draft-mahy-sip-remote-cc] to use SIP for remote call control—that is, for the manipulation of conversations by a UA that is not directly involved in those conversations.

Third party call control, the peer-to-peer approach, and remote call control will be tackled in the rest of the chapter.

Note: All the examples assume that the UAs are registered and that terminating calls are routed through the called party's inbound proxy. However, for the purpose of simplicity, in the call flows in this chapter, we will not show the SIP proxies and registrars involved in the scenarios.

17.2 Peer-to-Peer Call Control

The peer-to-peer model for call control fits well with the original approach of SIP, and with the general Internet paradigm that advocates letting state and intelligence sit at the edges of the network, in the end systems. There are no additional points of failure, and the services work end to end.

On the other hand, the fact that end systems need to have more functionality implies additional complexity in the User Agents. Also, this distributed model may pose some challenges to authentication aspects in some scenarios.

In order to support this model, User Agents need to support some call control primitives that are not included in the base SIP specification. A number of SIP extensions allow for the support of these additional primitives. Next we will describe some of these extensions:

- The REFER method
- The Referred-by mechanism
- The Replaces header
- The Join header

17.2.1 The REFER Method

[RFC 3515] defines a new SIP method, called REFER, that allows a User Agent to ask another User Agent to send a request on its behalf. It also provides a mechanism allowing the party sending the REFER to be notified of the outcome of the referenced request.

Scenarios where REFER is used involve three parties:

- The referrer: The UA asking for the request to be sent.
- The referee: The UA that is asked by the referrer to send the request.
- The refer target: The target of the referenced request.

In Figure 17.3, we can see these concepts. Let us imagine that John wants Alice to call Peter. John, acting as referrer, sends a REFER request to Alice. The REFER includes a new header, Refer-To, that indicates the URI of the refer target. When Alice receives the REFER, she creates a new INVITE, and copies the Refer-To URI in the REFER into the Request-URI of the INVITE.

The REFER method is quite general. It is used not only for call control; actually, it can be used to ask other UAs to send a request to any type of URI.

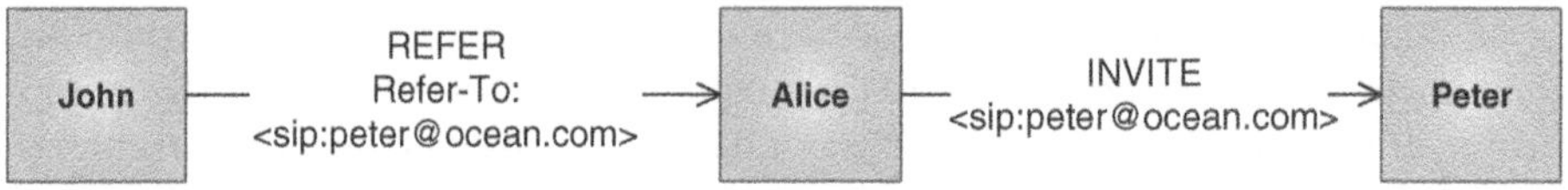

FIGURE 17.3

For instance, if John wanted Alice to look at the web page http://www.amazon.com, he might send a REFER to her with a Refer-To header field set to such a URI. This is depicted in Figure 17.4.

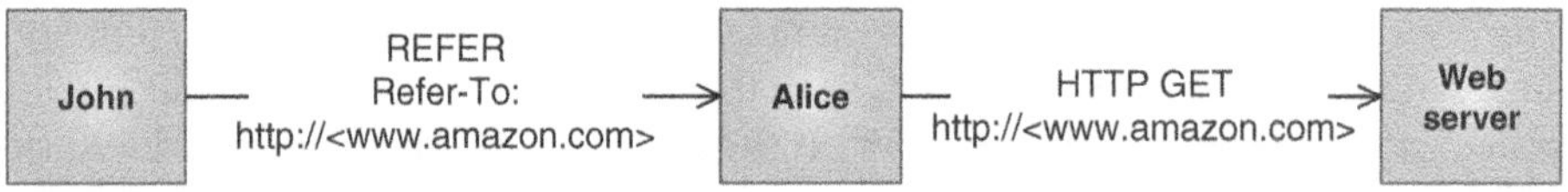

FIGURE 17.4

The REFER method also has the property to automatically establish a new subscription to the refer event. The refer event package is also defined in [RFC 3515]. The implicit subscription allows the referrer to receive NOTIFY messages that indicate the status of the referenced request. It is also possible to inhibit the implicit subscription to the refer event package by including the "norefersub" option tag in the Supported header field.

The refer event package defines that the way to indicate the status of the referenced request is by including in the NOTIFY requests a body of type "message/sipfrag" [RFC 3420]. Such a content type represents a fragment of a SIP message. The body in the NOTIFY must begin with a SIP Response Status-Line, and may be followed by other SIP headers that give more information about the outcome of the referenced request.

In order to illustrate these concepts, we will now show a practical use of the REFER method in order to implement the call transfer service.

Basic Call Transfer Example

Let us assume that John is already in a conversation with Alice. At some point in time, he decides to transfer the call to Peter so that Peter and Alice can talk together, and John leaves the call.

This simple scenario can be implemented by having John (the referrer) send a REFER request to Alice, including a Refer-To header that points to Peter.

As soon as the REFER reaches Alice, she will authorize the request and accept the request by sending a 202 (Accepted) response. At this moment, a subscription has been implicitly created to the refer event, so Alice immediately sends back a NOTIFY request to John, informing about the status of the referenced request.

Then Alice initiates a new INVITE request to Peter. As soon as it is accepted, she will send a new NOTIFY back to John, informing about the success of the

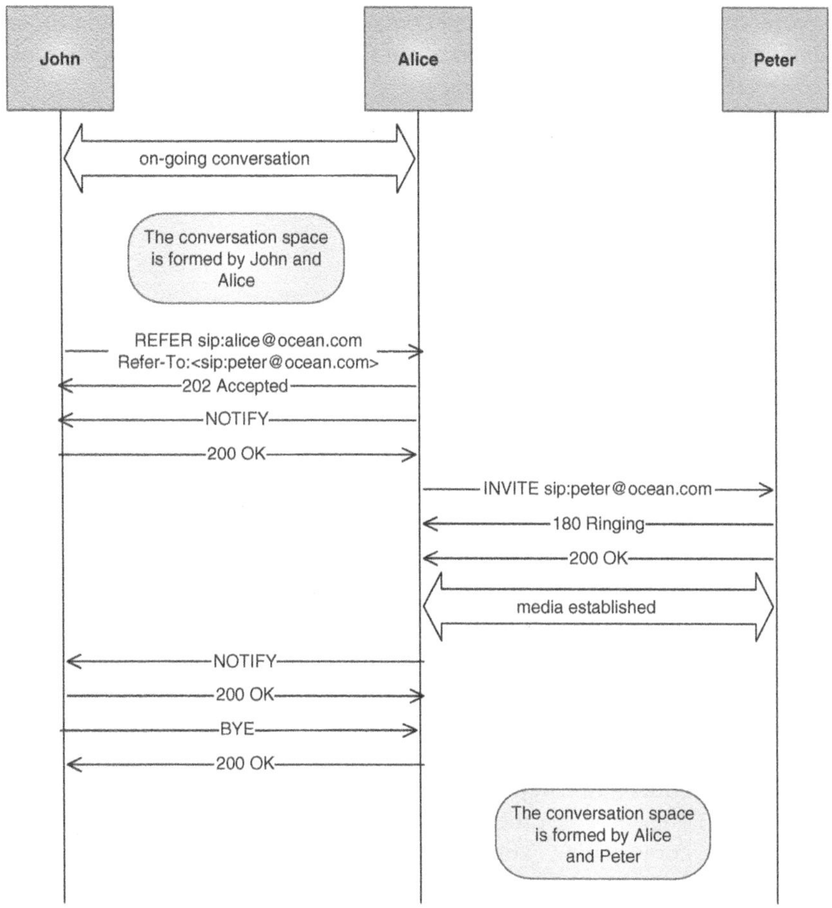

FIGURE 17.5

referenced request. John can, at this point, release the session with Alice.[3] Peter and Alice can now freely talk to each other. This example is shown in Figure 17.5.

For a thorough analysis of the implementation of call transfer using SIP, readers are referred to [draft-ietf-sipping-cc-transfer].

17.2.2 The Referred-By Mechanism

[RFC 3892] introduces the Referred-By header field. This header field allows the Refer-Target to:

- Know that the request he or she has received is a referenced request.
- Know the identity of the referrer.

[3] For a very short duration, Alice will have two SIP sessions active: one with John, and one with Peter. John may decide to keep the SIP session with Alice, but it's up to Alice's UA to cope with the two SIP sessions.

Therefore, the Referred-By header field contains the address-of-record of the referrer, and its presence in the request received by the Refer-Target allows him or her to know that this is a referenced request.

The way it works is quite simple. The referrer introduces the header field into the REFER request, and the referee copies the header field to the outgoing referenced request (e.g., INVITE). This is shown in Figure 17.6.

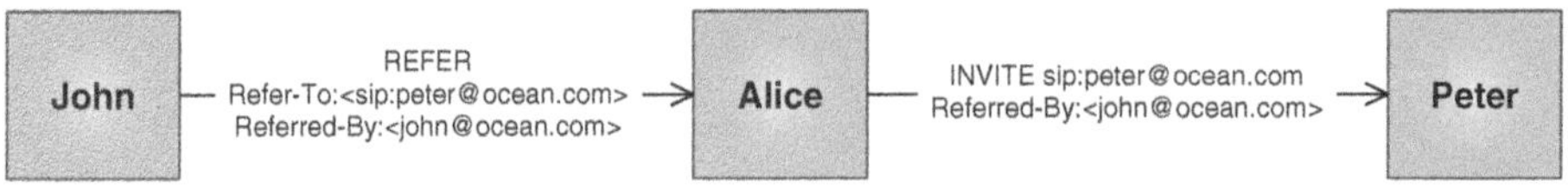

FIGURE 17.6

This header introduces some challenges as to how the User Agent acting as Refer-Target can authenticate the information in the Referred-By header. A malicious referee might modify such information. This is implemented using Authenticated Internet Bodies (AIB). Readers interested in learning how this works are referred to [RFC 3893].

17.2.3 The Replaces Header

[RFC 3891] introduces the Replaces header. The Replaces header can be used inside an INVITE request in order to replace one participant with another one in a multimedia conversation. This call control primitive enables services such as "Attended Transfer," "Call Pickup," and others.

In order to understand how the header is used, let us look at an example. Let us imagine that Alice works as a secretary. She is at the office and hears her boss's phone ring. Her boss is not currently at his desk, so Alice decides to take the call from her own phone. The call flow for this example is illustrated in Figure 17.7.

Alice subscribes to the session dialog event package of her boss's phone. Later on, Steve calls her boss, and Alice hears the phone ring. She also receives a NOTIFY including the identification of the early dialog established between Steve and her boss's phone. Because she knows her boss will not be able to take the call, Alice sends an INVITE to Steve including a Replaces header field set to the dialog identification obtained in the NOTIFY. When Steve receives the INVITE, he has to authorize Alice. If the authorization is successful, then the call is established between Alice and Steve, and Steve cancels the call to her boss.

The key to cause this behavior is the presence of the Replaces header in the INVITE. The header contains information used to match the existing early dialog between Steve and the phone of Alice's boss. In this example Alice has learned about the dialog identification because she subscribed to the session dialog event package, but she might also have learned it from some other out-of-band mechanism.

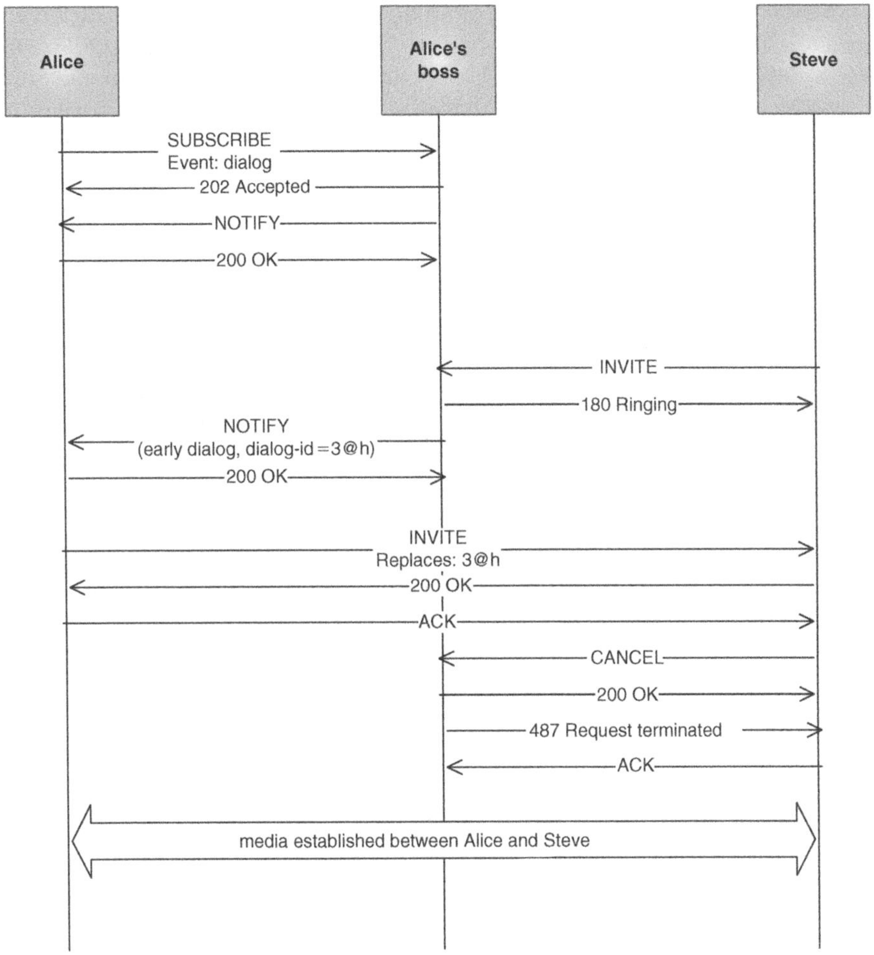

FIGURE 17.7

17.2.4 The Join Header

[RFC 3911] introduces the Join header. The Join header can be used inside an INVITE request in order to cause the joining of an existing SIP dialog with a new SIP dialog. This call control primitive enables services such as "Barge In," "Call Center Monitoring," and others.

In order to understand how the header is used, let us look at an example. Let us imagine that Alice is currently in a phone conversation with Steve, and uses some out-of-band mechanism (e.g., an email or an SMS) to ask John to join the conversation. John sends an INVITE with a Join header to Alice. The Join header must include the dialog information for the established dialog. John might have obtained this information from some other mechanism such as subscribing to the session dialog package from Alice's UA. When Alice receives the INVITE with the

Join header, she creates a conference bridge locally to mix the media. Then she issues a re-INVITE to Steve and responds to the INVITE from John, handling the session descriptions in such a way that she makes sure that both John and Steve are connected to the bridge. Given that now Alice is acting as the controller for the conference, the re-INVITE to Steve and the response to the INVITE from John will contain a new Contact header field set to a URI that represents the "controller" entity in Alice's UA. This is represented by the presence of the "isfocus" parameter in the Contact header field.[4]

This example is depicted in Figure 17.8.

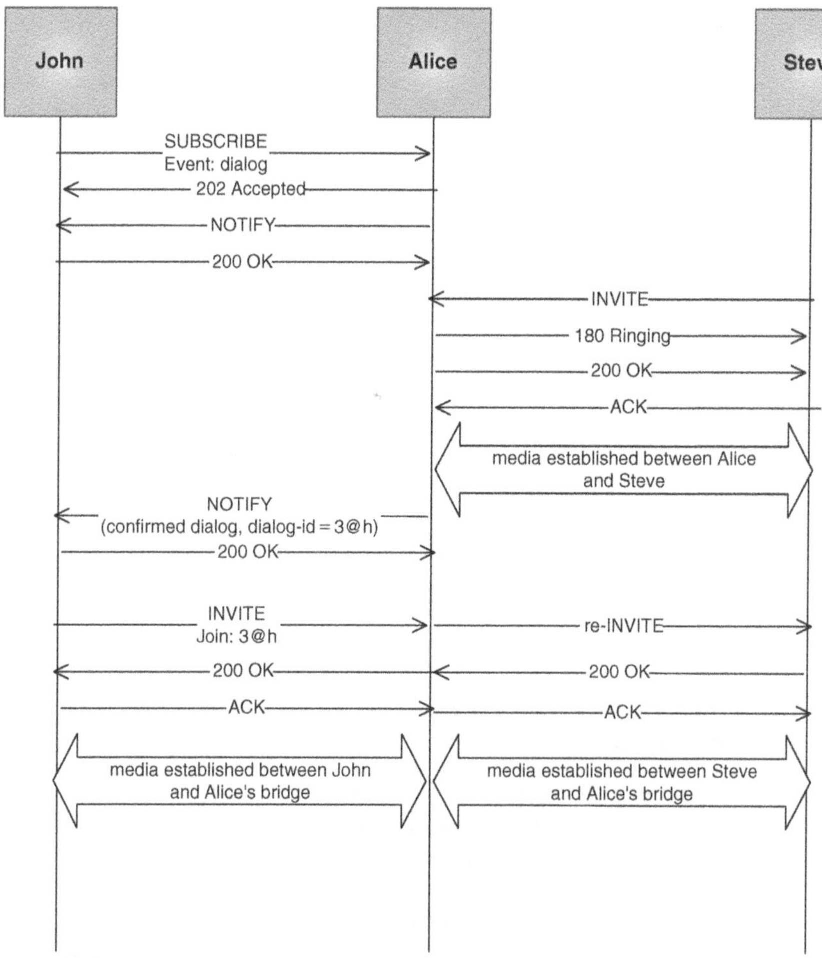

FIGURE 17.8

[4]In the terminology of the SIP conferencing framework, the conference controller is called the Focus. The SIP conferencing framework will be described in Chapter 19.

17.3 Third Party Call Control (3PCC)

Third party call control refers to the situation whereby a central controller (implemented as a B2BUA), is able to set up and manage the communication relationships between two or more parties. It can be used, for instance, for click-to-dial services, conferencing, short-number dialing, online charging, and others.

Click-to-dial services allow a user to click on a web page and be directly connected to customer care, for instance. When the user presses the button in the web page, the web server sends a command to the 3PCC controller, which would then create a call between the user and a customer-care representative.

In order to implement services with 3PCC, both the controller and the controlled UAs need to implement just the basic functionality defined in the core SIP spec in order to:

- Create a new dialog (INVITE).
- Modify a dialog (re-INVITE).
- Destroy a dialog (BYE).

Therefore 3PCC is useful in order to provide call control services in a homogeneous way irrespective of the type of SIP terminals that the users have. It is the ideal approach when dealing with dumb SIP terminals that do not support the extensions for advanced call control (refer, join, replaces), but that support just basic SIP. 3PCC is also used in scenarios where the service provider wants to maintain control over the services offered to the subscribers (e.g., for charging purposes). The 3PCC approach is the one used by the popular IP Centrex solutions[5] aimed at offering PBX-like features in the enterprise environment.

[RFC 3725] proposes some call flows for 3PCC. In Figure 17.9, we can see a possible way (there are others) to use 3PCC in a typical click-to-dial service. We assume that John is browsing through the web site of his bank. At some point, he has a question and wants to talk to a customer-care agent.

1. John clicks on a button in the web page in order to start a call (not shown) to customer care. This causes the controller to send an INVITE request to John. The message contains an SDP offer (offer1) with no media lines, meaning that the media will be established through a re-INVITE.
2. John accepts the call with a 200 OK that contains an SDP answer (answer1) with no media lines.
3. The B2BUA sends an ACK message.
4. The B2BUA sends an INVITE request with no SDP to customer care.
5. Customer care accepts the call with a 200 OK, and proposes an SDP offer (offer2).
6. The B2BUA generates a re-INVITE request toward John. This time, the request contains an SDP offer (offer2′) that is identical to offer2 but for the origin line (o=), which has to be coherent with the origin line in offer1.
7. John responds with a 200 OK that includes an SDP answer (answer2′).

[5] The IP Centrex concept is briefly explained in Chapter 1

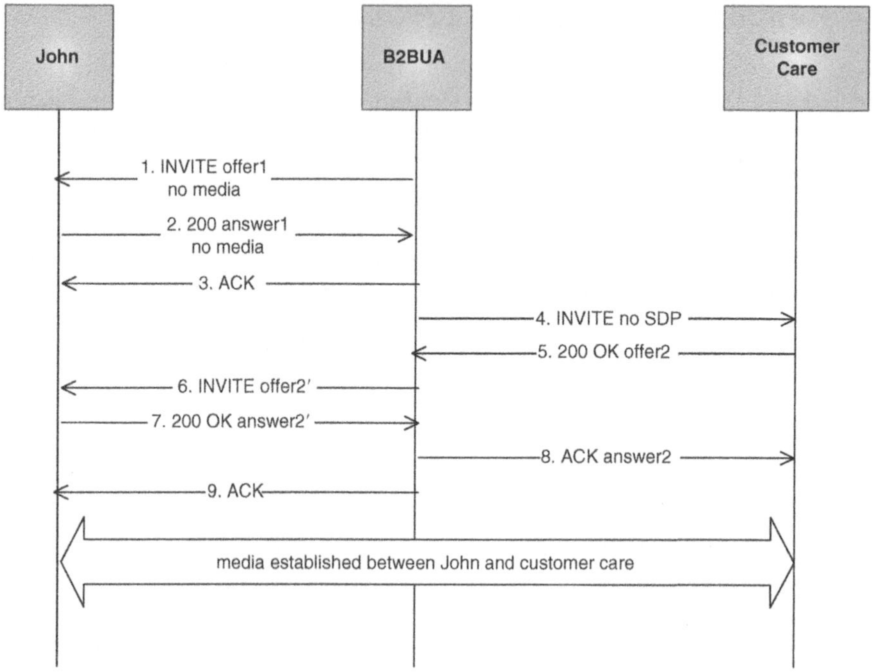

FIGURE 17.9

8. The B2BUA sends an ACK message to customer care including SDP answer2, which is almost identical to answer2′ (the difference resides in the fact that the m-lines in answer2 need to be organized in the same way as the m-lines in offer2).
9. The B2BUA sends the ACK to John.
10. At this point, the media is established between John and customer care.

A particular type of B2BUA is sometimes called transparent B2BUA. A transparent B2BUA is dedicated to forwarding SIP messages in a SIP proxy-like way, though it also leverages some features of a User Agent (UA) element. In addition to routing SIP messages, these B2BUAs can, among other things:

- Hide the user identity.
- Hide topology information.
- Modify the SIP body.

We will see in later chapters that transparent B2BUAs can be used to implement privacy services or some Session Border Controller functions.

17.4 Remote Call Control

Let us imagine that Alice works in the customer-care department of a company. She has a desktop SIP phone at her desk that she uses to make and receive calls, and also a computer from which she has access to her company's customer database. The program in her computer somehow controls the desk phone so that, when a call is received, the computer reads the identity of the caller, queries the customer database, and automatically displays information about the calling user. At that point, Alice, by clicking on some button in the user interface of the program, can decide, for example, whether to answer or redirect the call.

This scenario is possible because the program in Alice's computer is capable of controlling her desk phone. This is an example of remote call control (RCC). This may come in handy when, for instance, a user wants to combine different media (e.g., voice, a game, instant messaging) in the same conversation, but he or she does not have a single UA that is capable of handling all those media, but rather, three different UAs, each one specialized in a particular media. With remote call control, a UA specialized in voice can start a voice conversation, and then instruct, via RCC, a gaming UA to start a chess game.

As stated previously, there is work in progress in the IETF [draft-mahy-sip-remote-cc] to define a way to use SIP for remote call control scenarios. Remote call control is defined as the manipulation of conversations and session-oriented dialogs by a UA that is not directly involved in any of the relevant conversations, dialogs, or sessions.

The proposal in this draft is to use the REFER method to implement this functionality. Actually, the REFER method already has the semantics needed to implement remote call control. Let us remember that we can use the REFER method in order to instruct another UA to initiate a session.

Let us assume that John is at his computer, where he has an application capable of remotely controlling his SIP desk phone. He wants to make a call to Bob. John would send a REFER to his desk phone. The REFER request would include the URI of the resource to be contacted in the Refer-To header.

Refer-To: <sip:bob@pacific.com>

The recipient of the REFER will then generate an INVITE to Bob. In fact, the utilization of the REFER method is not limited to commanding a UA to send an INVITE. Actually, we could command a UA to send whatever method we may think of. We can also, by using REFER, instruct a UA to send a request in an already-existing dialog. In order to do that, we need to know the identity of the dialog within which we want to send the request. One way to obtain it is by subscribing to the session dialog event package.

In our previous example, John's computer application should be subscribed to the dialog package to his desk phone. So when the dialog is created, it would know the dialog id. Later on, if John wants to terminate the session, he would just need to send another REFER that includes a Refer-To header that contains Bob's contact address and also indicates the type of method to send:

Refer-To: <sip:deskphone@192.43.2.1;method=BYE> SIP/2.0

Additionally, the REFER request must also indicate the dialog id within which a BYE request needs to be sent. The dialog id will be included in the Refer-Target header field. The Refer-Target header field is defined in [RFC 4538].

In Figure 17.10, we can see the call flow for the previous example. In this case, we can see that John's computer already has an explicit subscription to the dialog event package of his phone, thus he sends the REFER commands with the "norefersub" option tag in the Supported header field, which inhibits the establishment of an (additional) implicit subscription to the dialog event package of John's phone. The "norefersub" option tag is defined in [RFC 4488].

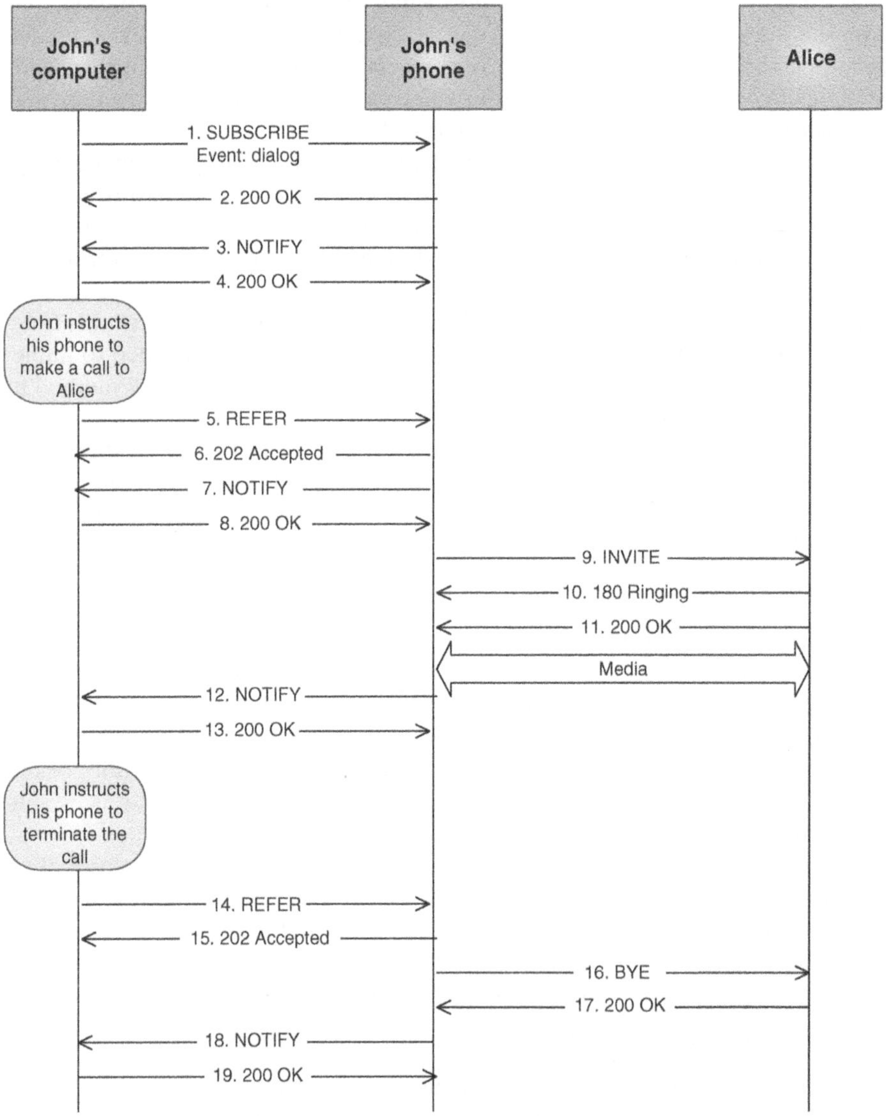

FIGURE 17.10

So far, we have seen how to remotely create and send requests. Actually, the REFER method can also be extended so as to incorporate the possibility to command the sending of responses. This would allow John, for instance, to answer from his computer an incoming call in his phone. For that, he would need to send a REFER including the following Refer-To header:

Refer-To:<sip:deskphone@192.43.2.1;method=INVITE;response=200> SIP/2.0

He would also need to include the Refer-Target header containing the dialog identification, for example:

Target-Dialog: 529;remote-tag=eed;local-tag=iuy

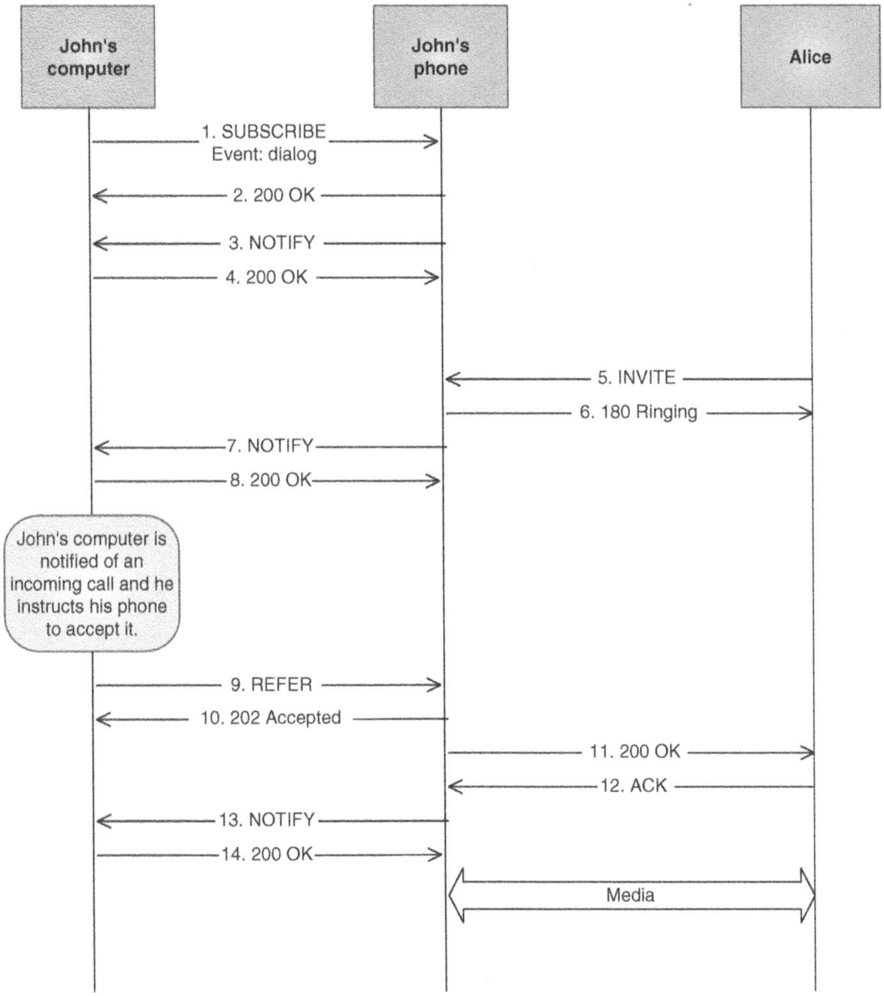

FIGURE 17.11

17.5 Summary

In this chapter, we have analyzed how to build advanced call control services in a pure SIP environment. The tools we learned in this chapter are typically used in the context of voice and video, though nothing precludes extending their utilization to other media as well.

In scenarios that involve voice, we need to make it possible that SIP users can also communicate with users in the legacy PSTN network. In the next chapter, we will look at the architectures that enable the interoperability between the IP and the PSTN environment.

CHAPTER

Interworking with PSTN/PLMN

18

In this chapter, we will tackle the integration of IP multimedia networks with the existing fixed (PSTN[1]) and mobile (PLMN[2]) circuit-switched networks in order to enable different types of communication scenarios. We begin the chapter by explaining what the motivation for the integration is. Then we present the high-level architecture that enables the identified scenarios. After that, we will look into specific aspects of the integration, such as addressing, protocol translation, and protocol encapsulation.

18.1 Motivation

We have seen that IP multimedia communications encompass the exchange of different types of media. Telephone calls can be seen as a type of multimedia sessions where just audio is exchanged. Although performing telephony call signaling and transporting the associated audio media over IP yields significant advantages over traditional circuit-switched telephony, we are not yet in the all-IP promised land; therefore, there is a need for IP communication networks to interwork with the existing PSTN and PLMN networks. We will assume that these mentioned circuit-switched networks offer, toward other networks, an ISDN User Part (ISUP)[3] interface in the signaling plane and a TDM[4] interface in the media plane. Henceforth, during this chapter, for the sake of simplicity, we will refer to just the interworking with PSTN, even though the same considerations would apply to the interworking with PLMN.

Such an IP/PSTN interworking can enable various types of communication scenarios:

- *Scenario 1.* IP origination–PSTN termination: A SIP UA calls a user in the PSTN network.

[1] PSTN stands for Public Switched Telephone Network.
[2] PLMN stands for Public Land Mobile Network.
[3] ISUP is the call-signaling protocol used between core network elements in PSTN and PLMN.
[4] TDM stands for Time Division Multiplexing. It is the type of multiplexing that is used in traditional circuit-switched networks. It is based on allocating a different time slot to each individual voice conversation.

- *Scenario 2.* PSTN origination–IP termination: A phone in the PSTN originates a call toward an IP user.
- *Scenario 3.* PSTN origination–IP transit–PSTN termination: A PSTN user calls another PSTN user, but the call is routed through an IP domain. There may be several reasons for this scenario, such as transmission costs optimization or provision of advanced voice services to PSTN users.

The first and second scenarios require that signaling and media are converted from the IP domain to the PSTN domain and vice versa. These scenarios require a "translation" function. The signaling protocols in the PSTN (e.g., ISUP) do not offer the same functionality as SIP—and, vice versa, SIP does not offer the same functionality as ISUP. Therefore, not all the protocol features and the services these protocols implement will be maintained when going from one domain to the other.

The third scenario, on the other hand, requires that all the original protocol features and services are preserved during the IP transit. That is, it requires that signaling information is passed transparently between the two PSTN domains. This is achieved through an "encapsulation" function.

[RFC 3372] describes the architectures needed to support the previous scenarios. These will be detailed in the next sections.

18.2 Architecture

Irrespective of the scenario, there is always a piece of equipment needed in order to perform the integration between the IP and PSTN domains. Such an element is called a *gateway*. A gateway is a device that has both circuit-switched and IP connectivity, and is capable of making the conversion between the protocols in one and the other domain. Figure 18.1 shows this idea.

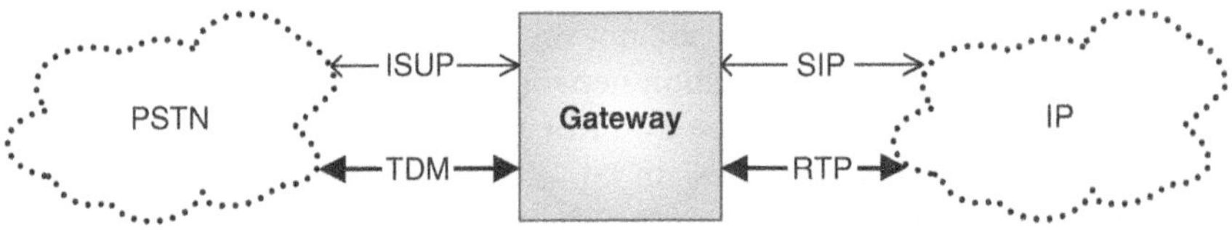

FIGURE 18.1

The protocol conversion in the gateway takes place at both the signaling plane and the media plane.

18.2.1 Signaling Plane

In the signaling plane, the protocol conversion occurs between SIP and ISUP (or BICC).[5]

[5]Some circuit-switched networks have evolved toward supporting other protocols, such as BICC (Bearer Independent Call Control). BICC is a call control protocol based on ISUP that allows us to offer the same narrowband services that ISUP supports, only over a broadband backbone network.

More specifically, an IP/PSTN gateway can perform two operations at the signaling plane:

- Protocol translation back and forth between ISUP and SIP.
- ISUP encapsulation in SIP messages, and ISUP decapsulation from SIP messages.

Both protocol translation and encapsulation are described in subsequent sections.

18.2.2 Media Plane

In the media plane, the conversion occurs between RTP, in the IP side, and TDM (Time Division Multiplex) in the PSTN side. It is worth mentioning that TDM and RTP will still contain PCM[6]-encoded voice.

18.2.3 Gateway Decomposition

An IP/PSTN gateway can be split into the following components:

- *The Media Gateway (MG[7]):* It is the entity that performs the interworking at the media plane between the IP and PSTN domains. It is controlled by the MGC.
- *The Media Gateway Controller (MGC)*: It is the entity that controls the Media Gateway. It also performs the mapping, at the application level between the signaling protocols (ISUP-SIP), in the IP and PSTN domains. The MGC is sometimes referred to as a "softswitch" or "call agent."
- *The Signaling Gateway (SGW)*: It is the entity that performs the signaling interworking at the transport level (MTP[8]-SCTP/IP) between the IP and PSTN domains.

The standard protocol used by the MGC to control the MG is called Gateway Control Protocol (GCP) specified in [RFC 3525] and [H.248.1].

The split-GW components are shown in Figure 18.2.

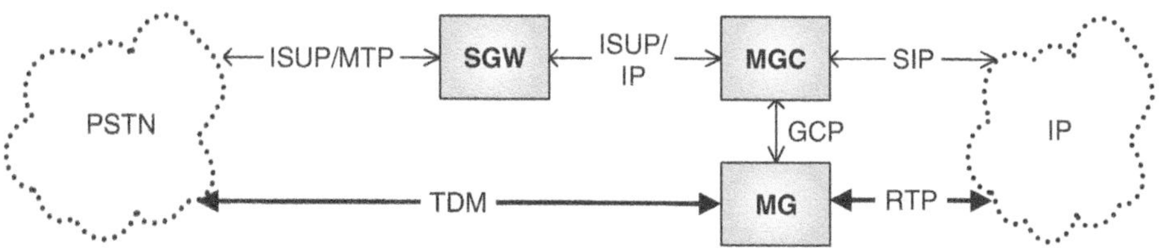

FIGURE 18.2

Let us now see the architecture for the different scenarios.

[6] PCM (Pulse Code Modulation) is a type of voice encoding that is traditionally used in telephone networks. It consists of sampling the voice signal at regular intervals (typically at 8,000 samples per second), and then digitizing each of the samples. PCM encoding can also be transported on RTP, as we saw in Chapter 10.

[7] MG is the terminology used in IETF specs to refer to a media gateway, though, in the industry jargon, it is more frequent to use the term MGW.

[8] MTP (Message Transfer Part) is the layer 2 (link) and 3 (network) protocol traditionally used in circuit-switched networks to carry signaling information.

18.2.4 Scenario 1 (IP to PSTN)

In this scenario, in addition to the need for a gateway that performs *protocol translation*, we need to tackle two additional aspects:

1. How to address a PSTN user from an IP endpoint.
2. How to route the call to the gateway.

The first aspect is resolved by having the IP endpoint use a new type of URI, the TEL URI, which will be discussed in the next sections.

Unless a SIP UA connects directly to a PSTN gateway, the second aspect is resolved by the SIP network, typically by the outbound SIP proxy for the originating user. The proxy translates the telephone like address (TEL URI) into a SIP URI, with the host part of that URI pointing to a gateway. There are several different options in order to implement such a translation:

1. The proxy server may translate all TEL URIs into the same SIP host name.
2. The proxy server may select a different gateway for different TEL URIs prefixes based on static configuration.[9]
3. The proxy server may use a gateway location protocol such as TRIP to select a gateway. TRIP (Telephony Routing over IP Protocol) is defined in [RFC 3219], and is part of the framework for gateway location defined in [RFC 2871].

Option 1 is used in small deployments. Option 2 is frequently used by VoIP service providers. Option 3 is conceived to cope with more-generic cases of Internet-wide provision of VoIP services and deployment of gateways.

Figure 18.3 shows the architecture for Scenario 1. In the figure, we refer to the legacy PSTN phones as POTS (Plain Old Telephone System) terminals, which is a common terminology.

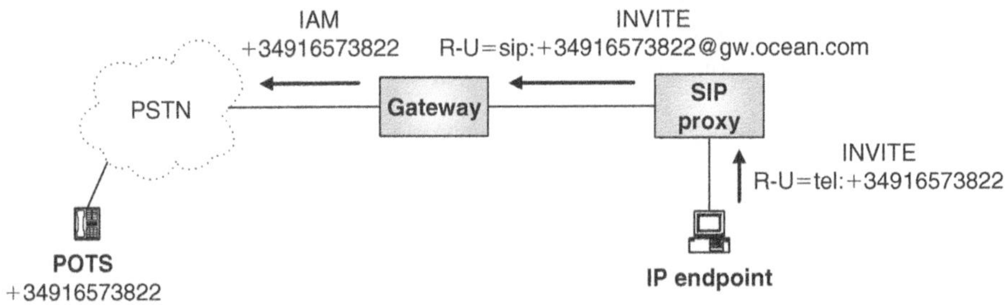

FIGURE 18.3

18.2.5 Scenario 2 (PSTN to Ip)

In this scenario, in addition to the need for a gateway that performs *protocol translation*, we also need to consider:

1. How to address an IP user from a PSTN telephone.
2. How to route the call from the gateway to the IP endpoint.

[9]For instance, based on the TEL URI prefix, different gateways could be selected for breakout to different national networks or to an international point of interconnection.

Regarding the first aspect, PSTN phones do not offer the capability of entering a sip or sips URI, but just a collection of digits that represent a telephone number. Therefore, in order to enable this scenario, we need to allocate telephone numbers to IP users who want to have the possibility of receiving calls from the PSTN. In other words, these users will need to have a TEL URI identity (possibly in addition to the SIP URI identity). The gateway would receive a telephone address, would convert it into a TEL URI, and would resolve the TEL URI into SIP URI by using an ENUM query. ENUM service is described in subsequent sections. Once the gateway has a SIP URI identifying the IP user, routing proceeds as per normal SIP mechanisms.

This scenario is depicted in Figure 18.4.

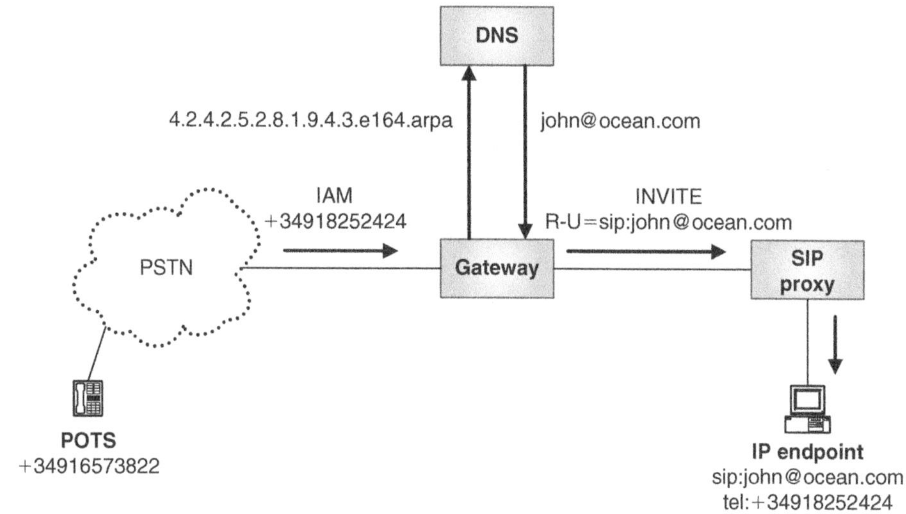

FIGURE 18.4

18.2.6 Scenario 3 (PSTN to PSTN via IP)

Scenario 3 implies that a call originated in the PSTN and addressed to a PSTN endpoint is transited through an IP infrastructure. A typical reason for doing this is for transmission cost optimization. Instead of using a TDM network to route the calls between PSTN users, the operator may want to leverage existing cheaper IP infrastructure (Figure 18.5). Another common reason is that the operator may want to apply enhanced telephony services to its customers (Figure 18.6). These services may be difficult to implement in a pure PSTN environment, whereas they might be easily enabled in an IP and SIP domain. As an example of this, just consider telephony services that require complex call leg manipulation. In the PSTN, the IN[10] standards needed to support those functions are not widely implemented or

[10] IN stands for Intelligent Network, and refers to a set of ITU standards for enabling circuit-switched networks (such as the PSTN) with enhanced and customizable call control capabilities. IN for PLMN is referred to as CAMEL and is defined by the 3GPP.

are very expensive, whereas SIP natively supports those functions, and SIP applications can be easily developed over cost-effective SIP application servers.

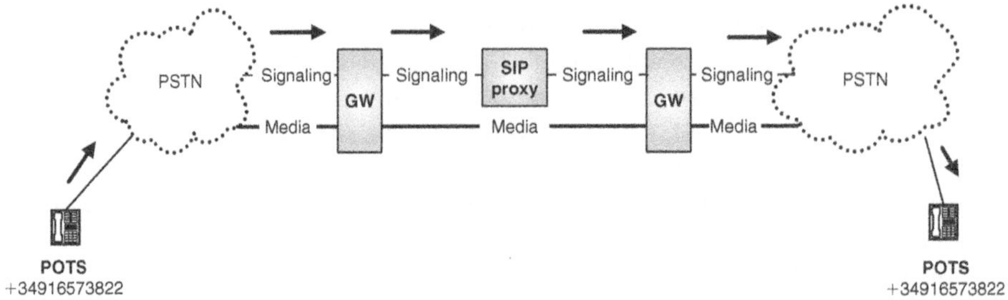

FIGURE 18.5

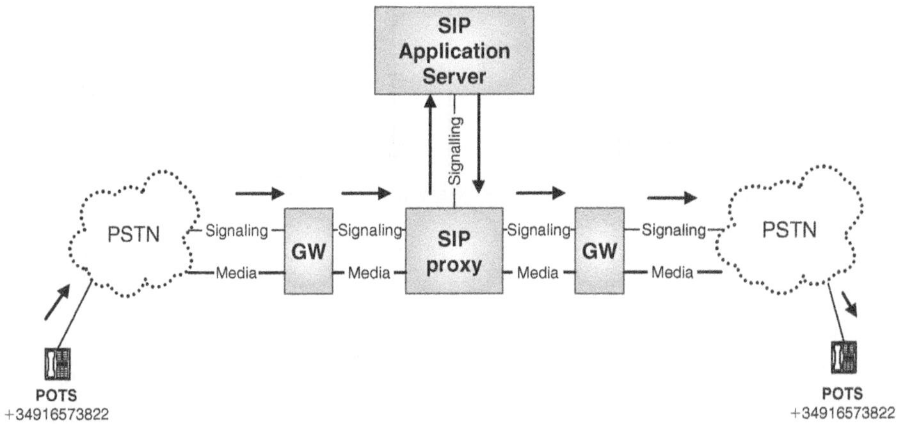

FIGURE 18.6

In this scenario, in addition to the protocol translation, addressing, and routing functions that we saw in previous scenarios, there is the need to transparently carry the ISUP signaling within SIP messages. That is referred to as the *protocol encapsulation* function, and it is critical so as not to lose any PSTN functionality during the IP transit. ISUP encapsulation is described in subsequent sections.

18.3 Telephone Addressing: The TEL URI

The TEL URI is a URI scheme defined by [RFC 3966]. It is used to describe resources identified by telephone numbers.

18.3.1 Motivation

Phone lines in the PSTN are identified by an [E.164] number. In order for a UA to be able to place a call to a PSTN user, it must somehow address the INVITE message to a telephone number. However, we have seen that addresses in SIP are in the form of URIs, mainly sip or sips URIs. In order to overcome this problem, [RFC 3966] defines a new URI scheme called the TEL URI. The TEL URI consists of a telephone number, and identifies a resource in the telephone network. An example of a TEL URI might be:

tel: +34610456822

Another use of TEL URIs is for allowing calls from PSTN to IP users. PSTN phones do not allow the user to introduce a sip URI in order to place a call to an IP user. In order to enable this scenario, IP users need to be given an identity in the form of a TEL URI so that they can be reached from the PSTN.[11]

18.3.2 TEL URI Format

A TEL URI complies with the following format:

"tel:" telephone-subscriber

where telephone-subscriber may indicate a global number or a local number.

Global numbers follow the E.164 recommendation from ITU, and are composed by the "+" character followed by a country code (CC) and national subscriber number (NSN). For example, the following URI points to a phone number in the United Kingdom (CC=44):

tel:+441259551634

Local numbers belong to private numbering plans, and have meaning only within a certain context. They may, for instance, represent extensions within a PBX, or telephones within a certain geographic area. The following example shows a TEL URI that represents an extension within a PBX at ocean.com. TEL URIs representing a local number must include the phone-context element:

tel: 4444; phone-context=pbx1.ocean.com

18.4 ENUM: The E.164 to URI Dynamic Delegation Discovery System

[RFC 3761] defines a mechanism for using the DNS for storage of E.164 numbers. This mechanism allows resolving telephone numbers into SIP addresses of record.

The solution uses an NAPTR resource record. NAPTR RRs were described in Chapter 6.

In order to illustrate how it works, let us consider a scenario where Mary, a PSTN user, calls John, who is a SIP user. John has two identities: a SIP URI and a TEL URI. The SIP URI is the identity that he gives to other multimedia users so

[11] The use of TEL URI to identify SIP users might also be for convenience. When a SIP-to-SIP call is established, the calling party may want to use a telephone number, simply because that's how he or she knows the other party. In addition, some people may not want to reveal their SIP URI (e.g., alice@ocean.com), but want to hide behind a number.

that they can reach him using SIP, whereas he advertises the TEL URI among his colleagues who, like Mary, still have only an old PSTN phone, so that they also can reach him for simple voice calls.

His TEL URI is:

tel:+12015551634

and his SIP URI is:

sip:john@ocean.com

Therefore, Mary dials +12015551634, and the call is routed by the PSTN operator, based on the analysis of the called-party number, to the PSTN/IP gateway. In order to translate the telephone number into a routable SIP URI, the gateway performs the following steps:

Step 1. Converts the received telephone number into an FQDN by applying the following rules:

a. Removes the "+" sign.
b. Puts dots between each digit.
c. Reverses the order of the digits.
d. Appends the string ".e164.arpa" to the end.

The resulting domain name would be: 4.3.6.1.5.5.5.1.0.2.1.e164.arpa.

Step 2. The gateway queries the DNS ENUM system for such a domain name.

Step 3. DNS ENUM returns a NAPTR record that includes the new sip URI:

sip:john@ocean.com

Figure 18.7 shows the different steps in this process.

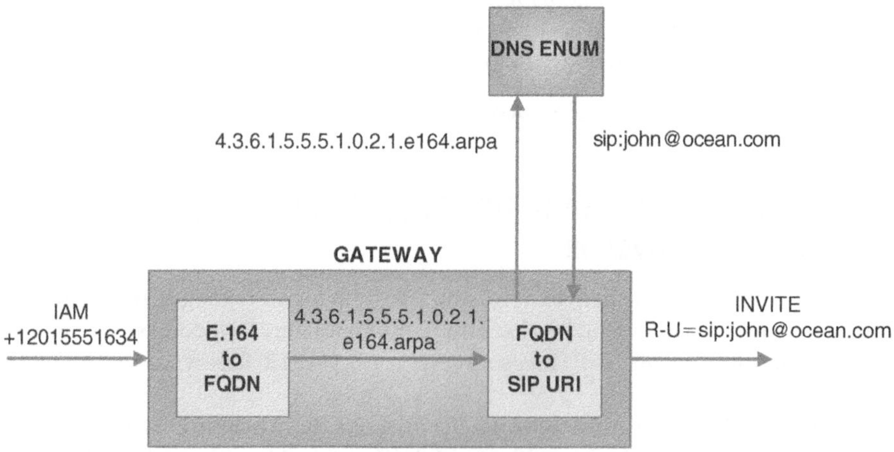

FIGURE 18.7

In order to allow the translation between telephone numbers and SIP addresses of record, [RFC 3761] defines an enumservice. The enumservice for SIP is "E2U+sip." Table 18.1 shows a possible NAPTR record for our previous example.

We can see that the NAPTR query returns a rewrite rule using the regexp field.

Table 18.1

Domain	TTL	Class	TP	Order	PRF	FL.	Service	Regexp
4.3.6.1.5 .5.5.1.0. 2.1.e164 .arpa	6000	IN	35	100	10	"U"	"E2U+sip"	"!^.*$!john@ ocean.com!"

18.5 Protocol Translation

In order to convert between SIP and ISUP and vice versa, three aspects need to be considered:

1. Message mapping
2. Parameter mapping
3. State machine alignment

18.5.1 Message Mapping

The gateway implements a set of rules that govern the mapping between SIP and ISUP at message level. For instance, one such rule might state that when an INVITE is received in the IP side, an IAM (Initial Address Message) should be sent in the PSTN side.[12] A potential mapping between ISUP and SIP messages has been described in [RFC 3398].

18.5.2 Parameter Mapping

Likewise, the gateway needs to decide how to map signaling parameters from one protocol to the other. Because the protocols do not offer exactly the same functionality, there will be parameters lost in the translation, or some parameters will have to be filled in by the gateway. There are, though, some parameters for which implementing the correct mapping is critical, such as those that carry routing information. For example, the Called Party Number could be mapped onto the SIP "To" header field and Request-URI, and so on.

The protocol translation topic is a complex one and, moreover, requires substantial knowledge about the protocols in the PSTN, which are not the focus of this book. Therefore, we will show just a couple of simple call flows that allow the reader to understand how the mapping works.

18.5.3 State Machine Alignment

The SIP and ISUP protocol state machines also need to be aligned because the message sequence in SIP is not exactly the same as the message sequence in ISUP.

[12] IAM is the name of the message used for initiating a call in ISUP.

18.5.4 Example 1: IP-to-PSTN Call

The gateway receives an INVITE message from the IP side, and translates it into an Initial Address Message (IAM). When the telephone rings, the PSTN generates an Address Complete Message (ACM) toward the gateway. The gateway translates it into an 18x provisional response. Later on, the PSTN user answers the call, and the PSTN generates an ANswer Message (ANM), which is translated by the gateway into a 200 OK final response. The IP endpoint will generate an ACK, which has no equivalent in the PSTN.

In order to terminate the session, the IP endpoint sends a BYE request that is converted by the gateway into an ISUP Release (REL) message. The gateway will acknowledge the BYE request as soon as it receives the request. The PSTN will generate a Release Complete (RLC) message as soon as it receives the REL message.

This scenario is shown in Figure 18.8.

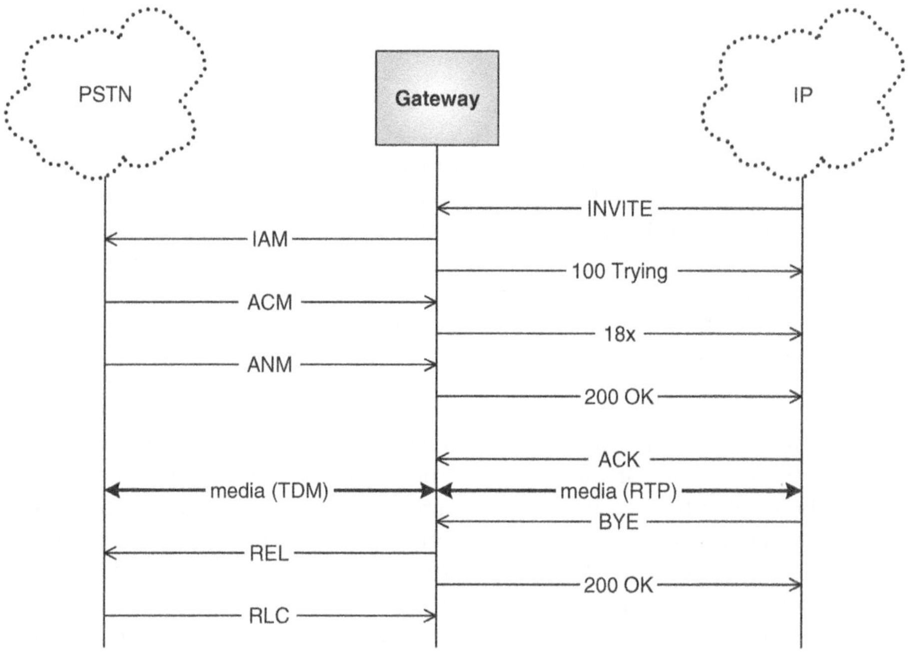

FIGURE 18.8

18.5.5 Example 2: PSTN-to-IP Call

Example 2 is shown in Figure 18.9.

18.5.6 Example 3: PSTN to PSTN via IP

Example 3 is depicted in Figure 18.10.

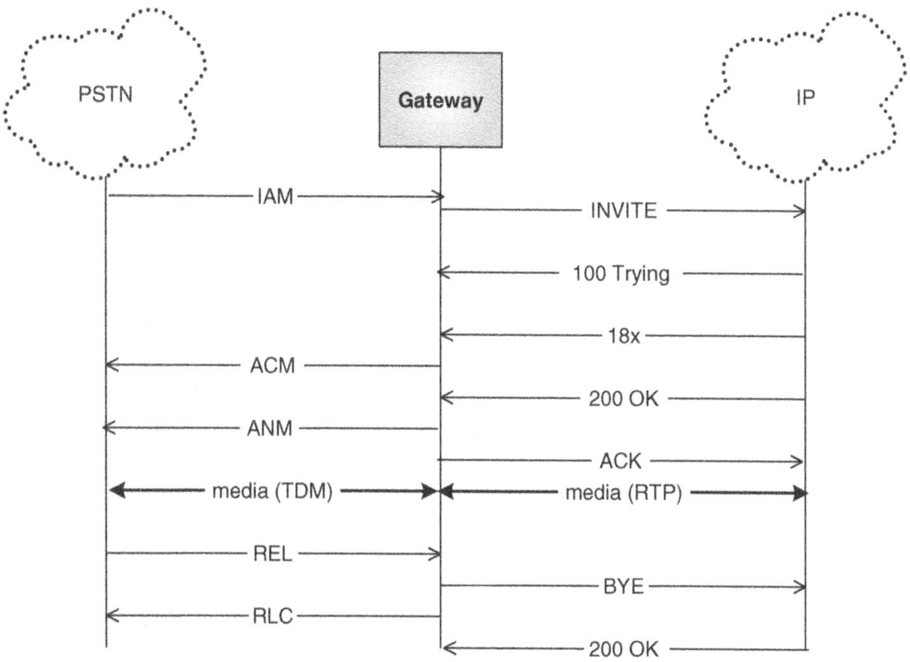

FIGURE 18.9

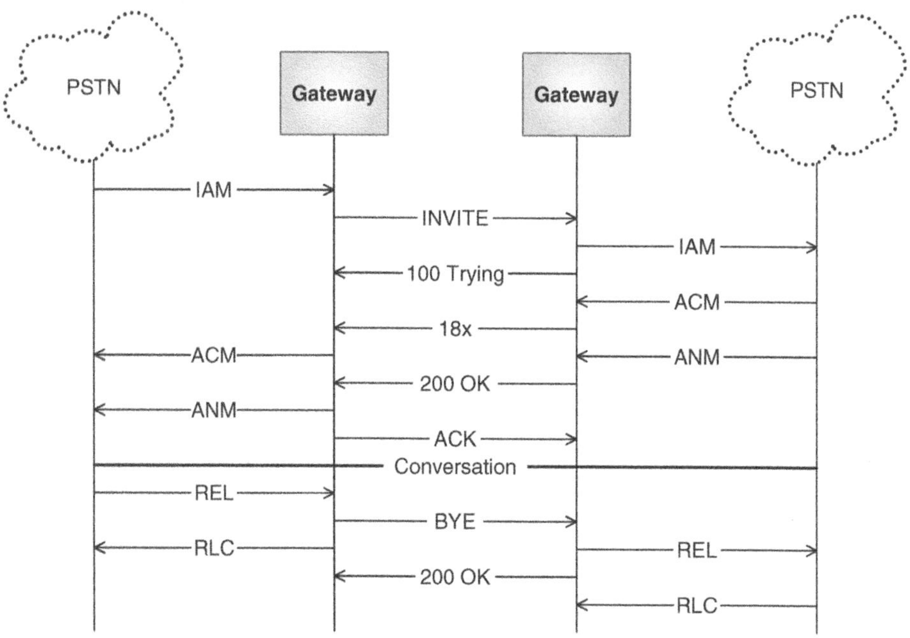

FIGURE 18.10

18.6 Protocol Encapsulation

As we saw before, Scenario 3 requires that the ISUP signaling is transparently carried between the ingress and egress gateways. In order to achieve this, the ISUP MIME media type has been defined [RFC 3204].

Therefore, ISUP signaling will be carried in the message body of SIP messages as a MIME object. Given that SIP also needs to transport the SDP content, the actual content carried on SIP will be of type multipart. This is shown in Figure 18.11.

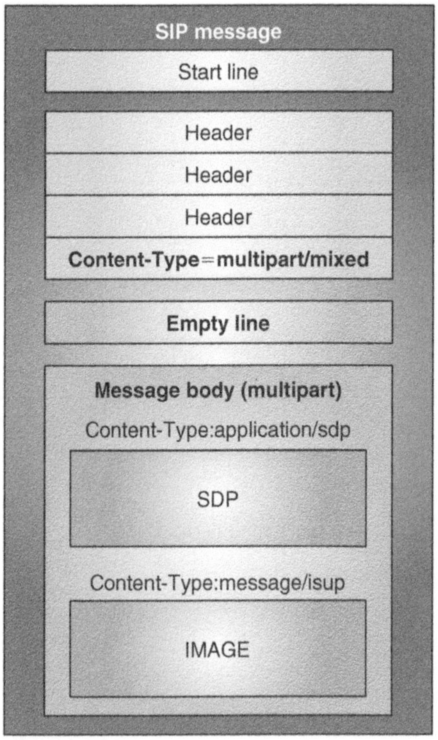

FIGURE 18.11

18.6.1 The INFO Method

In the protocol encapsulation scenarios, there are cases where a PSTN signaling message is received in the middle of a call and needs to be carried through the IP network to the egress gateway. The question here is: What SIP method to use in order to encapsulate the mid-call ISUP message?

The SIP core specification defines two methods that can be used in the middle of a session. One is re-INVITE, and the other one is BYE. The former updates the session parameters and also modifies the dialog state. The latter terminates the session. Therefore, these methods are not valid for our purposes. What we are looking for is a method that can be used for communicating mid-session signaling information along the signaling path of a call, and that modifies neither the session nor the dialog state.

[RFC 2976] defines a new SIP method, INFO, that can be used to solve this problem. It can be sent by SIP UAs at any moment during the session (provided the UAs support this extension), and it does not modify the dialog state. The mid-call ISUP message is carried in the body of the INFO message.[13] This is shown in Figure 18.12.

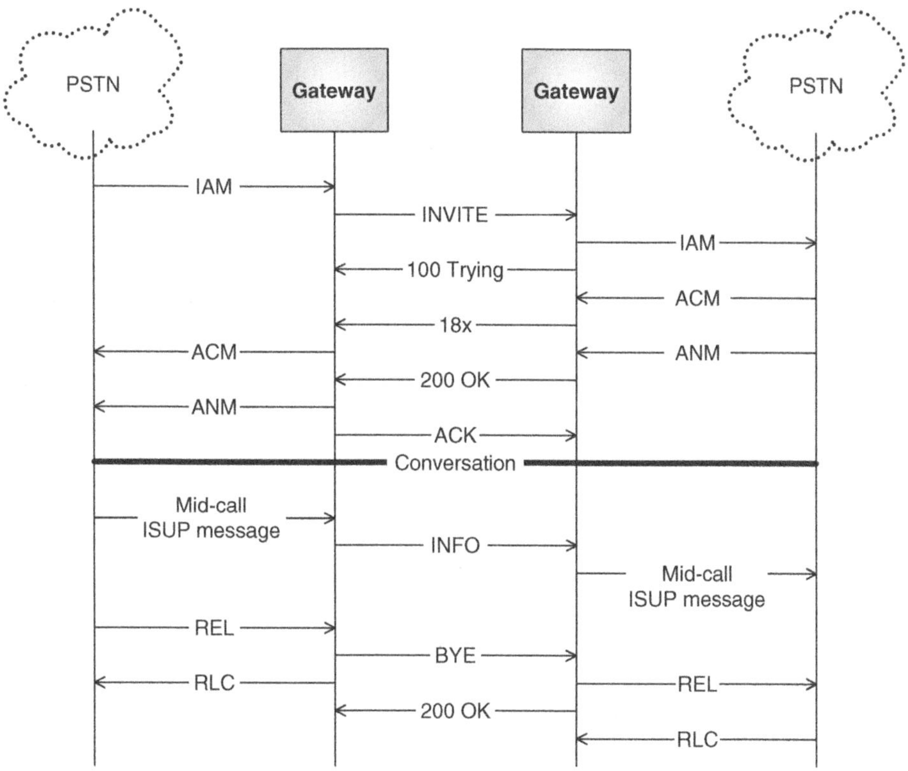

FIGURE 18.12

18.7 Translation or Encapsulation?

At this point, some reader might ask himself or herself: How does the gateway know whether it has to apply just protocol translation (as in Scenarios 1 and 2), or apply both translation and encapsulation (Scenario 3)?

[13] Some examples of ISUP mid-call message are:

- Call progress (CPG)
- Facility (FAC)
- User-to-User (UUS)

CPG and FAC may be used for Supplementary Services (e.g., to indicate call hold to remote party).

The answer to this question is that the gateway does not know—it will always apply both. This means that in Scenario 2, the User Agent will receive an encapsulated ISUP object that it does not understand. The approach taken by [RFC 3372] and [RFC 3398] is that if the UA does not understand ISUP, it should ignore the ISUP content in the SIP body.

18.8 Summary

In this chapter, we analyzed an aspect that is critical in order to offer SIP-based voice services: interoperability with the existing fixed (PSTN) and mobile (PLMN) circuit-switched networks. We focused mainly on voice, which is, by far, the main service offered in circuit-switched networks. However, PSTN (or, more precisely, ISDN) and PLMN can also offer circuit-switched-based video services. Video services in the circuit-switched network are considerably more complex than their voice counterparts because they require additional in-band signaling. Consequently, they were not covered in this chapter.

CHAPTER

Media Servers and Conferencing

19

In previous chapters (5 and 17), we saw how SIP application servers can be used to build SIP services. The service functionality was achieved through an intelligent manipulation of the SIP dialogs. Such manipulation managed to change the conversation space. A call transfer application is an example of such a service.

Nevertheless, not all the services delivered through SIP imply just manipulation of SIP dialogs. In fact, there are a lot of applications that also imply some processing at the media level. Take, for instance, a voice-mail service that requires the voice mail to play an announcement and record a message. Or think about services that require user input in the form of DTMF.[1] Also, conferencing services imply specific media processing so as to enable the mixing of different streams. All these services have in common the fact that, in addition to the manipulation of the SIP dialogs (i.e., manipulation of the signaling), they also involve some specific processing at the media level. Media-processing functions include, but are not limited to:

- play media, such as speech or video.
- record media, such as speech or video.
- prompt and collect media info from the user.
- mixing media streams.
- convert text to speech.
- speech recognition.
- transcoding media.

This chapter is devoted to describing different types of media services used in the context of Internet communications, and the architectures defined to support these media services. We will begin the chapter by looking at the basic media services and how to implement them by using SIP.

After the basic services, we will also tackle more-advanced media services such as advanced multimedia conferencing. This is a quite complex topic by itself, whose analysis would deserve a dedicated book. Therefore, we will just touch on the very key principles. References are given so that interested readers can dive more deeply into the subject.

[1] DTMF stands for Dual-Tone Multifrequency.

Advanced conferencing often requires the use of fully-featured media server control protocols. In the last section of this chapter, we will look at this currently hot topic in the industry and in the standardization committees.

19.1 Basic Media Services

By basic media services, we refer to three different types of functions:

- Playing announcements or video messages.
- Prompting and collecting information (user interaction).
- Mixing media (basic conferencing).

These are basic media services in nature that can be combined to provide interesting applications. Many of today's existing SIP applications use some or all of these media services.

Announcements are media played to the user. Think, for instance, of the case where Alice calls John, and she gets a user-busy announcement because John is engaged in another call. Another example could be an absence reason service such that whenever Alice calls John outside the working hours, an announcement is played to her indicating that he is not available just now, and giving information about the time of day when he can take calls again.

User interaction basically consists of prompting the user for some information—for example, in an announcement—and then collecting the user's response. For instance, a call to a company's number might result in an announcement being played that gives us several options depending on which is the department we want to speak with. The user provides, typically by pressing some keys on his or her IP phone, the desired option, and the application connects the user to the right destination. Also, as part of a user interaction basic service, it is common to have capabilities for recording the media input from the user. For instance, consider a basic voice-mail application that asks the calling user to leave a message. In order to implement this service, the voice mail would need to have the capability to record the media produced by the user. Media recording is also considered a media service.

Multiparty communication (i.e., conferencing) is one of the most complex topics in the general area of communication services. SIP can support many models of multiparty communications. Broadly speaking, we can classify conferences in SIP into three main groups:

- loosely coupled conferences.
- fully distributed multiparty conferences.
- tightly coupled conferences.

Loosely coupled conferences make use of multicast media groups. In this type of conference, there is no signaling relationship between the participants, and there is not a central point of control for the conference. Each participant subscribes to a particular multicast address where they receive the RTP streams from the rest of the participants. Participants also address their RTP streams to the multicast address. SIP may be used just to inform users of the multicast conference address, but also other mechanisms are available for that, such as email, web pages, or the Session Announcement Protocol (SAP). SAP is specified in [RFC 2974].

In fully distributed multiparty conferences, each participant maintains a signaling relationship with the other participants using SIP. There is no central point of control; it is completely distributed among the participants.

Tightly coupled conferences are characterized by the existence of a central point of control. Each participant establishes a signaling relationship to this central point, which provides a number of functions and may also perform media mixing.

In Figure 19.1, the architecture for the three different conferencing models is shown.

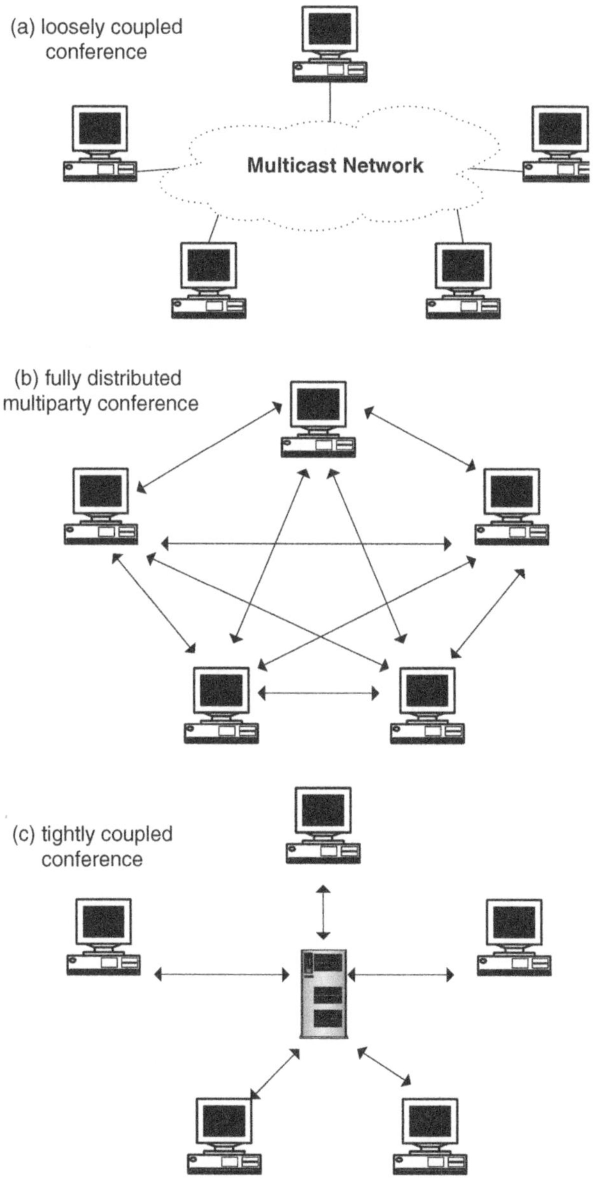

FIGURE 19.1

In this book, we will tackle only tightly coupled conferences, which is the most commonly used method. Therefore, from now on, we will use the term "conference" just to refer to "tightly coupled conferences." In this first section, we consider basic conferencing (that is, basic tightly coupled conferencing) as one of the three key basic media services.

Basic conferencing more or less equals a simple basic-media mixing function. It provides basic functions to create a conference, for a new user to join the conference, and for users to leave the conference. It does not address features such as floor control, gain control, muting, subconferences, and so on. These features are part of an enhanced conferencing service that will be examined in later sections.

19.1.1 Architecture for Basic Media Services

In addition to the manipulation of SIP dialogs according to some service logic (call control), many SIP applications also require media handling. From the functional perspective, we could consider that these applications are made up of two entities:

- *The service logic*, which triggers and drives the manipulation of the session dialogs. The service logic resides in the control plane.
- *The media-handling functions* (playing announcements, detecting DTMF, mixing streams, transcoding, and so on). The media-handling functions reside in the media plane.

In practice, this split is not just functional but also physical, given that media manipulation is a quite specific task that may require special types of hardware and software resources. In such a physical split, there are two types of servers (application platforms):

- The application server, which hosts the service logic to manipulate the dialogs.
- The media server, which is capable of media processing.

The presence of an application server may or may not be needed depending on the complexity of the service. For very simple applications, such as just playing an announcement at call setup, an architecture such as the one depicted in Figure 19.2 might be enough, whereas, for richer applications, there needs to

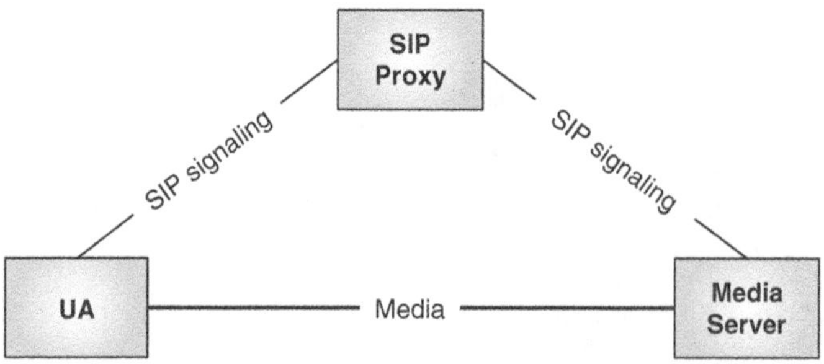

FIGURE 19.2

be a separate application server, as in Figure 19.3. We will consider the latter architecture as the reference in order to implement basic (and also advanced) media services.

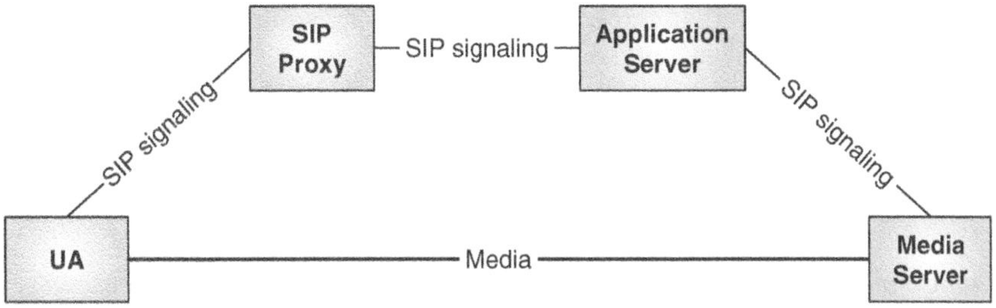

FIGURE 19.3

The way this architecture works is quite simple. In order to apply a service, the call (control plane) needs to be routed to the application server (AS). The application sever then executes the service logic and decides to invoke a media service on the media server. In order to invoke the media service (e.g., an announcement), the application server manipulates the Request-URI so that, instead of identifying a user, it identifies a service in the media server, and routes the call toward the media server. The media server receives the call, looks at the Request-URI, and determines what media service needs to be invoked.

The concept of addressing services as if they were users was introduced in [RFC 3087]. The utilization of this concept in order to invoke basic media services is described in [RFC 4240].

[RFC 4240] defines a format for the Request-URI so as to use it as a service indicator at the media server. More specifically, we take advantage of the fact that the standard SIP URI has a user part, but media servers do not have users. Therefore, we can use the user part in the SIP URI as a service indicator. In addition to the user part, it may also be necessary to add some other service-related information in the form of URI parameters.

In the next section, we will see how this is accomplished for the three basic media services described previously.

19.1.2 Implementation

[RFC 4240] defines a way to offer SIP-based basic media services using the simple architecture depicted in the previous section. It defines specific formats in the Request-URI that enable the invocation of the three basic services in media servers:

- announcements.
- user interaction.
- basic conferences.

Announcements

In order to invoke an announcement, the user part in the Request-URI is set to "annc." In addition to that, there also must be a "play" URI parameter that specifies the resource or announcement sequence to be played. There are also a bunch of other optional parameters that can specify aspects such as number of repetitions, maximum duration, language, and so forth.

The following URI identifies an announcement service (annc) at the media server (mediaserver.ocean.com), and gives the location (//fileserver.ocean.com) of the media file (welcome.wav).

sip:annc@mediaserver.ocean.com; play=file://fileserver.ocean.com/welcome.wav

User Interaction

The user interaction service is identified by the service indicator "dialog" contained in the user part of the Request-URI. In addition, the mandatory "voicexml" URI parameter must be present. It indicates the location of the VoiceXML script that needs to be executed. In practical deployments, the VoiceXML script may reside in the application server.

VoiceXML is an XML language used to describe voice (and now also video) interactions. The present book does not explain VoiceXML in detail. Interested readers are referred to the VoiceXML specification at [W3C_VOICEXML] for more information on the subject.

Nevertheless, in order to let the reader get the idea of what VoiceXML looks like, next we show a simple example VoiceXML script taken from the VoiceXML specification. This is used to ask the user for a choice of drink, and then that choice is submitted to a server script:

```
<?xml version="1.0" encoding="UTF-8"?>
<vxml xmlns="http://www.w3.org/2001/vxml" xmlns:xsi="http://www.w3.org/2001/
 XMLSchema-instance" xsi:schemaLocation="http://www.w3.org/2001/vxml
 http://www.w3.org/TR/voicexml20/vxml.xsd" version="2.0">
 <form>
  <field name="drink">
   <prompt>Would you like coffee, tea, milk, or nothing?</prompt>
   <grammar src="drink.grxml" type="application/srgs+xml"/>
  </field>
  <block>
   <submit next="http://www.drink.example.com/drink2.asp"/>
  </block>
 </form>
</vxml>
```

An example of Request-URI that causes the invocation of a user interaction service (dialog) at a media server (mediaserver.ocean.com) could be:

sip:dialog@mediaserver.ocean.com; play=file://fileserver.ocean.com/dialog.vxml

Basic Conferences

Basic conferencing provides mainly a simple media mixing service. A mixing service receives a number of RTP streams, combines them, and sends back the combination. Figure 19.4 shows the mixing of three incoming streams into the media server. For simplicity, only the media plane is shown.

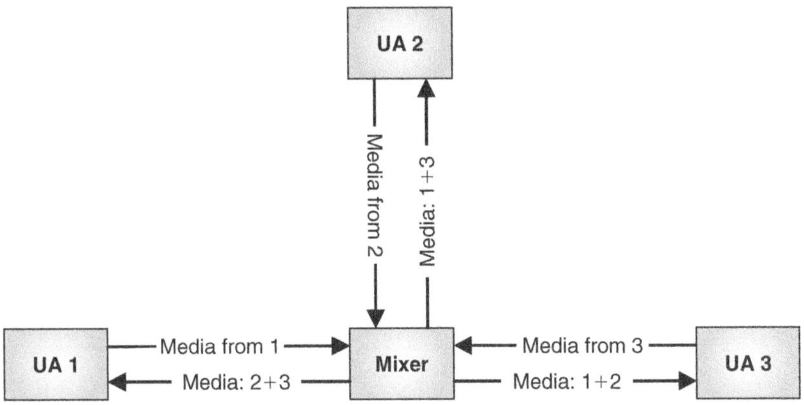

FIGURE 19.4

The user part in the Request-URI is again used to identify the particular media service: "conf." However, in this case, in addition to identifying that we want to use a conference, it is also necessary to identify the particular conference instance (i.e., the mixing instance) because many conference instances may exist at the media server. That is achieved by also including a unique identifier for the conference, separated with a "=" sign from the service indicator.

An example of Request-URI that invokes a conferencing service might be:

sip:conf=123@mediaserver.pacific.com

When the first INVITE request arrives at the media server, if a conference device associated with this URI does not yet exist, a mixing session is created that includes the seizing of a conference device. Subsequent INVITE requests for the same conference (i.e., same unique identifier) cause the media server to join them into the existing conference. If a user wants to abandon the conference, he or she just needs to send a BYE within the session they established with the media server.

When the last participant leaves the conference, the mixing session is destroyed in the media server.

19.1.3 Examples

Figure 19.5 shows the call flow for a simple absence reason service. John calls Alice, but Alice is in a meeting, so she has configured her absence reason[2] service to play the following announcement: "I am in a meeting until 10h00."

The call is routed from John to the application server.[3] The application server knows that Alice is in a meeting (because Alice configured such information), so it invokes an announcement service in the media server. The file that contains the announcement to be played is called "meeting.wav."[4]

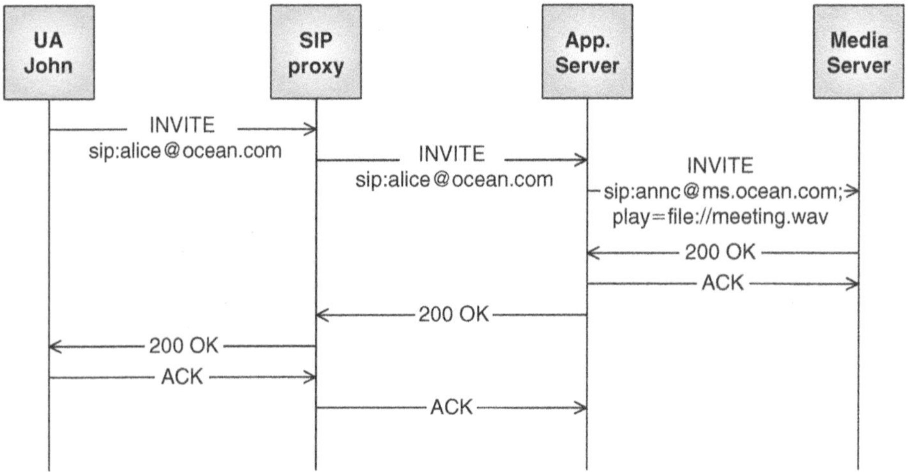

FIGURE 19.5

Figure 19.6 shows an example of a basic SIP conference. Participants make calls to a generic URI identifying a public conference, and the application server actually selects a particular identifier for the conference and modifies the Request-URI accordingly. John's INVITE request creates the conference, because his request is the first one. Subsequent INVITE requests to the same generic URI cause the respective participants to be joined to the conference.

[2]For instance, this information might be obtained from Microsoft Outlook.

[3]The actual mechanism by which the call is routed to the application server is not shown here. It might be through static configuration in the SIP proxy so that calls originated to a particular user are routed to the application server (by adding the application server URI to the Route header) or other mechanism.

[4]If a flexible announcement is played, then VoiceXML may be used. A flexible announcement may, for example, mention the time when you're in a meeting.

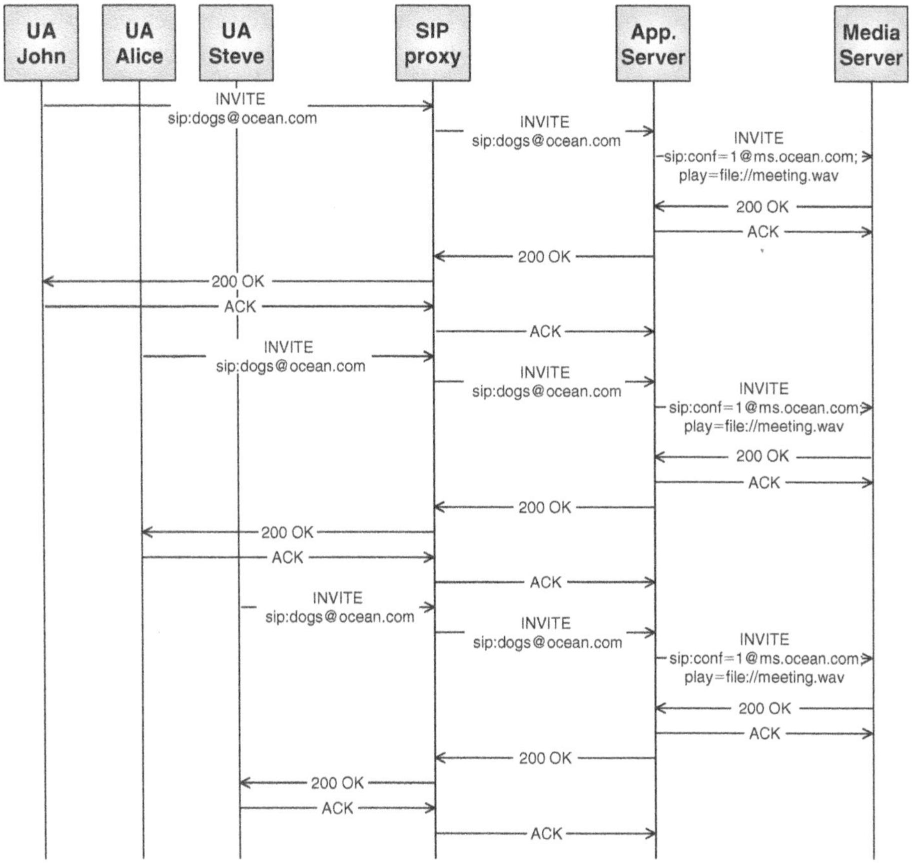

FIGURE 19.6

19.2 About KPML and the User Interaction Framework

In the previous section, we have seen that the basic media services architecture can be used to implement basic user interaction based on VoiceXML. There is currently work in progress in the IETF [draft-ietf-sipping-app-interaction-framework] in order to define a more generic framework for enabling the interaction of users with applications. The interaction of users with applications is implemented through the "user interface" concept. The framework defines two types of user interfaces: presentation-free UI and presentation-capable UI. The former is a UI that cannot prompt the user with information, whereas the latter can.

VoiceXML, for instance, may be used to enable a presentation-capable UI because it allows for both "collect information" and "prompt and collect for information." On the other hand, there are cases where only a presentation-free UI is available. An example of such an interface could be a gateway or media server that can just collect DTMF. In order to enable the collection of DTMF through presentation-free UIs,

[RFC 4730] defines the Key Press Markup Language (KPML) event package. KPML is an XML-based language that allows us to describe DTMF events. In order to receive notifications of DTMF events, an application server might subscribe the KPML event package to a media server. When the media server detects a DTMF tone in the media stream, it will send a NOTIFY request to the AS, including in the body a KPML document that describes the DTMF event produced.

KPML is a relatively recent standard. It might find acceptance in the remit of TDM/IP media gateways. When it comes to media servers, the current industry trend seems to go in the direction of implementing fully-featured media sever control protocols such as the ones we will describe in the last section of this chapter.

The application interaction framework does not tackle only media-based interaction. Actually, it is generic enough to accommodate any type of interaction, be it through media, web forms, or whatever. A thorough description of the framework is outside the scope of this book.

19.3 Enhanced Conferencing

The basic conference service depicted in the previous section offers very limited functionality. [RFC 4245] gives a high-level view of more-advanced requirements for tightly coupled conferences. These requirements will be extended by other forthcoming IETF specifications that will focus on particular areas. The requirements in [RFC 4245] include:

- conference creation.
- conference termination.
- dial-in: participants dial into the conference.
- dial-out: the "conference" calls the participants.
- third-party invitation: a user can invite other users to the conference.
- participant's removal: the "conference" can remove a participant.
- conference state dissemination (inform participants about conference info: number of participants, who the chair is, and so on).
- sidebar conferences: conferences within the conference—that is, a subgroup of participants can talk to each other without being heard by the other conference participants.

[RFC 4245] states that some of these requirements may be fulfilled by using SIP signaling, whereas others might need other means.

In order to meet these advanced requirements, the IETF, within the SIPPING Working Group, has defined a SIP conferencing framework, which is described in [RFC 4353]. This informational RFC proposes a SIP-centric framework and architecture to address the general requirements stated in [RFC 4245]. Most of the conferencing functions are, in this framework, implemented using the SIP protocol. Although it is stated that other functions will need non-SIP mechanisms, these mechanisms are not specified in [RFC 4353].

The SIP conferencing framework in [RFC 4353] represents an important advantage compared with the basic conferencing functionality of [RFC 4240], described in Section 19.1 "Basic Media Services." However, additional requirements, such as the ones described in [RFC 4376] (requirements for floor control) and [RFC 4597] (conferencing scenarios), and the need to have more-powerful conference management mechanisms, is driving the work, in the IETF XCON Working Group, on a new conferencing framework. The XCON conferencing framework, although still work in progress, is defining a more abstract model that could comply with the broadest set of conferencing requirements and is not necessarily SIP-centric. A lot of functions in the XCON framework can be achieved by using SIP (or other signaling protocols such as H.323, Jabber, ISUP, etc.), but there is also room in this model for other protocols in order to implement conference control or floor control.

In the next sections, we will review both conferencing frameworks.

19.4 Framework for Conferencing with SIP

RFC 4353 presents a general SIP-centric architectural model and terminology in order to address tightly coupled conferencing services.

The key element in this architecture is called the focus. The focus is a functional element that represents a SIP UA responsible for maintaining a SIP signaling relationship with each participant in the conference, and making sure, through the use of some mixers under its control, that the media is properly distributed among the participants.

For instance, in dial-in scenarios, the participants direct the session establishment signaling toward the focus, whereas, in dial-out scenarios, it is the focus establishing a SIP dialog with the participants.

There can only be one focus in a conference, but the focus can use more than one mixer. Figure 19.7 shows a functional architecture with just one mixer.

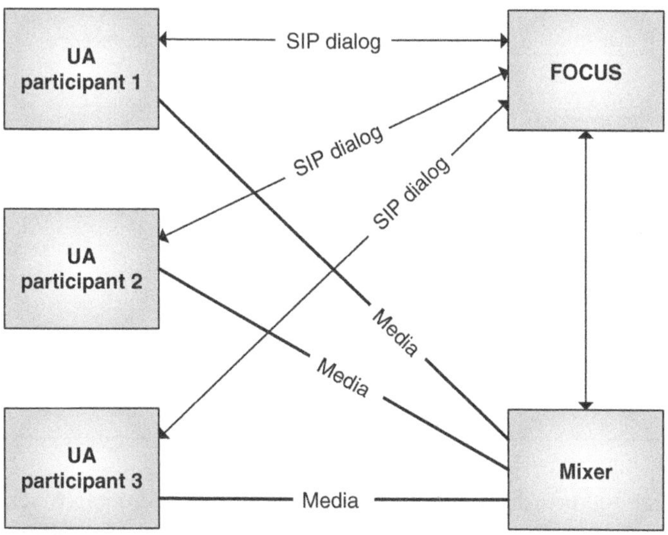

FIGURE 19.7

The focus can also, additionally, incorporate the functions of a conference notification service, accepting subscriptions from the participants and notifying them as soon as the conference state changes. The conference state represents general information about the conference—such as who is actually in the conference, who is the chairperson, what type of media is each participant using, and so on. [RFC 4575] defines a conference event package for this purpose. In order to subscribe to the conference state, a participant would send a SIP SUBSCRIBE message (see Chapter 15) toward the notification server. The notification server would then inform the participant about the conference state (e.g., who is currently in the conference) by sending back a SIP NOTIFY that reflects the current status. As soon as the status changes (e.g., new participants join or leave the conference), the participant would receive new NOTIFY messages.

In addition to the focus, the model also includes a conference policy. The conference policy contains the rules that guide the operation of the conference. For instance, a simple rule might contain the allowed participants to the conference, which the focus should check in order to authorize any attempt to join the conference. There may also be more-complex rules. The conference policy is stored in the conference policy database, and is accessed (read/write) through the conference policy server using non-SIP-specific means.

Figure 19.8 shows all the elements in the architecture and the interfaces between them.

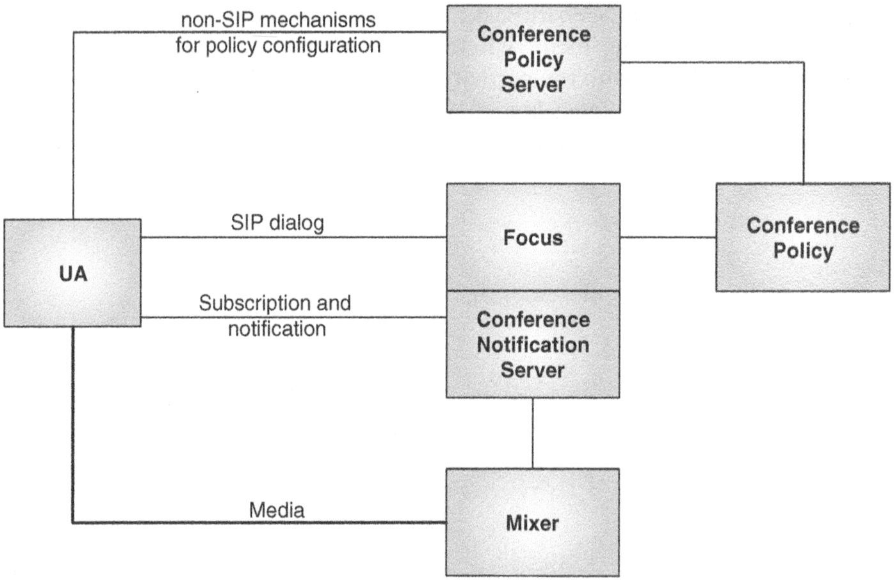

FIGURE 19.8

All the previous architecture diagrams show functional architectures. When grouping the functional entities into physical elements, there are various options. Figure 19.9 shows one such option in which the focus and conference policy elements are implemented in an application server and the mixer is a function of a media server. The interface between application server and media server for advanced conferencing applications will be discussed in subsequent sections.

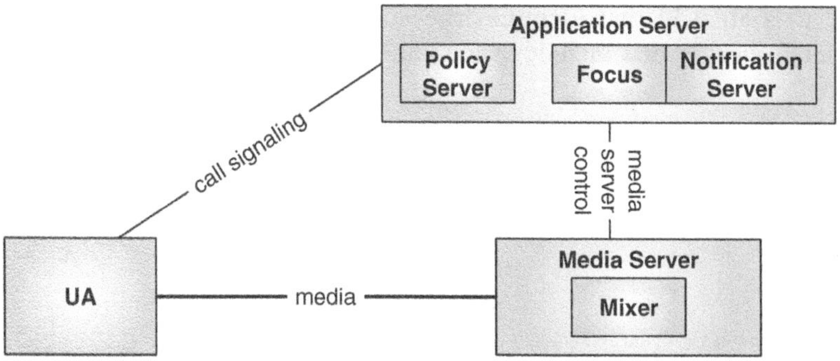

FIGURE 19.9

In Figure 19.10, another possible mapping is shown where all the functions sit on a conferencing server.

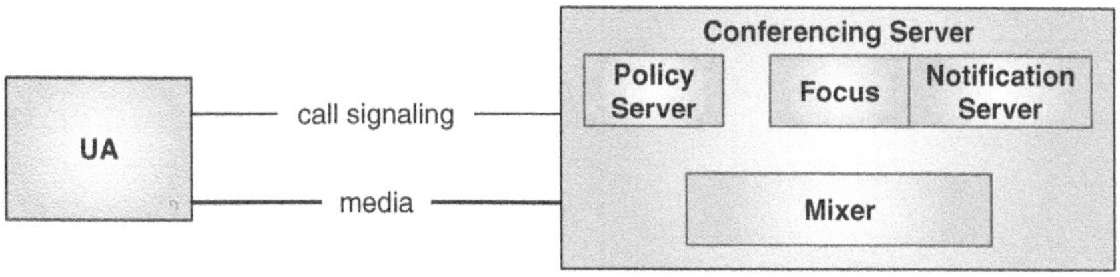

FIGURE 19.10

Next are a couple of examples that highlight some of the advanced conferencing use cases that can be implemented by using this framework. An extensive list of use cases supported by this architecture is contained in "SIP Conferencing for User Agents" [RFC 4579]. This RFC shows how the SIP protocol can be used to implement most of the conferencing features in the framework.

For the purpose of the following examples, and in order to focus the reader's attention on the signaling between the participants and the focus, the mixer and the focus appear as a single entity in the figures. Also, both examples assume that no participant is subscribed to the conference event package. The NOTIFY messages that appear in the call flow belong to the implicit subscription created by the REFER method, and give information about the status of the referred request (see Chapter 17 for an explanation of the REFER procedure).

19.4.1 Example 1: Dial-out to a New Participant

In this example, John, who is already participating in the conference, requests that the focus add Alice to the conference. All the steps in the scenario are implemented using SIP. The request from John is conveyed in a REFER method that, if accepted by the focus, will cause it to invite (dial-out) Alice to the conference. The focus will instruct the mixer to bring the new media from Alice into the conference and distribute it to the rest of participants. The REFER method would be addressed to a SIP URI that identifies the conference (Conf-ID), and would contain a Refer-To header that includes Alice's SIP URI. This example is shown in Figure 19.11.

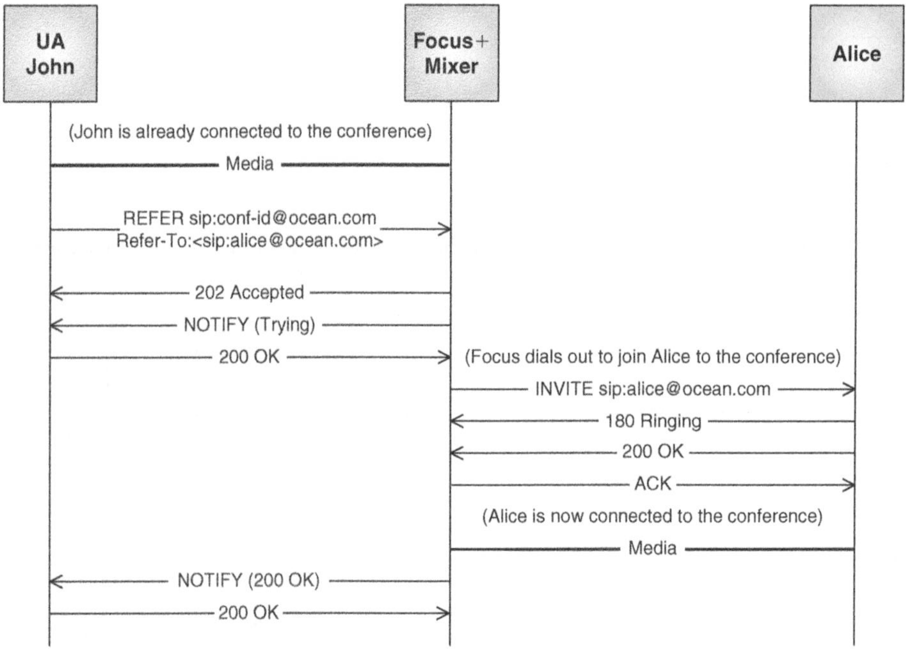

FIGURE 19.11

19.4.2 Example 2: Focus Removes a Participant

In this example, we assume that both John and Alice are connected to the conference. Then John asks the focus to remove Alice from the conference. He sends to the focus a REFER message that, if it is accepted, will cause the focus to send a BYE on the session it has with Alice. Then the focus will instruct the mixer to rearrange the way media is distributed among participants in order to reflect the new situation. The REFER method would be addressed to a SIP URI that identifies the conference (Conf-ID), and would contain a Refer-To header that includes Alice's SIP URI and an explicit indication of the method to be invoked, which is BYE in this case, so as to cause the termination of the session with Alice. This example is depicted in Figure 19.12.

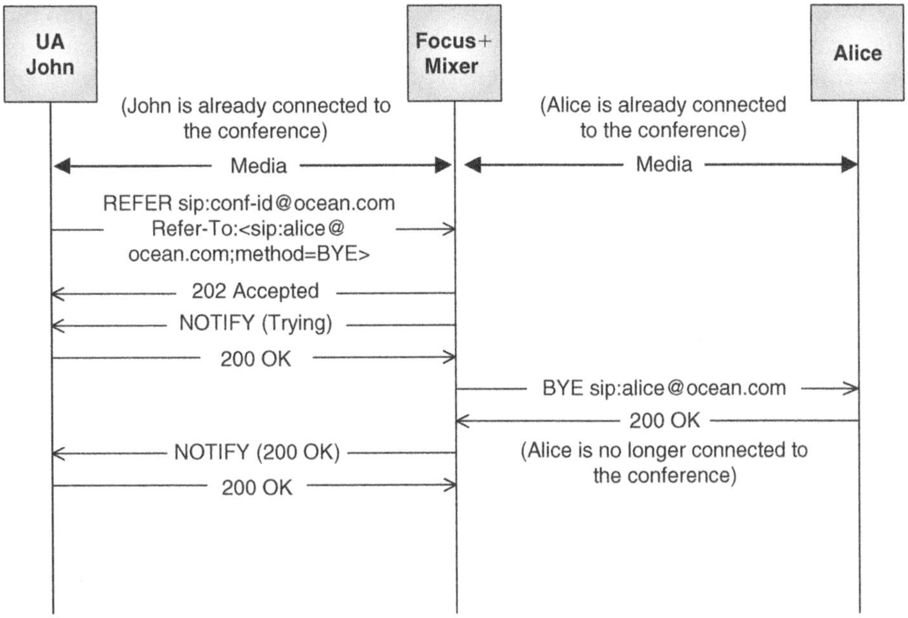

FIGURE 19.12

19.5 XCON Framework

19.5.1 Additional Requirements

As we stated before, the XCON framework for centralized conferencing [draft-ietf-xcon-framework] is being defined in order to cope with additional conferencing requirements such as enhanced conference management or floor control. The core requirements of advanced conferences are defined by [RFC 4245], but additional conferencing requirements are provided in [RFC 4376] and [RFC 4597].

Enhanced Conference Management

In previous sections, we saw how a conference could be created using the architecture for basic media services or the SIP conferencing framework. Basically, when the first user establishes the call against the conference server, the conference is created. This simple model allows for the creation of ad hoc and unmanaged conferences. However, there are cases where we need to have more control over the conference. For instance, we may want to create a scheduled conference or a recurring conference. We may also want to specify, at conference creation time, what is the maximum number of participants for the conference, or general information about the conference (subject, and so on) that might be queried by the participants, and so forth.

We also saw in previous sections how new participants might be added to the conference. The offered functionality allows just simple addition or deletion of participants. There are cases where there is a need to have more flexibility to manipulate participants. For instance, we might want to be able to define different roles for the conference participants (e.g., administrator, chairperson, moderator, participant, observer, and so on). We could then, for instance, add a new participant to the conference, specifying his or her role, which implies a certain level of privileges, and so on.

Another interesting application of enhanced conference management is the advanced manipulation of the media associated with the participants. For instance, the chairman of a conference might want to mute some participants whose background noise is very high. Or he or she might want to alter the gain associated with a media stream from one participant. In another example, the moderator of a video conference might want to change the video layout (i.e., the way the video media is combined by the mixer) from single view to dual view, and so on.

Another type of functionality that requires enhanced conference management is the creation and manipulation of sidebars. Sidebars are conferences within a conference. Imagine that John and Alice are participating in a large conference with other people. At one point in time, John and Alice want to exchange views on what is being said, but they do not want the other participants to listen to what they say to each other. John and Alice might create a sidebar with just themselves as participants. While the sidebar is active, they can talk to each other at the same time that they continue receiving the media from the main conference.

Sidebars can be used in many other scenarios. Think, for instance, of a call center application. Frequently, in this type of application, there is a requirement for having a supervisor listen to the conversation between an agent and a customer in order to do an evaluation of the agent. In more-advanced scenarios, the supervisor can also talk to the agent and give him or her instructions while both of them receive the audio from the customer. The customer would not hear what the supervisor says. These "observing and coaching" scenarios can be easily implemented by creating a particular sidebar between supervisor and agent.

All the previous scenarios are just some examples of functionalities that are enabled by enhanced conferencing management. As we will see in the next section, the XCON framework outlines a separate, non-SIP protocol between conference clients and conference systems in order to enable enhanced conference control.

Floor Control

In order to understand what floor control means, let us think of an "analyst briefing" conferencing scenario. The conference call has a panel of speakers who are allowed to talk in the main conference. In addition to the panel speaker, there are also a number of analysts who are not allowed to speak unless they have the floor (these are called floor participants). If they want to speak, they need to make a floor request to the floor chair (that is, the entity that manages the floor). The floor chair will grant or deny the request, and inform the floor participants about their status/position in the floor's queue.

Floor control represents an advanced conferencing requirement that was not supported either in the architecture for basic media services or in the SIP conferencing framework.

Requirements for floor control are covered in [RFC 4376].

As we will see in the next section, the XCON framework outlines a separate, non-SIP protocol between conference clients and conference systems in order to enable floor control.

Media Services for Enhanced Conferencing

Enhanced conferencing also requires other media-related features. It is common, for instance, that whenever new users joins the conference, they are asked to tell their name, which is then recorded and played to the rest of the participants. Also, when a participant leaves a conference, it is usual that an announcement is played to all the conference participants indicating who left the conference.

Another example could be the "whisper" functionality. This refers to a message targeted to a specific user or users—for example, when only the conference chair receives a warning that there is only five minutes left in the conference.

Therefore, the media services required for enhanced conferencing are:

- recording and playing participant names to the full conference.
- playing an announcement to a single user or to a conference mix.
- collecting DTMF from specific participants.

19.5.2 Architecture

Let us now look at XCON architecture, which supports the previous requirements.

The XCON framework defines some functional elements and outlines the interfaces between them. The framework is not SIP-centric, but SIP can be used as the call-signaling protocol within the framework and also for conference event notification.

The XCON framework is built around the fundamental concept of a conference object. The conference object represents the conference, and encapsulates the conference data throughout the different phases of a conference (creation, reservation, active, completed, and so on). The conference object is accessed through a number of servers:

- The conference control server.
- The floor control server.
- The focus.
- The notification server.

The conference participants include a specific client for each of these servers. Communication between clients and servers takes place via a number of protocols, as depicted in Figure 19.13.

Though not reflected in the architecture, the model also supports the existence of conference policies that define the set of rights, permissions, and limitations pertaining to operations being performed on a conference object.

Next we describe the main elements in the architecture.

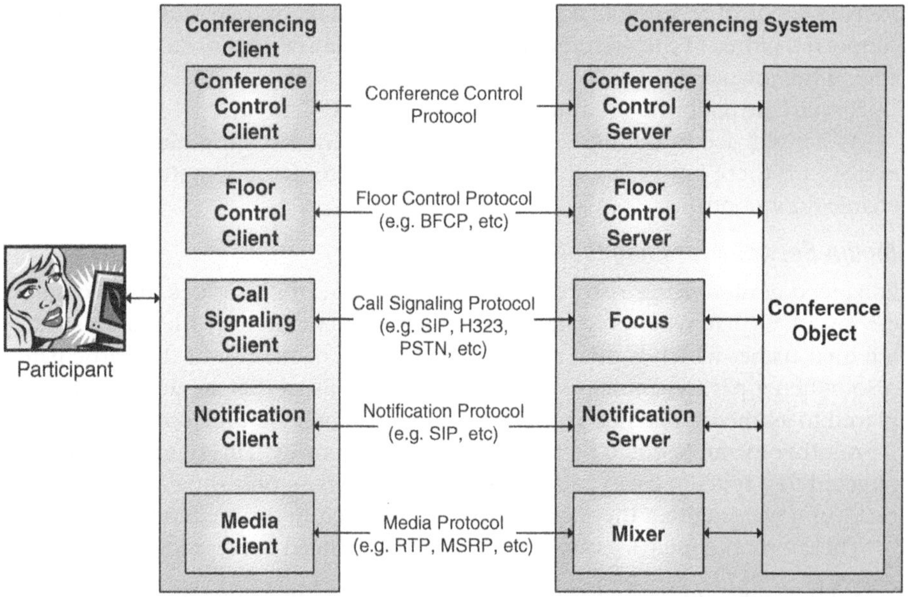

FIGURE 19.13

Conference Control

The conference control protocol provides for data manipulation and state retrieval from the conference object. It allows us to create/delete/modify conferences, add/delete users, add/delete/modify media, put participants on mute, alter the gain media streams, assign roles to participants, create sidebars, and so forth. The XCON framework does not specify a concrete conference control protocol. At the time of writing, there is not yet an IETF standard conference control protocol. An attempt to specify such a protocol was done in [draft-levin-xcon-cccp], which is now expired.

Much of the flexibility in the XCON architecture comes from the existence of a specific protocol for conference control. In the architecture for basic media services and in the SIP conferencing framework, there was no such protocol, and the conference management functions were performed by SIP. For instance, a conference was created when the first user joined; also, a participant was able to request that another user is joined to the conference by sending a REFER request to the focus. These capabilities are very limited in nature. Thanks to the utilization of a separate conference control protocol, much richer features can be offered.

Floor Control

Floor control refers to the capability to manage the access to shared resources—for instance, the determination of who in the audience has the right to talk, and so on. This may be accomplished through a separate, non-SIP protocol that is specified in [RFC 4582]. Again, Figure 19.13 shows specific client and server entities dedicated to floor control.

In the architecture for basic media services and in the SIP conferencing framework, there was no such protocol, and there was no way to offer floor control features.

The basic behavior of floor control is as follows:

- A participant who wants to get access to the floor sends a floor request to the floor control server.
- The floor control server checks with the floor chair—that is, with the entity (might be the moderator) that is responsible for granting access to the floor.
- The floor chair communicates its decision to the floor control server, and this, in turn, communicates the decision to the floor participant.
- At this point, the floor control server might send a notification to the rest of the floor participants to inform them about their position/status in the floor's queue.

This procedure is depicted in Figure 19.14.

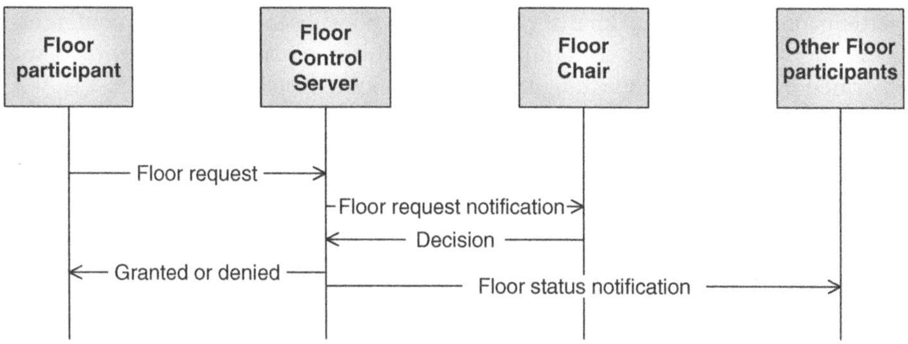

FIGURE 19.14

Focus

The focus in this framework has the same meaning as in the SIP conferencing framework, except that here it does not include the notification server. Another difference is that the call signaling protocol between the focus and the participant does not necessarily need to be SIP (it might be H.323, ISUP, and so on).

Conference Notification

It is a separate entity in this framework, with similar functions as in the SIP conferencing framework. The SIP event framework with the conference event package might be used for this function.

Mixer

It represents the entity that has the capability to combine different media inputs, and provides the media-handling capabilities to, for instance, mute participants, adjust voice gain, perform different video layouts, sidebars, and so on.

Next we will see some examples of utilization of the conference control protocol. We are not implying, in these examples, the usage of a particular conference control protocol. The intent is to let the reader understand the conference control functionality and its relation with other entities in the XCON architecture.

19.5.3 Example 1: Adding a New Participant to the Conference

In this example, we will see a possible way to add a new participant to the conference by using the conference control protocol. The scenario is shown in Figure 19.15.

Let us assume that John is in a conference and wants to join Alice to it. He would send to the conference control server a conference control request to join Alice to the conference. In the conference control request, John includes an XML file that contains the requested configuration for the new participant. For instance, he could indicate the role with which Alice should be joined to the conference. The conference control server would authorize the request, and instruct the focus to generate the necessary call signaling to join Alice. Additionally, if there are other participants (e.g., Peter) in the conference who subscribed to the conference state, they would receive a notification from the notification server (which was informed by the focus) indicating that Alice was joined to the conference.

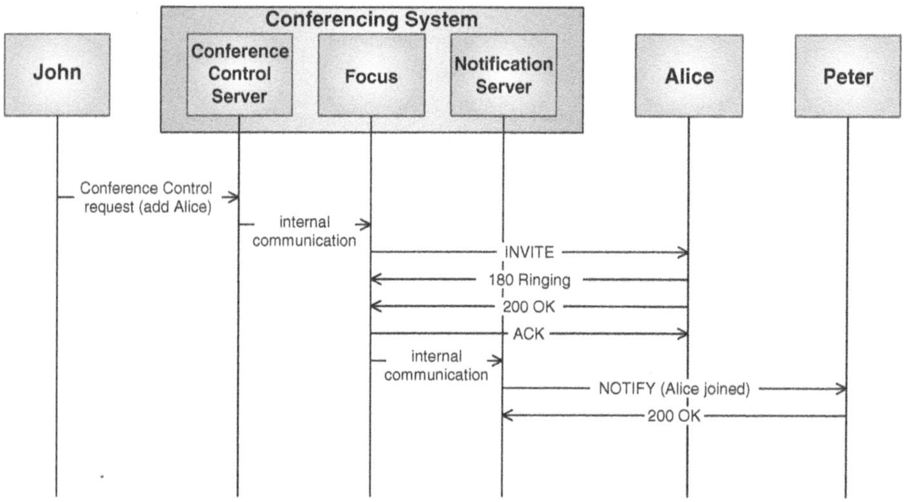

FIGURE 19.15

19.5.4 Example 2: Media Manipulation

In this example, we will see how a participant in the conference—John, who is the chairman—might cause another participant (Alice) to be muted because she is contributing a lot to the background noise, and she seems not to be listening to the conference. Additionally, if there are other participants (e.g., Peter) in the conference who subscribed to the conference state, they would receive a notification from the notification server indicating that Alice was put on mute. This example is shown in Figure 19.16.

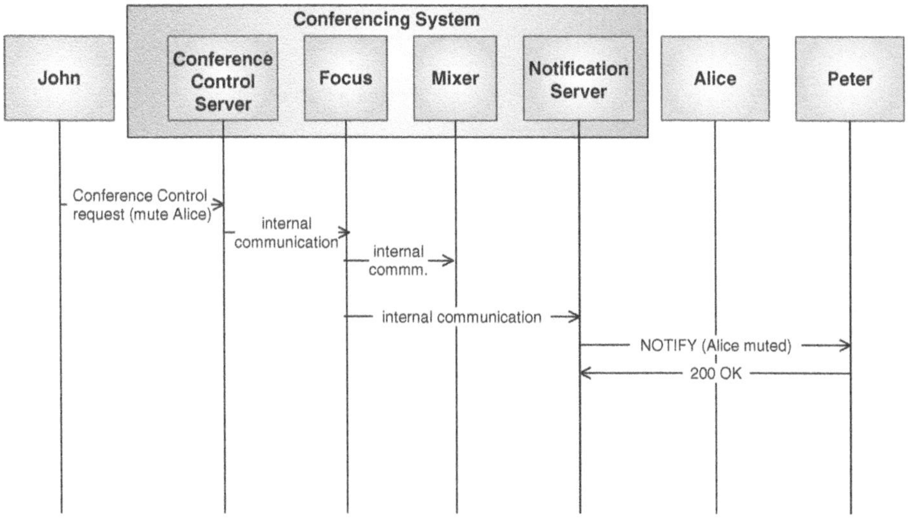

FIGURE 19.16

19.6 Media Server Control

19.6.1 Motivation

As we saw in previous sections, enhanced conferencing applications introduce a quite broad set of new requirements that cannot be met by the simple architectural approach used for basic services. In the previous two sections, we saw two frameworks to cope with these stringent requirements. These frameworks define a number of functional entities and the interfaces between them. There are different ways to group these entities into physical elements. In some cases, all the elements (focus, notification server, mixer, and so on) are implemented in the same box, whereas, in other approaches, all the entities except for the mixer sit at an application server, and the mixer is part of a separate media server. A possible physical instantiation of the XCON architecture following this second approach is shown in Figure 19.17. In this picture, we see an interface between the application server and the media server.

In the architecture for basic services, we already saw an interface between application server and media server. Actually, this interface was SIP, and the Request-URI was used to signal the type of the requested service. Although this approach is valid for simple conferences, it is not valid for enhanced conferencing. Let us just imagine that at one particular moment during the conference, we

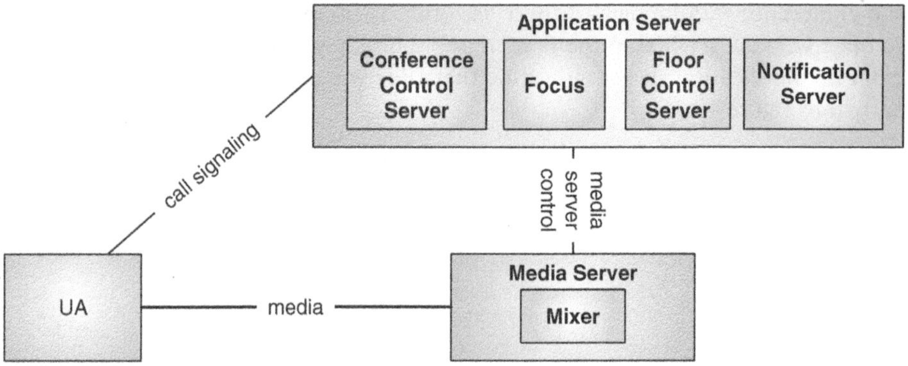

FIGURE 19.17

want to play an announcement to only some of the participants in the conference. This might be done by following the approach for basic services, which would imply that the focus uses third-party call control and issues re-INVITEs to all the participants that need to listen to the announcement on one hand, and also re-INVITEs to the media server indicating the requested resource (announcement) in the Request-URI. This would actually be a cumbersome and inefficient way to implement this function. Actually, the only thing needed here would be for the application server to tell the media server what is to be done (i.e., play announcement A to participants 1, 2, and 3 in conference Z), without the need to modify the established sessions. There are a lot of examples of features in enhanced conferencing scenarios that do not change the SIP dialogs or the sessions, but that do affect the media flow or the media processing of the server. For instance, imagine that we want to execute gain control on some of the participants in the conference, or that we wanted to create a sidebar conference. In order to implement these functions, we would just need a mechanism for the application server to instruct the media server to perform some action on the media without the need to modify the existing sessions.

So, the conclusion is that we also need to have the means to communicate other types of information in that interface so as to enable enhanced features.

These features would include:

- in-conference user interaction.
- creation of submixes.
- modification of the mix.
- recording the mix on a leg.
- play an announcement on a leg.
- alter the gain for a particular leg.
- mute a participant.

Now we will see what alternatives exist in order to convey the information between application server and media server needed to implement these functions.

19.6.2 Approaches

Protocols used between application server and media server for the sake of enabling these enhanced features are typically called media server control protocols. There is not, as of today, a unique standard for media server control. Several protocols compete in different deployments worldwide, and different companies push toward slightly different directions. A Working Group has been recently created in the IETF called MEDIACTRL, tasked precisely with the definition of the requirements for the media server control protocols and the protocol extensions needed to fulfill those requirements.

Knowing that this is a very hot and dynamic topic nowadays in the Internet, we will first describe some of the existing approaches for a media server control protocol. Then, in the next section, we will look at some of the possible trends for the future that are being discussed today in the MEDIACTRL Working Group.

First of all there are two very different approaches to media server control. The first one, usually referred to as the "device control" approach, models the media server as an entity providing low-level functions such as mixing media streams, playing media, transcoding, detecting tones, and so forth, along with the capability of connecting the media streams with them. This approach requires the application server to use a quite low-level protocol capable of indicating actions to be played on these resources. For instance, playing an announcement to a particular participant would imply that the application server needs to command several actions on the media server. These would include disconnecting the participant's stream from the mixer, allocating a media player, connecting the media player to the participant's stream, instructing the media player to start playing the media, waiting until the playing of the media has completed, releasing the media player resources, and then reconnecting the stream to the mixer.

The second approach is the "server control" approach. In this approach, the media server is modeled as an entity that provides high-level services such as playing announcements, interacting with the user, conferencing services, and so forth. In this case, the underlying media server resources are addressed using high-level application constructs.

The first model is exemplified by protocols such as MEGACO, and has gained quite some interest in the telecom domain, where it has been successfully used for controlling resources in TDM/IP gateways. The use of MEGACO to directly control media servers, on the other hand, has not yet found wide deployment. Telecom bodies such as 3GPP have proposed to use it as well in order to control media servers in the remit of IMS. However, its utilization in that remit has not yet found widespread deployment.

The second model has found wide acceptance in the Internet environment, where there was no legacy for application servers having to implement device control protocols, and where the usually preferred approach in order to foster the rapid development of applications is to use application-level protocols.

The two models have pros and cons. The first model, being so low level, is flexible enough in order to meet any present or future requirements. On the other hand, it requires application servers to speak a new, complex protocol such as

MEGACO. Moreover, it requires application developers to have an in-depth understanding of the low-level constructs and a different programming paradigm.

There is rough consensus in the Internet community to pursue the "server model" approach, and to reuse, to some extent, some of the functions existing in SIP (which anyhow needs to be present in the application servers) in order to handle the communication between application server and media server. There is also agreement in the Internet community to use an XML language in order to describe the control data exchanged between application server and media server. Virtually all the media server implementations in the Internet follow this approach.

More specifically, two different XML-based media server control protocols that use SIP as a transport cover all of the market. Neither of them is an Internet standard.[5] These are:

- MSCML: Media Server Control Markup Language [RFC 4722].
- MSML: Media Server Markup Language [draf-saleem-msml].

They differ in the XML language itself used to define the control of the media flows in the server. Both of them use SIP messages (INVITE and INFO) to carry the XML content.

Another point of difference between the two approaches is the way SIP is used. There are two ways to do this. The first is to carry the XML content in SIP messages within the same dialogs that established the media sessions with the media server—that is to say, reuse the existing signaling relationship. The other way is to establish a separate SIP dialog, which sets up no media, to carry the control messages.

The approach used by MSCML is to use the dedicated separate SIP dialog to carry commands that affect all the participants in the conference while using the session control connections for sending commands specific to a participant. For instance, closing the conference or playing an announcement to all the participants will be realized by sending commands on the dedicated SIP dialog.

On the other hand, MSML allows for the control messages to be sent on an individual connection even if they affect other participants. Therefore, the targets of MSML actions are not specified implicitly by the SIP dialog within which they are sent, but by specific identifiers carried in the XML data. Additionally, MSML also supports a dedicated control connection, with no media, to carry the XML content on the body of SIP messages.

Figure 19.18 shows an example with MSCML.

In this example, there is an already-established conference with three participants. Therefore, there exists one SIP signaling relationship between application sever and media server for each participant. In addition to that, there is another SIP dialog between application server and media server for the dedicated control channel. Commands sent on that channel will apply to the three participants, whereas commands sent on just an individual dialog will apply only to the corresponding participant.

In this example, the application server first plays an announcement to all the participants, therefore we can see it is sent on an INFO message pertaining to the

[5] [RFC 4722] is just an informational RFC (non-Standards Track).

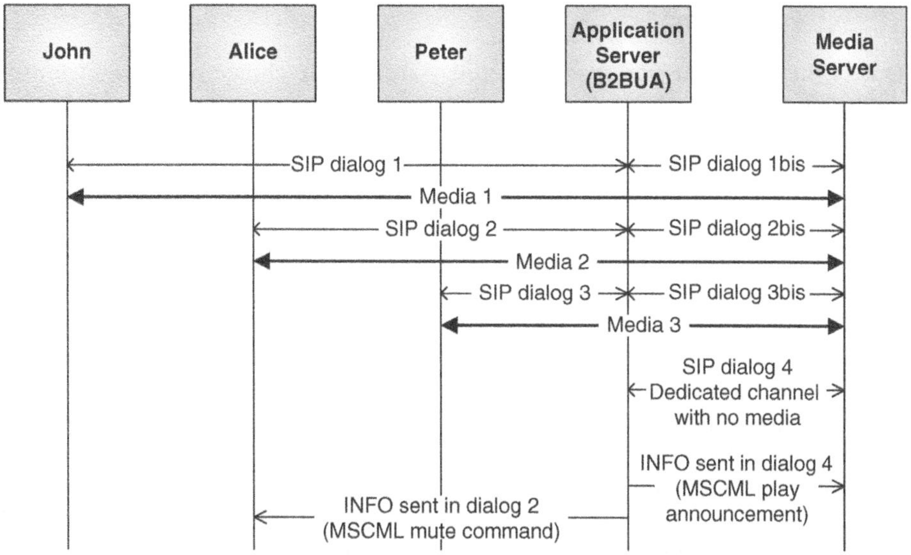

FIGURE 19.18

dedicated dialog (dialog 4). Later on, the application server mutes Alice, sending the mute command in just the SIP dialog that corresponds to Alice (dialog 2).

The XML content of the first INFO message (playing an announcement) might look like this:

```
<?xml version="1.0" encoding="utf-8"?>
<MediaServerControl version="1.0">
  <request>
    <play>
      <prompt>
        <audio url="http://announcements.ocean.com/welcome.wav"/>
      </prompt>
    </play>
  </request>
</MediaServerControl>
```

The XML content of the second INFO message (mute command) might look like this:

```
<?xml version="1.0" encoding="utf-8"?>
<MediaServerControl version="1.0">
  <request>
    <configure_leg mixmode="mute"/>
  </request>
</MediaServerControl>
```

19.6.3 Future Trends

Out of the hot discussion that exists today around the choice of the right protocol to implement media server control, there seems to be an agreement on some points:

- The use of SIP provides interesting capabilities for locating media servers, security, and so on.
- Carrying media server control data in INFO messages is not the best approach. Its main drawback relates to interoperability issues. There are no specific semantics associated with INFO; the semantics are typically defined in the message body. The SIP INFO method does not define any means by which the extensions contained in the message body can be used in an interoperable way.
- Using an XML language to carry the media server control data is a flexible and convenient approach.

With these considerations in mind, an approach has been proposed to use a dedicated control channel to carry the control messages. Moreover, the control information is now not carried on the SIP messages themselves, but on a transport connection that is established using SIP—very much following the approach defined in [RFC 4145], which we saw in Chapter 10 for TCP-based media transport. Figure 19.19 depicts this approach.

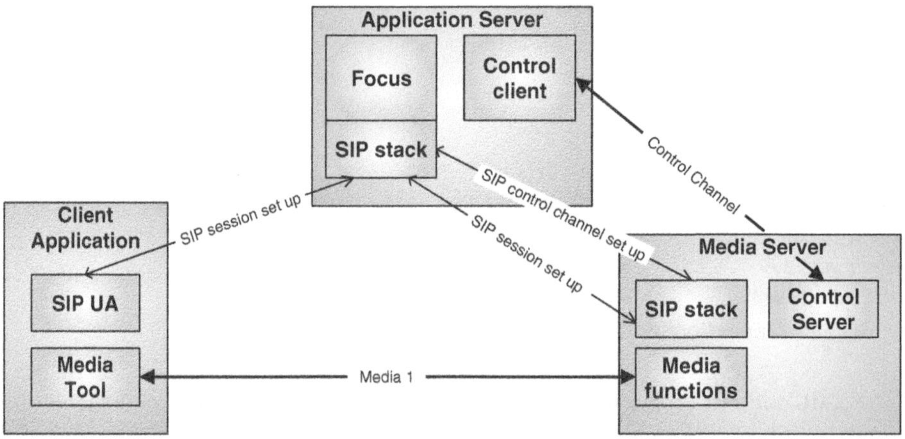

FIGURE 19.19

This approach is called "A Control Framework for the Session Initiation Protocol," and is still work in progress in the IETF [draft-boulton-sip-control-framework]. As its name implies, it defines just a framework for media server control. The framework defines how the dedicated control channel is established using SIP, and what are the messages exchanged on the transport connection established with SIP. More specifically, the framework defines several types of messages:

- SYNCH
- REPORT
- CONTROL
- K-ALIVE

The way these messages are used in order to deliver a specific functionality is left for additional extensions, called control packages, that build on top of the framework. Currently, there is ongoing work to define control packages for:

- basic interactive voice response [draft-boulton-ivr-control-package],
- advanced interactive voice response [draft-boulton-ivr-vxml-control-package],
- conference control [draft-boulton-conference-control-package].

19.7 Other Media Services

Some enhanced media applications also require functions such as Text-to-Speech or Automatic Speech Recognition. Imagine that John calls a customer-service number. As soon as the call is established, he hears an announcement asking him to say what department he wants to talk to. John says, "Sales," and the system applies some signal processing in order to translate the voice signal into text so that it can be used by the computer program that determines what to do next. Likewise, the computer program might have to dynamically build other announcements that are to be presented to the user as part of the execution of the interaction flow. Therefore, rather than having a recorded copy of all the possible combinations, it would be better if the server could automatically convert to speech a text string that has been constructed programmatically.

Text-to-speech (TTS) and Automatic Speech Recognition (ASR) are complex media functions that may be offered in media servers. These functions are highly specific, and therefore may be implemented physically separate from the media server itself. A possible protocol for allowing a client to control the ASR and TTS functions, called MRCP (Media Resource Control Protocol), was proposed in an informational Request For Comments [RFC 4463]. There is currently ongoing work to define MCRPv2 in [draft-ietf-speechsc-mrcpv2].

The MRCPv2 client is typically an application server or a media server. In Figure 19.20, we can see how the media server can act as client to a TTS/ASR server.

In a possible scenario, the media server would record a message from the User Agent and then pass the recorded message (e.g., in PCM-encoded format) to the ASR server, which would then translate it into text and send the text back to the media server.

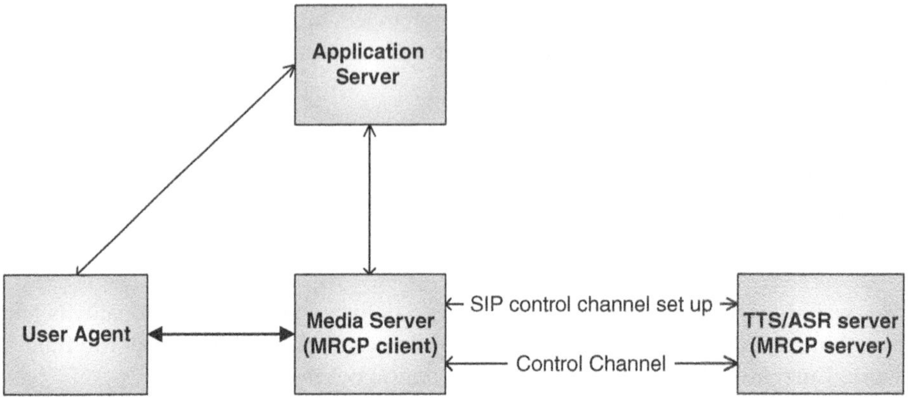

FIGURE 19.20

19.8 Summary

We learned in this chapter how media services can be implemented in SIP architectures. We saw that this is an area that is advancing at a rapid pace, so we may see new architectures and ideas being proposed in the near future.

In the next chapter, we change the topic a bit, and tackle the aspects related to SIP identity. We will cover two aspects that are very important in communication scenarios: the capability to convey an authenticated identity of the caller, and the capability to hide the identity of the caller. Both aspects are not successfully covered in the core SIP specifications, so new SIP extensions have been defined to cope with them.

CHAPTER

SIP Identity Aspects

20

This chapter covers some aspects regarding the management of the identity of SIP request originators. This includes aspects about how to assert such an identity—and also about how to hide it. First we present a general discussion about the topic, and then we describe three different approaches for identity management in SIP.

20.1 Identity Management in SIP

For the purpose of this chapter, we will use the expression "SIP identity management" to refer to the mechanisms for asserting and withholding the SIP identity of a user who is generating a request.

In the context of this discussion, two aspects are critical to our definition of SIP identity:

1. It is a "logical" concept, not a "physical" one (e.g., a user's identity is not his or her IP address).
2. It is not an alias; it is an identifier that allows other users to set up communications with the user represented by the identity.

Therefore, we do not consider an IP address to be a valid SIP identity for a user. On the other hand, an address of record would be a valid SIP identity.

In IP communication scenarios, it is important that, whenever John originates a SIP request, he has the means to voluntarily assert his identity. By asserting his identity, we mean that John is claiming that he can receive requests sent to that identity.

Asserting the requestor's identity provides mainly two features:

1. It gives information to the recipients of the request. They may use this information in several ways:
   - To be able to send new requests to the originator outside of the context of the current dialog.

- In the case of session-initiating requests, to influence their decision of whether or not to accept the session.

2. It gives information to SIP entities to determine which processing rules to apply to a request (for example, automatic call rejection).

Delivering the previous features implies at least two aspects. First there must be a header field in the SIP requests with the right semantics to express our concept of identity as stated above. Second, SIP entities that may use such a header field should be capable of authenticating its validity.

Another related topic is identity hiding (privacy). Sometimes when a user makes a multimedia call, he or she would like to withhold their identity from the called party. There may be several reasons for that. For instance, the user might not want to be associated with the information that they are going to impart, or they might not want to give information that allows the called party to call them back later on.

Obviously, when a user invokes identity privacy, he or she is inhibiting our feature No. 1. The effect of identity privacy in feature No. 2 is not so clear. For instance, a user may want to withhold his or her identity from the called party, but the user may still want some services to be applied on their behalf by some trusted entity. Such a trusted entity should have access to the user's authenticated identity in order to apply some service logic. In some cases—for instance, in a pure Internet environment—the user might want to hide his or her identity from any entity the call goes through, including (or not) the recipient. In yet other types of scenarios, such as those that may occur in SIP networks controlled by telecom operators, there may be other types of requirements (e.g., regulatory) that preclude the user's identity from being hidden from specific network nodes irrespective of the user's wishes.

Another aspect of the privacy topic is the fact that there are also other headers, different from the From header, in the SIP signaling that might also convey personal information about the originator of the request (e.g., Contact header, Via header, etc.). Moreover, the session traffic may also include parameters that convey personal information (e.g., IP addresses in RTP packets, and so on). A full solution for user privacy should address all these issues, as we will see in the next sections.

All in all, the identity-management problem is not an easy one, and is further complicated by the fact that there may be quite different scenarios for implementation of IP communication services ranging from a pure Internet environment to more-controlled SIP networks administered by a single entity (e.g., a telecom operator or a small company).

In the next sections, we will review three different approaches for SIP identity management. The first one, which we will call "Basic Identity Management," reflects the approach contained in the base SIP spec [RFC 3261], with the enhancements for privacy defined in [RFC 3323]. The second one, "Private Header for Network Asserted Identity" is an approach that has been defined to cope with identity-management requirements in the remit of networks composed of trusted nodes. It is defined in [RFC 3325]. The last one, "Enhanced Identity Management," defines a general-purpose mechanism to the problem-identity assertion that is appropriate for Internet-wide deployments.

20.2 Basic Identity Management

20.2.1 Assertion of the SIP Identity

We saw in Chapter 6 that the base SIP specification defines a mechanism for users to assert their identity by using the From header. The From header might be presented to the recipient of the request. Additionally, the From header might be used by SIP entities as an input parameter for service logic execution.

The base SIP specification also defines mechanisms for authenticating the senders of SIP requests by using, for instance, SIP digest (see Chapter 14).

From the above, one could conclude that the problem of asserting the identity in SIP is already solved in baseline SIP. However, the solution depicted above has some drawbacks. The first one is the semantics of the From header. The From header contains a logical identity, possibly an address of record, but nothing precludes the SIP user from introducing in the From header just an alias. If that were the case, the called user would not be able to return the call based on the identity in the From header. The second drawback has to do with authentication. The fact is that few User Agents today support the end-user certificates needed to authenticate themselves. Moreover, digest authentication is limited by the fact that the originator and the recipient must share a prearranged secret. This represents an issue because it is desirable that User Agents are able to send requests to users with whom they have no previous association, and still allow the recipient to have a reasonable assurance that the displayed identity truly represents the originator of the request.

In the next sections, we will see other approaches to the problem of identity management that solve these problems.

20.2.2 Privacy Mechanisms

Now we will see several approaches for dealing with privacy in the basic scenario we depicted in the previous section. The different approaches are tackled by [RFC 3323].

If a user wanted to hide his or her identity from the called party, the user might set the From header field to the following value:

"Anonymous" <sip:anonymous@anonymous.invalid>

This approach to obtain privacy by having the UA manipulate the header fields is typically referred to as user-provided privacy. User-provided privacy has two main drawbacks.

The first one refers to the fact that if the network gets no indication of the identity of the user, it would be impossible for the network to apply any services on behalf of that user.

The second drawback refers to the fact that there are other headers, in addition to the From header, that can convey personal information about the caller. For instance, the Contact header may contain the IP address of the calling party, or a hostname that resolves to that address. Likewise, the Via header also gives information about the IP address of the originator. Furthermore, the Record-Route header might also divulge information about the administrative domain of the caller. These headers, unlike what happens with the From header, are used in the routing of SIP responses or of subsequent requests. Therefore, so as not to cause improper routing of messages, they should not be modified by User Agents. Consequently, in order to hide the personal information implicit in these headers, there is a need to have support from the network. More specifically, a network-provided privacy service is needed. A User Agent, when sending a SIP request, might request such a service by including in the request a Privacy header field set to the value "header." The privacy header is a SIP extension defined in [RFC 3323].

The privacy service would implement at least the following three functions:

- Remove all Via headers that have been added to any received request prior to its arrival at the privacy service, and add a single Via header representing itself.
- Replace the value of the Contact header in received messages with a URI that does not refer to the originator of the message, but rather, to the privacy service itself.
- Strip any Record-Route headers that have been added to a request before it reaches the privacy service.

Obviously, the privacy service must locally persist the values of any of the above headers that are so removed. When further requests or responses associated with the dialog reach the privacy service, it must restore the values for the Via, Record-Route, and Contact headers that it has previously removed in the interests of privacy.

The privacy service could be implemented as a transparent B2BUA[1] that effectively terminates and reoriginates the messages that initiate a session.

Figure 20.1 shows a call flow with a privacy service implemented as a B2BUA.

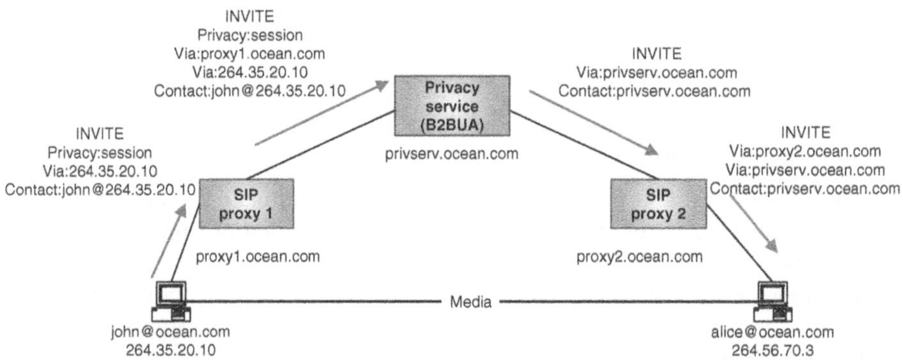

FIGURE 20.1

[1] A transparent B2BUA is a particular type of B2BUA that forwards SIP messages in a SIP proxy-like way, and that also benefits from some features of a User Agent (UA) element.

So far, we have referred only to the identities carried in the SIP signaling. But the media plane (the session) may also carry personal information about the caller, such as IP addresses and so on. In some cases, the calling party may also wish to hide such information. In order to withhold the identities (e.g., IP addresses) present in the media flows, there is a need for having in the media plane an intermediary entity that effectively terminates and reoriginates the media traffic. Such an entity would be controlled by the privacy service (B2BUA).

A User Agent might request such a session privacy service by including a Privacy header field set to the value "session." When the privacy server detects that session privacy is required, it would involve the media intermediary as appropriate. Figure 20.2 shows a call flow that illustrates the scenario for session privacy.

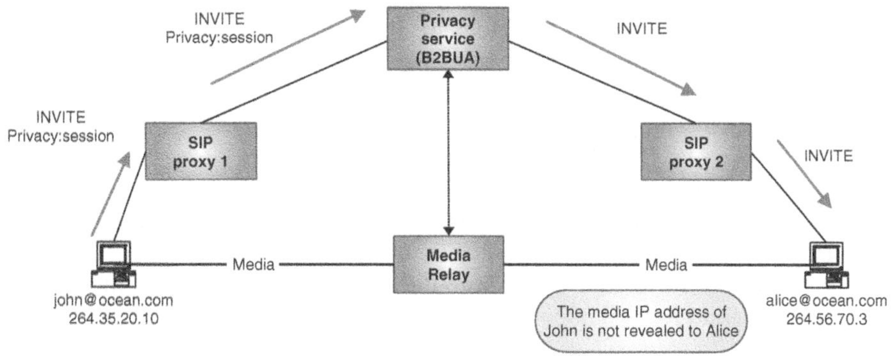

FIGURE 20.2

In addition to the values "header" and "session," the privacy header may also indicate that no privacy is to be applied ("none" value), or that it is critical that privacy is applied ("critical" value), therefore urging the privacy service to reject the call if, for whatever reason, it is unable to apply privacy.

20.3 Private Header for Network Asserted Identity

20.3.1 Assertion of Identity

As we saw in the previous section, the basic mechanism for assertion of identity in baseline SIP has two major drawbacks: the From header semantics and the authentication issue.

The problem of the From header semantics might be overcome by defining a new header field that carries a true SIP asserted identity. For deployments in controlled network environments (so-called Trust Domains), a solution to the second problem might also be found. That solution is described next.

The solution is based on having a bit of support from the network. We saw in previous chapters that, in order to obtain multimedia services, users typically need to subscribe to a service provider. In order to access SIP services, users will need to authenticate against their home SIP server. As a result of that process, the network can obtain an authenticated identity of the user. Such an identity is a SIP, SIPS, or TEL URI that, when used as the Request-URI of a SIP request, would cause the message to be routed to the user associated with that identity, possibly passing through one or more SIP servers or SIP proxies.

When John originates a call, first the network authenticates his identity. Once it is authenticated, the network can insert John's identity into the call signaling, and exchange it with other trusted nodes or with other User Agents that have secure connections to such a trusted node. User Agent servers that receive the asserted identity may render the value of the asserted identity to the called user.

A network of trusted nodes is referred to as a Trust Domain. A node can be a member of a Trust Domain, T, only if the node is known to be compliant to a certain set of specifications, Spec(T), which characterize the handling of the network asserted identity within the Trust Domain. Spec(T) is not a specification in the sense of a written document; rather, it is an agreed-upon set of information that all the elements in the Trust Domain are aware of.

Spec(T) specifies behavior for, among others, such things as:

- end-user authentication mechanisms.
- mechanisms to secure the communication among nodes in the Trusted Domain.
- mechanisms to secure the communication among nodes in the Trusted Domain and UAs.

The requirements for network asserted identity are specified in [RFC 3324]. Another document, [RFC 3325], defines a SIP extension for network asserted identity. This SIP extension introduces two new P-header fields:

- P-Asserted-Identity. It is the header field used to convey the authenticated identity of the originating user among trusted SIP entities. If the called party receives a P-Asserted-Identity from a node it trusts, the called party's User Agent may render the value of the P-Asserted-Identity to the user in order to show the identity of the caller.

- P-Preferred-Identity. In cases where the user has multiple identities, the user can use this header field in order to indicate to the network which particular identity he or she wishes to appear in the P-Asserted-Identity after authentication is performed.

Figures 20.3 and 20.4 show examples of the use of these two headers. In both examples, we assume that:

- Proxy1 and Proxy2 are proxies belonging to the Trust Domain.
- John and Suzanne have secure connections to Proxy1 and Proxy2 and are authenticated (authentication process is not shown).
- John has just one identity: sip:John@ocean.com.
- Suzanne has two identities: sip: Suzanne@ocean.com and Sussy@ocean.com.

Figure 20.3 shows a call from John to Suzanne. Figure 20.4 shows a call from Suzanne to John. Given that Suzanne has two identities, she chooses one to be presented to John by setting the P-Preferred-Identity header field to Sussy@ocean.com.

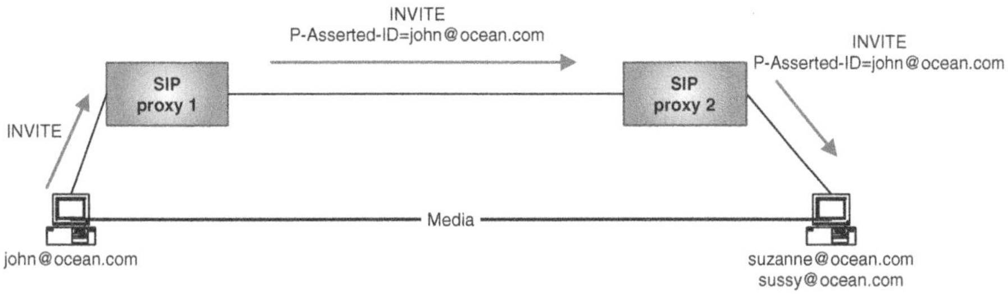

FIGURE 20.3

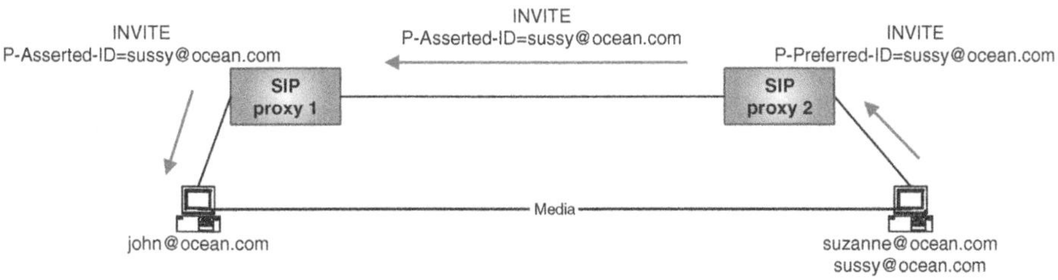

FIGURE 20.4

The P-Asserted-Identity header has found widespread deployment in spite of the fact that it is defined as a P-header (which implies that it has limited applicability).

20.3.2 Privacy Mechanisms

[RFC 3325] also defines the privacy value "id." A user may insert such a value into a Privacy header of a request if he or she wishes that network nodes forwarding the request to nontrusted entities remove the P-Asserted-Identity header. Figure 20.5 illustrates this behavior, where proxy1 and proxy2 belong to the same Trust Domain, whereas proxyA does not.

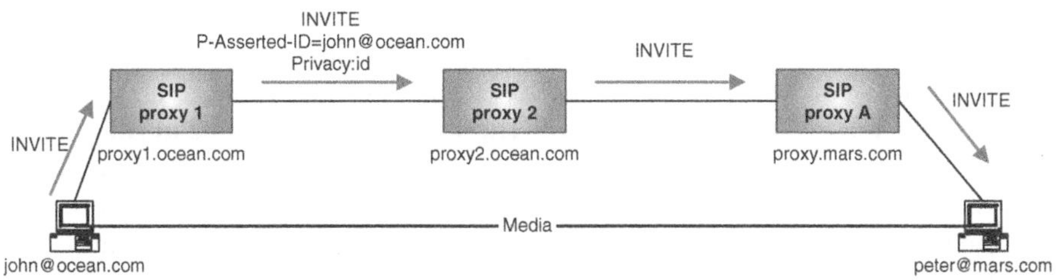

FIGURE 20.5

20.4 Enhanced Identity Management

20.4.1 Assertion of Identity

The previous approach for identity management assumes a managed network of nodes with strict mutual-trust relationships. Such an assumption is not compatible with widespread Internet deployment.

[RFC 4474] defines another approach to identity management based on specifying a means of sharing a cryptographic assurance of end-user SIP identity that is suitable for Internet-wide deployment.

It is based on an "authentication service" that would typically be instantiated by the user's outbound proxy. Let us see how it works.

Let us imagine that John makes an Internet call to Alice. Let us assume that they are registered with different service providers, and there is no trust relationship between the two domains. Still, John wants to assert his identity and let Alice have access to it at call initiation.

John generates an INVITE, and places his identity (possibly his address of record: sip:john@sea.com) in the From header field of the request. He sends the request over TLS to his outbound proxy. His outbound proxy instantiates an authentication service that authenticates John (SIP digest might be used for this), and validates that he is authorized to assert the identity that he placed in the From header field. John's outbound proxy then computes a hash over some particular headers, including the From header field and the bodies in the message. Then the proxy signs the hash with the certificate for John's domain (in our example, sea.com), and inserts it into a new header field in the SIP message, the "Identity" header. The proxy, as the holder of the private key of its domain, is asserting that the originator of this request has been authenticated, and that he is authorized to claim the identity that appears in the From header field. The proxy also inserts a companion header field, Identity-Info, that tells the recipient of the request how to acquire the certificate, if he or she doesn't already have it.

When Alice's inbound proxy receives the request, it verifies the signature provided in the Identity header. Therefore, it can validate that the domain present in the From header authenticated John, and also permitted him to assert the identity present in the From header. Once the request reaches Alices's UA, it might perform the same validation operation.

20.4.2 Privacy Mechanisms

The previous approach for enhanced identity management is, in principle, compatible with the privacy mechanisms defined in [RFC 3323]. There are, however, some aspects that need to be considered. These aspects are detailed in [RFC 4474]. For instance, when a user that desires privacy places the value anonymous@anonymous.invalid in the From header, it would be impossible to apply the previous mechanisms for identity assertion, because an authentication service must possess a certificate corresponding to the host portion ("anonymous.invalid" is not a real domain). Otherwise, if the user places the value anonymous@ocean.com, the mechanisms described before are perfectly applicable. The called party would learn that the originator of the request has been authenticated by ocean.com, and that the originator wants to withhold his or her identity.

20.5 Summary

In this chapter, we learned about several possible approaches to handle the identity aspects in the SIP protocol. The network asserted identity approach will prove to be instrumental for the delivery of multimedia services in controlled network environments such as IMS (Chapter 24).

Another aspect that is also crucial for the delivery of multimedia services is the quality of service. This is an aspect that can be used by service providers in order to offer a competitive advantage versus a pure Internet environment. In the next chapter, we will describe the possible architectures to offer quality of service in the remit of multimedia communications.

CHAPTER

Quality of Service

21

In this chapter, we will introduce the quality of service (QoS) topic as applicable to IP communication scenarios. QoS is a complex topic, and we will describe in this chapter just some basic ideas that allow the reader to understand the mechanisms and protocols that exist to provide quality of service.

We will start by looking at some of the available architectures at the IP transport level to provide QoS, such as integrated services and differentiated services. Then we will introduce the framework for policy control, which enables the introduction of more intelligence in the admission control decisions for QoS. Then we will see how these ideas are applied in a SIP-based communication scenario and what the necessary SIP extensions are in order to integrate the SIP/SDP session establishment process with the underlying IP transport-level processes for quality of service.

21.1 Quality of Service in IP Networks

Many communication scenarios involve the exchange of real-time traffic such as voice or video. We saw in Chapter 10 that in real-time traffic scenarios, it is critical that packets arrive at the destination no later than a certain time after they were transmitted by the source. If they arrive later, playback cannot happen and they have to be discarded. If the amount of packets arriving late increases, the quality of service perceived by the end user suffers, and, eventually, the received media (speech, video) may become unintelligible.

In a congested IP network, routers cannot cope with incoming packets as they come, so the routers are forced to queue the packets. This causes packet delay to increase, which, in turn, may cause real-time traffic packets to be discarded at the receiver. If congestion is severe, then the queue length limits are reached, and routers start to lose packets. In any case, a network congestion situation causes the end users to perceive a degraded quality of service.

In an unloaded IP network, this effect is not produced because packets are forwarded as soon as they are received, and therefore queues do not develop. Hence, an approach to provide quality of service for real-time communications has traditionally been, and still is, to overdimension IP networks. Obviously, one may argue that this is not the most cost-effective solution.

Our experience with the Internet of the 21st century tells us that Internet backbones are reasonably well dimensioned so as not to cause a problem for, for instance, voice transmission. Millions of people today around the world make telephone calls over the Internet with reasonably good quality. However, the explosion of high-bandwidth multimedia services, such as video, might pose a challenge in the future.

Even if there seems to be extra bandwidth in Internet backbones, there is still a point in the network where bandwidth is still limited: the access. Although xDSL technology has helped to overcome this issue in recent years, the issue still remains for access networks that are inherently limited in bandwidth, such as wireless networks.

There are, and there will be, cases where overdimensioning the network is not an option, and therefore it is critical to implement some kind of mechanism that helps preserve a certain quality of service for particular traffic flows and/or for particular users. If we assume that resources are limited, and that there is no endless extra capacity in the networks, assuring quality of service necessarily implies some way of prioritizing some packets over others. This calls for a different model from the traditionally egalitarian best-effort Internet model.

In general terms, prioritization could be implemented for those types of traffic (such as the real-time traffic) that have very stringent quality of service requirements. In that way, a router might prioritize a packet belonging to a real-time flow (e.g., UDP packet carrying voice) over a packet belonging to non-real-time flow (e.g., TCP packet carrying email). Another key aspect to consider here is charging. A network provider might want to charge for the provision of quality of service.

Even if the techniques to offer quality of service and policy control in an Internet environment have been defined for a long time, their implementation is marginal, as of today, in the public network. However, the concepts of quality of service and policy control are again becoming hot topics with the advent of telecommunication standards such as those produced by 3GPP and ETSI TISPAN. These standards, conceived for telecom operators, define the use of a controlled SIP-based private infrastructure in order to offer multimedia services (the so-called IMS, which will be described in Chapter 24). These standards build on the traditional Internet ideas for quality of service, taking them a step beyond, and allowing telecom operators to offer quality of service to their subscribers while at the same time providing the tools to enable charging for the use of QoS. The fact that, in some cases—for example, in wireless networks—bandwidth is limited, calls for such QoS mechanisms. Moreover, having the control of the access network—and thus, the key to the provision of quality of service—is a tool in the telecom operators' hands in order to compete with Internet multimedia service providers that cannot offer such a quality of service. All in all, it is therefore expected that the techniques for IP quality of service will gain relevance in the short term associated with the deployment of telecom operators' controlled multimedia networks.

Having said this, we will review in this chapter some of the traditional ideas around QoS in IP networks. These ideas will form the foundation that will allow the interested reader to understand the evolved QoS architectures that are now being defined—and, in some cases, deployed—in the remit of controlled 3GPP and ETSI TISPAN multimedia networks.

The approaches to QoS in IP networks are independent of the application layer—they all occur at IP level. This is a key design principle of the Internet, and has the tremendous advantage of allowing the two domains, application layer and transport layer, to evolve separately. Nevertheless, there is a need, at some point, to integrate the SIP application layer with the media transport layer, as we will see during this chapter.

The first sections in the present chapter will deal with the application-independent Internet approaches for providing quality of service and policy control. The last sections in this chapter will cover how to integrate the SIP layer (i.e., the control plane) with the previous approaches in an IETF-like multimedia network. Chapter 24 will touch upon how these concepts are used, slightly changed, in the Next Generation Networks (NGN) controlled by telecom operators.

21.2 Mechanisms for QoS

The IETF has developed extensions to the IP architecture and the best-effort service model in order to deliver quality of service. More specifically, two additional models have been defined:

- Integrated services (intserv)
- Differentiated services (diffserv)

21.2.1 Integrated Services

The integrated services approach is based on having the IP routers give preferential treatment to some IP flows over others. An IP flow is defined as a distinguishable stream of related datagrams that result from a single user activity and require the same QoS [RFC 1633]. In practice, an IP flow is distinguished by the combination of protocol, source and destination IP address, and source and destination port.

In order to implement a preferential treatment for some flows, IP routers would need to incorporate a couple of new functions:

- *the classifier*: That is, a component that inspects the incoming packet and marks it as entitled to receive a specific QoS treatment by the router. The classifier passes the packet to the scheduler.

- *the scheduler*: This component looks at the mark set by the classifier, and manages the forwarding of the packets in the different queues. The scheduler might, for instance, based on the mark, decide that a packet pertaining to a particular flow is forwarded before another packet pertaining to a different flow, even if the latter packet arrived earlier to the queue than the former.

The integrated services approach defines two different services:

- the controlled load service [RFC 2211]
- the guaranteed service [RFC 2212]

Both of them represent an enhanced quality of service as compared with the basic best-effort service provided by the Internet. The controlled load service provides users with a quality of service that closely resembles the QoS that they would receive from an unloaded network. Even if the network is congested with best-effort traffic, the controlled load service would give preference to packets subject to QoS, hence emulating the behavior of an unloaded network. The controlled load service does not offer a guarantee that the delay will be bounded for a particular flow; it just gives preferential treatment to some packets versus others.

The guaranteed service, on the other hand, provides a specific flow with the assurance of a bounded delay.

In order to implement integrated services, we need some additional pieces that we did not mention so far. First, clients need to have a mechanism to ask for resources to be reserved in routers so that they can assure a specific quality of service. Second, routers need to have the capability of accepting or rejecting new reservation requests based on their existing available resources. The first functionality is called resource reservation; the second is referred to as admission control.

Figure 21.1 represents the different functionalities in an IP router extended with intserv functionality.

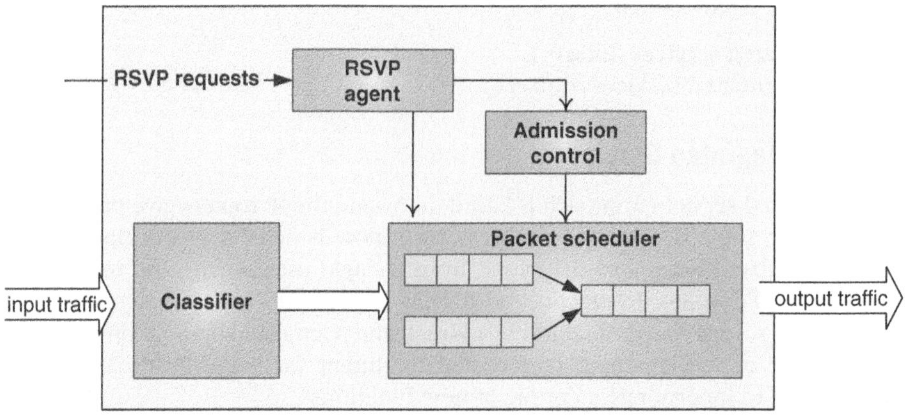

FIGURE 21.1

Resource reservation may be implemented with Resource Reservation Protocol (RSVP), defined in [RFC 2205]. Clients can, via the RSVP protocol, signal the routers the identification of the flow (protocol, source and destination IP address, and source and destination UDP/TCP port) and the required quality of service for it. Routers check if they have available resources to honor the request. If they have, then the packet classifier and scheduler are configured accordingly so as to give a specific treatment to the packets in the flow as soon as they arrive.

RSVP reservations are unidirectional; in order to reserve resources in both directions, two reservation processes need to be performed.

The way RSVP works is quite simple. In order to reserve resources in one direction, a two-step process is followed. First the transmitter sends an RSVP PATH message that is destined to the receiver (i.e., destination IP address is the receiver's address). As this message traverses the routers in the path to the recipient, it will store in each RSVP-enabled router the address of the previous RSVP router (conveyed in the RSVP PHOP parameter). When the PATH message reaches the receiver, the receiver will create an RESV message that is used to actually reserve the necessary resources in the routers. The RESV message will backward traverse all the routers previously traversed by the PATH message. Routing of the RESV message is performed in a hop-by-hop way using the state previously stored by the PATH message. In that way, it is assured that the resource reservation is done in the very routers that will handle the packets from transmitter to receiver, which will follow the same route taken by the PATH message.

This is shown in Figure 21.2.

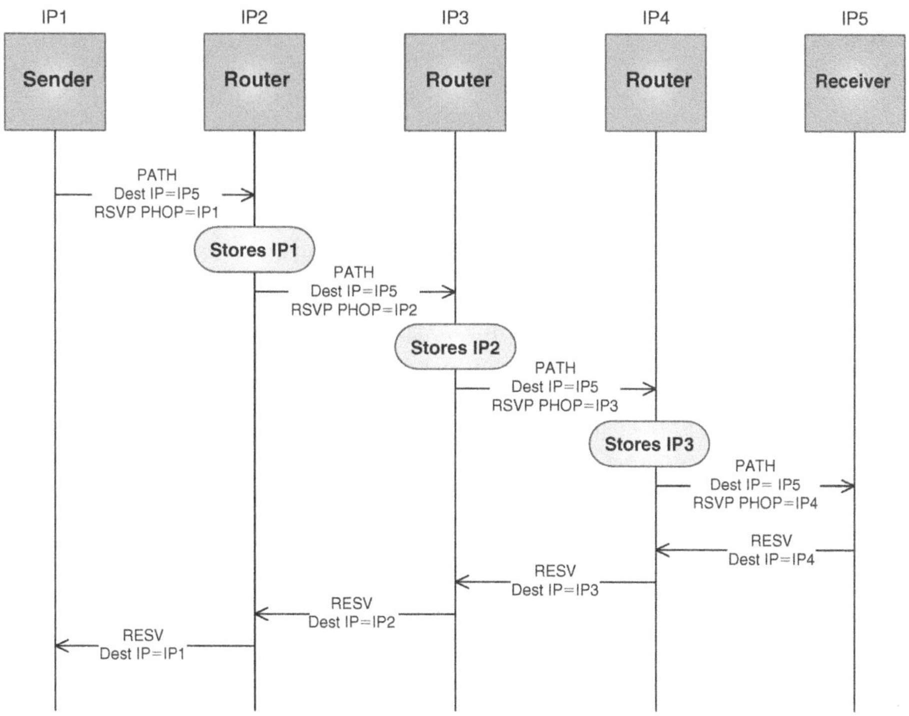

FIGURE 21.2

21.2.2 Differentiated Services

The differentiated services approach is also based on giving preferential treatment to some packets over others in the routers. However, instead of treating different flows separately, the diffserv approach relies on border routers marking the incoming packets with a tag called DSCP (differentiated services code point). Then the internal routers in the network just need to look at the DSCP in the packet and, based on it, apply a specific per-hop behavior (PHB) that is configured in the router. In other words, diffserv is based on applying specific treatment to aggregations of packets, rather than to specific flows, as in integrated services. This fact allows differentiated services to scale much better than integrated services. Figure 21.3 shows the differentiated services approach.

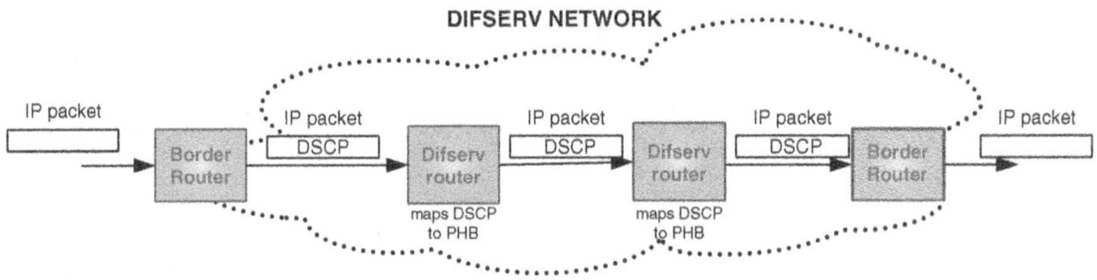

FIGURE 21.3

Differentiated services are defined in [RFC 2474], [RFC 2475], [RFC 2597], and [RFC 3260].

21.2.3 Integrated Services over diffserv Networks

The fact that the integrated services approach requires routers to classify different flows (and hence to look to several protocol fields in order to identify the flow) impacts its scalability. Thus, it is not considered a good approach for the core of the network, though it might be a good fit for the access network. For the core, the diffserv approach is a better choice. In this way, both mechanisms might prove to be complementary when offering end-to-end quality of service to end users. Moreover, RSVP might be used, not only to reserve resources in the access network, but also to signal to the edge router, between the access (intserv) and the core (diffserv) network, how to set the diffserv mark in packets pertaining to a particular flow. This approach is described in [RFC 2998]. Figure 21.4 shows a possible scenario.

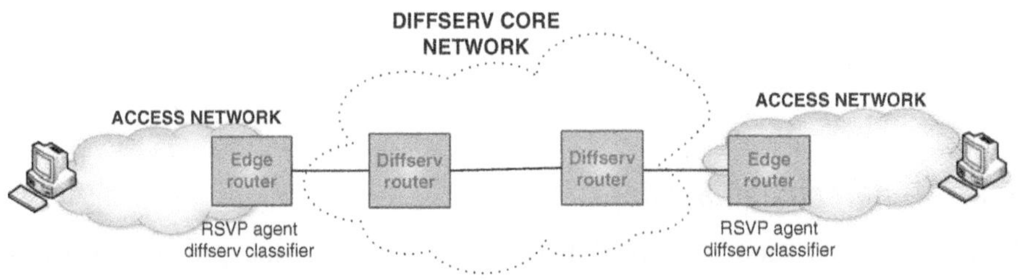

FIGURE 21.4

Variants of this approach are proposed for the newest IP-based next generation networks (3GPP IMS, TISPAN NGN), where, instead of RSVP, typically other protocols are used to signal the QoS requirements (e.g., 3GPP Generic Tunneling Protocol, GTP).

21.3 Policy-based Admission Control

We saw in the previous section that resource reservation requests need to undergo an admission control function. This function is typically implemented in the access network's edge router. The admission control component takes the decision to accept or reject the resource reservation request based on two factors:

- The requester's resource reservation request.
- The available capacity in the router.

Nevertheless, service providers might want to base the admission control decision also on other parameters, such as the requester's identity, his or her user profile, time of day or week, and so forth. For instance, the service provider might want to grant access to quality of service only to those users who have paid an extra amount.

[RFC 2753] specifies a framework for policy-based control over admission control decisions. The framework defines two functional entities: the policy enforcement point (PEP) and the policy decision point (PDP). The architecture is shown in Figure 21.5.

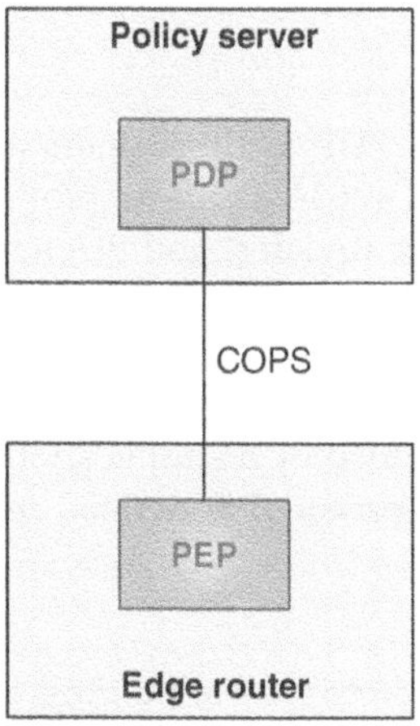

FIGURE 21.5

The PEP is a component located in a network node (e.g., router) that receives the resource reservation request. If that request requires a policy decision, the PEP will then formulate a request for a policy decision and send it to the PDP.

This request may contain information such as the description of the flow or the amount of requested bandwidth that was present in the original received request, plus additional information.

The PDP, when receiving the request, may look for additional info (e.g., might query a user profile database). Then the PDP makes a policy decision and communicates it back to the PEP.

The PEP receives the decision and enforces it—that is to say, accepts or rejects the original request. This is shown in Figure 21.6, where an incoming resource reservation request is rejected after a policy decision is made.

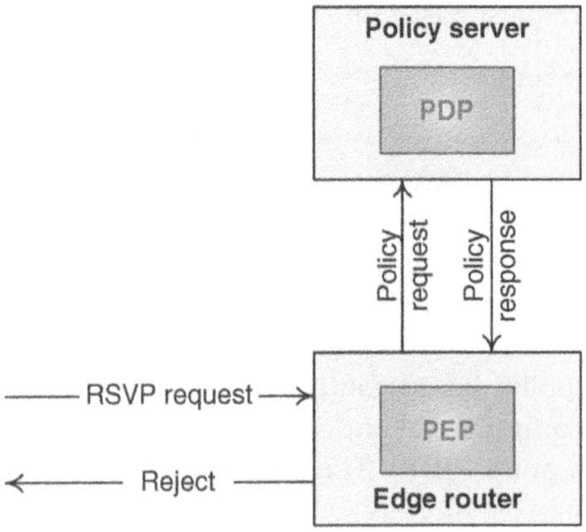

FIGURE 21.6

A possible option for the protocol between PEP and PDP is the Common Open Policy Service (COPS) protocol [RFC 2748] and [RFC 4261]. COPS employs a simple client/server model where the PEP sends requests, updates, and deletes to the PDP, and the PDP returns decisions back to the PEP. The COPS protocol uses TCP as a transport.

COPS was proposed for the communication between PEP and PDP in the first releases of 3GPP IMS. Since Release 7 (R7), it has been replaced by an application on top of the DIAMETER protocol. The DIAMETER base protocol is defined in [RFC 3588].

21.4 SIP Integration with Resource Reservation: The Preconditions framework

21.4.1 Motivation

Let us imagine that John wants to set up a voice call using SIP, and that he wants to use resource reservation so as to assure a certain quality of service. The reservation of network resources requires knowing the IP address, port, and session parameters of the called party (so as to identify the flow in the RSVP request). This information is obtained as a result of the SDP negotiation, in the SDP answer. Therefore, John will send the initial INVITE carrying the SDP offer. The INVITE request will cause Alice's UA to ring and respond with a 180 (Ringing) provisional response that includes the SDP answer. At this point, John starts the resource reservation process because he has all the session information to do that. Let us imagine that the resource reservation process fails because there is one router in the path that rejects the resource reservation request. The call would then be dropped, but Alice has already been alerted, therefore resulting in a negative end-user experience. This is shown in Figure 21.7.

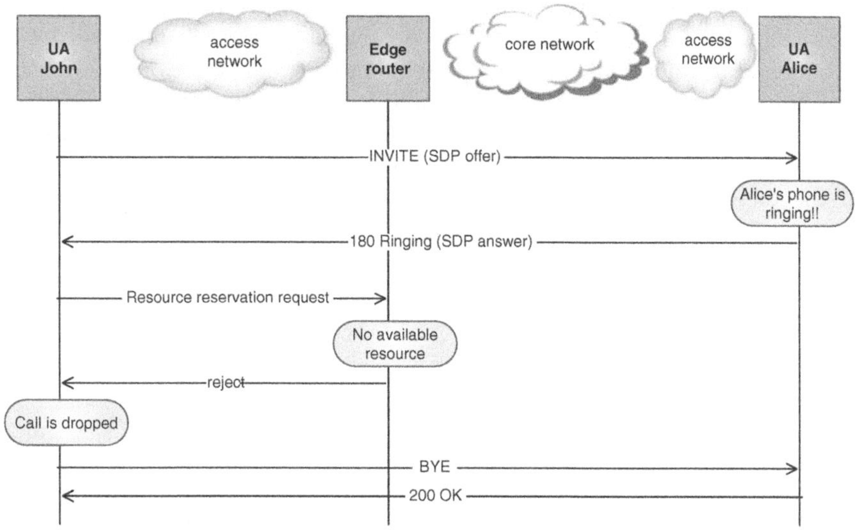

FIGURE 21.7

In order to avoid this problem, we need to make sure that the user is alerted only after network resources have been successfully reserved. This implies that SIP session establishment and resource reservation need to be somehow coordinated. The preconditions framework is a SIP extension defined in [RFC 3312] (the main spec) and [RFC 4032] (an update to the previous one) that specifies the way to integrate resource management with SIP and solve these issues. We will describe the usage of the framework for integrating QoS resources; however, the framework is general enough so as to be used for other types of resource management.

21.4.2 Overview

[RFC 3312] introduces the concept of a precondition. A precondition is a set of constraints about the session that need to be fulfilled before the called user can be alerted. The set of constraints is included in the SDP offer. When the called user receives the SDP offer, it generates an answer, but does not alert the user or proceed with session establishment. The recipient waits for the precondition to be met—that is, it waits for the resources to be reserved. As soon as the precondition is met, alerting can occur, and the session establishment can be resumed.

Figure 21.8 shows how this would work for a call between John and Alice. John does not want Alice to be alerted until network resources are reserved in both directions in order to assure quality of service. So he sends an INVITE request indicating that preconditions are required. This is indicated by:

- Including a SIP Require header field set to the option tag "precondition," and
- Including some additional attributes in the SDP offer (see next section).

When the INVITE reaches Alice's UA, the UA knows that Alice should not be alerted. Alice's UA agrees to reserve network resources. Alice will handle resource reservation in the direction Alice-to-John, but needs John to handle the John-to-Alice direction. Alice indicates this by sending back a 183 (Session Progress) response to John, asking him to start resource reservation and to confirm to her as soon as the John-to-Alice direction is ready for the session. Both John and Alice start resource reservation. Let us assume that Alice completes resource reservation in the Alice-to-John direction; she does not alert the user yet because network resources in both directions are needed. When John finishes reserving resources in the John-to-Alice direction, he sends an UPDATE request to Alice. She returns a 200 (OK) response for the UPDATE, indicating that all the preconditions for the

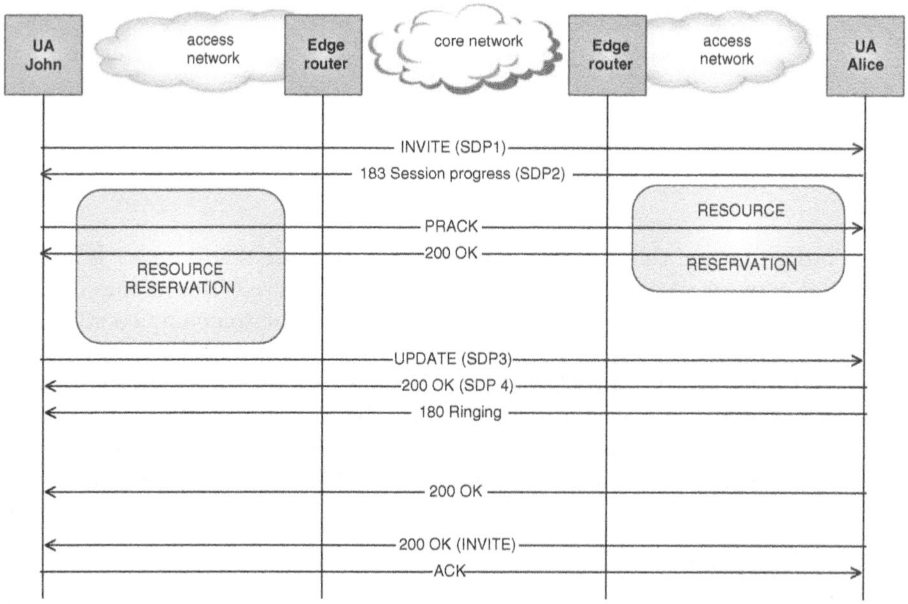

FIGURE 21.8

session have been met. At this point in time, Alice starts alerting the user, and session establishment completes normally.

21.4.3 Operation

We will now look a bit more in detail at how the SDP exchange works and what are the needed SDP attributes to handle preconditions.

From a User Agent's point of view, a precondition is characterized by the following parameters:

- *Type*: [RFC 3312] considers only the type "qos" (for quality of service). In the future, new types may be defined.[1]
- *Strength*: Indicates whether or not the called party can be alerted if the resources cannot be reserved.
- *Status-type*: Indicates whether the resource reservation needs to be done end to end or segmented.
- *Direction*: Indicates whether the resource reservation applies to one direction (send or receive) or to both.

An end-to-end precondition implies that resources are reserved all along the way between the two parties. A segmented precondition implies that end users need to reserve resources only in their corresponding access networks. From a User Agent's perspective, a segmented precondition can be local (if it applies to his or her own access network) or remote (if it applies to a peer's access network). Figures 21.9 and 21.10 illustrate the differences between end-to-end and segmented status-types.

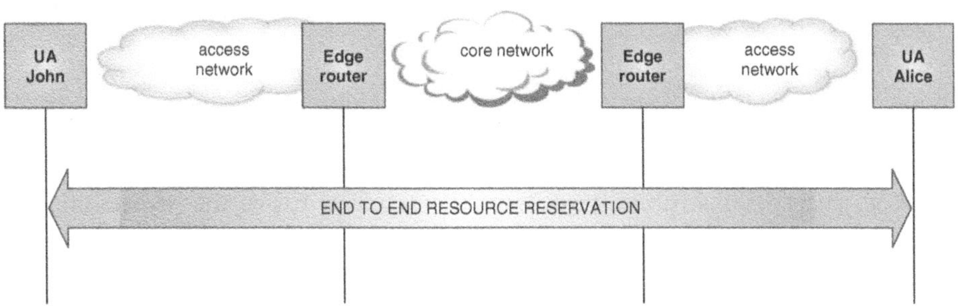

FIGURE 21.9

The strength tag can have the following values:

- mandatory: Alerting can only occur if resource reservation has been achieved.

[1]The IETF draft [draft-ietf-mmusic-securityprecondition], which, at the time of writing, is under evaluation, introduces a new type of preconditions: the security preconditions of type "sec".

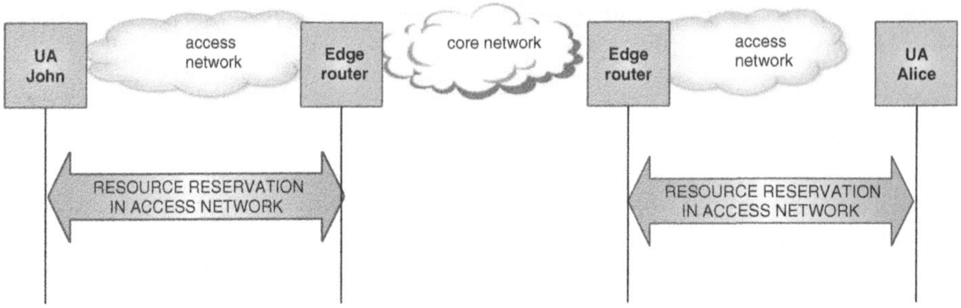

FIGURE 21.10

- optional: User Agents should try reserve resources, but the session can continue irrespective of whether or not the resource reservation was successfully accomplished.
- none: No resource reservation is needed,

The direction parameter can have the following values:

- sendrecv: Applies to both directions.
- send: Applies to the send direction (from the User Agent's point of view).
- recv: Applies to the receive direction (from the User Agent's point of view).
- none: Does not apply for any direction.

We have seen how a precondition is characterized; let us now see how this works.

When John, in our previous example, decides to call Alice using preconditions, he adds some additional media-level attributes to the SDP offer for each media type. One of those attributes is called the desired-status attribute (a=des). It represents the desired status for the required precondition. It might look like:

```
a=des:qos mandatory e2e sendrecv
```

What this means is that John requires a qos precondition, and that resource reservation must be done end to end and applied to both directions. In addition to the des attribute, John must also add another SDP attribute, the current-status attribute (a=curr). This attribute represents the actual status of the precondition—that is, the actual status of the resource reservation. Given that John cannot start resource reservation until he has received the SDP answer, the curr attribute will indicate that resources are not reserved in any direction. So the complete media-level content of SDP1 would be:

```
m=audio 20000 RTP/AVP 0
a=curr:qos e2e none
a=des:qos mandatory e2e sendrecv
```

The curr and des attribute must be present in any SDP offer/answer exchange that requires preconditions. The User Agent that receives the SDP offer compares curr and des; if they match (except for the Strength indication, which is sent only from calling party to called party), it means that the precondition is met, and alerting can proceed.

When the INVITE reaches Alice, she will create and send the SDP answer embedded in a 183 response, and start reserving resources in her sending direction. As was stated in Chapter 15, given that the 183 response contains an SDP answer, it must be sent reliably (that is, it will need to be acknowledged by a PRACK request). The SDP answer reflects the fact that Alice agrees to reserve resources for this session before alerting. She copies the received des attribute into the SDP answer, and includes a curr attribute that represents her view on the status of the precondition. In addition to those, she adds a new SDP attribute called confirm-status (a=conf), which represents a threshold on the status of the precondition. By including it in the response, Alice is indicating that she wants to be notified by John when the precondition reaches such a threshold.

SDP2 would look like (only the media-level):

```
m=audio 40000 RTP/AVP 0
a=curr:qos e2e none
a=des:qos mandatory e2e sendrecv
a=conf:qos e2e recv
```

When John receives this SDP, he will know that Alice agrees to reserve resources for this session (otherwise the SDP would have been rejected), so he initiates the resource reservation in his sending direction. The conf attribute in this SDP indicates to John that when he finishes reserving resources in his sending direction (which corresponds to Alice's receiving direction, as indicated by the "recv" parameter), he needs to communicate that situation to Alice.

Let us imagine that Alice completes resource reservation in her sending direction. Then she will wait to receive the confirmation from John about the precondition status for his sending direction (which corresponds to Alice's receiving direction).

When John completes resource reservation in his sending direction, he sends to Alice an UPDATE request that reflects the new status for the precondition. SDP3 would look like:

```
m=audio 20000 RTP/AVP 0
a=curr:qos e2e send
a=des:qos mandatory e2e sendrecv
```

We can see that now the current status indicates "send" direction, as opposed to "none," as appeared in SDP1.

At this point, Alice's UA knows that the precondition has been met, so she will include SDP4 in the body of the 200 (OK) response to the UPDATE, and ringing will start. SDP4 would look like:

```
m=audio 20000 RTP/AVP 0
a=curr:qos e2e sendrecv
a=des:qos mandatory e2e sendrecv
```

As we have seen from the example, the SIP preconditions extension requires that two additional SIP extensions are supported by User Agents: the PRACK and UPDATE methods. Therefore, the INVITE requests that require preconditions must additionally include the 100rel tag in the Supported header field, and should include an Allow header field with the "UPDATE" tag.

21.5 SIP Integration with Policy Control: Media and QoS Authorization

21.5.1 Motivation

In SIP communication scenarios, SDP is typically used to describe the desired session characteristics. SDP also allows a User Agent to indicate that QoS requirements must be met in order to successfully set up a session. However, we have seen that a different protocol, RSVP, is used to request the resources required to meet the end-to-end QoS of the media stream. Therefore, there is a need to assure that the resources requested through the resource reservation process match the resources that were requested and authorized as part of the SIP/SDP session establishment process. In other words, we need a mechanism to link the SIP and transport layer in order to assure that policies are correctly enforced. [RFC 3313] defines such a mechanism and will be described in the next subsection.

It is worth mentioning that this mechanism is again in contrast to general Internet principles, which completely separate data from applications. Thus, this solution is not applicable to the Internet at large, but does find a lot of applicability scenarios in networks under a single administrative domain. The SIP extension needed to implement these functions will then be defined as a private (P-) extension.

21.5.2 Architecture

[RFC 3521] and [RFC 3313] define the reference architecture for applying SIP sessions setup with media and QoS authorization, which is depicted in Figure 21.11.

The elements in the architecture are:

- *The End Host*: It is the user's device. It comprises a SIP UA, a RSVP client, and a media tool.
- *The Edge Router*: It is the router connecting the end host to the rest of the network. It includes the following three components:
  - The Policy Enforcement Point: that is the point where the policy decisions are enforced.
  - The RSVP Agent.
  - The data handler, which includes the packet classifier, packet scheduler and the admission control module.
- *The QoS-enabled SIP proxy*: That is, a SIP proxy that has the capability to interact with a PDP for the purpose of retrieving the media authorization token, as we will see later on.
- *The Policy Decision Point*: The point where the policy decisions are made.

Figure 21.12 depicts, at a high level, how the media authorization process works. During SIP session establishment, the QoS-enabled proxy will check if the user is authorized to receive QoS. If he or she is, the proxy will contact the PDP and

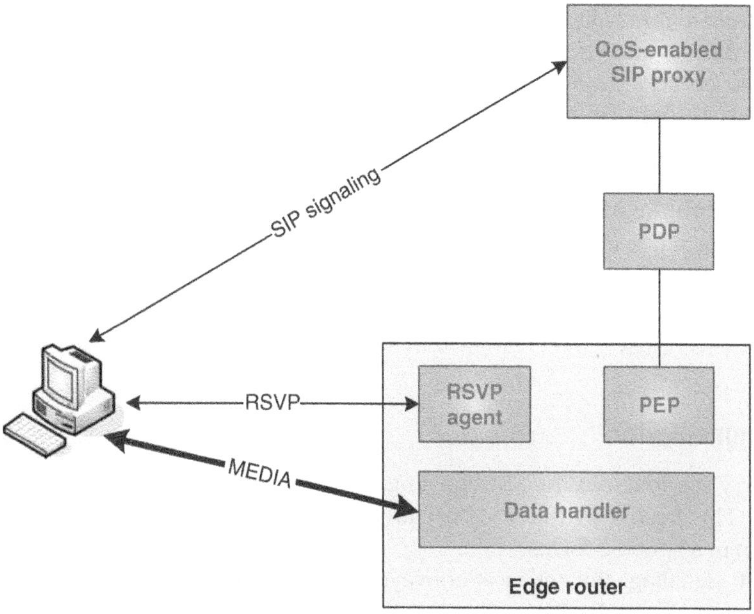

FIGURE 21.11

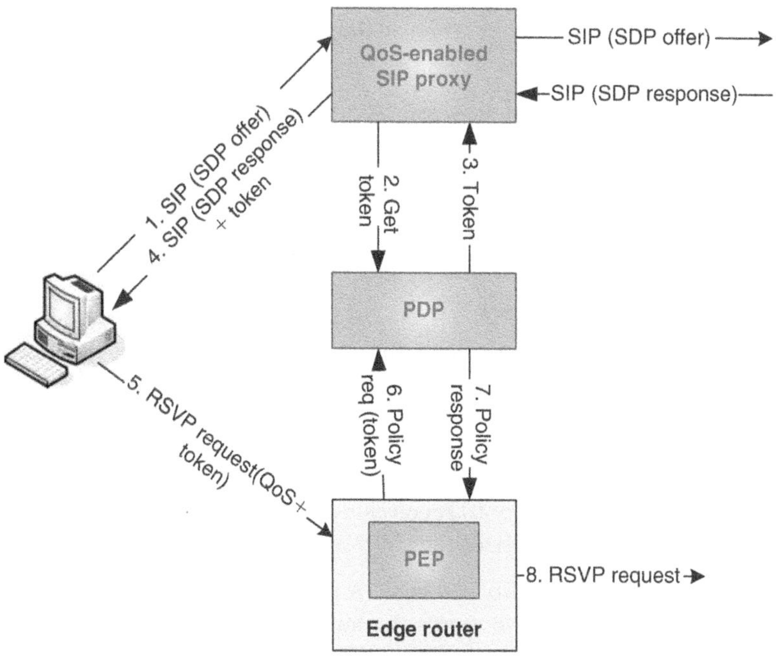

FIGURE 21.12

obtain an authorization token. The authorization token is stored in the PDP together with the negotiated session description. The proxy includes the token in the response back to the UA. The token contains all the information needed for the end host to perform resource reservation. Therefore, the end host initiates the resource reservation, including the token in the RSVP message requesting QoS. When this message is received by the Edge Router, the PEP will forward the token, together with the requested bandwidth, to the PDP. The PDP will check if the corresponding requested bandwidth is within the limit of what was negotiated in the SDP exchange. The PDP uses the token as the key to find the stored negotiated SDP. If the check is passed, the PDP sends back a positive response to the PEP, which reserves the resources and forwards the RSVP message.

21.5.3 Implementation

In order to carry the token in the SIP signaling, a new header is defined: P-Media-Authorization. This header includes a P-Media-Authorization-Token, which represents the token in a specific format.

In the RSVP signaling, the token is conveyed in an RSVP object called policy data—more specifically, in the Policy-Element field within that object, as defined in [RFC 2750], which is an extension to the base RSVP protocol defined in [RFC 2205].

21.5.4 Example

We will now see an end-to-end example for a session setup with media/QoS authorization and resource reservation. The call flow is shown in Figure 21.13.

We will assume that:

- John wants to set up a multimedia session with Alice.
- Both John and Alice have contracted QoS with their service provider.

1. John sends an INVITE to his QoS-enabled outbound proxy (proxy A). The INVITE request includes the SDP offer. The SDP offer contains the description of the media that John desires to use for this communication, and the bandwidth ("b" parameter) requested.
2. When the outbound proxy receives the INVITE message from the UAC, the proxy authenticates the caller and verifies that the caller is authorized to obtain QoS.
3. Proxy A forwards the INVITE.
4. Alice's inbound proxy (proxy B) receives the INVITE. It authenticates the originating proxy and authorizes the call.
5. Proxy B sends a Policy-Setup message (AuthProfile) to PDP-B including the media description. PDP-B stores the authorized media description in its local store, and generates an authentication token that points to this description.

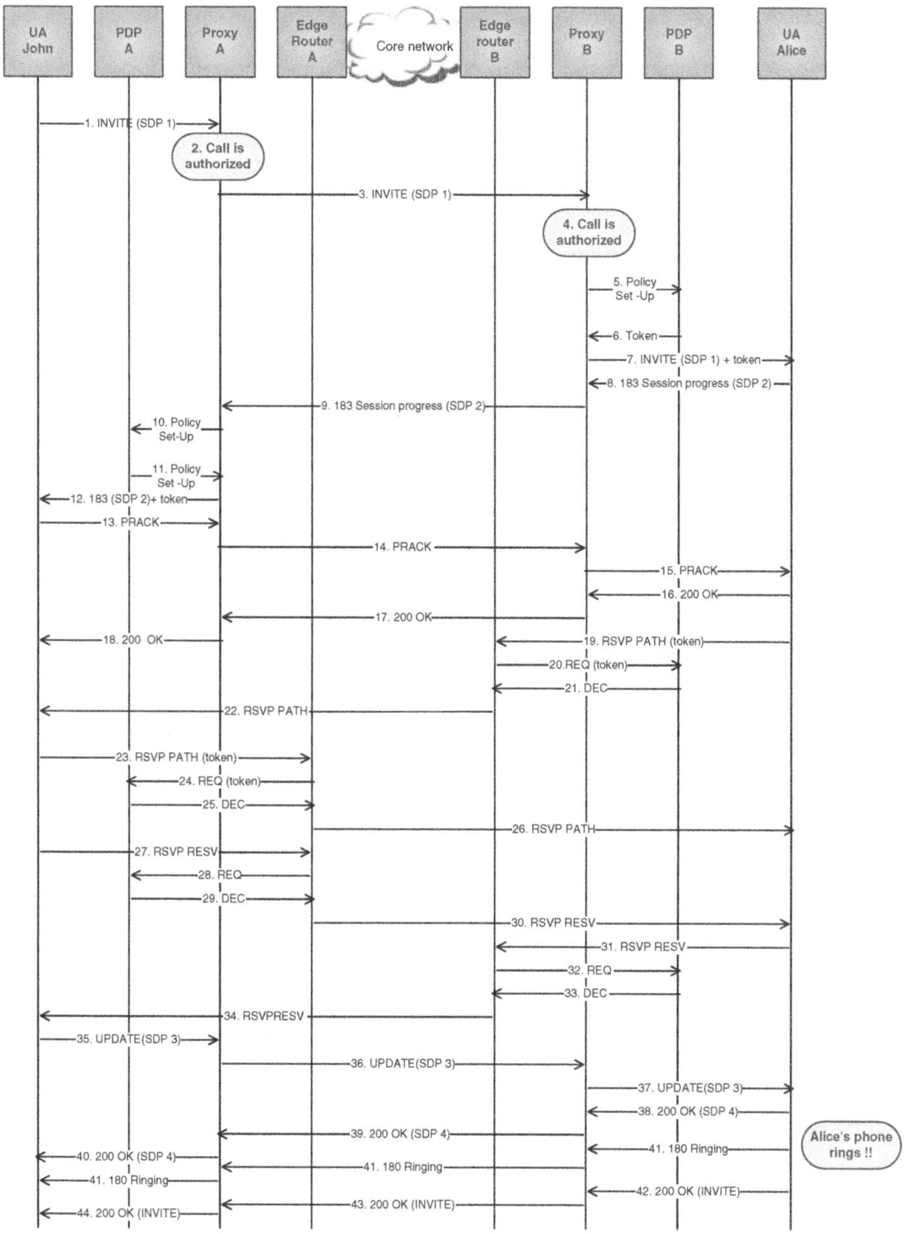
UA John
PDP A
Proxy A
Edge Router A
Core network
Edge router B
Proxy B
PDP B
UA Alice
1. INVITE (SDP 1)
2. Call is authorized
3. INVITE (SDP 1)
4. Call is authorized
5. Policy Set -Up
6. Token
7. INVITE (SDP 1) + token
8. 183 Session progress (SDP 2)
9. 183 Session progress (SDP 2)
10. Policy Set-Up
11. Policy Set -Up
12. 183 (SDP 2)+ token
13. PRACK
14. PRACK
15. PRACK
16. 200 OK
17. 200 OK
18. 200 OK
19. RSVP PATH (token)
20.REQ (token)
21. DEC
22. RSVP PATH
23. RSVP PATH (token)
24. REQ (token)
25. DEC
26. RSVP PATH
27. RSVP RESV
28. REQ
29. DEC
30. RSVP RESV
31. RSVP RESV
32. REQ
33. DEC
34. RSVPRESV
35. UPDATE(SDP 3)
36. UPDATE(SDP 3)
37. UPDATE(SDP 3)
38. 200 OK (SDP 4)
39. 200 OK (SDP 4)
Alice's phone rings !!
40. 200 OK (SDP 4)
41. 180 Ringing
41. 180 Ringing
41. 180 Ringing
42. 200 OK (INVITE)
43. 200 OK (INVITE)
44. 200 OK (INVITE)

FIGURE 21.13

6. PDP-B returns the authorization token to proxy B (AuthToken).

7. Proxy B places the token in the INVITE message and forwards it to Alice's UA.

8. Alice's UA sends a 183 response (including the SDP response) reliably.

9. Proxy B forwards the response to proxy A.

10. Proxy A sends a Policy-Setup message (AuthProfile) to PDP-A including the negotiated media description. PDP-A stores the authorized media description in its local store, and generates an authentication token that points to this description.

11. PDP-A returns the authorization token to proxy A (AuthToken).

12–18. Proxy A forwards the 183 response to John's UA. Then a PRACK transaction takes place to confirm delivery of the 183 response.

19. As soon as Alice has sent the 183 response (step 8), she can request QoS by sending a RSVP PATH message that includes the received token as a Policy Element.

20. The Edge Router B, acting as PEP for UA-B, upon receipt of the RSVP PATH message, sends a COPS message (REQ) to PDP-B. PDP-B checks the authorization using the stored authorized media description that was linked to the authorization token it returned to proxy B.

21. If the authorization is successful, PDP-B returns an "install" decision (DEC).

22. Edge Router B checks the admissibility of the request, and, if admission succeeds, it forwards the RSVP PATH message toward John.

23–26. As soon as John receives the 183 response (step 12), he can start requesting QoS by sending an RSVP PATH message. So, steps analogous to steps 20, 21, and 22 take place, but now on the originating side.

27. As soon as John receives the RSVP PATH message (step 22), he sends a RSVP RESV message to reserve resources on the network.

28. The Edge Router A, upon receipt of the RSVP RESV message, sends a COPS message (REQ) to PDP-A. PDP-A checks the authorization using the stored authorized media description that was linked to the authorization token it returned to proxy A.

29. If the authorization is successful, PDP A returns an "install" decision (DEC).

30. Edge Router A checks the admissibility of the request, and, if admission succeeds, it forwards the RSVP RESV message toward Alice.

31–34. As soon as Alice receives the RSVP PATH message, she sends the RSVP RESV message to reserve resources on the network. So, steps analogous to steps 28, 29, and 30 take place, but now on the terminating side.

35–40. As soon as John receives the RSVP RESV message, he sends an UPDATE to Alice to indicate that the preconditions are fulfilled. The UPDATE is acknowledged.

41. As soon as the UPDATE is received, Alice's UA starts ringing.

42. Alice accepts the call, and the media is established.

21.6 Summary

This chapter introduced a lot of concepts. As a summary, for the process to apply QoS in SIP communications, readers should remember:

- The User Agents (e.g., calling party and called party) *ask* for resources through SDP in SIP signaling.
- SIP proxies in the control plane then *permit* the media plane to allocate these resources.
- And then the clients must still *request* the routers in the media plane to actually *allocate* these resources.

The architectures around QoS are well known, though they have not yet been widely deployed. Broadband accesses and an Internet with increasing capacity have made these architectures not needed in many cases so far. However, with the advent of IP multimedia services for wireless, bandwidth-restricted accesses, these ideas recover importance, and we will see that they will play a crucial role in the IMS architecture for mobile operators (Chapter 24).

CHAPTER

NAT Traversal

22

In many real deployment scenarios, endpoints are located behind Network Address Translation (NAT) devices. The NAT functionality was designed sometime ago, when most of the Internet traffic was client to server. At that time, clients were just opening TCP connections to web or email servers in the public network, and the NAT device performed address translation and let the responses flow back to the client. Today, NAT devices are deployed everywhere—in enterprises connected to Internet, in end users who share the same public IP address among several devices, and so on. In this landscape, the new peer-to-peer multimedia services come into play, and we then find that NAT has pernicious effects on SIP and media traffic. There is no option to modify the NAT devices—they are already there. So we have to invent some ingenious mechanisms to overcome the problem. This chapter gives an overview of the problems caused by NAT, related specifically to SIP signaling and media transfer, and presents several possible solutions.

We start by reviewing the NAT fundamentals. Then we try to categorize the different NAT behaviors encountered in real deployments. This will help us to better address the NAT traversal problem. We will then focus on the issues associated with NAT traversal of SIP, and propose some solutions. After that, we will touch upon the issues and solutions for the media traversal problem. We will base our analysis of the previous topics on the work that is currently being conducted in several IETF WGs. We then, in the last section, present the Session Border Controllers, which represent the industry's response to solve, among others, the NAT traversal problem.

22.1 NAT Overview

Network Address Translation is a mechanism to connect an isolated internal realm with private IP addresses to an external realm with globally unique registered addresses. The NAT functionality is typically implemented in a private domain's edge router that connects to the public domain. This is shown in Figure 22.1.

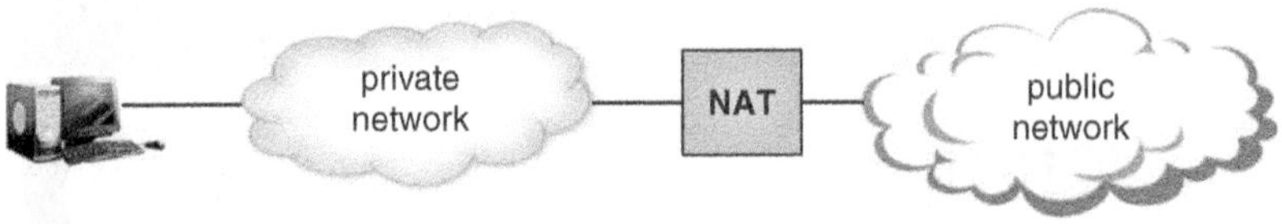

FIGURE 22.1

There are various types of NAT,[1] though the most widely deployed, by far, is the so-called Traditional NAT. Figure 22.2 shows the different types of NAT.

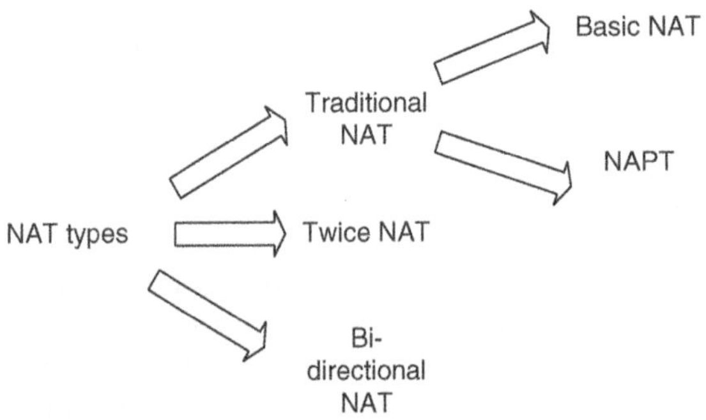

FIGURE 22.2

In this book, we will consider only Traditional NAT, and we will refer to it simply as NAT. Traditional NAT (or simply NAT) is further split into two types:

- Basic NAT
- Network Address and Port Translation (NAPT)

22.1.1 Basic NAT (Network Address Translation)

In Basic NAT, whenever an internal host sends a packet to an external host, the NAT device translates the internal (private) source IP address in the outgoing IP packet into an external (public) IP address owned by the NAT device. Similarly, for IP packets in the return path, the NAT device translates the public destination IP address in the incoming IP packet into the host's private address. This is depicted in Figure 22.3.

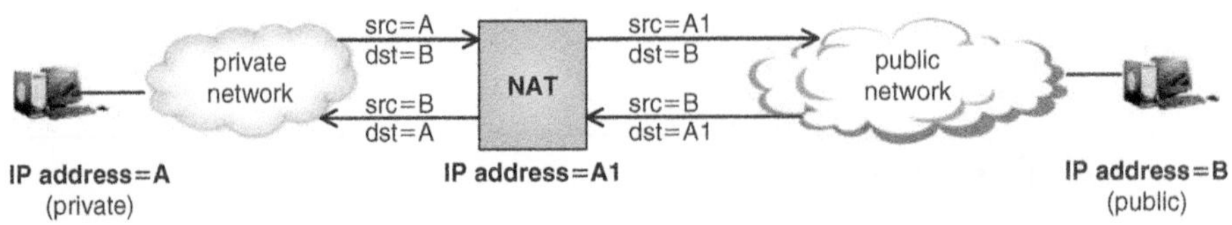

FIGURE 22.3

[1]See [RFC 2663] for a description of all the NAT types. Traditional NAT is described in [RFC 3022].

The mapping rule between private and public addresses can be static or can be dynamically created when the first packet from private address A to public address B traverses the NAT.

The mapping rule in the NAT could be expressed as:

- For outgoing packets (Table 22.1)

Table 22.1

Source	Destination	New Source
A	B	→ A1

- For incoming packets (Table 22.2)

Table 22.2

New Destination	Destination	Source
A←	A1	B

22.1.2 NAPT (Network Address and Port Translation)

NAPT is similar to Basic NAT, except for the fact that it also translates TCP/UDP ports. In this way, an NAPT device with only one public IP address can map all the internal private IP addresses and ports to the same external public IP address, but with different ports, which allows for a significant saving in public IP addresses to be owned by this NAPT device. Figure 22.4 shows:

- Internal host with private IP address "A" using source port "a" to communicate with port "b" in external host with IP address "B"
- Internal host with private IP address "C" using source port "c" to communicate with port "d" in external host with IP address "D"

As can be seen in Figure 22.4, the NAPT device uses the same public source IP address (A1), though with different ports (a1, a2) for the packets from A and C, respectively.

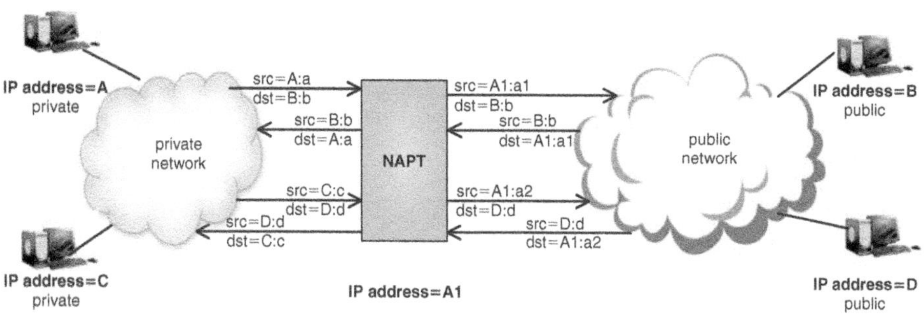

FIGURE 22.4

The mapping rule in the NAPT device could be expressed as follows—where uppercase letters represent IP addresses, and lowercase letters indicate ports:

- For outgoing packets (Table 22.3)

Table 22.3

Source	Destination	New Source
A:a	B:b	→A1:a1
C:c	D:d	→A1:a2

- For incoming packets (Table 22.4)

Table 22.4

New Destination	Destination	Source
A:a←	A1:a1	B:b
C:c←	A1:a2	D:d

NAT and NAPT functionalities may be combined in a single device that can manage a pool of IP addresses (instead of one), and can perform translations of both addresses and ports. During the rest of the chapter, we will use the term "NAT device" (or simply NAT) to refer to a device that supports both Basic NAT and NAPT functionalities (and their combination).

22.2 Behavior of NAT Devices

We have just described the very basic principles of NAT. Nevertheless, existing NAT devices, although fulfilling the basic functions, may exhibit different types of behaviors. Understanding these possible behaviors is crucial in order to successfully address the problems that NATs pose to peer-to-peer traffic (e.g., SIP and media).

NAT traversal of UDP traffic is particularly challenging, so it is important to understand what the NAT observed behavior for UDP traffic is with respect to two aspects:

- Address mapping
- Filtering

Filtering refers to the NAT's capability to block incoming traffic. Filtering behavior defines the security characteristics provided by the NAT.

The observed NAT behavior for UDP traffic is described in [RFC 4787].

22.2.1 Address Mapping Behavior for UDP Traffic

As we saw previously, when a first packet goes from A:a to B:b, a mapping is created in the NAT that maps the internal address A:a to the external one A1:a1. All subsequent packets from A:a to B:b will use this mapping.

Now, assume that a new packet is generated from A:a to a new destination C:c. What mapping will the NAT apply? Will it reuse the existing mapping, or will it create a new one? Different NATs behave differently regarding this point. More specifically, three different kinds of behaviors have been observed:

- Endpoint-independent mapping:
  The NAT reuses the same mapping for subsequent packets from the same internal IP address and port (A:a) to any external IP address and port (C:c).
- Address-dependent mapping:
  The NAT reuses the same mapping only for subsequent packets from the same internal IP address and port (A:a) to the same external IP address, irrespective of the destination port.
- Address- and port-dependent mapping:
  The NAT reuses the same mapping only for subsequent packets from the same internal IP address and port (A:a) to the same external IP address and port.

22.2.2 Filtering Behavior for UDP Traffic

When a mapping is created in the NAT, a filtering rule is associated with the mapping. The filtering rule defines the criteria used by the NAT to filter incoming packets from specific external endpoints. Three different behaviors have been observed:

- Endpoint-independent filtering:
  The NAT filters out only packets not destined to the internal address and port (A:a), regardless of the external source IP address and port.
- Address-dependent filtering:
  The NAT filters out packets not destined to the internal address and port (A:a). Additionally, it also filters out packets destined to the internal address (A:a) if they are not coming from B (that is, from the address to which A:a previously sent packets).
- Address- and port-dependent filtering:
  The NAT filters out packets not destined to the internal address and port (A:a). Additionally, it also filters out packets destined to the internal address (A:a) if they are not coming from B:b (that is, from the address and port to which A:a previously sent packets).

NAT devices that exhibit both endpoint-independent mapping and endpoint-independent filtering behavior are typically called endpoint-independent NATs.

Likewise, NAT devices that exhibit both address- and port-dependent mapping and address- and port-dependent filtering behavior are typically called address- and port-dependent NATs.

22.2.3 Examples

We will now see an example of a couple of different NAT behaviors for UDP traffic. For the time being, we will not refer to a particular application protocol—we will refer just to generic UDP packet exchange between different parties (these packets might represent, for instance, SIP or RTP traffic).

Endpoint-Independent NAT

Figure 22.5 depicts how this type of NAT behaves in different scenarios.

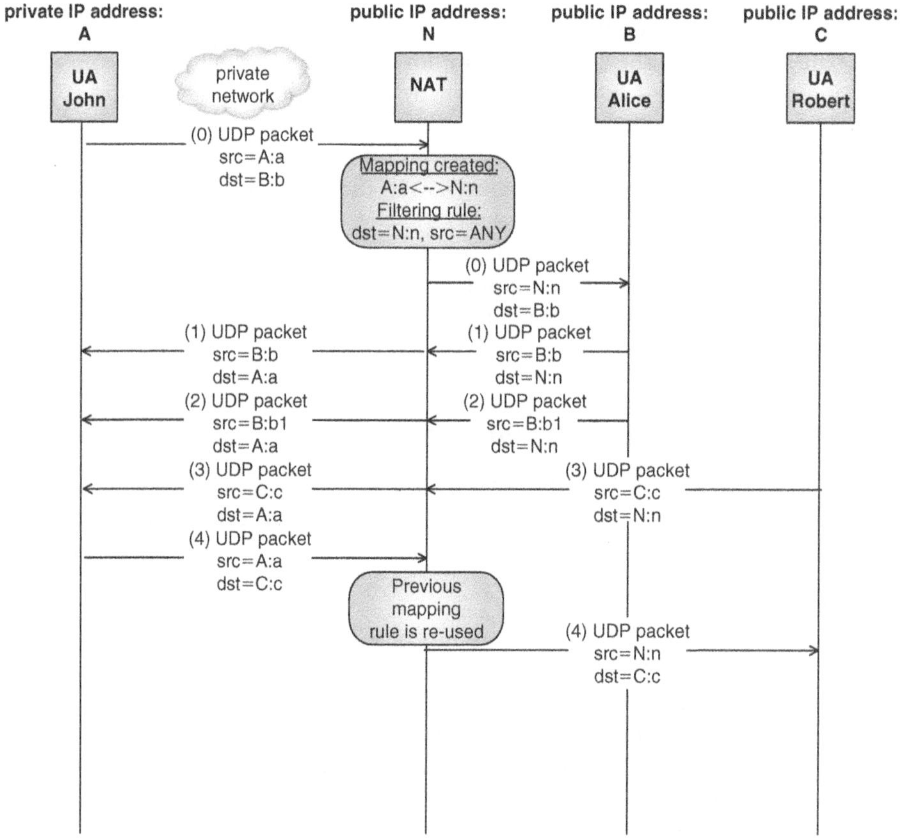

FIGURE 22.5

First, John sends to Alice a UDP packet (0) that opens a pinhole in the NAT.[2] The different scenarios shown in Figure 22.5 are:

1. Alice sends a packet to John with the same source address and port as the destination address in the received packet. The packet traverses NAT.

[2] In the industry jargon, the expression "open a pinhole" is frequently used to refer to the creation of a policy in the NAT that allows packets in a specific flow (internal IP address/port; external IP address/port) to traverse the NAT. As we have already seen, sending the first packet from internal IP address/port to external IP address/port would create a mapping in the NAT (together with its associated filtering rule) that would allow incoming packets in the flow to traverse the NAT.

Whatever the type of NAT is, this packet would always traverse the NAT because it is part of the virtual bidirectional UDP channel established in the NAT with the first outgoing packet.

2. Alice sends a packet to John with a source port that does not coincide with the destination port in the received packet. The packet traverses the NAT because the NAT exhibits an endpoint-independent filtering behavior—that is, whoever sends packets to John's destination address and port is sure to traverse the NAT.
3. Robert sends a packet to John from a different address and port. Again, the packet traverses the NAT.
4. John sends a new packet from the same IP address and port to Robert. Because the NAT exhibits an endpoint-independent addressing behavior, the previously created mapping is reused.

Address and Port-Dependent NAT

Figure 22.6 depicts how this type of NAT behaves in different scenarios.

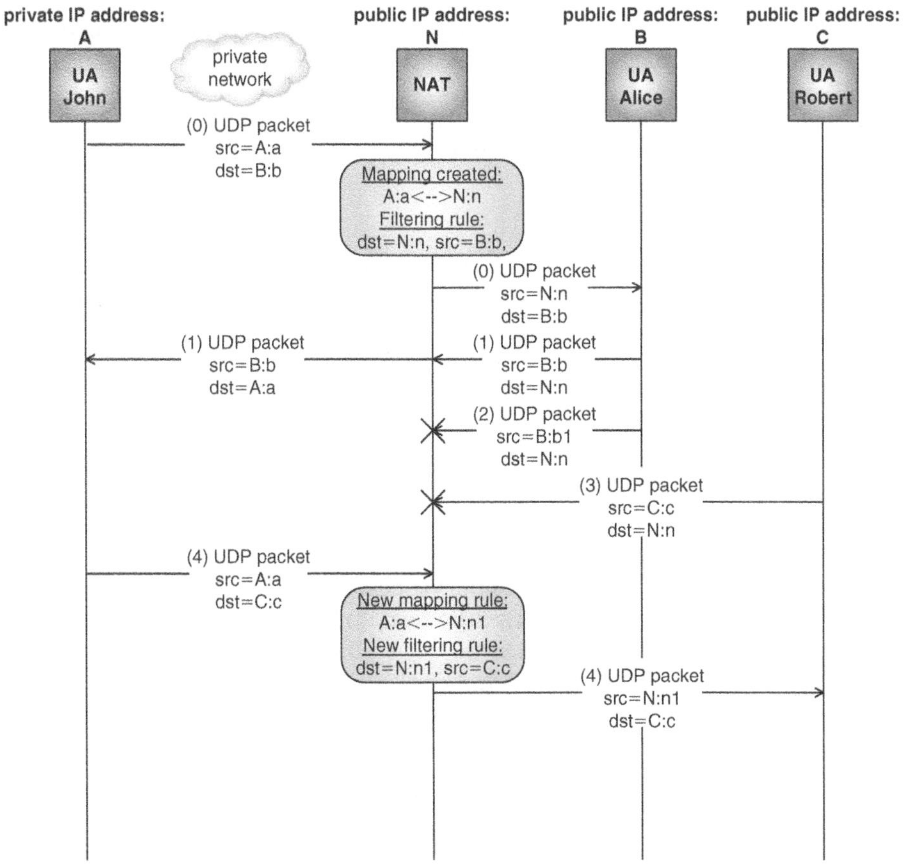

FIGURE 22.6

First, John sends to Alice a UDP packet (0) that opens a pinhole in the NAT. The different scenarios shown in Figure 22.6 are:

1. Alice sends a packet to John with the same source address and port as the destination address in the received packet. The packet traverses NAT. Whatever the type of NAT is, this packet would always traverse the NAT because it is part of the virtual bidirectional UDP channel established in the NAT with the first outgoing packet.
2. Alice sends a packet to John with a source port that does not coincide with the destination port in the received packet. The packet fails to traverse the NAT because the NAT exhibits an address- and port-independent filtering behavior, and, in this case, the port was changed.
3. Robert sends a packet to John from a different address and port. Again, the packet fails to traverse the NAT because neither port nor address coincides with the destination ones in the received packet (in this type of NAT, it would be sufficient that either the IP address or the port is changed so as to cause the packet to be filtered out in the NAT).
4. John sends a new packet from the same IP address and port to Robert. Because the NAT exhibits an address- and port-dependent addressing behavior, a new mapping is created in the NAT.

22.3 SIP Traversal through NAT

22.3.1 Issues

There are two main issues posed by NATs to SIP traversal:

1. Routing of SIP responses
2. Routing of incoming requests

Routing of SIP Responses

First we will tackle the case where UDP is used.

Let us recall from Chapter 7 how routing of responses in SIP works irrespective of the presence of NATs. This is depicted in Figure 22.7. In this figure, "src" and "dst" refer, respectively, to the source and destination addresses and ports present in the packet at the IP and UDP headers. When John wants to send a SIP request to Alice, he would set the sent-by field in the Via header to his own IP address (A) and port (5060) where he wants to receive the response to the request. This port may or may not coincide with the actual source UDP port (a) in the actual IP packet.

When the request gets to Alice's UA, her UA examines the origin IP address (in the IP header), and sets the "received"[3] parameter in the Via header to that value (A).

In order to send back a response, Alice directs it to the IP address in the "received" parameter (A) and to the port in the sent-by field (5060). As a consequence, the message is routed back to John.

[3]As was explained in Chapter 7, "received" is the name of a parameter in the Via header.

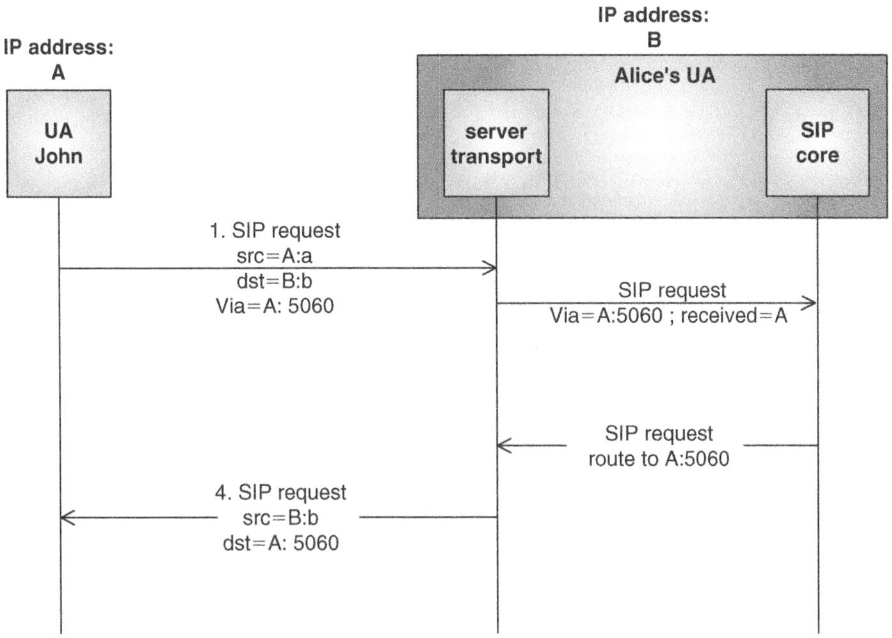

FIGURE 22.7

Let us assume now that John is in a private domain behind a NAT device, whereas Alice is in the public Internet. When John's request reaches the NAT, the NAT will replace the internal origin IP address and port with an external IP address and port. When Alice now tries to send the response back to John, the response will be directed to the address in the received parameter—which coincides with the external address allocated by the NAT, but to a port that was selected by John (different from the source port in the request). This port is not open in the NAT. Therefore, the response will be rejected by the NAT. Figure 22.8 shows this scenario.

If John uses TCP, this problem would not occur because Alice would send the response back through the TCP connection in which the request was sent. This connection is open in the NAT. This is shown in Figure 22.9.

Routing of Incoming Requests

The second issue refers to the routing of incoming requests. Let us assume that John is in a private domain behind a NAT device. In order to be able to receive calls, he first needs to register with his SIP server. So John generates a REGISTER message in which he indicates a contact address. The contact address contains John's private IP address and a port where he desires to receive incoming requests. Such a port in principle does not coincide with the source port used to send the REGISTER.

When an incoming request reaches the SIP server, it will retrieve the contact address and attempt to route the request toward a private IP address, which will fail.

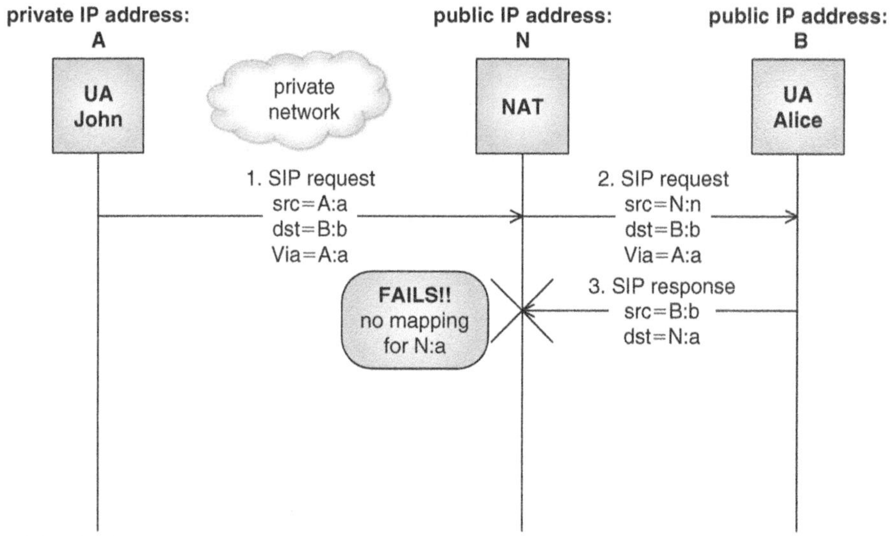

FIGURE 22.8

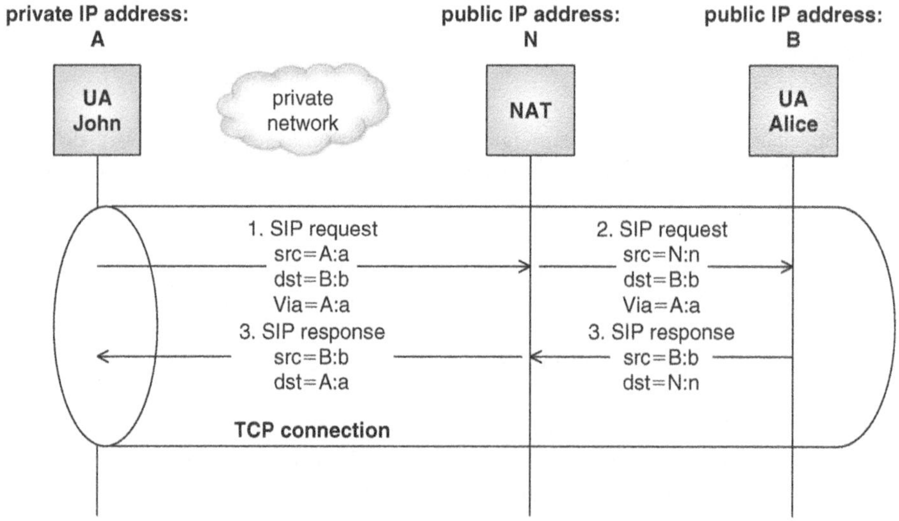

FIGURE 22.9

This problem exists irrespective of the transport protocol that is used (UDP or TCP). This is shown in Figure 22.10.

22.3.2 Proposed Solutions

Routing of Responses

The first of the previous problems (routing of responses) can be solved with a new SIP extension called "Symmetric response routing," described in [RFC 3581].

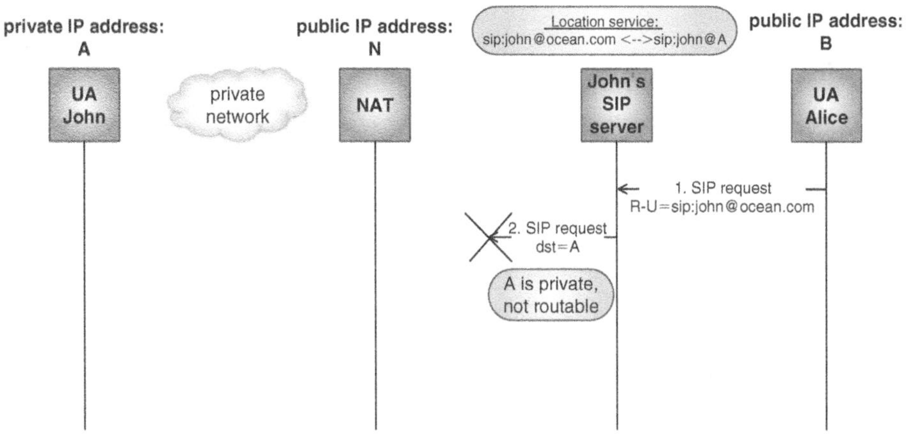

FIGURE 22.10

A client that supports this extension performs, when sending the request, two additional actions:

- Includes an "rport" parameter in the Via header. The parameter must have no value.
- Prepares itself to receive the response on the same IP address and port it used to populate the source IP address and source port of the request.

Likewise, a server that supports this extension will, when receiving the request, set the value of the "rport" parameter to the source port of the request. Moreover, in order to send the response back, it will:

- Send the response to the IP address indicated in the "received" parameter, and to the port indicated in the "rport" parameter.
- Send the response from the same IP address and port that the corresponding request was received on.

If both John and Alice support the previously described extension, routing of SIP responses through any type of NAT does not pose any problem. Effectively, the response will always be sent to an address that is open in the NAT and that is routed to John. Moreover, given that the source IP address and port of the response are the same as the destination IP address and port in the original request, the request will not be filtered out by "address-dependent" or "address- and port-dependent" NATs. This is depicted in Figure 22.11.

Routing of Incoming Requests

A solution to the second problem (routing of incoming requests) might be based on slightly modifying the core SIP registration process [draft-ietf-sip-outbound].

If UDP is used when a REGISTER is received, the SIP server might store the "flow" (that is, source IP/port and destination IP/port) on which the REGISTER was sent, and associate it with the AOR. The sending of the REGISTER would

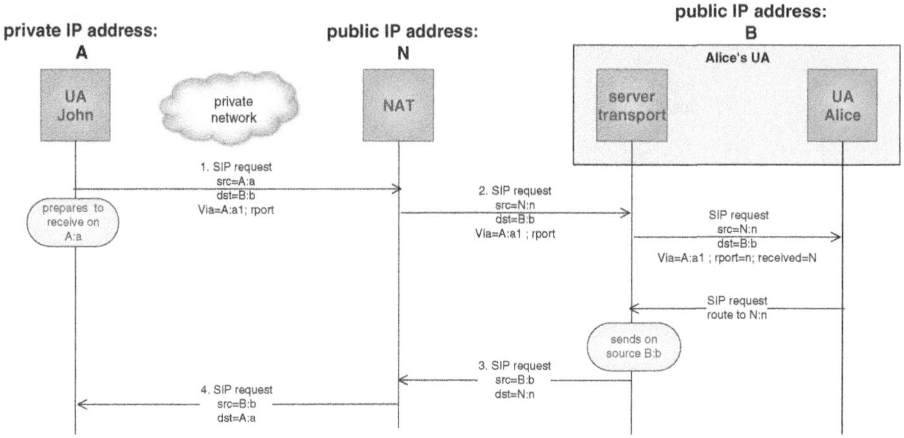

FIGURE 22.11

cause the NAT to open a pinhole for that flow. When a new request is received, the server will send the request within the same flow, therefore assuring that the request will traverse the NAT. This is shown in Figure 22.12.

If TCP is used, the TCP connection used for the registration opens a pinhole in the NAT. This connection should be kept open so that incoming requests can reuse it to traverse the NAT and reach the UA.

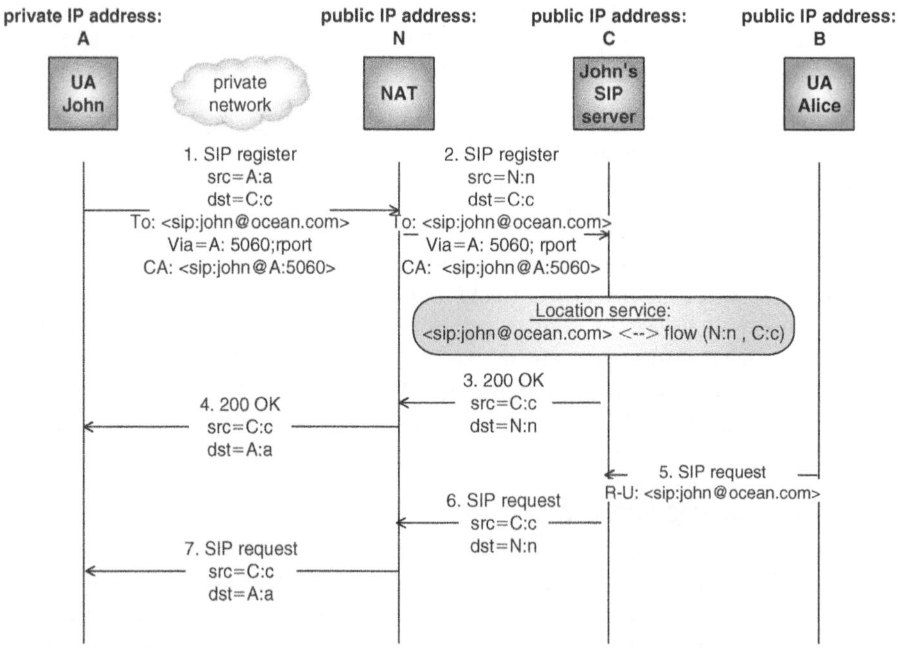

FIGURE 22.12

A problem associated with the mechanism described before refers to the fact that the mappings in the NAT expire after periods of inactivity. An incoming request might come a long time after the registration is done, so there is a need for a refresh mechanism that keeps the pinhole open. This might be done by having the client issue REGISTER requests after some timer expires or by sending other protocol messages (e.g., STUN messages[4]).

A best current practices (BCP) document for NAT traversal for SIP is actually in progress in the IETF [draft-ietf-sipping-nat-scenarios].

22.4 RTP Traversal through NAT

22.4.1 Issues

Let us consider that both John and Alice are located in private network domains behind respective NAT devices. Both domains are connected to the public Internet. The scenario is depicted in Figure 22.13.

FIGURE 22.13

Now John wants to call Alice. We will assume that the SIP signaling traverses NAT without problems, based on the solutions discussed before. During the SDP offer/response exchange, an IP address and port combination are specified by each UA for sending and receiving RTP media. Given that the endpoints are located in private domains, the IP addresses specified in the SDP are also private. Therefore, once the SDP exchange is completed, John and Alice will try to send packets to private addresses that are not resolvable in the Internet; thus, the submissions will fail. This situation is depicted in Figure 22.14.

22.4.2 Proposed Solutions

Though the RTP problem when traversing NAT is quite obvious, the solutions to overcome it are not so simple. Furthermore, different NAT topologies and different NAT behaviors increase the difficulty of proposing a single solution. We will now examine some NAT scenarios and their solutions. The focus of the scenarios is on the RTP traffic, so we will assume that the SIP signaling traversal of NAT has already been resolved.

[4] More specifically, the STUN binding keep-alive usage could be used for this purpose. STUN will be presented in subsequent sections.

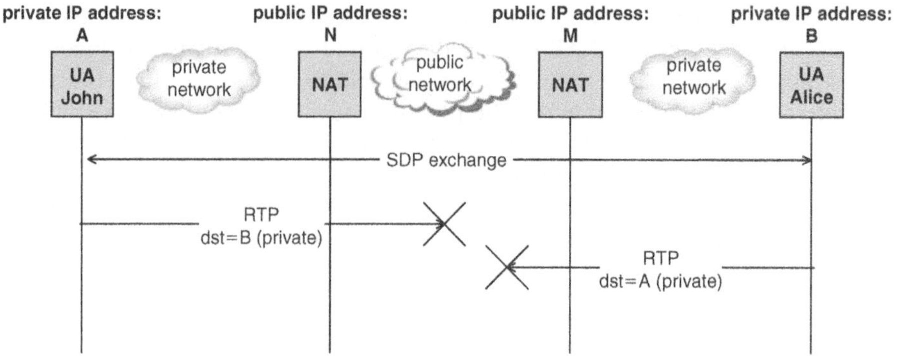

FIGURE 22.14

Scenario 1

In order to start with a simple scenario, let us assume that John is behind a NAT and wants to communicate with Alice, who is on the public Internet (and who definitively knows that she is on the public network).

The SDP offered by John contains a private address that is not routable, therefore no audio will flow from Alice to John. On the other hand, Alice's IP address in the SDP response is a public address, thus RTP packets can flow from John to Alice.

A possible mechanism to overcome this problem is to use "Symmetric RTP." This technique implies that John will transmit and receive RTP packets from the same IP address and port combination. Symmetric RTP is described in [RFC 4961].

Let us assume that both John's UA and Alice's UA support symmetric RTP. When John receives Alice's SDP, which contains a public IP address, John's UA will start transmitting RTP packets to that destination. Let us assume that the source IP address and port that he uses for sending the RTP packets are A:a. If John's UA supports symmetric RTP, it will then prepare itself to receive incoming packets in that same address and port (A:a).

When the outgoing RTP packet from John reaches the NAT, the NAT will select an external IP address and port (A1:a1), and will forward the packet to Alice. A pinhole has been created in the NAT. When the packet reaches Alice, there is an extra intelligence needed in Alice's UA such that, if her UA knows that it resides in the public Internet, the UA is able to detect that the source IP address and port of the received RTP packet do not coincide with the IP address and port indicated in the received SDP. Alice's UA will ignore the SDP information and start sending RTP packets to that address (A1:a1). Because Alice's UA also supports symmetric RTP, the source address and port of the packets that she sends back match the destination address and port of the incoming RTP packets. Therefore, when the RTP packets that she generates reach the NAT, there already exists a pinhole that lets the packets flow back to John.

This technique works for all the possible behaviors of NATs. This scenario is depicted in Figure 22.15.

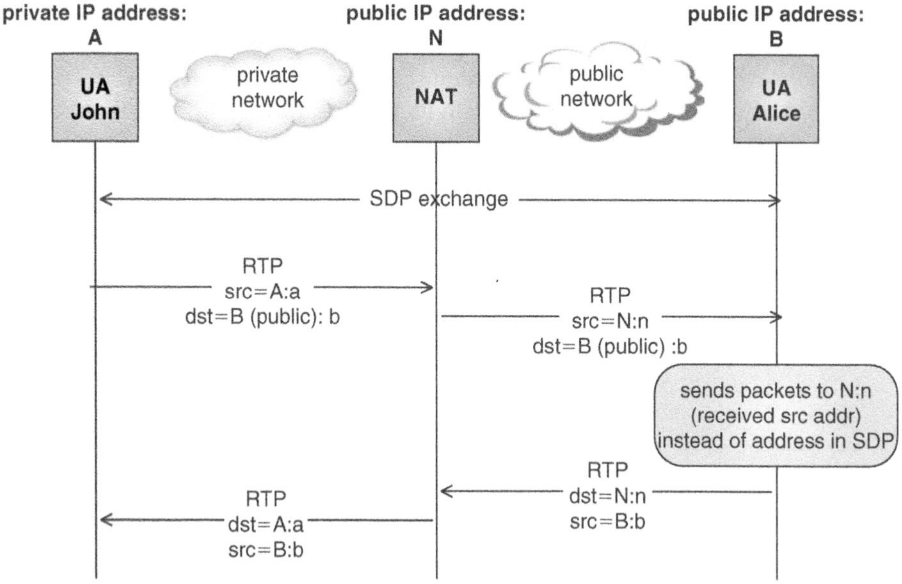

FIGURE 22.15

Scenario 2

We will consider now a more complex scenario in which both John and Alice are located in private networks behind respective NATs. Both networks are connected to a public network.

In this scenario, if both NATs exhibit an endpoint-independent behavior, there is a relatively simple way to overcome the NAT traversal problem. Such a solution consists of using the STUN protocol.

The STUN (Simple Traversal Utilities for NAT) protocol is a lightweight protocol that offers several tools to assist in NAT traversal. The different tools or functionalities that STUN offers are realized by using the protocol in specific ways, so-called STUN usages.

STUN was specified in [RFC 3489], though it is now under revision in [draft-ietf-behave-rfc3489bis]. Several STUN usages are being currently defined for STUN, such as:

- the binding discovery usage [draft-ietf-behave-rfc3489bis]
- the binding keep-alive usage [draft-ietf-behave-rfc3489bis]
- the short-term password usage [draft-ietf-behave-rfc3489bis]
- the relay usage [draft-ietf-behave-turn]
- the NAT-behavior discovery usage [draft-ietf-behave-nat-behavior-discovery]
- the connectivity check usage [draft-ietf-mmusic-ice]

In order to cope with Scenario 2, the STUN binding usage may be used. The STUN binding usage represents the classical usage of STUN. It allows a client behind a NAT device to learn what are the public address and port that the NAT will assign, as a source address, to the packets generated by the client. Once the client has obtained that information, it can then include the public address in whatever application-level (e.g., SDP) fields are required in order to achieve NAT traversal. This procedure allows the client to obtain its public address (the so-called "reflexive transport address") if the NAT is endpoint independent. If the NAT is endpoint dependent, this STUN usage is not helpful, as we will see in Scenario 3.

The simple architecture for STUN binding usage is depicted in Figure 22.16.

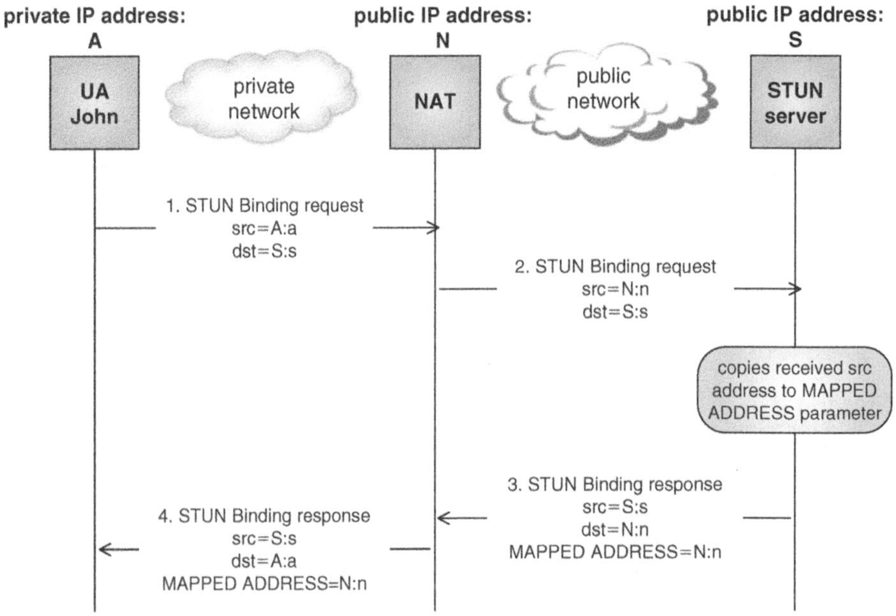

FIGURE 22.16

The client sends a STUN Binding request message to the STUN server, whose address is somehow known by the client (e.g., preconfigured). When the STUN request traverses the NAT, the STUN server changes the source address to A1:a1. The STUN server receives the request, and copies the source transport address into the MAPPED ADDRESS parameter of the STUN response. It sends back the message to the client to destination address A1:a1. The message traverses the NAT through the previously created pinhole, and is received by the client, who looks at the MAPPED ADDRESS parameter and learns its reflexive transport address.

Let us see now how the STUN binding discovery usage is used in the end-to-end scenario between John and Alice. Both UAs need to implement a STUN client. The way it works is quite simple. Before sending the SDP offer or SDP response, John and Alice just need to use STUN in order to obtain their respective reflexive transport addresses, which they will then include in the corresponding SDP offer and answer.

The addresses contained in the SDP offer/answer would now be a routable public address for which, moreover, there is a pinhole in the NAT that was opened during the STUN transaction. Therefore, RTP traffic can flow in both directions. This scenario is shown in Figure 22.17.

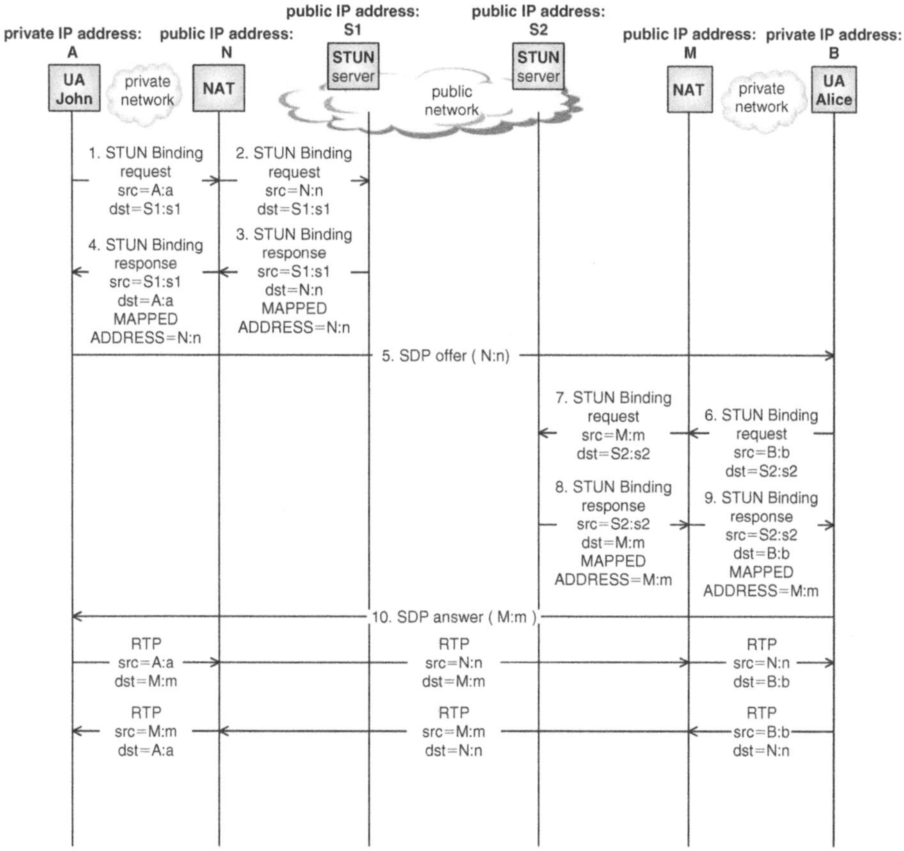

FIGURE 22.17

The flow shown before is purposely oversimplified so that the reader can focus on the crucial STUN functionality. More specifically, the flow does not show the STUN authentication process, which is a necessary aspect of the protocol. Another aspect that is not shown is the STUN Binding request, which is needed to obtain the client's reflexive transport address for RTCP traffic. In the picture, we showed only the Binding request for obtaining the RTP address, but it is also necessary to get the RTCP one. Because there is a NAT in between, it cannot be assumed that the RTCP port selected by the NAT will always be RTP port +1; thus, RTP and RTCP transport addresses need to be separately specified in the SDP. [RFC 3605] defines an extension attribute to SDP that can be used to carry the transport information for RTCP.

The scenario previously described is useful only to traverse endpoint-independent NATs.

Scenario 3

A more complex scenario occurs when both John and Alice are located behind address-dependent or address- and port-dependent NATs. In this case, the STUN binding usage does not help because the NAT would block all incoming packets that are not coming from the STUN server (after the sending of the STUN message, the client has only a bidirectional virtual UDP channel with the STUN server). In these cases, the only way to resolve the scenario is to use the STUN server as an RTP relay. For such purpose, the STUN relay usage has been defined, which allows the STUN client to obtain a "relay address" from the STUN server. The STUN request used to obtain a relay address is called "Allocate request." Both John's UA and Alice's UA will include such relay address in their respective SDPs, thus forcing the RTP traffic to traverse the STUN servers. Because all the RTP traffic traverses the STUN servers, it will use the pinhole open in the NAT for the virtual bidirectional UDP channel created in the first STUN transaction between UA and STUN server.

This scenario is depicted in Figure 22.18. When John sends media, the RTP packets are targeted at M:m, but they are encapsulated in a STUN message targeted at S1:s1, so that the NAT can be traversed. When the message arrives at John's STUN server, the server extracts the RTP packet and sends it to M:m, which is a relay address in Alice's STUN server.

Again, the diagram does not show either the STUN authentication or the Allocate request needed for the RTCP traffic.

Because the relay function consumes a lot of resources in the STUN server, it is recommended that this approach is used just where there are no other possible solutions—that is, only in case of endpoint-dependent NATs.

Putting It All Together

We have so far seen that RTP traversal through NAT is not a simple task. Moreover, different solutions are required depending on the scenario. What is needed is a kind of umbrella mechanism that can automatically discover what the NAT scenario is, and apply the right tool in order to solve it. An attempt to provide such a mechanism is being conducted in IETF. The mechanism is called ICE (Interactive Connectivity Establishment), and is an extension to the SDP offer/answer model that allows UAs to discover and agree on the right mechanism to use for NAT traversal.

The ICE mechanism is quite complex, and will not be analyzed in depth here. Interested readers are referred to the Internet draft where it is currently being defined [draft-ietf-mmusic-ice].

In essence, ICE works as follows. Before the SDP exchange takes place, both John's UA and Alice's UA employ the STUN binding and relay usages in order to obtain a mapped and a relay address. They then initiate the SDP exchange, including these addresses in the SDP body as CANDIDATE addresses (these are carried in new SDP attributes). Candidates are ordered in highest to lower priority, and

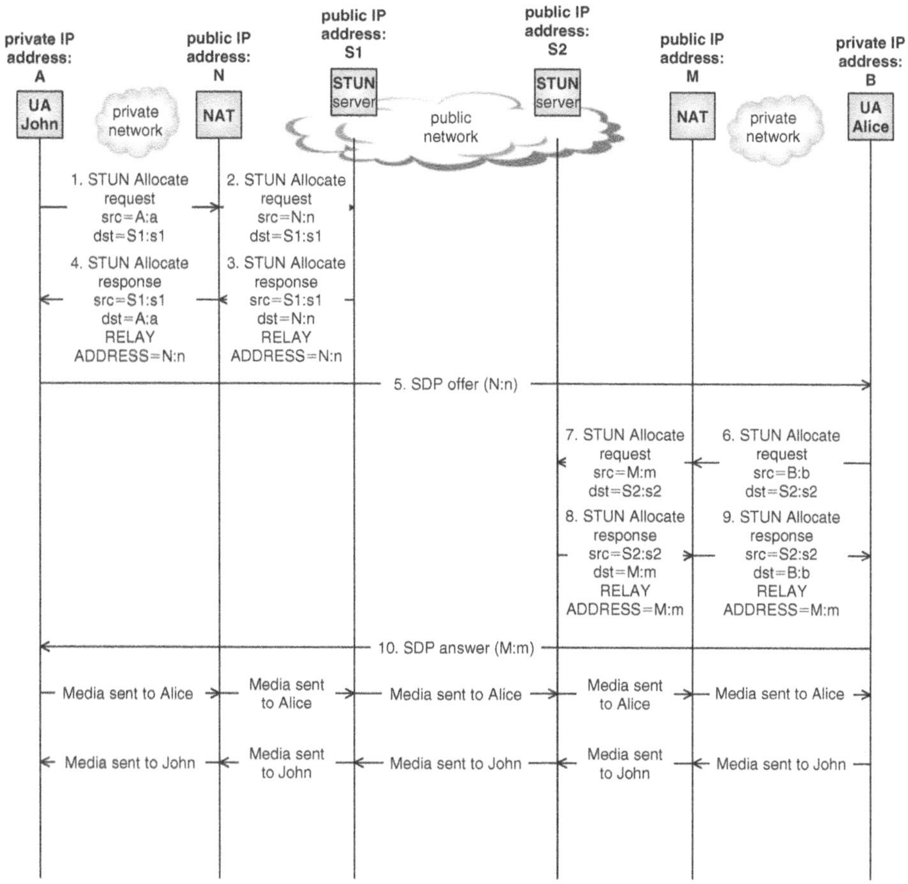

FIGURE 22.18

the UAs form pairs between their candidates and those of their peers. Once this is done, both UAs make use of the STUN connectivity check usage [draft-ietf-mmusic-ice] that allows them to determine which pairs of addresses permit NAT traversal. Once a pair is selected, John and Alice start sending traffic to those addresses. This scenario is depicted in Figure 22.19.

22.5 Session Border Controllers

We have seen that the traversal of SIP and SDP traffic through NAT devices is not a simple task. In particular, traversal of SDP does not have an easy solution, and the ICE protocol is really complex. Furthermore, ICE imposes extra requirements in User Agents who have to implement a full-fledged STUN client.

A different solution for NAT traversal proposed by the industry is currently very successful. It consists of making the NAT traversal function reside in a piece of equipment called a Session Border Controller (SBC).

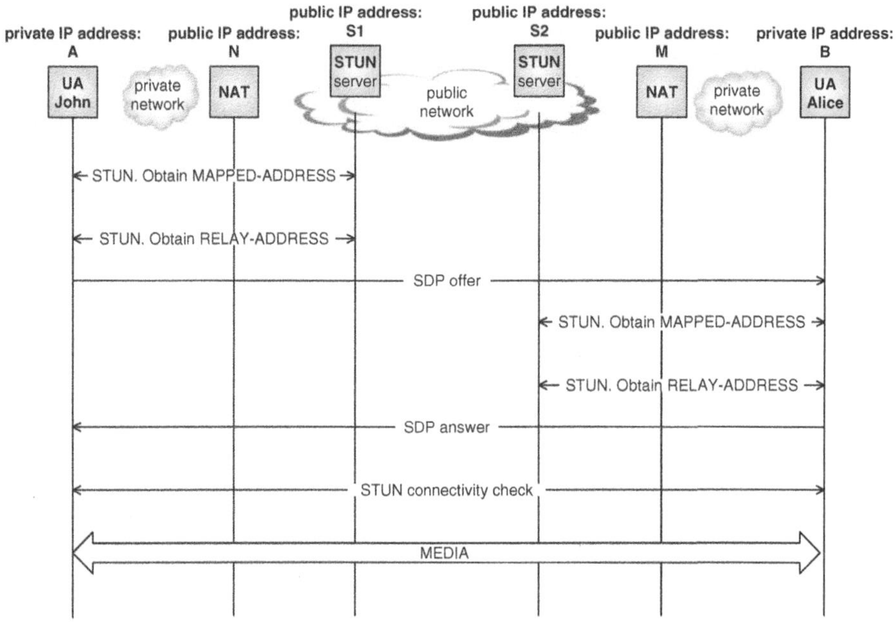

FIGURE 22.19

The term SBC has been coined by the industry to refer to signaling and media intermediaries that implement generic border control functions. Border control functions are functions needed at the border of IP-based communication networks. Two scenarios for SBC deployment exist:

- *Interconnect scenario*: The SBC sits between two service provider networks in a peering environment. In this case, SBCs are typically referred to as I-SBC (Interconnect SBC) or N-SBC (Network SBC).
- *Access scenario*: The SBC is placed at the border between the access network and the service provider's network. In this case, SBCs are typically referred to as A-SBC (Access SBC).

Both scenarios are shown in Figure 22.20.

SBCs typically handle both signaling and media. Regarding the SIP signaling, they act as Back-to-Back User Agents (B2BUAs). See Figure 22.21.

The most common border control functions implemented by SBCs[5] are:

1. *Topology hiding*: They can implement the header privacy service that we discussed in Chapter 20, thus avoiding the fact that the information in some

[5]A detailed description of SBC's functions is given in [draft-ietf-sipping-sbc-funcs].

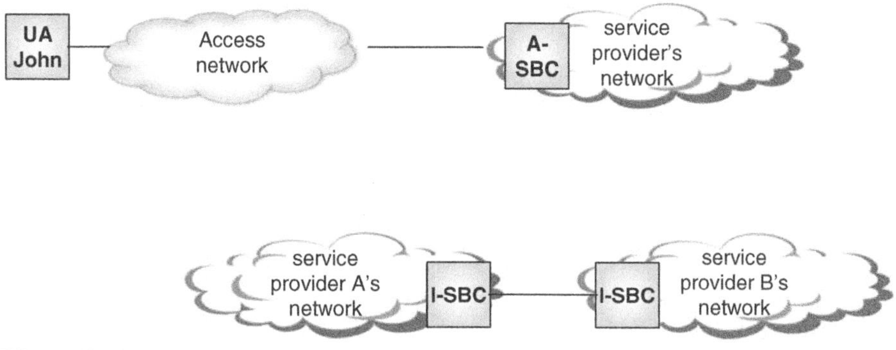

FIGURE 22.20

headers (e.g., Via, Record-Route, and so on), which can give information

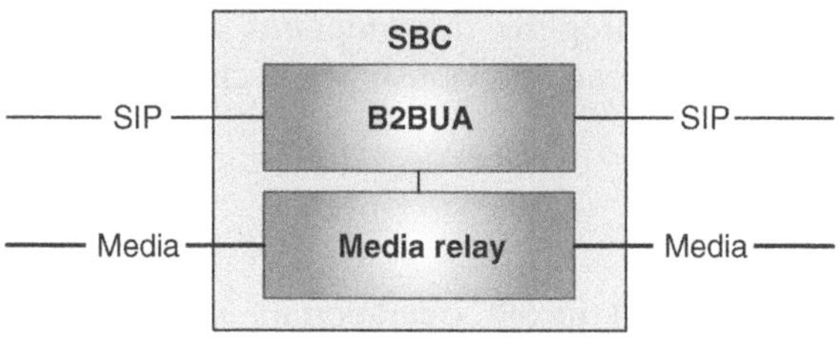

FIGURE 22.21

about the network topology, is provided to the other network. Additionally, they can also provide session privacy.

2. *DOS protection*: SBCs can protect from denial of service or other malicious attacks.
3. *Access control*: SBCs can be used to block traffic from unauthorized parties or from traffic that does not meet specific policies. For instance, the SBC can ensure that only media from authorized sessions is allowed to pass through the SBC.
4. *Media traffic control*: SBCs can implement a variety of functions related to controlling the media traffic—such as bandwidth control (checking that used bandwidth corresponds with what was negotiated in the SDP), bearer detection (detecting if media has stopped flowing, and consequently terminating the session), and so forth.
5. *Protocol repair*: So as to maximize interoperability, SBCs can repair protocol messages generated by clients that are not fully standard.
6. *Protocol interworking*: Allows us to bridge between different flavors of SIP (e.g., IETF and 3GPP). SIP extensions or methods that implement the same function differently can be interworked.

7. *Media encryption*: In those cases where encryption is required in the access network but not in the core network, an A-SBC can perform encryption/decryption at the edge of the network.
8. *Lawful interception*: In some scenarios, this may be necessary due to regulatory constraints (especially in telecom operators' deployments of SIP infrastructure).

In addition to these functions, SBC vendors also incorporate NAT traversal functions in the Session Border Controllers. Moreover, SBCs represent the most common solution taken by service providers in order to resolve the NAT traversal problem for SIP and RTP traffic.

Using SBCs to solve the NAT traversal issue has the advantage that it does not require the clients to support more or less complex STUN and ICE functionality. Moreover, it is able to resolve NAT traversal for all types of deployed NATs. Also, given that SBCs are already in both the signaling and the media path of the communications traffic in order to resolve other functions, using SBCs does not imply an extra intermediary.

For SBC-assisted NAT traversal to work properly, the endpoints must support the following extensions, which were mentioned previously in the chapter:

- symmetric SIP [RFC 3581]
- symmetric RTP [RFC 4961]
- RTCP attribute in SDP [RFC 3605]

In the next section, we will describe in detail the SBC operation for NAT traversal.

22.6 NAT Traversal Using SBCs

Let as assume that the endpoints are located behind a NAT, and are connected to a service provider's network. The service provider would deploy an access SBC at the border between its public network and the private network. The A-SBC may implement several border control functions, including NAT traversal. The basic architecture is shown in Figure 22.22.

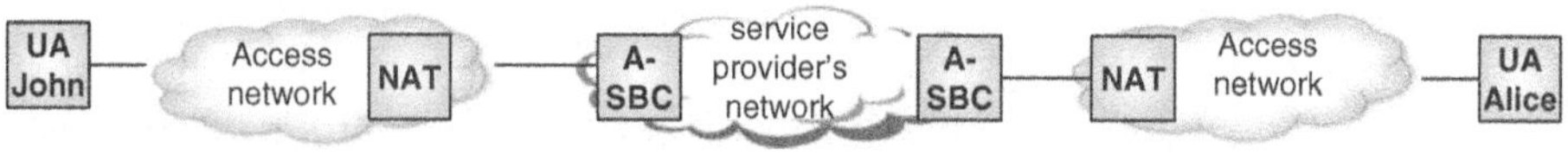

FIGURE 22.22

22.6.1 SBC-Based NAT Traversal of SIP Signaling

In order to assist in NAT traversal, the SBC acts as a B2BUA that is in the path of all signaling originated or terminated in the UA. The solution to NAT traversal is based in the following principles:

If TCP Is Used:

- Both client and SBC will maintain open the TCP connection created to deliver the REGISTER message. The SBC will transmit any incoming SIP request toward the UA through that TCP connection.
- The SBC will change the Expires header in the 200 OK response to the REGISTER request so as to force the UA to generate traffic that keeps the binding in the NAT alive. The SBC does not need to relay all the REGISTER requests received from the UA to the registrar. The SBC will instead respond autonomously to those requests until its own registration timer expires, at which point it will send the REGISTER to the registrar again.

If UDP Is Used:

- In this case, both UA and SBC have to support symmetric SIP so as to create a virtual bidirectional channel.
- Just as with TCP, the SBC will reduce the value in the Expires header in the 200 OK response that it sends to the UA so as to assure that the binding in the NAT is kept open.

Let us now see in more detail how this works. The call flow is depicted in Figure 22.23.

We will assume that the client is using UDP, but the flow for TCP is identical. Both John and SBC must support symmetric SIP.

1. John sends the REGISTER request to the SBC (configured as its outbound proxy). The REGISTER is intercepted by the NAT device, which will change the source IP address and port number, and forward the REGISTER to the SBC.
2. When the SBC receives the REGISTER request, it checks the address set by the UA in the Via header against the packet's source IP address. If they do not match, it means that there is a NAT between the UA and the SBC. Therefore, the SBC decides to assist the UA in NAT traversal.[6]
3. The B2BUA in the SBC creates a new REGISTER message setting the contact address to its own, and sends the REGISTER to the service provider's registrar. It will also store context information that maps the UA's received contact address with its own contact address.
4. The registrar sends back a 200 OK response including an Expires header set to 3600 (which is a typical value). The SBC changes the value of the "expires" parameter to 20 seconds, and forwards the response to the UA. By changing the "expires" value, the SBC forces the UA to generate frequent reregistrations (every 20 s) that will keep the NAT binding open.

[6]If the client uses TCP, and the SBC determines that the UA is not behind a NAT (because the Via header and source IP address match), then the SBC would close the TCP connection after the REGISTER transaction is completed because there is no need for assisting with NAT traversal.

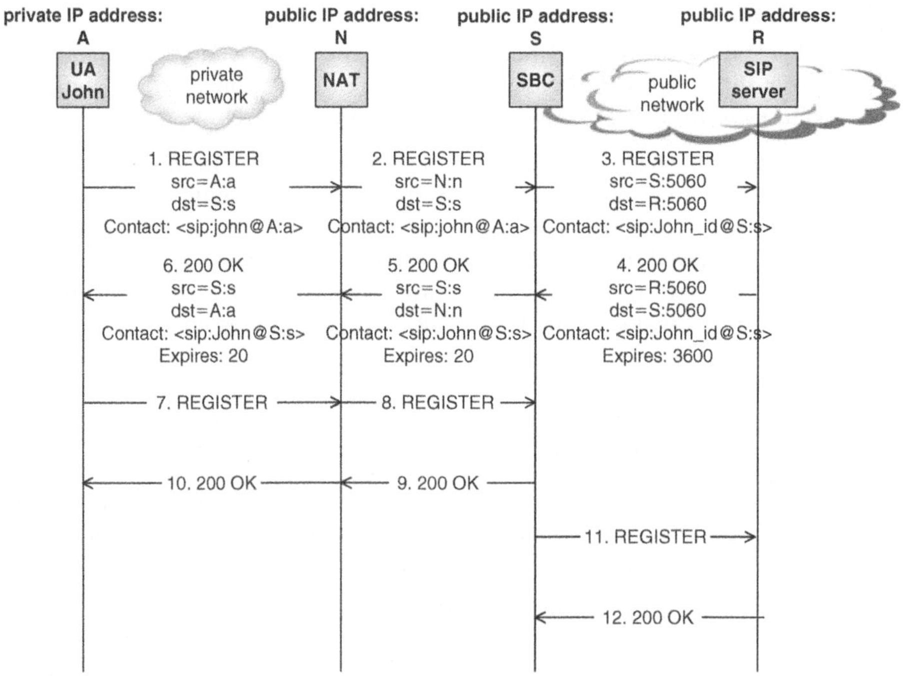

FIGURE 22.23

5. The 200 OK response reaches the NAT, and traverses it through the pin hole opened when the REGISTER was received.

6. The 200 OK reaches the UA.

7–10. When the registration timer expires in the UA, it will send a new REGISTER message, but it will not cause the SBC to relay this message to the registrar.

11. The SBC maintains its own registration timer. When this timer expires, the SBC sends a new REGISTER request to the registrar.

Once the UA is registered, it can receive incoming requests through the bidirectional UDP channel (or TCP connection), for which there exists a pinhole in the NAT. This is shown in Figure 22.24.

22.6.2 SBC-Based NAT Traversal of RTP Traffic

The problems posed by NAT traversal of RTP traffic might be overcome by:

1. Having the SBCs act as relays for both the incoming and the outgoing RTP traffic.
2. Having the endpoints support symmetric RTP.

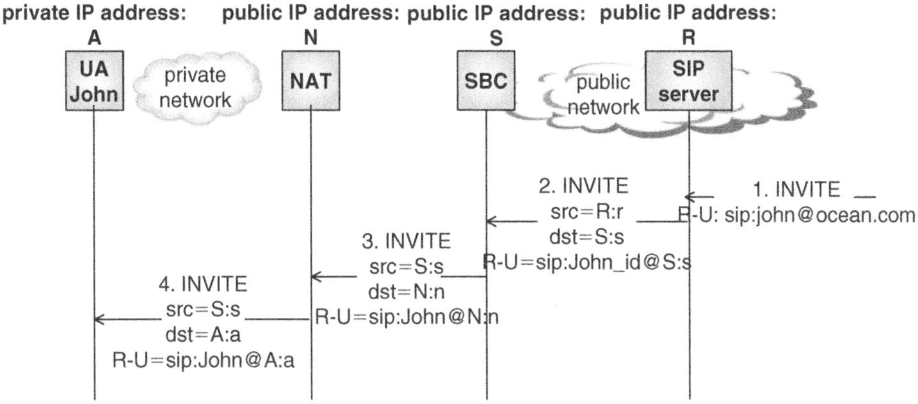

FIGURE 22.24

Effectively, if the SBC assisting a UA receives the outgoing RTP traffic from the endpoint, it may store the source IP address and port. Later, when the incoming RTP traffic is received, the SBC would set the destination address to the stored address, and then forward it to the endpoint. In that way, the incoming traffic would traverse the NAT through the pinhole created by the outgoing RTP traffic, and the endpoint would accept the incoming RTP packets because it supports symmetric RTP.

It is important to highlight the fact that until the SBC has received the first RTP packet in the uplink direction (i.e., from the local endpoint), it would not know how to route the incoming RTP packets in the downlink direction (i.e., from the remote endpoint) because the local endpoint's source address would not be stored in the SBC. Therefore, the SBC has to wait to start sending RTP packets to the local endpoint until it has received packets from the local endpoint. In order to facilitate this process, the local endpoint might send a first, "empty" RTP packet, even if no media has yet been produced, so that the SBC can learn the source address.

All in all, the problem boils down to forcing the RTP traffic (both outgoing and incoming) through the assisting SBC. Also, the SBC needs to be able to correlate the outgoing and incoming traffic so that it can perform the address manipulation explained above.

Given that the SBCs are in the path of the signaling, and that they are acting as B2BUAs, this can be easily achieved. When an SBC receives an SDP offer or response, it:

- Stores the SDP connection addresses and ports in an information context. This would allow the SBC to correlate the incoming and outgoing RTP streams.
- Sets the transport address in the outgoing SDP to its own address. The SBC addresses are public, so they can be conveyed in the SDP and then be used by the endpoints to send RTP traffic (i.e., they are routable addresses).

We can now look at the end-to-end scenario between John and Alice. Both of them are behind a NAT device, and both of them must support symmetric RTP. In this example, we will focus just on the traversal of RTP traffic, and will assume that the traversal of SIP traffic is already coped with by the SBCs based on the procedures discussed in the previous section.

This is depicted in Figure 22.25.

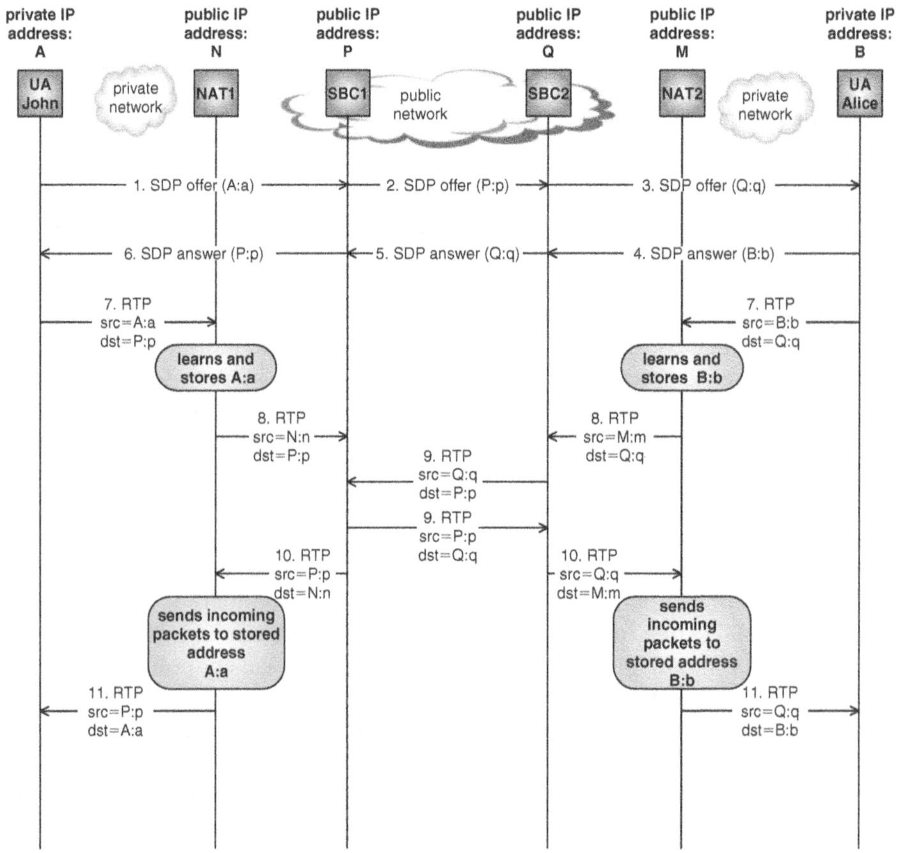

FIGURE 22.25

1. John offers an SDP containing its own private address. SBC1 stores the received SDP address, replaces that address with its own, and forwards the SDP to the network.
2. The SIP provider's network will route the SDP offer to SBC2, which will perform an action similar to that of SBC1 in step 1.
3. SBC2 forwards the SDP offer to Alice.
4. Alice's UA generates an SDP response and sends it to SBC2.

5. SBC2 stores the received SDP address, replaces that address with its own, and forwards the SDP answer to the network. The SIP provider's network will route the SDP answer to SBC1, which will perform an action similar to that of SBC2 in step 5.
6. SBC1 will send the SDP answer to John.
7. John and Alice start sending RTP to their respective assisting SBCs. When the traffic traverses the NAT, a pinhole is created.
8. The SBCs store the source IP address and port in the received RTP packets, and forward the packets to the remote SBCs.
9. The SBCs receive the RTP packets. They replace the destination IP address with the source address received in step 8.
10. The SBCs forward the RTP packet to the endpoint. It traverses the NAT through the pinhole created in step 8.
11. The RTP packets are received by the endpoints.

22.7 Summary

As the reader will have perceived, the NAT traversal topic is extremely complex. However, its relevance has been acknowledged by the IETF community, and that accounts for the hectic activity in this remit. In this area, we have also witnessed how the industry has been faster than the standards in proposing solutions; the proprietary, industry-coined SBC approach is, by far, the one more extensively used in order to overcome the NAT traversal issue.

At this point, we have covered most of the key advanced topics related to SIP. We are now in an ideal position to examine how some of the concepts learned so far can be applied in order to offer multimedia services not just in an Internet environment, but also in a controlled network environment. In the next chapter, we will look at the undefined, though thoroughly implemented, concept of "SIP network." We will set the basic ideas that will allow us to understand, in the last chapter of the book, the architecture of a particular instantiation of the "SIP network" concept, the IP Multimedia Subsystem (IMS).

CHAPTER

SIP Networks

23

In previous chapters, we saw some examples of functions implemented in the network, as opposed to in the endpoints, in order to deliver multimedia communication services. In this chapter, we will put these ideas into perspective and try to better understand what the role of the network is in this remit. The first section discusses the role of the network. Then we make a brief summary of the network functions analyzed throughout the book so far. This chapter focuses on the IETF perspective, and can be seen as a preparation for the next chapter about 3GPP IMS, where the ideas about an IP multimedia communications network are taken a step further and many new requirements are defined.

23.1 The Role of the Network

The original Internet paradigm advocates a scenario where the network is dumb and the endpoints are intelligent. The network should only provide is end-to-end connectivity. Moreover, it should keep as little state information as possible in order to make it robust and scalable. The state information should be moved to the periphery of the network.

Accordingly, the SIP design incorporated the Internet principles, and so it was defined as an end-to-end protocol that reflected the end-to-end nature of the underlying IP network. Nevertheless, soon in our discussion about SIP, we discovered that some additional functions at the SIP level were needed in order to properly address the mobility of the users and the routing of terminating calls to them. That is how the registrar and SIP proxy functions were born, which are considered to be SIP network functions—that is, application-level functions that are generic enough to be needed in any SIP implementation, and that require the introduction of new infrastructure in addition to the endpoints' hardware and software.

Starting from that point, we have seen throughout the book more and more functions incorporated into the architecture outside of the endpoints. These functions are not always needed. Depending on the deployment scenario, there may be more or fewer functions in the network. For instance, in Internet-wide deployments—that is, in interdomain and in heterogeneous environments—the network functions are kept to a minimum, and the trend is to do almost everything in an end-to-end fashion.

On the other hand, in controlled network deployments under the administration of a single entity (e.g., company, telecom operator, and so on), there can be a significant amount of additional network functions that allow us to deliver specific features. Private VoIP networks that intend to replicate (and enhance) existing services in the PSTN are an example of this.

23.1.1 Network Functions

As we saw in previous chapters, in the remit of Internet multimedia communications, when we talk about the network functions, we may be referring to two different concepts: the IP network and the SIP network. The former represents the traditional concept for a network that provides the end-to-end, packet-switched connectivity, and it consists mainly of the IP routers, domain name system (DNS) servers, and other elements that help to achieve the connectivity. The latter refers to some core and generic application-level functions that are not sitting on the endpoints, and that are necessary for delivering the communication service to the end users. The SIP network, being an "application-level network,"[1] sits on top of the IP network.

In both domains, IP network and SIP network, additional network functions are needed in order to provide Internet communication services. For instance, we saw in Chapter 21 that QoS provision requires a significant amount of extra functions in IP network on top of the basic routing function, such as packet classification and scheduling. Moreover, QoS scenarios also require us to have capabilities for admission control, policy control, and resource reservation that do call for the need to have extra functions in the network and to keep new pieces of state information. Although this represents a slight departure from the original Internet principle, it is implemented in such a way (e.g., using soft-states, and so on) so that the impact on scalability and robustness of the network is minimized.

On the other hand, in the SIP domain, and apart from the registrar and basic proxy functions, we also saw new additional functions needed at the SIP network level, such as authentication services, privacy services, and so on.

Actually, the functions of a SIP network can be broken down into several main areas:

- Mobility and routing
- Authentication, authorization, and accounting
- Assertion of identities
- Security

[1] The concept "application-level network" may seem a contradiction in itself, given that network and application are different levels in the TCP/IP stack. Still, the author has coined this term to reflect typical network functions—such as routing, mobility, and so forth—that may be sitting in the application layer (enabled by SIP).

- Interworking and border functions
- Provision of network-based services

We will now look at them a bit more in detail.

23.2 Mobility and Routing

The most basic functions in a SIP network, as we saw in Chapter 4, refer to the capability to route terminating calls to users who might be changing their location (i.e., their IP address). This is achieved through the introduction of three entities: the SIP registrar, the location service, and the SIP (inbound) proxy. The proxy functions are not limited to routing the terminating calls; they can also help in routing calls at origination. Thus, the SIP outbound proxy concept is born, which helps in routing the messages on behalf of the originating user.

In addition, SIP proxies may contain complex routing logic that takes a number of arbitrary input parameters into consideration, such as date, time of the day, presence information, and so forth.

23.3 Authentication, Authorization, and Accounting

We saw in Chapter 14 that in order to obtain an IP communications service, users need to subscribe to a service provider. Whenever the users want to take part in communications scenarios, they need to have previously registered with their home server, which authenticates them. Therefore, there is a need for an authentication function sitting in the network. Moreover, as we saw in Chapter 20, the authentication function can also incorporate additional functions for assertion of the user's identity. The authentication of the users, together with the assertion of their identities, is one of the key network functions.

User authorization is again a network function that can be implemented in proxies. User authorization may relate to very different aspects. Particularly relevant to our discussion are the aspects regarding media and quality of service authorization that we saw in Chapter 21. These functions allow the service provider to control the media and the QoS requested by the users, and to assure that network resources are used according to what was authorized. These functions are particularly relevant in controlled network scenarios where both SIP network and IP access network fall under the same administrative domain.

Also, accounting is an important network function, especially in scenarios with a tighter relationship between users and service providers, because these will most likely want to charge for offering the service. This function typically requires that the network infrastructure is able to monitor the entire duration of the call. Therefore, this function needs to be implemented in call-stateful proxies or in Back-to-Back-User-Agents. These network nodes might generate call records that include the identity of the caller, the destination address, time of day, call duration, and other information. These call records, when processed, allow the service provider to create bills for the users. This approach is called offline charging. Another approach allows for online charging, as is typical for prepaid applications.[2] In these cases, a Back-to-Back User Agent is required that has control over the call for the entire duration of the call, and that is able to query a charging server, obtain charging authorization from it, and release the call as soon as the credit is finished.

23.4 Security

Security is a broad topic in which the network plays an important role. We already mentioned the authentication service. Network functions are also concerned with securing the connections over which messages are sent that are addressed to SIPs URIs.

Privacy is another interesting security service that may be provided by the network, both at the control plane and at the media plane, as we saw in Chapter 20.

23.5 Interworking and Border Functions

Interworking with PSTN is yet another example of an issue that requires a network function to be resolved. IP communications service providers may offer an interconnect service with the PSTN. Some service providers offer calls just from the IP domain to the PSTN. Other service providers allow for calls in both directions. In any case, the service provider needs to come to an agreement with a telecom operator, and then deploy one or several gateways and connect them to the operator's PSTN infrastructure. The gateways are, in this case, network elements that contain, among others, the necessary conversion functions between the protocols in the two domains.

When interconnecting two different service providers' IP communication infrastructure, there is a need to provide additional functions that are implemented in the network and that involve the control plane and the media plane. These additional functions are typically offered by elements collectively known as Session Border Controllers (SBC). SBCs usually sit between two service provider networks in a peering environment, or between an access network and a backbone network to provide service to residential and/or enterprise customers. They provide a variety of functions to enable or enhance multimedia services. These functions include:

1. perimeter defense (access control, topology hiding, denial of service detection and prevention).
2. functionality not available in the endpoints (NAT traversal, protocol interworking or repair).
3. network management (traffic monitoring, traffic shaping, and QoS).

[2] Online charging can also used for postpaid—for example, for credit monitoring, call limit, dynamic charging, and so on.

SBCs typically handle both signaling and media traffic, and they include a SIP B2BUA. The privacy service that we saw in Chapter 20 might, as a matter of fact, be implemented in SBCs.

A detailed description of the functions of SBCs is given in [draft-ietf-sipping-sbc-funcs].

23.6 Provision of Network-Based Services

As we saw in Chapter 5, there are different approaches to deliver value-added services (VAS) in SIP. One approach is the end-to-end approach, where services are sitting in the endpoints. In such an approach, no service logic (or very limited service logic) is sitting in the network. An example of that could be a chess game or a plain voice call.

In another approach, the application is sitting in the network. Take, for instance, an application that provides enhanced voice call control services such as those required in an enterprise environment (hunting group, boss/secretary, call queuing, do not disturb, etc.).[3]

Network applications are provided in application servers that are typically implemented as SIP B2BUA. In order to provide these applications, Application Servers (AS) very often need to work alongside Media Servers. Both Application Servers and Media Servers are considered network infrastructure.

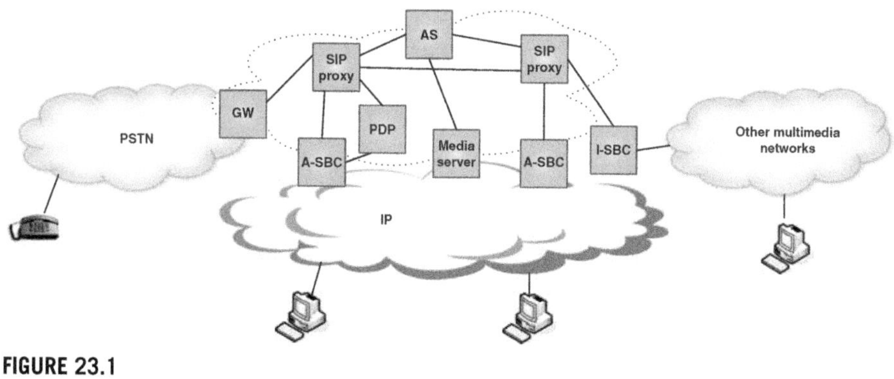

FIGURE 23.1

As a summary of the previous ideas, Figure 23.1 depicts a SIP network that incorporates most of the previous functions. This picture represents an IETF view. In the next chapter, we will see how this architecture may evolve, in order to cope with some telecom operator's requirements to build a controlled multimedia network under their administration (IMS).

[3] This type of SIP application that emulates the services provided by an enterprise PBX is collectively known as an IP Centrex application.

23.7 Summary

In this chapter, we have presented the basic functions in a SIP-based multimedia network. Even if the "SIP network" concept has not been explicitly tackled by the IETF, there are a lot of SIP extensions that allow building such a concept. Today, we can see many examples of IETF-like SIP networks deployed all around the world, either by service providers in the Internet or in enterprise environments.

In the next chapter, we will see an example of a particular SIP-based multimedia network specified by 3GPP: the IMS. Such a network is implemented by reusing the IETF concepts, though some extensions had to be developed in order to cope with new requirements.

CHAPTER

The IMS

24

In this chapter, we will introduce the 3GPP IP Multimedia Subsystem (IMS). The topic would deserve several books on its own, so in this chapter we will focus on just the key ideas. The main purpose of this chapter is to let the reader understand how the ideas around Internet multimedia that we learned throughout the book are applied in a concrete multimedia network intended for the telecom operators' environment.

In order to explain the IMS architecture, we will not follow a top-down approach, where the overwhelming IMS architecture with all its unintelligible names is presented first, and then the components are detailed. Instead, we will use our recently acquired knowledge of SIP and SIP network architectures to understand how, starting from a SIP network and adding IMS requirements, we end up with the IMS architecture.

First we begin by giving the reader a bit of background information about 3GPP, the standardization body that is responsible for the IMS specification. We will also introduce the high-level functional requirements for IMS. Next an overview of IMS and its architecture will be presented, following the bottom-up approach described before. We will then focus on some key IMS topics such as IMS identities and service control. A section in the chapter presents some new private SIP headers that are needed in order to support the IMS requirements. We will close the chapter by examining some present and future trends for the utilization of IMS, including the ETSI TISPAN NGN architecture and the work on IMS Centralized Services (ICS).

24.1 3GPP and IMS

The 3rd Generation Partnership Project (3GPP) is a collaboration agreement signed in 1999 by a number of telecommunications standards bodies—namely, ARIB, CCSA, ETSI, ATIS, TTA, and TTC.[1]

[1] ARIB (Association of Radio Industries and Business), CCSA (China Communications Standards Association), ETSI (European Telecommunications Standards Institute), ATIS (Alliance for Telecommunications Industry Solutions), TTA (Telecommunications Technology Association), TTC (Telecommunications Technology Committee).

The main goal of 3GPP is the specification of a third-generation mobile system comprising W-CDMA and TD-CDMA[2] radio access and an evolved GSM[3] core network. Such a third-generation mobile system is called UMTS (Universal Mobile Telecommunications System). The 3GPP is also responsible for maintaining and further developing the GSM specifications, which were originally developed by ETSI.

The UMTS architecture is broken down into access network (AN), which deals with the radio access, and the core network (CN). The core network can be further split into:

- The Circuit-Switched (CS) Domain
- The Packet-Switched (PS) Domain
- The Internet Multimedia Subsystem (IMS)

The UMTS architecture is shown in Figure 24.1.

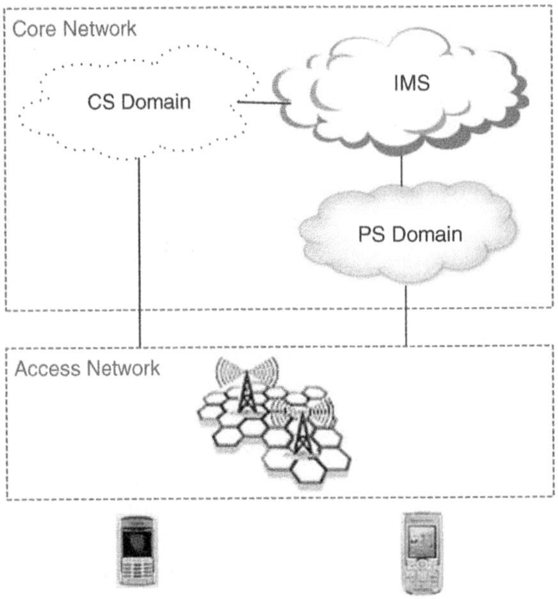

FIGURE 24.1

The CS Domain in UMTS is voice-centric (and video-centric) architecture similar to that of the second-generation (wireless) systems.

The PS Domain contains GPRS (General Packet Radio Service) [3GPP TS 23.060] infrastructure aimed at providing packet-based connectivity to mobile terminals. GPRS can be seen as a network providing IP connectivity. It does not provide any

[2] W-CDMA: Wideband Code Division Multiple Access, TD-CDMA: Time Division/Code Division Multiple Access.

[3] Global System for Mobile communications. It is representative of the so-called second-generation mobile systems (2G).

service itself beyond the pure connectivity. Services such as web, email, VoIP, and others have to be built on top.

The Internet Multimedia Subsystem is a network architecture that allows the provision of multimedia services. It relies on the IP connectivity provided by the PS domain. The IMS is based on the SIP protocol and architecture.

The complete solution for the support of IP multimedia applications consists of:

- IMS-enabled User Equipments (UEs).
- Access network and PS Domain providing IP connectivity.
- The IMS network, composed of a number of functional elements.

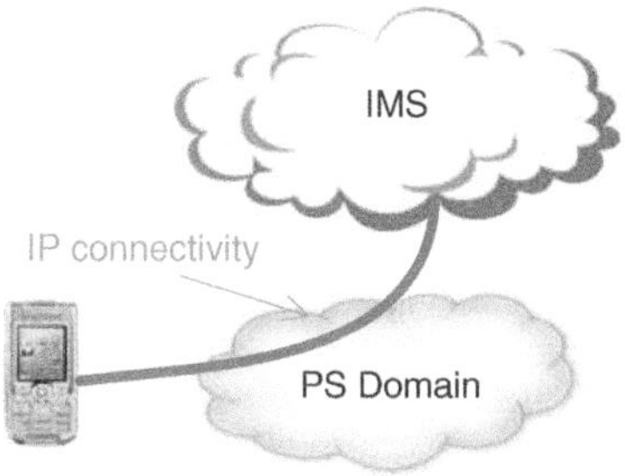

FIGURE 24.2

Several releases of the 3GPP specifications have been produced so far. The IMS, which is the purpose of this chapter, was included in 3GPP release 5 (R5), and has been further developed in R6, R7, and now in R8 as well. Table 24.1 lists these releases and the main IMS features in each of them.

Table 24.1

Release	Date	Info
R5	2002	IMS is introduced, focused mainly on GPRS access.
R6	2004	Enhancements to some interfaces
		IMS Group Management
		IMS Conferencing
		IMS Messaging
		Interworking between IMS and CS networks
		Interworking between IMS and non-IMS IP networks
		IMS charging
		PoC (Push to Talk Over Cellular)

(*Continued*)

Table 24.1 (*Cont.*)

Release	Date	Info
R7	2007	Emergency calls
		Combinational services
		Enhancements for fixed broadband access to IMS. TISPAN R1
		SMS over IP
		Evolution of Policy Control and Charging
		Voice call continuity
R8		IMS service brokering
		Multimedia Priority Service
		Enhancements for TISPAN R2
		Enhancements to support Packet Cable access
		Multimedia Conferencing
		Centralized IMS Service Control
		AS-MRFC media server control protocol

24.2 High-Level IMS Requirements

The IP Multimedia Core Network Subsystem (IMS) is an architecture designed to let telecom operators provide IP multimedia communication services to their customers. [3GPP TS 22.228] defines the service requirements for the IMS.

24.2.1 IP Connectivity

The 3GPP specifications state that both the endpoints and the IMS network elements must have IPv6 connectivity. However, they may in addition support IPv4 in initial IMS implementations and deployments [3GPP TS 23.221].

IP connectivity from the endpoints to the IMS is achieved through the so-called IP Connectivity Access Network (IP-CAN).

The main function of the IP-CAN is to provide the underlying IP transport connectivity between the user and the IMS. The IP-CAN is also responsible for dealing with the terminal mobility—that is, to maintain the service while the terminal moves, and to hide these moves from the IMS. The concept of "terminal mobility" should not be confused with "user mobility." The former refers to coping with movements of the terminal while still presenting the same IP address to the upper layers; it is the responsibility of the IP-CAN. The latter refers to allowing a user identified by a logical identity (e.g., SIP URI) to be reachable even if he or she changes the IP address; it is achieved through the SIP registration mechanism at the IMS layer.

Figure 24.3 represents a terminal mobility scenario, and Figure 24.4 represents the user mobility case.

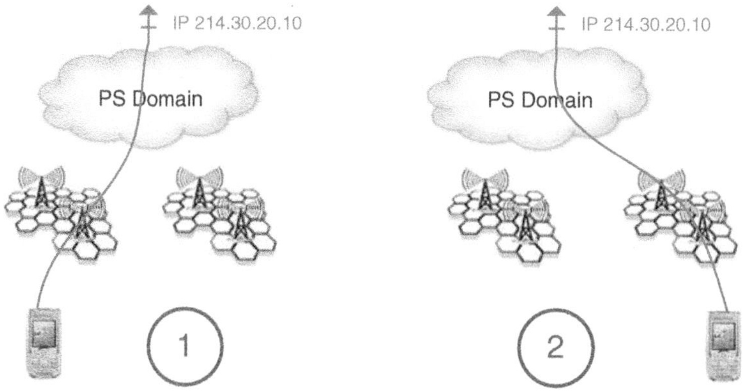

FIGURE 24.3

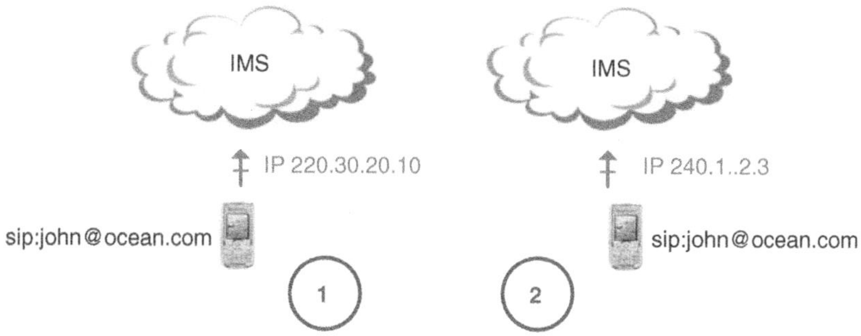

FIGURE 24.4

24.2.2 Access Independence

The IMS supports the principle of access independence so that IMS services can be provided over a variety of IP Connectivity Access Networks such as cellular (GPRS), xDSL, WLAN, cable, and so forth.

IMS Release 5 was fully orientated to its usage over a GPRS access. In Release 6, the possibility to use WLAN as an access network is introduced. In Release 7, specific aspects for the connection of xDSL access networks are also considered. Release 8 will tackle the support for Packet Cable accesses.

This principle is depicted in Figure 24.5.

Moreover, there is ongoing work [3GPP TR 22.892] to analyze the possibility of even considering the CS domain as another Connectivity Access Network so that even legacy terminals can gain access to a limited set of IMS applications. This is referred to as IMS centralized services.

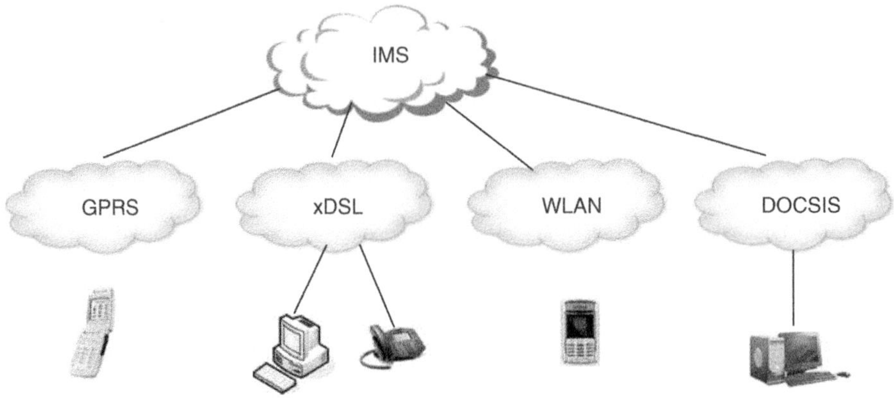

FIGURE 24.5

This idea is also present in the ETSI TISPAN architecture for PSTN/ISDN emulation where legacy terminals[4] are offered basic telephony services delivered through IMS. The ETSI TISPAN architecture is examined in subsequent sections.

24.2.3 Roaming Support

In mobile networks, there exists the fundamental concept of roaming. A user who wants to get mobile service needs to contract it with a mobile operator. The mobile operator offers mobile service to its customers in a defined country or region through its network. From the customer perspective, such a network is his or her home network. When the customer goes to another country or to another region where their operator does not have network infrastructure (specifically: no mobile radio coverage), they may still get mobile service through the mobile operator that offers service (i.e., mobile radio coverage) in that zone, provided that there is an agreement (a roaming agreement) between the customer's home network operator and the visited network operator.

IMS has also been designed to support roaming so that mobile users that are in a visited network can still have access to multimedia services. [3GPP TS 23.221] defines two possible ways to achieve roaming:

- In the first approach, the IP connectivity is provided by the visited network. It is the visited network that provides the IP address for the UE. Therefore, the roaming UE contacts the *visited IMS network* through the *visited access network*. The IMS signaling will be passed from the visited IMS network to the home IMS network where the service control resides. This scenario is depicted in Figure 24.6.

[4]Legacy phones, also called POTS (Plain Old Telephone System) phones, are connected to the PSTN using an analog (not digital) interface.

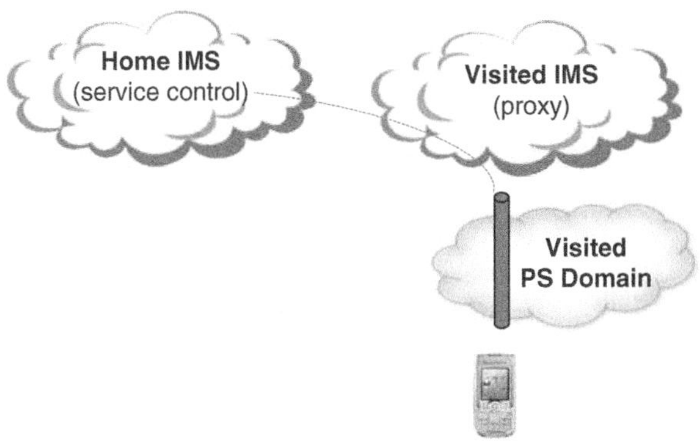

FIGURE 24.6

- In the second approach, the Connectivity Access Network is composed by both visited and home network elements, being the home network that provides the IP address. In this case, the UE contacts the home IMS network directly—that is, without the visited IMS network's involvement. This scenario is depicted in Figure 24.7.

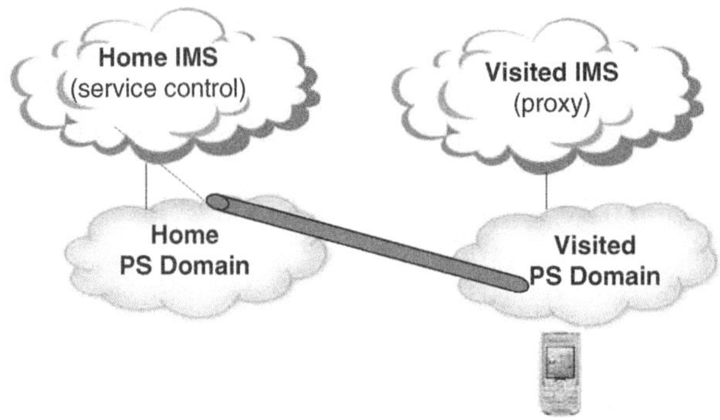

FIGURE 24.7

The first approach is better from the routing efficiency perspective because it does not force the media traffic to go all the way back to the home operator. In order to illustrate this idea, let us consider that both John and Alice, who belong to the same home IMS network, are roaming abroad in different visited IMS networks. John calls Alice. Figure 24.8 shows the path of both signaling and media traffic in each of the two approaches to achieve roaming.

It is important to highlight that in either of the two approaches for roaming, both the subscriber databases and the service control function reside in the home network. The service control function is in charge of invoking multimedia services on behalf of users based on subscription information. It will be further explained in subsequent sections.

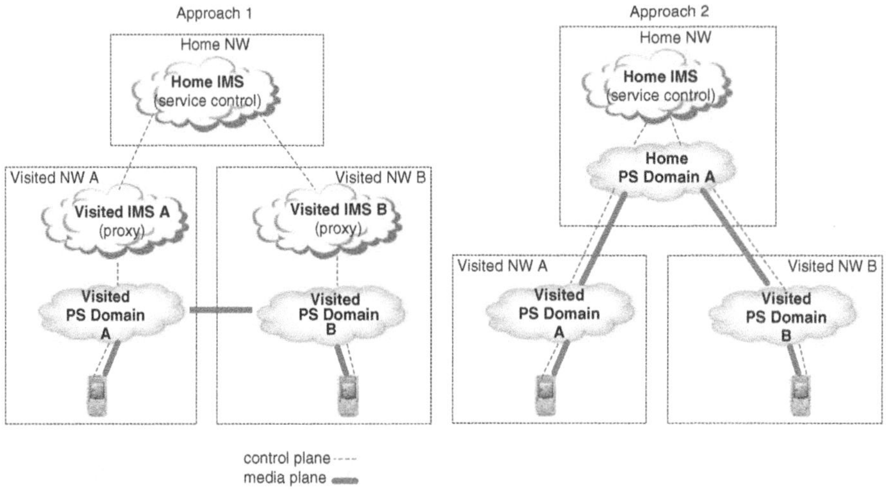

FIGURE 24.8

24.2.4 QoS Support

There is a requirement for the IMS, in conjunction with the underlying IP access and transport network, to provide quality of service. Moreover, it is stated [3GPP TS 22.228] that the end-to-end QoS for a VoIP call using IMS must be at least as good as that achieved in today's circuit-switched wireless networks.

Quality of service is seen as one of the aspects that telecom operators will use in order to differentiate their multimedia offerings from those of Internet service providers who in most cases do not have the means to provide QoS. This factor is particularly relevant when using limited-bandwidth accesses (e.g. wireless).

In order to offer quality of service, several aspects need to be considered:

1. The access network and the transport network must implement QoS mechanisms (packet classification, scheduling, admission control).
2. The operator may want to assure that the negotiated QoS at SIP/SDP level is enforced at the access and transport network level.
3. Resource reservation has to be realized in a coordinated manner with session establishment.

These three aspects amount to the need to use the architecture for quality of service that we presented in Chapter 21, which includes support for QoS policy control and QoS preconditions.

24.2.5 Support for Multiple Services

The IMS must be capable of supporting multiple multimedia applications within a single session. This requirement calls for a service control function in the IMS network that, based on subscription data, is able to identify per subscriber which applications need to be invoked for a call and in what order.

An important aspect is that the service control function is always located in the home network. So, in roaming scenarios, even if the IP connectivity is provided by the visited network, the IMS signaling (control plane) is routed back to the home network, where service control is applied. The decision to always base the service control (i.e., the service invocation) on the home network was one of the most crucial design decisions in the early days of IMS standardization. By having the service control reside in the home network, the architecture is made simpler, the interfaces between home and visited network are simplified, and the dependency for the delivery of services on the visited network is very much reduced.

24.2.6 Security

The IMS must provide the same level of security, authentication, and privacy services as the existing circuit-switched and GPRS networks.

In particular, IMS provides authentication, confidentiality, and integrity services at two levels:

- *access*: between the UEs and the IMS
- *network*: between two IMS networks or between the nodes of the same IMS network

This concept is illustrated in Figure 24.9.

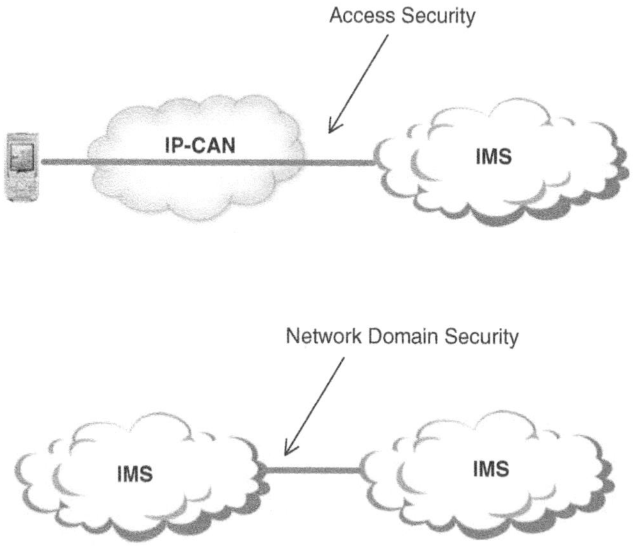

FIGURE 24.9

24.3 Overview of IMS Architecture

The Internet Multimedia Subsystem (IMS) is an architecture designed to let telecom operators provide multimedia communication services to their customers. 3GPP decided to base the IMS on the capabilities defined by IETF for multimedia session management—that is, on SIP. By doing so, it is expected that the Internet flexibility for delivering services can be brought to the telecom environment, and that the merger of mobile communications and Internet will create new services and business opportunities.

Nevertheless, given that the scope of IMS is centered on its use by telecom operators, the resulting IMS architecture makes some assumptions and addresses some requirements that are not applicable to the Internet at large. As an example, it is assumed that there is a tight relationship between the operator and the subscriber and that the operator's network is composed by a set of trusted nodes. Moreover, it is also assumed that quality of service and charging are crucial aspects of the solution.

Throughout this chapter, we will discover that the IMS, in addition to the core SIP specification, also incorporates many SIP extensions and SIP network functions. In some cases, these extensions already existed; in other cases, they have been defined based on specific IMS requirements. We will see that the IMS architecture is not, as a matter of fact, very different from the architecture of the full-fledged controlled SIP network that we saw in Chapter 23 (though the IMS elements are given new and sometimes obscure names).

It is important to highlight the fact that the architecture defined by 3GPP is a functional one.

Nothing precludes the operator from deploying several of those functions in the same box. Moreover, it is not surprising to see initial IMS deployments with just one box (or two, for redundancy reasons) including almost all the components.

The IMS architecture is defined in [3GPP TS 23.228].

Next we will present the different functional elements that compose the IMS architecture.

24.3.1 The Home SIP Server and the Subscriber Database

We learned throughout the book that the very basic SIP infrastructure consists of a SIP registrar and a SIP proxy. These two elements grouped together are typically referred to as a SIP server, and are necessary to provide user mobility and to route terminating calls to the user. Therefore, the first IMS element is the user's home SIP server—or, in IMS terminology, the Serving Call Session Control Function (S-CSCF).

The S-CSCF incorporates basic registrar and proxy functionality, but adds some additional functions. The main additional functions are described next.

1. Authentication

When the user registers with the S-CSCF, the S-CSCF may authenticate him or her. For that purpose, the S-CSCF contacts an authentication server from which it derives the authentication parameters that apply for this user (e.g., the authentication challenge, the expected response, etc.). The S-CSCF then challenges the user to provide authentication credentials. Once the user responds, the S-CSCF checks that the provided credentials are correct. The S-CSCF and the UE use SIP digest authentication with Authentication and Key Agreement (AKA) [RFC3310]. The AKA protocol will be explained in subsequent sections.

The authentication server used by the S-CSCF is called Home Subscriber Server (HSS). It holds the shared secret for each subscriber, among other subscriber data that we will see later on. The interface between S-CSCF and HSS is based on the Diameter base protocol.

2. User Profile

When the user registers and the authentication is confirmed, the S-CSCF again contacts the HSS in order to retrieve the user profile. The user profile contains information about the media types that the user is authorized to use, and about the services that are to be applied to the user (i.e., about the application servers that will need to be contacted whenever the user issues a request).

Therefore, the HSS, in addition to storing secret keys, also stores the service profile for each user.

3. Originating Calls

In IETF SIP, the end user needs to register in order to receive calls. However, the user might make outgoing calls without being registered. Moreover, he or she might even direct outgoing calls toward the recipient's SIP server without involving his or her own SIP server at all.

On the other hand, 3GPP mandates that the user also needs to be registered in order to make outgoing calls, and originating requests have to go through the user's S-CSCF. The main reason for that is to allow service execution and media authorization, in accordance with the user's profile downloaded from the HSS at registration, to be applied to the user when he or she originates calls. Later on, we will see how originating calls are forced through the S-CSCF.

4. Service Control

The service profile downloaded from the HSS contains a list of Application Servers (ASs) (identified by their URI) and some filtering rules. The filtering rules allow the S-CSCF to determine when received SIP requests need to be routed to a particular Application Server. In this way, customized services can be applied to the users, and a very neat separation is enforced between the basic SIP functions (S-CSCF) and the enhanced service logic (AS).

Service control aspects are further detailed in section 24.4.4.

5. Prohibition of Media Types

The user profile in the HSS, which is downloaded at registration, contains the list of media types that the user is allowed to utilize in multimedia sessions.

When an attempt to set up a session reaches the S-CSCF, the S-CSCF can reject the request if the session includes a nonallowed media type for the user (e.g., video).

Figure 24.10 depicts the three IMS entities discussed so far: S-CSCF, HSS, and AS.

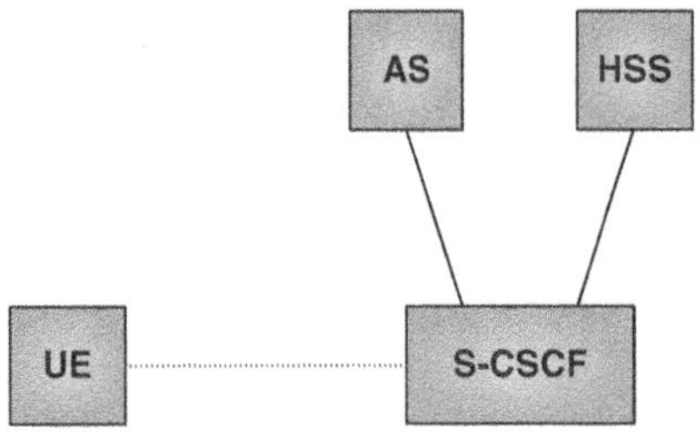

FIGURE 24.10

24.3.2 The Outbound/Inbound Proxy

We have seen that the S-CSCF incorporates the main functions of a home SIP server. However, there are some other needed SIP proxy functions that we have not yet mentioned.

1. Securing the Communication between UE and Network

One of the aspects that the S-CSCF deals with is the authentication of the users. In addition to the authentication itself, it is necessary to provide integrity and confidentiality protection between the user and the network. In Chapter 14, we saw the possibility to use TLS between the user and his or her SIP server in order to provide those functions. We mentioned that IPsec might be used as well. IMS specifies the use of IPsec security associations (SA) between the user and the network. Thus, we need a network function for maintaining such IPsec security associations.

2. Compression of SIP Messages

Another function that is very important, especially when dealing with bandwidth-limited-access networks such as cellular, is the signaling compression. There is, then, the need to have a network function responsible for compressing the SIP messages as they are sent to the user, and for uncompressing them when they are received by the network.

3. Prohibition of Codecs

The IMS network must have the capability to prohibit the use of specific codecs. For instance, some IMS networks might want to prohibit the use of codecs that consume a lot of bandwidth. This is particularly important when using IMS with cellular access, where bandwidth is limited.

4. Policy Control

In policy control architectures, such as the one we saw in Chapter 21, there is the need to have a QoS-enabled proxy that is responsible for interacting with the PDP in order to retrieve the authorization token and pass it to the user in the SIP signaling. Such a token is later on used by the endpoint to obtain authorization for resource reservation at media level.

Some of the functions mentioned above can benefit from closeness to the access network, whereas others require a significant amount of processing resources. Therefore, it was decided to logically separate these functions from the home SIP server and define another IMS functional element to cope with them. Such an element is a SIP proxy that, in IMS terminology, is called the P-CSCF (Proxy Call Session Control Function). It is the first contact point for users within the IMS, both for outgoing and incoming requests. Thus, our previous architecture in Figure 24.10 should rather look like Figure 24.11.

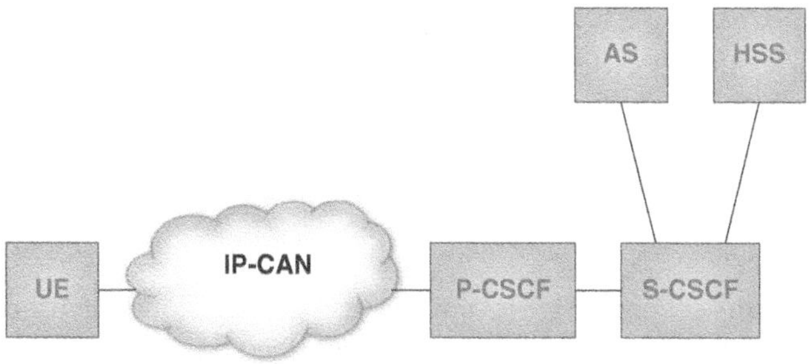

FIGURE 24.11

At this point, and given that the P-CSCF is the "single point of contact" for the user in the IMS, some readers might wonder how the user can determine its address. Two methods have been standardized for *P-CSCF discovery*:

- Use DHCP to provide the user with the domain name of a P-CSCF and the address of a DNS server that is capable of resolving the P-CSCF name. See Figure 24.12.
- Use means provided by the IP-CAN. Some IP-CANs provide the capability to derive the P-CSCF address as part of the access bearer establishment process.

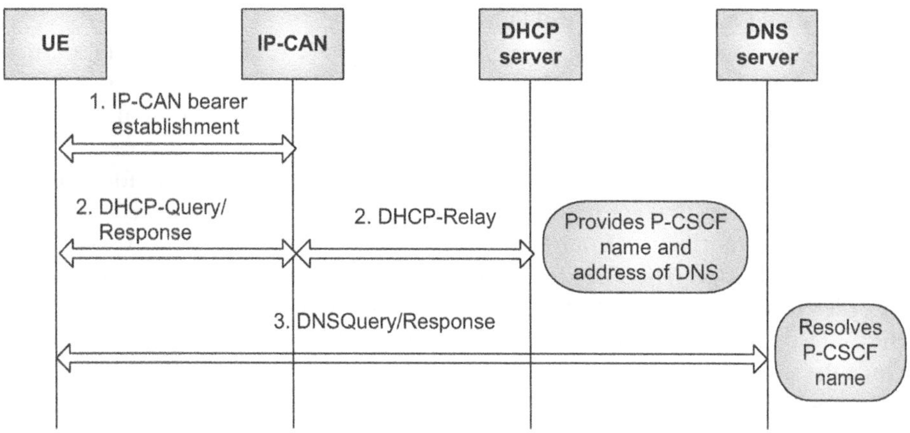

FIGURE 24.12

Another approach that, though not standardized, is used in some deployments consists of manually configuring the name or address of the P-CSCF in the terminal.

Once assigned to a user, the P-CSCF does not change while the user remains connected to the access network.

24.3.3 The Edge Proxy

An interesting aspect about the IMS architecture is the fact that it explicitly addresses network topologies where more than one S-CSCF may be needed. Moreover, users are not statically assigned a particular S-CSCF. The association between user and S-CSCF is dynamic and based on a number of criteria such as:

- S-CSCF capabilities that users need, according to their profile in HSS
- Operator's preferences on a per-user basis
- Load distribution

As we can see, the first and second criteria rely on using some kind of user-specific information in order to take the S-CSCF assignment decision.

Thus, two challenges are posed to the IMS architecture:

1. How to dynamically assign, at registration time, an S-CSCF to a user?
2. If users are distributed among several S-CSCFs based on user-level criteria, how can the IMS route incoming requests to the appropriate S-CSCF?

The solution to these challenges is based on having an additional SIP proxy function that:

- Receives both the registrations and the incoming requests.
- Interrogates the HSS to receive assistance for subsequent routing to the proper S-CSCF.
- Forwards the SIP requests to the corresponding S-CSCF.

Unsurprisingly, this new SIP proxy function is called, in IMS terminology, the Interrogating Call Session Control Function (I-CSCF).

The I-CSCF acts as an edge proxy, and requests are routed to it based on the home domain name. The I-CSCF is the entity in an IMS network that stands for the specific IMS domain (e.g., ocean.com) to which all registrations and incoming calls are directed.

In the registration case, the I-CSCF will interrogate the HSS for specific S-CSCF capabilities that are required for the registering user. When the I-CSCF has received that information from HSS, it will decide to which S-CSCF to route the REGISTER message. The I-CSCF uses internal configuration to select the S-CSCF. In order to force the routing to the appropriate S-CSCF, the I-CSCF will include the S-CSCF's name or address in the Route header field of the REGISTER request. Once the user is registered, the HSS will need to be informed of which S-CSCF the user has been assigned. This is important to cope with the routing of incoming requests, as we will see next. It is the assigned S-CSCF itself that, as soon as the authentication is successfully completed, informs the HSS about the assignment.

Figure 24.13 shows this scenario, which now includes all the CSCF types (S-, P- and I-) in action.

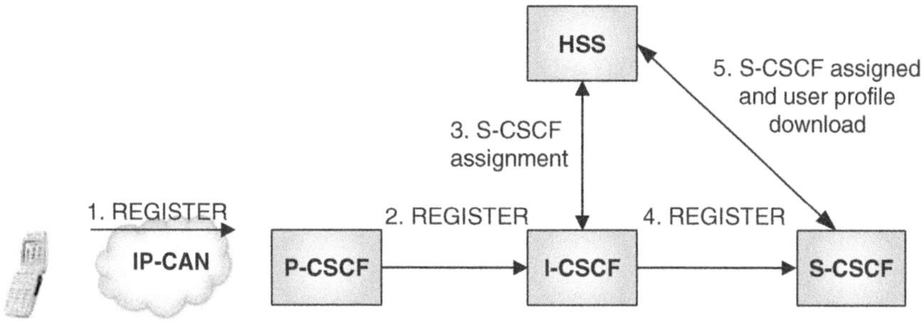

FIGURE 24.13

In the second case, when the I-CSCF receives an incoming request for john@ocean.com, the I-CSCF will interrogate the HSS for John in order to retrieve the name (or address) of the S-CSCF that John was assigned at registration time. Once the I-CSCF has obtained that information, it will include the S-CSCF name or address in the Route header of the request so that the request reaches the S-CSCF.

This scenario is shown in Figure 24.14.

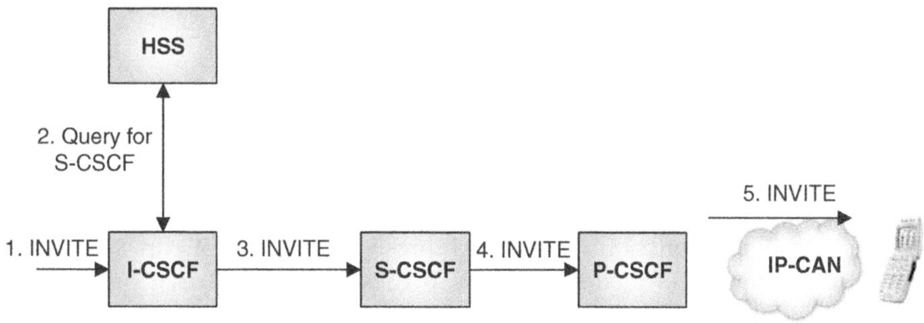

FIGURE 24.14

24.3.4 The Application Server and the Media Server

The SIP proxies that we saw before do not, just by themselves, deliver any added-value services. IMS applications are implemented in SIP application servers with the help, if needed, of media servers.

In the IMS architecture, it is the S-CSCF that, based on subscription information downloaded from the HSS, decides which Application Servers need to be involved and in what order, to handle a particular request. If the S-CSCF determines that an Application Server (AS) needs to be involved, the S-CSCF delegates control to that AS. The interface between the S-CSCF and the AS is SIP based, and is referred to as ISC (IMS Service Control).

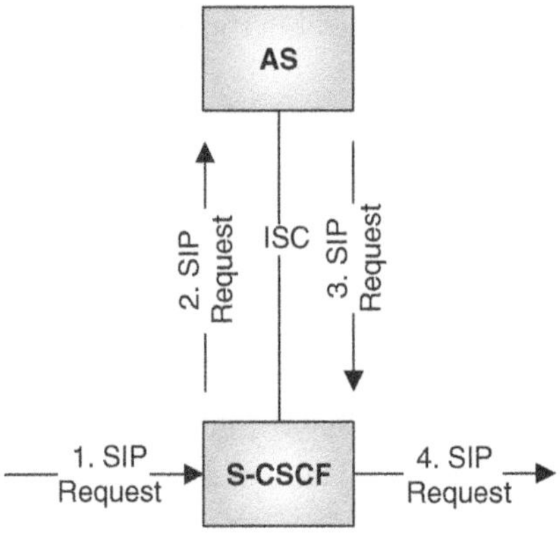

FIGURE 24.15

In the IMS terminology, the media server function is called MRF (Media Resource Function). The MRF is further split into two components:

- MRFP (Media Resource Function Processor)
- MRFC (Media Resource Function Controller)

MRFP

The Media Resource Function Processor provides the media-processing functions such as:

- media stream source
- media stream processing
- mixing of media streams

and offers its resources to be controlled by the MRFC.

MRFC

The Media Resource Function Controller represents the control part associated with the managements of media resources. It uses a MEGACO-based protocol to control the MRFP.

Figure 24.16 shows this architecture.

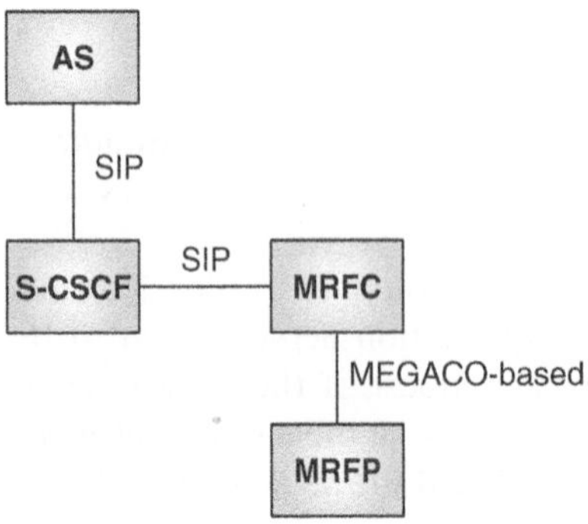

FIGURE 24.16

24.3.5 The PSTN Gateway

In order to interwork with the PSTN or PLMN, the IMS architecture also includes a gateway function. This function is split into MGC and MG according to the ideas discussed in Chapter 18. According to IMS terminology, the MGC is called MGCF (Media Gateway Control Function), and the MG is called IM-MGW (Internet Multimedia Gateway).

In addition to these functions, the IMS introduces a new SIP proxy function, the BGCF (Border Gateway Control Function), which is used in PSTN/PLMN breakout scenarios (call from IMS to PSTN). The reader may remember from our discussion in Chapter 18 that in these scenarios, there was a need to determine which gateway to use for the breakout. The BGCF is a SIP proxy responsible for selecting the gateway to be used for the breakout.

The IMS does not further specify how the BGCF obtains the information on which to base the decision to route to a particular gateway (it might be static configuration, based on a routing protocol, and so on).

If the breakout is not to occur in the operator's own IMS network, the BGCF may also select on which other IMS network the breakout is to happen, and route the call to a BGCF in the other network.

The architecture for PSTN interworking is shown in Figure 24.17.

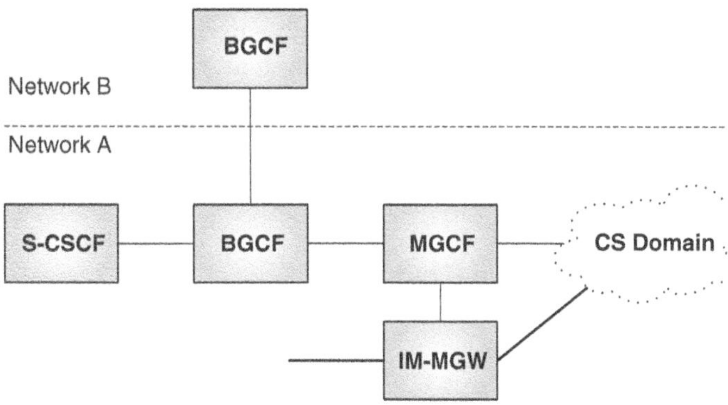

FIGURE 24.17

24.3.6 The Border Function

An operator's IMS network can also interwork with other operators' IMS networks or with other SIP-based multimedia networks. Border control functions may be applied in these cases, based on operator preference.

The border control functions are split, in the IMS architecture, into control plane and media plane. The control plane component is called Interconnect Border Control Function (IBCF), and the media component is called Transition Gateway (TrGW).

Some of the IBCF's functions are:

- IPv4/IPv6 address translation (i.e., it contains an Application Level Gateway, ALG)
- network topology hiding

- SIP signaling screening based on source/destination and operators' policy
- invoking an interworking function between different SIP profiles

As the reader can note, these functions are the ones that correspond to an I-SBC that we saw in Chapter 22. IBCF is the name that the IMS standards give to these functions, whereas I-SBC is a term coined by the industry to provide similar functions in SIP networks.

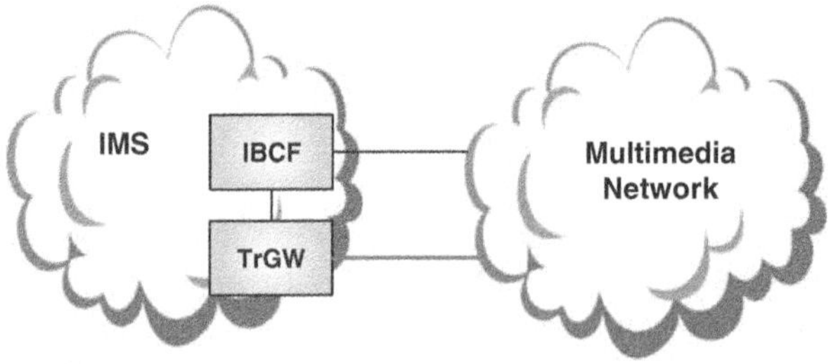

FIGURE 24.18

24.3.7 The IMS Architecture

With all we learned in the previous sections, we are now in a position to draw the architecture of the Internet Multimedia Core Network Subsystem and to understand its rationale. We have included the name that 3GPP gives to the interfaces between the functional elements. All the depicted interfaces are based on SIP, except for:

- Mn and Mp: based on MEGACO
- Cx and Sh: based on Diameter

The reference IMS architecture is shown in Figure 24.19.

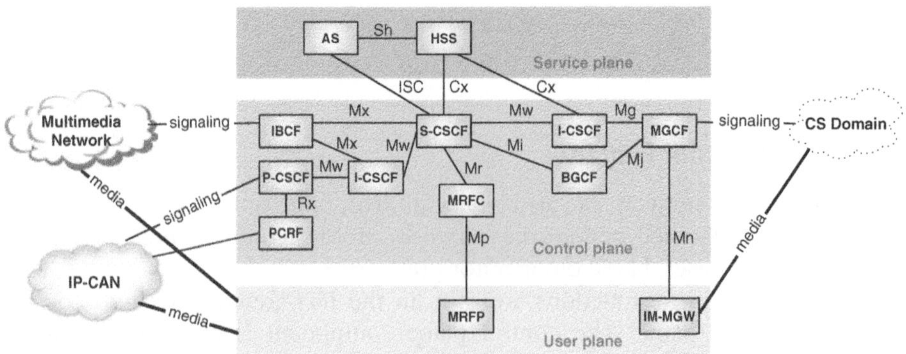

FIGURE 24.19

Next we present some representative IMS call flows that illustrate the IMS functions discussed so far.

24.3.8 Call Flows: Nonroaming Case

Registration

The call flow in Figure 24.20 shows John registering in his home network (network A).

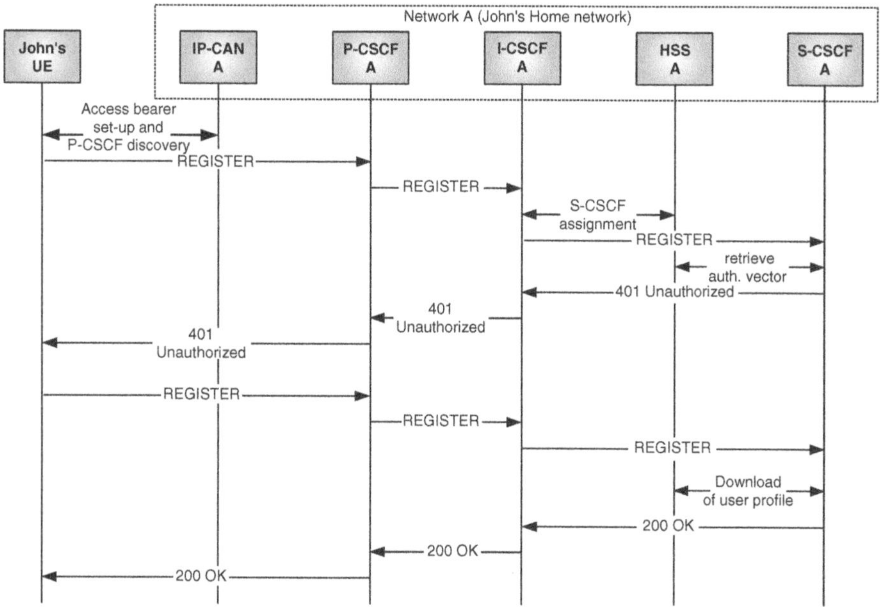

FIGURE 24.20

Call Setup

The call flow in Figure 24.21 shows John setting up a session with Alice. John's home network is network A. Alice's home network is network B.

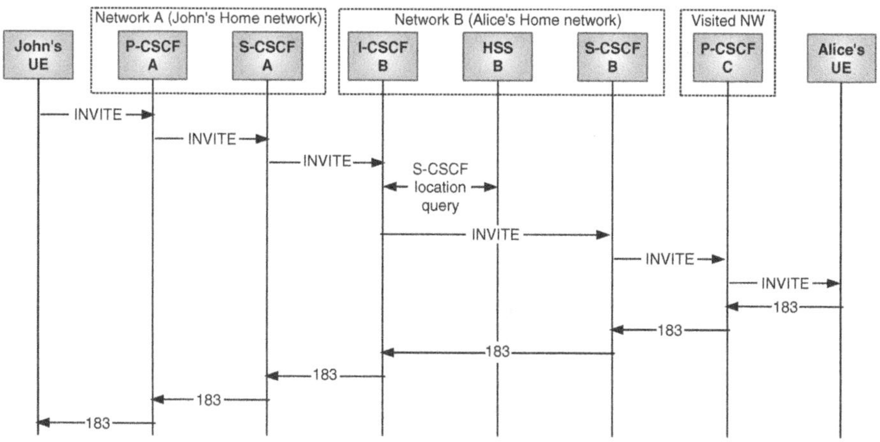

FIGURE 24.21

24.3.9 Call Flows: Roaming Case

In the following call flows, we consider Alice to be roaming in network C. We have considered a roaming approach such that Alice gains IP connectivity from network C, and her first point of contact in the IMS network is the P-CSCF in network C.

Registration

Figure 24.22 shows Alice registering in her home network (network B) while she is roaming in network C.

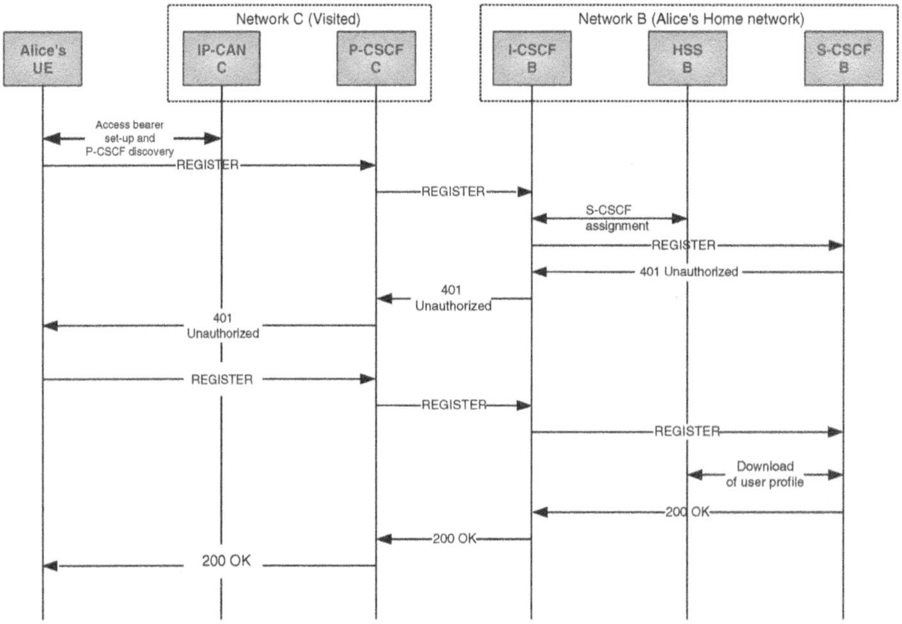

FIGURE 24.22

Call Setup

Figure 24.23 shows a call from John to Alice while Alice is roaming in network C.

A detailed explanation of various other IMS call flows can be found in [3GPP TS 24.228].[5]

24.4 IMS Concepts

In the previous section, we have seen that the IMS architecture implies certain additional functions on top of the architecture of a basic SIP network. Next we will describe in more detail some fundamental IMS concepts, and highlight what differences they represent as compared with a basic SIP network.

[5]For your information: [TS 24.228] is not continued after Release 5.

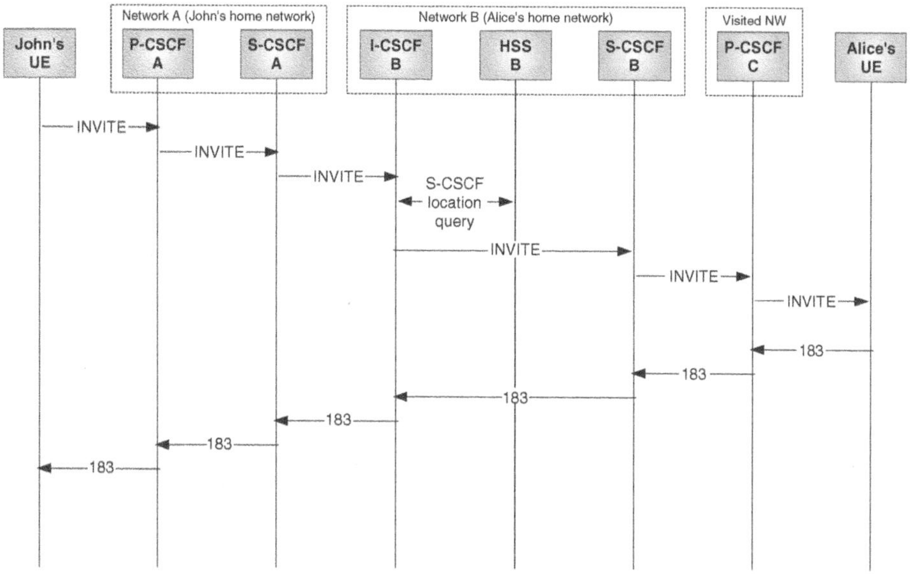

FIGURE 24.23

24.4.1 IMS Identities

In a basic SIP network, the end user is typically assigned a public identity and some security credentials. The public identity typically has the form of a SIP URI such as john@ocean.com. When John registers to his SIP server, he uses his public identity, which then is authenticated by the server. The public identity is also employed by other users in order to request communication with John.

In IMS, the end user is assigned two identities instead of just one. The first one is called the Private User Identity (IMPI), and represents the identity that is authenticated by the network. The second one is called Public User Identity (IMPU, sometimes also referred to as PUI), and is the one employed by other users to request communication with John.

In addition to public and private user identities, the IMS also defines support for GRUUs (Globally Routable User URIs). GRUUs were analyzed in Chapter 15.

Private User Identity

The Private User Identity is a unique global identity defined by the home network operator, which may be used within the home network to identify the user's subscription from a network perspective. It is valid for the complete duration of the user's subscription with the home network.

It is used mainly for authentication purposes during the registration phase. It can also be used for administration and charging purposes. It is not used for routing purposes.

The user does not have access to the Private User Identity. It is stored in the HSS and in the ISIM (IMS Subscriber Identity Module) application [3GPP TS 31.103].

The ISIM application resides on the UICC (Universal Integrated Circuit Card), which is a tamper-resistant device that can be inserted or removed from the User Equipment [3GPP TS 31.101].

The Private User Identity takes the form of an NAI, network access identifier [RFC 4282]. An example of Private User Identity is:

subscription1234@ocean.com

Public User Identity

In order to use the IMS, a user is assigned one or more Public User Identities. The Public User Identity is used by any user for requesting communications to other users. For example, it might be included on a business card.

The Public User Identity must be registered in the network before the user can start using the IMS.

The Public User Identity takes the form of a SIP URI or a TEL URI. It is stored in the HSS and on the ISIM.

Two examples of Public User Identity are:

sip:john@ocean.com and tel:+34610894471@ocean.com

24.4.2 IMS Security

IMS security encompasses two aspects:

- Access Security, described in [3GPP TS 33.203]
- Network Domain Security, described in [3GPP TS 33.210]

Access Security

This term refers to the provision of security services such as authentication, integrity, and confidentiality for the SIP signaling path between the user and the IMS network.

Mutual authentication between the user and the network is based on the UMTS Authentication and Key Agreement (AKA) protocol. As we saw in Chapter 14, SIP uses the HTTP Digest mechanism for authentication. Therefore, there is a need to map the AKA parameters onto HTTP Digest authentication. Such a mapping is described in [RFC 3310].

The AKA protocol works as follows:

- The ISIM and the network share a long-term secret (K).
- The network produces an authentication vector based on K and a sequence number SQN. The authentication vector contains:
  - A random challenge (RAND)
  - An authentication token (AUTN)
  - The expected authentication response (XRES)
  - Two session keys: an integrity key (IK) and a cipher key (CK)

- The authentication vector is downloaded from the HSS to the S-CSCF when the first REGISTER is received by the S-CSCF.
- The S-CSCF creates an authentication request containing RAND, AUTN, IK, and CK, and sends it to the user in the 401 (Unauthorized) response.
- The user verifies with the ISIM that the AUTN is correct. If the AUTN is correct, the network has been authenticated. The user then produces an authentication response using K and RAND, and sends the result (RES) to the S-CSCF in a second REGISTER message.
- The S-CSCF compares RES with XRES. If they match, authentication is successful.

As a by-product of the authentication process, two session keys have also been obtained (IK and CK). The UE and the P-CSCF use these session keys to secure the communication in the access by establishing two pairs of IPsec ESP security associations[6] through which the traffic is sent encrypted and integrity protected. Once the SAs are established, the P-CSCF will identify all the SIP requests coming through the corresponding SA as pertaining to the authenticated user.

Figure 24.24 depicts the whole process of authentication and SAs establishment. For brevity, the S-CSCF assignment process is not shown in the diagram.

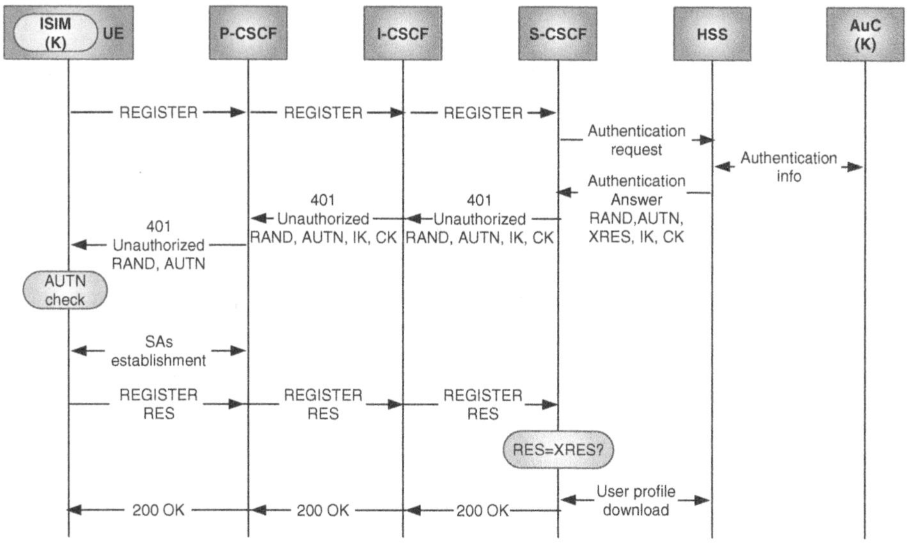

FIGURE 24.24

[6] The four security associations are:

sa1: for sending requests from UE to P-CSCF
sa2: for sending responses from P-CSCF to UE
sa3: for sending requests from P-CSCF to UE
sa4: for sending responses from UE to P-CSCF

Network Domain Security (NDS)

NDS refers to the provision of authentication, confidentiality, integrity, and replay protection between different IMS networks (security domains) or between nodes within the same security domain.

In order to achieve NDS, security gateways (SEG) are deployed in the interconnecting networks. Each SEG is responsible for setting up and maintaining security associations with its peer SEGs. The SAs are negotiated using the Internet Key Exchange (IKE) protocol defined in [RFC 4306]. The authentication is based on preshared secrets.

24.4.3 Identity Management

IMS uses the identity management procedures based on the P-Asserted-Identity that were described in Chapter 20 [RFC 3325]. The IMS home network is considered a trust domain.

Privacy mechanisms applicable in IMS are defined in [RFC 3323] and [RFC 3325], and were discussed in Chapter 20.

24.4.4 The IM Call Model

One of the most interesting concepts that IMS introduces as compared with a plain SIP network is that of the IM call model and service control function. The IM call model is described in [3GPP TS 23.218].

In IETF SIP, there is no standardized mechanism for service invocation. Following the IETF approach, a user might get access to multimedia services in different ways. For instance, the user might force his or her requests to traverse a particular Application Server (by introducing the AS URI in the Route header of outgoing requests), or they might rely on some proxy to do that function for them. But these mechanisms are not standardized.

Defining such mechanisms is critical in order to be able to provide users with a consistent service proposition that may be composed of different applications executing for the same call on behalf of the originating or the terminating user.

Moreover, standardizing those mechanisms is also crucial so that the IMS users can leverage applications deployed in the home operator, in the visited operator, or in a third party. The standardization of those mechanisms and of the interface between the S-CSCF and the Application Servers (ISC) is seen as a key element for the success of IMS. The IMS without services on top has very little value (if any), and operators cannot expect to themselves develop all the possible services that users may demand in the future. Telecom operators and Internet players may need to partner at some time, and the service control interface, or a higher-level interface (e.g., web services) may be the key for the integration.

Figure 24.25 shows an operator's IMS network through which users can access Application Servers owned by the IMS network operator, or external Application Servers not owned by the IMS operator (i.e., from another operator or a third party).

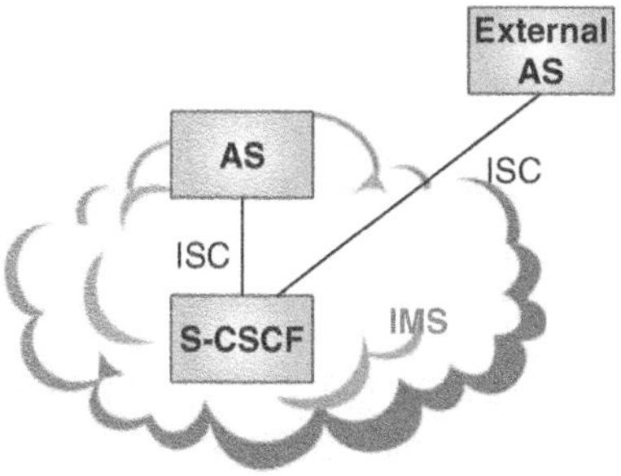

FIGURE 24.25

The IMS standards divide the call execution flow into two parts: originating and terminating. Associated with each part is a service control entity:

- The service control in the originating part is done by the home S-CSCF of the originator of the request.
- The service control in the terminating part is done by the home S-CSCF of the recipient of the request.

Therefore, the originating S-CSCF can invoke services on behalf of the requestor, and the terminating S-CSCF can invoke services on behalf of the recipient. This is depicted in Figure 24.26.

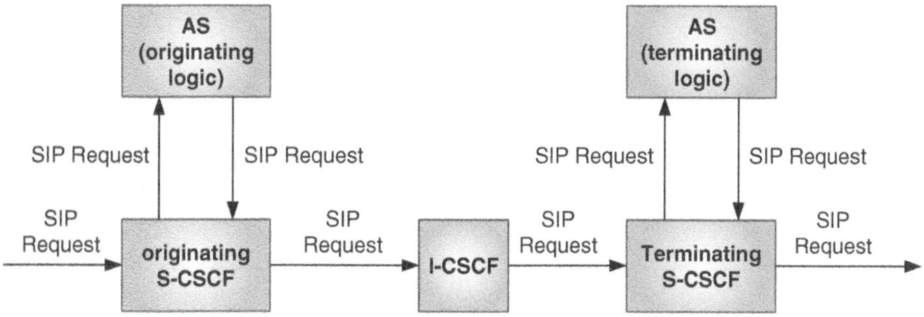

FIGURE 24.26

The services to invoke in both the originating and terminating side are defined by subscriber data stored in the HSS. This data is downloaded at registration.

Such data consists of a list of so-called Initial Filter Criteria (iFC). An iFC defines a set of conditions that, when met, will force the S-CSCF to delegate the control to an AS whose URI is also part of the iFC. The conditions can be based on whatever combination of values of SIP methods, SIP headers, SDPs, and so forth are present in the incoming request.

If more than one iFC is provisioned, this means that more than one AS may need to be involved in the processing of the request. Therefore, the subscription data also needs to specify in what order the Application Servers need to be invoked.

Next is an example of how service control works in an originating scenario. John is subscribed to four services, offered in respective Application Servers. John's user profile in the HSS contains four iFCs, one for each service. His profile also contains the iFCs' priority. The iFC with the highest priority is iFC1, whereas iFC4 has the least priority:

iFC1 > iFC2 > iFC3 > iFC4

When a new originating request reaches the S-CSCF, the S-CSCF will check John's service profile, and will determine if some of the iFCs are met. Imagine that iFC1, associated with AS1, is met. Then the S-CSCF forces the routing to AS1 and back to the S-CSCF.[7] Once the request is back to the S-CSCF, the S-CSCF will continue evaluating the remaining iFCs of lower priority for the new request that comes from the AS. So the S-CSCF will check if iFC2 is met, then iFC3, and then iFC4. Let us assume that in this particular case, iFC2 and iFC3 are not met, but iFC4 is. In that case, the S-CSCF will contact AS4. When the request comes back from AS4, the S-CSCF will know that there are no more iFCs to evaluate, and thus it will forward the request to the next network element. This is shown in Figure 24.27.

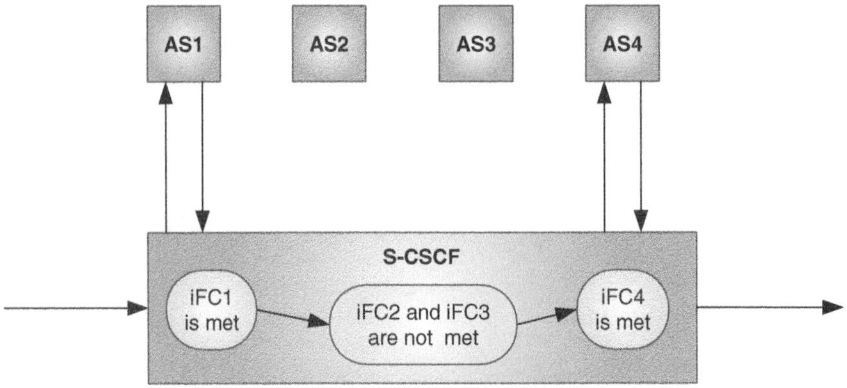

FIGURE 24.27

24.4.5 Charging

The charging architecture, charging principles, and charging data for IM CN subsystem are described in [3GPP TS 32.240] and [3GPP TS 32.260].

The IMS supports offline charging, online charging, and charging correlation. Charging correlation is briefly explained in the next section.

Offline Charging

Offline charging is a mechanism where charging information does not affect, in real-time, the service rendered.

[7]The GGSN (GPRS Gateway Support Node) is the network element within the UMTS Packet Switched (PS) domain that acts as a gateway between the wireless network and other networks such Internet or private networks.

All the IMS elements (P/I/S-CSCF, BGCF, MGCF, MRFC, SIP AS) can generate offline charging information. The charging information is sent via Diameter protocol to a Charging Collection Function (Rf interface). The CCF processes the received information, and generates billing records that are sent via FTP to the billing system (Bi interface). This is depicted in Figure 24.28.

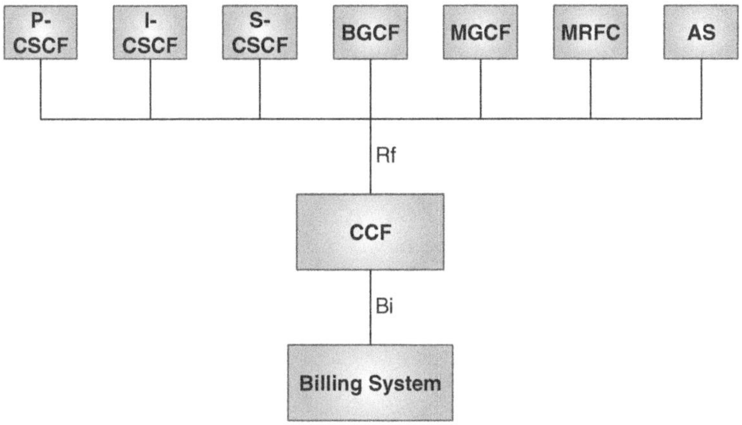

FIGURE 24.28

Online Charging

Online charging is a mechanism whereby charging information can affect, in realtime, the service rendered. Therefore, a direct interaction of the charging mechanism with the control of the network resource usage is required.

The S-CSCF, AS, and MRFC support a Diameter-based charging interface (Ro) toward an Online Charging Function (OCF). This is shown in Figure 24.29. The OCF is a functional element capable of charging in realtime. It performs mainly three functions:

- Charging control
- Account balance management
- Rating

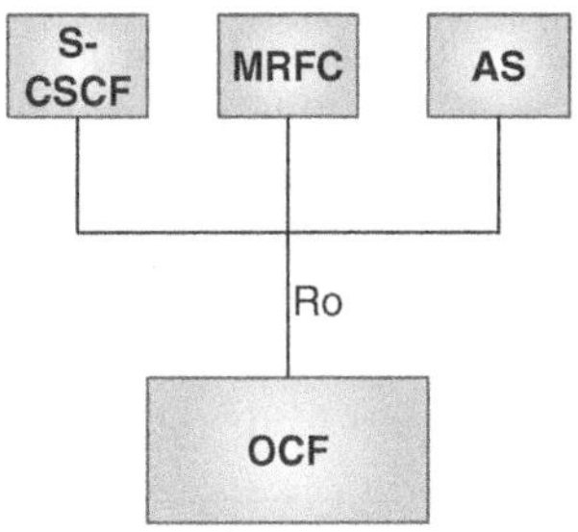

FIGURE 24.29

The OCF itself is not part of the IMS CN architecture. It is a horizontal function—that is, it can be used in other, non-IMS-related scenarios as well. The OCF is defined in [3GPP TS 32.296].

24.4.6 Policy and Charging Control

The IMS defines architecture for policy control that is similar to the one that we examined in Chapter 21. The main difference comes from the fact that, since R7, the architecture for policy control and charging control has converged into just one architecture. Therefore, there is no longer a PDF or a CRF—both are merged into a PCRF (Policy and Charging Rules Function).

Likewise, there is no longer a PEP (Policy Enforcement Point) or a TPF Transport Plane Function)—both are merged into the PCEF (Policy and Charging Enforcement Function).

Moreover, COPS is no longer used. The new Gx and Rx interfaces are used; they are based on Diameter.

This is depicted in Figure 24.30.

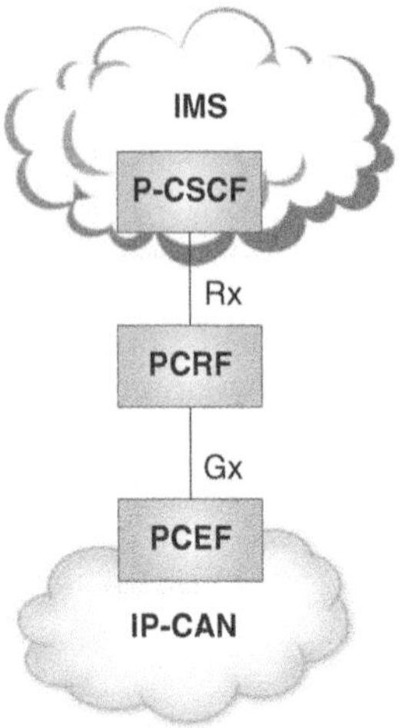

FIGURE 24.30

In addition to policy control and charging control, this architecture also supports charging correlation. Charging correlation consists of exchanging, through the PCRF, the charging identifiers generated at both IMS and IP-CAN levels so that the charging records generated at both levels can be correlated for billing purposes.

Charging control has not been explained in this book so far. It refers to a function that is targeted mainly at controlling the way in which IP flow-based charging on the traffic plane is realized. For that purpose, the PCRF is capable of installing rules in the traffic plane gateway, e.g., in the GPRS Gateway Support Node (GGSN).[8]

[8]In order to force the routing to the AS and back, the S-CSCF introduces the AS URI and its own URI into the Route header. The first value will be consumed for the routing between S-CSCF and AS, whereas the second one will be consumed in the way back from AS to S-CSCF.

An in-depth analysis of policy and charging control is out of the scope of this book. Interested readers are referred to [3GPP TS 29.214] and [3GPP TS 29.212].

24.5 New Requirements on SIP

In this section, and in order to make the book coverage on SIP as complete as possible, we will explain some new SIP extensions that are introduced due to IMS requirements.

24.5.1 Service Route Discovery During Registration

We saw earlier in this chapter that outgoing requests from a UE need to traverse the originating user's S-CSCF so that the S-CSCF can apply services on the user's behalf. We also learned that S-CSCFs are assigned to the users dynamically at registration.

Therefore, there is an issue that we have not yet tackled: How does the UE know which S-CSCF to use for originating requests, and how to get there? The UE has mechanisms (e.g., DHCP/DNS) to determine what P-CSCF to use for sending originating requests, but what about the S-CSCF?

This issue is resolved by a new SIP extension defined in [RFC 3608]. This extension defines the new Service-Route header field, which is generated by the registrar (i.e., the S-CSCF in the IMS case) and is included in successful responses to the REGISTER message. The Service-Route header conveys the name of the home service proxy (i.e., the S-CSCF) where the UA must direct its requests.

Once the UA has received the response (i.e., the 200 OK) to the REGISTER, it will include both the P-CSCF name and the S-CSCF name in the Route header of all outgoing requests.

This is shown in Figure 24.31.

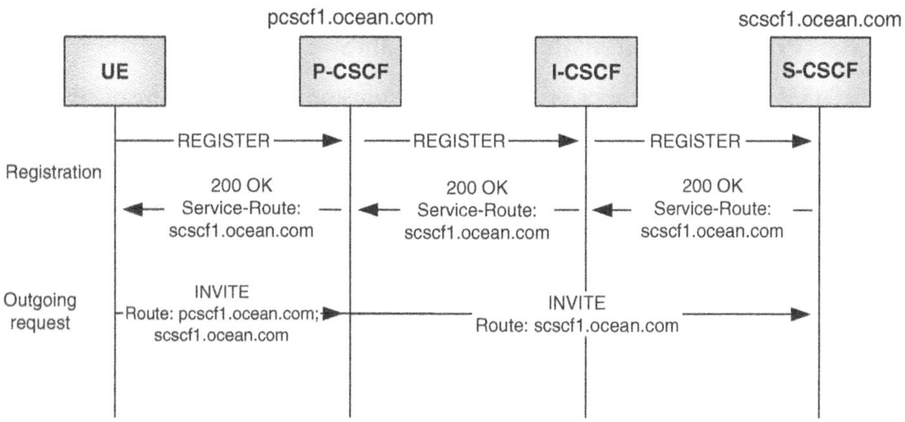

FIGURE 24.31

24.5.2 Discovering Adjacent Contacts

During our discussion of the IMS architecture, we said that the P-CSCF had to be involved in all originating and terminating requests. Because they are the elements that terminate the security associations toward the UE, it is critical that all traffic from and to the UE goes through them.

The originating scenario presents no difficulties—that is, we already saw that the UE can learn the address of the P-CSCF, and therefore force the routing of all outgoing requests through it.

In the terminating case, the terminating S-CSCF needs to know the name/ address of the recipient's P-CSCF so as to force the routing through it. The question now is: How can the S-CSCF know that information?

The answer to this issue comes again from a new SIP extension defined in [RFC 3327]. This extension defines the new Path header field, which the originating P-CSCF adds to the REGISTER message when the user registers. Therefore, as soon as the user is registered, the registrar (i.e., the S-CSCF) has the information as to the correct P-CSCF to which terminating requests to that user should be addressed.

This is shown in Figure 24.32.

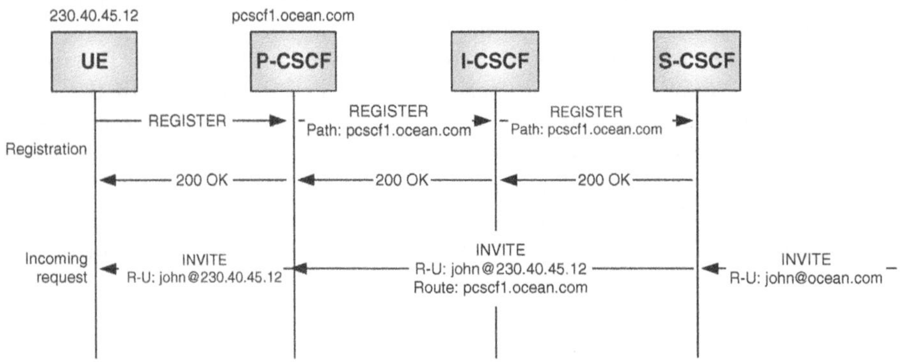

FIGURE 24.32

24.5.3 Private SIP Extensions for 3GPP IMS

[RFC 3455] defines a number of private SIP extensions to cope with specific IMS requirements. Next we briefly describe those extensions.

P-Visited-Network-ID Header

When a user roaming in a visited network attempts to register, there is a need to convey the information about the visited network to the home S-CSCF so that it can check if there exists a roaming agreement with the visited network. In order to convey this information, a new private header has been defined that contains a text string that identifies the visited network. The P-CSCF in the visited network adds this header into the REGISTER message that is sent to the home S-CSCF Example:.

P-Visited-Network-ID="Vodafone Italy"

P-Access-Network-Info Header

There are cases, especially when a wireless-access network is used, when the services to apply may depend on the technology of the access network or the location of the user (e.g., the cell from which a call or other IMS service originates). The new private P-Access-Network-Info header is capable of conveying that information from the UE to the IMS network. This header is populated by the UE based on the information it gets from other sources (for example, radio signaling).

P-Charging-Function-Address Header

The IMS architecture is distributed. Many functional elements are able to generate charging information. This charging information needs to be sent to either a Charging Collection Function (CCF), in the case of offline charging, or to an OCF (Online Charging Function), in the case of online charging. The addresses of these entities are conveyed via SIP signaling in the P-Charging-Function-Address header.

The CCF and OCF addresses are stored in the HSS, and are conveyed to the S-CSCF via the Cx interface. The charging function addresses are passed from the S-CSCF to the rest of the IMS entities in the home network so that they can know where to send the charging information.

P-Charging-Vector Header

The P-Charging-Vector header includes charging information that facilitates the task of the offline and online charging systems.

It includes three parameters:

- IMS Correlation ID (ICID)
- Access Network Charging Information
- Inter Operator Identifier (IOI)

IMS Correlation ID

The IMS is a distributed system. Many functional elements (e.g., P-CSCF, S-CSCF, AS, and so on) may be involved in processing a particular call or other IMS service. These elements may generate accounting information for the online and offline charging systems. The task of the charging systems would be much easier if they could easily identify different accounting information from different elements as pertaining to the same call. The IMS network facilitates this by providing a correlation ID.

The first IMS entity that is involved in a call will generate a globally unique ICID. It then passes the ICID in the SIP signaling, as part of the P-Charging-Vector header, to the rest of IMS entities in the IMS domain.

Access Network Charging Information

This parameter is provided by the access network via Gx and Rx to the P-CSCF, which includes it in the P-Charging-Vector header. It helps correlate charging information generated at IMS level, and the corresponding one generated at access network level (e.g., GPRS).

Inter Operator Identifier

It is a globally unique identifier that is shared, via SIP signaling, between sending and receiving networks. It is used to facilitate charging consolidation tasks for interconnection traffic.

P-Associated-URI

We saw in previous sections that an IMS user may be associated with more than one Public User Identity. When the user sends a REGISTER message to the network in order to register a particular Public User Identity, the S-CSCF responds with a 200 OK that includes the P-Associated-URI header that lists all the associated Public User Identities.

The presence of a URI in the P-Associated-ID does not mean that such a URI is registered, only that it is associated with the Public User Identity that has been registered.

P-Called-Party-ID

An IMS user may have various service profiles, each of them with its set of Public User Identities. For instance, John might have a personal profile with the URI: sip:johnny@ocean.com, and a business profile with the URI: sip:john.smith@ocean.com. The different profiles might have different services associated.

When John receives an incoming call or request, he might want to know if the caller is calling to his personal or business identity. For instance, he might want to apply a different ringing tone in each case, or perhaps his willingness to accept the call depends on what case it is. Unfortunately, there is no way to do this with plain SIP. Let us recall that when the call reaches the S-CSCF, the Request-URI does contain the original target identity, but the S-CSCF, after querying the location service, replaces it with the recipient's contact address, so the recipient does not have access to the identity the call was addressed to.

In order to overcome this problem, a new SIP header, the P-Called-Party-ID, is introduced by the S-CSCF in the requests toward the called party. The P-Called-Party-ID has the same value as the Request-URI of the terminating request received by the S-CSCF.

24.6 IMS Services

IMS being essentially a SIP-based multimedia network, most of the SIP services that we saw in previous chapters can be, in principle, offered over an IMS infrastructure. Furthermore, the combination of multimedia and wireless mobility creates new, compelling service scenarios. In many cases, and true to the end-to-end nature of SIP, IMS applications are located in the endpoints. That is the case of gaming applications, for instance. In other cases, the applications sit on Application Servers on top of the IMS network. An advanced IP telephony application such as "Follow-me" might belong to this category. Hybrid situations are also common.

The aim of 3GPP is not to standardize all the applications, but rather, to provide service capabilities. Nevertheless, there are some important applications that have been specified both by 3GPP and/or OMA, given the need to ensure interoperability and interworking across different operators' networks. Examples are:

- The presence service
- IMS messaging
- The Push to Talk over cellular (PoC) service
- The multimedia telephony services
- Combinational services
- Global Text Telephony (GTT)

24.6.1 The Presence Service

[3GPP TS 22.141], [3GPP TS 23.141], and [3GPP TS 24.141] define the IMS presence service that is based on the IETF SIP/SIMPLE. 3GPP defines a full-fledged, functional architecture for presence that is mapped to the IMS functional entities.

Figure 24.33 shows the elements and interfaces in the presence service architecture defined by 3GPP, whose explanation is outside of the scope of this book.

24.6.2 IMS Messaging

The requirements for IMS messaging are defined in [3GPP TS 22.340], and the technical realization is described in [3GPP TS 24.247].

IMS supports two types of online messaging services, which are referred to as:

- Immediate messaging
- Session-based messaging

In immediate messaging, the user can both send and receive messages without any prior actions. In session-based messaging, the user joins a messaging session before the message exchange can take place.

Immediate messaging is supported using just the SIP MESSAGE method (see Chapter 16), whereas session-based messaging is supported using SIP to establish the session, and MSRP for the messaging transfer in the media plane (see Chapters 10 and 16).

24.6.3 The PoC Service

Push to Talk over Cellular (PoC) service is a two-way form of communications that allows users to engage in immediate communication with one or more other users. The user experience for the PoC service is similar to a "walkie-talkie" application. When a user wants to initiate a talk session with an individual user or with a group of participants, he or she needs to press a button and then talk.

The implementation for this service is based on SIP Application Servers (and Media Resource Functions) sitting on the IMS network.

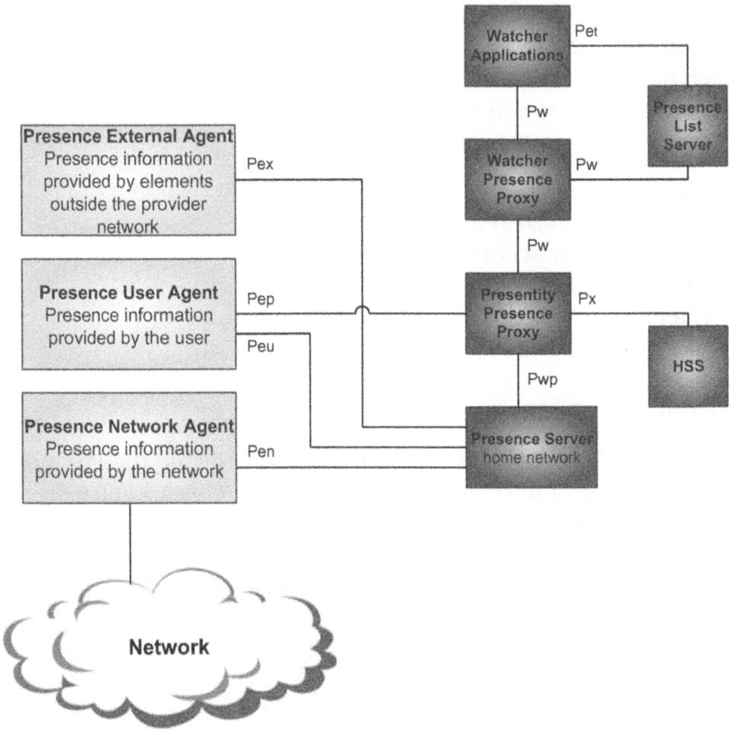

FIGURE 24.33

[OMA-AD-PoC] defines the architecture of the PoC service on top of a SIP/IP infrastructure. Such an infrastructure can be based on 3GPP IMS, as described in [3GPP TR 23.979].

24.6.4 The IMS Multimedia Telephony Service

The IMS Multimedia Telephony Service ([3GPP TS 22.173] and [3GPP TS 24.173]) allows multimedia conversational communications between two or more users, including different types of media such as speech, video, or other types of data. Associated with this service are a number of supplementary services, similar—but not identical—to the ones existing in 2G mobile networks and in ISDN.

The IMS multimedia telephony supplementary services are:

- Originating Identification Presentation (OIP)
- Originating Identification Restriction (OIR)
- Terminating Identification Presentation (TIP)
- Terminating Identification Restriction (TIR)
- Communication Diversion (CDIV)
- Communication Hold (HOLD)
- Communication Barring (CB)
- Message Waiting Indication (MWI)

- Conference (CONF)
- Explicit Communication Transfer (ECT)

The specification for these services is based on the TISPAN specification for PSTN simulation services [ETSI TS 181 002].[9]

The implementation for this service is based on SIP Application Servers (and media servers) sitting on the IMS network.

24.6.5 Combinational Services

It will yet take some time for mobile operators to replace the existing cellular circuit-switched voice service with cellular VoIP for the whole customer base. The reasons are technical (need for resource optimization, quality of service, and handset support) and commercial (huge investment in circuit-switching technology already done, need to make new investments on packet-switching infrastructure). However, in the meantime, the IMS network can be used to enable other services (ones that are not so bandwidth demanding) for wireless users. The possibility then arises to combine the cellular circuit-switched voice with other new fancy services such as picture sharing, video sharing, enriched alert, and so forth. The voice part would be carried by the Circuit-Switched domain, and the data part would be handled by the Packet-Switched domain and the IMS network. The voice part of the call and the data part of the call would be tied together into a single communication context at the terminal. Such types of services are referred to as Combinational Services [3GPP TS 22.279], [3GPP TS 23.279], and [3GPP TS 24.279].

Figure 24.34 depicts this idea.

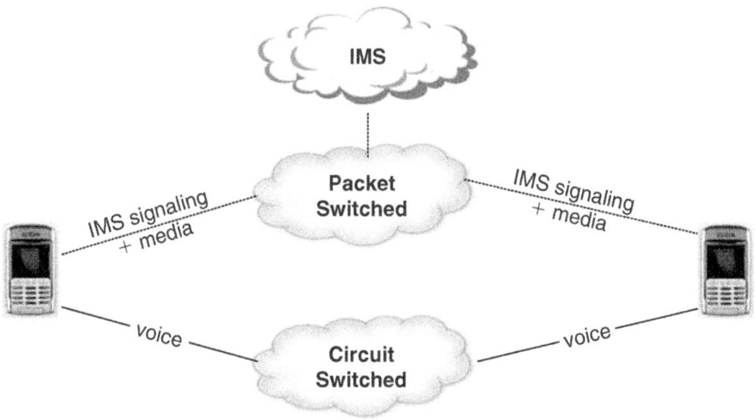

FIGURE 24.34

[9] TISPAN PSTN Simulation services provide PSTN-like service capabilities using session control over IP interfaces and infrastructure. This is not to be confused with TISPAN PSTN Emulation services, which provide PSTN services capabilities and interfaces using adaptation to an IP infrastructure.

Combinational services do not necessarily require network-based service logic. It is just the endpoints that need to have the proper service logic in order to generate the context that allows us to correlate the CS and IMS sides of the communication.

On the other hand, the terminal and the access network must facilitate simultaneous circuit-switched and packet-switched access. Hence, the access network must be UMTS (allows for simultaneous CS and PS access) or support Dual-Transfer Mode (DTM).

24.6.6 Global Text Telephony

The requirements for GTT are defined in [3GPP TS 22.226]. A possible utilization of the IMS architecture to deliver GTT services is described in [3GPP TS 23.226]. [3GPP TS 23.226] also defines other non-IMS-based architectures that can be used to deliver this service.

Global Text Telephony is a feature that adds the capability to use a real-time, character-by-character, text-conversation component in a session.

GTT in IMS is supported using SIP for the session management. Text is encoded according to [ITU T.140], and transported over RTP using the RTP text payload as specified in [RFC 4103]. This allows conversation in a selection of simultaneous media, such as text, video, and voice.

We have just seen some of the standardized IMS services. Nevertheless, the strength of SIP and IMS is that they offer the capability to create new communication services limited only by our imagination.

24.7 ETSI TISPAN NGN

TISPAN (Telecoms and Internet converged Services and Protocols for Advanced Networks) is a standardization body within ETSI (European Telecommunications Standards Institute) that specializes in fixed networks and Internet convergence.

TISPAN's aim is to define the architecture and provide technical specifications for a Next Generation Network (NGN).[10] TISPAN Release 1 was published in December 2005. The main focus of Release 1 was to define the reference architecture [ETSI ES 282 001] for the NGN, and to demonstrate its feasibility by specifying the details for two main objectives:

- To enable delivery of the services supported in a 3GPP IMS to broadband fixed lines.
- To enable PSTN/ISDN replacement (in whole or in part).

Interestingly enough, TISPAN has chosen the 3GPP IMS architecture (thus, a SIP-based network) to provide some core subsystems within the architecture. TISPAN and 3GPP have worked collaboratively in IMS R7 in order to specify wire-line

[10] The NGN concept is defined in [ITU Y.2001] and [ITU Y.2011], and refers to a packet-based network able to provide key capabilities to support a wide range of multimedia services.

access for an IMS network (let us recall that up to R6, 3GPP was focused mainly in wireless access).

So, 3GPP chose SIP as the basis for a wireless multimedia network (IMS), and now TISPAN chooses to adapt the IMS infrastructure (i.e., SIP based) for the evolved fixed network. Thus, both 3GPP and TISPAN are setting the grounds for a truly access-independent next-generation multimedia network that is based on SIP! Figure 24.35 shows the TISPAN reference architecture.

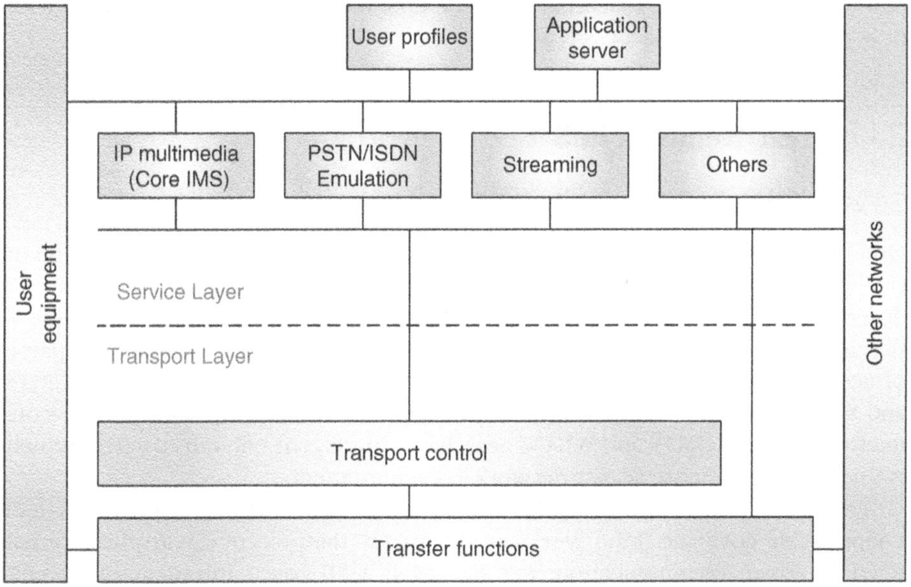

FIGURE 24.35

It comprises two layers:

- the transport layer
- the service layer

The transport layer provides the IP connectivity functions both in access and core, and the control functions associated with the transport (IP address assignment, resource and admission control, and so on). [ETSI ES 282 004] and [ETSI ES 282 003] describe the functional architecture for the transport-layer control functions.

The service layer is split into a set of subsystems, each of them specialized in a particular service area, plus a set of common components.

The subsystems are:

1. The core IP multimedia subsystem, targeted at providing multimedia services to TISPAN users [ETSI ES 282 007].
2. The PSTN/Emulation subsystem, aimed at providing PSTN features to legacy terminals over a SIP-based network, [ETSI TS 182 012] and [ETSI TS 183 043].

3. Streaming subsystem, to provide RTSP-based streaming services.
4. Other subsystems.

The common components are:

- User profile, where the user subscription information is stored (equivalent to the IMS HSS concept).
- Application Servers, where applications reside.

Subsystems 1 and 2 are based on the 3GPP IMS, but slightly adapted to cope with new requirements and access types.

24.8 Next Trends in IMS

24.8.1 Voice Call Continuity (VCC)

One of the key drivers for IMS deployment is to deliver fixed-mobile convergent (FMC) propositions. FMC is an overused term that different people use to refer to different concepts. Here, we will use the term to refer to terminal convergence—that is, to a service such that the end user can have one unique terminal, capable of accessing its services throughout a variety of access networks, mainly UMTS and WLAN. So, an FMC-enabled handset is a wireless handset that can have connectivity to both UMTS and WLAN, and that is intelligent enough to select which is the most appropriate access network at each moment.

For instance, consider that John is a customer of a UMTS operator that offers countrywide coverage. John works at a company that, to cope with the internal need for voice communication, has deployed a SIP-based infrastructure accessible via WLAN. So, ideally, John would like to use his company's infrastructure when at the office (it is "free"), and use the UMTS coverage when he is out of the office. An FMC application would enable this scenario for John. An FMC service consists basically of two parts:

- Some service logic in the terminal to decide in what network to perform the registration.
- Some service logic in the network to route terminating calls to John in the right domain (WLAN or UMTS).

A basic FMC proposition does not offer handover between the domains—that is, if John starts a conversation at his office and moves outside of it, the call would eventually drop (as WLAN coverage diminishes). Then its terminal would register to UMTS, and the call would need to be manually established again.

3GPP is designing a way to implement handover, the so-called Voice Call Continuity (VCC), in IMS-based FMC scenarios.

Support for VCC requires three main aspects:

- Support in the terminals.
- An application in the CS UMTS network capable of routing all CS-originated and terminated calls toward IMS.

- A network-based SIP Application Server that implements a 3PCC service (third party call control).

Interested readers can look at [3GPP TS 23.206] and [3GPP TS 24.206], where the solution is described in detail.

24.8.2 IMS Centralized Services

IMS centralized services (ICS), [3GPP TR 22.892], is a brand-new topic currently under investigation in 3GPP. ICS takes the access independence concept of IMS even further by considering the UMTS Circuit-Switched domain as just another access network. What this means is that the IMS would then be used to deliver services also for "legacy" circuit-switched users. This concept is shown in Figure 24.36.

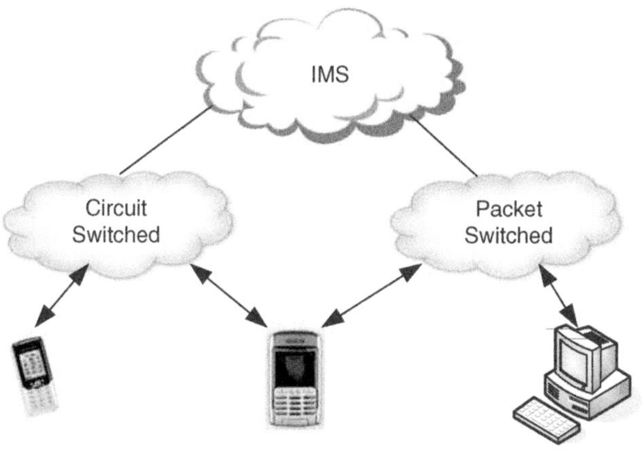

FIGURE 24.36

This idea is quite attractive to service providers, who could then base their service deployments on just one type of infrastructure (IMS). This would allow for a significant reduction in core network complexity, maintenance, and operation costs.

From the user's perspective, one of the key advantages of this approach is that they obtain a consistent user experience regardless of the domain (Circuit-Switched, Packet-Switched) they use.

24.9 Summary

In this chapter, we learned about the future of the telecommunication networks, both mobile and fixed. We saw that SIP plays a main role in this future. We are today at the brink of a new revolution. The convergence between Internet and the telecom domain is about to become a reality. Changes like this do not come often, and in the next 20 years, we will see advances of the sort nobody could dream of years ago. The way is being paved for the new era of total communications. For both enterprises and mainstream users to fully leverage the opportunities that these new technologies offer, it is key to be able to understand the new concepts and what new services they bring. We hope that, after going through this book, readers are better prepared for today's and tomorrow's challenges.

Source Code

All the source code for the practices and projects included in the book can be downloaded from the book's web site at http://books.elsevier.com/companions/9780123743008.

In order to run the code, readers need:

1. A computer with a soundcard and a webcam. The webcam is needed only if readers want to use video transmission/reception features in the soft-phone.
2. The Java Standard Platform (JSE), version 1.4 or later, installed in their computer. The Java platform can be freely downloaded at http://java.sun.com.
3. The JAIN SIP and JAIN SDP libraries. See Section A.1.
4. The JMF libraries. See Section A.2.
5. The code of the book's practices and projects. See Section A.3.

A.1 Obtaining the JAIN SIP and JAIN SDP Libraries

The NIST implementation of JAIN SIP and JAIN SDP can be obtained from https://jain-sip.dev.java.net. However, we also need other support libraries in order for JAIN SIP and JAIN SDP to work properly. So the best way to get all the needed libraries in just one shot is to download them from the SIP-communicator web page: http://sip-communicator.org. The sip-communicator project is an open-source initiative to build a fully featured and complex audio/video Internet phone and instant messenger. The sip-communicator project also uses JAIN SIP. After having understood the practices in this book, we encourage readers to take a look at the source code in the sip-communicator project. In order to download the JAIN SIP and SDP libraries, we have to download the whole project first, and then go to the lib folder and obtain the following jar files:

- JainSipApi1.2.jar and JainSipRi.1.2.jar (JAIN SIP libraries)
- nist-sdp-1.0.jar (JAIN SDP library)
- concurrent.jar, log4j-1.2.8.jar, jakarta-regexp-1.3.jar, and junit-3.8.1.jar (support libraries)

We will need to include these libraries in the classpath of our computer.

A.2 Obtaining the JMF Libraries

The JMF libraries can be downloaded at http://java.sun.com/products/java-media/jmf. The installation package installs the JMF libraries, some native libraries, and also the JMF Studio, an application that allows us to manage the JMF configuration and test the JMF implementation. Once installed, we can get the following jar files from the lib directory:

- jmf.jar
- customizer.jar
- mediaplayer.jar
- multiplayer.jar
- sound.jar

We will need to include these in the classpath.

A.3 The Book's Source Code

All throughout the book, the reader is guided to build six programming examples, several components, and four full-blown projects. These are:

- Practices
  - Example1: composing a SIP message (see Chapter 8)
  - Example2: stateless SIP messaging (see Chapter 8)
  - Example3: stateful SIP messaging (see Chapter 8)
  - Example4: creating SIP dialogs (see Chapter 8)
  - Example5: mid-dialog requests (see Chapter 8)
  - Example6: media transmission and reception (see Chapter 11)

- Projects
  - Softphone1 (see Chapter 12)
  - Softphone2 (see Chapter 13)
  - Sipproxy (see Chapter 13)
  - Softphone3 (see Chapter 16)

All the examples and practices (except for Example1, which is not truly a complete program) are composed of three Java classes. These are:

- *NameApp*: For instance, Example3App or Softphone1App. This is the class that contains the main() method, which we need to invoke in order to run the complete application.
- *NameGUI*: For instance, Example3GUI or Softphone1GUI. This is the class that contains the actual GUI.
- *NameListener*: This is the class that implements the SipListener interface and where the core application logic resides.

In addition to these, the soft-phone applications (1, 2, and 3) also use a number of other generic classes that were built throughout the book and that are grouped under the package called "splibraries." These classes are:

- SdpInfo (see Chapter 9)
- SdpManager (see Chapter 9)
- VoiceTool (see Chapter 11)
- VideoTool (see Chapter 11)
- TonesTool (see Chapter 11)
- Configuration (see Chapter 12)
- VideoFrame (see Chapter 11)

These need to be imported by the soft-phone applications. We need to include the splibraries in the classpath of our computer.

In addition to these homemade classes, the applications also need to import the external libraries for SIP, SDP, and JMF.

Acronyms

2G	Second-generation mobile system
3DES	Triple Data Encryption Standard
3G	Third-generation mobile system
3GPP	3rd Generation Partnership Project
3PCC	Third-Party Call Control
AAA	Authentication, Authorization, and Accounting
AAAA RR	IPv6 Address Resource Record
ABNF	Augmented Backus-Naur Form
ADSL	Asymmetric Digital Subscriber Line
AES	Advanced Encryption Standard
AH	Authentication Header
AIB	Authenticated Identity Body
AKA	Authentication and Key Agreement
AMR	Adaptative Multirate
AN	Access Network
AOR	Address of Record
API	Application Programming Interface
ARPA	Advanced Research Projects Agency
ARR	Address Resource Record
AS	Application Server
A-SBC	Access Session Border Controller
ASCII	American Standard Code for Information Interchange
ASR	Automatic Speech Recognition
ATM	Asynchronous Transfer Mode
AUTN	Authentication Token
AVP	Audio/Video Profile
B2BUA	Back-to-Back User Agent
BBN	(formerly Bolt Beranek and Newman)
BCP	Best Current Practice
BFCP	Binary Floor Control Protocol
BGCF	Breakout Gateway Control Function
BICC	Bearer Independent Call Control
B-ISDN	Broadband Integrated Services Digital Network
CA	Certificate Authority
CB	Communication Barring
CDIV	Communication Diversion
CDMA	Code Division Multiple Access
CK	Ciphering Key
CLIP	Calling Line Identification Presentation
CLIR	Calling Line Identification Restriction

CN	Core Network
CODEC	COder/DECoder
COPS	Common Open Policy Service
CPIM	Common Profile for Instant Messaging
CPP	Common Profile for Presence
CRLF	Carriage Return and Line Feed
CS	Circuit Switched
DES	Data Encryption Standard
DH	Diffie-Hellman
DHCP	Dynamic Host Configuration Protocol
DNS	Domain Name Service
DoS	Denial of Service
DSCP	DiffServ Code Point
DTM	Dual-Transfer Mode
DTMF	Dual-Tone Multifrequency
ECC	Elliptic Curve Cryptography
ECT	Explicit Communication Transfer
EKT	Encrypted Key Transport
ESP	Encapsulating Security Payload
ETSI	European Telecommunications Standards Institute
FMC	Fixed Mobile Convergence
FoIP	Fax over Internet Protocol
FQDN	Fully Qualified Domain Name
FTP	File Transfer Protocol
GCP	Gateway Control Protocol
GPRS	General Packet Radio Service
GRUU	Globally Routable User Agent URI
GSM	Global System for Mobile communications
GTP	Generic Tunneling Protocol
GTT	Global Text Telephony
GUI	Graphical User Interface
HMAC	Hash Message Authentication Code
HSS	Home Subscriber Server
HTML	Hypertext Markup Language
HTTP	Hypertext Transfer Protocol
I-BCF	Interconnect Border Control Function
ICE	Interactive Connectivity Establishment
ICID	IMS Correlation ID
ICS	IMS Centralized Services
I-CSCF	Interrogating Call Session Control Function
IDEA	International Data Encryption Algorithm
IETF	Internet Engineering Task Force
IFC	Initial Filtering Criteria
IK	Integrity Key

IKE	Internet Key Exchange
IMAP4	Internet Message Access Protocol version 4
IM-MGW	IP Multimedia Media Gateway
IMP	Interface Message Processor
IMPS	Instant Messaging and Presence Service
IMS	Internet Multimedia Subsystem
IOI	Inter Operator Identifier
IP	Internet Protocol
IP-CAN	Internet Protocol Connectivity Access Network
IPSEC	Internet Protocol Security
IPTV	Internet Protocol Television
I-SBC	Interconnect Session Border Controller
ISC	IMS Service Control
ISDN	Integrated Services Digital Network
ISIM	IMS Subscriber Identity Module
ISOC	Internet Society
ISUP	ISDN User Part
ITU	International Telecommunication Union
IVR	Interactive Voice Response
J2ME	Java 2 Micro Edition
J2SE	Java 2 Standard Edition
JAIN	Java APIs for Integrated Networks
JMF	Java Media Framework
JPEG	Joint Photographic Experts Group
JVM	Java Virtual Machine
KPML	Key Press Markup Language
LAN	Local Area Network
MAC	Message Authentication Code
MD	Message Digest
MEGACO	Media Gateway Control
MG	Media Gateway
MGC	Media Gateway Control
MGCF	Media Gateway Control Function
MIKEY	Multimedia Internet Keying
MIME	Multipurpose Internet Mail Extensions
MMAPI	Mobile Media API
MMS	Multimedia Messaging Service
MMTEL	Multimedia Telephony
MP3	MPEG-1 Layer 3
MPEG	Moving Picture Experts Group
MRCP	Media Resource Control Protocol
MRF	Media Resource Function
MRFC	Media Resource Function Controller
MRFP	Media Resource Function Processor

MSCML	Media Server Control Markup Language
MSML	Media Server Markup Language
MSRP	Message Session Relay Protocol
MTP	Message Transfer Part
MWI	Message Waiting Indication
NAPT	Network Address Port Translation
NAPTR RR	Naming Authority Pointer Resource Record
NAT	Network Address Translator
NDS	Network Domain Security
NGN	Next Generation Network
NIST	National Institute of Standards and Technology
N-SBC	Network Session Border Controller
OCF	Online Charging Function
OIP	Originating Identification Presentation
OIR	Originating Identification Restriction
OMA	Open Mobile Alliance
OPEX	Operational Expenditure
OSA	Open Service Architecture
PA	Presence Agent
PBX	Private Branch Exchange
PCEF	Policy and Charging Enforcement Function
PCM	Pulse-Code Modulation
PCRF	Policy and Charging Rules Function
P-CSCF	Proxy Call Session Control Function
PDP	Policy Decision Point
PEP	Policy Enforcement Point
PHB	Per-Hop Behavior
PIDF	Presence Information Data Format
PLMN	Public Land Mobile Network
PoC	Push-to-Talk over Cellular
POP3	Post Office Protocol version 3
POTS	Plain Old Telephone System
PSTN	Public Switched Telephone Network
PUA	Presence User Agent
QoS	Quality of Service
RC	Rivest's Cipher
RFC	Request for Comments
RLMI	Resource List Meta-Information
RLS	Resource List Server
RPID	Rich Presence Information Data format
RR	Resource Record
RSA	Rivest Shamir Adelman
RSVP	Resource Reservation Protocol

RTCP	Real-time Transport Control Protocol
RTP	Real-time Transport Protocol
RTSP	Real-time Streaming Protocol
SA	Security Association
SAP	Session Announcement Protocol
SBC	Session Border Controller
SCCP	Skinny Client Control Protocol
SCIP	Simple Conference Invitation Protocol
S-CSCF	Serving Call Session Control Function
SCTP	Stream Control Transmission Protocol
SDES	Source Description
SDP	Session Description Protocol
SEG	Security Gateway
SGW	Signaling Gateway
SIP	Session Initiation Protocol
S/MIME	Secure/Multipurpose Internet Mail Extensions
SMS	Short Message Service
SMTP	Simple Mail Transfer Protocol
SR	Sender Report
SRTP	Secure Real-time Transport Protocol
SRV RR	Service Resource Record
STUN	Simple Traversal Utilities for NAT
TCP	Transmission Control Protocol
TD-CDMA	Time Division–Code Division Multiple Access
TDM	Time Division Multiplex
TIP	Terminating Identification Presentation
TIR	Terminating Identification Restriction
TISPAN	Telecoms and Internet converged Services and Protocols for Advanced Networks
TLS	Transport Layer Security
ToIP	Text over Internet Protocol
TrGW	Transition Gateway
TRIP	Telephony Routing over Internet Protocol
TTS	Text-to-Speech
UA	User Agent
UAC	User Agent Client
UAS	User Agent Server
UDP	User Datagram Protocol
UE	User Equipment
UICC	Universal Integrated Circuit Card
UMTS	Universal Mobile Telecommunications System
URI	Universal Resource Identifier
URL	Universal Resource Locator

VCC	Voice Call Continuity
VFW	Video for Windows
VMS	Voice Mail System
VOD	Video-on-Demand
VoIP	Voice over Internet Protocol
VXML	Voice Extensible Markup Language
W-CDMA	Wideband Code Division Multiple Access
WDM	Windows Driver Model
WLAN	Wireless Local Area Network
WWW	World Wide Web
XCAP	XML Configuration Access Protocol
XHTML	Extensible Hypertext Markup Language
XML	Extensible Markup Language
XMPP	Extensible Messaging and Presence Protocol

References

IETF Documents

IETF documents can be found at www.ietf.org.

Requests for Comments

RFC 0741 Specifications for the Network Voice Protocol (NVP). D. Cohen. November 1977.

RFC 0768 User Datagram Protocol. J. Postel. August 1980.

RFC 0791 Internet Protocol. J. Postel. September 1981.

RFC 0793 Transmission Control Protocol. J. Postel. September 1981.

RFC 1633 Integrated Services in the Internet Architecture: An Overview. R. Braden, D. Clark, S. Shenker. June 1994.

RFC 1847 Security Multiparts for MIME: Multipart/Signed and Multipart/Encrypted. J. Galvin, S. Murphy, S. Crocker, N. Freed. October 1995.

RFC 1958 Architectural Principles of the Internet. B. Carpenter, ed. June 1996.

RFC 2026 The Internet Standards Process—Revision 3. S. Bradner. October 1996.

RFC 2045 Multipurpose Internet Mail Extensions (MIME) Part One: Format of Internet Message Bodies. N. Freed, N. Borenstein. November 1996.

RFC 2046 Multipurpose Internet Mail Extensions (MIME) Part Two: Media Types. N. Freed, N. Borenstein. November 1996.

RFC 2047 MIME (Multipurpose Internet Mail Extensions) Part Three: Message Header Extensions for Non-ASCII Text. K. Moore. November 1996.

RFC 2205 Resource ReSerVation Protocol (RSVP)—Version 1 Functional Specification. R. Braden, ed., L. Zhang, S. Berson, S. Herzog, S. Jamin. September 1997.

RFC 2211 Specification of the Controlled-Load Network Element Service. J. Wroclawski. September 1997.

RFC 2212 Specification of Guaranteed Quality of Service. S. Shenker, C. Partridge, R. Guerin. September 1997.

RFC 2326 Real Time Streaming Protocol (RTSP). H. Schulzrinne, A. Rao, R. Lanphier. April 1998.

RFC 2460 Internet Protocol, Version 6 (IPv6) Specification. S. Deering, R. Hinden. December 1998.

RFC 2474 Definition of the Differentiated Services Field (DS Field) in the IPv4 and IPv6 Headers. K. Nichols, S. Blake, F. Baker, D. Black. December 1998.

RFC 2475 An Architecture for Differentiated Service. S. Blake, D. Black, M. Carlson, E. Davies, Z. Wang, W. Weiss. December 1998.

RFC 2543 SIP: Session Initiation Protocol. M. Handley, H. Schulzrinne, E. Schooler, J. Rosenberg. March 1999.

RFC 2597 Assured Forwarding PHB Group. J. Heinanen, F. Baker, W. Weiss, J. Wroclawski. June 1999.

RFC 2617 HTTP Authentication: Basic and Digest Access Authentication. J. Franks, P. Hallam-Baker, J. Hostetler, S. Lawrence, P. Leach, A. Luotonen, L. Stewart. June 1999.

RFC 2663 IP Network Address Translator (NAT) Terminology and Considerations. P. Srisuresh, M. Holdrege. August 1999.

RFC 2748 The COPS (Common Open Policy Service) Protocol. D. Durham, ed., J. Boyle, R. Cohen, S. Herzog, R. Rajan, A. Sastry. January 2000.

RFC 2750 2750 RSVP Extensions for Policy Control. S. Herzog. January 2000.

RFC 2753 A Framework for Policy-based Admission Control. R. Yavatkar, D. Pendarakis, R. Guerin. January 2000.

RFC 2778 A Model for Presence and Instant Messaging. M. Day, J. Rosenberg, H. Sugano. February 2000.

RFC 2779 Instant Messaging/Presence Protocol Requirements. M. Day, S. Aggarwal, G. Mohr, J. Vincent. February 2000.

RFC 2871 A Framework for Telephony Routing over IP. J. Rosenberg, H. Schulzrinne. June 2000.

RFC 2960 Stream Control Transmission Protocol. R. Stewart, Q. Xie, K. Morneault, C. Sharp, H. Schwarzbauer, T. Taylor, I. Rytina, M. Kalla, L. Zhang, V. Paxson. October 2000.

RFC 2974 Session Announcement Protocol. M. Handley, C. Perkins, E. Whelan. October 2000.

RFC 2976 The SIP INFO Method. S. Donovan. October 2000.

RFC 3022 Traditional IP Network Address Translator (Traditional NAT). P. Srisuresh, K. Egevang. January 2001.

RFC 3204 MIME media types for ISUP and QSIG Objects. E. Zimmerer, J. Peterson, A. Vemuri, L. Ong, F. Audet, M. Watson, M. Zonoun. December 2001.

RFC 3219 Telephony Routing over IP (TRIP). J. Rosenberg, H. Salama, M. Squire. January 2002.

RFC 3233 Defining the IETF. P. Hoffman, S. Bradner. February 2002.

RFC 3258 Distributing Authoritative Name Servers via Shared Unicast Addresses. T. Hardie. April 2002.

RFC 3261 SIP: Session Initiation Protocol. J. Rosenberg, H. Schulzrinne, G. Camarillo, A. Johnston, J. Peterson, R. Sparks, M. Handley, E. Schooler. June 2002.

RFC 3262 Reliability of Provisional Responses in Session Initiation Protocol (SIP). J. Rosenberg, H. Schulzrinne. June 2002.

RFC 3263 Session Initiation Protocol (SIP): Locating SIP Servers. J. Rosenberg, H. Schulzrinne. June 2002.

RFC 3264 An Offer/Answer Model with Session Description Protocol (SDP). J. Rosenberg, H. Schulzrinne. June 2002.

RFC 3265 Session Initiation Protocol (SIP)-Specific Event Notification. A. B. Roach. June 2002.

RFC 3268 Advanced Encryption Standard (AES) Ciphersuites for Transport Layer Security (TLS). P. Chown. June 2002.

RFC 3286 An Introduction to the Stream Control Transmission Protocol (SCTP). L. Ong, J. Yoakum. May 2002.

RFC 3310 Hypertext Transfer Protocol (HTTP) Digest Authentication Using Authentication and Key Agreement (AKA). A. Niemi, J. Arkko, V. Torvinen. September 2002.

RFC 3311 The Session Initiation Protocol (SIP) UPDATE Method. J. Rosenberg. October 2002.

RFC 3312 Integration of Resource Management and Session Initiation Protocol (SIP). G. Camarillo, ed., W. Marshall, ed., J. Rosenberg. October 2002.

RFC 3313 Private Session Initiation Protocol (SIP) Extensions for Media Authorization. W. Marshall, ed. January 2003.

RFC 3323 A Privacy Mechanism for the Session Initiation Protocol (SIP). J. Peterson. November 2002.

RFC 3325 Private Extensions to the Session Initiation Protocol (SIP) for Asserted Identity within Trusted Networks. C. Jennings, J. Peterson, M. Watson. November 2002.

RFC 3326 The Reason Header Field for the Session Initiation Protocol (SIP). H. Schulzrinne, D. Oran, G. Camarillo. December 2002.

RFC 3327 Session Initiation Protocol (SIP) Extension Header Field for Registering Non-Adjacent Contacts. D. Willis, B. Hoeneisen. December 2002.

RFC 3351 User Requirements for the Session Initiation Protocol (SIP) in Support of Deaf, Hard of Hearing and Speech-impaired Individuals. N. Charlton, M. Gasson, G. Gybels, M. Spanner, A. van Wijk. August 2002.

RFC 3362 Real-time Facsimile (T.38)—image/t38 MIME Sub-type Registration. G. Parsons. August 2002.

RFC 3372 Session Initiation Protocol for Telephones (SIP-T): Context and Architectures. A. Vemuri, J. Peterson. September 2002.

RFC 3398 Integrated Services Digital Network (ISDN) User Part (ISUP) to Session Initiation Protocol (SIP) Mapping. G. Camarillo, A. B. Roach, J. Peterson, L. Ong. December 2002.

RFC 3420 Internet Media Type message/sipfrag. R. Sparks. November 2002.

RFC 3427 Change Process for the Session Initiation Protocol (SIP). A. Mankin, S. Bradner, R. Mahy, D. Willis, J. Ott, B. Rosen. December 2002.

RFC 3428 Session Initiation Protocol (SIP) Extension for Instant Messaging. B. Campbell, ed., J. Rosenberg, H. Schulzrinne, C. Huitema, D. Gurle. December 2002.

RFC 3439 Some Internet Architectural Guidelines and Philosophy. R. Bush, D. Meyer. December 2002.

RFC 3455 Private Header (P-Header) Extensions to the Session Initiation Protocol (SIP) for the 3rd-Generation Partnership Project (3GPP). M. Garcia-Martin, E. Henrikson, D. Mills. January 2003.

RFC 3489 STUN-Simple Traversal of User Datagram Protocol (UDP) Through Network Address Translators (NATs). J. Rosenberg, J. Weinberger, C. Huitema, R. Mahy. March 2003.

RFC 3515 The Session Initiation Protocol (SIP) Refer Method. R. Sparks. April 2003.

RFC 3521 Framework for Session Set-up with Media Authorization. L-N. Hamer, B. Gage, H. Shieh. April 2003.

RFC 3525 Gateway Control Protocol Version 1. C. Groves, M. Pantaleo, T. Anderson, T. Taylor, eds. June 2003.

RFC 3550 RTP: A Transport Protocol for Real-Time Applications. H. Schulzrinne, S. Casner, R. Frederick, V. Jacobson. July 2003.

RFC 3551 RTP Profile for Audio and Video Conferences with Minimal Control. H. Schulzrinne, S. Casner. July 2003.

RFC 3556 Session Description Protocol (SDP) Bandwidth Modifiers for RTP Control Protocol (RTCP) Bandwidth. S. Casner. July 2003.

RFC 3581 An Extension to the Session Initiation Protocol (SIP) for Symmetric Response Routing. J. Rosenberg, H. Schulzrinne. August 2003.

RFC 3588 Diameter Base Protocol. P. Calhoun, J. Loughney, E. Guttman, G. Zorn, J. Arkko. September 2003.

RFC 3605 Real Time Control Protocol (RTCP) attribute in Session Description Protocol (SDP). C. Huitema. October 2003.

RFC 3608 Session Initiation Protocol (SIP) Extension Header Field for Service Route Discovery During Registration. D. Willis, B. Hoeneisen. October 2003.

RFC 3665 Session Initiation Protocol (SIP) Basic Call Flow Examples. A. Johnston, S. Donovan, R. Sparks, C. Cunningham, K. Summers. December 2003.

RFC 3680 A Session Initiation Protocol (SIP) Event Package for Registrations. J. Rosenberg. March 2004.

RFC 3711 The Secure Real-time Transport Protocol (SRTP). M. Baugher, D. McGrew, M. Naslund, E. Carrara, K. Norrman. March 2004.

RFC 3725 Best Current Practices for Third Party Call Control (3pcc) in the Session Initiation Protocol (SIP). J. Rosenberg, J. Peterson, H. Schulzrinne, G. Camarillo. April 2004.

RFC 3761 The E.164 to Uniform Resource Identifiers (URI) Dynamic Delegation Discovery System (DDDS) Application (ENUM). P. Faltstrom, M. Mealling. April 2004.

RFC3830 MIKEY: Multimedia Internet KEYing. J. Arkko, E. Carrara, F. Lindholm, M. Naslund, K. Norrman. August 2004.

RFC 3840 Indicating User Agent Capabilities in the Session Initiation Protocol (SIP). J. Rosenberg, H. Schulzrinne, P. Kyzivat. August 2004.

RFC 3842 A Message Summary and Message Waiting Indication Event Package for the Session Initiation Protocol (SIP). R. Mahy. August 2004.

RFC 3850 Secure/Multipurpose Internet Mail Extensions (S/MIME) Version 3.1 Certificate Handling. B. Ramsdell, ed. July 2004.

RFC 3851 Secure/Multipurpose Internet Mail Extensions (S/MIME) Version 3.1 Message Specification. B. Ramsdell, ed. July 2004.

RFC 3856 A Presence Event Package for the Session Initiation Protocol (SIP). J.Rosenberg. August 2004.

RFC 3859 Common Profile for Presence (CPP). J. Peterson. August 2004.

RFC 3860 Common Profile for Instant Messaging (CPIM). J. Peterson. August 2004.

RFC 3861 Address Resolution for Instant Messaging and Presence. J. Peterson. August 2004.

RFC 3862 Common Presence and Instant Messaging (CPIM): Message Format. G. Klyne, D. Atkins. August 2004.

RFC 3863 Presence Information Data Format (PIDF). H. Sugano, S. Fujimoto, G. Klyne, A. Bateman, W. Carr, J. Peterson. August 2004.

RFC 3891 The Session Initiation Protocol (SIP) "Replaces" Header. R. Mahy, B. Biggs, R. Dean. September 2004.

RFC 3892 The Session Initiation Protocol (SIP) Referred-By Mechanism. R. Sparks. September 2004.

RFC 3893 Session Initiation Protocol (SIP) Authenticated Identity Body (AIB) Format. J. Peterson. September 2004.

RFC 3903 Session Initiation Protocol (SIP) Extension for Event State Publication. A. Niemi, ed. October 2004.

RFC 3911 The Session Initiation Protocol (SIP) "Join" Header. R. Mahy, D. Petrie. October 2004.

RFC 3966 The tel URI for Telephone Numbers. H. Schulzrinne. December 2004.

RFC 3986 Uniform Resource Identifier (URI): Generic Syntax. T. Berners-Lee, R. Fielding, L. Masinter. January 2005.

RFC 4032 Update to the Session Initiation Protocol (SIP) Preconditions Framework. G. Camarillo, P. Kyzivat. March 2005.

RFC 4083 Input 3rd-Generation Partnership Project (3GPP) Release 5 Requirements on the Session Initiation Protocol (SIP). M. Garcia-Martin. May 2005.

RFC 4103 RTP Payload for Text Conversation. G. Hellstrom, P. Jones. June 2005.

RFC 4145 TCP-Based Media Transport in the Session Description Protocol (SDP). D. Yon, G. Camarillo. September 2005.

RFC 4234 Augmented BNF for Syntax Specifications: ABNF. D. Crocker, ed., P. Overell. October 2005.

RFC 4235 An INVITE-Initiated Dialog Event Package for the Session Initiation Protocol (SIP). J. Rosenberg, H. Schulzrinne, R. Mahy, ed. November 2005.

RFC 4240 Basic Network Media Services with SIP. E. Burger, ed., J. Van Dyke, A. Spitzer. December 2005.

RFC 4244 An Extension to the Session Initiation Protocol (SIP) for Request History Information. M. Barnes, ed. November 2005.

RFC 4245 High-Level Requirements for Tightly Coupled SIP Conferencing. O. Levin, R. Even. November 2005.

RFC 4261 Common Open Policy Service (COPS) Over Transport Layer Security (TLS). J. Walker, A. Kulkarni, ed. December 2005.

RFC 4282 The Network Access Identifier. B. Aboba, M. Beadles, J. Arkko, P. Eronen. December 2005.

RFC 4301 Security Architecture for the Internet Protocol. S. Kent, K. Seo. December 2005.

RFC 4302 IP Authentication Header. S. Kent. December 2005.

RFC 4303 IP Encapsulating Security Payload (ESP). S. Kent. December 2005.

RFC 4306 Internet Key Exchange (IKEv2) Protocol. C. Kaufman, ed. December 2005.

RFC 4346 The Transport Layer Security (TLS) Protocol Version 1.1. T. Dierks, E. Rescorla. April 2006.

RFC 4347 Datagram Transport Layer Security. E. Rescorla, N. Modadugu. April 2006.

RFC 4353 A Framework for Conferencing with the Session Initiation Protocol (SIP). J. Rosenberg. February 2006.

RFC 4354 A Session Initiation Protocol (SIP) Event Package and Data Format for Various Settings in Support for the Push-to-Talk over Cellular (PoC) Service. M. Garcia-Martin. January 2006.

RFC 4366 Transport Layer Security (TLS) Extensions. S. Blake-Wilson, M. Nystrom, D. Hopwood, J. Mikkelsen, T. Wright. April 2006.

RFC 4376 Requirements for Floor Control Protocols. P. Koskelainen, J. Ott, H. Schulzrinne, X. Wu. February 2006.

RFC 4463 A Media Resource Control Protocol (MRCP) Developed by Cisco, Nuance, and Speechworks. S. Shanmugham, P. Monaco, B. Eberman. April 2006.

RFC 4474 Enhancements for Authenticated Identity Management in the Session Initiation Protocol (SIP). J. Peterson, C. Jennings. August 2006.

RFC 4480 RPID: Rich Presence Extensions to the Presence Information Data Format (PIDF). H. Schulzrinne, V. Gurbani, P. Kyzivat, J. Rosenberg. July 2006.

RFC 4481 Timed Presence Extensions to the Presence Information Data Format (PIDF) to Indicate Status Information for Past and Future Time Intervals. H. Schulzrinne. July 2006.

RFC 4482 CIPID: Contact Information for the Presence Information Data Format. H. Schulzrinne. July 2006.

RFC 4483 A Mechanism for Content Indirection in Session Initiation Protocol (SIP) Messages. E. Burger, ed. May 2006.

RFC 4485 Guidelines for Authors of Extensions to the Session Initiation Protocol (SIP). J. Rosenberg, H. Schulzrinne. May 2006.

RFC 4488 Suppression of Session Initiation Protocol (SIP) REFER Method Implicit Subscription. O. Levin. May 2006.

RFC 4566 SDP: Session Description Protocol. M. Handley, V. Jacobson, C. Perkins. July 2006.

RFC 4567 Key Management Extensions for Session Description Protocol (SDP) and Real Time Streaming Protocol (RTSP). J. Arkko, F. Lindholm, M. Naslund, K. Norrman, E. Carrara. July 2006.

RFC 4568 Session Description Protocol (SDP) Security Descriptions for Media Streams. F. Andreasen, M. Baugher, D. Wing. July 2006.

RFC 4572 Connection-Oriented Media Transport over the Transport Layer Security (TLS) Protocol in the Session Description Protocol (SDP). J. Lennox. July 2006.

RFC 4575 A Session Initiation Protocol (SIP) Event Package for Conference State. J. Rosenberg, H. Schulzrinne, O. Levin, ed. August 2006.

RFC 4579 Session Initiation Protocol (SIP) Call Control—Conferencing for User Agents. A. Johnston, O. Levin. August 2006.

RFC 4582 The Binary Floor Control Protocol (BFCP). G. Camarillo, J. Ott, K. Drage. November 2006.

RFC 4597 Conferencing Scenarios. R. Even, N. Ismail. August 2006.

RFC 4660 Functional Description of Event Notification Filtering. H. Khartabil, E. Leppanen, M. Lonnfors, J. Costa-Requena. September 2006.

RFC 4662 A Session Initiation Protocol (SIP) Event Notification Extension for Resource Lists. A. B. Roach, B. Campbell, J. Rosenberg. August 2006.

RFC 4680 TLS Handshake Message for Supplemental Data. S. Santesson. October 2006.

RFC 4681 TLS User Mapping Extension. S. Santesson, A. Medvinsky, J. Ball. October 2006.

RFC 4722 Media Server Control Markup Language (MSCML) and Protocol. J. Van Dyke, E. Burger, ed., A. Spitzer. November 2006.

RFC 4730 A Session Initiation Protocol (SIP) Event Package for Key Press Stimulus (KPML). E. Burger, M. Dolly. November 2006.

RFC 4733 RTP Payload for DTMF Digits, Telephony Tones, and Telephony Signals. H. Schulzrinne, T. Taylor. December 2006.

RFC 4734 Definition of Events for Modem, Fax, and Text Telephony Signals. H. Schulzrinne, T. Taylor. December 2006.

RFC 4738 MIKEY-RSA-R: An Additional Mode of Key Distribution in Multimedia Internet KEYing (MIKEY). D. Ignjatic, L. Dondeti, F. Audet, P. Lin. November 2006.

RFC 4787 Network Address Translation (NAT) Behavioral Requirements for Unicast UDP. F. Audet, ed., C. Jennings. January 2007.

RFC 4825 The Extensible Markup Language (XML) Configuration Access Protocol (XCAP). J. Rosenberg. May 2007.

RFC 4835 Cryptographic Algorithm Implementation Requirements for Encapsulating Security Payload (ESP) and Authentication Header (AH). V. Manral. April 2007.

RFC 4961 Symmetric RTP/RTP Control Protocol (RTCP). D. Wing. July 2007.

Internet Drafts

draft-boulton-conference-control-package
C. Boulton, T. Melanchuk, S. McGlashan, A. Shiratzky. "A Conference Control Package for the Session Initiation Protocol (SIP)."

draft-boulton-ivr-control-package
C. Boulton, T. Melanchuk, S. McGlashan, A. Shiratzky. "A Basic Interactive Voice Response (IVR) Control Package for the Session Initiation Protocol (SIP)."

draft-boulton-ivr-vxml-control-package
C. Boulton, T. Melanchuk, S. McGlashan, A. Shiratzky. "A VoiceXML Interactive Voice Response (IVR) Control Package for the Session Initiation Protocol (SIP)."

draft-boulton-sip-control-framework
C. Boulton, T. Melachnuk, S. McGlashan, A. Shiratzky. "A Control Framework for the Session Initiation Protocol (SIP)."

draft-fischl-sipping-media-dtls
J. Fischl, H. Tschofenig, E. Rescorla. "Datagram Transport Layer Security (DTLS) Protocol for Protection of Media Traffic Established with the Session Initiation Protocol."

draft-mcgrew-srtp-ekt
D. McGrew, F. Andreasen, L. Dondeti. "Encrypted Key Transport for Secure RTP."

draft-ietf-avt-dtls-srtp
D. McGrew, E. Rescorla. "Datagram Transport Layer Security (DTLS) Extension to Establish Keys for Secure Real-time Transport Protocol (SRTP)."

draft-ietf-behave-nat-behavior-discovery
D. MacDonald, B. Lowekamp. "NAT Behavior Discovery Using STUN." June 2007.

draft-ietf-behave-rfc3489bis
J. Rosenberg, C. Huitema, R. Mahy, D. Wing. "Session Traversal Utilities for (NAT) (STUN)."

draft-ietf-behave-turn
J. Rosenberg, R. Mahy, C. Huitema. "Obtaining Relay Addresses from Simple Traversal Underneath NAT (STUN)."

draft-ietf-mmusic-ice
J. Rosenberg. "Interactive Connectivity Establishment (ICE): A Methodology for Network Address Translator (NAT) Traversal for Offer/Answer Protocols."

draft-ietf-mmusic-securityprecondition
F. Andreasen, D. Wing. "Security Preconditions for Session Description Protocol (SDP) Media Streams."

draft-ietf-simple-message-sessions
B. Campbell, R. Mahy, C. Jenning. "The Message Session Relay Protocol."

draft-ietf-simple-msrp-relays
C. Jennings, R. Mahy, A. B. Roach. "Relay Extensions for the Message Sessions Relay Protocol."

draft-ietf-sip-gruu
J. Rosenberg. "Obtaining and Using Globally Routable User Agent (UA) URIs (GRUU) in the Session Initiation Protocol (SIP)."

draft-ietf-sip-outbound
B. Jennings, R. Mahy. "Managing Client Initiated Connections in the Session Initiation Protocol."

draft-ietf-sipping-app-interaction-framework
J. Rosenberg. "A Framework for Application Interaction in the Session Initiation Protocol (SIP)."

draft-ietf-sipping-cc-transfer
R. Sparks, A. Johnston, D. Petrie. "Session Initiation Protocol Call Control-Transfer

draft-ietf-sipping-gruu-reg-event
P. Kyzivat. "Registration Event Package Extension for Session Initiation Protocol (SIP) Globally Routable User Agent URIs (GRUUs)."

draft-ietf-sipping-nat-scenarios
C. Boulton, J. Rosenberg, G. Camarillo. "Best Current Practices for NAT Traversal for SIP."

draft-ietf-sipping-sbc-funcs
J. Hautakorpi, G. Camarillo, R. Penfield, A. Hawrylyshen, M. Bathia. "Requirements from SIP (Session Initiation Protocol) Session Border Controller Deployments."

draft-ietf-sipping-service-examples
A. Johnston, R. Sparks, C. Cunningham, S. Donovan, K. Summers. "Session Initiation Protocol Service Examples."

draft-ietf-speechsc-mrcpv2
S. Shanmugham, D. Burnett. "Media Resource Control Protocol Version 2 (MRCPv2)."

draft-ietf-xcon-framework
M. Barnes, C. Boulton, O. Levin. "A Framework and Data Model for Centralized Conferencing."

draft-levin-xcon-cccp
O. Levin, R. Even, P. Hagendorf. "Centralized Conference Control Protocol."

draft-mahy-sip-remote-cc
R. Mahy, C. Jennings. "Remote Call Control in the Session Initiation Protocol (SIP) using the REFER method and the session-oriented dialog package."

draft-saleem-msml
A. Saleem, Y. Xin, G. Sharratt. "Media Server Markup Language."

draft-zimmermann-avt-zrtp
P. Zimmermann, A. Johnston, J. Callas. "ZRTP: Media Path Key Agreement for Secure RTP."

draft-tiphon-background
S. Cadzow, P. Mart, P. Sijben. "TIPHON architecture background." (expired draft)

3GPP Documents

3GPP documents can be found at www.3gpp.org.

3GPP TS 22.141 Presence service; Stage 1

3GPP TS 22.173 IP Multimedia Core Network Subsystem (IMS) Multimedia Telephony Service and supplementary services; Stage 1

3GPP TS 22.226 Global text telephony (GTT); Stage 1: Service description

3GPP TS 22.228 Service requirements for the Internet Protocol (IP) multimedia core network subsystem (IMS); Stage 1

3GPP TS 22.250 IP Multimedia Subsystem (IMS) Group Management; Stage 1

3GPP TS 22.279 Combined Circuit Switched (CS) and IP Multimedia Subsystem (IMS) sessions; Stage 1

3GPP TS 22.340 IP Multimedia Subsystem (IMS) messaging; Stage 1

3GPP TR 22.892 Study on IMS centralized services (ICS) requirements

3GPP TS 23.060 General Packet Radio Service (GPRS); Service description; Stage 2

3GPP TS 23.141 Presence service; Architecture and functional description; Stage 2

3GPP TS 23.206 Voice Call Continuity (VCC) between Circuit Switched (CS) and IP Multimedia Subsystem (IMS); Stage 2

3GPP TS 23.218 IP Multimedia (IM) session handling; IM call model; Stage 2

3GPP TS 23.221 Architectural requirements

3GPP TS 23.226 Global text telephony (GTT); Stage 2: Architecture

3GPP TS 23.228 Multimedia Subsystem (IMS); Stage 2

3GPP TS 23.279 Combining Circuit Switched (CS) and IP Multimedia Subsystem (IMS) services; Stage 2

3GPP TR 23.979 3GPP enablers for Open Mobile Alliance (OMA) Push-to-talk over Cellular (PoC) services; Stage 2

3GPP TS 24.141 Presence service using the IP Multimedia (IM) Core Network (CN) subsystem; Stage 3

3GPP TS 24.173 IMS Multimedia telephony service and supplementary services; Stage 3

3GPP TS 24.206 Voice call continuity between Circuit Switched (CS) and IP Multimedia Subsystem (IMS); Stage 3

3GPP TS 24.228 Signalling flows for the IP multimedia call control based on Session Initiation Protocol (SIP) and Session Description Protocol (SDP); Stage 3

3GPP TS 24.229 Internet Protocol (IP) multimedia call control protocol based on Session Initiation Protocol (SIP) and Session Description Protocol (SDP); Stage 3

3GPP TS 24.247 Messaging service using the IP Multimedia (IM) Core Network (CN) subsystem; Stage 3

3GPP TS 24.279 Combining Circuit Switched (CS) and IP Multimedia Subsystem (IMS) services; Stage 3

3GPP TS 29.212 Policy and charging control over Gx reference point

3GPP TS 29.214 Policy and charging control over Rx reference point

3GPP TS 31.101 UICC-terminal interface; Physical and logical characteristics

3GPP TS 31.103 Characteristics of the IP Multimedia Services Identity Module (ISIM) application

3GPP TS 32.240 Telecommunication management; Charging management; IP Multimedia Subsystem (IMS) charging

3GPP TS 32.260 Telecommunication management; Charging management; Online Charging System (OCS): Applications and interfaces

3GPP TS 32.296 Telecommunication management; Charging management; Charging architecture and principles

3GPP TS 33.203 3G security; Access security for IP-based services

3GPP TS 33.210 3G security; Network Domain Security (NDS); IP network layer security

ETSI TISPAN Documents

TISPAN documents can be found at www.etsi.org/tispan/.

ETSI ES 282 001	NGN Functional Architecture Release 1. Overall architecture
ETSI ES 282 003	Resource and Admission Control Sub-system (RACS); Functional Architecture NGN RACS
ETSI ES 282 004	NGN Functional Architecture; Network Attachment Sub-System (NASS). NGN NASS
ETSI ES 282 007	IP Multimedia Subsystem (IMS); Functional architecture. NGN IMS Architecture
ETSI TS 181 002	Multimedia Telephony with PSTN/ISDN simulation services. NGN simulation services
ETSI TS 182 012	IMS-based PSTN/ISDN Emulation Subsystem; Functional architecture. IMS-based Emulation
ETSI TS 183 043	IMS-based PSTN/ISDN Emulation. Stage 3 specification. PES Stage 3

ITU Documents

The ITU official web site is www.itu.int.

ITU E.164	The international public telecommunication numbering plan
ITU F.700	Framework Recommendation for multimedia services
ITU G.711	Pulse code modulation (PCM) of voice frequencies
ITU G.723.1	Dual rate speech coder for multimedia communications transmitting at 5.3 and 6.3 kbit/s
ITU H.248.1	Gateway control protocol: Version 3
ITU H.261	Video codec for audiovisual services at p x 64 kbit/s
ITU H.263	Video coding for low bit rate communication
ITU T.38	Procedures for real-time Group 3 facsimile communication over IP networks
ITU Y.2001	General overview of NGN
ITU Y.2011	General principles and general reference model for Next Generation Networks

OMA Documents

OMA documents can be found at www.openmobilealliance.org.

OMA-AD-PoC Push to talk over Cellular (PoC)—Architecture. Approved Version 1.0.1-28 Nov 2006

W3C Documents

W3C documents can be found at www.w3c.org.

W3C_VOICEXML Voice Extensible Markup Language (VoiceXML) Version 2.0

W3C Recommendation 16 March 2004

Java Specification Requests

JSRs can be found at the JCP website: www.jcp.org.

JSR 22	JAIN SLEE API specification
JSR 32	JAIN SIP API specification
JSR 116	SIP Servlet API
JSR 135	Mobile Media API
JSR 165	SIMPLE Instant Messaging
JSR 180	SIP API for J2ME
JSR 240	JAIN SLEE v 1.1
JSR 289	SIP Servlet v 1.1
JSR 309	Media Server Control API
JSR908	Java Media Framework 2.2.1

Web Links

GSMA_MSRP	http://www.gsmworld.com/news/press_2007/press07_39.shtml
JIPLETS	http://www.cafesip.org/projects/jiplet/index.html
JSIP	https://jain-sip.dev.java.net/
MOVICENTS	https://mobicents.dev.java.net/
OPENSER	http://www.openser.org
PARLAY	www.parlay.org
PULVER	www.pulver.com
SIP FORUM	www.sipforum.org

Index

3GPP IMS (Internet Multimedia Subsystem), 322, 536
  private SIP extensions for, 530-532
3rd Generation Partnership Project (3GPP), 25, 501
  goal, 502

A

Access network (AN), 448, 452, 502, 505, 536
Access Network Charging Information, 531
Access Security, 522-523
ACK request, 93, 276, 287
  proxying requests, 304-305
  receiving, 292-293
`addReceiveStreamListener()`, 243
Address- and port-dependent mapping, 471, 473-474
Address-dependent mapping, 471
Address mapping, 471
`Address` object, 151
Address of Record (AOR), 77, 299, 323-324, 356, 439
`AddressFactory`, 151-152
`addSiplistener()`, 146
Alert.wav file, 279
Alerting signal, 279-280
Algorithm, 314, 317, 319, 322-323, 372
Allocate request, 484
Allow header, 343, 347
`appendLocationServiceDisplay(String newEntry)`, 296
`appendOngoingTransactionsDisplay (String newEntry)`, 296
Application-layer protocols, 36, 117
Application Programming Interfaces (APIs), 64, 225
Application Server (AS), 64, 358, 412, 413, 416, 418, 421, 429, 431-433, 515
ARPANET (Advanced Research Projects Agency Network), 21, 22, 26
`ArrayList`, 303
Asymmetric ciphers, 315-317
Asymmetric Digital Subscriber Line (ADSL), 8, 33-34
Attacks and threat models, in SIP
  message bodies, 320
  registration hijacking, 319
  server impersonation, 319-320
  service denial, 320
  tearing down and modification, of sessions, 319
Attributes (a-line), 183-184
Audio Video Profile (AVP), 208
Audio/Video Transport (AVT) Working Group, 20
`AudioFormat`, 230-231, 240
AUTH request, 214, 219
Authentication, 320, 510-511
  WWW-Authenticate header, 324-325
  WWW-Authorization header, 325-326
Authentication, Authorization, and Accounting (AAA), 41, 497-498
Authentication and Key Agreement (AKA) protocol, 322, 511, 522
Authorization header, 325-326
Automatic Speech Recognition (ASR), 435
AUTOMATIC_DIALOG_SUPPORT property, 300

B

Back-to-Back User Agents (B2BUA), 57-58, 61, 285, 358, 389-390, 498
Bandwidth (b-line), 182-183
Basic media services, 410-412
  architecture, 412-413
  implementation, 413
    announcements, 414
    basic conference, 415-416
    user interaction, 414-415
Best-effort delivery, 32
BGCF (Border Gateway Control Function), 517
BYE request, 82, 279, 285, 404
Byte-Range header field, 216

C

Call-blocking, 11
Call control, 11, 381-383
  peer-to-peer call control, 383-388
  remote call control, 390-393
  third party call control (3PCC), 389-390
Call flows, 103
  nonroaming case, 519
  roaming case, 520
Call Forwarding on Busy (CFB) service, 60
Call-forwarding service, 11, 284
Call-hold, 11
Call-ID header field, 88-89, 133
Call management
  and transactions, 275
Call pickup, 12
Call queuing, 12

Call stateful proxies, 289, 497
Call transfer, 11, 409
CANCEL request, 81-82, 89, 92, 93, 288
  proxying requests, 305
  receiving, 292
  treatment of, 273
`CaptureDeviceInfo`, 229, 237
CaptureDeviceManager, 229, 237
Carriage Return and Line Feed (CRLF), 83
Certificate Authority (CA), 318, 332
  see also Digital Certificates
Challenge-response mechanism, 324
Charging Collection Function (CCF), 527, 531
Cipher, 314
  see also Asymmetric ciphers; Cipher suites; Symmetric ciphers
Cipher suites, 318-319, 323
Ciphertext, 314
Circuit-Switched (CS) domain, 502, 535, 539
Classifier, 449
`clearLocationServiceDisplay()`, 296
`clearOngoingTransactionsDisplay()`, 296
Click-to-Dial (CTD) services, 12, 61, 389
Client transaction, 114, 117, 124, 130, 273, 287, 292
  and server transaction, 119
Client transport, 114, 129-130
`clone()`, 301
`close()`, 264
Closed-user group dialing, 12
CNAME, 208
Combinational services, 535-536
Command Sequence (CSeq) header field, 92-93, 135
Common Open Policy Service (COPS) protocol, 454
Common Profile for Instant Messaging (CPIM), 372
Common profile for presence (CPP), 364
Communication services, 4
  see also Offline communication; Online communication
Communicator applications, 13-14
Complementary protocols, 40-41
Conference control, 426-427
Conference notification, 427
Conferencing, 41
  basic, 412, 415-416
  enhanced conferencing, 418-419, 425
  framework, with SIP, 419-423
  services, 12-13
  see also XCON framework
Confidentiality, 320
Configuration/display area, 265-267
`configure`, 233, 240
Confirm-status attribute, 459
Connection information (c-line), 181, 186
Contact Addresses, 49, 77, 356, 358, 475
Contact header field, 77, 90-91, 103, 359, 439
Content-Disposition header field, 95, 343
Content-Encoding header field, 94-95
Content indirection, 374
Content-Length header field, 94
Content-Type header field, 94
`Context` class, 303, 304, 305, 306
Control Plane, 9, 498, 517
Controlled load services, 450
`ControllerListener` interface, 232, 239, 240, 255
`controllerUpdate()`, 255
Core network (CN), 502
Core protocol
  media, 40
  signaling, 39-40
Core sublayer, in SIP, 116
  transaction users, 117
  transport users, 117
`createCancel()`, 273
`createListeningpoint()`, 144
`createMediaDescription()`, 191
`createSdp`, 197, 261
`createSipStack()`, 144
Cryptography, 314
Curr and des attribute, 458

D

Data encryption, 316, 319
Data sink, 233-234
Data source, 229-230
  format class, 230-231
Datagram Transport Layer Security (DTLS) protocol, 332
`DataSink` interface, 234, 239
`DataSource`, 229-231, 233, 235, 236, 237, 238, 239, 241, 279
Demultiplexing, 227
Desired-status attribute, 458
Destination text field, 265
Dialogs, *see* SIP dialogs
Differentiated services model, 451-452
  and integrated services model, 452-453
Digital certificates, 318
Digital signatures, 317-318
Direct Call, 125-127
Direct-mode scenario, 100-101
Display-name field, 87, 88
`displayClient(String text)`, 296
`displayServer(String text)`, 296
DNS (Domain Name System), 45, 49, 97, 99, 102, 131

DSCP (differentiated services code point), 452
DTMF (Dual-Tone Multi-Frequency), 133, 184, 185, 209, 417-418

E

Early dialog, 135, 347
Edge Router, 460
Email, 4, 361-362
- end-user services, 35
- history, 22

Empty line, 83
Encrypted Key Transport (EKT), 330, 332
Encryption, 313
- asymmetric ciphers, 315-317
- cipher suites, 318-319
- cryptography, 314
- digital certificates, 318
- digital signatures, 317-318
- hash functions, 317
- symmetric ciphers, 314-315

End Host, 460, 462
End-to-end acknowledgement, 215
End-to-end delay, 203, 204
Endpoint-independent mapping, 471, 472-473
Enhanced client, 308-310
Enhanced conference management, 423-424
Enhanced conferencing, 418-419
- media services, 425

Enterprise total communication systems, 15
ESTABLISHED state, 270-271
ETSI TISPAN NGN, 536-538
Event-listener pattern, 143-144
Event packages, 350, 351
- for SIP dialogs, 353-354
- for SIP registrations, 352-353

Events, 147
`ExampleGUI`, 152-153, 155, 157
`ExampleListener`, 152-153, 155
Expires header, 78, 307, 350, 489
Extending SIP
- architectural principles, 338
- event packages, 351
  - for SIP dialogs, 353-354
  - for SIP registrations, 352
- Globally Routable User Agent URIs (GRUUs)
  - motivation, 356-359
  - work, 359-360
- History-Info
  - motivation, 355
  - work, 355-356
- with new content types, 343
- new extensions, 337-338
- with new headers, 339-343
- with new methods, 34
- provisional responses, reliability of
  - motivation, 344-345
  - work, 345-347
- specific event notification
  - motivation, 348-349
  - work, 349-351
- UPDATE, 347
  - motivation, 347
  - work, 347

Extensible Markup Language (XML), 352, 353, 432, 434
- *see also* VoiceXML; XCAP

F

Factory pattern, 141-143
Failure Report header field, 215-216, 217, 221
Fetchers, 364
Filtering, 470, 471
Fingerprint attribute, 333
Fixed-mobile convergent (FMC), 538
Floor control, 424-425, 426-427
Focus, 427
Forking, 55-56, 291
Format class
- `AudioFormat`, 230-231
- `VideoFormat`, 230, 231

FQDN (Fully Qualified Domain Name), 19, 44, 84
From header field, 78, 87, 273, 439-440, 441, 444
From-Path header field, 215, 219, 220
Fundamental data-processing model, 226

G

Gateway, 396, 399, 403, 498
- decomposition, 397

`getInstance()`, 144
`getSdp`, 198, 261
`getSupportedFormats()`, 251
`getVisualComponent()`, 252
Global Text Telephony (GTT), 536
Globally Routable User Agent URIs (GRUUs)
- motivation, 356-359
- work, 359-360

GPRS (General Packet Radio Service), 24, 502, 505
GSM (Global System for Mobile communications), 24, 230
Guaranteed services, 450
GUI (Graphical User Interface), 51, 155, 160, 267, 375
- configuration area
  - home domain text box, 297
  - "Off" button, 297
  - "On" button, 297
  - port text box, 298
  - record-route check box, 298

GUI (Graphical User Interface) (*Cont.*)
display area
location service display, 299
tracer display, 298
transaction display, 299, 300

H

H.323, 28-29
Hash functions, 317
Hash value, 317
HashMap object, 302
Header fields, 83, 86-94, 438
MSRP, 215-216
HeaderFactory, 149, 150, 151
History-Info
motivation, 355
work, 355-356
Home domain text box, 297
Home SIP server, *see* Serving Call Session Control Function
Home Subscriber Server (HSS), 511
Hop-by-hop acknowledgement, 215, 221
Hop-by-hop reliability mechanism, 286-289
HTML (Hypertext Markup Language), 22
HTTP (Hypertext Transfer Protocol), 22, 41, 75, 372
authentication, 324-326
Hunting groups, 12

I

ICE (Interactive Connectivity Establishment), 484
Identity management, in SIP, 437
basic identity management
assertion of SIP identity, 439
privacy mechanisms, 439-441
enhanced identity management, 444
assertion of identity, 444
privacy mechanisms, 444-445
network asserted identity, private header for, 441
assertion of identity, 441-443
privacy mechanisms, 443
Identity privacy, *see* Privacy service
IDLE state, 264, 268-270
IKE (Internet Key Exchange), 321-322, 524
IM-MGW (Internet Multimedia Gateway), 517
IMP (Interface Message Processor), 19, 21
IMPP (Instant Message and Presence Protocol), 363
IMS API, 67
IMS centralized services (ICS), 501, 539
IMS Correlation ID (ICID), 531
IMS Multimedia Telephony Service, 534-535
Inbound proxy, 54-55, 283-284
Info label, 265
Infotainment services, 4
Initial Filter Criteria (iFC), 525-526
initSession(), 235, 236, 243, 251
Instant messaging, 9, 10, 202, 210-211, 361, 372
content indirection, 374
MSRP, 185-186
and Presence, 362-363
servers, 374-375
see also IMPP
Integrated services model, 449-451
and differentiated services model, 452-453
Integrity, 320
Inter Operator Identifier, 532
Interactive voice response (IVR), 184
Interconnect Border Control Function (IBCF), 517-518
Interfaces
between SDPManager and SDP implementation, 262
between softphone1GUI and softphone1Listener, 260-261
between softphone1Listener and SDPManager, 261-262
between softphone1Listener and SIP implementation, 261
between softphone1Listener and VideoTool, 262-263
between softphone1Listener and VoiceTool, 262
softphone1Listener and TonesTool, 263
Internet Engineering Task Force (IETF), 16, 362
best current practice RFCs, 18
Internet Drafts (I-Ds), 18
non-standards track RFCs, 18
in SIP, 18-20
standard track RFCs, 17-18
see also XCAP; MEDIACTRL Working Group
Internet Multimedia
history, 26-29
Internet Multimedia Subsystem (IMS), 8, 24, 62, 503, 510
Internet paradigm, 33-34, 383, 495
Internet Protocol (IP) network, 3, 26, 32-33, 40, 41-42
architecture, 34-35
quality of service in, 447
Interrogating Call Session Control Function (I-CSCF), 514, 515
INVITE request, 78-80, 82, 132, 135, 169, 347, 386, 415
INVITE transactions, 123-124
IP address, 32, 97-100, 130, 187, 237, 469, 476
IP Centrex application, 15-16
IP communication sessions, 438, 498
attributes, 183

instant messages (MSRP), 185–186
online, 5
real-time text, 185
TCP content, 186–187
telephony tones, 184–185
voice and video, 184
IP Connectivity Access Network (IP-CAN), 504
IP Multimedia
architecture, 39–42
Internet concepts, 31–32
Internet paradigm, 33–34
Internet protocol, 32–33
TCP/IP Protocol architecture, 34–38
IP multimedia call, 10, 46
IP Multimedia Subsystem (IMS), 501
and 3GPP, 501–504
architecture, 510, 518
application server and media server, 515–516
border function, 517–518
call flows, 519–520
edge proxy, 514–515
outbound/inbound proxy, 512–514
PSTN Gateway, 517
Service Call Session Control Function, 510
concepts, 520
call model, 524–526
charging, 526
identities, 521–522
identity management, 524
policy and charging control, 528–529
security, 522–524
ETSI TISPAN NGN, 536–538
high-level requirements, 504
access independence, 505–506
IP connectivity, 504–505
multiple services, support for, 508–509
QoS support, 508
roaming support, 506–508
security, 509
IMS centralized services, 539
services, 532–533
combinational services, 535–536
global text telephony, 536
messaging, 533
PoC service, 533–534
presence service, 533
telephony service, 534–535
SIP requirements, 529
adjacent contacts discovery, 530
private extensions, 530–532
service route discovery, 529
voice call continuity, 538–539
IP multimedia communication services, 3
signaling and media, role of, 6–10
IP PBX applications, 14–15
IP Telephony (IPTEL) Working Group, 20
IPsec, 321–322, 331
ISC (IMS Service Control), 515
ISDN (Integrated Services Digital Network), 24, 25
ITU (International Telecommunication Union), 9, 25, 28

J

JAIN SDP, 66, 191–193
JAIN SIP, 137, 273
API standard, 65–66
architecture, 140–144
implementation, 307
initialization, 155–157, 299–300
interface
between listener and SIP implementation, 295
layering model, 139
version, 139–140
JAIN SLEE, 66
Java Media Framework (JMF), 70, 225
entities
data sink, 233–234
data source, 229–231
managers, 228–229
player, 231–233
processor, 233
session manager, 234–237
fundamental data-processing model, 226
high-level API, 226–227
implementation, 260
live media capturing, 237–238
media file capturing, 238
plug-in API, 226, 227
present media, 238–239
process media, 239–241
receive media from network, 241–245
RTP API, 225
send media over network, 241–245
send media to file, 239
Java Virtual Machine (JVM), 259
JNI (Java Native Interface), 138n
Join header, 387–388
`JTabbedPane`, 265, 298

K

Key-exchange algorithms, 318–319, 330, 331
Key-management protocols, for SDP, 331–332
KPML (Key Press Markup Language), 417–418

L

Layered approach, of protocol structure, 113
`ListeningPoint`, 140, 141, 142, 144, 156
Live media capturing, 237–238

Location Service, 45, 52-53, 77-78, 101, 327
  display, 299
  implementation, 302
`locationService HashMap`, 307
Loose routing, 96-97

M

MAC (message authentication code), 317
`Manager`, 228, 237
Managers, 228-229
Max-Forwards header field, 93, 290, 302
MBone (Multicast Backbone), 26, 27
Media and transport (m-line), 182, 186
Media file capturing, 238
Media Gateway (MG), 397
Media Gateway Controller (MGC), 397
Media locators, 241-243
Media plane, 9, 201-202, 397
  Messaging Service Relay Protocol, 209-211
    main features, 211-212
    message format, 213-216
    nodes, 212-213
    operation mode, 216-222
    security, 334
  programming, 225-227
    media streams, 227-228
  Real-time Transport Protocol, 202, 206-207
    motivation, 203-205
    RTCP, 207-208
    security, 330-332
  TCP-based media transport, 332-333
  TonesTool, 254-255
  VideoTool, 248-254
  VoiceTool, 245-248
  see also Java Media Framework (JMF)
Media-programming APIs, 69-70
Media servers, 60, 69, 409, 515
  basic media services, 410-412
    architecture, 412-413
    implementation, 413-417
  control
    approaches, 431-433
    motivation, 429-430
    trends, 434
    xml-based, 432
  KPML, 417-418
Media services, 12
Media stream, 179, 187, 227-228, 233, 236
  processing, 238-240
  sending to file, 239
Media transport protocols, 6, 7, 8, 9, 202
  Messaging Service Relay Protocol, 209-222, 334
  Real-time Transport Protocol, 206-209, 330-332
  TCP-based media transport, 332-333
MEDIACTRL Working Group, 431
Message body, 83, 94-95, 320
Message digest, 317
Message-ID header field, 215
Messages, *see* SIP messages
`MessageFactory`, 149, 150
Messaging Service Relay Protocol (MSRP), 9, 40, 185-186, 189, 202, 209-211, 334
  clients, 212, 217, 219
  main features, 211-212
  message format
    AUTH request, 214
    REPORT request, 213
    SEND request, 213
  nodes of, 212-213
  operation mode, 216
    reporting, 220-222
    with relays, 217, 219-220
    without relays, 217, 218
  see also MSRP header fields
Method name, 84
MGCF (Media Gateway Control Function), 517
MIME (Multipurpose Internet Mail Extensions), 94
Mixer, 427
Mobile Media API (MMAPI), 70
Mosaic, 22
MRFC (Media Resource Function Controller), 516
MRFP (Media Resource Function Processor), 516
MSCML (Media Server Control Markup Language), 432
MSML (Media Server Markup Language), 432
MSRP header fields, 214
  Byte-Range, 216
  From-Path, 215
  Message-ID, 215
  Status, 216
  Success Report
    and Failure Report, 215-216
  To-Path, 215
MSRP URI, 211-202, 219
Multidevice service, 358
Multimedia communications security, 313
  basic encryption concepts
    asymmetric ciphers, 315-317
    cipher suites, 318-319
    cryptography, 314
    digital certificates, 318
    digital signatures, 317-318
    hash functions, 317
    symmetric ciphers, 314-315
  media plane security
    Message Service Relay Protocol, 334
    Real-time Transport Protocol, 330-332
    TCP-based media transport, 332-333
  security mechanisms, for SIP, 320-321

best practices on, 327–330
HTTP authentication, 324–326
network-layer security, 321–322
S/MIME, 326–327
transport-layer security, 322–323
URI scheme, 323–324
security service, for SIP, 320
SIP, attack and threat models in
message bodies, 320
registration hijacking, 319
server impersonation, 319–320
service denial, 320
tearing down and modification, of sessions, 319
Multimedia Conference Control (MMCC), 27
Multimedia Internet KEYing (MIKEY), 331
Multimedia-service creation
customer-based SIP services, 62–64
media-programming APIs, 69–70
SIP programming interfaces, 64–69
SIP services, 59
and SIP entities, 60–61
Multiparty Multimedia Session Control (MMUSIC) Working Group, 19
Multiparty communication, *see* Conferencing
Multiplexed tracks, 227

N

NAPT (Network Address and Port Translation), 469–470
NAPTR RR (Naming Authority Pointer Resource Record), 99
Network, *see* SIP network
Network Address Translation (NAT) traversal, 41, 467
basic, 468–469
behaviors, 470
address mapping, 471
filtering, 471
session border controllers, 485–488
of SIP signaling, 488–490
of RTP traffic, 490–493
see also NAPT; RTP traversal; SIP traversal
Network Domain Security (NDS), 524
Network-layer security, 321–322
see also IPsec
New content type, 343
New header fields, 339, 349, 355, 441, 444
`NewReceiveStreamEvent`, 242
NGN (Next Generation Network), 25
"No" button, 265
Non-ACK requests
and non-CANCEL requests, 301–304
Non-INVITE transactions, 122–123, 124
Nonce, 324, 325
NOTIFY, 349, 351, 418, 420
NVP (Network Voice Protocol), 26

O

OCF (Online Charging Function), 527–528, 531
"Off" button, 264, 297
Offer/answer model, with SDP, 187
MSRP, 189
TCP content, 190–191
voice/video, 188–189
Offline charging, 497, 526–527
Offline communication, 4
see also Email
"On" button, 264, 297
Online charging, 498, 527–528
Online communication, 4, 5, 362
see also Instant messaging; IP multimedia communication services; Prestored image; Voice call
Opaque, 325
Open Mobile Alliance (OMA), 363
Open-source implementation, 69
Option tags, 342, 345
OPTIONS request, 82–83, 339, 343
Origin (o-line), 181
OSA/Parlay, 67, 68
Outbound proxy, 53–54, 284, 512–514

P

P-Access-Network-Info header, 531
P-Asserted-Identity header, 442, 443
P-Associated-URI, 532
P-Called-Party-ID, 532
P-Charging-Function-Address header, 531
P-Charging-Vector header, 531
P-headers, 343, 443
P-Preferred-Identity header, 442, 443
P-Visited-Network-ID header, 530
Packet-Based Multimedia Communications Systems, 28
Packet-Switched (PS) domain, 24, 25, 502–503, 535
Page-mode messaging, 211, 372
`Parameters` interface, 151
Parlay X, 68
Payload type (PT), 182, 183, 207, 208, 209
PCEF (Policy and Charging Enforcement Function), 528
PCRF (Policy and Charging Rules Function), 528
Peer-provider pattern, 140–141
Peer-to-peer call control, 382, 383
Join header, 387–388
REFER method, 383–385
Referred-by mechanism, 385–386
Replaces header, 386–387

PIDF (Presence Information Data Format), 364, 368
content, 369
PKI (Public Key Infrastructure), 318
Plaintext, 314
Player, 231-233
`Player` interface, 231, 232, 238, 239, 252, 255
`playTone()`, 255
Policy-based admission control, 453-454
Policy control, 41, 512-514, 528
Policy decision point (PDP), 453-454, 460, 462
Policy enforcement point (PEP), 453-454, 462, 528
Port text box, 298
POTS (Plain Old Telephone System), 398
`prepareTone()`, 254, 263, 279
Presence
address resolution, 370
information, 368-370
model, 363-365
notification, 367-368
resource lists, 370-371
with SIP, 365
information publication, 365-366
subscribing information, 366-367
XCAP, 372
Presence Agent (PA), 365
Presence service, 13, 361, 364, 370, 533
Presence User Agent (PUA), 365
Prestored image, 5
Privacy service, 438, 440, 498
Private key, 315, 317, 444
Private User Identity (IMPI), 521-522
`Processor`, 233, 240, 251
Processor, 233
`processRequest()`, 147, 163, 166, 169, 173
`processResponse()`, 147, 167, 174
`processTransactionTerminated`, 307
Protocol encapsulation, 400, 406
INFO method, 406-407
Protocol operation, of SIP
mode of operation
responses, 76
requests, 76-83
SIP detailed call flows
call, 105-112
registration, 103-105
SIP message format, 83
header fields, 86-94
message body, 94-95
responses, 85-86
SIP requests, 84-85
SIP routing, 95
IP address, port and transport, determination, 97-100
next-hop SIP URI, determination, 96-97
routing scenarios, 100-103
Protocol structure, of SIP
layered approach, 113
SIP core sublayer
transaction users, 117
transport users, 117
SIP dialogs, 132-136
identification of, 133-134
information, 134-135
working of, 135-136
SIP entities, 114-116
SIP sublayers, 114
SIP syntax and encoding function, 132
SIP transaction sublayer
behavior of, 125-129
client and server transaction, 119
transaction-layer functions, 119-121
SIP transport sublayer
client transport, 129-130
server transport, 130-132
Protocol translation, 397, 398, 407
message mapping, 403
parameter mapping, 403
state machine alignment, 403
Protocol version (v-line), 84, 85, 181
Provisional responses, reliability of
motivation, 344-345
work, 345-347
Proxies, *see* SIP proxies
Proxy-assisted-mode scenarios, 100, 101-103
Proxy server, 52, 53, 398
forking, 55-56
inbound proxy, 54-55
outbound proxy, 53-54
Proxying requests, 300, 306
non-ACK requests
and non-CANCEL requests, 301-304
PSTN (Public Switched Telephony Network), 184, 498
emulation applications, 16
gateway, 517
PSTN/PLMN
architecture, 396
gateway decomposition, 397
IP to PSTN, 398
media plane, 397
PSTN to IP, 398-399
PSTN to PSTN via IP, 399-400
signaling plane, 396-397
ENUM, 401-403
motivation, 395-396
protocol encapsulation, 406-407
protocol translation, 403
TEL URI, 400-401

Public key, 315, 318, 326
Public User Identity (IMPU), 522
Pulse Code Modulation (PCM), 27, 79
Push To Talk over Cellular (PoC) service, 533-534
`put()`, 307

Q

Qop-options, 325
Quality of Service (QoS), 40, 447
  in IP networks, 447
  mechanisms for, 449
    differentiated services, 451-452
    integrated services, 449-451, 452-453
  policy-based admission control, 453-454
  SIP integration, with policy control, 460
    architecture460-462
    implementation, 462
    motivation, 460
  SIP integration, with resource reservation
    motivation, 454-455
    operation, 457-458
    overview, 455-457
  SIP proxy, 460
  support, 508

R

Realm, 325
Real-time communication, 6, 178
Real-time text, 185, 209
Real-time Transport Control Protocol (RTCP), 207-208, 243, 483
Real-time Transport Protocol (RTP), 6, 9, 40, 78, 202, 206-207, 257, 330-331
  application examples, 208-209
  Datagram Transport Layer Security protocol, 332
  EKT, 332
  key-management extensions, for SDP, 331-332
  motivation
    end-to-end delay, 203-204
    jitter, 204-205
    out-of-sequence delivery, 204
    packet loss, 203
  payload format specification, 207
  profile specification, 207
  RTCP, 207-208
  SDP security descriptions, 331
  streams, 235, 410, 415
  traffic, 322, 490-493
  ZRTP, 332
Reason phrase, 85
`ReceiveStreamEvent`, 235, 242, 243, 246
`ReceiveStreamListener`, 235, 242, 245, 247
Record-route check box, 298
Record-Route header field, 91-92, 103, 135, 302
recordRoute Boolean variable, 302
Redirect Servers, 57
REFER method, 383-385, 391, 393, 422
Referred-by mechanism, 385-386
REGISTER request, 77-78, 307-308, 328, 359, 489
Registrar, 52, 101, 115, 328, 359
Registration hijacking, 319
Re-INVITE request, 80, 347, 388, 430
Reliable Delivery, 121-122
Remote call control, 383, 390-393
`RemoteListener`, 235
`remove()`, 307
Replaces header, 386-387
REPORT request, 213, 221
Request line, 84, 149
Request URI, 78, 84, 96, 100, 101, 135, 301, 329, 355, 365, 413, 415, 442, 532
Request/Response Correlation, 121
Requests, in SIP, 76, 84-85
  ACK, 80-81
  BYE, 82
  CANCEL, 81-82
  INVITE, 78-80
  OPTIONS, 82-83
  REGISTER, 77-78
Resource List Server (RLS), 371
Resource Records (RRs), 99
Resource Reservation Protocol (RSVP), 450-451, 460, 462
Responses, in SIP, 76, 85-86
Retargeting, 355
Retransmissions, 274-275
Ring.wav file, 279
RINGING state, 271, 275
Roaming, 506-508, 530
Route header field, 91, 96, 135, 290, 514, 524
RTP traversal
  issues, 479
  proposed solutions, 479
RTSP (Real Time Streaming Protocol), 40, 42, 178
`run()`, 275

S

S/MIME, 326-327
Scheduler, 449
SCTP (Stream Control Transmission Protocol), 36, 38, 98
SDES (Source DEScription), 208
`SdpFactory`, 191, 197
`SdpInfo`, 196
`SdpManager`, 196, 197
Secure Real-time Transport Protocol (SRTP), 330, 331, 332

SecureRandom class, 273-274
Security, 498, 509
Security mechanisms, for SIP, 320-321
  HTTP authentication, 324-326
  network-layer security, 321-322
  S/MIME, 326-327
  transport-layer security, 322-323
  URI scheme, 323-324
Security services, for SIP, 320
SEND request, 213, 215, 216, 221
SendStreamListener, 235
Server transaction, 114, 119, 123-124, 173, 285
Server transport, 114, 130-132
Service denial, 320
Service-Route header, 529
Services, enabled by SIP
  application
    enterprise total communication systems, 15
    IP Centrex application, 15-16
    IP PBX applications, 14-15
    PSTN emulation applications, 16
    SIP communicator applications, 13-14
  basic session management services, 10-11
  conferencing services, 12-13
  enhanced control services, 11-12
  IETF, 18-20
  media services, 12
  presence services, 13
Serving Call Session Control Function (S-CSCF), 510, 515, 525, 526, 529, 532
  authentication, 510-511
  media types prohibition, 511-512
  originating calls, 511
  service control, 511
  user profile, 511
Session Announcement Protocol (SAP), 27, 40, 178
Session border controllers (SBC), 485-488, 498
  functions, 486-488
  of RTP traffic, 490-493
  of SIP signaling, 488-490
Session description
  IP communication sessions, 184-187
  purpose, 177-178
  offer/answer model, with SDP, 187-191
  Session Description Protocol (SDP), 179-184
    programming, 199-199
Session Description Protocol (SDP), 11, 39-40, 43, 78
  answer
    receiving, 278-279
    sending, 278
  attributes (a-line), 183-184
  bandwidth (b-line), 182-183
  connection information (c-line), 181
  implementation, 259
  IP communication sessions, 184-187
  manager, 259
  media and transport (m-line), 182
  message, 179-180
    encoding, 193-194
    parsing, 194-195
  offer, 79
    sending, 277
    receiving, 277-278
  offer/answer model, 187, 276-279
  origin (o-line), 181
  practice, 195-199
  programming, 191-199
    encoding SDP messages, 193-194
    JAIN SDP, 191-193
    parsing SDP messages, 194-195
    SDP practice, 195-199
  protocol version (v-line), 181
  security descriptions, 331
  session name (s-line), 181
  time line (t-line), 182
Session Initiation Protocol (SIP), 113
  addressing, 44-45
  definition, 43
  entities
    Back-to-Back User Agents, 57-58
    Location Service, 52-53
    proxy servers, 53-56
    Redirect Servers, 57
    registrar, 52
    user agents, 50-52
  functions, 45
    session setup, termination, and modification, 46-48
    user location, 48-50
  implementation, 259
SIPPING WG, 19
SIP WG, 19
Session-mode messaging, 211, 372
Session name (s-line), 181
Session termination, 279
SessionAddress, 236-237
SessionDescription interface, 191
SessionListener, 235, 236
SessionManager, 234, 242-244
  listeners, 235
  operation, 235-236
  RTP streams, 235
  SessionAddress, 236-237
setContent(), 193
setFormat(), 240
setMediaDescriptions(), 193
showInfo(), 265
showStatus(), 261
Signaling Gateway (SGW), 397

Signaling plane, 396-397
Simple Conference Invitation Protocol (SCIP), 27
SIMPLE Instant Messaging, 66
SIMPLE Working Group, 19
Simultaneous ringing, 12
SIP dialogs, 79-80
  identification of, 133-134
  information, 134-135
  usage of, 132-133
  working of, 135-136
SIP entities, 114-116
  registrar, 115, 116
  SIP User Agent, 115
  stateful proxy, 115, 116
  stateless proxy, 115, 116
SIP practice
  `AddressFactory`, 151-152
  applications, Structure of, 152-155
  `HeaderFactory`, 149-151
  JAIN SIP Initialization, 155-157
  JAIN SIP, 137
    JAIN SIP architecture, 140-144
    version, 139-140
  `ListeningPoint`, 144
  `MessageFactory`, 149
  `SipListener`, 144, 146-148
  `SipProvider`, 144
  `SipStack`, 144
  testing of, 157
SIP messages, 83
  header fields, 86-94
  message body, 94-95
  SIP requests, 84-85
  SIP responses, 85-86
SIP network, 495
  authentication, authorization, and accounting, 497-498
  interworking and border functions, 498-499
  mobility and routing, 497
  network-based services, 499
  role of, 495-496
    functions, 496-497
  security, 498
SIP protocol sublayers, 114, 115
SIP proxies
  routing, 283-285
  SIP server
    architecture, 295-296
    end-to-end SIP communication example, 310-312
    enhanced client, 308-310
    handling registrations, 307-308
    JAIN SIP initialization, 299-300
    management console, 297-299
    proxying requests, 300-305
    proxying responses, 306
    scope, 294-295
    terminated transactions, 307
  stateful proxies, 285-286
    behavior, 289-293
    call stateful proxies, 289
    treatment of, 286-289
  transaction stateless proxies, 293-294
  types, 285
SIP registration, 103-105
SIP routing, 95, 283-285
  IP address, port and transport, determination, 97-100
  next-hop SIP URI, determination, 96-97
  routing scenarios, 100-103
SIP security, best practices on, 326-330
SIP server
  architecture, 295-296
  end-to-end communication example, 310-312
  enhanced client, 308-310
  handling registrations, 307-308
  JAIN SIP initialization, 299-300
  management console, 297-299
  proxying request, 300-305
  proxying responses, 306
  scope of, 294-295
  terminated transactions, 307
SIP servlets, 66
SIP session, 219
SIP syntax and encoding function, 132
SIP transaction sublayer
  client and server transaction, 119
    behavior of, 125-129
  transaction-layer functions, 119-121
SIP transport sublayer, 114
  client transport, 129-130
  server transport, 130-132
SIP trapezoid, 127-129
SIP traversal
  issues
    incoming requests routing, 475-476
    routing responses, 474-475
  proposed solutions
    incoming requests routing, 477-479
    routing responses, 476-477
SIP UA, 50-52
SIP UDP port, 266
SIP URI, 44, 323-324
SipFactory, 142, 144, 145
`SipListener`, 143, 144, 146-148, 295
`SipProvider`, 140, 142, 146, 267
`SipproxyGUI`, 296
`SipproxyListener`, 296, 299
`SipStack` interface, 140, 142, 145, 146
SipStack property RETRANSMISSION_FILTER, 274

SipURI object, 151
Soft-phone
  architecture, 258-259
    components, 259-260
    interfaces, 260-263
  configuration/display area, 265-267
  implementation aspects, 271
    call management and transactions, 275
    CANCEL request treatment, 273
    code running, 280
    configuration, 272
    error conditions and timeouts, 274
    retransmissions, 274-275
    SDP handling and media tool utilization, 276-279
    session termination, 279
    tag calculation and management, 273-274
    tones and signals playing, 279-280
  scope, 257-258
  state model, 267-268
    ESTABLISHED state, 270-271
    IDLE state, 268-270
    RINGING state, 271
    WAIT_ACK state, 271
    WAIT_FINAL state, 270
    WAIT_PROV state, 270
  user interface, 264-265
Soft-phone application core logic, 259
Softphone1Listener, 262, 263, 267, 279
Softphone1Listener(), 261
Softphone2, 308
Softphone2GUI, 308, 309
Softphone2Listener, 308-310
Softphone3, 375-379
Software CODEC, 8
Spec(T), 442
Specific event notification
  motivation, 348-349
  work, 349-351
SR (Sender Report), 208
SRV RR (Service Resource Record), 99
Start line, 83, 84, 85
start(), 238
startMedia(), 245-247, 248, 249-252, 262
startSession(), 235, 243-244
State model, 267-268
  ESTABLISHED state, 270-271
  IDLE state, 268-270
  RINGING state, 271
  WAIT_ACK state, 271
  WAIT_FINAL state, 270
  WAIT_PROV state, 270
Stateful proxies, 285-286
  behavior, 289
    ACK request, receiving, 292-293
    CANCEL request, receiving, 292
    requests treatment, 290-292
    response processing, 292
  call stateful proxies, 289
  treatment, 286-289
Stateless proxies, 293-294
Status code, 85
Status header field, 216
Status line, 85
stopMedia(), 247-248, 249, 253-254, 262
stopTone(), 255, 263
Stream Control Transmission Protocol (SCTP), 38
Streaming services, 4
Strict routing, 96
  vs loose routing, 96-97
STUN (Simple Traversal Utilities for NAT), 481-484
SUBSCRIBE, 349, 350
Subscribers, 364
Success Report header field, 215-216
Supported header, 340
Symmetric ciphers, 314-315
  and asymmetric ciphers, 316

T

T.38 fax transmission over UDP, 202
Tag calculation
  and management, 273-274
"Tag" parameter, 87
TCP (Transmission Control Protocol), 37-38, 40, 98, 202
TCP-based media transport, 332-333
TCP content, 186-187, 190-191
TCP/IP Protocol architecture, 34-35
  application-layer protocols, 36
  transport-layer protocols, 36-38
TCP/TLS, 333
Tearing down and modification, of sessions, 319
TEL URI
  format, 401
  motivation, 400-401
Telephone NUmber Mapping (ENUM) Working Group, 19
"Telephone-event", 209
Telephony tones, 184-185, 209
TelURL object, 151
Terminated transactions, 307
Text over Internet Protocol (ToIP), 209
"Text/t140" RTP payload type, 209
Text-to-speech (TTS), 435
Third party call control (3PCC), 382, 389-390
Third-party registration, 78
Tightly coupled conferences, *see* Conferencing
Time line (t-line), 182
Time to live (TTL), 242

TimerTask class, 275
To header field, 88
TonesTool class, 279
TonesTool, 260
  playTone(), 255
  prepareTone(), 254
  stopTone(), 255
To-Path header field, 215, 220
Tracer display, 298
TrackControl interface, 240, 251
Tracks, 227
Transaction, 75
Transaction display, 299, 300
Transaction-layer functions, 119–124
Transaction stateful proxies, *see* Stateful proxies
Transaction stateless proxies, *see* Stateless proxies
transactionContext ArrayList, 305
transactionContext, 303, 305, 306, 307
TransactionTerminatedEvent, 307
Transition Gateway (TrGW), 517
Transparent B2BUA, 390
Transport layer, 114
Transport-layer protocols, 36–38
  Stream Control Transmission Protocol (SCTP), 38
  Transmission Control Protocol (TCP), 37–38
  User Datagram Protocol, 36–37
Transport-layer security (TLS), 129, 322–323, 332, 334
Trust Domain, 442

U

UMTS (Universal Mobile Telecommunications System), 24, 502
Unsupported header, 342
update(), 244, 245, 249, 252–253
UPDATE, 347
  motivation, 347
  work, 347
updateConfiguration(), 261, 272
URI (Universal Resource Identifier), 131
  SipURI interfaces, 151
  TelURL interfaces, 151
URL (Uniform Resource Locator), 22, 75
User Agent Client (UAC), 50, 75, 114, 154
User Agent Server (UAS), 50, 75, 114, 154
User Agents (UAs), 113
User Datagram Protocol (UDP), 36–37, 81, 98
User identity, 266
User interaction area
  destination text field, 265
  info label, 265
  "No" button, 265
  "Off" button, 264
  "On" button, 264
  "Yes" button, 265
User interface, 259
  and configuration, 263
    and display area, 265–267
    user interaction area, 264–265
  configuration area
    "Off" button, 297
    "On" button, 297
    home domain text box, 297
    port text box, 298
    record-route check box, 298
  display area
    location service display, 299
    tracer display, 298
    transaction display, 299, 300
User name, 266
userInput(), 152, 272

V

Value-added services (VAP), 499
VAT (Visual Audio Tool), 26
VFW (Video for Windows) interface, 249
Via header field, 89–90, 439
Video codecs, 267
Video RTP port, 266
Video-telephony, 10
VideoFormat, 230, 231
VideoTool, 248–249, 260
  startMedia(), 248, 249–252
  stopMedia(), 248, 253–254
  update(), 249, 252–253
Voice and video, 184, 188
Voice call, 4
Voice Call Continuity (VCC), 538–539
Voice codecs, 267
Voice Mail System (VMS), 12, 78, 133
Voice over Internet Protocol (VoIP), 26
Voice RTP port, 266
VoiceTool, 245, 259
  startMedia(), 245–247
  stopMedia(), 247–248
  update(), 247
VoiceXML, 414, 417

W

WAIT_ACK state, 271
WAIT_FINAL state, 270, 273
WAIT_PROV state, 270
Watchers, 364, 365, 366
  see also Subscribers; Fetchers
World Wide Web
  history, 22–23

WWW-Authenticate header, 324-325
WWW-Authorization header, 325-326

X

XCAP (XML Configuration Access Protocol), 372
XCON framework, 419
  architecture, 425-428
  enhanced conference management, 423-424
  floor control, 424-425
  media services, 425

Y

"Yes" button, 265

Z

ZRTP, 332

Printed and bound by CPI Group (UK) Ltd, Croydon, CR0 4YY
03/10/2024
01040314-0008